Ray & McLaughlin
Practical Inheritance Tax
Planning

Ray & McLaughlin's Practical Inheritance Tax Planning

Eleventh edition

Mark McLaughlin CTA (Fellow) ATT TEP

Geoffrey A Shindler OBE MA LLM (Cantab) TEP

Paul Davies CTA TEP, Solicitor

Ralph Ray CTA (Fellow) TEP BSc (Econ)

Bloomsbury Professional

Bloomsbury Professional Ltd, Maxwelton House, 41–43 Boltro Road, Haywards Heath, West Sussex, RH16 1BJ

© Bloomsbury Professional Ltd 2013

Bloomsbury Professional, an imprint of Bloomsbury Publishing Plc

A CIP Catalogue record for this book is available from the British Library.

ISBN: 978 1 84766 968 1

Typeset by Phoenix Photosetting, Chatham, Kent
Printed and bound by CPI Group (UK) Ltd, Croydon, CR0 4YY

Preface

It is not very long ago since Mark McLaughlin welcomed readers to the tenth edition of *Practical Inheritance Tax Planning*. Once upon a time, changes in inheritance tax legislation and legal decisions came at a steady, sometimes imperceptible, pace. Not so now.

Like many other taxes, the world of inheritance tax moves at an ever accelerating rate. Government which is short of money introduces new legislation to block what it regards as existing unfair and unwanted loopholes and introduces new legislation to try and block loopholes that have not yet been thought of, taxpayers are forever testing the boundaries of this new legislation, judges are forced to focus their minds precisely what it is that the legislation has achieved and Parliamentarians are going through one of those eras of moral outrage (hoping that many of us will have forgotten their own previous suspect activities in the world of tax arrangements).

This eleventh edition of *Practical Inheritance Tax Planning* deals with what has now become the most important budget of the year, namely the December statement. It has been necessary to tinker with large parts of this book to take account of the proposals outlined in the 2012 December statement accompanied as it was in many respects by draft legislation. As the work suggests, the legislation is still draft so practitioners are left in the unsatisfactory position of saying that this is what we think the law will be but it has not been enacted, so could change.

The three of us have attempted to be faithful to Ralph Ray's original concept of practical planning rather than to write a theoretical, learned work. But, one cannot understand the practice without understanding the underlying theory, so theory has to take its place in a book which is intended ultimately to be practical for those working in the world of inheritance planning on a day to day basis.

I would like to express my thanks to Mark and to Paul for bearing the largest part of the burden of rewriting where required. Also to Bloomsbury and our editors for their help assistance and extraordinarily adept handling of our manuscripts in the shortest possible time to give our readership fully up to date material from which to work.

Preface

The law in this book is stated as at 1 December 2012.

Geoffrey A Shindler OBE, MA, LLM (Cantab) TEP
Manchester
January 2013

Contents

Table of statutes

Table of statutes

Table of statutes

Table of statutory instruments and other guidance

[All references are to paragraph numbers and appendices]

Table of cases

H

Chapter 1

Introduction and outline

INTRODUCTION

1.1   Later chapters of this book treat the subject of inheritance tax (IHT) mainly from a practical approach, not being directly or primarily concerned with summarising the law, whilst **Chapters 1** and **2** introduce the following basic aspects of IHT:

- the basis of IHT and property chargeable, especially the concept of PETs and the gift with reservation provisions (see **1.3–1.11**);

- calculation of IHT; scale and rates; the extent of the cumulative principle; and the grossing-up concept (see **1.12–1.19**);

- main anti-avoidance provisions (see **1.20–1.34**);

- exemptions and reliefs and excluded property (see **1.35–1.37**);

- IHT compliance issues (**2.1–2.27**);

- payment by instalments (see **2.28–2.32**);

- main valuation rules (see **2.33–2.45**);

- key administration aspects (see **2.46–2.75**);

- practical approach and future of the tax (see **2.76–2.79**).

IHT has its origins in the Finance Act (hereafter 'FA') 1975 which introduced the capital transfer tax (CTT) regime. The CTT legislation was modified in subsequent Finance Acts and eventually consolidated in what was the Capital Transfer Tax Act 1984 which took effect on 1 January 1985. In FA 1986, the CTT regime was replaced by the IHT regime with effect from 18 March 1986.

In practice, and with later modification, this meant that, until FA 2006, most lifetime gifts were outside the reach of IHT, with these main exceptions:

- gifts on general discretionary trusts;

- certain gifts via companies; and

- outright gifts to individuals where the donor dies within seven years (or dies outside that period when he has reserved some sort of benefit).

The IHT regime, although retaining the basic framework and administrative provisions of CTT, had an affinity in some respects with the old estate duty. The consolidated legislation in CTTA 1984, as subsequently amended, is now known as the Inheritance Tax Act 1984 (IHTA 1984). References throughout this book are generally to IHTA 1984, unless otherwise stated.

IHT thresholds

1.2   There has been a recent trend of IHT thresholds being set well in advance. In FA 2005, the IHT thresholds were set for the next three years. The thresholds set were £275,000 for 2005–06, £285,000 for 2006–07, and £300,000 for 2007–08. Furthermore, FA 2006 set the IHT threshold at £312,000 for 2008–09 and £325,000 for 2009–10. FA 2007 originally extended the threshold to £350,000 for 2010–11. However, it was subsequently announced in the Budget on 24 March 2010 that the nil rate band would remain at its 2009–10 level of £325,000 for 2010–11, and also for the tax years 2011–12 to 2014–15 inclusive. This 'freezing' of the nil rate band was subsequently enacted in FA 2010, s 8.

In addition, it was announced in Budget 2011 that the default indexation factor for direct taxes, including IHT, will move from the retail price index to the consumer price index (CPI). Legislation to that effect was subsequently included in FA 2012, with effect from 6 April 2015. In the meantime, as indicated above, the IHT nil rate band is frozen until 5 April 2015. Automatic indexation of the nil rate band using the CPI is subject to override if Parliament determines that a different amount should apply s 8). For example, the nil rate band for 2015/16 is to increase by 1% (rounded up), from £325,000 to £329,000.

BASIS OF IHT AND PROPERTY CHARGEABLE

The types of transfer

1.3   IHT is a direct tax on transfers of capital (eg gifts) made on or after 18 March 1986. Subject to a few exceptions, it is a cumulative charge on chargeable transfers made within any seven-year period and on death. It is important at the outset to distinguish between different types of gift and to see their effect for IHT:

●   Outright gifts (transfers of value) between individuals: these are initially exempt from IHT and are termed 'potentially exempt transfers' (they are referred to as PETs).

- Prior to 22 March 2006, gifts by an individual into accumulation and maintenance trusts (s 71) or into disabled trusts (s 89) and into 'interest in possession' trusts were also PETs.

- However, gifts into trust were significantly affected by changes in FA 2006. A gift into a discretionary trust was always excluded from the PET regime (which had a countervailing advantage as regards CGT hold-over relief; see **1.12**), but since 22 March 2006 almost all lifetime gifts into trust (other than for disabled persons) are chargeable transfers; and where such trusts are not settlor-interested, hold-over relief should be available.

- PETs which turn out to have been made within seven years of the donor's death become liable to IHT ('failed PETs'). These are charged at death rates. However, taper relief is available, where the donor survives at least three years after the gift. For example, if the donor makes his gift five and a half years before his death, the rate of tax charged on the gift is reduced to 16% (40% of 40%). Where the gift was within the nil rate band, there is no saving.

- Lifetime gifts by individuals into most settlements and to companies (though only close companies would ever be likely to receive gifts): these are chargeable transfers attracting an immediate charge at lifetime rates (20%) (adjusted to the full rate, but subject to a measure of taper relief, if the donor dies within seven years).

- Gifts where the donor has reserved some benefit enjoyed within the seven-year period before his death. Here the donor is treated for IHT purposes as still being the beneficial owner at his death (this provision does not apply to gifts before 18 March 1986, even if there is reservation after then).

- There are occasions when one is *treated* as making a chargeable transfer. For example, if an individual's interest in a (pre FA 2006) interest in possession settlement is terminated, he can be treated as making a chargeable transfer if the property in question remains in trust.

The transfer on death

1.4 Apart from lifetime chargeable gifts, tax is charged on the value of the deceased's estate immediately before death. Certain key aspects of IHT may be pointed out:

- The first £325,000 (for 2012–13, and also 2013–14 and 2014–15) is liable at a nil rate of IHT. Thereafter, there is a single rate of 40% in the case of a transfer on death, and 20% in the case of a lifetime transfer. The nil rate band is an important planning tool.

- The IHT legislation is concerned primarily with individuals, although trusts are covered in ss 43–93 and close companies in ss 94–102.

- The all-important charging provisions are contained in ss 1, 2, 3, 3A (for PETs) and 10. Particular note must be taken of s 10(1) in relation to the associated operations provisions of s 268.

- The nil rate band and the seven-year cut-off point can be important planning tools, particularly where CGT can be minimised or excluded.

- Certain reversionary interests are excluded from the scope of IHT and thus can give rise to planning possibilities.

The IHT regime gives considerable scope for tax mitigation. Careful use of the nil rate band, exemptions and PETs (watching the interaction with CGT) can significantly reduce an IHT charge. However, the risk that the present government might build on the FA 2006 changes to bring back a comprehensive lifetime gifts tax regime, and the fact that annual exemptions once lost can never be recouped, add some urgency to IHT planning.

Another reason to 'do it now' is the risk that reliefs may be cut back by the government. The possible income tax implications of IHT planning as applied to benefits received by former owners etc (commonly known as the 'pre-owned assets tax' or POAT) must also be considered (see **Chapter 13**).

Meaning of 'chargeable transfer' and 'transfer of value'

1.5   IHTA 1984, s 1 provides that IHT shall be charged on the value transferred by a chargeable transfer. A 'chargeable transfer' is a transfer of value which is not an exempt transfer (eg a gift to a UK-domiciled spouse). Section 3(1) defines 'transfer of value' as a disposition made by the transferor as a result of which the value of the transferor's estate immediately after the disposition is less than it would be but for the disposition. In other words, the value transferred is represented by the fall in the value of the transferor's estate. This 'consequential loss' formula is one of the most important principles of IHT. It is used to determine the extent of chargeable transfers made during lifetime.

The idea of a transfer of value on death is of course rather more artificial. By virtue of IHTA 1984, s 4(1), tax is charged on the deceased's estate as if, immediately before his death, he had made a transfer of value and the value transferred by it had been equal to the value of his estate immediately before his death. The following example shows how the IHT method of valuation works in practice and how it can be used to the advantage of the transferor.

Example 1.1 – 'Loss to estate' principle

Mr Gold holds 80% of the issued share capital of Private Ltd which, let us assume, does not qualify for business relief (see **Chapter 15**). He gives 45% to his son and dies within seven years. The method is not to value a separate 45% parcel, but to charge IHT on the difference between 80% held immediately *before* the transfer and the 35% remaining afterwards.

If Mr Gold holds 80% of the issued share capital of Private Ltd and instead of the above single transfer decides to give 15% to each of his three children, he can (again assuming no business relief) make the gifts on three separate days and then three separate calculations (and four valuations: 80%, 65%, 50% and 35%) are required:

(1) First Disposition	Value of estate before, ie including 80% holding; less value of estate after, including only 65% holding
(2) Second Disposition	Value before, including 65% holding, less value after, including 50% holding
(3) Third Disposition	Value before, including 50% holding, less value after, including 35% holding

Order of gifts

1.6   On the footing that each donee bears his own IHT, the order specified can be particularly relevant. In such cases, the value transferred depends on the order in which the gifts are made: if gifts are made on the same day, they are treated as made in the order which produces the lowest chargeable value (s 266).

The effect of the 'related property' provision (in IHTA 1984, s 161) should be considered where appropriate. The decision in *Arkwright and another (Personal Representatives of Williams, deceased) v IRC* [2004] STC 1323 offered the IHT planner some hope of mitigating the effects of this valuation rule, at least initially (see **1.24**). In that case, the Special Commissioner held that HM Revenue & Customs (HMRC) could not rely on the valuation rule in s 161(4) for shares of land.

However, HMRC subsequently stated (in Revenue & Customs Brief 71/07) that, following legal advice, they would apply s 161(4) when valuing shares of land as related property in cases received after publication of that Brief (27 November 2007) and would consider litigation in appropriate cases, but that any existing cases would be dealt with on the basis of the Special Commissioner's decision in the *Arkwright* case as it relates to the interpretation of s 161(4).

In *Price v Revenue & Customs* [2010] UKFTT 474 (TC) (see **1.24**), the tribunal declined to rely on the Special Commissioner's analysis in *Arkwright*, but held that the two property interests under consideration must be valued as though they were offered for sale and at the same time. If that approach resulted in a greater price being achieved, it must be attributed to the two interests by applying the formula in s 161(3).

The estate on death

1.7   As noted above, a disposition only gives rise to IHT if there has been a reduction in the value of the transferor's estate or because, on death, the deceased is treated as having made a transfer of value equal to the value of his estate immediately before death. But what comprises an 'estate'? Essentially, an estate is the aggregate of all the property to which the person is beneficially entitled, after deducting excluded property and other allowable deductions. Tangible property, equitable rights, debts, choses in action, are all included in the term 'property'.

A person who has a 'general power' (or would have if he were *sui juris*), to dispose of, or to charge money on, any property other than settled property is treated as beneficially entitled to the money or property. 'General power' means a power or authority enabling a person by whom it is exercisable to appoint or dispose of property as he thinks fit (IHTA 1984, s 5).

A practical approach was taken by the Special Commissioner in *O'Neill and others v IRC* [1998] STC (SCD) 110 (SpC 0154) to the question of whether the deceased had a 'general power' to dispose of property within the meaning of s 5(2). The deceased had set up a bank account in Jersey in the joint names of himself and his daughter. The existence of the bank accounts was a secret known only to himself – not his daughter, his estranged wife, or the Inland Revenue (now HM Revenue & Customs). The Special Commissioner accepted that on the facts the deceased had a general power and that the daughter had no present beneficial interest in the bank account during her father's lifetime. Notwithstanding that the bank accounts passed to the daughter on the father's death through survivorship.

Subsequently, in *Taylor and another v Revenue and Customs Commissioners* [2008] SpC 704, the deceased was held to have a general power enabling her to dispose of the whole of two joint accounts, within s 5(2). This was on the footing (among other reasons) that there was no evidence that the other joint account holder was to benefit from the accounts on the particular facts of the case, and that the deceased was able to dispose of the whole balance in those accounts.

In *MB Smith v HMRC (and related appeals)* [2009] SpC 742, the deceased transferred a building society account into joint names with her son, on the basis that she would be entitled to the interest and he would become entitled to the capital when she died. The funds in that account were held to be settled property, and the person held to be liable for IHT in respect of it was the son, in his capacity as both the trustee and recipient of it.

In *Matthews v Revenue & Customs Commissioners* [2012] UKFTT 658 (TC), the deceased opened a joint account with her son, and provided all the funds. Monies could be withdrawn without each other's consent, and each party declared half of the interest credited to the account on their personal tax return. The tribunal held on the facts that the whole of the funds in the account were liable to IHT as part of the deceased's estate. For a discussion of when interests in, and powers over, trust property amount to a beneficial entitlement, see for example the decision in *Stow and others v Stow and others* [2008] ChD 14 March 2008, considered at **7.18**.

The share of the deceased in jointly held property is part of his estate. In the common situation where the other joint owner is a spouse or civil partner who is domiciled in the UK, the value will be covered by relief. Still, the value must be taken into account. This has implications for compliance, as discussed in the next chapter.

The transfer: the 'consequential loss' principle

1.8 IHT is charged by reference to the transferor and not the recipient. This means that the value to the recipient of the transferred property is irrelevant. The valuation of shareholdings is an important area which illustrates the point.

The transfer of a 2% shareholding by A to B might change B from a minority to majority shareholder, thereby giving the 2% interest a high value. This is irrelevant to A's IHT. What is important is the effect of the loss of 2% shareholding on the value of A's overall shareholding and thus on A's estate.

The consequential loss formula and the related property provisions of s 161 (regarding which reference should be made to the decision in the *Arkwright* case and HMRC Business Brief 71/07: see above and **1.24**) have made the need for valuations based on a majority shareholding more common. This is particularly true for private limited companies where the value transferred may be calculated as between a controlling interest before and a minority interest thereafter, though the introduction of 100% and 50% business relief as from 10 March 1992 (see **Chapter 15**) greatly mitigated this problem. There can be a substantial IHT liability (potential or actual) even as between one majority holding (say, over 75%) and another (being less than 75% after the transfer), because the former carries certain powers for company law purposes.

In all such transfers of shares, the precise impact and percentage level of business property relief available must be checked very carefully before the transaction is made. Practitioners should always bear in mind when negotiating values with HMRC or the District Valuer that, apart from contingent CGT or other taxes within the company itself, the IHT considerations (such as the availability of business relief) may be a factor in arriving at business or other values.

For future reference, the IHT method of valuation could well be followed if ever any government decides to introduce a wealth tax.

The consequential loss formula also applies to the trustees of relevant property trusts (s 65(1)(b)) and to transfer out of heritage maintenance funds.

Transfer made without intent to benefit

1.9   When an individual makes a transfer of value, unless it is an exempt transfer or a transfer of excluded property (see **1.35**), it is either a lifetime chargeable transfer or a PET. However, not all dispositions by the transferor will amount to a transfer of value. The test under s 10(1) is whether the transferor has intended a gratuitous benefit to pass to the transferee directly or indirectly. A gratuitous intent does not have to be in favour of the transferee. There will be no such gratuitous benefit if the transaction is at arm's length between persons not connected with each other (so that a mere bad bargain does not attract an IHT charge) or, should they be connected, if it was such as might be expected to be made in a transaction at arm's length between persons not connected with each other.

Again, a bad bargain does not itself entail that the transaction was not at arm's length. In *IRC v Spencer-Nairn* [1991] STC 60, which was concerned with the sale of a farm to a connected person, the disparity between the actual sale price and the open market value was held to be no more than a single factor to be taken into account in all the circumstances, and the Crown's appeal was dismissed. Connected persons should arm themselves with evidence of commerciality in order to withstand any attack.

Ex gratia benefits to employees may be excluded from IHT provided they are made for business purposes and are allowable in computing the employer's profits. In the case of unquoted shares or unquoted debentures, there is the additional requirement that 'a price' must have been 'freely negotiated' at the time of sale. Otherwise, the sale must be at a price such as might be expected to have been freely negotiated at the time of sale. It is arguable that an exchange of such securities is not a 'sale' for this purpose. 'Connected persons' are defined in s 270 broadly on the same lines as for CGT to cover transfers between husband and wife and other close relatives, trustees and settlor, and between partners (except bona fide sales or purchases of partnership assets). As regards relatives, however, the definition extends to uncles, aunts, nephews, nieces, or such relatives' spouses. In the case of 'connected persons', the onus is much more heavily placed on the taxpayer to show that a transfer was not gratuitous.

Associated operations

1.10   In addition to the provisions concerning 'connected persons', s 272 defines a 'disposition' to include dispositions effected by associated operations. 'Associated operations' are defined in s 268 and cover the case where, for example, A wants to grant the freehold to B and does so by granting a lease and then the reversion. Rather than value the two transactions at their separate and lower values, HMRC will want to tax the total value of the unencumbered freehold (see also **1.20**).

The possibility of avoiding IHT by means of bets or wagers has been aired from time to time. For example, a father might lose considerable sums to his son on a round of golf or in a game of poker, in the knowledge, presumably, that the son is a far more proficient player. This type of arrangement is hardly likely to avoid IHT, because there is still the underlying intention to benefit. The real gamble is therefore whether or not HMRC will be convinced, which is hardly sound tax planning!

However, where a winning football coupon or National Lottery ticket has been submitted in the name of one person and so he receives all the winnings from the promoter, HMRC have indicated that IHT will not be charged on a division of the winnings among others, provided the monies are paid out on the basis of a pre-existing enforceable arrangement among the members of a syndicate (SP E14). In such a case, evidence might be hard to come by.

Basis of liability

1.11   The liability to IHT is based on domicile (including deemed domicile), as discussed in **Chapter 17**.

CALCULATION OF IHT; SCALE, RATES AND TAPER RELIEF; THE CUMULATIVE PRINCIPLE; THE GROSSING-UP CONCEPT

Scale, rates and taper relief

1.12   For transfers from 6 April 2012, there is no IHT payable until the cumulative total reaches £325,000; this IHT threshold is unchanged from the tax years 2009–10 to 2011–12 inclusive, and is to remain unchanged up to and including 2014–15 (note – the threshold is set to increase to £329,000 for 2015–16). This first tranche is commonly called the 'nil rate band'. The IHT rate thereafter is 40% (Sch 1).

However, following legislation introduced in FA 2012, a lower IHT rate of 36% applies to a deceased person's estate in certain circumstances involving charitable legacies. The lower rate broadly applies where 10% or more of a deceased's net estate (after deducting liabilities, exemptions, reliefs and the nil rate band) is left to charity or a registered community amateur sports club. In such cases, the normal 40% rate is reduced to 36% (Sch 1A). The lower rate has effect for deaths on or after 6 April 2012. For further commentary on gifts to charity etc charged at the lower rate, see **5.26**.

Unless Parliament decides otherwise, the nil rate band is increased each year by indexation (s 8(1)). However, as indicated at **1.2**, from 6 April 2015 the default indexation assumption changes from the retail price index (RPI) to the consumer price index (CPI), although the Government announced on 5 December 2012 that the nil rate band for 2015–16 is to be £329,000.

Lifetime chargeable transfers (eg gifts into discretionary trusts) are taxed in the first instance at one half the normal rate, so that, where the nil rate band has been used up by earlier chargeable transfers brought into cumulation, the initial rate will be 20%.

If the transferor then dies within seven years the IHT is recalculated by reference to the full rate, but with the benefit of any reduction in the scale between the gift and the death (s 9 and Sch 2, para 2). The recalculation may have to take into account any one or more earlier PETs, now chargeable because made within seven years of the death.

Finally, taper relief may be due if the chargeable gift was outside three years of the death (s 7(4)). Under this relief the *value* of the transfer stays the same, but the full rate(s) of IHT charged are reduced to a percentage of those rates on the following scale:

Transfer more than three but not more than four years before death: 80% rate reduced to:

Transfer more than four but not more than five years before death: 60% rate reduced to:

Transfer more than five but not more than six years before death: 40% rate reduced to:

Transfer more than six but not more than seven years before death: 20% rate reduced to:

If, however, the tax on a lifetime chargeable transfer is recalculated on death with the benefit of taper relief and produces a lower tax figure than the tax at half rate initially calculated, the earlier half rate figure stands (s 7(5)), but with the benefit of the rates at the date of death. This means that the chargeable transfer cannot obtain taper relief on death after five years because there is no rebate of the 20% (half of normal 40% in lifetime) tax paid. As a result, a transfer that was originally chargeable is taxed more heavily than one which was originally potentially exempt but which becomes chargeable (ie a failed PET).

Example 1.2 – Recalculation with tapering

Mr A is a widower and makes a gift of £359,000 on discretionary trusts six and a half years before his death. He leaves an estate of £400,000 (for illustration purposes, assume 2012–13 IHT rates and thresholds throughout).

IHT on gift:	£
on first £325,000	Nil
on £34,000 at half 40%	6,800
	6,800
Recalculation at death (full 40% rate tapers to 20% thereof = 8%)	2,720

The payment of £6,800 must stand. The estate of £400,000 bears IHT of £160,000.

There can be no taper relief where the gift in question is within the nil rate band. This is a potential disadvantage since a failed PET will use up part of the deceased's available nil rate band.

As regards PETs, if the donor survives the PET by seven years it becomes an exempt transfer; but if he dies within seven years of making the PET, it is converted into a chargeable transfer (s 3A). IHT then becomes payable at the full rate on the death (on the value at the time of the gift) with taper relief if the gift took place between three and seven years of the death.

Example 1.3 – Chargeable PET

Mr B makes an outright gift of £359,000 to his nephew and dies three and a half years later with an estate of £223,000 (assume 2012–13 rates).

IHT on gift:	
on first £325,000	Nil
on £34,000 at full 40% tapered to 80% thereof (= 32%)	£10,880

The estate bears 40% tax on £223,000, ie £89,200.

11

It follows that, in the case of lifetime gifts, whether initially PETs or lifetime chargeable transfers, the donees or trustees should make a reserve for the necessary (additional) IHT that would become payable by them should the donor die within seven years. Alternatively, the donees or trustees might consider insuring the donor's life on a term basis, see **14.16**. In considering the possible IHT charge on gifts, the donor must also take into account the fact that capital gains tax hold-over relief is restricted to a narrow range of cases, including gifts:

- of business and agricultural assets;

- of shares in trading companies (see TCGA 1992, s 165);

- of heritage property;

- to political parties; and

- transactions constituting immediate lifetime chargeable transfers, most commonly those to discretionary trusts (see TCGA 1992, s 260).

In the last of these cases, note that hold-over relief can be obtained even if the gift falls within the nil rate band. The relief is not, however, available to PETs which later become chargeable transfers. Any relief for the (ultimate) payment of both IHT and CGT (see s 165(1) and TCGA 1992, s 260(7)) is given only by way of reduction of value or gain, and not by set-off of one tax against the other, so that two taxes (at rates of 40% (IHT) and 18% or 28% (CGT)) may become payable. Bearing in mind that an individual's assets acquire a new base value for CGT on death, the narrow range of gifts covered by hold-over relief means very great care must be taken in making gifts in order to avoid unnecessary pitfalls (see **11.3** onwards).

In the case of husband and wife or civil partners (cp) it may be appropriate to leave the bulk of the estate (ie over the nil rate band) by will to the surviving spouse/cp outright or by way of life interest, thereby obtaining the CGT exemption and market value uplift on death and then relying on the surviving spouse/cp to make PETs. This is particularly suitable where the survivor is younger and/or in good health. Note however that by FA 1986, s 102ZA the scope to sidestep the GWR code has been curtailed: see in greater detail at **1.34**.

The cumulation principle and seven-year cut-off

1.13   The scheme of IHT is based on the simple principle of the cumulation of successive chargeable transfers to form a ladder in order to determine the rate of tax on the latest. There is a seven-year cut-off period (s 7(1)) so that the last chargeable transfer is aggregated with those chargeable transfers made within the previous seven years, and becomes the highest part of them. There are, however, a number of features to bear in mind which can affect and retrospectively upset this cumulative ladder.

First, PETs (outright gifts to individuals or to favoured trusts) are initially treated as exempt. Where an individual makes a lifetime chargeable transfer (eg a gift on discretionary trusts) there fall to be cumulated with that chargeable transfer only those transfers in the preceding seven years which are themselves lifetime chargeable transfers: PETs are left out of account.

When the donor dies, the cumulative ladder at that point will comprise all chargeable transfers within the previous seven years. These chargeable transfers will now include not merely the lifetime chargeable transfers on which IHT was paid at the time but also any 'failed PETs' (ie those within seven years of death which now become chargeable transfers and which have to be slotted into the ladder at the right chronological point). This causes the total of lifetime chargeable transfers to be re-cumulated.

Each chargeable transfer (including former PETs within seven years of death) will then have its own cumulative ladder of chargeable transfers within seven years of itself. A former PET now chargeable because made, say, just inside seven years of the donor's death has to cumulate chargeable transfers within the seven years preceding its own date. Because of this 'knock-on' effect cumulation can be a 14-year problem even though the cut-off is seven years. PETs made in that earlier seven years, however, because outside seven years of death, will have become permanently, not merely potentially, exempt and can be ignored.

Example 1.4 – Cumulation of transfers

Year 1	Settlement on discretionary trusts	Chargeable transfer
Year 3	Outright gift to X	PET
Year 5	Gift to company	Chargeable transfer
Year 7	Outright gift to Y	PET
Year 9	Further settlement on discretionary trusts	Chargeable transfer
Year 11	Outright gift to Z	PET
Year 13	Donor dies	Chargeable estate

On the donor's death the PETs in years 7 and 11 become chargeable, so that the estate is cumulated with the successive gifts in years 7, 9 and 11.

The PET in year 11 becomes chargeable and is cumulated with the gifts in years 5, 7 (PET now chargeable) and 9.

The settlement in year 9 is cumulated on a revised basis with the gift in year 5 and the former PET in year 7, but not with the PET in year 3 which has become permanently exempt as outside seven years of the death.

The former PET in year 7 is now chargeable and is cumulated with the chargeable transfers in years 1 and 5, but the now permanently exempt gift in year 3 is ignored.

The additional cumulation for the settlement in year 9 by reason of the PET in year 7 becoming chargeable could affect the exit charge on a capital distribution from the settlement.

Avoidance of double charge

1.14   The structure of IHT means that in certain circumstances the same property can be charged twice and enter twice into the cumulation of chargeable transfers as a result of a transferor's death. The Board of Inland Revenue (now HM Revenue & Customs) made regulations (Inheritance Tax (Double Charges Relief) Regulations 1987, SI 1987/1130) which provide for relief in these circumstances. These are here called 'the 1987 Regulations' to distinguish them from the newer ones mentioned below. FA 1986, s 104 empowered the Board to make provision by regulations for avoiding in certain circumstances double charges to IHT in respect of transfers of value and other events occurring on or after 18 March 1986.

The 'pre-owned assets' legislation also provides a measure of relief from IHT in certain very specific circumstances, where the taxpayer elects for those provisions not to apply and if two IHT charges may arise on the same underlying asset value (see Charge to Income Tax by Reference to Enjoyment of Property Previously Owned Regulations 2005, SI 2005/724, reg 6). These are here called 'the POAT Regulations' and should not be confused with other almost contemporaneous legislation, the Inheritance Tax (Double Charges Relief) Regulations 2005, SI 2005/3441, here called 'the POAT Relief Regulations'. See also **Chapter 13**.

The 1987 Regulations

1.15   These regulations provide for the avoidance of double charges arising in specified circumstances.

Regulation 1 provides the title and commencement date.

Regulation 2 contains definitions.

Regulation 3 describes the scope of the regulations.

Regulation 4 provides for the avoidance of a double charge where property given by a PET is subsequently returned (otherwise than for full consideration) by the donee to the transferor, and as a result of the transferor's death, both that property and the PET become chargeable to tax. If charging the property as part of the death estate produces a higher amount of tax than would be payable if the charge on the PET was taken instead, the value transferred by the original transfer (the PET) is reduced by reference to the amount of the value of that property which is included in the chargeable transfer on the death. Conversely, the PET is charged if that produces the higher amount of tax, with a corresponding reduction in the value of that property which is included in the chargeable transfer on the death. To avoid the value of the same property entering twice into the tax calculations this reduction applies for all purposes of the tax.

Example 1.5 – Death within seven years

A gives B a house; B dies and leaves the house to A; A dies within seven years of his gift to B. The gift of the house from A to B is chargeable, because it is made within seven years of death, and the house is also chargeable as part of A's death estate.

There appears to be scope to use regulation 4 for tax avoidance. This is because, to the extent that partial consideration is paid by the transferor in buying back an asset previously gifted to the transferee, the value of his estate is diminished. The regulation allows HMRC to bring into charge either:

- the PET; or
- the value of the property comprised in the transferor's estate immediately before his death;

whichever produces the greater liability to IHT, *but not both.*

Example 1.6 – Partial consideration

A gives his house worth £200,000 to B in 2010. He does not continue to reside there because the gift with reservation provisions would then apply. Shortly before his death in 2012 he buys the property back from B for partial consideration of £175,000. He then dies. Assuming the value of the property increases to £225,000 by A's death this amount will be brought into charge, but the PET will not. A's estate has been reduced by the £175,000 consideration paid, less the increase in value of the property of £25,000 giving a net reduction of £150,000.

If, following its repurchase, the house became A's residence again, POAT could be in issue because the contribution condition would be satisfied. If A does not live there, POAT should not be a problem.

Regulation 5 provides for the avoidance of a double charge where there is a transfer of value by way of gift of property which is or subsequently becomes a chargeable transfer, and the property is (by virtue of the provisions relating to gifts with reservation) subject to a further transfer which is chargeable as a result of the transferor's death. As under regulation 4, whichever transfer produces the higher amount of tax as a result of the death remains chargeable, and the value of the other transfer is reduced by reference to the value of the transfer which produced that amount.

However, this reduction in value does not apply for the purposes of any relevant property trust charges arising before the transferor's death if the transfer by way of gift was chargeable to tax when it was made. Further, provision is made for credit to be given on account of any tax already paid on the transfer by way of gift against so much of the tax payable on the other transfer as relates to the value of the property in question.

Example 1.7 – Gift with reservation

C gives D a house, but reserves the right to continue to live in it, and does so until he dies five years later. There is a charge on the gift from C to D because it is within seven years of death, but because this is a gift with reservation the house is also charged as part of C's death estate.

Under the regulations, IHT is calculated, first, ignoring the value of the house at the date of death, and second ignoring the value of the lifetime gift. IHT is charged based on whichever of the two scenarios yields a higher tax charge, but a double charge on the same asset is avoided.

Regulation 6 provides for the avoidance of a double charge where a transfer of value is or subsequently becomes a chargeable transfer, and at the transferor's death his estate owes to the transferee a debt which (under the rules relating to such liabilities; see below) falls to be abated or disallowed in determining the value of the estate chargeable on the death.

Two separate calculations of tax payable as a result of the death are made. In the first, the amount of the transfer of value is reduced by the amount of the debt which is disallowed or abated. In the second, the amounts of the transfer of value and of the debt are both taken into account. The higher amount of tax is payable, but relief is given either by reducing the value of the transfer of value or by allowing the debt and charging the transfer of value in full. As under regulation 5, the reduction in value does not apply for the purposes of any charges on discretionary trusts arising before the death if the transfer of value was a chargeable transfer when it was made. Credit is allowed for some or all of the tax already paid on that transfer against the tax payable on the transferor's estate at death.

Example 1.8 – Gift and loan back

E gives F £100,000; F lends it back to E; and E dies three years later with the debt outstanding.

There is a charge on the gift from E to F, and the debt of £100,000 is not allowed against E's death estate (FA 1986, s 103) as the consideration for it was property derived from E.

The double charges relief regulations include worked examples to illustrate how regulation 6 applies in gift and loan back circumstances.

Regulation 7 provides for the avoidance of a double charge where property given by a transfer of value which is chargeable when made, is returned (otherwise than for full consideration) by the donee to the transferor, and that property is also chargeable as part of the transferor's estate on his death. It provides the same relief as is provided under regulation 4 in the case where the transfer of value was a PET when it was made, but credit is available for tax already paid. The reduction in value does not apply for the purposes of discretionary trust charges arising before the death.

Regulation 8 provides a rule to determine which of two equal amounts under regulations 4(4), 5(3), 6(3) or 7(4) is to be treated as the higher amount for the purposes of each of those regulations.

Regulation 9 introduces the Schedule, which contains a number of very helpful examples illustrating the operation of the regulations.

Finally, there is no 'pre-owned assets tax' charge if the reservation of benefit provisions apply, or if an election is made (under FA 2004, Sch 15, para 21) effectively to 'opt out' of the income tax charge and into the reservation of benefit rules for IHT purposes (see **Chapter 13**). This is where the POAT provisions and the POAT Relief Regulations come into play.

The estate rate

1.16   As discussed at **1.12**, IHT is calculated on the basis of successive bands. An example of the application of the bands to the calculation of IHT is as follows:

Example 1.9 – The estate rate

Mr A was a widower who died on 1 September 2012. He had made no previous chargeable transfers but left an estate of £259,000 and had an 'old' interest in possession under his father's will trust in £150,000.

	£
Estate for IHT purposes:	409,000
Charged at 0%	(325,000)
Balance chargeable	84,000
Tax at 40%	33,600

The estate rate would be calculated, for apportioning between the estate and the will trust, and between the beneficiaries, as follows:

$$\frac{33,600 \times 100}{409,000} = 8.215\%$$

The 'grossing-up' concept

1.17   The position for lifetime chargeable transfers (eg any settlement for an individual other than a disabled person after 22 March 2006, or a gift to a company) is that the transferor is primarily accountable for IHT (ss 199(1) and 204(6)). If the transferor wishes to make a gift to the recipient which is net of IHT, the transferor must also make a further gift of the IHT which is paid to HMRC. In other words, the difference between a gross transfer and a net transfer is as follows.

- In the case of a gross transfer, it is the transferee who pays the tax, so he will be left with the after tax amount.

- In the case of a net transfer, where the transferor himself wishes to pay the IHT so that the transferee receives and keeps the net transfer, grossing up of that net transfer is necessary, in order to ascertain the gross amount on which the tax payable (by the transferor) will reduce that gross amount to the net transfer in the hands of the transferee.

This concept of grossing up is a direct corollary of the consequential loss formula; namely, one does not measure the benefit received by the donee, but the loss suffered by the donor and in calculating such loss pursuant to s 5(3) and (4) the IHT liability increases the amount of the loss to the donor.

Explaining this concept in more detail:

- The value transferred is the amount by which the transferor's estate is reduced.

- Therefore, one must value his estate *before and after* the transfer.

- In valuing the transferor's estate, certain (but not all) liabilities may be deducted.

- Among such deductible liabilities is his liability to pay IHT.

- If the transferor pays IHT his estate is therefore reduced by the actual gift and by the IHT on that gift.

- The transferor accordingly makes a transfer of (gift plus tax) such a sum as after deduction of the IHT leaves the net amount with the donee.

Example 1.10 – Grossing up of gift (1)

Mr B has already used up his nil rate band and makes a net lifetime gift of £80,000 to his son's company, and wishes to pay the IHT himself. The IHT rate (ie half the normal 40% rate for a chargeable lifetime transfer) is 20%. The value of the gift is accordingly multiplied by 100/80 to gross it up and make it £100,000; and this latter figure is the amount to be added on to Mr B's cumulative ladder. IHT at 20% on £100,000 reduces the amount to the net sum of £80,000 received by the donee company.

If, on the other hand, there had been an arrangement for the company to bear the tax, Mr B could either have given £100,000, so that after paying the tax the company would have retained a net £80,000 (value of gift on Mr B's cumulative 'ladder' £100,000); or given the company £80,000 only so that after paying the tax of £16,000 the company would have been left with £64,000 (£80,000 on Mr B's ladder).

Of course, the result of the donor not bearing IHT on a chargeable gift is that the value of the gift on the cumulative ladder is reduced. It is always possible to arrange that the donee is not out of pocket by giving him further unrelated cash gifts which are exempt (eg up to the annual exemption of £3,000, or 'normal income' gifts within s 21).

Compared to the days when there were several ascending rate bands, and special tables had to be employed in order to calculate the grossing up, with rules to cancel value in respect of 'mutual transfers' the process is now comparatively simple, with a single uniform rate of 40% (or half that during lifetime) over the nil rate band (although a lower rate of 36% may apply in certain circumstances; see **1.12**). This relative simplicity is something that would-be reformers should bear in mind: some have advocated a lower general tax rate for modest estates and one or more higher rates. It is practitioners and HMRC staff who would bear the burden of any extra complexity.

If the nil rate band has been exhausted so that the relevant lifetime chargeable gift is liable at 20% the process of grossing up consists of multiplying the amount of the straight gift by 100/80 or one and a quarter. If the amount of the net gift straddles the top of the nil rate band, then the process is first to deduct from the value of the gift the balance remaining of the nil rate band and then to multiply the excess by 100/80.

Example 1.11 – Grossing-up of gift (2)

Mr C settles £325,000 on discretionary trusts in 2012–13. He wants to pay the IHT himself. He made a chargeable transfer of £165,000 gross and net in 2010–11, so he has unused £160,000 of the nil rate band. Of the present gift, the nil rate band shelters £160,000. Against the balance of £165,000 may be set any unused £3,000 exemption for this year and last; but assuming for simplicity that no annual exemption is available, £165,000 is multiplied by 100/80 giving a figure of £206,250.

The grossed-up gift is therefore (£160,000 plus £206,250) £366,250.

To check the calculation: gross transfer: £366,250:

	£
Deduct balance of nil rate band:	160,000
Chargeable	206,250
Tax at 20%	41,250
Net gift (£366,250 – £41,250)	325,000

The gross transfer of £366,250 is added to Mr B's cumulative ladder, which is now £165,000 plus £366,250, a total of £531,250.

There is, of course, no grossing up of exempt gifts (eg the annual £3,000 exemption (s 19) or exempt wedding gifts (s 22)). Equally, grossing up is avoided, or reduced, where the value of a transfer is reduced by reliefs, for example business/agricultural property relief at 100% or 50% (see **Chapter 15**).

Example 1.12 – Effect of business property relief

Assume in the example above that the gift was of assets worth £325,000 which were used in a business in which the donor was a partner, so that 50% relief was available (based on 2012–13 rates).

	£
Value of gift net of relief	162,500
Prior transfers	165,000
Total, partly offset by nil rate band	327,500

The nil rate band is £325,000, leaving £2,500 chargeable. This figure is grossed up by 100/80 to produce an IHT charge of:

£3,125 × 20% = £625

Check: £162,500 + £625 = £163,125 + £165,000 = £328,125 – £325,000 = £3,125 × 20% = £625.

The position when the donor dies within seven years, both for PETs which then become chargeable transfers and in respect of additional IHT on lifetime chargeable transfers, is that the donee is primarily liable for tax payable as a result of the death; and the liability of the donor's personal representatives remains secondary and relevant insofar as the donee has not paid the tax within 12 months of the death (s 204(8)); see **2.47** and **11.48** for indemnity position. This rule can be exploited in unhappy family situations.

Example 1.13 – Effect of aggregation

Fred left his house, worth £375,000, and cash of £100,000 on interest in possession trusts for his (second) wife Melanie with remainder to the children of his first marriage, Alan and Belinda. Fred had made chargeable lifetime gifts to utilise his nil rate band.

Melanie has a daughter from an earlier relationship, Celia. Melanie made lifetime gifts within the last three years of £200,000, and has an estate of £250,000. She has been advised that on her death Celia will suffer IHT because the £250,000 will be aggregated with the £475,000. Melanie gives Celia £225,000 (all of which Celia soon spent), but dies within six months.

On Melanie's death in 2012–13, the calculation is:

	£
Trust fund	475,000
Free estate	25,000
Aggregable gift	225,000
	725,000
Nil rate band 2012–13 (£325,000 – £200,000)	(125,000)
Balance	600,000
Tax at 40%	240,000

Although the tax should be 'spread', Celia will refuse to contribute towards the tax bill, claiming that, *when made*, the gift to her was free of tax because it was within the nil rate band. That is correct, although Melanie's lifetime gifts became chargeable transfers on her death within seven years, which utilised part of her nil rate band. The trustees will pay it from the trust fund as far as it will go. The executors will be left to pick up any balance: see s 204(8).

The above is an illustration of the potential unfairness which can arise due to the nil rate band being set against lifetime transfers, as opposed to setting it against lifetime transfers and the death estate proportionately.

In the case of PETs, therefore, where the donor dies within seven years, the donee will normally be liable for IHT on the amount of the gifts as made, with no grossing up. As for any additional IHT on death in respect of lifetime chargeable gifts, this tax is payable on the amount of the lifetime transfer, so that if the amount was then grossed up because the donor paid the lifetime tax, it is the amount of the grossed-up gift upon which the additional IHT at death will be charged which the donee is called upon to pay. If the lifetime tax was paid by the donee so that the value of the gift was not originally grossed up, the additional IHT on death is calculated on that same 'ungrossed-up' value (see s 204(7)).

Order of gifts

1.18   Where two or more chargeable transfers are made on the same day the tax is calculated as if there had been a single transfer and the IHT apportioned pro rata (s 266(2)).

Example 1.14 – Gifts on the same day

David Brown, having used his annual exemptions, on 1 August 2012 gave £179,500 to his sister's discretionary trust and £179,500 to his brother's company. Both gifts are lifetime chargeable transfers. IHT on a gift of £359,000 would be £6,800 (half of 40% on excess of £359,000 over the nil rate band of £325,000) giving an average rate of 1.894%. Tax payable by the sister's trustees and the brother's company is therefore 1.894% of £359,000 or £3,400 each.

If David had made the gifts on consecutive days, then if the first gift had been to the sister's discretionary trust, it would have been free of IHT being within the £325,000 exemption, and IHT of £6,800 would have been payable in respect of the gift to the brother's company.

It should be noted that this provision governing chargeable transfers made on the same day does not apply on death. Moreover, if the value transferred depends upon the order in which the transfers are made, for example, because one transfer is a gross amount and the other a net amount, then s 266(1) provides that the transfers taking place on the same day are deemed to take place in the order which produces the lowest level of IHT.

Getting the order right

1.19   Where the transferor is proposing to make two gifts, one a PET and the other a lifetime chargeable transfer, look at:

● the respective values and amounts; and

● the likely tax charge that would arise if the transferor did not survive seven years.

On death of the transferor within seven years, the chargeable transfer cannot obtain taper relief in years six and seven because it has already suffered 50% (ie half) of the normal IHT rate (s 7(5)). That might suggest that the PET should come first.

However, this view can be complicated by factors including:

● the possible increase in rate on the ten-year periodic and exit charges if the chargeable transfer is to a relevant property trust;

● the fact that, in HMRC's view, the annual IHT exemption is allocated against PETs when made (IHTM14143), which could therefore distort the IHT position of the later chargeable transfer upon the PET becoming chargeable.

● the undoubted usefulness of the nil rate band for chargeable transfers.

Do the sums: do not just rely on intuition. A general rule emerges that if there is a chargeable lifetime transfer, for example into most lifetime trusts after

22 March 2006, together with other transfers (eg PETs), the gift into the trust should be made *first* so as to minimise ten-yearly charges and exit charges.

MAIN ANTI-AVOIDANCE PROVISIONS

1.20   The IHT legislation contains some far-reaching anti-avoidance provisions, the main ones being summarised in this section (see also **2.77**). Certain 'targeted' anti-avoidance rules are covered elsewhere in this book, such as those introduced in FA 2012 to block specific avoidance schemes which broadly involved a UK-domiciled individual acquiring an interest in settled excluded property, where the arrangements resulted in a reduction in the individual's estate for IHT purposes (see **7.109**). See also **Chapter 11** for specific discussion of the 'anti-*Ingram*' legislation. Practitioners should always give proper regard to these anti-avoidance provisions, particularly associated operations (s 268).

Wherever possible, use available exemptions and reliefs in as straightforward a manner as possible, rather than sophisticated and artificial schemes which will be opposed by HMRC. It should be noted that the disclosure of tax avoidance schemes provisions introduced in FA 2004 (ss 306–319) now apply for IHT purposes as well (see **2.78**).

For an academic discussion of the '*Ramsay*' principle, look first at the judgment of the House of Lords in *W T Ramsay Ltd v IRC* [1981] STC 174. Those ideas were developed in *Furniss v Dawson* [1984] STC 153, but were relaxed slightly in *Craven v White, IRC v Bowater Property Developments Ltd* and *Baylis v Gregory* (all at [1988] STC 476). The idea that one may disregard some steps in a complicated transaction to 'drill down' to the essential and taxable event was developed further in *Fitzwilliam v IRC* [1993] STC 502, *Hatton v IRC* [1992] STC 140 and *IRC v McGuckian* [1997] STC 908.

A further formulation of the '*Ramsay* principle' can be found in the House of Lords decision in *MacNiven v Westmoreland Investments* [2001] STC 237. Subsequently, the *Ramsay* principle was considered in cases including *Hong Kong Collector of Stamp Revenue v Arrowtown Assets Ltd*, FCA(HK) 2003, 6 ITLR 454, *CIR v Scottish Provident Institution* [2005] STC 1 and *Mawson v Barclays Mercantile Finance Ltd* [2005] STC 11: see **2.77**.

The more recent cases on the subject of tax avoidance have tended towards adopting a purposive construction of the legislation, and the *Ramsay* principle could perhaps now be better described as a rule of statutory construction, rather than a definitive statement on the subject.

As indicated at **2.77**, two separate tax avoidance strategies fared rather differently in *Astall and others v HMRC* [2009] EWCA Civ 1010 and *Mayes* *v HMRC* [2009] EWHC 2443 (Ch). In the latter case, a subsequent appeal by HMRC was unsuccessful (*Revenue & Customs v Mayes* [2011] EWCA Civ 407). The Court of Appeal noted that *Ramsay* does not lay down a special doctrine of revenue law striking down avoidance schemes on the ground that they are artificial composite transactions and that parts of them can be disregarded for fiscal purposes because they are self-cancelling and were inserted solely for tax avoidance purposes and for no commercial purpose.

The government announced at Budget 2012 that it intends to introduce a general anti-abuse rule (GAAR) in FA 2013, which will be targeted at 'artificial and abusive tax avoidance schemes'. The draft Finance Bill 2013 legislation was subsequently published on 11 December 2012. However, it may still be necessary to consider the *Ramsay* doctrine and the rule of statutory construction, because cases where the application or otherwise of the GAAR will no doubt come before the tribunal and judges will need to look at the legislation realistically.

Associated operations

1.21   We have already seen that, in general terms, a transfer of value is any disposition made by a person as a result of which the value of his estate immediately after the disposition is less than it would be but for the disposition; and the amount by which it is less is the value transferred by the transfer (s 3(1)). As mentioned above, 'disposition' is defined by s 272 to include a disposition effected by associated operations.

The definition of 'associated operations' in s 268 closely follows the wide estate duty definition (FA 1940, s 59) and enables transactions to be treated as gifts whether made directly or indirectly and made by way of two or more operations.

There is, however, one IHT addition. Under s 3(3) where a person's estate is diminished by an omission to exercise a right, he may be deemed to have made a gift unless 'the omission was not deliberate'. Under s 268(1) an omission can be one of the associated operations (reversing *Nichols v IRC* [1975] STC 278, CA). Instances of such omissions could include failing to take up a favourable rights issue; foregoing the right to sue or contest a will; or failing to apply for a new statutory tenancy.

In the context of pension schemes, prior to changes introduced in FA 2011 an IHT charge could arise where a scheme member omitted to take their pension entitlement, such as where the member chose not to do so whilst in ill health and then died (see *DM Fryer & others (Personal Representatives of Ms P Arnold) v HMRC* [2010] UKFTT 87 (TC), TC00398). However, from 6 April 2011 a charge under s 3(3) is disapplied (by s 12(2ZA)) where a member of a registered pension scheme (or qualifying non-UK pension scheme or s 615(3) scheme) omits to exercise pension rights under the scheme.

The Special Commissioners' decision *Reynaud v IRC* [1999] STC (SCD) 18 usefully reminds us that it is not enough to show that two operations are associated. It must be shown that there is a 'disposition effected by associated operations'.

The associated operations rules are frequently brought into estate planning discussions and it is important therefore to try to understand them. Examples can be helpful. A Revenue letter in the *Law Society Gazette* of 1 March 1978 posed two cases. In the first, A sold an asset to B for £20,000. The price was left outstanding on loan, and the loan was released in yearly stages by £2,000 each year (the then annual exemption). The view was expressed that the sale and the subsequent releases of parts of the loan were associated, with the result that the Revenue might have regard to the value of the asset at the date of release of the last part of the debt.

The second case involved a controlling shareholder of a company who gave all his shares to his son on the footing that his son would pay the tax by instalments of £2,000 per annum. The father then made gifts of £2,000 a year to his son so that he could pay the instalments. Here the Revenue accepted that s 268 would not apply. The fact that the father made subsequent gifts to his son did not call for the original chargeable transfer of shares to be reviewed. These two cases are difficult to reconcile.

Other helpful examples are those posed by counsel for the taxpayer, together with the comments of counsel for the Crown, in the case stated by the Special Commissioners set out in the report of *IRC v Brandenburg* [1982] STC 555.

Generally, HMRC will regard operations as associated with each other if the prime reason for each of them taking place is that the other will also take place, or indeed has already done so. Channelling operations between spouses are not normally regarded as associated (IHTM14833). However, it would be dangerous to rely on this exception if there is clear evidence that the transfer from one spouse to the other was subject to a condition that the donee spouse made particular gifts in an agreed direction.

A general conclusion on associated operations would be that a carefully laid down series of steps accompanied by an understanding or expectation that they will all take place is almost bound to run into HMRC opposition; whereas a number of disparate transactions, each entered into separately for its own particular reasons at the time, may escape attack. For that reason many advisers recommend that there be 'a decent interval' between the transfer between spouses/civil partners before the recipient spouse/civil partner makes an onward gift. Thus, it is wise for the recipient at least to receive some income from the asset, return it as such and enjoy it (net of the tax) before disposing of any of it (though see the rule in *Pigott v Staines* below).

Another possibility, for couples of reasonable wealth, is for the 'poorer' of the two to make an unconditional gift from his or her existing resources and, some time later, to be reimbursed by the richer of the two, though perhaps not in an identical sum. Proof that the transactions were unconnected may rest in simple details, as where (in the scenario just described):

- it was urgent to make the gift, perhaps to help a child in trouble;
- the fund from which the gift had been made was an instant access account; and
- the fund from which partial reimbursement is made could not be available, if at all, until some time later.

In deciding whether two operations might be associated under s 268, proximity in time might be an important factor. In this respect it is helpful to note that s 268(2) states that a lease for full consideration is not treated as associated with any operation effected more than three years later. There is also the five-year charity rule in the related property provisions in s 161 (see **1.24**). Comparison might also be drawn with the anti-avoidance case *Pigott v Staines Investments Co Ltd* [1995] STC 114, which established that there is no mechanistic time period after which transactions cannot be linked and even steps taken ten months apart could be linked. It is also interesting to note the income tax case of *Bambridge v IRC* (1955) 36 TC 313, HL which indicates that death itself is not an 'associated operation' for the purposes of what is now ITA 2007, ss 721 and 719 (*dicta* in the Court of Appeal (1954) 36 TC 313), although the execution of a will can be.

In the context of the family company, HMRC are likely to attack artificial arrangements designed to mitigate the diminution in value formula where there is loss of control. For example, ignoring business relief, A owns 51% of the shares of a company and transfers 2% to his wife who thereupon gifts that 2% interest to her son. This could incur a (manageable) related property charge on 2/51 × 51% of the value of these shares; and thereafter A could proceed to make a gift out of a 49% holding (ie valued on a minority basis). HMRC are likely to attack this arrangement as being an associated operation, and ignore the intermediate gift from A to his wife with the result that A's gift is out of a 51% controlling interest, not out of a 49% holding.

How does the *Ramsay* principle apply to IHT in the context of associated operations? Do we really need s 268? It is wider in its effect than the *dicta* of Lord Brightman in *Furniss* because the operations merely have to affect the same property or property representing that property, or one operation be effected with reference to the other.

In the CTT cases of *Brandenburg* and *IRC v Trustees of Sir John Aird's Settlement* [1983] STC 700, CA the courts ignored arguments on associated operations, and decided the cases on other grounds. Thus in *Sir John Aird's* case an attempt to structure a 'contingent' interest in possession failed: the contingency was somewhat artificial, namely that the intended beneficiary should survive a 'designated person', who was identified as the first whose name should appear in the obituaries of *The Times* or the *Daily Telegraph* for 1 December 1975. The Court of Appeal held that the trust interest did not depend on survival, but merely on the publication of the newspaper: there was no real possibility that no name would appear in the obituary column of one of the papers for that day. All this would seem to indicate a reluctance to resort to the s 268 code where there is another basis for proceeding with the problem.

Compare that with the unchallenged view of Lord Jauncey in *Macpherson v IRC* [1988] STC 362 HL, a case about a discretionary trust fund which included paintings. There, the Crown had accepted that, since the associated operations rules in (what is now) s 268 could cover a multitude of events affecting the same property, some limitation had to be placed on them. Reference had been made to the earlier case of *IRC v Herdman* (1967) 45 TC 394 (Northern Ireland CA), an income tax case concerned with the transfer of assets abroad provisions (under what is now ITA 2007, ss 716ff), which also contain associated operations provisions; see in particular ITA 2007, s 719. There the court had decided that the only associated operations which were relevant were those by which, in conjunction with the transfer, the income of the assets could be enjoyed, and did not include those associated operations taking place after the taxpayer had obtained the power to enjoy the income.

Lord Jauncey then quoted the definition of 'disposition' in (what is now) s 10(3) and referred to 'a series of transactions and any associated operations'. In his view, gratuitous benefit qualified both 'transactions' and 'associated operations'. Thus, if an associated operation:

- was not intended to confer such a benefit; or
- did not form part of and contribute to a scheme which did confer such a benefit,

it was not relevant. This House of Lords decision is helpful to practitioners. It narrows the scope of associated operations to clearly relevant transactions. It also provides a clear working hypothesis in this difficult area, although actually applying the hypothesis to particular circumstances may be difficult.

If we may apply the associated operations code in a practical way, there seems to be no need to rely on *Ramsay*. In *Kwok Chi Leung Karl v Comr of Estate Duty* [1988] STC 728, a Privy Council case from Hong Kong, Lord Oliver expressed surprise that *Ramsay* arguments had not been put forward. There was no reference in that case to any Hong Kong associated operations rules.

In *Fitzwilliam v IRC* [1993] STC 502, HL, the Revenue made no serious attempt to use the associated operations argument. The Crown referred to the associated operations provisions at an early stage but then abandoned any intention to rely on the code and based their case wholly on *Ramsay*.

Can we use multiple discretionary trusts to maximise the availability of nil rate bands? Yes: this should not normally be challenged by HMRC on the basis of *Ramsay* or associated operations: see *Rysaffe Trustees (CI) Ltd v IRC* [2003] STC 536. The Court of Appeal held that five separate settlements created on different dates, albeit on very similar terms, constituted separate settlements for the purposes of the ten-year anniversary charge under s 64. The Revenue's contention that there was only a single settlement, existing by associated operations, was firmly rejected. The settlor intended separate settlements and that intention was paramount. Hence, each settlement was eligible for its own nil rate band. Each settlement had been created by a 'disposition' within s 43.

Restriction on freedom to dispose

1.22   Provisions in a contract whereby the right to dispose has in some way been excluded or restricted are to be ignored in valuing the transfer to the extent that such exclusion or restriction is not for a consideration in money or money's worth (s 163).

This anti-avoidance provision is particularly designed to deter artificial arrangements in partnership agreements, for instance, as regards options below market value and transfers of goodwill, and pre-emption provisions in articles of association of a company which aim at artificially reducing the market value of the shares.

Artificial reductions in the value of settled property – depreciatory transactions

1.23   Transactions between the trustees and the beneficiaries (or persons connected with the beneficiaries) will be assessed as:

- a transfer of value in an 'estate' interest in possession trust; or

- the occasion of an interim or 'exit' charge in a relevant property (eg discretionary) trust,

where the transaction results in a reduction in value of the trust fund, for example, the creation of a lease designed to reduce the freehold value, or value-shifting operations with company shares (ss 52(3), 65(1)(b)) (see also **8.3**).

The 'related property' provisions

1.24   These provisions (s 161) give rise to particularly sinister valuation problems because of a special rule in respect of property held by husband and wife (or civil partner), or transferred by either of them to a charity or public body within the last five years. The period of five years in the case of a transfer to a charity or public body still continues from the date of transfer whether or not the transferee is still holding the property, and thus inhibits planning.

The section provides that property in a spouse's estate is related to property comprised in the estate of his spouse, or property which is or has been within the preceding five years the property of a charity or public body. The effect of the section is that when the spouse transfers his property and the value of that property is less than the value of the 'appropriate portion' of that property and the related property, then that appropriate portion of the aggregate value is the value transferred. This rule applies in general to lifetime transfers and dispositions on death and can have particular application to private company shares, freehold and leasehold properties, and to jointly held sets or collections of valuable objects.

It is far less likely to have application to quoted securities. HMRC are of course able to (and do) make use of Companies House records for this purpose. For instance, in Example 1.1, if Mr Gold had owned only 50% and Mrs Gold 30%, the position would still have been as in that example, namely, as if Mr Gold had been disposing of a proportion of an 80% holding.

Of course, in view of 100% business relief (alongside 50% relief) for transfers of relevant business property on or after 10 March 1992 (see **Chapter 15**), the problems associated with transfers out of related property are no longer so formidable. Nevertheless, care is still required, not least because business relief is not available in respect of all companies or businesses (see s 105(3)–(7)).

The rules on related property have a most unfortunate retrospective effect where a family company has been set up before the IHT (or CTT) era and the shares issued to husband and wife, and where the shares have now become valuable. Having regard to the related property provisions, any transfer of shares, however small, will involve a valuation of the aggregate shareholding owned by the spouses. Although the aim of the related property provisions is to avoid fragmentation of values, its application is much wider; thus the fact that the spouse in question has acquired an asset independently and for full consideration is irrelevant.

The related property provisions actually extend beyond s 161 because by virtue of s 49(1) a person beneficially entitled to an interest in possession is treated as beneficially entitled to the property in which the interest subsists (see also **7.8** and **7.14**). This would indicate that a holding of family company shares in an individual's estate is related always to a holding of similar shares in which the individual has such an interest in possession under a settlement.

However, following a statement by the Revenue (Press Release, 9 May 1990), this aggregation is not considered to apply when an interest in possession comes to an end during the lifetime of the individual entitled to it. Under s 52(1) the value for IHT is 'equal to the value of the property in which his interest subsisted'. The statement went on to say that the settled property 'should be valued *in isolation* without reference to any similar property'. The statement concluded that the practice was without prejudice to the application of the *Ramsay* principle or the associated operations code in any appropriate case. The statement does not apply to excluded property (see **1.36**).

This practice applies only to the valuation of settled property on the termination of an interest in possession *in lifetime* (which is normally a PET and becomes chargeable only on the death of the former life tenant within seven years), and is based purely on the peculiar wording of s 52(1). Section 52 applies to interests in possession that were in existence before FA 2006 and to the coming to an end of such an interest if it is an IPDI, a DPI or a TSI. All these terms are discussed more fully later. It does not apply to an interest in possession terminating on death, where the related property provisions still apply, or to the valuation of property (aggregation) which is part of an individual's free estate. It is only settled property in which an interest in possession subsists and which is terminated *in lifetime* where valuation in isolation from other related property (eg part of the individual's own estate) is in point.

In *Arkwright and another (Personal Representatives of Williams, deceased) v IRC* [2004] STC 1323, Mr and Mrs W owned a freehold property as tenants in common. Mr W died, leaving Mrs W a life interest in his 50% share of the property, remainder to his daughters. Mrs W and the daughters executed a deed of variation so that Mrs W's interest in the property vested in his daughters. The Revenue determined that IHT was due on 50% of the property's agreed open market value. Mrs W's daughters (the personal representatives) appealed to the Special Commissioners, contending that Mrs W's interest should be valued at less than 50% of the vacant possession value, because his widow had the right to occupy the property and not have it sold without her consent.

The Commissioner accepted this contention and allowed the appeal in principle, holding that the value of Mrs W's interest should be determined in accordance with s 161(3), ie on the basis that both shares in the property were related, and that their values should therefore be aggregated. The Court of Appeal subsequently held that the Commissioner was also entitled to conclude that the value of the deceased's interest in the property was not inevitably a mathematical one half of the 'vacant possession value, rejecting the Revenue's argument that s 161(4) applied to treat the land as 'units' and that the valuation ratio was one half. However, the Court considered that it was a step too far for the Commissioner to determine, as a matter of fact, that the value of Mr W's interest was less than a mathematical one half of the vacant possession value. Rather, this was a question for the Lands Tribunal to determine. As stated at **1.6**, following the *Arkwright* case, HMRC subsequently stated (in *Revenue & Customs Brief 71/07*) that, following legal advice, they would apply s 161(4) when valuing shares of land as related property in cases received after publication of that Brief (27 November 2007).

Subsequently, in *Price v Revenue and Customs Commissioners* [2010] UKFTT 474 (TC), the appellant (the executor and trustee of his late wife's estate) appealed against an IHT determination in respect of a property owned in equal half shares by husband and wife as tenants in common. The entire property was valued at £1.5 million, whereas the half shares of the property, valued independently, amounted to £637,500 each. The appellant argued (among other things) that 'the value of that and any related property' in s 161(1) meant the value of the two property interests valued independently of each other. HMRC argued that the above expression meant the totality of both interests treated as a single item of property. The tribunal held that the related property provisions hypothesise a notional sale and that the property interests were to be valued on the basis that they are offered for sale together and at the same time. If this resulted in a greater price than if the interests had been offered individually, then (if the sale would not have required undue effort or expense) the greater price must be attributed to the two items by applying the formula in s 161(3). The appeal was therefore dismissed.

Despite the possible availability of business relief, great care should be taken to consider future planning possibilities when making a gift of property such as company shares. Subject to the *Ramsay* principle, it may well be better to give part of a shareholding to the donee outright and part to him by way of settlement on an interest in possession trust. The donee will then in the future have the flexibility to terminate his interest in possession without an aggregate valuation. This planning idea remains relevant notwithstanding the changes to trust taxation introduced by FA 2006. In many cases, the trust will be a relevant property trust and there is no possibility of aggregation with the estate of the life tenant.

It is doubted whether different interests in land, such as a leasehold interest and a freehold reversion, constitute related property. Similarly, different classes of shares held by, say, husband and wife, with different rights attaching thereto, may not be related property.

Example 1.15 – Transfer of related property

Hawker sold 10% of the shares in his family company on 17 November 2010 to his nephew for £20,000 (par) and died on 1 October 2012. Hawker previously held 41% of the shares and his wife 39%. It was agreed with HMRC Shares & Assets Valuation that 80% of the shares were worth £1,000,000, 70% were worth £800,000, and 10% were worth £50,000.

Hawker is connected with his nephew within the meaning of s 270 and the sale was not at an arm's-length price under s 10 (Note: the position might be different if Hawker's nephew had paid full market value (£50,000) for the shares, on the basis that there was no intention to confer a gratuitous benefit (s 10).)

The transfer has to be valued at: the value before the gift, namely:

	£
41/80ths × £1,000,000 =	512,500
Less the value after, 31/70ths × £800,000 =	354,285

ie £158,215 under the related assets provisions of s 161.

	£
The transfer (ignoring business relief) is:	158,215
Less: consideration paid	(20,000)
Net	138,215

In particular, where husband and wife together have voting control of a company, and it is proposed to reduce their combined holdings so that control is lost, it is generally preferable for the spouse with the lower holding of shares to make the gift that loses control. If this situation is contrived, the s 268 rules on associated operations are likely to be applied, but if the inequality is a given, long-standing state of affairs, s 268 should not be applicable.

It is therefore wise to plan the allocation of shareholdings in a new company, when the shares are worth their initial subscription price only, with great care. It is at that stage that plans can be laid for a future transaction whereby control of the company can be relinquished with least impact for IHT. The broad principle (which will vary in individual circumstances) is that shares should be spread around (eg 45% to the husband, 15% to the wife and, say, 40% to children (in a settlement if amount and relief allows, which it may well do)).

If, later, it is desired to make a gift of a 15% shareholding (bringing the related holdings of husband and wife down to 45%), the IHT charge will reflect a diminution in value from a control aggregate holding to a minority. A gift by the wife of her 15% will involve the loss of a 15% holding (a quarter of the value of the combined 60%); but the diminution in value of the husband's shareholding because control has been lost escapes possible IHT. If the 60%

had been in his sole name and he had made the 15% gift, the IHT charge would have been on the whole diminution in value of a 45% as against a 60% holding.

Example 1.16 – Gift by spouse

The value *per share* of a 60% holding in X Ltd (1,000 shares issued) is £1,500. The value per share of a minority 45% holding is £500. If the 60% holding is in the husband's sole name, and there is no related property, a gift of 15% (150 out of the 600 shares) will produce a diminution of £675,000 for the husband (£900,000 down to £225,000).

If the shares are held 45% by the husband and 15% by the wife, and the wife gives away her 15%, the diminution is of £225,000 only (ie 150 × £1,500). The accompanying diminution of £450,000 in the husband's estate (from 45% on a control basis to 45% on a minority basis) is not caught. Business relief has been ignored in this illustration.

For private trading companies the problems associated with related property are undoubtedly eased by the availability of 100% business relief (together with the 50% relief) for transfers and other events on or after 10 March 1992 (see **Chapter 15**). Nevertheless, difficulties still remain and great care is necessary in considering both IHT and the attendant CGT results.

A further possibility may be worth noting, particularly where the combined husband and wife holding just spans control, say 51%; that is, to sell a small holding of shares, say 2%, at arm's length without any gratuitous intent (see s 10). The purchaser might well be a trusted employee, who should take separate advice both as regards the consideration as well as the effect on him of the employment income legislation, particularly employment-related securities.

In the context of disposals between connected persons careful consideration should also be given to the CGT aspects having regard in particular to the CGT rules on disposals of assets in a series of transactions to connected persons (see TCGA 1992, s 19). These rules apply to the fragmentation of an asset (for example, when an individual splits up a large shareholding in a private company by disposing of parts to two or more relatives etc within a six-year period), and the greater value of the undivided asset can be substituted.

Tax chargeable in respect of certain future payments

1.25   This anti-avoidance provision (s 262) acts as a deterrent against the sort of transaction where, for example, there is a sale for partial consideration (ie a transfer of value) on which the purchaser pays the agreed price more than one year after the original transaction; or the vendor delivers the subject matter of the contract more than one year after the original disposal.

It applies where either the purchaser pays more than the market value of the asset (ie a disguised gift of cash) or the vendor receives a lower purchase price than the true value of the asset (ie a disguised partial gift of the asset).

In these circumstances s 262 assumes that the chargeable transfer is made at the time the payment is made or the asset is transferred; but at the current value on each occasion. The section is an anti-avoidance measure to prevent the making of a transfer of value in advance where an asset is likely to increase in value.

Example 1.17 – Sale of house in stages

Father sells house to son for £60,000, payable by six annual instalments of £10,000 each (discounted present value of instalments, say £40,000). The market value on sale is £180,000 and the gift element therefore £140,000. By the time the third instalment is paid, the value of the house has increased to £240,000.

The formula to be applied to this instalment for s 262 purposes is as follows:

$$\frac{\text{Value of asset transferred}}{\text{Total value at time of gift}} \times \text{original gift element}$$

$$\frac{240,000}{6} \times \frac{140,000}{180,000} = £31,111$$

This is grossed up and taxed as a gift at the date of the third instalment payment. One-sixth share of the house passes with each instalment (and a separate similar calculation is done for each instalment).

It should be emphasised, however, that although s 262 applies to a situation where the father agrees to transfer an asset in stages to B, it does not apply where the father simply sells an asset to B at market value with payment by instalments.

Since s 262(1) provides that 'tax (if any) shall be charged as if' it would follow from s 3A(6) that the instalment dispositions cannot be PETs and must therefore be taxed as lifetime chargeable transfers. In these circumstances, it would seem far better to replace the instalment transaction by a simple PET, avoiding the traps of the section.

As future payments are treated as separate dispositions, the availability of IHT exemptions must be considered at the time of each payment. Thus the annual, small gifts or normal expenditure out of income exemptions can potentially be claimed on each disposition (IHTM14873).

Free loans etc

1.26 An interest-free loan can be virtually as beneficial to the borrower as a gift. Accordingly, at an earlier stage of the legislation, a tax charge was imposed on the notional interest forgone on an interest-free or cheap loan. The same principle applied for use or occupation of land or chattels at a non-commercial rent or hire. These provisions were, however, abolished as from 6 April 1981, presumably because in most cases the interest etc forgone would have been exempt from (the then) CTT as normal expenditure. The general use of loans, etc, is discussed in **Chapter 11**.

The loan principle has been used in what are known as 'inheritance trusts' of single premium policies, mentioned at **11.53**. Following the changes in FA 2006 that treat lifetime gifts into most trusts as chargeable transfers, these trusts appear less attractive than before in the sense that the trust will be subject to the relevant property trust regime, with its attendant complications. FA 2006 contains a measure of transitional relief in respect of TSIs of settled property comprising life assurance policies entered into before 22 March 2006 (IHTA 1984, s 49E).

'Back-to-back' life policies

1.27 Sections 21(2) and (3) and 263 operate to disqualify so-called 'back-to-back' arrangements from benefiting from the 'normal expenditure' relief. The offending arrangement is one where an individual purchases one or more annuities to enable him to take out one or more life policies in favour of beneficiary(ies) which under normal circumstances would not have been an accepted risk by an insurance company except at weighted premiums.

HMRC practice (as for estate duty) is not to disqualify the gifts under the normal expenditure exemption where it can be shown that the life policy was issued on 'normal' terms. This means that full evidence of health must have been obtained and that the terms on which the policy was issued would have been the same even if the annuity had not been bought (SP E4). In such circumstances the transactions will not be associated operations. In the case of back-to-back life policy arrangements involving husband and wife (or civil partners), full medical evidence should be obtained in respect of both parties (*Smith and others v Revenue and Customs Commissioners* [2008] STC 1649; see **14.20**).

For IHT, there is one major drawback which makes these sorts of back-to-back arrangements largely impractical; namely that the capital element of the annuity is not regarded as income for the normal expenditure exemption.

The value chargeable where such back-to-back operations have taken place is not to exceed the lesser of:

- the cost of the annuity and the premiums paid to date; and

- the value of the greatest benefit capable of being conferred at any time by the policy.

The latter part of the formula is capable of quantification for non-profit life policies but problems arise in the case of with-profit, equity and unit linked policies.

PETA policies

1.28   The above provisions have acted as a deterrent against the linked use of an annuity and a policy as a deathbed planning scheme. Attempts were made to achieve similar ends on slightly different lines. This was the PETA plan whereby the individual effected two policies. The first was a single premium pure endowment policy (giving regular annual withdrawals of capital to the individual). The second was a term assurance for the specified beneficiary who (because maturity of the endowment was set at age 105) could be expected to take the remaining capital on the individual's death.

Use of this plan together with the old-style 'inheritance trust' arrangements was terminated by FA 1986, Sch 20, para 7, which brought them within the gifts with reservation regime (a simpler new style inheritance trust, avoiding the reservation problems, has now been brought forward – see **14.30**). HMRC are likely to consider any pre-existing PETA policies closely (see IHTM20410).

It should be noted that the back-to-back arrangement contemplates a purchased life annuity, bought out of the individual's own resources. The anti-avoidance provisions do not apply where the individual becomes entitled to a pension annuity under registered pension scheme arrangements. Here all the pension instalments are subject to income tax (there is no untaxed 'capital content' proportion as with a purchased annuity). The result is that the individual is free to regard the whole of his pension income as available (over and above his living expenses) for normal income exempted gifts (see **12.4**) providing him with a useful opportunity to effect an IHT-free policy in trust for his beneficiaries (see **14.10** onwards).

Finally, certain insurance policies call into question whether a 'pre-owned assets' income tax charge potentially arises. Following correspondence with the Association of British Insurers, HMRC issued a technical note 'Income Tax and Pre-Owned Assets Guidance' dealing with insurance policies, which was superseded by guidance in the Inheritance Tax Manual. The guidance broadly indicates that 'discounted gift trusts' (IHTM44112) and 'loan trusts' (IHTM44113) are not normally caught by the pre-owned assets regime, but that business trusts (or partnership policies) are potentially affected by the rules (IHTM44115). For further information on pre-owned assets, see **Chapter 13**.

Again, the use of these trusts was threatened by FA 2006 as originally drafted. Strong representations achieved some amelioration of the rules, at least for existing policies: see **1.26**.

Close companies

1.29   The provisions dealing with close companies are contained in ss 94–102 and 202. Where a close company as defined for corporation tax (covering the normal family type of company), and whether or not UK resident (s 102(1)), makes a transfer of value, the amount transferred is apportioned among the participators (meaning broadly the shareholders). They are then charged on the grossed-up equivalent of such amount according to their rights and interests in the company. The deemed transfer is however reduced by the amount by which the value of the estate of the participator is *increased* by the company's transfer (s 94(1)). However, for this purpose we must exclude any rights or interests in the company, for example, allotment of shares in the company.

Having regard to this permitted reduction, the section operates only rarely. It is largely restricted to extending the meaning of 'transfer' in s 98. Thus, a transfer can include:

- any alteration or extinguishment of unquoted company shares or loan capital, for example the variation of rights attaching to shares so that the estate owner's equity is watered down; or

- the redemption of debentures, thereby increasing the equity capital; or

- a mere issue of new shares, for example, to an outsider, especially if at a favourable price.

Depending on the circumstances, however, it might be possible to argue on the basis of s 10 that the transfer was not intended to confer gratuitous benefit, but was part of the commercial arrangements to secure the transferee's services.

Moreover, there will be no liability to the extent that the transferee suffers income tax or corporation tax (eg as an income distribution by the company); or where a participator is domiciled abroad in respect of foreign assets. Transfers of value can be traced through another close company, but there is protection against a double charge where a participator holds shares in both companies (s 95).

Liability for the s 94 tax

1.30   A liability under s 94 is primarily that of the company. The purchasers of shares of such a company should obtain an appropriate warranty from the vendors. Secondarily liable are the participators themselves, the value becoming part of their cumulative total grossed up. There is an exception to this last rule that applies to a person to whom not more than 5% of the value transferred is apportioned. In that case the company remains solely liable. The value is not part of such person's cumulative total. The charge is also adapted in respect of trustee participators.

No part of the transfer of value is apportioned to preference shares if the transfer of value 'has only a small effect on the value' of those shares compared with its effect on the value of other parts of the company's share capital. As a result, they are normally left out of account (s 96).

Where a close company surrenders losses by way of group relief under CTA 2010, s 99, such a transaction does not give rise to any charge to IHT (s 94(3)).

Certain actual or deemed transfers within a group of companies under TCGA 1992, s 171 or s 171A are ignored for purpose of apportionment amongst certain minority participators (s 97).

Charges under s 94 benefit by virtue of s 94(5) from the £3,000 per annum exemption referred to in **12.2**. A decrease in value resulting from an alteration of share etc rights under s 98(1) is ignored for the purpose of assessing a person's estate on death in view of s 171(2). It is made clear that bearing in mind the consequential loss formula of s 3(1), alteration of share etc rights only reduces the value *after* the disposition, not before. If it applied both before and after there would be no chargeable fall in value. In the case of a wholly owned subsidiary of a close company which makes a transfer of an asset at an undervalue to its parent or to a wholly owned sister subsidiary; or in the case of a dividend paid by such subsidiary to its parent company; HMRC do not regard it as a transfer of value, so that s 94 does not operate. This is less clear where the parent–subsidiary relationship is not a 100% ownership.

When a close company makes a transfer of value, IHT is charged *as if* each participator has made a transfer (s 94(1)). The transfers attributed to the participators cannot, therefore, be treated as PETs (s 3A(6)). They constitute immediate lifetime chargeable transfers of the grossed-up amounts apportioned to the respective participators by reference to their rights and interests in the company immediately after the transfer (IHTM14852).

Example 1.18 – Company property sale at undervalue

There are two shareholders in X Ltd, Mr A with 20% and Mr B with 80%. X Ltd sells a house worth £500,000 to a close friend of Mr A and Mr B for £50,000, thereby making a transfer of value of £450,000.

Of the company's transfer, £90,000 is therefore apportioned to A, and £360,000 is apportioned to B.

The £90,000 apportioned to A falls within his available nil rate band, so there is no IHT payable.

As regards B to whom £360,000 is apportioned, the calculation of IHT (applying 2012–13 rates) is as follows:

	£
First £325,000 of £360,000 (the nil rate band) gross and net	325,000
Excess £35,000 × 100/80	
(representing grossing-up fraction for half of 40% = 20% rate)	43,750
Gross transfer	368,750
IHT on that gross transfer (being 20% on excess of £43,750 over the nil rate band of £325,000)	(8,750)
Net transfer by B	360,000

If it seems odd that Mr B, who has received no benefit, is treated as making a chargeable transfer, then that is a reflection, via the see-through provisions of s 94(1), of the consequential loss principle on which IHT is based (s 3(1)).

Settlement powers

1.31   The term 'settlement power' was introduced in FA 2002, in response to the Court of Appeal's decision in *Melville and others v IRC* [2001] STC 1271, that in determining the value of transfers to a discretionary settlement, a general power of appointment over the settled property should be taken into account for IHT purposes. Subsequent legislation inserted by FA 2002 was intended to combat the substantial number of *Melville* schemes that followed the court's judgment (see **11.5**). HMRC had contended in *Melville* that the power was not 'property' within s 272. The definition of property in s 272 includes rights and interests of any description (as before), but now specifically excludes a settlement power. The term 'settlement power' is defined as any power over, or in relation to, settled property or a settlement (s 47A).

But for specific anti-avoidance legislation, it would have been possible to achieve IHT savings and simultaneously benefit another person by purchasing a settlement power. Such a power would not form part of the purchaser's estate for IHT purposes, due to its specific exclusion from the definition of 'property' in s 272. Provisions dealing with purchased settlement powers (s 55A) were therefore introduced in FA 2002 to counter this planning possibility. The rules bite where a person makes a disposition acquiring a settlement power for money or money's worth. If s 55A applies, the acquisition is precluded from being a disposition not intended to confer gratuitous benefit (see s 10(1)). The purchaser is treated as making a transfer of value, which does not take into account the value of the settlement power acquired. In addition, various exemptions (ie the spouse exemption, and the exemptions for gifts to charities, political parties, housing associations, for national purposes and to maintenance funds for historic buildings) do not apply in relation to the transfer (s 55A(1)).

Variants of the *Melville* scheme followed, which were not affected by these anti-avoidance provisions. One such '*Melville Mark II*' arrangement involved a settlor settling property on trust for an initial discretionary period (typically 100 days), following which the trust fund reverted to the settlor absolutely. The existence of this reversionary interest devalued the initial transfer of value, upon which gifts hold-over relief would be claimed for capital gains tax purposes (TCGA 1992, s 260). During the discretionary trust period, the settlor gifted his reversionary interest (eg to an interest in possession or accumulation and maintenance trust). This would be a potentially exempt transfer. However, FA 2004, s 116 and Sch 21 introduced restrictions to hold-over relief in respect of 'settlor interested' trusts with effect from 10 December 2003, thus generally rendering such *Melville* schemes unattractive (TCGA 1992, ss 169B–169E). In practice, these rules, coupled with the redefinition of all trusts for minors as 'settlor interested' in FA 2006, have curtailed many other transactions that may have been less offensive than 'son of *Melville*' schemes.

Reversionary interests

1.32 The use of arrangements involving reversionary interests such as *Melville* schemes (see above) was adversely affected by an anti-avoidance rule introduced in FA 2010. Since the FA 2006 changes to the IHT treatment of trusts, the lifetime creation of an interest in possession settlement is (subject to certain limited exceptions) an immediately chargeable transfer, with the settlement falling within the relevant property regime. However, a reversionary interest is not initially an interest in possession. In addition, a life interest does not normally form part of an individual's estate (s 5(1A)), whereas a purchased reversionary interest or a settlor's reversionary interest does.

The anti-avoidance rule (s 81A) broadly provides that if a reversionary interest in relevant property has been purchased for consideration in money or money's worth, or is held by the settlor or spouse or civil partner, a deemed disposal arises for IHT purposes when the reversionary interest ends and entitlement to an interest in possession begins. The resulting IHT charge is based on the value of the reversionary interest immediately before it ended. A gift of such a reversionary interest is prevented from being a PET. This rule applies to reversionary interests arising from 9 December 2009, but does not affect interests in possession outside the 'relevant property' regime, such as a disabled person's interest.

Interests in possession under s 5(1B)

1.33   A further anti-avoidance rule was introduced in FA 2010, broadly affecting purchased interests in possession. As noted at **1.32**, following FA 2006 the lifetime creation of an interest in possession settlement (other than a disabled person's interest) does not generally form part of the estate of the person beneficially entitled to the interest. Without an anti-avoidance rule, the arm's-length purchase of such an interest in possession could therefore have resulted in that interest falling outside a person's estate.

However, s 5(1B) provides that the interest forms part of the estate of a person who was domiciled in the UK upon becoming beneficially entitled to it, if that entitlement arose by virtue of a disposition within s 10 ('Dispositions not intended to confer gratuitous benefit'). In addition, the lifetime termination of such an interest is an immediately chargeable transfer, since it is prevented from being a PET (s 3A(6A)).

Gifts with reservation: Eversden schemes

1.34   Legislation was introduced in FA 2003 to block '*Eversden* schemes' resulting from the Court of Appeal's decision in *IRC v Eversden and another (executors of Greenstock, deceased)* [2003] STC 822. In that case, a married woman (W) settled a 5% interest in the family home she owned for herself absolutely. The other 95% was settled on an interest in possession trust to benefit her husband (H) for his life, following which the trust fund would be held on discretionary trusts for a class of beneficiaries including W. They continued to occupy the property until H's death four years later. The property was sold a year later, and a replacement property was bought together with an investment bond. The 5% and 95% interests held by W and the settlement remained unchanged. W died five years later.

The Revenue issued a notice of determination on the basis that the settled property fell to be treated as W's property on her death by virtue of the gifts with reservation provisions in FA 1986, s 102. However, the Special Commissioner, High Court and the Court of Appeal all held that the original gift of the property was an exempt transfer between spouses under IHTA 1984, s 18. The effect of FA 1986, s 102(5)(a) as originally enacted was that the spouse exemption was to be considered at the date of the original gift into settlement, not (as the Revenue had argued) at the date of W's death.

FA 2003 subsequently amended FA 1986, s 102, by introducing s 102(5A)–(5C). If the initial disposal by the donor was made on or after 20 June 2003, the effect of these changes is that the donor is treated as making a gift when the life interest of his or her spouse terminates. This means that if the donor subsequently occupies or enjoys a benefit from the settled property, the gift is one to which the reservation of benefit rules apply. Not only are *Eversden* arrangements curtailed by this legislation for IHT purposes, but they are also subject to the 'pre-owned assets' income tax charge from 6 April 2005 (see **Chapter 13**). In any event, however, one of the consequences of the FA 2006 changes was to make new *Eversden* arrangements impossible, unless the spouse who will receive a life interest qualifies as a 'disabled person' within s 89.

The anti-avoidance rules were further extended by FA 2006, introducing FA 1986, s 102ZA to counter the perceived abuse whereby a life interest in property was terminated though the occupier of it remained there. The termination of the life interest is now classified as a 'gift' to trigger the GWR provisions of FA 1986, s 102.

EXEMPTIONS, RELIEFS AND EXCLUDED PROPERTY

1.35   The table below outlines in two parts the main current exemptions and reliefs available for IHT. The first part covers the main *exemptions* (and also dispositions that are not transfers of value), namely a *full* release from IHT (or as otherwise stated); and the second part deals with the main *reliefs*, namely where there is a *partial* release or allowance. Only brief details of the exemptions and reliefs are given in the third column of the table, either by way of cross-references to other parts of this book or a short summary of the provisions. The reader's attention is drawn to the statutory references in the second column as later amended in some instances, and to the available textbooks.

The material is listed in alphabetical order so as to act as a checklist.

PART I: EXEMPTIONS

Type/Transaction	Statutory reference	Application: Lifetime only = L; Death only = D; Both = L+D	Brief summary or cross-reference
Active service, killed on	s 154	D	Applies to death from wounds, accident or disease resulting from active service; not restricted to battlefield. A wound etc need only be a contributory factor in the death: *Barty-King v Ministry of Defence* [1979] STC 218. Covered Falkland hostilities and would also apply to Gulf War and those in Afghanistan. By concession F5 covered deaths of the RUC resulting from terrorist activities
Cash options under approved personal pension and annuity schemes (from 6 April 2006, registered , qualifying non-UK or ICTA 1988, s 615(3) pension schemes)	s 152	D	**10.49**. Exercise of cash option under (typically) personal pension or retirement annuity scheme not a chargeable transfer
Charities or registered clubs, gifts to (including charitable deeds of covenant or, more commonly, Gift Aid payments)	s 23	L+D	**12.21**
Covenants, deeds of	ss 5(5), 21	L	**12.4**. The covenanted payments should generally qualify as exempt normal income expenditure (Note that income tax relief was abolished for non-charitable deeds of covenant executed on or after 15 March 1988)

Type/Transaction	Statutory reference	Application: Lifetime only = L; Death only = D; Both = L+D	Brief summary or cross-reference
Domicile abroad of transferor, settlor or deceased – as to foreign assets	ss 6(1), 48(3), 267	L+D	**17.6, 17.11**. Excluded property but note restrictive definitions of s 267 ('Persons treated as domiciled in United Kingdom')
Failure of interest in settled property before possession	ss 47, 48 and effect of s 49	L+D	Where person has a future life interest subject to a previous *subsisting* life interest and that person surrenders or assigns – no charge (NB see also 'Reversionary interests' below)
Family maintenance, dispositions for	s 11	L (HMRC's view)	**12.14**
First slice – the 'nil rate band'	ss 7–8A	L or D but cumulatively (seven years)	**1.12**. Charged at nil rate (not strictly an exemption) but very useful in planning, particularly following the introduction of transferable nil rate band facility for spouses and civil partners (in FA 2008). NB future indexation of rate bands by reference to the CPI.
Funeral expenses	s 172	D	Reasonable funeral expenses allowed (including cost of tombstone or gravestone: SP 7/87). Concession F1 allowing reasonable mourning expenses withdrawn from 9 December 2009, but potentially allowable in practice (IHTM10375)

Type/Transaction	Statutory reference	Application: Lifetime only = L; Death only = D; Both = L+D	Brief summary or cross-reference
Government-exempted securities, National Savings etc for Channel Island and Isle of Man individuals and other non-UK domiciled individuals	s 6(2), (3) s 48(4) s 267(2)	L+D	Certain government securities are exempted from IHT (as for ED) if the transferor or deceased beneficial owner was domiciled (general definition, ie not restricted by s 267(1)) and ordinarily resident abroad (NB as to ordinary residence and domicile requirements, see **17.26**)
Housing associations	s 24A	L+D	**12.21**. Covers land in UK given to registered housing association
Marriage (or civil partnership) gifts and settlements	ss 22, 57	L	**7.91**. Exemptions £5,000, £2,500, £1,000; also available on termination of interests in possession in settled property
National purposes, gifts for, (eg, museums, local authorities, government departments, universities, etc)	s 25(1), Sch 3	L+D	**12.22**
Normal income expenditure (ie not reducing standard of living)	s 21	L	**12.4**. See in particular *Bennett v IRC* [1995] STC 54
Pensions, generally (NB from 6 April 2006, arrangements with potential IHT avoidance may be challenged)	ss 151, 152	L+D	**9.28**. Most pensions to dependants (whether capitalised or not), and most lump sums on death, should give rise to no IHT charge

Type/Transaction	Statutory reference	Application: Lifetime only = L; Death only = D; Both = L+D	Brief summary or cross-reference
Pensions overseas	s 153	D	Most pensions payable by governments of former colonies or protectorates
PETs outside seven years of death of transferor	s 3A(4)	L+D	**1.3**. Not most lifetime gifts into trust (from 22 March 2006, following FA 2006)
Political parties, gifts to	s 24	L+D	Without any limit on size since 15 March 1988 (FA 1988, s 137)
Public benefit, gifts for	ss 26, 26A	L+D	**12.23**. Covers land, buildings, contents, works of art, maintenance funds, on direction of Treasury NB s 26 repealed for transfers after 16 March 1998
Reversionary interest (= excluded property)	ss 3(2), 48(1), (3) s 55(1)	L+D	**12.18** (but subject to anti-avoidance provisions in s 81A – see **1.32**)
Reverter to settlor or spouse	s 54	L+D	**7.49**. NB Restricted in respect of beneficial entitlements from 22 March 2006 Must revert during settlor's lifetime and not acquired for consideration. Interest in possession trusts only
Sales, not gifts	s 10	L	**11.49**. Applies where no gratuitous intent – arm's length

Type/Transaction	Statutory reference	Application: Lifetime only = L; Death only = D; Both = L+D	Brief summary or cross-reference
Settlements – certain exempt situations including:			
interest in possession – beneficiary becomes entitled absolutely (or to another interest in possession, subject to restrictions following FA 2006)	s 53(2)	L	**7.58**
termination of interest in possession disposal to extent consideration in money or money's worth	s 52(2)	L	**7.58**. NB Restricted in respect of beneficial entitlements from 22 March 2006
inter-spouse trusts	s 18	D	**7.90**. NB lifetime interests in possession from 22 March 2006 are not generally subject to the spouse exemption
accumulation and maintenance trusts	s 71	L+D	**7.13** (but not from 22 March 2006, although note the subsequent regime for 'bereaved minor's trusts' (s 71A) and '18 to 25' trusts (s 71D)
superannuation schemes (from 6 April 2006 registered, qualifying non-UK or ICTA 1988, s 615(3) pension schemes)	ss 151–153	L+D	**7.98**
trusts for benefit of employees	ss 28, 86	L+D	**7.101**

Type/Transaction	Statutory reference	Application: Lifetime only = L; Death only = D; Both = L+D	Brief summary or cross-reference
Settlements – *contd* charitable trust	s 23	L+D	**7.106**
annual exemption: £3,000 pa (ie per tax year)	ss 19, 57(1), 94(5)	L	**12.2.** Cumulative for one tax year only; to the extent that full value of exemption not used up, the shortfall can be carried over to the next year only; available on termination of an interest in possession in a settlement
£250 pa outright per donee per tax year	s 20	L	**12.3.** Outright, ie not *into* settlement, and not the first £250 of a larger gift (whether exempt or not); not on termination of an interest in a settlement
Spouses, transfers between	s 18	L+D	**6.3.** If transferor spouse UK domiciled and transferee spouse non-domiciled, exemption limited (by s 18(2)) on a cumulative basis (see **6.4**)
Surviving spouse exemption – IHT relief for settled property where first spouse died pre-13 November 1974 and ED paid on his/her death	s 18; and Sch 6, para 2	L+D	**7.61**
Trading expense transfers etc	s 12(1)	L+D	Exempt if allowed for income tax, etc purposes, eg, provision of some pensions by employers for employees
Trustee and personal representative, property held by transferor or deceased as	s 204	L+D	Exemption applies if the property held purely in a *fiduciary* capacity

Type/Transaction	Statutory reference	Application: Lifetime only = L; Death only = D; Both = L+D	Brief summary or cross-reference
Trustees' remuneration	s 90	L	Reasonable remuneration to a trustee not assessable to IHT
Visiting forces (excluded property)	ss 6(4), 155	L+D	Limited exemption, eg US forces and civilian auxiliaries
Voidable transfers	s 150	L+D	**12.24**. IHT cancelled where a transfer set aside by a rule of law or enactment (eg bankruptcy or a gift made under undue influence)
Waivers of remuneration and dividends	ss 14, 15	L+D	**9.12**, **9.13**. NB such waivers must be by *deed*, as there is no consideration
Interests in authorised unit trust and open ended investment company held or settled by non-domiciled individual	ss 6(1A), 48(3A)	L+D	**17.27**

PART II: RELIEFS

Type/Transaction	Statutory reference	Application: Lifetime only = L; Death only = D; Both = L+D	Brief summary or cross-reference
Alteration of dispositions taking effect on death	s 142	D	**5.32**
Art etc, works of	s 230	L+D	Certain transfers to eg HMRC in satisfaction of tax due are exempt transfers (SP 6/87)
	ss 30–35A	L+D	**16.12.** Conditional exemption. Treasury approval necessary
Agricultural property	ss 115–124C		**15.43.** Value of agricultural property reduced by 100% (primarily if owner occupied or let on a tenancy after 1 September 1995) and 50% for other cases
Business property	ss 103–114	L+D	**15.1.** Reduction of value for interest in a business – 100%; unquoted securities which by themselves or together with other such shares or securities gave control – 100%; unquoted shares – 100%; quoted shares or securities which by themselves or together with other such shares or securities gave control – 50%; property used by company controlled by transferor or by his partnership – 50%; and settled property used in business by beneficiary of settlement with qualifying interest in possession – 50%

Type/Transaction	Statutory reference	Application: Lifetime only = L; Death only = D; Both = L+D	Brief summary or cross-reference
Commorientes, rule (as to survivorship)	ss 4(2), 92	D	**5.1**. Need for survivorship clauses in defined circumstances
Double taxation relief	ss 158, 159	L+D	Application of relevant double taxation agreement or available unilateral relief
Instalment payments	s 227	L+D	**2.28**
Quick succession reliefs: interest in possession	s 141	L+D	Occurrence of chargeable events in a 5-year period with decreasing relief; relief of tax against tax already paid
cash or identifiable asset		D	As above
Quoted securities etc: Sale within 12 months of death	ss 178–189	D	**2.35**. Adjustment of value
Taper relief	s 7(4)	D	**1.12**. Relief is against tax paid, so not applicable where nil rate band available
Valuation reliefs – others: transfers of any property within 7 years *before* death	ss 131–140	D	**2.34**
falls in value of land 3 years after death (sometimes 4 years)	ss 190–198	D	**2.37** (See *Jones v IRC* [1997] STC 358)
Sales of related property within 3 years after a death	s 176	D	**2.40**
Woodlands	ss 125–130	D	**16.1**

Excluded property

1.36   Various categories of property are taken outside the ambit of the IHT charge as 'excluded property'. No account is to be taken of a disposal of excluded property in measuring the diminution in the value of a person's estate (s 3(2)) and it is left out of an estate for the purpose of a charge on death (ss 4(1) and 5(1)). The main categories of excluded property are:

- property situated abroad belonging to a person not domiciled or treated as domiciled in the UK (see **17.11**), or settled by such non-domiciled person; and

- reversionary interests not acquired for a consideration in money or money's worth or to which the settlor or his spouse is not or has not been entitled (s 48(1)).

The separate treatment of excluded property from exemptions appears in practice to be mainly a difference without a distinction in respect of a *death* situation. In the case of *lifetime* dispositions, however, where the estate includes assets required to be valued in conjunction with the excluded property, the consequential loss in value of those other assets could be considerably higher than if no excluded property existed.

Example 1.19 – Planning with excluded property

A owns absolutely 30% of the shares of an overseas company, and also has a life interest in a further 25% of such shares as settled by a non-domiciled individual. Although the 25% holding by way of interest in possession is excluded property, if A gives away 6% of his absolute holding he is losing control because he is treated as holding 55% of the shares in that company.

Depending on the circumstances, it may be that A should first terminate his interest in possession in, say, 6% of the excluded settled holding (no IHT consequences) so that the aggregate of the shares falls below 50% before he comes to make a gift out of his own holding. Note that because this interest in possession is excluded property, the May 1990 Revenue statement (see **1.24**) is not applicable.

CGT reliefs and inheritance tax

1.37   The art of estate planning is to combine capital gains tax and inheritance tax reliefs and exemptions. To deal with these taxes in isolation can often be of little avail.

For example, whilst the gift of an asset may reduce a donor's estate on death, any capital gains tax uplift in the value of that asset which would have been available had the donor retained the asset until death is lost.

APPENDIX 1.1 – IHT RATE SCALE

The following scale applies for transfers made between 6 April 2009 and 5 April 2015 (see below):

Band	Rate	Cumulative tax
Up to		
£	%	£
325,000	Nil	Nil
Over 325,000	40%	

Note: The mechanism in IHTA 1984, s 8 provides for annual upgrading of tax bands by reference to indexation, unless in any year Parliament should decide otherwise. FA 2006 increased the IHT threshold by more than expected statutory indexation, to £325,000 for 2009–10. In addition, FA 2007 initially set the threshold for 2010–11 at £350,000. However, it was subsequently announced in the Budget on 24 March 2010 that the nil rate band would be frozen at £325,000 for the tax years 2010–11 to 2014–15 inclusive.

Furthermore, following changes introduced in FA 2012, the default indexation assumption for the nil rate band will move from the retail price index to the consumer price index, with effect for chargeable transfers made from 6 April 2015. Until then, as mentioned above, the nil rate band is frozen at £325,000 (FA 2010, s 8). However, the government announced on 5 December 2012 that the nil rate band will increase by 1% (rounded up) to £329,000 in 2015–16.

Lifetime rate: With just the one positive rate of 40%, it is only the ceiling of the nil rate band that may be indexed. For lifetime chargeable transfers the normal rate of 40% is halved to 20% under s 7(2). If, however, the transferor dies within seven years, the tax is recalculated under s 7(4) using the normal 40% rate, subject to any taper relief due.

Grossing up: For lifetime chargeable gifts the transferor can either leave the donees (say, the trustees of a discretionary trust) to pay the immediate IHT out of the gift itself, or he can pay the tax himself so that the donees keep the amount given. In this latter case the gift has to be grossed up.

The example below illustrates the 'grossing up' principle (see also Examples 1.10 and 1.11).

Example 1.20 – 'Grossing up' for IHT

Mr A has already made lifetime chargeable gifts totalling £350,000 gross on 6 April 2012. On 10 May 2012 he makes another lifetime chargeable gift by transferring £100,000 on discretionary trusts. He wants to pay the IHT of 20% himself so that the trustees are left with a net £100,000.

The gift of £100,000 is therefore grossed up by a factor of 100/80 = £125,000. The IHT at 20% is £25,000, which Mr A pays. The gift for the cumulative ladder is the gross £125,000: see **1.16**.

APPENDIX 1.2 – TAPERED RATES

The rates below apply to gifts made within seven years of death. The taper relief is given by charging the percentage below of the normal death rate (ie in the fourth year before death the rate is 80% × 40% = 32% on the gift (s 7(4)).

Years before death	Percentage of death rate
0–3	100%
3–4	80%
4–5	60%
5–6	40%
6–7	20%

Examples

Note In these examples it is assumed:

(i)   No annual exemptions

(ii)   No change in rates of IHT from those in force for 2012–13.

Example 1.21 – All property passes on death or is treated as so passing

Estate of £644,000 (NB no charitable legacies)

	£		£
IHT payable on	325,000	=	Nil
on next	319,000 @ 40%	=	127,600
Total IHT		=	127,600

Example 1.22 – PET and taper

Estate of £644,000

Assume gift (eg outright to individual) of £344,000 made in the 7th year before death.

IHT payable at 20% of death rate on first £344,000.

	£		£
First	325,000	=	Nil
Next	19,000 @ 20% of 40%	=	1,520
IHT payable on remaining estate at death: £300,000 @ 40%		=	120,000
Total IHT			121,520

APPENDIX 1.3 – EXPECTATION OF LIFE

Information on life expectancy can be obtained from the Government Actuary's Department (GAD) website: www.gad.gov.uk/Demography%20Data/Life%20 Tables/Period_and_cohort_eol.html

National life tables are produced by the Office for National Statistics. Current and historic life tables are available via the GAD website: www.gad.gov.uk/ Demography%20Data/Life%20Tables/index.html

Chapter 2

Compliance

COMPLIANCE AND TAX PLANNING

2.1   There has traditionally always been something of a divide, both intellectually and in professional offices, between 'policy' and 'compliance', with the sharper minds being drawn to the former. In the days, if they ever existed, when so-called junior staff 'knew their place' and aspired to nothing higher than the implementation of plans sent down to them by the senior partner, it was quite possible for a qualified man never to get down to the business of filling in forms.

That attitude is no longer good enough. The sweeping changes to the IHT treatment of trusts brought in by FA 2006 forced some practitioners, for the first time, to look at form IHT100. That duty has been softened, retrospectively, by the regulations described in this section, but epitomises the approach now required. HMRC have given careful thought to the process by which trusts are created and taxed: they have constructed a 'tube map' which attempts to show in diagrammatic form the process by which:

- transactions evolve that can give rise to a tax charge;

- returns are (or should be) made; and

- tax is charged.

The whole process is being tightened up, with a commendable amount of consultation with the professions. The 'toolkit' approach, which has already been applied to CGT, has been extended to IHT for the form IHT400, giving practitioners easy links to guidance and showing clients, if interested, just what standards are expected (and what they are or should be paying for).

An otherwise good scheme to save a family much of the burden of IHT can easily be frustrated by poor execution. That can be through sloppy drafting, but just as easily by failure to follow through with timely and accurate completion of the appropriate forms to register new trusts and notify HMRC as appropriate. For the detail, see for example *Trust Drafting and Precedents* (Bloomsbury Professional).

Forms

2.2   The main control documents are IHT100, the account for the lifetime transfer of value already mentioned, and IHT400, the account for IHT following death. In many situations they will not be required, as where on death an estate is of substantial size, but no tax is in fact chargeable. Always use the most recent version, downloading from the HMRC website at: www.hmrc.gov.uk/inheritancetax/iht-probate-forms/find-right-forms.htm.

The IHT400 series is better laid out and perhaps better adapted to electronic capture of the information than the predecessor IHT200 series. The IHT400 series takes account of common practices such as the gift of personal effects to charity, which is specifically catered for by form IHT400, box 35, and form IHT408 (see below). Extra information, which was hitherto set out in a supplemental sheet, can now fit into pages 15 and 16 of this slightly longer return. The IHT400 series asks for greater detail in respect of domicile than did the IHT200 series.

Form IHT407 ('Household and personal goods') looks more user friendly than the form it replaced, but its proper completion will be much more intrusive than most families will expect or enjoy. Form IHT408 ('Household and personal goods given to charity') completes the investigation of this part of the estate.

The duty of notification on creation of offshore trusts stipulated by s 218 should not be overlooked. Those concerned with the creation of such trusts, except barristers, must inform HMRC within three months. A letter is usually enough; see **2.54**.

Compliance

2.3   The compliance landscape of the tax system was changed significantly by FA 2007 and subsequent legislation. FA 2008, Part 7 and Schedules 36, 37, 39 and 40 (as originally enacted) introduced rules for income tax, capital gains tax, corporation tax, self-assessment and PAYE. HMRC's powers were subsequently extended by legislation introduced in FA 2009, Part 7 and Schedules 47–57, and apply to other taxes and duties, including IHT.

The effect for IHT purposes can broadly be summarised as follows:

- The penalty regime for inaccuracies in returns, which was introduced in FA 2007 (s 97, Sch 24) was extended (in FA 2008, s 122, Sch 40) to include IHT (and certain other taxes), with effect for all chargeable events occurring on or after 1 April 2009 (see **2.59** onwards).

- HMRC's information and inspection powers (which were introduced in FA 2008, s 113, Sch 36) were extended (by FA 2009, s 96, Sch 48) to cover IHT (and other taxes) from 1 April 2010 (SI 2009/3054, art 2).

- Record-keeping obligations are set out in FA 2008, Sch 37. These rules were subsequently extended (eg by FA 2010, Sch 1, para 34), but do not cover IHT as yet.

- A harmonised late payment interest charge regime applying to IHT (and most other taxes and duties) was introduced in FA 2009 (s 101, Sch 53), with effect from 12 August 2009 (SI 2009/2032) (see **2.52**).

- Similarly, a unified regime for HMRC payments of interest on overpayments of IHT (and most other taxes and duties) was introduced in FA 2009 (s 102, Sch 54), from 12 August 2009 (SI 2009/2032).

- The penalty regime for the late payment of various taxes, including IHT, was introduced by FA 2009, s 107, Sch 56. The provisions relating to IHT are not yet in force.

- The penalty provisions for failure to notify etc were introduced for most taxes and duties (by FA 2008, s 123, Sch 41) with effect from 1 April 2010, but are not yet in force for IHT purposes.

- Provisions to align the time limits for HMRC assessments and taxpayer claims, which were originally introduced in FA 2008 (s 118, Sch 39), were extended (by FA 2009, s 98, Sch 51) to include IHT and certain other taxes, from 1 April 2011 (SI 2010/867, art 2(2)).

The general scope of the legislation is to amend and align the different compliance regimes that previously applied to the various taxes and duties, by applying rules on record keeping, information and inspection powers, penalties (ie for inaccuracies, the late filing of returns etc and the late payments of tax) and time limits for assessments, claims and elections. This major task was a staged process, with the first stage mostly concentrating on income tax, capital gains tax, corporation tax and VAT, and the second stage 'mopping up' other taxes and duties, including IHT. Government thinking on errors in returns etc, based on international research is that, although the majority of mistakes are simple errors, a minority think that detection of understatements is unlikely.

Taxpayers should understand what records are needed in order to calculate the tax due and for example, in the context of the administration of estates, the preparation of proper executorship accounts must come high on the list. Checks are being introduced to find out, and correct, errors of understanding of the law. Practitioners are urged not to rush completion of IHT400 but to take time to find out the facts. Conversely clients want to make progress quickly; obtaining a grant of representation is the litmus test for perceiving that progress is being made. Only after the grant has been obtained can the personal representatives get their hands on the deceased's assets. Conversely the beneficiaries want the administration process to be as quick as possible and will press for early distributions.

The checks are also intended to expose deliberate understatement of tax. The whole approach is risk based. Thus, taxpayers in a particular category or holding a particular type of asset may be getting returns wrong in a particular way that can be corrected through work with representative bodies or trade organisations. The change that brings the interest rate for IHT in line with other taxes may come as something of a shock to practitioners.

But see *Robertson v IRC (No 1)* [2002] STC (SCD) 182 and *Robertson v IRC No 2* [2002] WTLR 907 (referred to in **2.60**) for mitigation of the extreme position granted to the taxpayer following an intransigent, and wrong view taken by HMRC. See also *Cairns v HMRC* [2009] WTLR 793.

Amendments to the IHT400 form and IHT calculations will often be necessary following submission of the IHT account. HMRC are not resourced to deal with numerous amendments in respect of the same estate. Thus it is not necessary to notify HMRC every time there is an amendment. Provided the changes do not:

- amount to more than £50,000 in total;
- comprise items of land/realty or unquoted shares;
- comprise loss on sale of land or shares claims;
- relate to a case that is subject to a compliance check; or
- relate to a deliberate inaccuracy,

HMRC only need to be informed within 18 months from the date of death or at the point the estate is finalised, whichever is earlier (HMRC Trusts & Estates Newsletter, April 2012).

Penalties for late payments

2.4 The penalty provisions for failure to make tax payments on time (FA 2009, Sch 56) are likely to be a real practical problem in many cases, when they are eventually implemented for IHT purposes. For example, in the case of an account of an individual's estate on death, the due date for payment of IHT is generally six months after the end of the month of death or, if earlier, the delivery of an IHT account by the personal representatives (s 226(1), (2)). By contrast, the filing date for a return on death is normally within 12 months from the end of the month of death or, if later, three months from when the personal representatives first act as such (s 216(6)(a)).

Many personal representatives of larger estates in particular will therefore be faced with a race to complete the first part of the administration of the estate, finalising the IHT liability. They may make estimated payments on account in the hope that it will cover the eventual liability, or they may simply be unable to do so because of circumstances beyond their control. Actually raising the funds may be a major problem, despite the instalment option.

The initial late payment penalty under the FA 2009 regime is 5% of the unpaid tax, with a further 5% penalty if the tax is still unpaid five months after the penalty date, and another 5% penalty if non-payment continues after 11 months (FA 2009, Sch 56, para 3).

However, penalties may be subject to mitigation as follows:

● a 'special reduction' at HMRC's discretion because of 'special circumstances' (Sch 56, para 9);

● suspension of penalties during an agreement for deferred payment (para 10); and

● a 'reasonable excuse' exception (although insufficiency of funds is not a reasonable excuse unless this is attributable to events beyond the person's control) (para 16).

In the case of IHT instalments under s 227 (land, shares and businesses) and s 229 (woodlands) other than the first instalment, there is a 30-day 'period of grace' after the normal due date, before the first penalty is incurred.

Perhaps the major change is that families who, through grief or lack of business or clerical skills, simply delay will be penalised. They should, of course, seek professional help; but not all will do so. Specifically, delay through disputes as to who is to prove the will, or which will is valid, do not delay liability to tax and interest: see *Richardson v Revenue and Customs Commissioners* [2009] STC (SCD) 202, where an argument by the taxpayer as to fairness failed. Even though the delay was not the fault of the personal representative, full tax and interest was due. It was no fault on the part of HMRC that no statements of interest had been sent to the taxpayer.

Lifetime transfers

2.5   No account is needed of a PET but a chargeable transfer above certain limits must be reported even though, being made in lifetime, seven years may elapse before the death of the transferor. Where the transfer is immediately chargeable and not exempt from reporting under the rules described below, the account must be delivered by the transferor. If he does not pay the IHT by the due date, other persons become liable such as donees, trustees and beneficiaries under settlements, but they do not have to deliver the account themselves. In the rare cases where a close company makes a transfer of value, it becomes liable for IHT on it, but need not deliver an account. IHT is charged as if the participators in the company had made the transfer (ss 94, 202).

FA 2006 greatly increased the number of transactions that are chargeable transfers, but many will be within the nil rate band so there will be no immediate tax results. To prevent swamping of HMRC with returns that yielded no tax, and no doubt partly to reduce the burden on taxpayers, the level of disclosure was revised and reduced by the Inheritance Tax (Delivery of Accounts) (Excepted Transfers and Excepted Terminations) Regulations 2008 (SI 2008/605) and the Inheritance Tax (Delivery of Accounts) (Excepted Settlements) Regulations 2008 (SI 2008/606).

Excepted transfers and terminations

2.6   The regulations as to excepted transfers and excepted terminations came into force on 6 April 2008. They remove the obligation to deliver an account in certain circumstances, unless HMRC serve a notice requiring one. For some purposes they are retrospective to 6 April 2007. Trustees must still file an account in respect of failed PETs. Trustees and others must file an account on the termination of a settlement which would have been a PET, but fails under the seven-year rule. A return must be filed where the parties thought that the transfer was excepted within the current rules and it turns out not to be.

Excepted transfers

2.7   An excepted transfer under the current rules is one:

- made by an individual; and
- an actual transfer, not a deemed transfer.

There are two categories.

'Fixed-value' transfers: the 100% rule

2.8   Where the transfer is either cash or quoted shares or securities, the transfer will be excepted if (disregarding APR and BPR) the value transferred, together with values of chargeable transfers by that transferor in the preceding seven years, do not exceed the current nil rate band.

Transfers of uncertain value: the 80% rule

2.9   Where the transfer includes assets other than cash or quoted shares or securities, the transfer is exempt where (again disregarding APR and BPR):

- its value, together with other transfers by that transferor in the preceding seven years, do not exceed 80% of the nil rate band; and

- the value transferred by the transfer of value giving rise to this particular transfer does not exceed the nil rate band after deducting the value of all the previous chargeable transfers (in other words, the nil rate band available when the disposal takes place).

HMRC guidance (at IHTM06104) includes an example where the first of the above conditions is satisfied, but the second is not.

Example 2.1 – Gift of shares

Arthur owns 76% of the family company. Arguably it is a trading company, but BPR is disregarded for this purpose. The net asset value of the company is £1,100,000 and is the appropriate measure of value of the shares. He has already used his annual exemptions but to celebrate Christmas 2012 he wished to settle 10% of the company on his grandchildren. A discount of 15% applies to his holding, so it is worth £710,600.

He settled the shares, which might seem to be a gift of £110,000 but for the loss to estate rule. Before the transfer his estate includes shares carrying control over the structure of the company; after, he has 66%, which is a majority but cannot vary the Articles of Association and should be discounted by, say, 40%, being therefore worth (£1,100,000 × 66% × 60%) £435,600. The loss to his estate is £275,000.

Applying the 80% rule to the nil rate band for 2012–13 of £325,000, the limit above which the transfer must be reported is £260,000. Arthur's transfer must be reported; it is not £110,000, which would have been within the limit, but £275,000.

Example 2.2 – A series of gifts

Belinda, having used her annual exemptions, set up several small trusts for her nephews, all discretionary, totalling £39,500 in the years 2006 to 2010. All of the settlements were cash, and all were below the old filing rules.

Towards the end of 2012, she proposes to settle another £280,000 in cash and quoted securities. By then, she will also have used her annual exemption. Her cumulative total of gifts will be £319,500, well over the limit under the old rules.

Under the current regulations, the relevant limit will be the nil rate band £325,000, of which Belinda still has £285,500 unused, so she need not file an IHT100.

Excepted terminations

2.10   The rules as to excepted terminations apply only to:

- interest in possession trusts that existed before Budget Day 2006;
- trusts for bereaved minors under s 71A(c);
- IPDI trusts within s 49A(d);
- disabled persons trusts; or
- TSI trusts within ss 49B–49E.

The termination of an interest in possession in a trust can be a chargeable transfer, but it need not be reported in one of three circumstances, as set out below.

(i) Small or exempt transfers

The transfer may be small, for example within the annual exemption, and the life tenant may have served notice under s 57(3) that an exemption is available. If the amount of the transfer is within the specified exemption, there is no need for a return.

(ii) Nil rate band: fixed value fund

Where the trust property is cash or quoted securities and the value of the fund in respect of which the termination takes place, and the value of transfers by the tenant for life of any other kind together are within the nil rate band, there is no need for an account.

(iii) Variable value funds

Where the trust fund does not consist wholly of cash or quoted securities there is still no need to file a return if the value of the 'termination fund' and of previous chargeable transfers by the life tenant in the previous seven years do not exceed 80% of the nil rate band.

As with the rules for excepted settlements, these termination rules take no account of APR or of BPR. The 2008 regulations replace those made in 2002 in relation to lifetime transfers made on or after 6 April 2007.

Excepted settlements

2.11   The rules as to excepted settlements (SI 2008/606) reduce the filing requirements in respect of pilot trusts and small settlements. There is no need to file a return in respect of a pilot trust, ie a settlement made with UK trustees, who stay in the UK, of cash of £1,000 or less where there are no related settlements.

Apart from such pilot trusts, the regulations remove the obligation to file a return in respect of:

- UK trusts (which remain in the UK);
- settlors who are domiciled in the UK at the time the settlement is made;
- settlors who remain domiciled here until either the chargeable event or the death of the settlor whichever first happens;
- where there are no related settlements; and
- one of the following extra conditions are met.

Extra condition 1: from the ten-year charge.

The trust is excepted where the value in the trust is not more than 80% of the nil rate band (disregarding liabilities or reliefs such as APR or BPR). In arriving at the notional aggregate chargeable transfer of value any previous transfers from the trust that were themselves excepted from delivering an account must also be included before deduction of any relief or liabilities (IHTM06124).

Extra condition 2: from the exit charge in the first ten years of the trust.

Regulation 4(5) concerns the value transferred by the notional chargeable transfer which readers will remember is one element of calculation of the exit charge in the first ten years of the relevant property trust. For a transfer to be excepted, the calculation of value disregards liabilities or reliefs such as APR and BPR. On an exit charge in the first ten years of a relevant property trust, no return need be filed if the value released from the trust does not exceed 80% of the nil rate band.

Extra condition 3: from an exit charge after the first ten-year anniversary.

There is no need to file a return if the value of the transfer does not exceed 80% of the nil rate band.

Extra condition 4: from an exit charge from an 18-to-25 trust.

There is no need for a return where the chargeable transfer is within 80% of the nil rate band.

A 'heffalump' trap

2.12　Note with care the situation described in IHTM06130 which arises on the death of a transferor. Trustees may have received sums which are well within the nil rate band. They may have appointed funds out, again well within the levels that are now exempt from reporting. If this is the only chargeable transfer made by the settlor, there is no problem.

However, on taking office, trustees should enquire whether the settlor had made other transfers, such as PETs, in the seven years before the transfer to their trust. If the transferor dies within seven years of those prior transfers, those PETs will fail on his death. There will be a 'knock-on' effect on the trust because, when seen in the context of the failed PETs, the transfers that were previously exempt from reporting must now be shown in an account. Depending on the value, there might not be any extra tax to pay, but the return must be filed.

Example 2.3 – Death affecting prior transactions

Carrie gave her daughter Delia a block of lock-up garages in 2008. This was a PET, so no return was made. There was some prospect that Delia could get planning permission to redevelop the land, but she and her mother assumed that the value of the gift was £60,000. On 1 August 2011, Carrie settled £240,000 being partly cash and partly quoted securities. Seen in isolation that was an 'excepted transfer' and there was no need to report it.

On 15 June 2012, the trustees advanced £80,000 to David, a beneficiary, to help him buy a house. The settlement was within the nil rate band when Carrie made it, so there would normally be no exit charge. The nil rate band is then £325,000 so, under the current filing rules, 80% of that is £260,000; so an appointment which is an occasion for an exit charge need not be reported under the current rules because in this example the original fund, at £240,000, is well within the reporting limits.

Carrie died on 6 August 2012, so the PET to Delia fails. The tax charges on the settlement must now be reviewed. The value of the transfer of the garages must be agreed. If the value is indeed £60,000, the notional aggregate of chargeable transfers goes up to £300,000. That is still within the nil rate band, so there will be no exit charge on the appointment made by the trustees, but the figures now exceed the limits in the current regulations, so the trustees will have to deliver an account.

Matters will become more difficult for the trustees, if not for Delia, if it turns out that, with hope value, the true value of the garages was much more than £60,000 when Carrie gave them. A significant increase in their value could easily bring the tax rates applicable to the trust up to the level where an exit charge would be due on the £80,000 that was advanced to John.

The regulations are complex, but probably as simple as IHT rules will allow. Practitioners should read the detailed and useful draft guidance, with further illustrations, inserted into the IHT Manual at IHTM06100–IHTM06130. These show, for example at IHTM06105, how discounted gift schemes are valued. If it turns out that the discount has been claimed at too high a level, a duty to file within six months may arise on discovery.

Settlors sometimes try to get around the chargeable transfer rules using the s 21 'normal expenditure out of income' exemption. Under the current regulations, there is no duty to file a return if the transfers are within the nil rate band, but if more value than that is involved we must assume that the transfers are chargeable, and report them. HMRC have not been satisfied that the exemption applies. It may well do, but it must be 'shown' to; see IHTM06106, which is effectively a note about statutory clearance.

A taxpayer may have thought that a transfer was outside the filing rules and, either on his own or with the benefit of advice, realise the error later. If so, he has six months to put things right. Practitioners who see their clients regularly, as when filing income tax returns, should remember to ask if there have been gifts that should have been reported.

Transfers on death and failed PETs

2.13   As just seen in relation to Carrie (in Example 2.3), a lifetime transfer may become chargeable if death occurs within seven years, what is termed a failed PET. The primary duty to complete returns rests with the personal representatives. They must complete the return to the best of their knowledge and belief, subject to a test of reasonableness. HMRC's 'Inheritance Tax:

Customer Guide' contains guidance to encourage consistency between HMRC's approach to the penalty legislation for IHT (www.hmrc.gov.uk/cto/customerguide/page22.htm).

Example 2.4 – Accounting for a gift

Ellis died on 7 July 2012, leaving his personal effects and half his estate to his daughter Frances and the remainder to his son George. Whilst still well enough to manage his affairs, he had made simple, outright, cash lifetime gifts as follows:

1: January 2005	£25,000 to Frances
2: August 2005	£26,000 to George
3: December 2005	£3,000 between his grandchildren
4: December 2006	£3,000 as before
5: December 2007	£3,000 as before
6: May 2008	£10,000 to the National Trust
7: December 2008	£3,000 as before
8: December 2009	£3,000 as before
9: May 2010	£20,000 to George
10: December 2010	£3,000 as before

Ellis's health and faculties deteriorated and he had to move to a nursing home. Under a lasting power of attorney, George continued the pattern of gifts at Christmas and also made gifts, on behalf of his father, as follows:

11: January 2011	£15,000 (personal effects to Frances at the time of sale of the house)
12: May 2012	£25,000 between grandchildren

But beware the overriding rules relating to enduring and lasting powers of attorney. They cannot authorise major gifts, often wanted as part of a tax-planning exercise. Authority from the Court of Protection is required. See *McDowall v IRC* [2004] WTLR 221 for the disasters that can occur. All unauthorised gifts, even those made more than seven years before death, were ineffective for IHT purposes, and their value added back to the taxable estate on death.

The executors can claim relief under s 21 (ie normal expenditure out of income) for all the Christmas gifts up to and including 2010. Gift 1 is more than seven years before death and out of the reckoning. Gift 2 enjoys £6,000 of annual exemption, so is a failed PET of £20,000 net. It is set against the nil rate band. Gift 6 is to a charity and exempt. Gift 9 benefits from two annual exemptions, leaving £14,000 to go against the nil rate band.

Of the gifts under the power of attorney, those at Christmas 2011 are probably exempt both under s 21 and because they were habitual and therefore reasonable for the attorney to continue. Gift 11 was reasonable within the terms of the power: Ellis had bequeathed the items to Frances and the alternative was to sell the chattels, which would adeem the bequest. Gift 12 fails in every sense. It goes beyond what is reasonable under a power, unless there was specific authority, and (as it turns out) half the cheques were in fact still unpresented at the date of death and, thus, were not effective gifts.

Lasting powers of attorney

2.14   The authorities, it seems, initially seriously underestimated the work, cost and registration requirements for lasting powers of attorney (LPAs) as required under the Mental Capacity Act 2005. This fully justified the rush to sign enduring powers before expiry of the deadline. To be fair, the LPA forms were subsequently simplified and many individuals of average intelligence and diligence will be able to complete them without much professional help, as was always intended. The power of an attorney under an LPA is more closely defined than used to be the case under an EPA: see MCA 2005, s 12, which provides that there is no general power to make gifts but that, subject to any express limitation in the power, the attorney may make gifts on customary occasions to persons related to or connected with the donor, including the grantee of the power; and may make certain charitable gifts. 'Customary occasion' means births, birthdays, marriage, formation of civil partnership or any other customary occasion, which allows cultural flexibility.

Reporting lifetime transfers after death: the duty of care

2.15   Personal representatives should enquire into the history of lifetime transfers by the deceased. The approach of HMRC is all about the risk of loss to the public purse. Personal representatives should establish the exact nature, value and extent of the property remaining in the estate at death. They should, in all substantial cases, call for back statements on bank and similar accounts to check the pattern of withdrawals. They should ask relatives, professional advisors and close business colleagues about the way the deceased ran his affairs.

History shows that death can uncover affairs of the heart as well as of a financial nature. If, in the course of their enquiries, the suspicions of the executors are raised that gifts may have been made that were not disclosed by other papers of the deceased, they should continue to search through the papers until they are reasonably sure that they have identified the gifts made by the deceased.

There is a particular problem over the date and nature of the gifts. In relation to 'old' gifts, their date will be material, perhaps to show that a gift was made more than seven years before death. When was the gift truly made, in the sense that it was perfected by transfer of title? What was the value at the transfer date? A gift may have been made out of property that was at that time held jointly with some other person who has since died. The gift may therefore have been of only one half or some other fraction of the property given away.

Lifetime gifts may qualify for exemption under ss 18, 19, 20, 21, 22 or 23 and following. Form IHT403 describes the information that should be maintained, and includes tables in a spreadsheet style. As an alternative for the practitioner's own use, the following (partly completed) table may be prepared as a spreadsheet to help to calculate the amount of nil rate band available after the lifetime gifts have been brought into account on death.

Example 2.5 – Calculating the unused nil rate band

Hannah died on 17 December 2012 having made many lifetime gifts. Her income was steady, at about £36,000 per annum after tax. She lived frugally, taking a holiday (cost £3,000) only occasionally. Her living expenses were £17,000 per annum in the 'non-holiday years'. The following table, which should be created as a spreadsheet, can be used to sort the gifts and to claim the reliefs before completing IHT400:

Period	Income	Gifts	Annual exemption	s 21 claim	Other claims	Gift after reliefs, etc	NRB to use	Balance of NRB
18.12.2005– 5.4.2006	4,375	10,000	6,000			4,000	325,000	321,000
Year to 5.4.2007	16,000	3,000	3,000			Nil		321,000
Year to 5.4.2008	19,000							
Year to 5.4.2009	16,000							
Year to 5.4.2010	19,000							
Year to 5.4.2011	16,000							
Year to 5.4.2012	19,000							
6.4.2012– 17.12.2012	12,500							

The table shows that (unless death was on 5 April) there are actually eight periods for consideration if the form is completed by tax years, as is contemplated by the form. The nil rate band at date of death was £325,000. If Hannah made an isolated gift of £10,000 in September 2005, that gift falls entirely out of account, with the result that the annual exemption is still available for that year, and for the previous year. Therefore, a gift in February 2006 of £10,000 may be reduced by two annual exemptions, leaving only £4,000 to be set against the nil rate band.

Normal expenditure out of income

2.16   Claims under s 21 (normal expenditure out of income) meet resistance from HMRC where the evidence is, frankly, thin. The taxpayer must show that:

- the gift was made as part of normal expenditure (see below);

- it was made out of income; and

- the transferor was left with enough to live on.

Form IHT403 requires nursing home fees to be shown as an expense to be met out of income. This is consistent with the decision in *Nadin v IRC* [1997] STC (SCD) 107, but takes no account of the views expressed in *Stevenson (Inspector of Taxes) v Wishart* [1987] STC 266, where nursing home fees were substantial. The issue causes regular difficulty.

It is not necessary to set gifts against the annual exemption in priority in making an s 21 claim. Thus, in Example 2.5, if Hannah made gifts up to 5 April 2007 that used up the annual exemption for that year, she could make gifts in the following year of £3,000 and make further gifts in respect of which an s 21 claim was made.

To be treated as normal expenditure there must be:

- regularity;

- a pattern of gifts; or

- a commitment to make regular gifts;

and preferably all three.

There is scope for 'overs and shorts' under s 21(1)(b), but it is interpreted narrowly by HMRC, who will resist claims to relief based on carrying forward income over a number of years that was not used up on gifts. They strongly resist claims based on averages which rely on bringing back into a year the income of a later period. However, the legislation only requires the taxpayer to show 'that (taking one year with another) [the gift] was made out of [the taxpayer's] income'.

The normal expenditure out of income exemption in s 21 is covered in more detail at **12.5** onwards.

Personal effects

2.17   HMRC consider that there may previously have been insufficient disclosure of value, so this is another 'risk area'. The true value to be shown is governed by the market value rule in s 160. The tone of official notices suggests that HMRC wish to dislodge the ingrained habit in taxpayers and their advisers of systemic undervaluation of chattels.

It is good practice to ensure that a professional valuer, whether for chattels or other assets, always signs off his valuation with an express statement that he has followed the principles set out in s 160.

There is no such thing as 'probate value': the value to be disclosed is 'the price which the property might reasonably be expected to fetch if sold in the open market' or 'the value in accordance with IHTA 1984, s 160' at the date of death. That is the gross selling price, not the net.

Here, in particular, form IHT407 ('Household and personal goods') asks much more searching questions than its predecessors, even down to the registration number of the deceased's car; whether chattels that have been sold were purchased by relatives; and how the value of other chattels was arrived at. A point to watch is that if the deceased was in business on his own account, working from home, certain assets at the premises, such as his car, may actually appear in the balance sheet of the business and should therefore not be included as personal effects. This is actually a point for will drafters to watch, since the definition of 'personal chattels' in the Statutory Will Forms can include assets used in a business carried on at home, which may not be what the testator would have wanted, if asked.

Estimates and 'taking a view'

2.18   There is statutory authority in s 216(3A) for the use of estimates. The personal representatives must make very full enquiries but, if unable to arrive at the exact value, must:

- say that they have made full enquiries;
- supply a provisional estimate of the value; and

●   undertake to deliver a further account as soon as the value is ascertained.

For an example of litigation on these issues and on the costs of the litigation itself, see *Robertson v IRC (No 1)* [2002] STC (SCD) 182, and *Robertson v IRC (No 2)* [2002] STC (SCD) 242. HMRC's view is that although s 216(3A) provides for actual figures to be submitted as soon as the value is ascertained, it is not cost-effective for amendments to be notified on a piecemeal basis. It is suggested that amendments to estimates should be treated in the same way as any other corrections to the return. As to HMRC's preferred approach in respect of multiple amendments to the IHT account, see **2.3**.

More difficult is the situation where a relief may be available but the basis might be disputed; or the validity of a gift might be challenged. Form IHT400 has no exact parallel to the 'white space' in a return under income and capital gains self-assessment, so practitioners may feel that they have to send in a covering letter to point out areas of difficulty. The claiming of a relief can lead to penalties if there is no justification for the claim. The safe course is to ensure that the IHT400 contains enough detail for the examiner to realise what the issues are. If a gift was for some reason conditional when made, the full facts should be disclosed.

It may be tempting to include an estimated asset valuation on the IHT return and subsequently submit a corrective account, particularly due to the threat of penalties for late IHT returns, and also in view of the new interest and penalty regimes outlined at **2.3**. In the IHT & Trusts Newsletter for August 2009, HMRC pointed out that, as interest starts to accrue six months after the end of the month in which the relevant death occurs, IHT400 returns are often submitted with estimates to pre-empt the date for interest charges, even though the deadline for the return itself is 12 months from the end of the month in which the death occurs. However, if an application for an IHT reference is made in good time during the six-month period, a payment on account of the final liability can be made, allowing the IHT400 possibly to be submitted with accurate figures at a later time within the 12-month filing period.

HMRC also indicate that communicating any difficulties in obtaining actual figures to them at an early stage will help to demonstrate that everything reasonable is being done to deal with the matter. This would seem to imply that HMRC may view the case sympathetically if penalties later become an issue.

HMRC's 'Inheritance Tax Toolkit' cites valuation as 'an area of very high risk for HMRC' and offers guidance on mitigating that risk, such as engaging a qualified, independent valuer, explaining the context of the valuation and drawing attention to the definition of market value in s 160 (see www.hmrc. gov.uk/agents/toolkits/iht.pdf).

EXCEPTED ESTATES

Bare trusts

2.19   Bare trusts, created by mere declaration, have long been popular with accountants because the document is short. No substantive trust is created, thus avoiding the relevant property regime for IHT. Where the value was large, some advisers tried to build in safeguards and in doing so went to the limit of what might be considered to be a bare trust. HMRC revealed that they were considering whether there was a substantive trust (and thus a potential IHT charge) if, either expressly or by implication, the trustees were under a duty to accumulate the income. A second issue was whether the power of advancement under Trustee Act 1925, s 32 might be used to make settled advances, which would again allow ongoing trusts of precisely the kind eschewed by FA 2006.

Professional advisers did not agree, although as far as the authors are aware no case has yet been brought on the effect of s 43(2)(b), which refers to accumulations. There was perceived to be an inconsistency between the established treatment of bare trusts for income tax (see for example Trusts, Settlements and Estates Manual at TSEM1563) and what was proposed for IHT. If drafting a bare trust it seemed wise to exclude TA 1925, s 31, so as to weaken the suggestion that there was a substantive trust.

The argument that active duties are the hallmark of a substantive trust may have some validity in the area of family trust arrangements but from an intellectual point of view it sits ill with, for example, the position of unit trusts, where the trustees are active and which are nevertheless bare trusts. The present position is that a bare trust of capital for a minor beneficiary is not settled property and thus cannot be relevant property.

The law was clarified in the exchange between STEP and CIOT and HMRC following FA 2006. HMRC stated, in response to questions raised:

> 'We confirm that our view is that where assets are held on an absolute trust (ie a bare trust) for a minor the assets so held will not be settled property within the meaning of section 43 IHTA 1984 and that this will be the case whether or not the provisions of section 31 Trustee Act 1925 have been excluded.'

Transfers on death

2.20   There are three categories of excepted estate, see Inheritance Tax (Delivery of Accounts) (Excepted Estates) Regulations 2004 (SI 2004/2543), as amended. Many practitioners fail to take advantage of the regulations, using form IHT400 where it is not needed. This is not encouraged by HMRC, because it just makes for unnecessary work that yields no tax.

Similarly, HMRC have previously reported that a large number of letters are received about transfers and settlements that are excepted under the IHT Regulations (see IHT & Trusts Newsletter, December 2008). HMRC point out that the purpose of the regulations is to reduce the number of reports made, and urge practitioners not to do this.

The reporting levels were increased by Inheritance Tax (Delivery of Accounts) (Excepted Estates) (Amendment) Regulations 2006 (SI 2006/2141) with effect from 1 September 2006.

The excepted estate regulations were further amended by The Inheritance Tax (Delivery of Accounts) (Excepted Estates) (Amendment) Regulations, SI 2011/214, with effect for deaths occurring from 6 April 2010, to take account of the 'transferable nil rate band' provisions (IHTA 1984, s 8A). The regulations provide (inter alia) for the 'IHT threshold' (as defined) to be increased to £650,000 (for 2012–13), subject to a claim being made to increase the nil rate band by 100% on the basis of the full nil rate band being available to transfer from not more than one earlier deceased spouse or civil partner, and subject to certain other conditions being satisfied. Where a claim for unused nil rate band is required, an excepted estate return (form IHT205, or C5 in Scotland) must also be made. HMRC guidance on excepted estates, the transferable nil rate band and other changes are included in HMRC Trusts & Estates Newsletter (April 2011).

Perhaps from an abundance of caution, agents also often notify HMRC on form IHT100 of distributions out of discretionary will trusts even though s 144 applies to relate the transfers back to the death. One such occasion will be the family who appoint the nil rate fund to the surviving spouse so as to maximise the transferable nil rate band, in the hope that it will increase over time and be more valuable on the second death. There is no need for this: moreover it wastes HMRC resources.

Category One: small estates: the traditional form

2.21   The conditions are that:

- The deceased, UK domiciled, died on or after 1 September 2006.

- The estate relates to property in the following categories:

    - it passes under the will of the deceased or on his intestacy;

    - it passes under nomination taking effect on death;

    - it is contained in one settlement only in which the deceased had an interest in possession; or

    –   it was joint property and passes by survivorship (or in Scotland by survivorship in a special destination).

- Of the property passing on death:

    –   no more than £100,000 was situated overseas; and

    –   no more than £150,000 was trust property.

- In the seven years before death the deceased made transfers which, before deduction of business or agricultural relief, did not exceed £150,000.

- The whole estate, including certain categories of transfer, did not exceed the IHT threshold. Note for this purpose that, if the deceased died after 5 April but before 6 August in the year and an application for grant of representation is made before 6 August, the relevant threshold is the 'old' one from the tax year before that in which the deceased died.

In addition, the deceased must not have made any gifts with reservation, and no charge must arise under the 'alternatively secured pension' (ASP) rules in IHTA 1984, ss 151A–151C. This liability has been abolished by FA 2011. There are two categories of transfers referred to in the fifth bullet point above. 'Specified transfers' are defined in SI 2004/2543, reg 4(6) to mean chargeable transfers in the seven years up to death consisting only of:

- cash;

- personal chattels or moveable property;

- quoted shares or securities; or

- interest in land (with qualifications).

The same regulations define 'specified exempt transfers' as those made in the seven years up to death which are exempt under one of the following headings:

- transfers between spouses;

- charities;

- political parties;

- gifts to housing associations;

- gifts to maintenance funds for historic buildings;

- employee trusts.

Category Two estates: spouse/charity exemption

2.22   SI 2004/2543 created a new category of excepted estate of a gross value of up to £1 million where, after spouse or charity exemption, the estate was still within the IHT threshold. To comply with this category the following conditions must be satisfied (reg 4(3)):

- UK domicile, death on or after 6 April 2004.

- The estate includes only property passing:

    - by will or on intestacy;

    - under a nomination taking effect on death;

    - under a single settlement of which the deceased was tenant for life; or

    - joint property passing by survivorship or in Scotland by survivorship in a special destination.

- The estate included:

    - not more than £100,000 foreign property;

    - not more than £150,000 of settled property but ignoring settled property that on death passes to a spouse or to charity; and

    - that in the seven years leading up to death the deceased did not make chargeable transfers other than specified transfers not exceeding £150,000 before deduction of business or agricultural relief.

- The estate did not exceed £1,000,000, including within that figure:

    - the gross value of the estate;

    - the value transferred by specified transfers;

    - the value transferred by specified exempt transfers.

- Applying the formula A − (B + C), the total does not exceed the IHT threshold. For this purpose:

    - A is the aggregate of the estate, specified transfers and the specified exempt transfers;

    - B is the total value transferred on death that qualifies for exemption as passing to a spouse or charity, but subject to qualification of that rule in relation to Scotland; and

    - C is the total liabilities of the estate.

The same comments regarding gifts with reservation and ASP charges apply as for Category One above.

Category Three: small foreign estates

2.23   This is the category of estate where (see reg 4(5)):

- the deceased was domiciled outside the UK on death, and was never domiciled or deemed to be domiciled in the UK; and

- the estate in the UK comprises only cash or quoted shares or securities with a total value not exceeding £150,000.

Remember to state the value of the worldwide estate. If below the IHT threshold, domicile is less likely to be examined in detail; there is no point. The personal representatives of an excepted estate are not entirely excused from supplying information. In all such cases they must complete the short form IHT205. This may in any event serve a separate function by offering some protection to beneficiaries, especially charities, because without IHT205 there might actually be no formal inventory of the estate.

PARTICULAR COMPLIANCE POINTS

Excepted estates generally

2.24   The scheme of excepted estates is attractive: it enables executors to make rapid progress, which may be very important where, for example, a business is owned for which the executors need the extra security of a grant to secure funding; or an asset in the estate is falling in value; or severe illness of a main beneficiary adds urgency. However, statistical analysis has tended to show that a disproportionate number of estates 'seem' to fall just below the threshold in value for an estate to be excepted. Hitherto, random selection of estates usually meant that, if you heard nothing within a couple of months after obtaining a grant, you could relax.

However, in the IHT & Trusts Newsletter for August 2008, HMRC explained that a process comparing data drawn from lifetime records and the estate in question with the criteria for an excepted estate may take a little longer than the random system, so statutory clearance will not be given after 35–60 days, as before. HMRC will only pursue the most suspicious cases; but, if the trial shows systemic failings in the way that agents prepare applications, HMRC will discuss the process itself with representative bodies.

Example 2.6 – Estate enquiry

Ian worked in the building trade and managed to keep turnover just below the VAT threshold, but eventually some third-party disclosures in matrimonial proceedings ('what about Dad's real money, the money in the safe deposit box?') resulted in a full enquiry.

The statement of assets produced for that enquiry, showing ownership (free of mortgage) of the family home, a workshop, accounts in Jersey, a collection of classic cars, and substantial other assets formed a useful benchmark for HMRC when Ian's executors tried to obtain probate of his will. Virtually none of the expected assets were shown; there was no business interest, nor the level of bank deposit that might suggest its recent sale.

The executors, one of whom was Ian's companion in his later years and whose view was perhaps somewhat biased, explained that the former wife and the children had 'taken him to the cleaners' but that was not confirmed by the terms of the final court order. Even allowing for the costs of a long and acrimonious divorce, there was a substantial shortfall.

She, the companion, had had the money; lifetime gifts had not been fully disclosed; since she was not married to him, spouse exemption could not apply. She and their baby boy Henry may have been all the family Ian still had when he died, but that did not bring her within the disposition for maintenance of family provisions (IHTA 1984, s 11(1)(a)). The best that could be salvaged was a claim, which would have been better made earlier, to some relief for the cost of Henry's upbringing under s 11(4) incurred whilst Ian was still alive, and under Inheritance (Provision for Family and Dependants) Act 1975.

Transferable nil rate band

2.25   Following the announcement of the transferable nil rate band (TNRB) facility in the Pre-Budget Report 2007, HMRC reported that lay taxpayers had completed satisfactory returns. By contrast, some 80% of agents initially failed to adhere strictly to the filing requirements of form IHT216 (subsequently replaced by form IHT402), resulting in their rejection and failure (HMRC IHT & Trusts Newsletter, August 2008). Often, it seems, the agents were just careless, failing to supply documents that were already in their possession and were needed to support the claim.

This is the type of systemic error that HMRC wish to prevent through the use of an IHT toolkit (as to which, see at **2.67**).

Annuities

2.26   There will seldom be any residual value of an annuity, but where payments do continue after death, as where the annuitant dies before the end of the guaranteed period, the right to the income stream must be valued. Whilst personal representatives may value as they think fit, many will want to make use of the HMRC calculator for guaranteed annuities on their website (www. hmrc.gov.uk/cto/forms/g_annuity.pdf), giving a reasonable estimate of the value under s 160.

Joint property

2.27 Property owned as joint tenants passes to the survivor by the *ius accrescendi* (survivorship), without the need for a grant of representation. That does not mean, however, that no IHT is due. If the surviving joint owner is neither the spouse nor the civil partner, the value may be taxable. Form IHT400 will be appropriate, with form IHT404 ('Jointly owned assets') annexed.

The deceased may have opened an account jointly with a child, perhaps for convenience through frailty or failing intellect. Payment of money into such an account is not necessarily a gift of half to the child: but the withdrawal of funds by the child for her own purposes will usually be a transfer for IHT and should be brought into account. HMRC explained, in the IHT Newsletter for December 2006, that they look critically at accounts opened shortly before death.

There is good reason for this: it seems that the number of grants of representation taken out by lawyers is falling, whilst the number of deaths and of personal applications is steady; so what accounts for the shortfall? Undeclared inheritance of jointly held assets may be one factor.

PAYMENT BY INSTALMENTS

2.28 Cash flow is always an important factor, especially where the transaction gives rise to a 'dry' tax charge, ie in circumstances where there is no liquidity as a result of what has happened. Here the right to pay IHT by instalments can be of great value (ss 227, 228), as it will be in the case of farmers and shareholders of family companies, subject to the availability of business or agricultural property relief. This right is, however, subject to stringent conditions which vary depending on whether IHT liability arises on death or by way of lifetime transfers. Personal representatives remain personally liable for any unpaid tax instalments, even after the relevant assets have been transferred to the beneficiary (*Howarth's Executors v IRC* [1997] STC (SCD) 162).

The position on death

2.29   Six types of property are eligible:

(1)   land (including buildings of any description, wherever situated);

(2)   shares or securities of a company which gave the deceased control of the company immediately before his death;

(3)   shares or securities of a company which did *not* give such control but which are unquoted, if either the '20% rule' (see below) applies or HMRC are satisfied that payment otherwise than by instalments would cause undue hardship;

(4)   shares of a company (not securities) which did not give such control and which are unquoted where the '£20,000/10% rule' (see below) applies;

(5)   the net value of business interests provided they are carried on for gain and not as a hobby; and

(6)   trees or underwood (s 229).

Under s 269, a person has 'control' of a company for the above purpose at any time if he then has the control of powers of voting on all questions. However class rights giving voting powers in certain cases, for example, on liquidation or on matters affecting shares of that class are ignored.

The definition of 'unquoted' comprises shares which are not listed on a recognised stock exchange. Accordingly, shares quoted only on the Alternative Investment Market or on PLUS (formerly OFEX) are unquoted for s 227. Beware the situation where a company has a second listing elsewhere on an exchange which is 'recognised'. Following FA 2007 (s 109, Sch 26), HMRC are empowered to add or amend the list of recognised stock exchanges, with consequential implications for various tax purposes.

As regards the '20% rule', the condition requires that the party accountable for the IHT is liable for at least 20% of the total tax for which he is accountable (in the same capacity) for the *defined assets*, namely assets numbered 1 to 5 inclusive above.

The '£20,000/10% rule' is that:

●   the value of the shares transferred exceeds £20,000; *and*

●   either the nominal value of the shares is not less than 10% of the nominal value of all shares of the company at the time of death (it is assumed that this refers to issued shares); or

●   the shares are ordinary shares (ie the equity) and that their nominal value is not less than 10% of the nominal value of all ordinary shares of the company at the time of death.

As regards business interests, including professions or vocations, this term covers the net value of the business interests, net value being the principal value of the assets used in the business (including any goodwill) reduced by the aggregate liabilities incurred for the purpose of the business.

If the relevant conditions are met, the taxpayer can elect to pay the IHT by ten equal yearly instalments, the first becoming payable six months following the end of the month in which the death occurs (s 227(3)(a)).

Interest

2.30 Historically, the rate of interest on IHT has been lower than that charged on other taxes. However, as indicated above (see **2.3**), a harmonised late payment interest charge regime applying to IHT (and most other taxes and duties) was introduced in FA 2009, Sch 53, which has effectively resulted in IHT 'catching up' with certain other taxes in terms of the interest rate charged.

The aligned interest rules provide that the late payment dates for certain IHT instalments run from the date on which the instalment is due to be paid. This applies to the following (Sch 53, para 7):

- any IHT payable on instalments in respect of woodlands (under s 229); and

- IHT payable on instalments (under s 227) relating to:

  - shares or securities within s 228, or business interests; or

  - agricultural property (ie within Pt 5, Ch 2).

Shares or securities within the second bullet above are excluded if the company's business consists wholly or mainly of dealing in securities, stocks or shares, land or buildings, or making or holding investments (ie those companies in respect of which business property relief is precluded by s 105(3)). However, shares or securities may nevertheless be eligible if the company's business wholly or mainly consists of being a 'holding company' (as defined in CA 2006, s 1159) of a company not within an excluded category, or if its business is carried on in the UK wholly as a market maker or discount house (FA 2009, Sch 53, para 7).

Similarly, if an order is made to tax under certain provisions relating to family and dependants (eg s 146(1)), late payment interest does not begin to run until the order is made. If HMRC accept property in lieu of IHT (under s 230), late payment interest will cease from the date that the property is valued (FA 2009, Sch 53, paras 8, 14).

Other occasions for relief

2.31   Under s 227(1A) and (1C), the instalment provisions apply in two other circumstances. The first is a PET which becomes chargeable by reason of the transferor's death within seven years of the transfer. The second is where there is additional IHT assessable on a lifetime chargeable transfer because the transferor dies within seven years. Either way, the instalment option is subject to the condition that:

- *either* the relevant property is owned throughout by the transferee from the date of the transfer to the death of the transferor (or if earlier the death of the transferee);

- *or* the property qualifies as 'replacement property' for business or agricultural property relief purposes (s 113B or 124B; see **15.27**);

and

- in the case of shares or securities, they remain unquoted from the transfer to the transferor's death (or that of the transferee, if earlier).

Payment by instalments – lifetime chargeable transfer

2.32   The above rules are adapted for lifetime chargeable transfers in the following ways:

- In the case of a lifetime gift, the right is only available if the *donee* pays or bears the tax (s 227(1)(b)).

- Where the property is settled, the right is only available so long as the asset is retained as settled property by the trustees (s 227(1)(c)).

- The date of the lifetime chargeable transfer of value is substituted for the date of death.

- The '20% rule' does not apply (effect of s 228(1)(b), (2)).

The interest is not deductible for tax purposes.

Example 2.7 – Payments by instalments

James made a gift of shares on discretionary trusts (an immediate chargeable transfer) on 17 May 2011. The shares were valued (after business relief) at £400,000 and represented 15% of the ordinary share capital in an unquoted company. The gift was on condition that the donee/trustees paid the IHT. James had previously made a PET of £100,000 on 20 December 2009, which can at present be ignored, but had made no previous chargeable transfers. He had used his annual exemption.

The IHT payable on the gift of shares is accordingly (£325,000 at the nil rate and the balance at 20% amounting to) £15,000, which may be paid by instalments. Under s 227(3), £1,500 was due on 30 April 2012 (s 226(1)) followed by nine similar payments at yearly intervals. Interest is not charged on the outstanding balance if payment is made on the due dates. If the trustees were at any point to sell the shares, the tax then outstanding, plus any accrued interest, would be payable forthwith (s 227(4)).

MAIN VALUATION RULES

The open market price (s 160)

2.33   As for CGT, the general rule, in the absence of special valuation rules, is that the value at any time of any property shall be the price which the property might reasonably be expected to fetch if sold in the open market at that time. No allowance is made on the ground that the whole property is to be placed on the market at one and the same time, namely that the market is being 'flooded'. On the other hand, one might argue that the mere existence of overhanging IHT makes an asset less valuable.

In order to reach the hypothetical value of the hypothetical property a fiction is created of a sale between hypothetical partners of the hypothetical property. This does not mean, however, that evidence of actual transactions is inadmissible, although it is a question of fact, how much, if any, weight is given to the evidence (*IRC v Stenhouse's Trustees* [1992] STC 103, Ct of Session).

This 'statutory hypothesis' is helpfully summarised by Hoffmann LJ in *IRC v Gray* [1994] STC 360, CA, at pp 371–2. This case is also relevant to the valuation of agricultural property (see **15.77** and *Walton v IRC* [1996] STC 68, CA).

Transfers within seven years before death (ss 131–140)

2.34   The additional tax payable on transfers of any property (former PETs or lifetime chargeable transfers) made within seven years before death may be relieved where the value of the gift has fallen between the time the gift was made and death. If the market value of the transferred property at the time of the chargeable transfer (ie date of gift) exceeds its market value at 'the relevant date' (normally the date of death), the additional tax is to be calculated as if the value transferred were *reduced* by the amount of that excess. Thus, in effect the lower value is substituted.

'Relevant date' means:

- the date of death, where the transferee or his spouse still holds that property; or

- if that property is sold before the transferor's death, the date of a qualifying sale, namely an open market, arm's-length arrangement.

Example 2.8 – 'Fall in value' relief

Kenneth gives some commercial property to his daughter Lisa in 2008; it is then worth £300,000. This crystallises the initial potential IHT value. If Kenneth dies in 2012 when the value has fallen to, say, £200,000, this value can be substituted.

However, if Lisa had sold the property in 2010 for £250,000, that would represent the substituted value instead (s 131(1)).

Common-sense rules apply to changes in the property. Thus capital receipts on shares are added to the market value of the transferred property, whereas calls on shares reduce it. Adjustments must also be made for reorganisation and alterations of share capital and demergers as well as changes in interest in land and leases not exceeding 50 years.

The relief does not apply to tangible property that is a wasting asset, ie plant and machinery and other assets of a predictable useful life not exceeding 50 years (s 132).

As to PETs which become chargeable on the death of the transferor within seven years and the application of taper relief, see **1.11** and the examples there set out.

Valuation of certain securities sold within 12 months of death (ss 178–189)

2.35 Relief is available where:

- quoted shares and securities (NASDAQ shares are included; see IHTM34131);

- authorised unit trust holdings;

- shares in an open-ended investment company; or

- holdings in a common investment fund established under the Administration of Justice Act 1982, s 42 are sold within 12 months of a death at a genuinely lower level. The persons accountable for IHT, normally the personal representatives, may in effect claim that the total of the sale prices be substituted for the date of death values.

This relief is limited in two ways. First, any gains made in the same period must be set off against the losses. Secondly, repurchases by the claimant of any of the investments in the same capacity in which they were sold will reduce the relief. This restriction applies to repurchases at any time during the period beginning on the date of the death in question and ending two months after the date of the last sale (ie a maximum of 14 months from the date of death). The loss on sale is then reduced on a pro rata basis as set out in s 180(1).

Where the 'appropriate persons', ie the claimants, are personal representatives or trustees the purchase in such capacity of *any* qualifying investments would restrict the relief. For other accountable persons, for example, donees, the relief is only restricted if an investment of the same description is made (a share separately quoted from another share is not of the same description for this purpose).

Where personal representatives distribute cash to the beneficiaries the rule may be avoided. Even if the beneficiaries themselves acquire qualifying investments (whether of the same description or not), there will be no restriction of the loss relief. The purchase by the beneficiaries will not have been in the same capacity as the holdings of the personal representatives. Thus personal representatives should 'cherry pick' for sale the securities that have fallen and should appropriate those that have risen to the beneficiaries *in specie*. Such beneficiaries must remember that for capital gains tax purposes they have acquired the securities at their market value on the deceased's death.

This 'fall in value' relief has been adapted to other losses. Where investments are cancelled during the 12-month period or where listing on a recognised stock exchange or dealing is suspended and remains so to the end of the 12 months (see ss 186A, 186B), relief is allowed. This adaptation applies to deaths on or after 16 March 1992.

These rules deal with losses incurred on investments within 12 months of death. Should an investment become worthless in the second year after the death, consideration might be given to a variation of the will within two years of death under s 142 (see **5.35** onwards). The now worthless shares could be given to an exempt beneficiary such as the spouse or a charity so as to save the IHT on the value of the shares at death.

The valuation of quoted shares and securities on the '1/4 up' rule as provided for CGT (TCGA 1992, s 272) will in practice apply for IHT, although there is no corresponding statutory provision.

In the IHT & Trusts Newsletter for December 2008, HMRC reminded claimants that AIM shares are not qualifying investments, and should not be included on form IHT35 ('Claim for relief: Loss on sale of shares'), although the shares may qualify for business property relief. HMRC also indicated that the forms were not always being completed correctly, and reference was made to guidance at IHTM34000.

The claim form IHT35 can be downloaded from HMRC's website: (www. hmrc.gov.uk/cto/forms/iht35.pdf).

Development value of land

2.36   *Prosser v IRC* (DET/1/2000) shows that the value of land for IHT must take limited account of 'hope' value. There a plot of garden ground, in respect of which planning permission was eventually obtained, was held to be worth 25% of its ultimate value for probate purposes. The IHT Newsletter (April 2006) stressed that development value must be accounted for, and that the value of a house should reflect any feature that makes it attractive to a builder or developer. If new information comes to light that enhances the value at the date of death, the personal representatives should declare it, on pain of penalties for failure to do so.

But this is really only an example of the working out of the general s 160 valuation rule.

Falls in value of land four years after death (ss 190–198)

2.37   These provisions apply similar relief to that set out in **2.35** to land. The relief applies where an interest in land (including buildings) in a person's estate immediately before death is sold by 'the appropriate person', ie the person liable for the IHT thereon (normally the personal representatives), within three years of the death at a genuinely lower value. That value is then to be the taxable value subject to certain conditions. These conditions include a *de minimis* rule if the difference is only £1,000 or 5% of death value, whichever is the lower; and various anti-avoidance provisions are introduced where the purchaser is 'associated'.

The meaning of the word 'sold' was considered in *Jones v IRC* [1997] STC 358 where Lightman J held that in the context of ss 190–198 it is 'clear beyond question that "sold" means "conveyed or transferred on completion of a sale"' (ie an exchange of contracts which does not result in completion of the sale (for whatever reason) denies the relief).

Where the appropriate person has received other land from the estate and sells it, the claim must be for all or none of the land (this perhaps affords a loophole in so far as the sale of the profitable land can be left until later after the four-year period). There are similar adjustments for changes (as described in **2.35**) as well as adjustments for further purchases up to four months from the last sale.

2.38   Where the claimant purchases any interest in land in the *same capacity* the claim is reduced, ie the sale price is increased by the following addition:

$$\frac{\text{Date of death value minus sale price}}{\text{The aggregate sale prices}} \times \text{Aggregate purchase prices}$$

The aim is that the relief is to apply only to the *net* loss. Note the importance of the relief only being restricted where the sales and purchases are in the same capacity.

2.39   The earlier relief period was three years. In recognition of difficulties in selling land, a new s 197A was introduced by FA 1993, s 199, applying to deaths on or after 16 March 1990, whereby a sale (not by compulsory purchase) of land at a loss in the fourth year after death is treated as a sale within the first three years. Putting such a fourth-year loss back into the initial three years, rather than merely extending the period from three to four years excludes any problems with other fourth-year sales either at a profit or to associated persons which could otherwise limit the relief on the loss.

The requirement in s 191(1)(a) that the 'appropriate person' (ie the person liable for inheritance tax attributable to the value of the land interest) must make the relief claim was considered in *Stonor and another (executors of Dickinson, deceased) v IRC* [2001] STC (SCD) 199. In that case, a claim made by the executors of the deceased's estate to *increase* the valuation of properties in that estate (ie to increase their base cost for CGT purposes) was refused, as there was no appropriate person to make the claim. The deceased's residuary estate, which included freehold properties, was left to charity (ie an exempt transfer). The value of the deceased's non-residuary estate did not exceed the available nil rate band. There was no tax payable, and hence no appropriate person was liable to pay the tax.

A claim can result in values being increased (unlike with shares), and therefore a higher IHT liability. The position is stated accurately in HMRC's guidance (IHTM33010): 'When an interest in land ... is sold for a price different to its date of death value within four years of the death, relief may be available'. There are no provisions allowing for a claim to be withdrawn once it is made (see IHTM33013). Consideration should therefore be given to delaying the making of a claim if possible until the position becomes clear, ie until it becomes certain that there will be no further sales.

Form IHT38 ('Claim for relief – loss on sale of land') can be downloaded from HMRC's website: (www.hmrc.gov.uk/cto/forms/iht38.pdf).

Sales of related property within three years after death (s 176)

2.40 This relief applies where, within three years after a person's death, there is a sale of any property comprised in his estate immediately before his death which was valued for IHT purposes under the rule in s 161 with related property. It also applies in conjunction with property which was also comprised in the estate but has not at any time since death been vested in the vendors, for example the deceased's interest in possession. For a discussion on related property following the *Arkwright* case, see **1.24**.

A claim (under s 176(2)) can then be made that the property at the death be valued freed from the related etc property provisions. There are conditions:

- the vendors must be the persons in whom the property is vested or the deceased's personal representatives;
- the sale must be at arm's length (s 176(3)(b)), and not in conjunction with other related property sales;
- the vendor and the purchaser must not be associated or connected;
- the vendor must have no right to have the property sold back to him; and
- the relief is not available if there has been an alteration of shares or rights under s 94 between the death and the sale.

Example 2.9 – Related property relief

Malcolm died on 3 August 2011. His estate included 2,000 shares (20%) in Leatherhead Ltd, an unquoted company. His wife held 40% of the shares. His shares were valued, under the related property rules of s 161 at £100 per share, ie £200,000.

On 15 September 2012, the shares were sold by his executors to a venture capital company for £25 per share on an arm's-length sale, thus realising £50,000. The executors claimed to have the original valuation amended to value the shares as unrelated property at death. On that basis, it was agreed that at that time the value was £20 per share, ie a total of £40,000, on the basis of a 20% shareholding.

£40,000 is therefore substituted for the related property value of £200,000.

Business relief has been ignored in the above example. Where shares which qualified for business or agricultural relief on the footing that the deceased had control of the company are then revalued under these provisions, business relief may be lost. It will be available only if the shares subject to the revaluation would themselves have given the deceased control without taking into account any other shares with which they were valued (ss 105(2) and 122(2)).

Undivided or joint shares

2.41   The discount for the lower marketability of assets such as land and buildings held in joint shares continues to be reflected in IHT valuations (a 10% reduction is fairly normal). This position may not, however, exist in strictness where the related property provisions apply, ie between husband and wife or where held by a charity within five years of a transfer from either of them (see **1.24**). Moreover, the loss on the *creation* of such an interest would be *greater* and taxed at that time.

Example 2.10 – Joint property

Nigel, a widower, whose late wife had used her nil rate band, on 7 August 2008 transferred his house into joint names of himself and Olive, his carer, having earlier that financial year used his annual and other allowances. Before the transfer the house was worth, say, £200,000; afterwards Nigel's half share is worth, say, £90,000.

On the consequential loss formula Nigel's transfer of value was £110,000. Olive lived with Nigel, so there was no reservation of benefit (FA 1986, s 102B(4)). (The only problem for Olive was in persuading Nigel's family, after Nigel's death on 4 September 2012, that there had been no improper influence on Nigel to make the gift: the burden of proof will almost certainly be on her, not on the family.)

Whatever the outcome of litigation, the value remaining in Nigel's estate in respect of the house is the reduced value of a share in the house, which in September 2012 is worth £249,995: using the same fraction as at the time of the gift of 50% (but valued at 90% of that for tax purposes), his estate will contain: a share worth £112,498; and any other assets, such as chattels.

The nil rate band available will be £325,000 reduced by £110,000, ie £215,000.

For a detailed discussion of the valuation of the value of an interest in an agricultural tenancy, see **15.77** (*IRC v Gray*; *Walton v IRC*).

Unquoted shares and unquoted securities

2.42   Here the open market value position applies. However, in many cases, particularly where loss of control is involved, the consequential loss formula may produce a different valuation than applies for CGT. Subject to this, s 168 provides that it shall be assumed that there is available to any prospective purchaser of the shares or securities all the information which a prudent prospective purchaser of the shares or securities might reasonably require if he were proposing to purchase them from a willing vendor by private treaty and at arm's length. The concept of consequential loss is so fundamental to IHT that it is perhaps worth illustrating again.

Example 2.11 – Consequential loss to estate

Peter, on 3 September 2012, gave to his No 1 discretionary trust 10% of the shares in Altitude Ltd (a property investment company without business property relief), reducing his holding from 55% to 45%, and to his No 2 discretionary trust a Ming vase, one of a pair, valued on its own at £8,000. Both sets of trustees are to pay the tax.

HMRC agreed the following values of the shares (the remaining 45% were held by non-related parties):

55%	£240,000
45%	£160,000
10%	£10,000

The Ming vases were valued as a pair at £23,000.

There was one previous chargeable transfer. Peter had used up his annual exemptions and nil rate band, so that the present transfers were in the taxable band.

Chargeable transfers

	£
Shares (£240,000 – £160,000)	80,000
Vase (£23,000 – £8,000)	15,000
	95,000
Tax payable thereon at 20%	19,000

However, if Peter had given cash of, say, £10,000 to the No 1 discretionary trust and £8,000 to the No 2 trust, there is at least an argument that the respective trustees could have used the money at a later date to buy the shares and vase. The transfers of assets are sales rather than transfers of value in view of s 10, and are therefore not chargeable transfers under s 3.

The difficulty would be in showing that the sales were at market value and were not intended to confer any gratuitous benefit and that the operations were not associated transactions under s 268. That would be hard to prove, in respect of the shares, unless it could be shown that, in the prevailing financial climate, there was little or no market in property companies. It would also be hard to justify on market value grounds the destruction of value involved in selling one vase of a pair to a connected person: why not sell both at arm's length and use part of the proceeds to buy a singleton?

Debts due to the transferor/estate owner

2.43   The assumption is made in s 166 that any debt will be discharged in full, the onus being on the taxpayer to show that recovery is impossible or not reasonably practicable. It must therefore be brought into account at its face value unless the taxpayer can produce evidence to the contrary. See below as to the complicated issues that may arise. This concept is important in the context of interest-free loans (see **11.53**).

Provided such loans are repayable on demand no IHT liability on the consequential loss formula should arise when they are made. However, if a debt forming part of a deceased person's estate is not *currently* due, it should still be possible to argue that its value for IHT on the death must be discounted. If after death (but in the administration period) a debt previously considered to be irrecoverable is in fact paid, the deceased's estate will be increased by that amount.

Example 2.12 – Discounted liability?

Quentin, a pharmacist, founded a research company and gave his life's study to a rare tropical disease and its cure. He made some progress in 2000, but the ideas required funding. In 2002, he inherited from his parents and, being a bachelor without dependants, he used capital to expand the research.

He subscribed £300,000 on 10 August 2002 for new shares in the company and at the same time lent a further £200,000. By 30 March 2011, the company was again in difficulties, so Quentin agreed to a dilution of his equity below 50%, converted the loan into more shares and subscribed for £1,250,000 unsecured loan stock which would carry votes in certain circumstances but no interest until certain banking covenants had been fulfilled.

Sadly, Quentin's hopes for a breakthrough were unfulfilled at the time of his death on 31 August 2012. The company was still in difficulties and, without Quentin's leadership, the accumulated expenditure on research had little realisable value. The shares were worth little more than par, and the loan stock, with impending breach of banking covenants, was worth only 20p in the pound.

For IHT purposes, the shares bought in 2002 carry BPR, for what it is worth. The shares arising on conversion in 2011 have not been held long enough and do not give control under s 105(1)(b) so enjoy no relief. Since the investment of £1,250,000 only 18 months before death has lost much of its value, the question arises whether, when lending the money, Quentin must have known that he was throwing good money after bad and was making at that time a chargeable transfer.

Deductible liabilities and restrictions on deduction

2.44   The basic provisions in relation to deductibility on death are contained in s 5(5). Except for liabilities imposed by law, a liability incurred by a transferor shall be taken into account only to the extent that it was incurred for a consideration in money or money's worth, (eg a voluntary covenant to X is not a deductible debt and is ignored).

Deficiencies in the deceased's estate may not be 'netted off' as liabilities against the value of interests in settled property. In *St Barbe Green & another v CIR* Ch D [2005] STC 288, the deceased held a life interest in funds in two settlements, but his estate was insolvent. The Revenue rejected the settlement trustees' claims to deduct the estate deficiencies against the value of the settlement interests. The High Court held that free estate liabilities could only reduce the value of the free estate, and that if the personal estate was reduced to zero there was nothing else to offset any excess liabilities against. A harsh case as, if both the free estate and the trust estate were of value, they would be aggregated to establish the total taxable estate.

The provisions concerning liabilities were tightened to counter the ease of making PETs and as an adjunct to the reservation of benefit rules (see FA 1986, s 103). This gives rise to an abatement of the deductible liabilities in certain circumstances.

Abatement (ie full or partial disallowance of deductibility against the deceased's estate) applies:

- Where, and to the extent that, consideration received by the deceased (ie the money or other property advanced to him giving rise to the debt or encumbrance) consists of 'property derived from the deceased'. Examples would include:

–   annual or periodical payments made by the deceased which are lent back to him; or

–   the case where a donor transfers an asset to the donee and the donee sells it back to the donor leaving the purchase price outstanding on loan; or

–   the case where the donee sells the original asset, buys another, and sells that one to the donor on a loan arrangement; and

● Where, and to the extent that, the consideration is given by anyone who was at any time 'entitled' to, or whose resources at any time included, property derived from the deceased. An example would be where A gives Blackacre to B; B sells Blackacre to C; C sells it to D; C sells Whiteacre to A leaving the sale price on loan. It appears that the loan would not be deductible in A's estate.

For the meaning of 'property derived from the deceased', see FA 1986, s 103(4), which covers circumstances where the arrangements are in concert, or are direct/indirect/intermediate dispositions.

The following points should be borne in mind:

● *McDougal's Trustees v IRC* [1952] SLT 337. In this case, M bought park land and donated it to Edinburgh City Council, from which he borrowed the purchase price. On M's death, the loan due to the council was not deductible because the consideration for the loan by the council was in respect of property derived from the deceased.

● These provisions undermine most 'old style' inheritance trust schemes. 'Modern' inheritance trust arrangements seek to avoid the trap: see **14.30**.

● The abatement provisions are avoided if the person receiving the property derived from the deceased received it in a different capacity to that in which the consideration for the debt is given; or the disposition was not made with reference to or with a view to enabling or facilitating the giving of the consideration.

● Abatement will not be applied to the extent that consideration exceeds the value of the property derived from the deceased.

● If and to the extent that the estate owner discharges non-deductible liabilities, he is treated as having made a PET (FA 1986, s 103(5)). Such discharges should be by deed.

There are specific provisions on life policies under FA 1986, s 103(7), which deny relief for a deduction claimed against a deceased's estate relating to a life policy issued on or after 1 July 1986 unless the whole proceeds form part of the deceased's estate. These provisions counter:

- The decision in *Re Whitfield's Estate, IRC v Whitfield* [1976] STC 89, CA. In that case a deathbed life assurance arrangement was allowed as an ED deduction as the debt was incurred for 'full consideration in money or money's worth wholly for the deceased's own use and benefit' as between the lender and the deceased even though applied by way of gift.

- Schemes whereby an individual took out life assurance in trust for beneficiaries and paid a small initial premium, the substantial part of the premium being payable after death and claimed to be a deduction from the estate.

These restrictions on deductibility may give rise to a double charge of IHT (eg where property given by a PET is lent back by the donee and both the property and the PET become chargeable to IHT because the transferor of the PET dies within seven years). In such cases, relief may be obtainable under regulations (Inheritance Tax (Double Charges Relief) Regulations 1987, SI 1987/1130) issued under FA 1986, s 104, for the avoidance of double charges: see **1.14**.

The issue of deductibility was considered in *Alexander v IRC* [1991] STC 112. A council flat had been sold to the tenant under the 'right to buy' legislation with an obligation on the tenant to repay a percentage of the discount on the price if a disposal occurred within five years. The tenant died within that period. The Court of Appeal directed the Lands Tribunal to determine the value for (what was then) CTT on the owner's death after taking into account the liability to repay. The tribunal was to fix the amount a hypothetical purchaser would pay to stand in the shoes of the deceased, being subject to the obligation. This followed *IRC v Crossman* [1937] AC 26, HL dealing with restrictions on transfer of shares in a private company.

Demutualisation and nationalisation: IHT consequences

2.45   The Special Commissioners held in *Ward v IRC* [1999] STC (SCD) that rights to windfall payments which arose on the conversion of a building society into a public limited company should be included as part of the deceased's death estate. In this case, although the deceased had died shortly before the society's flotation was confirmed, under the terms of the transfer document the first named executor under her will was entitled to the shares on behalf of her estate. The CTO (as it then was) published guidance on how to value the rights to the shares. The guidance includes a valuation table to help calculate the open market value of deceased members' shares and lists the various building societies which had converted in previous years. See *Tax Bulletin Issue 34*, April 1998.

A special rule applies in relation to holdings in Northern Rock Building Society (NR), which got into financial difficulties and was bailed out by the taxpayer. Former NR shareholders who died on or after 22 February 2008 no longer held NR shares, but were instead entitled to compensation for the loss of their shares. Where the right to compensation relates to a holding of 1,000 shares or less in NR, HMRC will accept the values offered in IHT400 returns without enquiry, including a value of nil. For holdings of more than 1,000 shares, any valuation is likely to be referred to HMRC Shares and Assets Valuation. Similar treatment applies in respect of former shareholders of Bradford & Bingley who died on or after 29 September 2008, and were entitled to compensation for the loss of their shares (IHTM10073).

KEY ADMINISTRATION ASPECTS

The burden of IHT

2.46   The relevant rules are in ss 199–214, and are more detailed than many practitioners realise. Generally, the persons liable for tax due on a chargeable transfer are:

- the transferor;
- the transferee;
- any person in whom the property is vested at any time after the transfer;
- any person beneficially entitled to an interest in possession in the property; and
- where the chargeable transfer results in property being comprised in a settlement, any person for whose benefit the property or its income is applied.

Certain key aspects in relation to personal representatives are summarised below.

Administration and liability for IHT

2.47   The tax due on a PET, or the extra tax due as a result of the transferor's death within seven years of a chargeable transfer, is due primarily from the donee and secondly from the personal representatives of the transferor (see s 199(2)).

The position of the personal representatives in more detail is as follows:

(1)   If the donee of a PET which becomes chargeable fails to pay the IHT within 12 months from the end of the month of death, the personal

representatives become liable for the IHT (ss 199(2), 204(8)) plus interest due after six months. The personal representatives have no indemnity against the donee.

(2)   Likewise the additional rate charge on the donee of a chargeable lifetime transfer.

(3)   Contrast the position where there is a gift with reservation (FA 1986, s 102(3)) and the donee fails to pay the IHT. Here the personal representatives do have an indemnity against the donee under s 211(3)).

(4)   Practical problems arise where the personal representatives have completed the administration of the estate and/or hold a certificate of discharge (see s 239). It seems that a certificate may not wholly protect the personal representatives from increased liability to IHT as a result, say, of the discovery of a hitherto unknown PET, because s 239(4) nullifies a certificate in case of fraud or 'failure to disclose material facts'. An innocent failure to disclose is still a failure and ostensibly could take away the protection of the certificate.

(5)   Prudent action by the donor and/or personal representatives could avoid the problems of (4) above:

   (a)   The personal representatives should retain sufficient funds for the tax. But how can you retain funds to pay IHT in respect of an asset of the deceased which you, as personal representative, did not know existed?

   (b)   The donor should always obtain a specific indemnity on making PETs or chargeable lifetime transfers (see the precedent at **11.48**).

   (c)   The personal representatives could insure against the liability (maximum to be the liability in the estate). See the comments in (a) above.

   (d)   If the donee of a PET also benefits under the deceased's will or intestacy, the personal representatives could set off their IHT liability against the donee's share of the estate.

Even these precautions cannot entirely cover the situation: see the comments at (7) below.

(6)   Further practical problems arise because the account must be delivered, and tax due paid, before grant of representation can be obtained. Indeed, an IHT reference number and payslip must be obtained before any IHT is paid. This means that money must be raised to pay IHT before the personal representative is in a position to obtain and deal with the deceased's property. Solutions include:

   (a)   *Direct Payment Scheme (DPS)*: The DPS was introduced to allow personal representatives to draw on money held in the deceased's bank or building society accounts in order to pay the IHT due on delivery of the IHT account (see IHT Newsletter, April 2003). The scheme applies to credit balances on accounts in the deceased's sole name, and involves applying to HMRC Inheritance Tax for a reference number. All taxpaying estates must obtain an IHT reference before the IHT400 account is submitted. The application can be made online via HMRC's website (www. hmrc.gov.uk/inheritancetax/online.htm) or by posting form IHT422 ('Application for Inheritance Tax reference'). HMRC will then send the new reference by post, which must be noted on the IHT account (IHT & Trusts Newsletter, December 2007). Form IHT422 can be downloaded from HMRC's website (www.hmrc. gov.uk/inheritancetax/iht422.pdf).

The application should be made at least three weeks before form IHT400 is to be submitted. When the tax liability has been calculated, form IHT423 ('Direct Payment Scheme bank or building society account') should be completed and signed by the personal representatives in respect of each account from which a transfer is to be made. The bank or building society should be contacted beforehand to ensure that they participate in the DPS. When the personal representatives wish to apply for grant, form IHT423 should be sent to the bank or building society, and the IHT400 form (and supplementary pages) submitted to HMRC.

When HMRC receive notification of the electronic payment, it will be attributed to the IHT400 form and, if everything is in order, form IHT421 ('Probate summary') (or form C1 ('Confirmation' in Scotland)) will be stamped and returned. Detailed instructions on paying IHT from the deceased's bank account are available from HMRC's website: (www.hmrc.gov.uk/inheritancetax/paying-iht/ find-money-to-pay/direct-payment-scheme.htm).

(b)   *The building society method*: One way around the funding problem involves forward planning. The estate owner, during his lifetime, moves appropriate funds from his bank account to a building society account. This helps because as a general rule most building societies will transfer funds out of an account in satisfaction of tax on death without probate or letters of administration. For example, the production of a death certificate and will may suffice. Banks are not generally so amenable. In any case, a building society may well pay a better rate of interest.

Alternatively, it may be possible for the estate owner to negotiate a similar facility with the bank (especially when they realise that a transfer out of the funds is the alternative). However, these arrangements, ie the transfer of funds to the building society or negotiation with the bank, must be done prior to the death of the estate owner. Written assurance should be obtained during the estate owner's lifetime that the arrangements referred to will have the required effect. If the individual has entered into a (lasting) power of attorney, the attorneys will be in a position to arrange matters.

(c) *Lifetime arrangements*: Alternatively, appropriate bank accounts could be set up during the lifetime of the estate owner. For example, a husband and wife or the proposed beneficiary could hold separate bank accounts containing the required amounts. As between spouses, the account could be a joint account, with each party having full signing power and/or a mandate. This latter proposal is not to be recommended as between non-spouses because HMRC are likely to assess the entire balance in the joint account on the first death. In view of the inter-spouse exemption this is not relevant as between husband and wife. See in this connection *O'Neill (O'Neill's Executors) v CIR* [1998] SSCD 110 (SpC 154) or *Sillars and another v CIR* [2004] STC (SCD) 180 (SpC 401). See also *Ms s Taylor (Executrix of Mrs K Boland) v HMRC* [2008] (SpC 704).

In *Smith v HMRC* [2009] SpC 742, [2009] WTLR 691, the lifetime transfer by the deceased of a building society account into joint names with her son was held to constitute a settlement for IHT purposes within s 43. As Mrs Smith was entitled to the income from the property, she was beneficially entitled to an interest in possession (IIP) in settled property. Under the 'old' (pre-FA 2006) rules on the IHT treatment of lifetime IIP settlements which applied in this case, Mrs Smith was beneficially entitled to the property itself, and it therefore formed part of her taxable estate when she died.

In *Matthews v Revenue & Customs Commissioners* [2012] UKFTT 658 (TC), Mrs Matthews died in January 2007. She initially held funds in an account in her sole name. In 1999, she opened a new account with her son at Abbey plc. Mrs Matthews withdrew all the monies in the account in her sole name, and deposited them in the new joint account. The account instructions included that either Mrs Matthews or her son could withdraw monies from the account without the other's signature being required, although no withdrawals were actually made prior to Mrs Matthews' death. The only deposits after the deceased's initial transfer into it consisted of interest credited, and small account bonuses. Mrs Matthews and her son each declared half of the interest earned in their income tax returns. The IHT account on Mrs Matthews' death also indicated that her share of funds in the account passed by survivorship to her son. The tribunal held that the whole of the funds in the account were liable to IHT as part of the deceased's estate under s 5(2), or alternatively under the gift with reservation anti-avoidance provisions (FA 1986, s 102).

(d) *Insurance solution*: Another option is to take out appropriate whole life, endowment or term insurance cover. For example, this could be done under the Married Women's Property Acts, other trust policies, or joint survivor trust policies. The establishment of such trusts are (from 22 March 2006) a chargeable transfer, but the value may be negligible. It is of primary importance that the policies are written in trust in favour of the intended beneficiary(ies) so as not to swell the estate of the individual whose life is being assured. As mentioned (see **1.27**), certain insurance solutions (eg partnership insurance policies, but not normally 'discounted gift trusts' and 'loan trusts') may give rise to potential 'pre-owned assets' income tax issues. For further information on pre-owned assets, see **Chapter 13**.

(7) However, although personal representatives still need to exercise prudence, it would appear that HMRC will act reasonably in genuine cases. In a letter to the Law Society (published in the *Law Society Gazette*, 13 March 1991) they indicated their practice in the following terms:

'The capital taxes offices will not usually pursue for inheritance tax personal representatives who:

– after making the fullest enquiries that are reasonably practicable in the circumstances to discover lifetime transfers, and so

– having done all in their power to make full disclosure of them to the Board of Inland Revenue

have obtained a certificate of discharge and distributed the estate before a chargeable lifetime transfer comes to light.

This statement of the Board's position is made without prejudice to the application in an appropriate case of IHTA 1984, s 199(2).'

This statement is reproduced in the Inheritance Tax Manual, which also instructs HMRC officers as follows (at IHTM30044):

'You must remember that the facility to have recourse to the transferor's personal representatives is not to be regarded as a soft option. We are to make all the attempts at recovering from the persons liable under Section 199(1) IHTA 1984 that we would presently contemplate in a similar situation against any liable person.'

On this footing, personal representatives may feel a little more comforted. The case of *Howarth's Executors v IRC* [1997] STC (SCD) 162 deals with the personal liability of executors – a lesson to be learnt! The executors distributed the estate, the beneficiary agreeing to settle the outstanding IHT instalments. When he went bankrupt, the remaining executor became personally liable for the IHT.

In *Smith v HMRC* (see 6(c) above), the question of the incidence and liability to IHT arose in respect of the 'settlement' of a building society account into joint names. The person liable for the IHT attributable to the settled property was the deceased's son as trustee and as recipient of it. He was also liable as executor of the estate for any additional tax due and which was attributable to the assets returned in the original IHT return. The appeals in that case were allowed in part, and Notices of Determination in respect of other family members (in their capacities as executor and recipient of residue) were adjusted accordingly.

Certificate of discharge

2.48   Pursuant to s 214, HMRC on application must issue a certificate of the amount of IHT recoverable where a person has paid or borne tax attributable to the value of any property, but for which he is not ultimately liable (eg trustees). Under s 239, there are provisions for the issue of a certificate of discharge to a person liable for any IHT. HMRC must issue a certificate if the person liable applies in circumstances where the transfer is on death or the transferor has died, but issue of a certificate is discretionary in other circumstances.

It seems that strictly a certificate may not protect personal representatives, although HMRC have adopted a reasonable stance: see **2.47**. See also **3.12** regarding clearance certificates in the context of the transferable nil rate band.

The HMRC charge

2.49   Under ss 237 and 238, HMRC have an enforceable charge, subject to certain limits, in respect of unpaid IHT and interest, the charge being imposed on the property itself. The charge does not affect purchasers without notice, nor does it arise in respect of any personal or moveable property, if the property was beneficially owned by the deceased immediately before his death and the transfer was made on death. Personal property does not include leaseholds which may be charged by HMRC (ie in relation to deaths occurring on or after 9 March 1999, following FA 1999).

Recovery from spouse

2.50   Under s 203, when a transferor has made a transfer of value to his spouse, IHT otherwise payable by the transferor, for example on chargeable transfers to a third party, may be recovered from such transferor's spouse up to the market value of the assets transferred to that spouse at the date of that spouse transfer. (This may cause some matrimonial consternation: for example, a wife could be liable for the IHT in respect of a discretionary settlement set up by her husband for his mistress!) The section enables the transferee spouse to apply a lower valuation to the gifted property received, particularly if the market value of the gift to that spouse has fallen by the time the chargeable transfer to the third party is made.

Delivery of accounts and payment of interest

Accounts

2.51   The transferor or trustee of a settlement need no longer submit an account of chargeable transfers that fall within the nil rate band, as outlined at **2.7**, but above that level must account unless some other person liable for tax (eg the transferee) has done so. Where the account is still required, it should include transfers which are exempt or within the nil rate band. Delivery to HMRC, where required, must be made within 12 months or, if later, three months from the date on which the liability to tax arises.

Personal representatives must deliver an account within 12 months of the death or, if later, within three months of beginning to act as such. In cases where no grant of representation has been obtained within 12 months of death, those in whom the property is vested (at the time of death or at any time after), or those beneficially entitled to an interest in possession, are under a duty to account under s 216(2).

Late payment interest and penalties

2.52   A contradictory position exists in that, whereas an account of chargeable transfers must be rendered only within 12 months from the end of the month in which the death occurs or the chargeable transfer is made (s 216), tax is due and interest accrues at the current rate six months after the end of the month in which death occurs or the transfer is made (subject to the right to pay by instalments; see **2.30**).

This applies in respect of transfers other than on death between 1 October and the following 5 April. For transfers after 5 April but before 1 October in any year, the IHT is due on 30 April of the next year. This can in theory be exploited as a cash-flow exercise. Thus a chargeable gift made on 5 April 2012 is due for payment on 1 November 2012, whereas tax on a gift on 6 April 2012 is not due until 30 April 2013. In practice, the timing of gifts is usually governed by other factors. The rules as to lifetime chargeable transfers apply to trustees.

Interest on the IHT is generally non-deductible for income tax purposes. Thus, for example, for lifetime transfers the true rate of interest of 4% for a taxpayer who pays income tax at the rate of 40% is 6.66%; the rate, which had been reduced to 0% at the height of the recession, was increased to 3% from 29 September 2009. As indicated at **2.3**, FA 2009 introduced provisions to align interest rates on underpayments and overpayments of IHT with other taxes (FA 2009, ss 101, 102, Schs 53, 54).

The Taxes and Duties (Interest Rate) Amendment Regulations 2009, SI 2009/2032, which came into effect on 12 August 2009, provide that the rate for charging interest on unpaid tax is the Bank of England base rate plus 2.5%. The rate of interest on repayments of tax is the Bank of England base rate minus 1%, subject to a lower limit of 0.5%. Interest generally runs on late paid IHT, from the due date to the date of payment or set-off. Repayment interest runs from a defined 'start date' to the date of repayment. Hardly a level playing field, it might be thought!

A new penalty regime in respect of the late payment of IHT liabilities was also included in FA 2009, to be introduced from a date to be appointed (see **2.3**). Under this regime, IHT liabilities generally begin to incur penalties if remaining unpaid by the filing date (within s 216) for the relevant account. The same applies to IHT determinations if there is a failure to submit an IHT return under s 216 or 217 by the due date and the return would show an amount payable.

In the case of amendments or corrections of IHT returns, penalties are due in respect of IHT unpaid after the filing date or, if later, more than 30 days after the amendment or correction. The same applies in respect of HMRC determinations other than those mentioned above.

For late paid instalments under s 227 (land shares and businesses; see **2.28**) or s 229 (woodlands), penalties generally apply in respect of the first instalment if it remains unpaid after the filing date for the relevant IHT account, or more than 30 days after the due date for subsequent instalments paid late (FA 2009, Sch 56, paras 1, 2).

The penalties regime

2.53   Penalties may be incurred for failing to deliver an account, to make a return or to comply with a notice seeking information. Fraud or negligence in the provision of information or accounts and returns may also be penalised. Any penalty is in addition to tax and interest. FA 2007 applied, in Schedule 24, the penalty regime for taxes other than IHT. FA 2008, Schedule 40, took that further. The changes apply with effect for all chargeable events occurring on or after 1 April 2009, and are described at **2.57** onwards, after noting rules that are specific to IHT.

A penalty of up to £100 may be charged under s 245(2) for a failure to deliver an IHT account (or a corrective account). If the account has still not been delivered within six months following the filing date and no proceedings for declaration of the failure have commenced, there is a liability to a further penalty of up to £100. These penalties are restricted in total to the IHT liability if the taxpayer can prove that the tax liability is lower. Formerly, it was rare for these penalties to be claimed, but it is now commonplace, as the application of penalties becomes more uniform across all taxes.

There is a further penalty of up to £60 for each day following that on which the failure has been declared by a court or the First-tier Tribunal and before the day on which the account is delivered. If a person has a reasonable excuse for failing to deliver the account, he is not liable to a penalty if he delivers the account without unreasonable delay after the excuse has ceased (s 245).

The penalty is not imposed where the taxpayer can show reasonable excuse, but the penalty will be charged unless the taxpayer delivers the account without unreasonable delay after the excuse has ceased: see s 245(7). The mere fact that the estate is complicated is not itself a factor; there must be some other element.

Example 2.13 – Inexcusable delay

Roger's estate comprised his various UK business interests, investments and properties. His executors were his son Tom, who had worked with him, and his friend Ursula, a registered Trust and Estate Practitioner. Roger died on 11 September 2010 and the normal filing date under s 216(6)(a) for form IHT400 was therefore 30 September 2011.

The account was late. A handwritten 'codicil' was discovered under which Sarah, a former friend and companion of Roger was appointed executrix, but the document was not admitted to probate, as was clear by 1 May 2011. Had Sarah become an executrix, she could have argued, under the 'three-month' rule in s 216(6)(a), that time did not run against her until appointed, but she did not act.

Tom and Ursula, as the executors, were jointly liable for penalties, so should have delivered the account and had no excuse. The size and complication of the estate are not excuses *per se*; Tom knew all about the assets, and Ursula had the specialist knowledge to deal with the account.

Notification of offshore settlements

2.54   Any person (other than a barrister) involved in the course of his trade or profession in the making of an offshore settlement (except in a will) must deliver a return to HMRC. This must be done within three months of its making, if he knows or has reason to believe that the settlor was UK domiciled and that the trustees are not resident in the UK (s 218).

The penalty for failing to comply is up to £300, plus a further penalty of up to £60 for every day after that on which the failure has been declared by the First-tier Tribunal and before the day on which the account is delivered (s 245A(1)).

Production of information etc

2.55   As indicated at **2.3**, HMRC's information and inspection powers (FA 2008, s 113, Sch 36) were introduced for IHT purposes from 1 April 2010 (SI 2009/3054, art 2). Penalties may arise for failing to comply with an information notice, or deliberately obstructing an inspection that has been approved by the tribunal, or concealing, destroying or otherwise disposing of documents, or providing inaccurate information or a document containing an inaccuracy in response to an information notice (FA 2008, Sch 36, paras 39–40A). There is a right of appeal against the imposition of a penalty, or the amount of a penalty (para 47).

With regard to the first two offences above (ie failure to comply or obstruction), there is an initial penalty of £300 (Sch 36, para 39). If the failure or obstruction continues, further penalties of up to £60 per day may be imposed (para 40). However, no fixed or daily penalty arises if there is a reasonable excuse for the failure (para 45).

Furthermore, HMRC may apply to the tribunal for an increased daily penalty of up to £1,000 per day, if there is a continuing failure to comply with an 'identity unknown' notice (Sch 36, para 49A).

A tax-related penalty can be imposed by the Upper Tribunal where a person fails to comply with an information notice, or deliberately instructs an inspection, and that failure continues after an initial penalty has been imposed (Sch 36, para 50). HMRC must make an application to the Upper Tribunal for the tax-related penalty within 12 months of a defined 'relevant date'. Such a penalty is only sought broadly where a significant amount of tax is considered to be at risk.

Daily, increased daily or tax-related penalties cannot be charged unless an initial penalty in respect of the failure, obstruction or concealment etc has been imposed. The increased daily penalty cannot be charged unless daily penalties have already been charged.

If inaccurate information is provided, or an inaccurate document is produced in response to an information notice, penalties can arise if the inaccuracy is careless or deliberate, or if the inaccuracy is later discovered but reasonable steps are not taken to inform HMRC. The maximum penalty is £3,000 for each inaccuracy (Sch 36, para 40A).

Last but not least, there is a criminal offence of concealing or destroying documents which are, or which HMRC consider may be, required by an information notice that has been approved by the tribunal. This offence applies in the most serious cases, and can result in a fine and/or imprisonment (Sch 36, Pt 8).

In relation to notices requiring information under s 219 ('Power to require information') or s 219A ('Power to call for documents etc) given before 1 April 2010, the appeal facility under s 219B ('Appeal against requirement to produce documents etc') and the penalty regime under s 245A ('Failure to provide information etc') continue to have effect. Readers are referred to the previous edition of this work for commentary on penalties under s 245A.

Incorrect return

2.56   For periods prior to the introduction (by FA 2008, Sch 40) of the penalty regime for inaccuracies in tax returns for IHT purposes, a person liable for the tax who fraudulently or negligently supplied an incorrect account, information or document to HMRC was liable to a penalty. The maximum penalty is 100% of the tax potentially lost (ie broadly the difference between the amount of tax correctly payable, and the amount of tax payable based on the incorrect return etc (s 247(1), (2)). For incorrect returns etc delivered between 22 July 1999 and 22 July 2004, the penalty for fraud was up to £3,000 plus a maximum amount equal to the additional tax based on the correct information. For neglect, the penalty was up to £1,500 plus a maximum amount equal to the additional tax based on the correct information (see IHTM36103). The rules as to calculation and mitigation of penalties as they applied under the previous penalty regime allowed practitioners to negotiate mitigation of the penalty by up to 30% for disclosure, up to 40% for cooperation and up to 40% in respect of seriousness (ie size and gravity); but all that has changed since the provisions described later in this chapter came into force.

The current penalty regime applies for IHT purposes to all chargeable events occurring from 1 April 2009, but the old provisions outlined above continue to apply to events before that date.

A person not liable for the tax (eg an agent or adviser) who fraudulently or negligently supplies any incorrect document or information in connection with a chargeable transfer is liable to a penalty of up to £3,000. A person who assists in or induces the supply of any account, information or document he knows to be incorrect is liable to a penalty of up to £3,000 (s 247(3), (4)). For such accounts, documents or information delivered between 22 July 1999 and 22 July 2004, the maximum penalty for fraud is £3,000, and £1,500 for negligence (see IHTM36104). These provisions are unaffected by the changes introduced by FA 2008, Sch 40.

A person liable to the tax may have supplied an account, information or document without fraud or negligence. He may subsequently discover that it is 'materially' incorrect (eg if the total tax arising from the correction(s) amounts to £1,000 or more; see IHTM09088). In such a case, the return is treated as having been negligently supplied unless the error is remedied without unreasonable delay. If another person (eg an agent or adviser) supplied the account, information or document and the person liable to the tax discovers that it is incorrect, he must inform the Board of the error without unreasonable delay. Otherwise, he is liable to a penalty as if he personally had negligently supplied the incorrect account, information or document (s 248).

2.57   Whereas other aspects of the modernisation of penalties do not specifically concern IHT, that tax is included in FA 2008,s 122 and Sch 40. The intention of the legislation is to address five areas of concern:

- incorrect returns;

- failure to notify a new taxable activity;

- late filing and late payment;

- failure to keep records, and powers to seek information; and

- other regulatory failures.

The penalty regime for errors in returns etc (FA 2007, Sch 24) was amended and extended (by FA 2008, Sch 40) so as to include accounts under IHTA 1984, ss 216 and 217, information or documents required by IHTA 1984, s 256 and statements or declarations in connection with deductions, exemptions or reliefs.

2.58   In IHT situations, there is often shared responsibility for information gathering, most obviously in relation to lifetime gifts. The rules apply to errors on returns for tax events and periods beginning on or after 1 April 2009, where the filing date is 1 April 2010 or later (although, if information or a document is produced under s 256 ('Regulations about accounts, etc') from 1 April 2009, the tax period must begin on or after that date), and the examples that follow are framed as if the rules apply to them.

Example 2.14 – A difficult estate to administer

Vera, a travel writer, led a long and colourful life. A liaison with a tax adviser whilst at college produced a daughter, Winifred, whom she brought up until old enough for Winifred's father to place her in the English public school system. Vera left for South America, married and had a son, Xavier, and daughter, Yolande. Following divorce, Vera returned to the UK, living off royalties and rental income and working as a nanny, mainly for cash. She ended her days living with Zoltan.

Vera's South American will appointed two friends in Buenos Aires as executors, and under the Law Reform (Succession) Act 1995 the will took effect as if the former husband had died on the date of decree absolute, but the rest of the will was still valid and made no provision for Zoltan.

In old age Vera sought some reconciliation with each of her children, in particular Winifred, now a journalist who (she later said) had cared for her mother in her later years. Vera's mental powers were failing; shortly before the deadline of 30 September 2007 she signed an enduring power of attorney in favour of Winifred. By the time of Vera's death serious differences had arisen between Winifred, Xavier, Yolande and Zoltan. The estate was complicated, involving UK and American assets and succession rights to royalties. Serious issues arose as to whether certain gifts had or had not been made and whether, at the time of gifts, Vera had had capacity to make them.

The executors in Buenos Aires faced very significant difficulties in discharging their obligation under IHTA 1984, s 216 to deliver an account that specifies all the appropriate property and its value. This is addressed by FA 2007, Sch 24, para 1A. Most of that schedule concerns the obligations of a person identified in para 1(1) as 'P'. The penalties in para 1A concern a different person, 'T'. A penalty may be due where the inaccuracy in the return made by P is attributable to false information deliberately supplied, either directly or indirectly, by T or where T deliberately withholds information from P.

The inaccuracy is one which results in:

- an understatement by P of the liability to tax; or

- a false or inflated statement of a loss (which would not normally apply to IHT though debts at death have a similar effect); or

- a false or inflated claim to repayment of tax.

Thus, in the example of Vera, the obligations would be shared by the executors and the family; and if, for example, it transpired that Vera had made a substantial gift to Winifred, which Winifred kept quiet about, the burden would lie on Winifred.

Degrees of culpability

2.59   It should be noted under the current penalty regime that there is no penalty in the case of an 'innocent error' (ie broadly where a person has taken reasonable care in completing the return, and has taken reasonable steps to notify errors if appropriate). This 'reasonable care' requirement replaces the 'negligence' test under the previous rules. HMRC consider that the deceased's personal representatives will have taken reasonable care where, for example, they:

- follow the guidance provided about filling in forms such as the IHT400;

- make suitable enquiries of asset holders and other people (as suggested in the guidance) to establish the extent of the deceased's estate;

- ensure correct instructions are given to valuers when valuing assets;

- seek advice about anything they are unsure of;

- follow up inconsistencies in information they receive from asset holders, valuers and other people; and

- identify any estimated values included on the form.

If an agent is acting, HMRC expect the PRs to check through the form before signing it and to question anything that does not accord with what they know about the deceased. Simply signing an account completed by an agent is not considered by HMRC to be taking reasonable care. It was explained by HMRC to practitioners, when the 'toolkit' for CGT was under consultation, that (proven) use of the toolkit would be regarded as the taking of reasonable care. However, this does not appear to be the stance that HMRC have subsequently adopted (see **2.67**).

If IHT is payable other than on death, HMRC expect the transferor (or trustees) to deliver a full and complete return of the transaction concerned, and to have sought professional advice as necessary. Again, simply signing an account completed by an agent is not taking reasonable care in HMRC's view (Inheritance Tax and Trusts Newsletter April 2009).

There are three behaviour types or degrees of culpability:

- The lowest level of culpability, described as 'careless', is where the taxpayer fails to take reasonable care in completing the return.

- The 'middle' level of culpability is 'deliberate but not concealed' where the return is wrong and results from the deliberate action of the taxpayer, but the taxpayer makes no arrangements to conceal the inaccuracy.

- Finally, the most serious level of wrongdoing is that which is 'deliberate and concealed' where the taxpayer has deliberately sent in a wrong return and deliberately tries to conceal the parts of the return that are wrong, for example by submitting false evidence in support of false figures.

When a return proves to be inaccurate, the taxpayer will be treated as careless, even though he may not have been so at the time of the return, if he discovers the inaccuracy some time later and does not take reasonable steps to inform HMRC (FA 2007, Sch 24, para 2). In this summary, the word 'return' is used, but the rules apply in the much wider context of documents that, whether or not returns, fix the liability to tax.

The level of penalties

2.60   The following maximum levels were established by FA 2007, Sch 24, but as mentioned their scope was extended by FA 2008:

- The 30% rate: 30% of the potential lost revenue, where the taxpayer was careless.

- The 70% rate: 70%, where the action of the taxpayer was deliberate but not concealed.

- The 100% rate: 100%, where the action of the taxpayer was deliberate and concealed. This can apply in two circumstances. Under FA 2007, Sch 24, para 4(1)(c) the full penalty could apply to 'deliberate and concealed action'. That penalty is extended to cover 'third party' acts such as might apply to the family of Vera in Example 2.14 (Sch 24, para 4B). The collection of tax lost through third-party inaccuracy is extended to include any inaccuracy resulting from the supply of false information or the withholding of information.

Where there are various errors, as could easily apply in the administration of an estate, careless inaccuracies are corrected before deliberate inaccuracies; and deliberate but not concealed inaccuracies are corrected before deliberate and concealed inaccuracies. In calculating the lost tax, account is taken of any overstatement in any document given by the taxpayer that relates to the same tax period.

Probate practice has long been seen as something of a legal backwater, to which perhaps under-employed conveyancers may turn in troubled times. The tax in issue on death can greatly exceed what an ordinary family person would be likely to incur in respect of any other tax or on any other occasion. Preparation of the IHT400 should fully reflect the tax in issue and the professional risks involved.

Example 2.15 – Too casual an approach to compliance

Alice, a widow whose late husband had used his nil rate band, died leaving a house, a share in an investment partnership and personal effects. Her daughter Brenda, as sole executor, knew that Alice had always used her annual exemption and was aware of lump-sum gifts of £80,000. Brenda completed the IHT400 thus:

house	300,000
partnership share	150,000
personal effects	15,000
gifts	80,000
	545,000
Less: funeral, etc	(2,500)
	542,500
less nil rate band	(325,000)
taxable	217,500
tax liability	87,000

Brenda had been in a hurry to get a grant of probate, anxious to catch the property market before her mother's house fell in value. She did not get a professional valuation, thinking that she knew property prices in the area. It turned out that an area of land to the side of the house had realistic prospect of development and that, if sold separately, with the benefit of planning permission, it might realise £100,000 without taking any value off the house. Applying the valuation rule in *Prosser v IRC*, that added £25,000 to the estate and £10,000 to the tax liability.

It also transpired that the investment partnership had made certain losses in respect of which it was entitled to a refund of tax, so £20,000 would be added to the value of the estate when the returns were settled. Brenda told HMRC as soon as she had the right figures. No business relief was available in respect of the investment partnership, so this added £8,000 to the eventual liability.

Brenda knew that Alice had given her sister, Celia, the family campervan, some eight or nine years before her death. It had then been worth £43,000. Brenda had not the slightest interest in camping and had never been concerned with the arrangement between her mother and her sister, and assumed that the gift need not be disclosed because it was outside the seven-year period.

Brenda did know that her mother continued to tour Italy but thought it was with her sister and her family, so it never occurred to Brenda that that might constitute a reservation of benefit out of the gift within *Revenue Interpretation*

55. Celia did complain occasionally that she had to bear all the costs of running the vehicle whilst her busy life as a mother and matrimonial lawyer prevented her from taking time off, whereas her mother in retirement made extensive use of it. When the reservation of benefit point was raised in correspondence on another aspect of the estate, Brenda immediately realised that there was a problem and disclosed the gift.

Brenda was less forthcoming about the cheques that she had signed in her capacity as attorney for her mother. For the last four years of her mother's life, acting under an enduring power of attorney which had not been registered despite Alice's failing powers, Brenda had regularly drawn off £1,000 per month into a separate account and had used the money towards the cost of her children's education.

Brenda thought that the gifts would be covered by the IHTA 1984, s 21 exemption for normal and reasonable expenditure of the deceased, even though the gifts went well beyond what Brenda had power to make under her powers of attorney. It was only when HMRC called for copy bank statements that the £48,000 of gifts were discovered and even then Brenda offered a number of implausible reasons that the sums should not be taxable. Adding them back to the estate increased the tax liability by £19,200.

The valuation error was careless. It was held in *Robertson v CIR* [2002] STC (SCD) 182 that a material understatement of value did not there trigger penalties, but in that case the executor had indicated in the return that the value was an estimate and was therefore, in *Robertson v CIR (No. 2)* [2002] SSCD 242, able to recover handsomely from HMRC. In the present case, a penalty of up to £3,000 arises because the error is not simply the difference between one person's view of a value and that of another; there is a fundamental error in the basis of valuation which would have been avoided if Brenda had been in less of a hurry and had obtained a proper valuation in the first place.

The restatement of value of the partnership interest probably does not attract a penalty at all. Brenda showed the value of the partnership as she understood it at the date of death, and it is only after some negotiation with another branch of HMRC that the tax refund materialises. Brenda has disclosed the change as soon as aware of it, so it is simply a case of paying the tax and interest, but not of a penalty.

Brenda did not disclose the reservation of benefit in connection with the campervan, which was careless because she should have thought about the issue and the form of the return contains ample prompts on the issue. It might have been different if Alice had taken Celia's children off her hands for the summer holidays: Revenue Interpretation 55 refers to 'babysitting' and might cover the point. Celia made no secret of the fact that her mother had some benefit from the vehicle that she had given away, so Celia is not to blame. Tax is chargeable subject to negotiation as to value, remembering the option of HMRC to treat the gift as a chargeable transfer or to treat it as part of the estate at death. Where an asset falls in value, HMRC will probably prefer to treat the gift as a failed PET and tax the value at the time of the gift. On that basis, there is extra tax of £12,000 to find.

In relation to the school fees, Brenda's action is deliberate and concealed, so the possible penalty (subject to the observations below) is 100% of the tax: an extra £19,200.

FA 2007, Sch 24, para 6 requires an initial calculation of the careless inaccuracies, here the £10,000 on the valuation issue and possibly the £8,000 in respect of the business. Next in gravity comes the £12,000 on the van and finally the £19,200 on the school fees. As to mitigation, see below.

Reduction in penalties for disclosure

2.61   FA 2007, Sch 24, para 4 sets bands of penalties, and para 9 allows for a reduction within the bands but not total reduction in the more serious cases. The penalty is reduced where a person, including a third party, discloses inaccuracy in a tax document. This may be by simply telling HMRC about the situation; or giving HMRC reasonable help to quantify the inaccuracy; or allowing HMRC access to records to enable the inaccuracy to be corrected.

Where the disclosure is made by the taxpayer at a time when he has no reason to believe that HMRC have discovered or are about to discover the inaccuracy, that disclosure is classified as 'unprompted'. The effect of this is that an unprompted disclosure of a careless error can reduce the penalty to nil. Applying Example 2.15, the revaluation of the business following the obtaining of the tax refund, if disclosed promptly, may avoid a penalty entirely.

Mitigation of 30% penalties

2.62   Where the disclosure is prompted, a careless error, attracting a penalty of 30%, may be reduced, but not below 15% (unless there are 'special circumstances'; see FA 2007, Sch 24, para 11). The error in valuing the house in Example 2.15 was careless. If notified to HMRC as soon as it was discovered, that might be treated as an unprompted disclosure. However, the mechanism of valuation in deceased estates relies on disclosure which in turn includes answering the question whether the property is to be offered for sale. The value of the property is routinely referred to the Valuation Office Agency.

If it is known that a property is to be sold within a reasonably short time of the death, then it is quite common for the gross sale proceeds to be taken as the value at the date of death.

Brenda could argue that she merely offered an opinion of the value of the property that turned out to be wrong and that she was, in effect, disclosing as part of the estate whatever price would eventually be received on sale, on the basis that the sale price would be substituted for the valuation. However, that is a weak argument and, by her carelessness, Brenda has certainly risked a penalty of at least £1,500 (ie £10,000 × 15%).

Mitigation of 70% penalties

2.63   Where the action of the taxpayer was deliberate but not concealed, the starting point for penalties is 70% but it may be reduced under FA 2007, Sch 24, para 10(3), to a minimum of 20%. The mitigation will depend on the 'quality' of the disclosure, defined by FA 2007, Sch 24, para 9(3) to include timing, nature and extent.

In Example 2.15, the failure to disclose the gift with reservation was careless, but not actually concealed or unprompted, arising from the detailed correspondence on the administration of the estate. Had Brenda volunteered details of the gift (ie an unprompted disclosure), the penalty could have been reduced to 20%, but under FA 2007, Sch 24, para 10(4) a penalty that is otherwise chargeable at 70% cannot be reduced below 35% if the disclosure is prompted. On the face of it, therefore, Brenda will be at risk of a penalty of £4,200 in respect of the van (ie £12,000 × 35%).

Mitigation of 100% penalties

2.64   Similar rules apply to errors that fall into the 100% regime, but they will be harsher. For unprompted disclosure, the minimum penalty is 30%, but where the disclosure arises only after HMRC have raised questions the penalty cannot be less than 50%. In relation to the undisclosed, unauthorised transfers to pay school fees in Example 2.15, Brenda has done nothing to help HMRC. She did finally supply copies of her mother's bank statements, but only after she had been asked a couple of times. She attempted to 'explain away' the payments and will be fortunate to escape with a penalty of much less than, say, £18,000.

As indicated at **2.62**, there is facility in FA 2007, Sch 24, para 11 for 'special reduction' of a penalty if HMRC think it right because of 'special circumstances', but that does not include inability to pay, nor the fact that the increased liability of one taxpayer may reduce the liability of another.

There is a 100% cap on penalties (see FA 2007, Sch 24, para 12(4)), to cover the situation where a penalty could be charged against both the taxpayer and a third party. Thus, in Example 2.15, if Celia had kept quiet about her mother's use of the van and Brenda had been careless about the issue of reservation of benefit, a penalty could apply to both of them, but either way it would not exceed 100% of the tax in issue.

2.65   Penalties will not be claimed from a deceased person who had not been compliant, but that in no way exonerates delinquent personal representatives.

Valuations and penalties

2.66   Asset valuations, and the valuation of land and buildings in particular, often give rise to difficulties. HMRC perceive valuation as a key area of risk. This increases the risk of a successful challenge, where the valuation appears to HMRC to be too low (*Hatton v Revenue and Customs Commissioners* [2010] UKUT 195 (LC); although by contrast, see *Chadwick & another v Revenue and Customs Commissioners* [2010] UKUT 82 (LC)). In addition, a substantial undervaluation may result in the imposition of penalties.

Penalty issues can and do arise if an incorrect valuation included in a return results in an IHT liability being understated, and there has been a lack of reasonable care in that valuation. HMRC's Inheritance Tax & Trusts Newsletter (August 2009) features a report on its Annual Probate Section Conference, which indicates that if instructions for the valuation of a property are given on the correct basis, any uplift in value subsequently agreed is 'unlikely' to attract a penalty. The 'correct basis' is defined as:

'… a hypothetical sale in the open market under normal market conditions and marketed property with no discounts for a quick sale or for the time of year etc.'

The suggestion was made that in order to be confident that 'reasonable care' had been demonstrated, three valuations from different estate agents would be preferable, or a professional (ie Royal Institute of Chartered Surveyors) valuation if a definitive valuation was necessary. But if three different valuations are received what is the personal representative to do? Take the lowest one and incur the wrath of HMRC? Take the highest one and have an angry client? Or just take the middle one, though both the client and also HMRC will be unhappy? And are all three valuations to be disclosed? The three valuation idea is neither practical nor sensible. Even if there were three valuations obtained, HMRC said that this would only 'go a long way' to demonstrating reasonable care. HMRC stated that they would also look at what steps were actually taken, and would consider:

●   Was professional advice sought?

- Were instructions given on the correct basis?

- Was the valuer's attention drawn to particular features of the property (eg development potential)?

- Was anything unusual about the valuation questioned?

Clearly, this implies a high standard of care, and could perhaps be in response to the decision in *Cairns v Revenue & Customs Commissioners* [2009] UKFTT 67 (TC). In that case, HMRC imposed a penalty on Mr Cairns, a solicitor acting as a personal representative. The penalty related to a valuation of £400,000 in respect of the deceased's residence, as returned on form IHT200. This was a valuation by chartered surveyors in January 2004, which was stated to be an '… arbitrary figure pending investigations as to costs involved in upgrading'. The valuation was heavily qualified due to the poor state of the property. Mr Cairns was uncertain of the property's value, but considered that the existing valuation was sufficient meantime. The District Valuer subsequently valued the property at £600,000 as at the date of death, which was also the amount for which the property was sold. The Special Commissioner was asked to consider whether Mr Cairns submitted an incorrect IHT account, and whether he had acted negligently. The Special Commissioner held: '… the mere failure to obtain another valuation when it has not been established that a second valuation would have led to a different figure being inserted in the statutory form does not constitute negligent delivery of an incorrect account'. He added: 'On the evidence before me, even if it were concluded that an incorrect account was delivered or furnished, it is simply not possible to conclude that it was negligently delivered or furnished except in one minor respect'. The minor matter referred to related to the fact that the valuation obtained had been heavily qualified, and was a provisional estimate. Mr Cairns had not disclosed this in the IHT account. The omission to do so was a careless error. However, the Commissioner added that '… it was minor, technical and of no consequence whatsoever'.

The Commissioner concluded that there had been a 'narrow, technical failure …'. The account was incorrect. The sum of £400,000 should have been described as a provisional estimate. Whilst that failure was negligent, it was held to be a 'failure of the merest technicality'. Mr Cairns was held to have acted 'perfectly sensibly and reasonably throughout'. The summons against Mr Cairns was dismissed. The Commissioner added that even if he had been wrong to dismiss it, he would have reduced the penalty to a nominal amount or recommended that it be so reduced.

That case predates the new penalty regime, but nevertheless may offer some comfort to the personal representatives of a deceased person's estate on the circumstances in which penalties can be imposed for an incorrect IHT return. However, it also provides a warning as to the degree of disclosure required in respect of provisional valuations and estimates to avoid an accusation by HMRC of careless behaviour. In general, provision of good, detailed information in support of values will often achieve earlier agreement with HMRC.

Even if a professional valuation is obtained, HMRC may expect it to be revisited in certain circumstances. HMRC's Trusts & Estates Newsletter (August 2010) states the following:

> 'If, having obtained a valuation and before you apply for a grant, you find out about other information that casts doubts on the initial valuation, you must reconsider it. For example, if you have a valuation that shows the property was worth £250,000, but when you try to sell the property you market it at £270,000 and receive some offers at that figure or more, it suggests that the open market value for the property may be more like £270,000.

> In these circumstances, HMRC recommends that you ask the valuer to reconsider and, if appropriate, amend the date of death value, taking into account such things as the length of time since the death and movements in the property market.'

In the context of valuations of residential property in the UK, the following five key points have been offered to help minimise the scope for liability if an incorrect valuation is submitted (STEP Journal, July 2012):

- Ensure that any valuation is prepared both in accordance with the Royal Institute of Chartered Surveyors' Valuation Professional Standards ('The Red Book') and by an appropriately qualified and, in applicable cases, registered valuer.

- Beware of the potential conflict of interest for firms instructed to market the property and to also value for IHT purposes.

- Provide clear instructions to the valuer.

- Check all assumptions made by the valuer in their report.

- No 'quick fix' estimate is likely to be sufficient, even if property is to be sold immediately after grant is obtained.

Toolkits

2.67   The above comments in the Trusts and Estates Newsletter and the *Cairns* case deal with asset valuations in IHT returns, but should also perhaps be considered in the context of tax returns for individuals and companies as well. HMRC has produced a series of 'toolkits' for agents. These provide guidance on compliance risks, and aim '… to set out how agents can reduce the likelihood of mistakes occurring in the returns'. The toolkits cover risks in areas including CGT (land and property), CGT for trusts and IHT. The IHT toolkit is aimed at tax agents, advisers, trustees, personal representatives and others when completing form IHT400. The toolkit can be downloaded from HMRC's website (www.hmrc.gov.uk/agents/toolkits/iht.pdf).

It was originally understood that the use of these toolkits would constitute reasonable care, which therefore suggested that an error in a return on a subject covered by a toolkit would not be careless for penalty purposes if the guidance in the toolkit had been followed properly. Unfortunately, HMRC's website currently includes the following caveat (www.hmrc.gov.uk/agents/toolkits-essential-info.htm): 'Whether reasonable care has been taken in any particular case will be a question of fact and will not depend on whether a toolkit has or has not been used'. Nevertheless, best practice for anyone who does not complete a large number of IHT accounts would probably be to use the IHT toolkit.

HMRC initially stated that using the toolkits will '... reduce the potential risk of an HMRC enquiry or inspection that could result after an error has been made'. This indicates that the toolkits will also make it more difficult for HMRC to make a 'discovery' outside the normal tax return enquiry window. However, this point has yet to be tested before the tribunal. In the meantime, guidance is available on finality and discovery in self-assessment returns in HMRC's Statement of Practice 1/2006.

File management

2.68 It is in the nature of probate work that the full story does not emerge immediately. That is recognised in the provisions for the use of estimates and in connection with the delivery of an account which turns out to be wrong; and in the advice from HMRC not to rush completion of the form of account. Errors must be put right without 'unreasonable delay': see ss 217 and 248(1). If not, the person liable to deliver the account suffers the same penalty as someone who delivers an account negligently. Correction may be made on form C4 but, if there are a number of small changes and the overall value is not significant, the changes can be dealt with by correspondence.

At their Open Day in 2000, Inland Revenue Capital Taxes (as they then were) suggested that penalties could be avoided by putting errors right quickly. 'Quickly' means within six months in relation to accounts and within 30 days in relation to other information and documents. Where an error arises which, on correction, generates £1,000 or more of tax, the error should be notified immediately.

However, in some cases involving multiple amendments to the IHT400 return, HMRC will only need to be informed within 18 months after the date of death or at the point the estate is finalised, whichever is earlier (HMRC Trusts & Estates Newsletter, April 2012; see **2.3**).

Interest

2.69   Historically, probate lawyers never worried much about interest on IHT. It was just a normal expense of administration: the work would be done as and when the lawyer got round to it. The level at which interest is charged on IHT was traditionally less than the charge in respect of other taxes, although that position has changed following the introduction of aligned interest rates in FA 2009 (see **2.52**). Personal representatives and beneficiaries are now much less tolerant of this easy-going attitude on the part of lawyers. Clients expect lawyers to administer estates more promptly to mitigate the burden of interest. It can be avoided by the use of the direct payment scheme mentioned at **2.47**, which is given prominence in form IHT400.

Interest is chargeable where payment of the tax itself is made by instalments. Where tax and interest arise on death, s 233(1)(b) charges interest from the end of six months beginning with the end of the month in which the death occurred. There are special rules in relation to specialised forms of property, as mentioned earlier in this chapter.

Interest charged by HMRC is not allowable as a deduction in calculating any income profits or losses for any tax purposes. However, that is different from the situation where the executors have taken out a loan specifically in order to pay IHT (ie where they have not used the direct payment scheme). Where a specific loan account is taken out (but not an overdraft), the interest for the first year may be deductible in calculating the income tax liability of the executors (ITA 2007, s 403). This facility relates only to the initial loan to fund the tax payable before a grant of representation can issue and does not relate to any further loans taken out by the personal representatives at any other time.

Suspension of penalties

2.70   The new penalty regime includes an 'enabling' facility to encourage better compliance, where the error in a return is careless and results from a faulty procedure or misunderstanding on the part of the taxpayer that can be put right.

Penalties can be suspended for a careless inaccuracy where, by notice under FA 2007, Sch 24, para 14, HMRC specify the action to be taken and the period for which it must be taken.

However, this is unlikely to apply to family members who act as executor.

Shifting the blame onto the adviser

2.71   Taxpayers often say that 'I left it to the accountant/solicitor/adviser to get the forms right.' The prevalent reluctance of taxpayers either to pay tax or to give sufficient time to form filling may indicate that such a complaint is unjustified. FA 2007, Sch 24, para 18(3) exonerates the taxpayer only if he can show that he took reasonable care to avoid inaccuracy or unreasonable failure.

Reliance on an agent was held to be taking reasonable care to avoid an inaccuracy in *Hanson v Revenue & Customs Commissioners* [2012] UKFTT 314 (TC), albeit that this case concerned an error in the taxpayer's self-assessment return in the context of capital gains tax. However, in *Shakoor v Revenue & Customs Commissioners* [2012] UKFTT 532 (TC), the tribunal held that the advice given by the taxpayer's accountant was obviously wrong, and that the taxpayer should have realised that it was wrong, or so potentially wrong to call for further explanation or justification.

RECORD KEEPING

2.72   The absence of records can be a major headache for personal representatives. Specific instances arise where the executors have a duty to notify HMRC of events of which they have had no personal knowledge. It is good practice for any person who has an estate that may on his death become taxable to maintain personal records of gifts etc in a form that will be intelligible to the personal representatives. That has become more important as many more lifetime transfers have been treated as chargeable since 22 March 2006.

Capital taxation long enjoyed a separate and more relaxed compliance regime than now applies, for example, under self-assessment, but (as indicated at **2.55**) the information-gathering powers of HMRC for IHT purposes have now largely been subsumed into FA 2008, Sch 36, replacing the previous powers to require information under s 219, to call for documents under s 219A and to inspect property under s 220.

Practitioners will usually keep probate and trust files for a very long time. In relation to trusts, the papers will be kept because of the ongoing nature of the matter and because of the record-keeping requirements under self-assessment. In relation to estates, it is not uncommon that queries will arise some time later, for example where assets have been appropriated to beneficiaries *in specie* and where the probate value has not been notified to the beneficiary or, if it has, the beneficiary has lost the record. The value for tax purposes at which the beneficiary acquired the asset will normally be its probate value under the rule in TCGA 1992, s 274 (where the value was 'ascertained' for IHT), although note the exception to this general rule at **3.13** in respect of the transferable nil rate band. In this context see the Law Society's recommendations issued on 6 October 2011: www.lawsociety.org.uk/advice/practice-notes/file-retention-wills-probate/.

FA 2008, Sch 37 contains obligations as to record keeping. However, at the time of writing these provisions do not have effect for IHT purposes (see **2.3**).

Hold-over on gifts

2.73   Restrictions on capital gains tax hold-over relief were introduced in FA 2004 (s 116, Sch 21) in relation to gifts to settlor-interested trusts. FA 2006 extended the definition of 'settlor interested' so that it now includes any trust for the minor child of the settlor. Apart from those restrictions, which are considerable, hold-over relief remains available under TCGA 1992, s 165 to shelter gifts of shares in trading companies and holding companies of trading groups where either:

- the shares are not listed on a recognised stock exchange (nor dealt in on the former USM); or

- the company concerned (including a quoted or a USM company) is the transferor's personal company (ie at least 5% of the voting rights are exercisable by him): see s 165(2)(b).

Hold-over relief for CGT is also available under TCGA 1992, s 260 in cases of IHT lifetime chargeable transfers (eg any lifetime gift into trust after 22 March 2006), even those within the IHT nil rate band or covered by the annual exemption under s 19. However, as with TCGA 1992, s 165, restrictions in gifts hold-over relief under s 260 were introduced by FA 2004 (ss 116, 117, Schs 21, 22).

Under SP 8/92, a taxpayer, when applying to hold over a gain, can elect not to compute the gain itself. This means that valuations for purposes other than IHT are unlikely. If it is wished to finalise the valuation as quickly as possible, the appropriate IHT return should be accompanied by a professional valuation.

'Snoopers charter' and the issue of professional privilege

2.74   As noted at **2.54**, under s 218 *any* professional person (other than a barrister) must report a (post-26 March 1974) settlement in which he is concerned 'with the making' where the settlor is domiciled in the UK but the trustees are or will be non-resident. A person is absolved from reporting the settlement where the settlement is one made by will, or where someone else has already delivered an account or return.

HMRC have very wide powers of obtaining information, including from third parties (FA 2008, Sch 36); although, in the case of a barrister or solicitor, privileged information is excluded (see below) unless the consent of the client is obtained. A solicitor may nevertheless be required to give the name and address of the client and, if non-resident, his UK associates (see also TCGA 1992, Sch 5, para 10, and Sch 5A in relation to settlements with a foreign element for CGT).

In FA 2008, Sch 36 the issue of privilege is addressed, but in a way that does not suit all professions involved with IHT. Schedule 36, para 23 excuses a person from providing information which, for the purposes only of Sch 36 is treated (see para 23(2)) as privileged:

'if it is information or a document in respect of which a claim to legal professional privilege, or (in Scotland) to confidentiality of communications as between client and professional legal adviser, could be maintained in legal proceedings.'

This rule did not, in the opinion of CIOT, recognise the observations of Lord Hoffmann in *R (on the application of Morgan Grenfell & Co Ltd) v Special Commissioner of Income Tax* [2002] STC 786, at p 796 para 39. He considered that any changes in the then law would only be compatible with the European Convention on Human Rights, Art 8 if they pursued a legitimate aim that was necessary in a democratic society, doubting that the public interest in collecting taxes was a good enough reason for such a change.

Legal and professional privilege does not generally apply to skilled advice about tax law from an accountant as opposed to a lawyer. This principle was reinforced in *R (oao Prudential plc) v Special Commissioner (and related applications) QB* [2009] EWHC 2494 (Admin). In that case, a Special Commissioner had given consent for notices under TMA 1970, s 20 to be issued to two associated insurance companies. The companies applied for judicial review, contending that some of the documents were subject to legal professional privilege. However, the court dismissed the applications, and held that, for legal professional privilege to apply to legal advice and assistance, it must generally be given by a member of the legal profession. That decision was subsequently upheld by the Court of Appeal ([2010] EWCA Civ 1094). At the time of writing, the decision of the Supreme Court in the *Prudential* case is awaited.

However, tax advisers (and auditors) get limited protection from Schedule 36, paras 24–25. Paragraph 25 defines 'tax adviser' as 'a person appointed to give advice about the tax affairs of another person (whether appointed directly by that person or by another tax adviser of that person)', but does not provide protection for such of the advice of the tax adviser as is in the hands of the taxpayer.

TAX TRIBUNALS AND INTERNAL REVIEWS

2.75   The First-tier and Upper Tax Tribunals replaced the General and Special Commissioners with effect from 1 April 2009. An internal review system was also introduced by HMRC, to coincide with the introduction of the tax tribunals (TMA 1970, ss 49A–49I). Under the tribunals regime, the appellant must notify an appeal to HMRC in writing and apply to the tribunal for the appeal to be heard, rather than relying on HMRC to arrange for the appeal to be listed for hearing.

Most IHT appeals will initially be heard by the First-tier Tribunal, with appeals being heard by the Upper Tribunal. Appeals from the Upper Tribunal are generally to the High Court (or Court of Session in Scotland). For IHT cases, there is a right of appeal to the High Court on issues substantially confined to questions of law (see HMRC Inheritance Tax and Trusts Newsletter, April 2009).

Internal reviews are available for appealable HMRC decisions. If an appeal has been submitted to HMRC and the issue cannot be settled, the taxpayer can notify the appeal to the tribunal. Alternatively, the taxpayer may require HMRC to review the point at issue, or HMRC may offer the taxpayer a review. The taxpayer and HMRC meet their own costs of an internal review.

If the taxpayer asks for a review, it is conducted by an HMRC 'review officer'. HMRC must respond to the taxpayer by stating the review officer's view of the matter within 30 days, or possibly a longer period if this is reasonable. Alternatively, if HMRC notify the taxpayer of their current view and offer a review, the taxpayer has 30 days in which to accept. Otherwise, HMRC's original view generally stands. If a review takes place, HMRC's original view of the matter may be upheld, varied or cancelled, and HMRC must generally notify the taxpayer of this conclusion within the following 45 days, or other agreed period. If the review is not concluded and the taxpayer advised of the review conclusion within these time limits, then unless an extension has been agreed, HMRC's view is treated as upheld and the taxpayer must be notified accordingly.

If HMRC's review is unfavourable and the taxpayer does not wish to accept it, an appeal must be notified to the tribunal within 30 days, or outside this period with the tribunal's permission. Otherwise, HMRC's review conclusions are treated as having been agreed.

Some practitioners were sceptical about the internal reviews system prior to its introduction, on the basis that (as the name suggests) internal reviews could not be entirely impartial. However, internal reviews provide an opportunity to resolve disputes with HMRC without the need for a tribunal hearing, and anecdotal evidence indicates that the system is working better than many expected.

PRACTICAL APPROACH AND FUTURE OF THE TAX

Lifetime loopholes

2.76 Clients want simple, cheap but effective solutions to tax issues. While the adviser must gather detailed facts as to individual circumstances, for example, assets, age, health, family, business, previous transfers of value etc and his planning proposals, this must be done in an efficient, economical way. An outline agenda of such preliminary discussion is set out in **Appendix 2.1** at the end of this chapter but should be used with imagination, not slavishly asking questions that are irrelevant. This agenda can later be edited to become the basis of recommendations submitted to the client for approval.

There is scope for minimising IHT by using exemptions and reliefs, and taking advantage of the seven-year cut-off for cumulation. There is always a political risk of changes in the law when undertaking future planning, such as the major changes in FA 2006, and opportunities which are available now may disappear in the future, so 'use it or lose it'.

Even at a minor level, the failure to use one annual IHT exemption of £3,000 incurs (at 40%) a 'penalty' of £1,200. At higher levels, failure to plan incurs much larger costs.

Playing with fire: the application of the Ramsay principle

2.77 Tax planning which relies on artificial technical loopholes is questionable. In the case of *W T Ramsay Ltd v IRC* [1981] STC 174, Lord Wilberforce stated:

> 'It is the task of the court to ascertain the legal nature of any transaction to which it is sought to attach a tax or a tax consequence and if that emerges from a series or combination of transactions, intended to operate as such, it is that series or combination which may be regarded.'

The '*Ramsay* approach' was applied by the House of Lords in *IRC v Burmah Oil Co Ltd* [1982] STC 30 in relation to 'a pre-ordained series of transactions (whether or not they include the achievement of a legitimate commercial end) into which there are inserted steps that have no commercial purpose apart from the avoidance of a liability to tax which in the absence of these particular steps would have been payable'.

This approach was confirmed by the House of Lords in *Furniss v Dawson* [1984] STC 153, adding that 'no commercial purpose' meant 'no commercial (business) purpose', *not* 'no commercial (business) *effect*'. In the words of Lord Brightman:

'The formulation, therefore, involves two findings of fact, first whether there was a preordained series of transactions, ie a single composite transaction. Secondly, whether that transaction contained steps which were inserted without any commercial or business purpose apart from a tax advantage.'

A swing of the pendulum back towards the taxpayer emerged from the House of Lords in three appeals, *Craven v White*, *IRC v Bowater Property Developments Ltd* and *Baylis v Gregory* [1988] STC 476.

In *Fitzwilliam v IRC* [1993] STC 502, HL, Lord Keith further clarified the *Ramsay* test. In the leading speech, he held that steps 2–5 taken in that case by the trustees were pre-ordained, but the pre-ordained nature of the steps could not negative the application of the exempting provisions. The correct approach was to ask whether steps 2–5 realistically constituted a simple and indivisible whole in which one or more of them was simply an element without independent effect, and to ask whether it was intellectually possible to so treat them. He concluded it was not so possible in the case of *Fitzwilliam*.

Hatton v IRC [1992] STC 140, another mutual gifts/reverter to settlor scheme, was decided by the High Court in favour of the Crown on *Ramsay* grounds, again the sole argument taken. Unlike *Fitzwilliam*, *Hatton* involved a marketed scheme.

The House of Lords in *Macniven v Westmoreland Investments* [2001] STC 237 held that *Ramsay* is relevant only where the statutory words refer to commercial concepts such as 'loss', 'gain' and 'disposal'. In *Ramsay,* where these concepts had been in issue, this approach meant that the legislation could be applied to a pre-planned series of transactions by reference to the overall effect rather than the various distinct parts of that series. However, not all statutory words refer to commercial concepts. If the statutory word is a legal (or juristic) concept such as 'conveyance or transfer on sale', *Ramsay* will not apply to determine whether, commercially, a sale was effected.

This test was applied in *Westmoreland* where, under ICTA 1988, s 338, payments of interest could be set against profits and any excess carried forward under s 75. Westmoreland owed a group pension scheme a substantial amount of accrued interest under loans; if it paid that interest, that amount would be available for relief (and Westmoreland could be sold to a purchaser with income profits that needed sheltering). In order to fund repayment of the interest, the pension scheme made a further loan. The Revenue contended that a circular payment such as this should be ignored for tax purposes. Their Lordships, however, held that Westmoreland had made a 'payment' of interest within the normal (legal or juristic) meaning of that word and that there was nothing in the legislation to justify a different meaning.

How should we apply the *Ramsay* principle to IHT? We must decide, when construing IHTA 1984, FA 1986 or FA 2006, whether a given word has, in context, a 'commercial' or a 'juristic' meaning. Some words will have no recognised legal meaning. In such cases, a commercial or 'ordinary business' approach must be adopted.

In other cases the statutory language may clearly be 'juristic': 'conveyance on sale' was an example of a term that lawyers, rather than businessmen, would recognise. The term 'property' in relation to reservation of benefit is also likely to be a juristic term, given the decision of the House of Lords in *Ingram*. Other cases will be more difficult: what about 'interest in land' in s 102A; does that include a debt which is practically certain to be charged on land one week after the date of the gift?

In *CIR v Scottish Provident Institution* [2005] STC 15, the House of Lords ruled against the taxpayer in connection with a series of transactions involving options over gilts designed as a tax avoidance scheme to produce a deemed loss for tax purposes. Their Lordships held that:

> 'We think that it would destroy the value of the *Ramsay* principle of construing provisions … as referring to the effect of composite transactions if their composite effect had to be disregarded simply because the parties had deliberately included a commercially irrelevant contingency, creating an acceptable risk that the scheme might not work as planned. We would be back in the world of artificial tax schemes, now equipped with anti-*Ramsay* devices. The composite effect of such a scheme should be considered as it was intended to operate and without regard to the possibility that, contrary to the intention and expectations of the parties, it might not work as planned.'

However, in *Barclays Mercantile Business Finance Ltd v Mawson* [2005] STC 1, the House of Lords ruled in favour of the taxpayer. The appeal concerned a capital allowances scheme involving a sale and leaseback with security arrangements. Whilst it was recognised that the series of transactions was preordained, the *Ramsay* principle was not considered to apply. There was a genuine business purpose for the asset (a pipeline) in respect of which the disputed capital allowances claim was made. Lord Nicholls of Birkenhead commented that disregarding transactions or elements of transactions with no commercial purpose was going too far. He added (at para 36):

> 'Cases such as [*Burmah Oil, Furniss v Dawson* and *Carreras*] gave rise to the view that, in the application of any taxing statute, transactions or elements of transactions which had no commercial purpose were to be disregarded. But that is going too far. It elides the two steps which are necessary in the application of any statutory provision; first, to decide, on a purposive construction, exactly what transaction will answer to the statutory description and secondly, to decide whether the transaction in question does so.'

Whilst these cases provide further guidance on the application of the *Ramsay* principle, it seems likely that the approach of the courts in future cases will result in the principle evolving still further. As noted by their Lordships in the *Barclays Mercantile* case:

'It is no doubt too much to expect that any exposition will remove all difficulties in the application of the principles because it is in the nature of questions of construction that there will be borderline cases about which people will have different views. It should however be possible to achieve some clarity about basic principles.'

More recently, the *Ramsay* principle was considered in *Astall and others v HMRC* [2009] EWCA Civ 1010 and *HMRC v Mayes CA* [2011] EWCA Civ 407. In *Astall*, the court adopted a purposive construction of a tax avoidance scheme in dismissing the taxpayer's appeal. However, in *Mayes*, an avoidance scheme (known as 'SHIPS 2') succeeded on the basis that the relevant legislation adopted a formulaic and prescriptive approach.

Some practitioners think that there are periods of time when the judiciary seem to favour the taxpayer even on complex tax avoidance schemes; and there are other periods when the judiciary seem very strongly in favour of HMRC. Quite often, the planning takes place in a relaxed era but the court decision comes when there is an entirely different, and harsher, judicial approach.

This judicial attitude is manifested when the difference between tax planning and legal tax avoidance is removed so that some avoidance works and some does not. When does planning become ineffective, but legal, avoidance?

A general anti-abuse rule (GAAR) is to be introduced in FA 2013, which will be targeted at 'artificial and abusive tax avoidance schemes'. However, as indicated at **1.20**, it may still be necessary to consider the *Ramsay* doctrine and the rule of statutory construction, in terms of whether schemes or arrangements are abusive.

As to the disclosure of IHT planning arrangements, see the next section.

DISCLOSURE OF TAX AVOIDANCE SCHEMES (DOTAS)

2.78   The provisions requiring the disclosure of tax avoidance schemes introduced in FA 2004 (ss 306–319), which initially applied to arrangements prescribed in regulations relating to schemes involving income tax, corporation tax and capital gains tax, were subsequently extended to IHT, with effect from 6 April 2011 (Inheritance Tax Avoidance Schemes (Prescribed Descriptions of Arrangements) Regulations 2011, SI 2011/170, and Tax Avoidance Schemes (Information) (Amendment) Regulations 2011, SI 2011/171).

See HMRC's website for a summary list of the legislation to which the disclosure provisions apply (www.hmrc.gov.uk/aiu/legislation.htm).

For IHT purposes, the subordinate legislation is broadly aimed at arrangements resulting in assets being transferred to relevant property trusts with a main benefit of obtaining a reduction in the IHT entry charge that would otherwise arise (ie essentially *Melville*-type schemes).

However, the disclosure of such arrangements is subject to transitional 'grandfathering' provisions. Thus, HMRC's revised DOTAS Guidance (February 2012) (available at www.hmrc.gov.uk/aiu/dotas.pdf) confirms (at para 11.6) that arrangements are excepted from disclosure under the regulations if they are:

'the same or substantially the same description as arrangements:

(a) which were first made available for implementation before 6 April 2011;

(b) in relation to which the date of any transaction forming part of the arrangements falls before 6 April 2011; or

(c) in relation to which a promoter first made a firm approach to another person before 6 April 2011.'

The guidance goes on to state:

'It is a matter of fact whether an arrangement is grandfathered. Evidence of grandfathering would include:

● the existence and substance of the arrangement being clearly described in tax manuals or publications;

● the production of an affidavit where evidence that the grandfathering rule applies is subject to legal professional privilege;

● a practitioner's own record as to when they made, or learnt that competitors were making, an arrangement available.'

A 'white list' of grandfathered schemes and schemes that are not within the regulations is included in the HMRC guidance (para 11.7). The list includes:

● the purchase of business assets with a view to transferring the assets into a relevant property trust after two years;

● the creation of pilot trusts;

● discounted gift trusts/schemes; and

● transfers of the nil rate band every seven years.

Conclusion

2.79   An estate owner intent on planning should first make maximum use of his annual and other exemptions. Then he should make PETs of assets with no or a low liability for CGT. Beyond that, he should consider making use of the nil rate band for chargeable transfers of assets that have risen in value, so that gains can be held over, but he should remember that any unused nil rate band may be worth more on the later death of his spouse or civil partner than it is now.

From 22 March 2006, a lifetime transfer to any kind of trust (other than a bare trust) is chargeable. If the settlor is not yet sure of ultimate destination then a discretionary trust will serve as well as any type. CGT hold-over can still at present be obtained, broadly unless the trust is/or becomes 'settlor-interested' or is for the settlor's minor children. Some comfort can be obtained where CGT has to be paid on an outright gift that, unlike hold-over, the donee does get a market value uplift.

It will be more appropriate now than historically to use the inter-spouse exemption to pass assets by will to the (perhaps younger) surviving spouse with CGT uplift on death, so that the transferable nil rate band facility can be considered, and the survivor can then consider making PETs. The main advantages to be gained, however, would be the availability of the new cumulative clock after seven years (including a new nil rate band) and the ability to transfer appreciating assets to the transferee. On the downside is the fact that, whether CGT is paid or deferred, one will not get the market value uplift and exemption that would apply on death of the surviving spouse in respect of the assets in question. The government could revoke the seven-year cumulation period but it would be particularly harsh if that period has started, and the legislation was retrospective.

Complex lifetime planning gets more and more difficult. The 'pre-owned assets' income tax charge, the (previous) Labour Government's inclination towards retroactive legislation and the FA 2006 changes are just three examples of this potential complexity. The best estate planning may therefore revolve around the death estate, particularly with the ability to make variations and disclaimers (see **Chapter 5**), which can be useful in the context of pre-owned assets.

TAX PRACTITIONERS AND ADVISERS

2.80   What is the duty of care? The adviser may feel that he is between a rock and a hard place. On the one hand, anti-avoidance provisions are often drafted very widely, so as to potentially exclude legitimate tax planning, or at least cause some uncertainty. Equally, there is usually as part of the retainer a duty to the client to mitigate tax burdens.

Two cases, *Cancer Research Campaign v Brown* [1997] STC 1425 and *Hurlingham Estate Limited v Wilde & Partners* [1997] STC 627, illustrate the duty to clients. In *Hurlingham* the judge held that a reasonably competent conveyancer and commercial lawyer owed a duty to his client to advise on the tax implications of the transaction unless his retainer was limited or it was apparent that advice was not needed by the client.

The facts in *Cancer Research Campaign* were as follows. N died on 11 December 1986 leaving a will dated 21 October 1985 giving his residuary estate to his sister, the testatrix, who died on 28 May 1988. There was much delay. The sister left her estate to seven charities, who later sued the solicitors for negligence. They also sued P, a legal executive employed by them and principal executor of both wills. They claimed that, by reason of the defendants' negligence, they were unable to take advantage of a deed of arrangement under IHTA 1984, s 142, because the two-year period for doing so expired before they knew of the inheritance.

That had cost the charities some £200,000 of unnecessarily paid IHT on N's estate. They argued that the defendants were in breach of their duty of care in two ways. During the testatrix's lifetime the solicitors failed to advise her of the possibility of executing a deed of variation of N's bequests. Further, in breach of their duty of care, following her death, the solicitors failed to notify the charities of their prospective legacies.

The decision may surprise the 'average' practitioner. Harman J held (dismissing the action) that although it was established that a solicitor was under a duty to take care to ensure that an intended beneficiary received the benefit intended, there was no duty to advise an intended testator about the tax avoidance schemes of another estate. In the instant case the defendants' retainer was to draw the testatrix's will. Their duty was limited to drawing that will and to ensuring that it was properly executed, both of which they had done. There was no duty to the residuary beneficiaries to consider and advise the testatrix about possible ways of rearranging the dispositions under N's will.

A second argument against the charities rested on the issue of loss. No duty of care arose in tort in favour of an intended beneficiary unless and until the client had (a) decided to confer on the intended beneficiary a particular intended testamentary benefit (being the benefit for the loss of which the intended beneficiary sought to hold the solicitor liable); and (b) retained the solicitor for that purpose. Here, no particular testamentary benefit was intended by the testatrix for the plaintiffs out of the net assets of N's estate which would come to her. As a result, that loss could not be recovered by the plaintiffs against the solicitors.

The defendants therefore owed no duty to the plaintiffs during the testatrix's life to advise her that she could or might execute a deed of variation pursuant to s 142 so as to confer the benefits which she would get out of N's estate on the plaintiffs. Even if there had been such a duty, the plaintiffs had to satisfy the court that, on a balance of probabilities, they would have received benefits under the putative deed of variation.

That could not be proved. The most likely result of discussion between the testatrix and her solicitors would have been her decision that, not knowing what the future held, she would retain N's estate. The plaintiffs had not proved that they had suffered any damage. *White v Jones* [1995] 2 AC 207 and *Trusted v Clifford Chance (a firm)* Ch D, [2000] WTLR 1219 applied.

There was no duty, either on the solicitors or on the executor after the testatrix's death, to communicate with the residuary beneficiaries and thereby enable them to arrange and execute a deed of variation themselves. The solicitors owed no direct duty to the plaintiffs: there was no separate duty to legatees under the will they were helping to administer. An executor's duty was to collect the assets: he was under no obligation to inform a legatee that there was a prospective legacy. *Re Lewis* [1904] 2 Ch 656, *Chauncy v Graydon* (1843) 2 Atk 616 and *Re Mackay* [1906] 1 Ch 25 followed.

It was a regrettable feature of the *Brown* case that everything took so long. Had the solicitors acted more promptly in proving either of the wills, the charities would probably have known of the chance of a variation in time to effect it. Perhaps the duty of care is also higher now than it was in 1997, though the cardinal principle remains that the solicitor owes a duty to his client first and foremost and that no duty to third parties should be imputed to him except where necessary under the *White v Jones* principle to fill a lacuna in the law. The facility of saving tax by deed of variation is more widely recognised, even by general practitioners, than it once was. Harman J very fairly expected a lesser standard of knowledge of a provincial practitioner in a small firm than of a London specialist: again, the fact that many practitioners in this area of law undertake extra and specialised forms of training no doubt raises the bar.

Having said that, there is a point of good policy in the decision. If an adviser can easily be sued for not putting a tax-saving scheme in place, he will at all times be anxious not only to comply with the law but also to exploit it. That only stretches the law yet further. Anti-avoidance legislation proliferates. Few benefit long term, other than the lawyers.

In *Vinton and others v Fladgate Fielder and another* [2010] EWHC 904 (Ch), a family sued their advisers in respect of a flawed IHT planning scheme, as the personal representatives of the deceased, as the prospective executors, and as the residuary beneficiaries under her will. They sought to recover the tax lost and the costs of an unsuccessful tax appeal. The lawyers argued that they had been engaged only to deal with a capital-raising project for the family company, not to advise on tax; and that their liability was to the deceased, not to her estate, nor to her personal representatives, nor to the beneficiaries. However, the court held that, insofar as the claims lay in contract, there was a serious claim on which to adjudicate. It was clear that tax was a significant consideration in the proposed transaction on which advice had been sought. Insofar as the claims lay in tort, ie relied on allegations of negligence, it was inappropriate to strike them out; the claims were not fanciful.

Finally, it is generally important to ensure that the scope of any tax advice to be provided by a professional adviser is fully and clearly set out in an engagement letter or retainer. In *Swain Mason & ors v Mills & Reeve (A Firm)* [2012] EWCA Civ 498, the claimants were executors of their late father's estate. The deceased (Mr Swain) was the shareholder of a company which was the subject of a management buyout (MBO). Mr Swain had a history of ill-health, and he sadly died during a heart procedure. The proceeds from the sale of the deceased's shares became liable to IHT; whereas, if he had died while still owning the shares, no IHT liability would have arisen due to business property relief. A claim of professional negligence was made against the defendant firm, on the basis that the advice given was deficient, and that, had the correct advice been given, completion of the MBO would have been deferred until after the heart procedure. However, the claim was dismissed. The court held (inter alia) that the defendant firm's retainer did not extend to advising the shareholders how the MBO fitted into their personal financial and tax-planning positions. There had been no breach of duty.

More detailed discussion of the principles involved can be obtained from a specialist textbook on professional negligence.

APPENDIX 2.1 – PERSONAL DATA SHEET

Notes for the practitioner

This appendix is intended partly as an instruction sheet and as a 'practitioner's toolkit' (to steal a concept from HMRC), to help the client to leave his affairs in good order. Financial affairs and products get ever more complex; nothing is simple. The problem becomes more acute on a death; however, difficulties can be eased by keeping good records.

This form becomes relevant as soon as an individual has expectations or assets of substance. The details should be updated regularly, ideally annually, when completing the tax return. About every five years, the client should review his will (see **Chapter 4**).

This form cannot cover every circumstance and should be adapted accordingly. In particular, detailed and numbered schedules/inventories can be attached. Try not to let the form become cluttered; only the more important information, the main assets and liabilities need be noted. Use schedules for the detail or refer to the source of the information, eg solicitor, accountant, stockbroker or others mentioned in section 2 of the form. Section 10 'Miscellaneous items' can then be used to indicate where further details can be obtained, with appropriate cross-references to section 2.

The completed form should be kept with the individual's file. If the client keeps a copy, it should be with his private papers and the next-of-kin (eg wife, husband or civil partner) perhaps informed of its contents and whereabouts.

[Here personalise the form with your firm's logo, office address, contact details etc, to encourage your client to return to you for advice in future.]

Information re estate and assets of:

Name:

Address:

Former addresses in the last ten years:

Other names by which the client is known or in which he holds assets (useful later when proving the will).

Dates of:

Birth

marriage (1)

divorce (1)

marriage (2)

divorce (2)

marriage (3)

divorce (3)

National Insurance/Social Security number:

Unique Taxpayer Reference number:

1.   Immediate, essential information

     1.1   Location of will

     1.2   Funeral wishes (cremation, burial, no flowers, etc)

1.3   Other wishes, eg anatomical use

1.4   Details of any lasting power of attorney provisions as to healthcare decisions

2.   Relevant personal information

2.1   Executors

2.2   Solicitor or will writer

2.3   Accountant or tax adviser

2.4   Stockbroker or other financial adviser

2.5   Bankers (see also 3.6)

2.6   HM Revenue & Customs

Address:

Location of copy tax returns (copy attached):

2.7   Doctor

2.8   Others, eg local authority; public utilities

2.9   Location of personal documents, eg birth/marriage certificates, credit cards (details of safe deposit box)

3.   Assets and liabilities

3.1   Main residence

Address:

Sole name or jointly: Does it pass by survivorship? YES/NO

Subject to/free of mortgage: £

Mortgagee lender:

Address:

Reference no:

Estimated value (net of mortgage):

Council tax band:

3.2   Other properties

Sole name or jointly: Does it pass by survivorship? YES/NO

Subject to/free of mortgage: £

Mortgage lender:

Address:

Reference no:

Estimated value (net of mortgage):

Council tax band:

Location of deeds re 3.1 and 3.2

3.3 Stock Exchange/government securities (state if held jointly):

3.4 Family company/unquoted shares

3.5 Other investments, eg Premium Bonds, National Savings, ISAs

3.6 Bank accounts/building society accounts

Bank/Society:

Type of account:

Account no:

Mandate/signing powers/? Joint:

3.7 Other business, agricultural assets

3.8 Miscellaneous assets

3.9 Liabilities eg bank overdraft arrangements, loans

4. Pension/insurance arrangements

4.1 Pension schemes

Insurance company	*Policy number*	*Details*	*Location of policy*

Details of any assignments of rights

4.2 Employee's pension (or life) schemes. Brief details. NB what rearrangements have been made for nominating death benefit (eg letter of wishes to the trustees)?

5.   Cancellation/notification/alteration

    5.1   Membership or subscriptions to:

           Professional/trade associations

           Clubs

           Other organisations, eg AA

    5.2   Offices held (eg Company Secretary, Treasurer, Chairman, Trusteeships, Executorships, Guardianships, etc)

    5.3   Credit cards/bank, retail store/cash dispenser cards:

           Type

           Number

    5.4   Direct debits/standing orders (see also 3.6)

    5.5   Registration documents for vehicles

    5.6   Deeds of covenant ceasing on death

    5.7   Agreements/licences, etc (eg hire purchase, car, TV and other contents of home)

    5.8   Gift Aid arrangements

Date	Donee	Location of document	Renewal date (if applicable)

6.   Family settlements

    6.1   Set up by the individual

Date of trust	*Type*	*Trustees' names & addresses*	*(Main) Beneficiaries' names & addresses*	*Location of original deed*	*UTR and IHT reference, if known*

    6.2   Details of any settlements where the individual is a beneficiary

        Type: (eg life interest, discretionary)

        Approx value of trust fund

        Date of trust deed and whereabouts of the deed (or copy)

7.   IHT history

Transaction	Date	Value transferred (approx)	Name & address of donee

8.   Transferable nil rate band

Note: A separate checklist is included as **Appendix 3.1** ('Record for use of the nil rate band for IHT purposes') at the end of **Chapter 3**.

9.   If you are non-UK domiciled

Are there assets situated in UK (= IHT chargeable)?

Consider remedial steps (ie for the assets to be abroad), eg

–   sale and remitting proceeds abroad (but beware CGT)

–   transfer abroad, eg chattels, bank accounts, bearer shares

–   exploiting the spouse exemption

–   gifting fixed assets, eg land/buildings to a foreign company (but beware CGT and income tax)

–   borrowing cash secured on UK assets and depositing the cash abroad

10.   Miscellaneous items

Signed ……………………..

Dated ……………………. 20—……………………..

Chapter 3

Transferable nil rate band

INTRODUCTION

3.1   Tax planners need to be prepared and to expect the unexpected. The Pre-Budget 2007 announcement regarding the transfer of unused nil rate bands between spouses (or civil partners) was a typical case in point. The proposed changes, which were subsequently enacted in FA 2008, came as a complete surprise to most IHT practitioners. However, some had previously advocated the proposed changes as a means of simplifying IHT planning, in terms of allowing for the unused nil rate band of the first to die to be used in the context of a married couple or civil partnership without requiring relatively complicated IHT planning to achieve that objective.

BACKGROUND AND STRUCTURE OF THE RULES

3.2   Estate planning for many married couples and civil partnerships has been simplified by the provisions in IHTA 1984, ss 8A–8C, which allow a claim for all or part of an unused nil rate band on the death of a spouse or civil partner to be transferred to a surviving spouse or civil partner who dies on or after 9 October 2007. The rules apply in the same way whether the survivor leaves a will, or dies intestate. The facility to make claims for the transfer of unused nil rate band remains very useful, despite the nil rate band being frozen at its 2009–10 level of £325,000 for the tax years 2010–11 to 2014–15 inclusive.

As mentioned, the facility to transfer unused nil rate band is available where the surviving spouse or civil partner dies on or after 9 October 2007. For married couples, the first death can have occurred at any time before or after that date. However, for civil partners the first death must have occurred on or after 5 December 2005, the date the Civil Partnership Act became law in the UK. If a civil partnership was entered into in another country before that date, the parties to the relationship are treated as having formed a civil partnership in the UK on the date the Act came into force (IHTM43001).

Background

3.3   Before transferable nil rate bands were introduced, it was generally important for IHT purposes to ensure that the estates of spouses or civil partners were sufficient to utilise their available IHT thresholds (or 'nil rate bands') if possible, and that optimum use was made of the nil rate band on the first death. If each spouse or civil partner owned sufficient assets to constitute their nil rate bands, the estates of each individual could be sheltered from IHT up to an amount equal to the nil rate band multiplied by the 40% rate on death. This was often achieved by legacies to a discretionary trust up to the available nil rate band ('NRB trusts').

There is a complete exemption (in s 18) for transfers between UK-domiciled spouses or civil partners during lifetime and on death. Thus, if a deceased spouse or civil partner leaves their entire estate to the surviving spouse, then (unless the recipient spouse or civil partner is non-UK domiciled, as to which see below), the legacy will normally be wholly exempt from IHT. However, the estate of the survivor increases accordingly. Before the FA 2008 changes, such exempt legacies between spouses or civil partners often resulted in a higher IHT liability on the second death, and a higher IHT liability overall. Therefore, IHT planning for married couples or civil partners typically involved ensuring that an amount up to the available nil rate band was left to non-exempt legatees (eg adult children), or, say, to a family NRB trust in which the surviving spouse was included among the class of beneficiaries.

This planning was relatively straightforward and simple to implement if each spouse or civil partner owned sufficient 'liquid' assets (eg cash, shares or other investments) to constitute their nil rate bands. However, lifetime transfers between spouses or civil partners were often necessary to achieve this result on death. In some cases, the only asset of any substantial value would be an interest in the family home. This often resulted in relatively complicated and artificial arrangements involving an interest in the family home to constitute the nil rate band, such as 'debt' or 'charge' schemes.

It should be noted that the usefulness of the transferable nil rate band has hitherto been rather limited for legacies to non-UK domiciled spouses or civil partners, as the spouse or civil partner exemption is limited to £55,000 in such cases (s 18(2)), thus potentially reducing the transferable nil rate band on death in the case of larger legacies. However, the government announced on Budget Day 2012 (21 March 2012) that it intends to increase the £55,000 exempt amount that a UK-domiciled individual can transfer to their non-domiciled spouse or civil partner. It is also proposed that non-UK domiciled individuals with a UK-domiciled spouse or civil partner will be allowed to elect to be treated as UK domiciled for IHT purposes. Those changes were subsequently included in the draft Finance Bill 2013 clauses published on 11 December

2012. The intended increase in the spouse or civil partner exemption in s 18(2) is from £55,000 to the amount of the nil rate band at the time of transfer, and will have effect for transfers of value made on or after 6 April 2013.

Effectively, couples who made simple wills leaving everything to each other, with remainder to children on the second death, are now in at least as good a position as those who took the trouble to obtain tax advice before FA 2008 and who used the nil rate band trust route. As will be seen, in some circumstances those who did not take tax advice are now potentially better off than those who did. Much will depend on the increase in value of the nil rate band trust assets, compared with increases in the nil rate band over the survivor's remaining life. Interestingly, it does not matter how small an estate was left by the first spouse to die; we are concerned only with the extent to which that spouse used the nil rate band.

It should be noted that transferable nil rate band claims cannot be made by co-habiting couples who are not legally married or civil partners (see *Executor of Holland deceased v IRC* [2003] SpC 350), or by family members who occupy the same property, such as siblings (see *Burden and another v United Kingdom* [2008] All ER (D) 391 (Apr)). In addition, whilst nil rate band legacies to chargeable (non-exempt) beneficiaries on the first spouse or civil partner to die are probably much less common or popular than before the introduction of the transferable nil rate band, there may be circumstances in which such legacies are necessary or preferred, such as where the property occupants are unmarried, or to make provision for offspring. There may also be non-IHT considerations for the nil rate band to be left on trust (eg due to concerns about care fees or divorce).

It is not necessary for assets to have passed to the spouse or civil partner on the first death. Thus, property that passed as an IHT exempt transfer (eg a qualifying gift to charity), or subject to IHT relief (eg business or agricultural property subject to 100% relief) may result in unused nil rate band being available. It is only possible for unused nil rate band to be transferred from one spouse (or civil partner) to the survivor when the relationship is ended by the death of one party to the relationship. If the relationship was ended by an earlier divorce (or dissolution of the civil partnership), the facility to transfer unused nil rate band is lost unless the parties remarried (or entered into a new civil partnership).

Structure and methodology

3.4   The transferable nil rate band legislation forms IHTA 1984, ss 8A–8C (and amended s 151BA prior to its repeal from 6 April 2011), with consequential changes elsewhere in the legislation. The transfer of any unused nil rate band requires a formal claim, and the provisions broadly work by increasing the nil rate band of the second spouse (or civil partner) to die on or after 9 October 2007; the general level of the nil rate band is unaffected. It does not matter if the unused nil rate band arises because no assets were owned on death. However, note that if both spouses died before 9 October 2007, it is not possible to take advantage of the transferable nil rate band facility. Similarly, as mentioned, the relief in respect of civil partners can apply only if the earlier death occurred after 5 December 2005, because that was the first date on which a person could be a civil partner.

HMRC have published guidance in the Inheritance Tax Manual (at IHTM43001–IHTM43068) on the transferable nil rate band facility and related issues. In this chapter it is referred to as 'HMRC's guidance'. It defines the requirements for a valid marriage at IHTM43003.

HMRC have also published an 'Inheritance Tax Toolkit' to assist tax agents and advisers in the preparation of IHT account form IHT400 (www.hmrc. gov.uk/agents/toolkits/iht.pdf). The toolkit identifies various areas of risk for completing IHT400. The 'risk' in respect of the transferable nil rate band is 'If full details of any pre-deceased spouse or civil partner have not been obtained the transferable nil rate band may be overlooked or not applied correctly'. The toolkit goes on to suggest various ways to mitigate this risk.

The amount of increase in nil rate band on the later death is fixed as a percentage (which cannot exceed 100) of the nil rate band (or, where there was more than one former spouse, bands) not used on any previous occasion. The percentage increase is applied to the nil rate band in operation on the death of the surviving spouse.

There are potentially complicated rules for dealing with the transfer of the nil rate band and the calculation of IHT when certain IHT and capital transfer tax deferred charges (ie on heritage assets and woodlands) are triggered, where the deferred IHT is calculated by reference to the earlier deceased spouse (s 8C). The provisions dealing with alternatively secured pensions (ss 151A–151E) also included rules (at s 151BA) to determine the amount of nil rate band to be applied in calculating IHT where a dependant who inherits an alternatively secured pension fund dies or ceases to be a dependant. However, those pension provisions were repealed for deaths occurring from 6 April 2011.

The method of determining the unused nil rate band percentage requires the use of formulae, involving such factors as 'M' and 'VT'. All of this can appear somewhat complex, and is potentially off-putting. This book is concerned with IHT planning, and what follows is therefore more concerned with the principles and planning issues regarding the transferable nil rate band, rather than the underlying methodology. However, whilst in many cases it may be possible to 'do the sums' in one's head, the formulae and terminology used in the legislation may be useful in more complicated situations. The terminology and formulae used in the basic calculation of the transferable nil rate band (s 8A) is therefore reproduced below:

Unused nil rate band on death (s 8A(2)):

M > VT, where:

- M is the maximum amount that could be transferred by a chargeable transfer made on the person's death if it were to be wholly chargeable to tax at the rate of nil per cent (in other words, the nil rate band on the first death, less any chargeable lifetime transfers); and

- VT is the value actually transferred by the chargeable transfer so made (or nil, if applicable). This value includes any gift with reservation assets and any trust assets forming part of the deceased's estate on death.

The percentage increase in the survivor's nil rate band maximum (NB this is subject to an overriding maximum of 100% (s 8A(5)), and to the 'clawback' rules (s 8C) in respect of heritage property and woodlands relief (see **3.6**)):

$$\left(\frac{E}{NRBMD}\right) \times 100$$

Where:

- E is the amount by which M is greater than VT in the case of the deceased person; and

- NRBMD is the nil rate band maximum at the time of the deceased person's death.

In HMRC's view, the percentage should be taken to four decimal places, if necessary.

Those wishing to become more familiar with the methodology in the legislation may find the HMRC guidance mentioned above useful (see IHTM43020 and following). However, Examples 3.1 and 3.2 illustrate how they apply in practice.

Example 3.1 – Unused nil rate band (1)

Cynthia died on 6 May 2011. She had made gifts in the last seven years of her life of £50,000. By her will she left £30,000 to her sister and £50,000 to her daughter Jessica, with residue to her husband Wilfred. Wilfred had not made any lifetime gifts. He died on 13 October 2011 leaving an estate of £400,000 and nominating Jessica as his executrix.

Jessica may claim the relief. Wilfred's nil rate band would have been £325,000, but there is still £195,000 unused from Cynthia's estate, so the total nil rate band available (£520,000) is more than enough to exclude Wilfred's estate from an IHT liability.

This is seen by applying the formula:

M > VT (the unused nil rate band on Cynthia's death):

£325,000 – £130,000 = £195,000

Example 3.2 – Unused nil rate band (2)

Take the facts in the above example, except that Wilfred died on 6 April 2012 and his estate was £600,000. If Jessica makes a claim, the nil rate band available for 2012–13 will be £325,000 plus a figure in respect of the unused nil rate band available to Cynthia. She used 40% of the band, so 60% is left. At the rates applicable for 2012–13 that will amount to £195,000 as before, so Wilfred's nil rate band will be £520,000.

Applying the formula (on Cynthia's death):

$$\left(\frac{E}{NRBMD}\right) \times 100$$

Where: E = (£325,000 – £130,000) = £195,000

NRBMD = £325,000

$$\left(\frac{£195,000}{£325,000}\right) \times 100 = 60\%$$

Wilfred's nil rate band is therefore: £325,000 + (£325,000 × 60%) = £520,000.

The transferable nil rate band applies 'for the purposes of the charge to tax on the death of the survivor' (s 8A(3)). Thus in addition to reducing IHT on the survivor's free estate, the ability to transfer the unused nil rate band on the first death has the potential to reduce the IHT liability on any gifts with reservation upon death, or in respect of qualifying (eg pre-22 March 2006) interest in possession property, or any additional tax on a chargeable lifetime transfer or IHT on a failed PET.

Surviving spouses or civil partners who try to utilise an additional nil rate band on a chargeable lifetime transfer (eg to a discretionary trust) will be faced with an IHT liability, although on the survivor's death within seven years an extra nil rate band may then be available, albeit that there would be no refund of any lifetime IHT paid.

CLAIM TO THE RELIEF

3.5   The relief is available on the making of a claim to HMRC Inheritance Tax on Schedule IHT402 ('Claim to transfer unused nil rate band'), which can be downloaded (in pdf format) from the HMRC website: www.hmrc.gov.uk/inheritancetax/iht402.pdf. This Schedule replaced form IHT216 in respect of deceased estates, following the introduction of the IHT400 Inheritance Tax Account. However, if the personal representatives of the deceased's estate do not make a claim to transfer unused nil rate band (eg if there is no need to take out a grant), any other person liable for tax on the survivor's death (eg the trustees of a settlement or the donee of a gift) may make a claim, but only when the initial period for claim by the personal representatives has passed (see below). In those cases, the claimant should use form IHT216 (IHTM43006).

The requirement to make the claim is in s 8A(3). The rules for claims are in s 8B. It should be noted that more than one Schedule IHT402 may be required, as a separate claim is required for each spouse or civil partner who died, as appropriate.

The claim is to be made by the personal representative of the surviving spouse or civil partner within the permitted period (see below), but the HMRC Commissioners may allow a longer period. If no claim has been made by the personal representatives, a claim can be made by any other person who is liable to IHT on the survivor's death, outside the normal two-year time limit. The legislation permits such late claims at HMRC's discretion (s 8B(1)(b)).

The 'permitted period' is two years from the end of the month in which the survivor dies or, if later, three months from the date on which the personal representatives first act as such (see s 8B(3)).

HMRC may admit claims submitted late due to reasons beyond the claimant's control on a discretionary basis, such as in the following circumstances (see IHTM43009):

- if there is a dispute over the estate, which must be resolved before the personal representatives can be identified;
- unforeseen postal disruptions resulting in the loss or delay of a claim;
- the loss of records supporting a claim due to fire, flood or theft, where the records could not be replaced in time for a claim within the permitted period;

- serious illness of the claimant (or possibly a close relative or partner, depending on the circumstances);

- the death of a close relative or partner shortly before the end of the permitted period, where necessary steps had already been taken to make the claim on time;

- the claimant can show that they were not aware (and could not reasonably have been aware) of their entitlement to make a claim.

Example 3.3 – Claiming the relief

Jake was 'a bit of a lad', and quite late in life was divorced from his wife and went to live with Caroline. He showered presents on her and took her away for romantic weekends and for holidays in flats above chip shops in Malaga. Caroline loved it and, to some extent, him, and whilst they were enjoying the winter sunshine in Spain arranged for Jake to sign a will. No lawyer being readily to hand, she wrote the will out herself and got a couple of people at a neighbouring table in the local café to act as witnesses.

Jake's children were not impressed. Before Caroline could even apply for a grant of probate they had lodged caveats. After the usual lengthy and expensive correspondence between solicitors, culminating in a meeting with a mediator, a settlement was reached which allowed Caroline to apply for a grant of probate. The mediation itself took place on the second anniversary of Jake's death and it was two more months before Caroline had the HMRC account ready. She discovered that Jake had actually been married twice before, and that his first wife had died, leaving everything to him. As a result, there was a possibility of a claim to increase the nil rate band available on Jake's estate. Caroline had one month in which to put in the claim, as the deadline for making the claim in her capacity as personal representative is three months from the date she first acts as such (s 8B(3)(a); see IHTM43007).

The failure to make a claim on an earlier death could have an unfortunate knock-on effect on the amount of nil rate band that may subsequently be claimed. However, the legislation provides for some possible relief. For example, when a surviving spouse ('C') dies and C's personal representatives discover that no claim was made on the death of the deceased spouse ('B') in respect of the death of an earlier spouse ('A'), a claim is allowed in respect of A's death as well as B's death, if the original IHT position of A is unaffected (s 8B(2)).

Once a claim is made it can be withdrawn, but no later than one month after the end of the permitted claim period (s 8B(4)).

Heritage and woodland relief

3.6   Under certain circumstances, it becomes necessary in relation to heritage relief and woodland relief to look back to an earlier death to establish the tax charge. As may be imagined, the availability of the nil rate band can affect that tax charge. Section 8C takes account of this, where a heritage or woodland clawback charge applies.

Clawback of heritage or woodlands relief whilst surviving spouse still alive

3.7   If the event triggering the charge happens before the death of the surviving spouse, it becomes necessary to recalculate the available (or used) nil rate band.

To apply the legislation, first find the nil rate band for the first spouse to die, defined as in s 8A(4) 'NRBMD'. Next, find the current nil rate band, ie that in force at the time of the event triggering the charge. This is defined by s 8C(2) as 'NRBME'.

Next establish 'E'. This is the excess of the nil rate band over the chargeable transfer at the first death; effectively, the unused nil rate band.

Finally (for this stage of the computation) calculate 'TA': this is the amount on which the clawback is charged.

Then apply the formula:

$$\left(\frac{E}{NRBMD} - \frac{TA}{NRBME} \right) \times 100$$

The result represents the percentage of the nil rate band in respect of which a claim may be made. HMRC's guidance includes a worked example (IHTM43045).

Example 3.4 – Effect of heritage relief clawback (1)

Lady Penelope's pink Rolls Royce, worth £100,000, was the subject of an undertaking under IHTA 1984, s 30 when she died in November 2007. Her son had the car re-sprayed in May 2012 which destroyed the essential character of the vehicle and which was in breach of the undertaking, triggering a s 32 charge. Lady Penelope had made chargeable lifetime transfers of £25,000 and left her estate, apart from the car, to Parker, whom she had married late in life.

Nil rate band – November 2007 (NRBMD): £300,000

Nil rate band – May 2012 (NRBME): £325,000

Unused nil rate band, November 2007:

applying the formula in s 8A(2) and (4) (E): £275,000 viz

M = £300,000

VT = £25,000

E = (M – VT) = £275,000

TA: £100,000

Computation:

$$\left(\frac{£275,000}{£300,000} - \frac{£100,000}{£325,000} \right) \times 100 = 60.8975\% \text{ of Lady Penelope's nil rate band remains available.}$$

An alternative way of looking at this is to say that Lady Penelope's estate used up 8.3333% of the nil rate band when Lady Penelope died; on the breach of undertaking a further 30.7692% of the nil rate band in effect at that time was used up (ie 39.1025% in total), leaving 60.8975% available.

If there is more than one breach of undertaking, or where there are several woodland clawback charges, the nil rate band that may be transferred is reduced by the proportion of the nil rate band clawed back by all the deferred charges (ie by the aggregate of TA/NRBME in respect of each triggering event) (s 8C(3)).

Clawback of heritage or woodlands relief after the second death

3.8   If a deferred charge is triggered after the nil rate band has been transferred, s 8C(4) reduces the nil rate band of the first spouse to die. The mechanics of the adjustment are set out in s 8C(5). The nil rate band of the first to die of the spouses or civil partners is first adjusted by applying Sch 2 (the uprating provisions that give the benefit of any reduction in the tax that applies because the nil rate band has been increased over time).

That up-rated nil rate band is then potentially both increased and decreased. The increase can apply where the first spouse to die might himself have more than one nil rate band available, perhaps being a widower. The reduction is the amount of any increase in that band by virtue of the nil band transfer rules. The language of the legislation is rather convoluted; it was with greater optimism than truth that the Explanatory Note to Finance Bill 2008 suggested that s 8C(5) 'makes [it] clear' at all; but the following example may illustrate it.

Example 3.5 – Effect of heritage relief clawback (2)

Sir James was first married to Zuleika who became UK domiciled in 1978 and who left her estate to Sir James when she died in March 1996. Zuleika did not use her nil rate band. In 2000 Sir James married Sally and on his death in November 2012 he left her his estate, having made only one chargeable transfer of £50,000 (a failed PET). The family seat qualified as heritage property, but a sale of amenity land for £200,000 to meet Lady Sally's debts after her death in March 2014 triggered a clawback charge under the 'associated property' provisions of s 32A.

The nil rate band in 1995–96 was £154,000 but none of it was used. In November 2012 it was £325,000, so the total nil rate band available to Sir James's executor is (£325,000 – £50,000 = £275,000 + £325,000) £600,000. The nil rate band when the property was sold and at Sally's death is £325,000. The clawback charge is on £200,000.

Sir James's estate now has available a reduced (double) nil rate band of (£600,000 – £200,000): £400,000.

Any clawback charge after the death of the survivor (Sally) under s 8C(5) would depend upon the extent (if any) to which the nil rate band transferred from Sir James's estate was required to keep Sally's estate free of IHT.

[NB If a Scottish law claim to 'legitim' is made after a claim to transfer unused nil rate band following the death of the second parent, HMRC may adjust the claim in respect of the unused nil rate band accordingly (s 147(10); see IHTM43041).]

HMRC's guidance includes a further illustration of a clawback charge arising after the survivor's death (IHTM43046).

Unexhausted pension funds

3.9   The IHT provisions relating to alternatively secured pensions (ASPs) (in ss 151A–151E) ceased to apply (subject to transitional provisions) following legislation in FA 2011, which amended the pension rules (in FA 2004, Part 4) relating to registered pension schemes applying to individuals reaching the age of 75. The changes broadly removed the effective requirement to buy an annuity by the age of 75. From 6 April 2011, IHT will not generally apply to drawdown pension funds remaining under a registered pension scheme, including where the individual dies after reaching the age of 75.

Whilst the IHT rules affecting the transferable nil rate band were repealed with effect for deaths occurring from 6 April 2011, they still need to be considered in respect of deaths prior to that date. The background to these rules is the IHT charge that arises (under s 151B) on that part of an alternatively secured pension (ASP) fund which has not been used in benefits for the fund member and his dependants. In broad terms, the unexhausted fund is treated as the 'top slice' of the member's estate for IHT purposes. Section 151BA(5) uprates the nil rate band that is to be applied. The provisions were modified in FA 2008 by the introduction of s 151BA(6) and (7).

Once again, a formula first requires the taxpayer to establish certain values.

E, as before, is the unused excess nil rate band available; and NRBM is the nil rate band in force when the member died.

The legislation provides the formula:

$$100 - \left(\frac{E}{NRBMD} \right) \times 100$$

This produces 'the used-up percentage' (ie the fraction by which the nil rate band otherwise available to the member is to be reduced).

Example 3.6 – 'Used-up percentage' of nil rate band

Mabel died in July 2009, when the nil rate band was £325,000. She had made no lifetime gifts but left £25,000 to her son and the rest of her estate, including her pension rights, to her husband, David. He did not draw the entire pension. He had no dependants. The unexhausted portion of the pension fund, at his death on 6 January 2011, was £100,000. For Mabel's estate:

E = £300,000 (£325,000 – £25,000);

NRBM = £325,000; and

the 'used-up percentage' is $100 - (300 / 325) \times 100$ ie $100 - 92.3077 = 7.6923\%$. This is the part of Mabel's nil rate band that has been used.

A section of HMRC's Inheritance Tax Manual is devoted to the interaction of ASP charges with the transfer of unused nil rate band (IHTM43047 to IHTM43052), and a full worked example where the deceased's estate includes funds in an ASP is included at IHTM43048–IHTM43050.

Matters become more complicated where the pension fund is still not exhausted by the death of the second person benefiting from it. This follows from s 151BA(8)–(12), which was introduced in FA 2008. First, the situation is addressed where there has been an IHT charge on an ASP fund by reference to the first to die of husband and wife (or civil partner). This affects the person's nil rate band and restricts the amount available for transfer later: it is 'appropriately reduced' under s 151BA(9) where the chargeable event occurred after the death of the surviving spouse. If, however, the surviving spouse is still alive when the chargeable event happens, tax is charged when the survivor dies by adjusting the member's transferable nil rate band using a formula (see s 151BA(12)) which compares the 'adjusted excess' with the 'adjusted nil rate band maximum', expressed as a percentage.

The detail of the calculation may have been enough to cow pensioners into submission – in the form of drawing income to exhaust the fund. Thus, where the charge arose after both spouses died, each may have used part of his or her nil rate band, so there may have been less available to meet the IHT charge under s 151B; see s 151BA(9), as augmented by the definitions set out in s 151BA(10).

Where the charge arises whilst the surviving spouse is still alive, the formula in s 151BA(12) applies. This restricts the nil rate band available later. 'AE', the adjusted excess, deducts from the maximum nil rate band the value transferred by chargeable transfers after calculating the taxable amount and after adjusting the nil rate band itself: ANRBM. 'ANRBM' is the nil rate band, adjusted for ASP charges under s 151B.

A detailed consideration of the interaction of the transferable nil rate band with the ASP provisions is (fortunately, perhaps) outside the scope of this book. However, HMRC guidance contains detailed examples on the interaction (IHTM43048–IHTM43052).

The foreign element

3.10 The examples have so far concerned couples based in the UK. However, these days even provincial practitioners regularly have to advise in situations where the foreign element adds complications such as if, for example, the surviving spouse was not domiciled in the UK (see **3.26**).

Where a deceased husband or wife was domiciled abroad, the available nil rate band of the surviving spouse will depend on the circumstances, as illustrated in HMRC's Inheritance Tax Manual (at IHTM43042 and IHTM43043). The starting principle is that everyone (whether domiciled in the UK or not) is entitled to a nil rate band that may be set against the value of assets otherwise subject to IHT.

Practitioners must also be familiar with the rules as to *situs* of assets and exemptions and exclusions, as shown in the next example.

Example 3.7 – Foreigner whose foreign widow moves to the UK

(This example is adapted from IHTM43042.)

Manfred was married to Silke, both being domiciled in Germany. Manfred had an estate in Germany but since Silke was well provided for, he left his estate to his son Christoph, living in England. Manfred also had a bank account denominated in Euros, the contents of which he also left to Christoph. After Manfred died, Silke decided to leave Germany permanently and moved to live with Christoph.

We may ignore assets outside the UK, as being excluded property; similarly the Euro account qualifies as excluded property under s 157(5); so, in leaving assets (including the bank account) to Christoph, Manfred used none of his nil rate band.

Silke acquired a domicile of choice in the UK. Her personal representative may claim two nil rate bands.

The restricted spouse exemption applies where the *recipient* spouse is non-UK domiciled, as illustrated below.

Example 3.8 – UK-domiciled person leaving non-UK domiciled widower

(This example is adapted from IHTM43043.)

Jennie was domiciled in England and Wales and retained that domicile though married to Jaap, a Dutchman and living with him in Rotterdam. Jennie had given Jaap £41,000 in 2008, setting against that gift two annual exemptions and £35,000 of the (restricted) spouse exemption. At her death in February 2012, she left Jaap her estate valued at £320,000.

The nil rate band at date of death, M, was £325,000.

The available spouse relief is (£55,000 – £35,000): £20,000

The value transferred, VT, is (£320,000 – £20,000): £300,000

M (£325,000) is greater than VT (£300,000), so there is unused nil rate band of £25,000 to transfer.

The rules work remarkably favourably where the surviving spouse dies in the UK with local assets. To that extent, the UK may be regarded as something of a tax haven.

Example 3.9 – UK-domiciled person leaving widow with UK estate

(This example is also adapted from IHTM43043.)

Mike had estate in the UK of £240,000 that on his death in December 2012 he left to his Italian wife Antonia, not having made any previous gifts to her, nor any chargeable gifts to anyone else.

The nil rate band at date of death is £325,000. The spouse exemption is restricted to £55,000 (s 18(2)).

The value transferred (£240,000 – £55,000): £185,000, which as a fraction of what was available is 56.92%, leaving 43.08% unused. Using the formula in s 8A(4):

E, the unused proportion, is (£325,000 – £185,000): £140,000.

NRBMD is £325,000.

The transferable band is (140,000 / 325,000) × 100 = 43.0769%.

Supposing Antonia retains her foreign domicile but owns assets in the UK: her personal representatives will enjoy 143.0769% of the nil rate band. Likewise, if as time passes she becomes deemed domiciled in the UK, the enhanced nil rate band may be set against her estate otherwise subject to IHT.

COMPLIANCE

The importance of records

3.11   Whilst historians of tax changes will all agree that the introduction of the transferable nil rate band has been (like the Roman Conquest in '*1066 and All That*') a 'Good Thing', the exercise of claiming it requires some discipline on the part of surviving spouses or civil partners and their personal representatives, in terms of keeping and maintaining records in respect of the first spouse or civil partner to die and their estate.

In HMRC's 'frequently asked questions' soon after the introduction of the transferable nil rate band, it was pointed out that 'The information and documents about the claim could be very valuable to the second estate and it will be important to keep them safe'.

Unfortunately, the importance of submitting full information was apparently lost on most professional firms submitting claims on behalf of their clients, following the introduction of the transferable nil rate band facility. In the 'IHT & Trusts Newsletter' (August 2008), HMRC commented:

> 'One disappointing feature since the introduction of these new provisions is the very high initial failure rate by agents to provide the supporting details we ask for. The IHT216 claim form lists the documents that we want to see to support the claim for relief, and in only 20 per cent of cases submitted by agents are all the requested documents provided. This is in stark contrast to claims made by unrepresented taxpayers who manage to provide all the documents at the first time of asking.'

HMRC warned that, if all the necessary documents are not submitted, claims cannot be processed, resulting in delays and increased costs.

Schedule IHT402 ('Claim to transfer unused Inheritance Tax nil rate band'), which replaced IHT216 and is one of the supplementary schedules to the IHT400 account, includes a list of the following documents to be copied and sent with the claim form:

- copy of the grant of representation (confirmation in Scotland) to the estate of the spouse or civil partner (or if no grant has been taken out, a copy of the death certificate);

- if the first spouse or civil partner to die left a will, a copy of it; and

- if a Deed of Variation or other similar document was executed to change the people who inherited the estate of the spouse or civil partner, a copy of it.

Particularly in 'older' cases where the earlier spouse or civil partner died some time ago, there may be gaps in the information and documentation available. In those circumstances, the survivor's personal representatives will need to complete the claim form to the best of their knowledge and ability, attaching whatever documents are available, and explaining to HMRC the reason for any omission. Alternatively, if there is a delay in obtaining the necessary documentation, HMRC may allow the personal representatives to make a provisional claim to transfer unused nil rate band (IHTM43006).

However, it will clearly be preferable if personal representatives of the earlier spouse or civil partner can undertake the preparatory work for a possible future claim on the survivor's death, such as by packaging together the required information and documents and passing them to the survivor for safe keeping. In cases where the first spouse or civil partner has died on or after 9 October 2007, HMRC point out that their published guidance has advised taxpayers to keep the following records (IHTM43012):

- a copy of the IHT200/IHT400, IHT205 (C5 in Scotland) or full written details of the assets in the estate and their values;

- the death certificate;

- the marriage or civil partnership certificate for the couple;

- a copy of the grant of representation (Confirmation in Scotland);

- a copy of the will, if there was one;

- a note of how the estate passed if there was no will;

- a copy of any Deed of Variation or other similar document if one was executed to change the people who inherited the estate;

- any valuation(s) of assets that pass under will or intestacy other than to the surviving spouse or civil partner;

- the value of any other assets that also passed on the death of the first spouse or civil partner, for example jointly owned assets, assets held in trust in which the deceased had a qualifying interest in possession and gifts made in the seven years prior to death;

- any evidence to support the availability of relief (such as agricultural or business relief) where the relievable assets pass to someone other than to the surviving spouse or civil partner.

However, the guidance assures taxpayers that HMRC do not expect them to provide all this material in support of a claim, although it would be much easier to make the claim if they did.

Practical difficulties have arisen as a result of the transferable nil rate band facility. For example, HMRC's policy used to be not to check claims for 100% BPR or APR where there is no immediate IHT liability, such as where personal representatives claim the relief on an individual's death and no IHT liability would arise on the death regardless of the availability of BPR or APR, due to the deceased's available NRB. However, such an issue will now be relevant in determining the unused NRB available to the surviving spouse or civil partner. Practitioners have experienced delays in the issue of form IHT421 ('Probate summary', which replaced form D18) or C1 ('Confirmation'). The HMRC guidance at IHTM43011 is clear: 'You should review the claim and correct any obvious errors, including collecting any additional tax due as a result, before releasing form IHT421/C1.' It goes on to state: 'Provided the documents show the claim is valid and any tax due has been paid, you can release form IHT421/C1'.

The same guidance instructs the Inspector, *after* release of form IHT421/ C1, 'to consider the risk to tax in deciding whether or not to accept the claim as offered'. It would seem that it is at this point that HMRC will test the availability of BPR or APR on the second death. Where the claim to TNRB had not been accepted by the risk assessors, Compliance Group at HMRC will investigate it as part of an enquiry (see IHTM43014). Close attention is likely to be paid to the situation where relievable property has been left to chargeable beneficiaries. The HMRC guidance recognises that, in 'old' cases, evidence may be very limited.

In HMRC's previously published 'frequently asked questions' on the transferable NRB, the comment was made that '… if a farm is left to, say, a son and the personal representatives of the first death consider that agricultural relief is due against the whole property, the extent to which the relief is due will be established, if it is necessary, on the second death'.

Problems may also arise if HMRC did not formally agree asset valuations on the first death for the same reason. All this should be seen in the context of HMRC's information and inspection powers, which were introduced in FA 2008 (s 113, Sch 36), and extended to include IHT in FA 2009 (s 95, Sch 48) from 1 April 2010. The earlier HMRC Consultation document 'Compliance Checks: The Next Stage' focused quite specifically on the way that IHT could be drawn into the new framework of checks as to record keeping, indicating in particular that records may in future need to be kept after an event on which IHT is chargeable, even where no return or account is required.

A sample checklist for nil rate band claims is included as **Appendix 3.1** at the end of this chapter.

Clearance certificates

3.12   A 'certificate of discharge' (or clearance certificate) confirms HMRC's satisfaction that all the IHT due in a particular case has been (or will be) paid (s 239).

Inevitably, there is a risk that tax charges will be missed. As a result, the clearance certificate issued by HMRC in respect of an estate will not guarantee freedom from IHT charges where the amount of the nil rate band that was transferred must be adjusted. Section 239(4) was qualified with effect from 9 October 2007, so that if too little IHT has been paid because of adjustment to the nil rate band, those persons who are accountable remain liable to pay the balance. If HMRC clearance was given by letter rather than a clearance certificate, the clearance is similarly disapplied if it is subsequently shown that too much nil rate band has been transferred.

Penalties

3.13   Penalties may be imposed on a wide range of people including (see **2.56**) someone other than the person in default (FA 2007, Sch 24, para 1A, formerly s 247(2)), if incorrect information has been supplied in connection with a claim to transfer unused nil rate band, for example by failure to cut down the nil rate band of the first spouse to die to reflect a part of that band used by him or her.

As to compliance and penalties generally, see **Chapter 2**.

Personal representatives of the surviving spouse or civil partner must therefore be mindful of the potential risk when making claims to transfer unused nil rate bands from an earlier death.

HMRC's IHT Toolkit defines the transferable nil rate band as an area of risk, if full details of any pre-deceased spouse or civil partner have not been obtained, and advocates thorough research on their background. The Toolkit also highlights a number of 'common points often overlooked' in connection with claims to transfer unused nil rate band. The IHT Toolkit is available via the HMRC website at www.hmrc.gov.uk/agents/toolkits/iht.pdf.

Valuations

3.14   The 'value ascertained' capital gains tax rule in TCGA 1992, s 274 ('Value determined for inheritance tax') under which values ascertained for IHT purposes apply for capital gains tax purposes was amended in FA 2008. The effect is that an asset valuation for the purposes of calculating the amount of transferable nil rate band (as opposed to calculating the amount of any IHT on death) cannot be treated as having been agreed for CGT purposes as well.

Managing risk

3.15   Compliance issues such as those mentioned above add to the burden of personal representatives and their advisers. It may in the past have been common for them simply to obtain a signature from the residuary beneficiary on the estate account in lieu of any formal discharge. Some advisers, not relishing the task of preparing proper accounts, may even have dispensed with as much formality as that. They will simply have issued a client account cheque. Experience tells us, however, that the kind of problem that might invalidate a discharge (on form IHT30 ('Application for a clearance certificate')) is most likely to arise in the administration of the estate of a member of a 'difficult' family! It may be precisely the beneficiaries of such a deceased who are impatient with the formality of probate and administration and who put the adviser under pressure simply to release the funds. Remembering the fate that befell the adviser in *Howarth's Executors v IRC* [1997] STC (SCD) 162, the adviser who is also an executor should insist on a formal release if he is in any doubt.

One important self-help procedure, which will cut down that risk, will be for widows and widowers to make and keep a record of the extent to which their late spouses had used the nil rate band. A simple form, along the lines of **Appendix 3.1** at the end of this chapter, might be placed with the survivor's will. A certain amount of documentary evidence may be required. By way of illustration, the nil rate band on 1 October 1977 was £15,000. It may be difficult to ascertain, in relation to deaths many years ago, how much of that band was in fact used. The 'statutory legacy' on intestacy at that time was £25,000.

HOW SHOULD PRACTITIONERS ADVISE?

3.16   As indicated at **3.3**, prior to the introduction of the transferable nil rate band facility, the thinking behind utilising the nil rate band on the first death was to leave it to chargeable beneficiaries. However, many testators really wanted the primary benefit to go to the surviving spouse or civil partner, so the trustees of a discretionary nil rate band trust were encouraged to regard the surviving spouse as the primary beneficiary, with the deceased spouse or civil partner typically leaving a sum equivalent to the upper limit of the nil rate band upon a discretionary trust so that the surviving spouse could have the benefit of the fund and at the same time the nil rate band could be utilised and not wasted. Distributions could be made in favour of the surviving spouse in case of need; and if they were of capital any exit charge under the discretionary trust regime in the first ten years would be by reference to the nil rate band on the testator's death.

However, much of that thinking has been rendered obsolete by the transferable nil rate band legislation. In many cases the emphasis is on not using the nil rate band on the first death, in the hope that the transferable band will be larger on the second death, when it will really be needed. Note, though, the problems of a '28-day' or similar survivorship clause discussed at **3.25**.

Some individuals will prefer to 'bank' the nil rate band, rather than rely on its availability on the survivor's death. In addition, there are still special circumstances where a will should contain a nil rate band trust, as will be seen below.

Advice where both spouses are still alive

3.17   Husband and wife (or civil partners) are both still alive and have made wills that incorporate nil rate band discretionary trusts. What should they do?

If they feel uncomfortable with the relative complexity of trusts in their wills, they could consider making new wills, although codicils to their existing wills may well be sufficient to dispense with the nil rate band legacy. Alternatively, there is scope (under s 144) for the trustees of a relevant property trust to appoint funds or assets to beneficiaries within two years of the death. To avoid the difficulty suffered in *Frankland v IRC* [1997] STC 1450, trustees should not normally (but see below) take any action until three months have elapsed from the date of death. Between the fourth and the twenty-fourth month, however, a distribution from the discretionary trust will take effect as if it had been a gift under the terms of the will and not a distribution from the relevant property trust.

Therefore, subject to the survivorship point below, there is no need to change the will. On the death of the first to die of husband and wife, the trustees simply wait at least three months and appoint the whole of the nil rate band to the surviving spouse (note there is no need to wait three months if the effect of the deed of appointment is to create an immediate post-death interest (IPDI), only if the interest created is an absolute one). If the will of the *surviving* spouse is drafted in common form, the provision as to the nil rate band will not apply on the second death assuming it has been excluded where the surviving spouse is not married at the date of death. In this scenario, therefore, all that is needed is a deed of appointment by the trustees of the nil rate band set up by the will of the first spouse to die.

However, not everyone is familiar with the drafting of deeds of appointment of assets out of discretionary trusts. Things can get left. If one of the executors is a professional person, there is a significant risk that he or she will be liable in negligence for not being up to date with tax law, and/or for failing to do what is right for the family in terms of IHT. If the executors are all family members and if they miss the various deadlines, they could be worse off than if they had simpler wills.

In this context, it is useful to review the difficulties that arose in the unfortunate case of *RSPCA v Sharp and others* where the will contained, first, a gift of the nil rate band; then a gift of an asset to a chargeable beneficiary, followed by the gift of residue to a charity. It was a case on construction: the charity claimed that the second gift should operate to reduce the first, so that together they took up only the nil rate band. The High Court disagreed ([2010] EWHC 268 (Ch)), and criticised the charity for bringing the case. However, the charity's subsequent appeal was successful (*RSPCA v Sharp & others* [2010] EWCA

Civ 1474). Overall, the case serves as a lesson about the problems which can arise if there is any ambiguity in the drafting of wills where legacies to charity are involved.

The 'debt' or 'charge' schemes were difficult to explain properly. Where there was a problem under FA 1986, s 103, as illustrated by the *Phizackerley* case (*Phizackerley (Personal Representative of Phizackerley, deceased) v Revenue and Customs Comrs* [2007] SpC 591) (see **5.17** onwards), it became quite difficult to explain the scheme to clients. Many people may have been slightly uncomfortable with the complexity of wills containing nil rate band discretionary trusts and they may feel much happier with simple new wills, even though that will (of course!) involve paying a new fee to have them prepared.

Nil rate band trusts may still be useful in certain circumstances, such as are more fully explored in **Chapter 4**. They will be appropriate where the surviving spouse already has an additional nil rate band available (ie for remarried spouses, following the death of a spouse), and for other reasons which are not related to IHT. Possible reasons include the following:

● where future care costs are a concern, as outlined below; or

● for asset protection purposes (eg in the event of financial or marriage failure); or

● where it is likely that the survivor may remarry (note in some cases, up to four nil rate bands are potentially available; see **3.23**); or

● if the value of an asset is likely to increase faster than increases in the nil rate band; or

● if the asset qualifies for business or agricultural property relief (ie to 'bank' the relief in the event of any future reduction or withdrawal of it). As indicated at **6.12**, where business or agricultural property relief at 100% is available, the value of the gift on top of the nil rate band is unlimited, whereas relief at 50% effectively doubles the nil rate band (in either case, the trust is not really a 'nil rate band' trust in the normal sense of the term).

Advice where one spouse or civil partner died some time ago

3.18   Suppose that the husband died five years ago but the widow is still alive and that there is a nil rate band discretionary trust in place. In this situation, nothing can or should be done. By putting in place a nil rate band discretionary trust, the husband used his NRB and, since five years have elapsed since his death, it is now too late to make any changes relying on s 144. It is also too late to consider a deed of variation because to be effective, that must also be made within two years of death to claim relief under s 142.

Therefore the only nil rate band available to the widow (unless she remarries and survives her second husband!) is the single nil rate band. It would be totally wrong for the family to assume that 'we just don't need that silly scheme now' and to appoint all the funds in the discretionary trust to the widow. That would just increase her estate without giving her back her late husband's nil rate band.

Most difficult will be the vague situations, often encountered in practice, where the family cannot positively show that they have implemented the terms of the will.

Example 3.10 – The effect of sloth

Father died, having left the nil rate band on the usual trusts for his immediate family; mother still lives in the family home, which was held as tenants in common; dividends from stocks and shares, in so far as they have been collected by the slow-moving executors, have been bundled up in payments to mother; the proceeds of insurance bonds and policies have been used to buy mother a new and more efficient car than father's aging limo; but there is, by the second anniversary of his death, absolutely nothing on paper to show that the trustees have even considered the discretion given them by the will trust, let alone exercised it.

What has happened here? The decision in *Judge* suggests that where trustees do not even consider the exercise of discretion they have not exercised it. It will be hard for the trustees to argue that, in effect, there have been distributions from the nil rate band trust to mother within s 144. More likely the end result may be only partial use of father's nil rate band, cutting down what can be transferred by the trustees, and mother's estate has since been increased for IHT purposes. Someone has probably been negligent.

Advice where one spouse died recently

3.19   Suppose that, although the husband died last year, his widow is still alive and in good health. This is a situation that will affect many families, and must be approached with care. The results can be seen with an extended and detailed example. Note in particular the rule in *Russell* v *CIR* (Ch D [1988] STC 195) as to 'only one bite of the cherry' where there has already been a variation of a will.

Example 3.11 – Spouse died recently

Fred made a will in standard form, leaving a nil rate band discretionary trust for the benefit of his close family, with residue to his wife Hannah. The main asset was their house, worth £800,000, held by them as tenants in common in equal shares. Fred had £100,000 of savings. He died on 3 January 2012, having made no chargeable lifetime transfers.

It was agreed that Hannah would sell the family home and move to something much less expensive nearer her daughter, Angela. The house was sold by the executor and Hannah for £900,000. Fred's estate was administered promptly and the nil rate band of £325,000 was satisfied with £100,000 from his savings and £225,000 from the sale of the house. Hannah soon realised that she need not rely on any of the nil rate band and told Angela that she would be much happier if all of the money could be released to Angela straightaway.

The family understood that, since they were still within two years of Fred's death, they could effectively rewrite Fred's will so that all of his estate went to Hannah. That way, the whole of Fred's nil rate band would still be available. The assets that were to be transferred to Angela would not now, for IHT purposes, be coming to her from the discretionary trust. They would be treated as gifts from Hannah and, if Hannah lived seven years, those gifts would fall out of account anyway.

The family decided that, despite the fact that Fred's estate was almost completely administered, it would be worthwhile unscrambling everything, and rewriting the will so that Fred's nil rate band had not been used on his death. Hannah hoped that perhaps a future government might increase the nil rate band and that her executors would then reap double benefit.

New instructions: the 'put together' family

3.20   In order to make a claim to transfer the unused nil rate band, the surviving spouse must have been married to the deceased on the first death. Divorce therefore severs the ability to transfer the nil rate band. Subject to that, where a 'second husband' marries a 'second wife' a careful balance must be struck between tax considerations and what the family want. Suppose that each party to the new marriage has both assets derived from, and obligations to the children of, former marriages. The transferable nil rate band facility will allow the executors of the survivor husband and wife each to enjoy an amount equal to not more than double the nil rate band where he or she has been married more than once.

Example 3.12 – Death, divorce and remarriage

David was married to Liz. They had two children. David's best friend was Edward, married to Jill. They had one son. Tragically, Edward died intestate on

Boxing Day 2006. Jill put in place a deed of variation under which £142,500 was set aside for their son, and the rest of the estate, about £350,000, passed to Jill. That effectively used half of Edward's nil rate band.

David's comforting of Jill in her bereavement led to his divorce from Liz. As a preamble to, but not part of, the divorce, in summer 2010 David voluntarily settled £81,250 on their children. That settlement was not relieved by IHTA 1984, s 10 or 11. David then married Jill, but died on 1 August 2012, leaving all his estate to her. Jill died on 17 October 2012.

Jill's executor can make claims in respect of the nil rate band that was available to Edward and to David. As far as Edward is concerned, the provision that Jill arranged in respect of his estate used half the nil rate band (ie £285,000 for 2006–07), so half the nil rate band is still available, which (at 2012–13 rates) is £162,500.

As far as David's estate is concerned, the chargeable gift of £81,250 reduced the nil rate band available at the date of his death from £325,000 by one-quarter. So three-quarters of the nil rate band is potentially available, ie £243,750.

However, Jill's executor cannot enjoy more than one total extra nil rate band, so the nil rate band available at Jill's death is £650,000.

Tax planning to 'recycle' APR or BPR

3.21   A discretionary trust may still be a useful vehicle to hold assets that are within the NRB because their value is wholly or partly reduced for IHT by property reliefs.

Example 3.13 – Recycling BPR (or APR)

Julian was a successful engineer. By his will, he left all his assets attracting relief from IHT at 100% to a discretionary trust for his children, and the residue of his estate to Delia, his wife, who had always taken a keen interest in the family business. At the date of Julian's death, his shares in his engineering business attracted 100% BPR and were worth £900,000. Delia received the parts of the estate that did not qualify for any relief. She also received substantial cash from insurance policies and death in service benefits.

Delia used the cash to buy the shares from the trustees. That gave the trustees far more, in real terms, than the nil rate band, so effectively the children received more than Julian could have given in simple cash terms.

If Delia lives two years from her purchase of the shares, BPR will again be available.

Meanwhile, there is control over the children's inheritance.

Care fees considerations

3.22   Many couples are more concerned about the likely burden of care fees than about IHT. Care fees considerations are outside the scope of this book. However, a discretionary trust, properly run, can be expensive (eg as compliance procedures such as anti-money laundering (AML) rules in the UK are detailed and potentially complex), but can shelter from fees the estate of the first spouse, who is often cared for by the spouse who survives but who thereafter also needs care.

Alternatively, a simple IPDI will protect the capital and might be cheaper to run.

Companionship in old age

3.23   In certain situations, it is quite conceivable that four nil rate bands may be available. This could happen if, for example, a co-habiting couple who had each been married before left their respective estates to chargeable legatees such as adult children (or to the survivor), in order to utilise both their own nil rate band and the transferred nil rate band of their deceased spouse.

However, following marriage their overall IHT position could dramatically worsen.

Example 3.14 – Marriage or co-habitation?

Doris, widowed with one daughter, had inherited from her husband all his modest estate. Her part of London had become fashionable and their former council house was now worth £525,000. She had worked on the checkout at a very successful supermarket and had always taken up any employee share offers, so she now had a holding worth £150,000.

Eric, a jobbing builder until his retirement, had also inherited all of his late wife's estate and intended to leave everything, amounting to £700,000 in value, to their two sons.

Eric and Doris met on a long journey on a coach holiday in Tuscany. They decided to set up home together, letting Eric's house, and consulted their friend, a tax adviser, about getting married and leaving their estates to each other. Their friend was as discouraging as Dr Johnson had been to the young man in Streatham. It was not that, for Eric and Doris, second marriage would be the triumph of hope over experience; far from it. However, leaving their estates to each other would not only result in the nil rate band of either Eric or Doris being wasted on the first death, but also the unused nil rate band of the spouse from their first marriage.

Marrying each other may well create a further unused nil rate band on the first of Eric or Doris to die, but it could not be transferred to the survivor, whose maximum nil rate band entitlement had already been reached. The deceased spouse's additional nil rate band entitlement from their first marriage could not be transferred either.

In the above example, if Eric and Doris did marry, consideration could be given to including a legacy to chargeable beneficiaries (eg to adult children or a discretionary will trust) on the first death, sufficient to use the deceased's nil rate band plus the transferred nil rate band from that person's first marriage.

Nil rate band relevant property trusts

3.24   As indicated at **3.17**, despite the transferable nil rate band provisions, a nil rate band relevant property trust may still be considered desirable for various reasons. However, some care is required in respect of wills drafted before the introduction of the transferable nil rate band provisions, and also when drafting new wills that incorporate such trusts of the nil rate band.

For example, if the will of a surviving spouse or civil partner leaves a sum 'that is equal to an amount that will not give rise to an IHT charge' on a relevant property trust, in HMRC's view that amount will include nil rate band that has been transferred. The effect when calculating an exit charge before the first ten-year anniversary of the trust is that there will be a positive rate of tax under s 68(1), and an IHT liability arises on the exit.

HMRC's guidance (at IHTM43065) helpfully includes examples of typical wording in wills, and their likely effect:

- 'I give free of tax to my trustees such sum as at my death equals the maximum amount which could be given to them by this Will without inheritance tax becoming payable in respect of my estate' – this will allow the uprated nil rate band to be transferred.

- 'To my trustees such sum as I could leave immediately before my death without IHT becoming payable' – this will only transfer the single nil rate band available on the deceased's death, because any nil rate band that may transferred is not available immediately before death.

- 'I give free of tax to my trustees an amount equal to the upper limit of the nil per cent rate band in the table of rates in Schedule 1' – this will only transfer a single nil rate band.

- 'To my trustees an amount equal to the nil rate band in force at my death' – this again will only transfer a single nil rate band.'

The inclusion of the transferred nil rate band from the first death with the survivor's own nil rate band legacy could also adversely affect charities (ie where the survivor's residuary estate after the nil rate band legacy has been left to a charity).

Such difficulties could be prevented by limiting the nil rate band legacy on the survivor's death by reference to the nil rate band in force at the date of death, rather than by reference to an amount that does not give rise to an IHT charge.

Survivorship clauses

3.25 In wills drafted without tax in mind it is common to include words such as 'If my wife shall survive me by 28 days but not otherwise I give her all my estate', with the intention of saving the family the trouble of passing assets from one spouse to the other only then to have to pass them to the next generation.

However, that wording fails to make use of the transferable nil rate band. Where there is substantial property held as joint tenants, the rules of survivorship may ensure that part of the estate is not a chargeable transfer.

For consideration of how a survivorship clause can cause an increased charge to IHT to arise on the estate of a married couple, and how a deed of variation might be used to improve the position, see Example 5.11.

Death of non-domiciled spouse or civil partner

3.26 As indicated at **3.10**, both domiciled and non-domiciled spouses and civil partners are entitled to a nil rate band in respect of their UK assets. In terms of maximising the amount of unused nil rate band available on the death of the survivor, a non-domiciled spouse or civil partner should ensure that his estate comprises non-UK *situs* assets as far as possible. Excluded property (within ss 6, 48(3), 48(3A), including certain UK investments) not attracting an

IHT charge can be left to otherwise chargeable legatees (eg children) or exempt ones (eg the surviving spouse or civil partner), leaving the nil rate band intact and subject to a transfer claim on the death of the survivor.

Care needs to be taken on the death of a spouse or civil partner if the survivor was not domiciled in the UK, as the exemption for assets passing to the surviving spouse or civil partner is subject to an upper limit. At the time of writing, that upper limit is £55,000 (s 18(2)), although it is set to increase to the amount of the nil rate band at the time of transfer (subject to an election for the transferee spouse or civil partner to be treated as domiciled in the UK for IHT purposes), following changes to be introduced in Finance Act 2013. If the entire estate passes to the surviving spouse or civil partner, any excess over £55,000 is a chargeable legacy. If the net estate is above the nil rate band plus £55,000, there will be no nil rate band available to transfer to the surviving spouse.

Example 3.15 – Non-domiciled surviving spouse

Sarah died on 2 September 2010, leaving an estate of £217,500 to Karim, her non-UK domiciled husband. Karim dies on 13 December 2012, leaving a UK estate of £700,000.

The IHT nil rate band at Sarah's death was £325,000. Her chargeable estate was £162,500 (ie her estate of £217,500 less the restricted spouse exemption of £55,000 (s 18(2)).

The unused nil rate band is therefore £162,500 (ie £325,000 – £162,500). The transferable nil rate band percentage is: (£162,500 / £325,000) × 100 = 50%.

On Karim's death, his nil rate band is increased by 50% to £487,500 (ie £325,000 + (£325,000 × 50%)), which can be deducted from his UK estate.

For further commentary on domicile, see **Chapter 17**.

DEATHS BEFORE 25 JULY 1986

3.27   IHT was introduced in 1986. However, the transferable nil rate band provisions are adapted in cases where an earlier spouse died before 25 July 1986, and the surviving spouse died on or after 9 October 2007. FA 2008 adapted s 8A accordingly, so that the rules apply for capital transfer tax purposes where the spouse died between 1 January 1985 and 24 July 1986, or between 13 March 1975 and 31 December 1984, as appropriate (FA 2008, Sch 4, para 10(2), (3)).

Similarly, the transferable nil rate band provisions are adapted for estate duty purposes where the spouse died between 16 April 1969 and 12 March 1975, or before 16 April 1969, as appropriate (FA 2008, Sch 4, para 10(4), (5)).

Prior to 22 March 1972, there was no spouse exemption at all. Thus, if property was left to a spouse, an estate duty charge would have arisen. If the estate was large enough for duty to be paid, the equivalent of the nil rate band would have been exhausted, so that there would be nothing left to transfer.

Between 22 March 1972 and 12 November 1974, the spouse exemption was limited to £15,000, and it was therefore possible that the estate may have been liable to estate duty.

From 13 November 1974, the exemption for spouses who died domiciled in the UK was unlimited.

Example 3.16 – A real life situation

Lest readers should think that the above commentary is academic, this example (suitably changed) is based on actual facts.

By his will dated 1963, Cedric gave to his wife Irene a legacy of £500 and the family home. He left the residue of his estate on trust for Irene for life with remainder to their children, Jennifer and Alice. Cedric died in June 1971.

Let us assume that Irene, aged no less than 101, still lives in the family home, worth £350,000. She has capital of £150,000. Meanwhile, the trust fund had grown over the intervening years and now stands at £750,000. The trustees achieved this growth applying the principles of Warren Buffett, in that there have been very few transactions with the result that one half of the value of the fund is capital gain.

Irene is concerned to mitigate the burden of IHT on her estate, though she does realise that she may have left things rather late. She wondered if it would be appropriate for her to give up her interest in the trust so that Jennifer and Alice could at last inherit under their father's will.

Irene was advised that under no circumstances should this be done. The trust fund is free of IHT by virtue of the estate duty surviving spouse exemption (Sch 6, para 2), so no saving of IHT would be achieved by any distribution from the fund. In any case, all the gains would be 'washed' on Irene's eventual death, whilst any dealing with the capital of the fund during Irene's lifetime would trigger CGT charges.

The trustees should leave well alone. Irene could consider transactions in relation to her personal estate, in particular gifts out of any surplus income, though it will take time to establish a pattern. It would probably be too late to contemplate 'conventional' gifts which would require Irene to live until nearly 109. If still in good health, she might consider investing some of her savings in an 'IHT portfolio' (ie securities on AIM or similar that, after two years, would qualify for BPR at 100%).

Alice wondered if there might be available a transferable nil rate band, but there will not. Cedric's legacy to Irene and his gift of the house will have amounted together to more than the nil rate band applicable in 1971, so there is no nil rate band to transfer. The maximum exposure to IHT, if Irene does nothing, and if she still has the whole of her personal nil rate band for 2012–13 of £325,000, is £70,000.

As far as Jennifer and Alice are concerned, if they inherit from their mother, they will suffer an effective tax rate of only 5.6% (ie (£70,000 / £350,000 + £150,000 + £750,000) × 100).

The 'clawback' provisions dealing with the interaction of the transferable nil rate band and IHT or capital transfer tax charges in respect of heritage relief and woodland relief (see **3.6**) are also adapted accordingly, where the surviving spouse died on or after 9 October 2007 and the earlier spouse died between 13 March 1975 and 24 July 1986, or between 1 January 1985 and 24 July 1986, or between 7 April 1976 and 31 December 1984, or between 13 March 1975 and 6 April 1976, so that the clawback rules in s 8C apply to the appropriate capital transfer tax legislation (FA 2008, Sch 4, para 11).

The nil rate band in force upon the spouse or civil partner's death can be found in the form IHT400 Rates and tables (www.hmrc.gov.uk/inheritancetax/iht400-rates-tables.pdf). However, the form only lists the nil rate bands in operation from 18 March 1986. A list of rates applicable for earlier years can be obtained via HMRC's website at www.hmrc.gov.uk/rates/iht-thresholds.htm.

Other points

3.28
- The estate duty surviving spouse exemption (Sch 6, para 2) was unaffected by the introduction of the transferable nil rate band facility. Practitioners should do nothing to disturb that very useful situation, which confers freedom from both IHT and CGT.

- An 'immediate post-death' interest (see **4.12**) in favour of the surviving spouse or civil partner may be a suitable option if, for example, asset protection is a concern. Such a legacy is subject to the spouse or civil partner exemption, resulting in the deceased's unused nil rate band being available on the survivor's death.

- Practitioners should note the effect of s 143 ('Compliance with testator's request') and take care to avoid accidental use of the 'first' nil rate band where, for example, the surviving spouse trades down after the first death and shares out the contents of the old home.

- For commentary on *commorientes* situations and the effect on the transferable nil rate band, see **5.3** and following.

APPENDIX 3.1 – RECORD OF USE OF THE NIL RATE BAND FOR IHT PURPOSES

[Note: In this record, the terms 'married' and 'widowed' include being a member of a registered civil partnership and still being such a member when the civil partner died.]

The purpose of this record is to show whether a deceased spouse or civil partner made transfers that used all or any part of the nil rate band for inheritance tax that was available at death.

Part 1: Your relationship to the deceased person(s)

1   Have you been married?

2   If so, how many times?

3   Did your marriage end only on the death of your spouse?

4   If so, state the date your spouse died.

5   If you have been widowed more than once, state the date that each spouse died.

Part 2: Details of transfers and of the nil rate band available

6   If you know it, state the amount of the nil rate band when your spouse died (or when each spouse died).

7   Do you have a copy of the will that your spouse made?

8   Was that will (if any) varied within two years of death? If so, do you have a copy?

9   Did your spouse leave all his estate to you?

10   If not, state the value given by your late spouse to others, and specify if any was left exempt (for example, to charity).

11   Did your spouse make gifts to others in the seven years before death?

12   If so, state the amount given and to whom (again noting any gifts that were exempt for any reason).

Part 3: Checklist of documents that may be required for each claim to transfer the nil rate band (ie one claim for each deceased spouse of the survivor)

13   Death certificate of deceased spouse (DS).

14   Copy of the marriage certificate.

15   Copy of the grant or representation (Confirmation in Scotland) to the estate of the DS.

16   Copy of DS's will (if there is one).

17   Details of how the estate of DS passed (if there was no will).

18   Copy of any instrument varying DS's will.

19   Copy IHT400 or IHT200 (or equivalent return under CTT or Estate Duty).

20   Any other documentary evidence in support of the claim. This might be, for example:

–   a copy of form IHT205 'Return of Estate Information' (C5 in Scotland) if appropriate, accounts of the administration of the estate of DS, etc;

–   asset valuations (if any), eg of assets that passed under the will or intestacy other than to you, or any jointly owned assets, assets held in trust and gifts made in the seven years before death;

–   evidence to support the availability of any IHT relief (eg business or agricultural property relief), where the assets in question passed to someone other than you.

Chapter 4

Appropriate will planning

INTRODUCTION

4.1   As a will operates from the date of death, it might seem more appropriate to make this the concluding chapter. There are two reasons for dealing with this subject early in this book.

First, it is often only when an individual is thinking of making his will that the idea of estate planning occurs to him, and it is at that stage that the wider IHT issues can be explored.

Secondly, estate planning avoids the 'pre-owned assets' income tax problems associated with lifetime planning. Although the will is a key vehicle in planning, it is also a very personal document. Sometimes the tax advantages have to compete with the personal aims and feelings of the individual, which may have to receive priority.

Great care should be taken when receiving and taking instructions for a will and a suggested 'Instruction Sheet' is set out as **Appendix 5.1** at the end of **Chapter 5**.

Factors in will drafting

4.2   Choosing the correct type of will can achieve substantial IHT mitigation, particularly if advantage is taken of business and agricultural property reliefs and the exemption between spouses. The law keeps changing: see *Re Benham* [1995] STC 210 as later clarified by *Re Ratcliffe* [1999] STC 262 and *Phizackerley v HMRC* [2007] STC (SCD) 328, SpC 00591, reviewed in depth in an earlier edition of this work but now of less relevance following the FA 2008 changes that introduced the transferable nil rate band (TNRB) facility (see **Chapter 3**). This means that the will must be kept under regular review.

Seven key issues should be remembered:

- First, the importance of reciprocity, namely that husband and wife (or civil partners – see below) should each make appropriate wills. It may well be appropriate to leave business or agricultural assets specifically to chargeable parties, such as a discretionary trust.

- Second, wills are ambulatory, ie they operate as from death and in respect of the assets *then owned* by the testator or testatrix.

- Third, the need to draft wills with the maximum flexibility.

- Fourth, the liquidity of the estate: debts and liabilities will need to be paid as well as the IHT. The estate will often be tied up in the matrimonial home, in unquoted shares or in other business assets.

- Fifth, in preparing a will, the tax aspect is only one factor to be taken into consideration and must be subject to particular family and other circumstances.

- Sixth, a subsequent marriage, or entry into a civil partnership (see below) revokes a will (unless the will was expressly made in contemplation of that marriage or partnership) and the matter of the revocation of gifts made in a will to a spouse/partner will arise on the termination of the marriage/partnership (see **Appendix 5.1**).

- The seventh aspect, which is not limited to the question of wills, is that detailed records should be maintained of lifetime gifts, whether PETs or (as will increasingly now be the case) immediately chargeable transfers.

Civil partnerships and other relationships

4.3   The Civil Partnership Act 2005 came into force on 5 December 2005, enabling same-sex couples to have the relationship legally recognised through the formation of a civil partnership. For tax purposes, FA 2005, s 103 paved the way for regulations to change tax legislation to ensure that civil partnerships are treated the same as married couples for tax purposes, including IHT. The existence of a civil partnership therefore needs to be taken into account if appropriate when considering wills and estate planning. For example, if two individuals enter into a civil partnership, that 'marriage' revokes their wills unless made in contemplation of it. References in this chapter (and indeed this book) to spouses and married couples can normally be taken to include civil partnerships.

4.4   Despite the patient and determined efforts of the Burden sisters, siblings cannot achieve for their relationship the same protection as spouses or civil partners. In *Burden v UK* EHCR [2008] App No 13378/05, [2008] STC 1305, the sisters, who had all their lives lived together in a stable, committed and mutually supportive relationship, argued that their human rights had been violated by the refusal of the UK government to allow them IHT spouse relief.

The likely result of that refusal would eventually be that the survivor of them would have to sell the family home to pay the IHT.

It was held, by the Grand Chamber of the EHCR, that there had been no breach of their human rights. Their relationship was different from marriage or civil partnership, being based on consanguinity, whereas one of the defining characteristics of marriage or civil partnership was that it was forbidden to close family members. This is an area where logic is perhaps hard to maintain and where in truth there was simply a policy decision to allow the UK to tax as it pleased.

Why make a will?

4.5   There are six main advantages of leaving a will rather than dying without one (ie intestate):

- choice of executors;
- ability to act immediately after death;
- guardians;
- extending trust rules;
- limiting trust rules; and
- getting the entitlement right and at the right time or age. As to the provisions dealing with intestate estates, see **4.8**.

Executors

4.6   Choosing one's own executors and trustees is important because persons entitled to the equivalent office on intestacy (ie 'administrators') may be inappropriate.

An executor's functions include collecting in the deceased's property, paying off any debts, and distributing to those persons entitled under the will. When the executors have collected in the deceased's estate and paid the liabilities, it is common for the will to provide that they will then become trustees. The change in capacity is necessary if the will is to contain gifts to minors conditional on attaining a defined age; or where certain assets may be held in their present state pending sale – 'a trust for sale'.

Assets are transferred from the executors to trustees (even if these are the same individuals) by means of an assent. An assent can be informal, except in the case of land where a written document is necessary (*Re King's Will Trusts* [1964] 1 All ER 833). The assets retained in the administration could be those assets pregnant with a high capital gain, which could then in due course be transferred to the legatees free of CGT.

The trustees' responsibilities include:

- ensuring that the property subject to the trust is transferred to the beneficiaries at the appropriate time or occasion;
- exercising various powers given them by statute or in the will;
- managing assets of the estate (eg land) subject to the trust;
- distributing income or capital from the trust fund; and
- exercising appropriate discretions.

It is possible to appoint individuals or institutions as executors and trustees. In practice at least two individuals will be appointed with, possibly, a provision that if one dies before the testator or does not accept the office, a third person should be appointed in his stead.

Note the difficulties that arose where a firm of solicitors had become an LLP in *Re Rogers Deceased* [2006] EWHC 753 (Ch). The clause appointing executors was in the common form of 'the partners at the date of my death in the firm of …' and was intended to provide succession to office. However, the words 'or in the firm which at that date has succeeded to and carried on its practice' was perhaps inappropriate as a reference to what had now become an LLP.

Lightman J, whilst construing the will so as to allow the LLP to prove, that being the intention of the testatrix, suggested that to avoid doubt in the future:

' … testators will be well advised to make express provision whether on the conversion of any appointed firm of solicitors or successor firm and (if this is desired) for the appointment of employee (as well as profit sharing) members as executors.'

Administrators

4.7   These are persons appointed pursuant to statute to deal with the affairs of a deceased person, in circumstances where:

- the deceased has died intestate (ie leaving no will); or
- he has left a will which fails to appoint (or effectively appoint) any executors; or
- he has left a will appointing executors none of whom take a grant of probate, for whatever reason. An administrator's functions are similar to those of an executor.

Administrators are persons having an interest in the estate of a deceased person who wish to become involved in dealing with the deceased's affairs. They obtain grant of letters of administration (contrast grant of probate) which is appropriate in the circumstances referred to above.

To a considerable extent, executors can act before grant of probate. An executor derives his power and appointment under the will and can act in that capacity from the moment the testator dies. The executor can do many other things, eg arrange the funeral and generally take over the deceased's affairs including the running of his business and terminating any continuing liability, such as tenancy and disposing of chattels (eg furniture and effects, jewellery or cars). He should also take immediate possession of any valuables and secure their safety and arrange insurances where necessary since, his responsibility begins from the moment the deceased dies.

By contrast, an administrator has no such power although the next of kin or proposed administrator should prudently take some of the steps mentioned such as arranging the funeral, preserving the assets, etc.

Under the terms of a will, guardians of infant children can be appointed: clearly a most important provision. Normally, the need to appoint guardians arises only when both parents are dead but either parent of a legitimate minor can appoint a guardian to act jointly with the surviving parent.

Powers granted or extended by the will

4.8   The trustees' implied powers under the Trustee Act 1925 can be appropriately extended: for example, the power of applying the whole of a beneficiary's potential entitlement to capital instead of only one half as permitted under s 32 of the Act.

Special requirements can be embodied in a will, for example, powers of appointment (ie distributing capital funds); options (eg on shares of a family company); avoiding complex apportionments; directions as to burial or cremation etc.

The predetermined entitlement of next of kin under an intestacy may be entirely inappropriate. This is because the entitlements are based on statutory provisions designed to meet the likely wishes of the average family man. As everyone has special likes and dislikes and no family is typical, this average is bound to be unsatisfactory to a degree. In any event, family life has moved on: for example, marriage is no longer necessarily the norm. This is the subject of a consultation by the Law Commission, which has put forward several ideas for change. These ideas tend to favour the surviving spouse over the children and even contemplate a statutory right of inheritance for long-term companions to whom the deceased was not married.

Under the Family Provision (Intestate Succession) Order 2009, SI 2009/135, the statutory legacy for the surviving spouse (or civil partner) is, at the time of writing, £250,000 where issue also survive, and £450,000 where no issue survive, but there is a surviving parent, brother or sister. These levels were increased with effect from 1 February 2009 (previously, the limits were £125,000 and £200,000 respectively, in the cases of deaths between 1 December 1993 and 31 December 2009). Different rules apply in Scotland.

Example 4.1 – Distribution of intestate estate

Adam had done better than the rest of his family, but had no children. He did not bother to make a will. 'Everything will go to my wife Eve in any case', he asserted. *Wrong*!

He died on 7 March 2012, leaving an estate of £550,000. Eve and two jealous brothers survived him.

Eve got the 'personal chattels', ie furniture, etc, £450,000 and a life interest in half of the balance, ie £50,000. The brothers took £25,000 each.

4.9   When an individual considers the terms of his will, it may be appropriate at that stage to consider suitable lifetime tax planning measures. For example:

- making potentially exempt transfers (PETs);

- using or transferring the nil and lower lifetime rates of IHT;

- setting up appropriate family trusts; and

- undertaking suitable insurance and pension arrangements.

See further **Chapter 11**.

Claims under the Inheritance (Provision for Family and Dependants) Act 1975

4.10   Under English law (in contrast to certain continental systems), there is no community of goods between husband and wife (or civil partners). However, the Inheritance (Provision for Family and Dependants) Act 1975 ('the 1975 Act') restricts the free disposal of property by will so that, provided the deceased was at death domiciled in one of the countries forming the

UK, the deceased's dependants are provided for. It does so by giving certain dependants of the deceased (including spouses, ex-spouses who have not remarried, common law wives, children, etc) the right to make a claim to the court if they consider that the deceased has not made reasonable provision in his/her will or in accordance with the intestacy rules. The court is given a very wide discretion to direct income and/or capital of the deceased's estate to the claimant, but a claim must be made within six months of the grant of probate.

As with intestate succession, the rules under the 1975 Act are being reviewed by the Law Commission as part of their current consultation. The Commission has put forward several very sensible recommendations in this area.

This chapter treats the subject matter of wills under the following headings:

- making the correct type of will with particular emphasis on the flexibility gained by wills with life interests;

- the will that is appropriate to the relevant IHT circumstances; and

- incidence of IHT and treatment of specific gifts including legacies (s 38).

The next chapter considers the practical aspects:

- will drafting: legacies and bequests (ss 36–42);

- ancillary aspects of wills; and

- variations and disclaimers – post-death planning (s 142).

The Trusts of Land and Appointment of Trustees Act 1996

4.11   All wills of persons dying after the commencement of the Trusts of Land and Appointment of Trustees Act 1996 (TLATA 1996) (namely 1 January 1997) are subject to the regime governing trusts relating to land. The few practitioners who still understand the 'old' Settled Land Act precedents must desist from their use. Some trust for sale precedents need altering. Trusts involving land are now called 'trusts of land'. The distinction between Settled Land Act settlements and trusts for sale disappears. Now every such trust of land has an implied power to postpone sale, which cannot be excluded by the trust instrument. The doctrine of conversion no longer applies.

It is essential for the will draftsman to decide whether an interest in possession in a property is desired; and if it is, to use appropriate words. It is quite possible that the idiosyncratic wording of the will examined in *re Judge (Walden's executors) v HMRC* [2005] STC (SCD) 863, discussed at **4.13**, owed part of its genesis to a desire to use a form of words that would not create a strict settlement.

Part II of TLATA 1996 contains administrative provisions. Section 18 of the Act includes within the provisions personal representatives of estates in the course of administration in respect of deaths after commencement of the Act. Part II of the Act applies to trusts of land and personalty, Part I only to trusts of land.

MAKING THE CORRECT TYPE OF WILL

4.12   There are three basic types of will:

(1)   A will disposing of the estate by one or more interests which, in the case of adult beneficiaries, are absolute. In that case the recipients, on reaching 18, will have unfettered control of the assets on which no conditions can be attached.

(2)   A will by which a life interest, ie an immediate post-death interest (IPDI), is given by one spouse to another in the whole or part of the estate, followed by or containing one or more outright, absolute interests.

(3)   A will whereby the surviving spouse receives a life interest, but full and unrestricted powers are vested in the trustees. These powers enable them to advance capital and to make loans to that spouse. Alternatively, the trustees can appoint the capital or income onto new trusts, thus terminating the spouse's life interest in whole or part.

Such a 'type 3' will might also include an appropriate discretionary trust fund as described below. Accordingly, such a 'type 3' will could contain three main clauses:

• income to widow(er) for life;

• if no widow(er), then discretionary trust of income and capital;

• notwithstanding the two previous provisions, a wide overriding power of appointment.

Relevant aspects of life interest wills

4.13   The term 'life interest' is used here because it is widely understood, though tax planners will commonly refer to 'interest in possession' or to the new terminology spawned by FA 2006 such as IPDI. Notwithstanding FA 2006, a life interest will should be drawn flexibly. The executors/trustees ('the trustees') should be given wide, overriding powers of appointment, so that they can either appoint the capital in whole or part to the surviving spouse absolutely and/or terminate the life interest in whole or part and appoint the capital to one or more of the other beneficiaries named or referred to in the will, eg children or grandchildren. It should be noted that FA 2006, by introducing FA 1986, s 102ZA, has limited the original scope of this tactic.

When drafting the will trust, ensure that it is clear as to whether the surviving spouse has an interest in possession in the deceased's share of the home. In *IRC v Lloyds Private Banking* [1998] STC 559, the Special Commissioner decided that the provisions in the deceased's will in relation to the deceased's share of the matrimonial home were not dispositive (ie they did not make a disposition of an interest in the deceased's half share to the survivor); they were merely administrative. Lightman J reversed the decision on appeal to the High Court. The key provision which Lightman J held to be dispositive was that no objection, restriction or disturbance was to be made to the survivor's continued residence so long as he desired to remain there. Such dispositive provision clearly gives the surviving spouse security as to occupation of the home, but at the cost of IHT on the entirety, on the death of the survivor, as contrasted with, say, only a half share.

See also *Faulkner (trustee of Adams, deceased) v Inland Revenue Commissioners* [2001] STC (SCD) 112 where directions in a will to the trustees to permit two persons to occupy a house constituted a present right of present enjoyment, and gave those persons a chargeable interest in possession, not a mere licence.

If the beneficiaries under the will are the persons entitled to the property, they are likely to have interests in possession in any event: see *Woodhall v IRC* [2000] STC (SCD) 558. This was a case where the testator gave his children the right to occupy the house and gave the trustees administrative powers to permit the children, or any of them, to occupy. The result was that each child had an interest in possession in the property (the value divided between them).

The issue was subsequently considered in *Judge and anor (personal representatives of Walden, dec'd) v HMRC* [2005] STC (SCD) 863, SpC 506. Mr W owned the matrimonial home prior to his death. His will declared (*inter alia*) that the trustees during the lifetime of Mrs W should permit her the use and enjoyment of the property 'for such period or periods as they shall in their absolute discretion think fit'. When Mrs W later died, HMRC issued a Notice of Determination that she had an interest in possession of the residence.

The appeal by Mrs W's personal representatives was allowed. The Special Commissioner held that Mrs W had no right to occupy the property, but that the trustees had discretion (but not a duty) to allow her to occupy. These words were clear and unambiguous, and effect had to be given to them. Mrs W did not have an interest in possession. It therefore appears that any entitlement to occupy should be avoided (see *IRC v Lloyds Private Banking* [1998] STC 559) above.

The decision in *Judge* would seem to call into question the correctness of SP 10/79, which indicates that HMRC will normally regard the exercise of trust powers to create a permanent home for a beneficiary as constituting an interest in possession. It is argued by HMRC that SP 10/79 was not in point in *Judge*, but many advisers consider that it was relevant.

The chief lessons to be learned from *Judge* are:

- do not cobble a will together from different precedents; and

- read through it carefully before sending it out for signature.

For an illustration of drafting of a deed to vary a will which paid particular attention to the difference between dispositive and administrative powers, see *Oakley and another (Personal Representatives of Jossaume deceased) v IRC* [2005] SpC 460. The issue there was whether an interest in possession had been granted to the widow, as HMRC argued, or to the family company, as was argued by the executors of the widow and with whom the Commissioner agreed. It was relevant that the deed of variation of the late husband's will directed the trustees of the property not to require payment of any rent from the company during the subsistence of the trusts, which came to an end on the death of the widow.

It was held that the interest granted to the company abated the interest of the widow. The trustees were directed, not merely empowered, not to ask for rent, so it was no mere administrative power. When the husband had died, spouse exemption had been claimed on the transfer to the widow; as a result of the decision, tax became due on the husband's estate but the overall burden was lower than if the executors of the widow had not pursued the appeal.

In November 2007, HMRC provided guidance on interests in possession and SP 10/79 in response to queries raised by STEP and CIOT, which included the following points:

- The circumstances in which HMRC would not regard the trustees as having exercised their power to give a beneficiary an exclusive right of occupation (ie so as not to create an interest in possession) are 'rare', but might include instances where there was no evidence of (or significant doubt as to) the intentions of the trustees.

- An SP 10/79 interest in possession generally arises if there is evidence that the trustees have knowingly exercised their powers so as to give a beneficiary exclusive occupation of the property.

- If the trustees have intended to grant a beneficiary the right to occupy a specific, named property owned by the trust, the beneficiary's interest in possession would end when the property was sold.

The guidance on SP 10/79 and interests in possession can be accessed via the STEP website at www.step.org/pdf/874668_1(PCL2).pdf.

Advantages of life interest wills

4.14   A will which confers a life interest on the surviving spouse has the following advantages:

- IHT flexibility 'in lieu' of variations

  Instruments of variation under s 142 remain a useful fallback for cases where proper IHT planning has failed (usually because circumstances have changed by the date of death), but they are always second best. Family members may not wish to disturb the last wishes of the deceased, merely to secure a tax advantage. Besides, there are restrictions on the s 142 variation (and it is always possible that the relief will be curtailed by legislation). Therefore, a will which includes a flexible life interest with wide powers of appointment has the best of both worlds: the will itself is flexible and can be adapted to changed circumstances but a s 142 variation remains an option where necessary and available.

  Inclusion of a flexible life interest, together with wide powers of appointment written into the will itself, means that s 142 powers of variation can be avoided.

  It must be said that though flexibility is desirable, it can create uncertainty. If the widow is the life tenant and is not a trustee but the trustees do have overriding powers those powers can be exercised to deprive the widow of her interest without her being consulted even less being in agreement with the exercise of the overriding powers.

- Reversionary interests and their re-settlement

  The creation of the life interest will also create the subsequent interest in reversion. Prior to FA 2006, this enabled the parties to achieve substantial IHT, CGT and SDLT savings. This was done by the reversioner as described in **5.23** and following, but the scope for this has been cut down by the fact that the creation of virtually all new lifetime settlements are, since 22 March 2006, treated as chargeable transfers.

- Practical use of life interests

  Life interest trusts have an important practical use in retaining the capital assets in the estate for the eventual benefit of the testator's children in circumstances where it cannot be guaranteed that the surviving spouse will retain or use the assets for the benefit of the testator's children. For example, where the spouse or civil partner remarries or enters a new civil partnership, there is a danger that the assets will be diverted by the new husband, wife or partner to their side of the family. Similarly, with second or subsequent marriages, the testator spouse can provide for the surviving spouse by way of a life interest trust and ensure that the capital is left to his own children as appropriate.

Moreover with a life interest, as trustees will be involved (of whom the widow(er) may well be one), opportunity can be taken to ensure that he/she will receive proper financial and investment advice.

● Keeping them waiting

It is a curious feature of the FA 2006 regime that, if a testator gives a fund on trust for a young beneficiary 'if she shall attain 25', there will be a form of relevant property trust for the period from attaining 18 until 25, whilst the gift of the same fund on IPDI trusts does not, even though it may be accompanied by powers to advance capital at (surprise, surprise) 25.

Ancillary aspects of life interests

4.15   If the surviving spouse's 'old' life interest (ie one that existed before 22 March 2006) is terminated (in whole or part), the spouse is treated as making a transfer. Where the trustees appoint funds away from the spouse in favour of issue absolutely, the surviving spouse will still be treated as having made a potentially exempt transfer (PET). That will normally give rise to no IHT, provided that she survives seven years. Taper relief may be available at the rate of 20% per annum after surviving three years (s 3A(7)), although transfers are set first against the nil rate band.

Avoid automatic termination of the life interest on remarriage, because such termination can give rise to (i) a CGT liability (subject to the possible, somewhat restricted, hold-over relief under TCGA 1992, s 165); and (ii) a possible IHT liability, ie a failed PET if the spouse does not survive seven years from the remarriage.

Prior to the enactment of FA 2006, the creation of the life interest in favour of the surviving spouse, as for an absolute interest, would normally obtain the benefit of the IHT inter-spouse exemption under s 18. On the survivor's death, if still then owning the life interest, it was the capital supporting that interest that would be assessed and added to that surviving spouse's own estate to arrive at the amount and rate of IHT. The rules are now more complex, and are examined in detail at **4.16** and following.

THE APPROPRIATE WILL TO THE RELEVANT IHT CIRCUMSTANCES

4.16   Suggestions are made below for several different circumstances. Remember that all families have their own peculiarities.

Couples who are married or in civil partnership, but who have no issue

4.17 Here the usual suggestion would be to provide an absolute interest (or possibly a life interest) for the surviving spouse or partner. An immediate post-death interest may be preferable in terms of protecting capital (eg for the benefit of children from an earlier marriage, or where nursing home fees are a potential issue).

This retains the advantage of the transferable nil rate band (TNRB). There will no doubt be minor exceptions, for example, legacies and bequests to relatives, charities, etc. Provisions may be included for alternative gifts over to others if one spouse does not survive the other by, say, one month, but:

- an advantage can be secured by providing that this is not to apply in a commorientes situation; and
- a survivorship clause will prevent transfer of the nil rate band: see **3.25**.

Married couples – with issue – unlikely to remarry – small/ medium estate

4.18 For a small or medium estate (say, £350,000–£500,000) that does not include business or agricultural property, consider using an absolute interest (and/or possibly an immediate post-death interest) will in favour of the surviving spouse.

Contrary to previous (pre-FA 2008) practice, generally speaking the will should not ensure that up to the full amount of the available nil rate band for IHT goes to the children or other issue, either directly or by way of a mini discretionary trust (see below), but instead the nil rate band should be left unused so that its benefit may be transferred to the executors of the surviving spouse or civil partner.

For 2012–13, the first £325,000 of chargeable transfers (which include chargeable lifetime gifts in the previous seven years) is in effect exempt from IHT. The nil rate band can normally be expected to increase annually by reference to the retail price index (but see below). The increase in the retail price index in September in each year is to apply to the rates of chargeable transfers made on or after 6 April in the following year (s 8). However, Parliament may determine the nil rate band otherwise than by reference to the retail price index, and in recent Finance Acts have done so.

It was announced in Budget 2011 that, from April 2012, the default indexation factor for direct taxes, including IHT, will move from the retail price index to the consumer price index. However, as the IHT nil rate band is frozen until 5 April 2015, the consumer price index will have no effect until after that date.

Consider carefully whether or not to include a 28-day or similar survivorship clause, bearing in mind the comments at **3.25**.

Married – with issue – quite likely to remarry – medium estate

4.19   Here it may be best to use the nil rate band to protect the inheritance of the children, on the basis that the executors of the survivor might otherwise have available to them more than one TNRB, from more than one spouse, so part of the relief might be lost.

Consider the use of a mini-discretionary trust, drafted so as to give to chargeable beneficiaries as much of the nil rate band (or unused balance) as is still available at the death. A maximum could be imposed, to ensure a particular beneficiary does not obtain more than the testator contemplated. Take care to avoid the uncertainties of drafting highlighted in *RSPCA v Sharp* [2010] WTLR 855 ChD, [2011] WTLR 311 CA and noted at **3.17**.

Married – with issue – estate including business or agricultural property

4.20   Here again it may be best to use the nil rate band, to achieve the 'double dip' effect described in **15.55**. A trust of the nil rate band is included into which the executors may transfer assets qualifying for relief that would exceed the nil rate band in value, but for the relief. Where the bulk of the estate is in farming or business assets, you must address the issue and decide whether the gift of all the value that can pass within the nil rate band will, actually, be a gift of too great a value.

The beneficiaries are, mainly, the chargeable beneficiaries, eg children, grandchildren but the surviving spouse can (and normally should) also be a beneficiary (see also Example 15.7).

Married – big house – not much cash – might remarry

4.21   If the matrimonial home is jointly owned (as tenants in common) the deceased might leave his share to the children (using the nil rate band). The surviving spouse may continue to occupy by reason of his/her own beneficial share in the home. Substantial protection of his/her occupation is given by the Trusts of Land and Appointment of Trustees Act 1996, in particular ss 12 and 13, so the will should not contain further restrictions. See the reference to the *Lloyds Private Banking* and other cases mentioned in **4.13**.

Married – with issue – larger estate

4.22 For the larger estate (say, more than £500,000), there will be greater emphasis on the advantages of a life interest will (see **4.14**).

Equalisation of estates

4.23 Should wills be drafted so as to equalise estates? This was desirable under the progressive rates of tax that applied under estate duty but for the time being, there is little need. This is because for deaths after 15 March 1988 there has been only one rate, currently 40%, that applies on death; and therefore IHT is no longer a progressive tax beyond the nil rate band (ie there is only one rate thereafter).

This is subject to considering the availability of exemptions (eg to charities), or reliefs (eg for business or agricultural property). However, there are proposals for more rates from time to time, so it is an issue to remember.

Example 4.2 – Tax rates

Husband has an estate of £800,000, wife of £200,000. Husband dies first, in 2006–07, and leaves £50,000 to each of his two children and the balance of £700,000 to his wife (by way of life interest or absolute interest) and she dies in 2012–13. IHT, assuming no change in the value of assets in respect of the two deaths:

Charge on husband's death =	NIL
Nil rate band unused: (£163,000 / £263,000) × 100	61.9771%
Charge on wife's death:	
Total estate of wife (£700,000 + £200,000)	£900,000
Chargeable estate for IHT =	900,000
Nil rate band available (£325,000 × 161.9771%)	526,425
IHT: £373,575 × 40% =	£149,430

Example 4.3 – Effect of equalisation

Another husband and wife with the same aggregate assets, based on archaic advice, equalise their estates during lifetime, ie each has an estate of £500,000.

Husband dies in 2004–05 and leaves his estate direct to children. Wife dies in 2012–13:

IHT on husband's estate:	500,000
Less nil rate band	263,000
	237,000
£237,000 × 40% =	94,800
IHT on wife's estate:	500,000
Less nil rate band	325,000
	175,000
£175,000 × 40%	70,000
Total IHT suffered (£94,800 + £70,000)	164,800

The second family pay £15,370 more in tax and, most importantly when inflation may be in issue, pay it earlier. Before the TNRB facility was introduced, the tax would have been the same in each example. Note also that, in Example 4.2, the surviving spouse has greater opportunity to make PETs or enjoy a greater income, or (for example) make exempt gifts by normal expenditure out of income.

Some steps towards lifetime equalisation between husband and wife used to be necessary to ensure that *each* spouse could use his/her nil rate band, whoever dies first, but following the TNRB that is generally unnecessary.

Therefore under the present regime the main IHT purpose of giving assets to chargeable parties up to or beyond the nil rate band is that those assets are expected to appreciate substantially. Putting appreciating assets in the hands of the younger generation should defer IHT for a longer period than would be the case if they were given to the surviving spouse. Even that advantage may well be countered by the ability of the surviving spouse (or the will trustees) to make/arrange PETs.

Policy changes

4.24   We cannot look too far ahead: IHT is a 'political football' and when one political party loses dominance, each puts forward vote-catching ideas which might well become law. As part of a move to increase the nil rate band so as to exclude 'Middle England' from suffering IHT (particularly in respect of their parents' home), differential or progressive rates of IHT may well be re-introduced. During the testator's lifetime the will should be subject to regular review. Different motives also apply to business and agricultural property, see **Chapter 15**.

Other reasons to equalise estates

4.25   For income tax purposes, husband and wife have long been taxed independently on all income (earned and unearned) and gains. Married women are fully responsible for the tax on their income and gains have their own allowances. To the younger reader it must now seem unthinkable that it was ever otherwise! Therefore, equalisation of income-producing assets has long been relevant for income tax and capital gains tax rather than IHT. Much use is now made of ISA accounts to hold stocks and shares to shelter the income and gains from taxation.

Note the anti-avoidance provisions of ITTOIA 2005, ss 624–628. In a common form of inter vivos trust, a husband gives his wife a life interest right to the income, followed by a gift of capital in remainder to the children. The income of that trust will not be treated as the wife's, but will be treated as the husband's during his lifetime, on the basis that the husband retains an interest in the settlement (s 624(1)).

Why leave it to 'the wife'?

4.26   At this level (ie for larger estates and subject to business/agricultural property relief) five motivating factors favour provisions whereby the bulk of the testator's estate passes, probably by way of flexible life interest to the surviving spouse. This is particularly true where he/she has reasonable prospects of surviving the vulnerable seven-year period. These factors are:

(a)   the TNRB facility;

(b)   IHT can be deferred until the death of the surviving spouse, a clear cash-flow advantage;

(c)   the surviving spouse can make IHT-effective gifts, especially PETs (ie by way of the trustees' termination of the life interest trust; or by way of absolute gifts by the surviving spouse);

(d)   since IHT is currently not a progressive tax beyond the nil rate band, there is no present incentive to use up lower rates for chargeable parties;

(e)   there is greater opportunity to make gifts by normal expenditure out of income, particularly paying premiums on life policies. In relation to lifetime gifts be particularly careful, having regard to the draconian income tax charge by way of the pre-owned asset regime (see **Chapter 13**).

For CGT purposes, there are circumstances where it can be very beneficial to transfer assets, initially during lifetime, between spouses.

Example 4.4 – Deathbed planning

Michael is married to Susan. She suffers from a wasting disease and is expected to live only another year. She is domiciled in the UK. Michael owns a portfolio of let properties standing at a considerable gain and would like to make outright gifts to their children, but is hindered from doing so because the value of the properties greatly exceeds his available nil rate band, so the use of a lifetime trust to hold over the gains is not appropriate. A simple gift would trigger a CGT charge.

Michael therefore transfers the properties to Susan free of CGT and IHT. By her will, Susan leaves her estate to Michael.

Susan (dutifully) dies before Michael (death is not an 'associated operation', though a will might be).

Michael receives back the assets free of CGT on Susan's death, uplifted to the then market value. Michael is now able to make outright gifts of the properties to his children free of CGT and, if he survives seven years, free of IHT.

Such arrangements should be carried out subtly and with *Ramsay* in mind. To avoid that challenge, where the gain is a large percentage of the value but the overall value is within the nil rate band, consider an adaptation of the above example whereby Susan leaves the assets to someone other than Michael (eg children, grandchildren, or discretionary trust for the family) such as one that exploits s 144 (see **5.6**).

Such a gift will also avoid CGT, but IHT will be payable on the death unless it is within the nil rate band, either due to its gross value or because the gift attracts business or agricultural property relief.

Single (unmarried) persons

4.27 Largely non-tax considerations are applicable here, but exempt transfers may be appropriate, eg nil rate band to relatives, gifts to charities, etc.

Widow(er) or divorced persons

4.28   Consider, in this situation, using a trust. Before FA 2006, this might have been an accumulation and maintenance trust but that, in its simplest form, is no longer possible. The choice is now between:

- a bereaved minor's trust (BMT); this is the option apparently preferred by the previous Labour Government, judging from comments in Parliament, giving entitlement to capital at 18 and no further IHT cost or complications;

- an '18-to-25' trust: this is more flexible than the BMT, though that flexibility comes at a (moderate) cost in terms of IHT on the fund; and

- a full discretionary trust. If the fund is large, say £400,000 or more, this may be the preferred choice, giving much flexibility at only moderate tax cost, though the administration may reflect the size of the fund and the complexity.

The undecided testator

4.29   Consider the various uses of discretionary will trusts under **5.6–5.10**. As noted above, even a will that does no more than appoint executors may be better than no will at all.

Sharing an estate between spouses and issue – assets qualifying for relief

4.30   It is always relevant in sharing an estate between a spouse and issue to consider whether any of the assets qualify for reliefs, and whether any reliefs are being wasted. This is particularly significant where the 100% business and agricultural property relief applies.

Example 4.5 – Bequests of business property

A testator has an estate comprising a business interest worth £400,000, eligible for 100% business property relief, which he leaves to the widow (by way of life interest or outright), and general investments worth £400,000 left to children. The widow will receive something worth £400,000 (or a life interest therein) which will be exempt in any case (ie the business relief is wasted). IHT will be payable on the £400,000 given to the children.

If, on the other hand, the bequests are switched round, so that the children get the business and the widow the investments (or a life interest therein), no IHT will be payable at all having regard to the operation of the 100% business and inter-spouse exemption.

Alternatively, if the children need cash (as they so often do) or if the widow needs to benefit from such business assets, they could be bequeathed in the will by way of a discretionary trust in respect of which the widow would be one of the beneficiaries. Although the disposition of the trust assets would be at the discretion of the trustees, they might release some, or even most, of the income.

If, in due course, the spouse was treated as enjoying an interest in possession in the business assets, that might not matter. If she had enjoyed that interest for two years, BPR would be available.

If the business assets are eligible for the 50% relief only, a similar formula should be considered. This would have the result that IHT would be payable only on the reduced value of the business assets passing to the children (of £200,000 in the above example). That would probably be within the nil rate band. Consider, however, the complications of s 39A (see **4.36**).

Some businesses are personal in nature, such as those requiring specific qualifications (eg a doctor, pharmacist, lawyer or accountant). There is an argument that, on the death of the qualified person, the business must cease and that no relief should therefore be allowed on the value of the business assets on any later transfer. Where valuable assets were owned in such a business (eg office premises) business relief would not be available to the transferee on any later transfer if those assets were left to an individual who was unable to satisfy the relevant conditions on their death (eg if the spouse let out the business premises).

It may be better for the professionally qualified testator to leave such assets to a discretionary trust so that, on the death of the spouse, the transfer is free from IHT and the asset is not part of the surviving spouse's estate on death.

Let the surviving spouse receive wasting assets, thereby avoiding or at least reducing the bunching effect on the survivor's death.

Pension benefits

4.31   The death in service amount of a pension or insurance policy could be nominated at the discretion of the trustees to the deceased's children free of tax. That sum could be used to purchase from the surviving spouse illiquid assets left to her in the will, eg family company shares.

The maximum death benefit now payable before retirement benefits are drawn is a lump sum equal to the lifetime allowance. Registered pension schemes can broadly allow members to draw income from age 50 (or 55 from 2010), or possibly to defer drawing benefits.

For the provisions relating to the position of a member of a pension scheme who has attained 75 but not taken either a lump sum or a pension annuity, see FA 2011 and the discussion in **9.25**.

INCIDENCE OF IHT AND TREATMENT OF SPECIFIC GIFTS INCLUDING LEGACIES

Incidence of IHT: Re Dougal and s 211

4.32   The incidence of IHT (ie who bears the tax) varies according to whether the gifts are made subject to IHT (so that the recipient bears the tax) or free of IHT (so that the residuary estate bears the IHT). It is most important that the will should state whether any particular gift in a will is to be subject to or free of IHT. If the will is silent on the point IHT will normally be payable out of the residue. As a result, unless there are provisions to the contrary, specific gifts are free of IHT whether or not the asset in question is land.

Section 211 expressly provides that in the absence of contrary intention shown by the deceased in his will, the IHT will be payable as part of the general testamentary and administrative expenses of the estate. Section 211 applies where:

- the PRs are liable for IHT on a death;

- in respect of any UK property (ie real or personal) which vests in the PRs;

- property was not immediately before the death settled property; and

- subject to any contrary intention in the will;

the IHT plus any interest thereon is treated 'as part of the general testamentary and administrative expenses of the estate' (ie the gift is free of IHT payable out of residue).

In other cases (eg settled property; property abroad; and property held as joint tenants, where the survivor takes automatically under the *jus accrescendi*), IHT is to be borne 'where occasion requires' by the person in whom the property vests, eg trustees of settled property, beneficial owner of overseas property, or surviving co-owner.

4.33   *Re Dougal* [1981] STC 514 was a Scottish case where it was held that, in Scotland in the absence of express provisions in the will, capital transfer tax (CTT) on realty (as well as CTT on personalty) was payable out of residue. It is considered that *Re Dougal* also applies in England and Wales and for IHT purposes.

The 'golden rule' is to ensure that all gifts in wills indicate expressly whether they are free of or subject to IHT. Bear in mind that, if the nil rate band has been exhausted by other gifts, any further gift 'free of tax' must be grossed up unless to an exempt beneficiary (see below). See also *RSPCA v Sharp* [2010] WTLR 855 ChD, [2011] WTLR 311, CA.

Treatment of specific gifts including legacies (s 38)

4.34   Where a transfer (normally the transfer of the whole of the individual's property on death by will) is only partially exempt (because, for instance, he is leaving part of his estate to his spouse or to charity), it is necessary to have provisions which determine the extent and the impact of IHT liabilities on that part or proportion which is not exempt. The rules governing the allocation of exemptions in such circumstances are set out in ss 36–42.

Planning aspects of ss 36–42

4.35   Where residue goes in whole or part to an exempt party, such as the surviving spouse or charity, then legacies which are expressed to be free of IHT must be grossed up either among themselves (if the entire residue goes to the exempt parties) or additionally re-grossed at the estate rate of the whole chargeable estate (eg if part of the residue goes to a non-exempt party). Consider the alternatives, for example making legacies which are expressed to be subject to IHT; or converting legacies into a share of residue.

The problem need not arise where the 100% business/agricultural property relief applies. Section s 39A provides that relief relating to business or agricultural property which is not specifically given is apportioned rateably between the exempt and non-exempt parts of the gross estate.

Therefore, it is normally good estate planning to make specific gifts of business and agricultural assets which attract 100% relief to chargeable parties (eg children), in addition to the nil rate band, free of IHT.

Section 39A and the nil rate band complication

4.36   Section 39A also applies where there are specific gifts of *non*-business or *non*-agricultural assets (eg cash gifts to chargeable parties) and residuary gifts (eg to a surviving spouse) which include business or agricultural assets. In that case the specific gifts of *non*-BPR/APR assets will be entitled to a due proportion of the BPR/APR. This is particularly relevant where the nil rate band is given to chargeable parties, eg to children or into a mini-discretionary trust.

Example 4.6 – Section 39A 'trap'

Albert intends to leave the nil rate band to his children and the residue to his widow Victoria. His will gives the children 'the largest sum at the date of my death as shall not incur any liability for the payment of tax by reason of my death …'. Albert has an estate of £1.5 million, including a 30% shareholding in the family trading company, Albert Widgets Ltd, valued at £1.2 million. He died on 1 August 2012.

The children will in fact receive much more than the then nil rate band of £325,000 (in fact, up to £1,500,000) and Victoria gets nothing.

This is calculated as follows (see s 39A):

Proportion of estate which consists of taxable property is:

$$\frac{£300,000}{£1,500,000} = 1/5$$

Proportion of the estate which consists of 100% relief property is:

$$\frac{£1.2m}{£1.5m} = 4/5$$

The value of the property which therefore passes under the pecuniary gift of the nil rate band free of IHT (inclusive of the 100% relieved BPR/APR) is therefore:

£325,000 × 5 = £1,625,000 (but abated to the value of the estate, ie £1,500,000).

Note: The multiplier of 5 applies because the 100% relief is spread over the value of the dispositions of property comprised in the estate under s 39A, so that for every £1 of property which is taxable (at a nil rate) passing under the nil band, a further £4 of property which is 100% relieved also passes.

WILL DRAFTING: LEGACIES AND BEQUESTS

4.37   Remember that, when redrafting a will, TLATA 1996 will apply. Any old provisions requiring a 'trust for sale' should be removed. The ability of joint owners to apply for property to be sold is now affected by considerations such as the original purpose of the trust under which the joint property is held.

Where a transfer is only partially exempt (because, for instance, the testator leaves part of his estate to his spouse or to charity) it is necessary to have provisions which determine the extent and the impact of IHT liabilities on that part or proportion which is not exempt. The rules governing the allocation of exemptions in such circumstances are set out in ss 36–42. This area has been the subject of judicial consideration in *Re Benham's Will Trusts* [1995] STC 210 and *Re Ratcliffe* [1999] STC 262 (see **4.39**).

The present IHT rules and formula

4.38   *Apart* from exempt gifts which can be specific *or* of residue, chargeable gifts would be:

Type (1) – Specific and bearing own tax (ie subject to IHT)

This would cover gifts expressed to bear their own tax (see **4.34**); for example:

> 'I give [to my son … a] [legacy of £x] and direct that [the said legacy] shall be subject to the payment of any IHT attributable thereto.'

Note also that a testator *cannot* place the burden of IHT onto gifts which are exempt transfers to a spouse, a charity, a political party, or for national purposes or public benefit (s 41 applies 'notwithstanding the terms of any disposition').

Type (2) – Specific gift with tax falling on residue (ie free of IHT)

This could be realty and personalty where there is no direction that the asset in question is to bear its own tax.

Type (3) – Residue or a share or fraction thereof

For gifts within Type (1) above, the value of the gifts is *not* re-grossed. The value taken is the *actual* value. This type of gift is therefore generally the simplest method.

Gifts within Type (2) are re-grossed. All such gifts are added together and the *total* then re-grossed (s 38(3)). If *only* gifts within Type (2) (free of IHT) are comprised in the estate apart from exempt gifts, then s 38(3) alone applies and these gifts are only grossed up *inter se* with no further re-grossing.

However, if there are any chargeable gifts within Type (1) (subject to IHT) and/ or Type (3) (residue), then s 38(4) and (5) operate, forcing the practitioner to 'double gross'. The formula and the stages are as follows:

(a)   Aggregate all gifts within Type (2) as if a separate transfer and gross up for IHT thereon. In the example below, £334,000 + IHT £6,000 = £340,000.

(b)   Deduct the above, ie £340,000, from total estate £740,000, leaving £400,000. The *balance* is divided between:

    (i)   exempt specific gifts;

    (ii)   exempt residuary gifts; and

    (iii) gifts within Type (1) and Type (3) above.

(c)   Add to grossed-up figure under (a), ie the £340,000, the *actual value* of gifts under Type (1) and Type (3) above. This gives a new total of taxable gifts.

(d)   Calculate the IHT on new total. This is the *amount* of IHT calculated to this stage. It is notional only.

(e)   Make a fraction:

    the numerator is the notional amount of IHT; and

    the denominator is the notional new total of taxable gifts.

(f)   Express the above fraction as a percentage. This gives the new *assumed* or estate rate.

(g)   Go back to actual value of gifts within Type (2) (free of IHT) and make *second* re-gross and calculate by new assumed rate. *Second* re-grossed figure: note it.

(h)   Deduct the *second* figure from *true* total estate and split balance between exempt and taxable estate.

(i)   Now calculate *final estate rate* on taxable estate, giving true IHT payable.

Example 4.7 – Incidence of IHT

Estate of £740,000 on death in 2012–13.

Specific legacies of:

(a)   £284,000 to son;

(b)   £20,000 to each of two nephews; and

(c)   £10,000 to a friend.

None of the specific legacies is to bear its own tax.

Residue to be shared equally between widow (exempt) and daughter (non-exempt).

4.38 *Appropriate will planning*

No chargeable transfers in the previous seven years.

Values must be attributed to the specific legacies in accordance with s 38, and to residue in accordance with s 39. The specific gifts are not the only gifts which are or might be chargeable: the daughter's share of residue is chargeable. This means that the assumptions described in s 38(5) must be used to work out the 'assumed rate' of tax.

(1) Attribute a hypothetical value to the specific gifts as if they were the only chargeable transfers. This means grossing up the legacies of £334,000. After the nil rate band of £325,000, the grossed-up amount would be £340,000 (ie £334,000 plus the grossing-up amount, viz (£334,000 – £325,000 × 2/3), £6,000 = £340,000).

The hypothetical value attributable to residue is determined accordingly, ie £740,000 – £340,000 = £400,000.

(2) The assumed amount of tax based on the hypothesis in (1) must now be calculated. This is calculated by aggregating the chargeable transfers: £340,000 (the value currently attributed to the chargeable legacies) + £200,000 (the chargeable half of the value currently attributed to residue), ie £540,000.

The tax on £540,000 would be (0% × £325,000) + (40% × £215,000) = £86,000. That is the 'assumed amount of tax'. Accordingly, the 'assumed rate' is:

$$\frac{£86,000}{£540,000} = 15.926\%$$

(3) A value is now attributed to the legacies in accordance with s 38(4), by grossing them up at the assumed rate:

$$£334,000 \times \frac{100}{(100 - 15.926)} = £397,269$$

(4) Having attributed a value to the specific gifts, the value of residue can be worked out, ie £740,000 – £397,269 = £342,731. Half of the residue (ie £171,366) is exempt.

(5) The total chargeable estate is therefore made up of £171,365 (the other, chargeable half of the residue) + £397,269 (the value attributed to specific gifts) = £568,634.

(6) The tax on the chargeable part of the estate is (0% × £325,000) + (40% × £243,634) = £97,453. This is an effective rate of 17.138%.

Tax on gross legacy £397,269 × 17.138% = £68,084

Tax on chargeable residue £171,365 × 17.138% = £29,369

The residue is:

Estate	£740,000
Gross legacy (£334,000 + £68,084)	£402,084
Residue	£337,916
Exempt residue: Widow (50%)	£168,958
Chargeable residue: Daughter (50%)	£168,958

Assuming a *Ratcliffe* rather than *Benham* distribution of residue (as to which, see below), and ignoring other administration expenses, the estate would be paid out in the following way:

Son:	£284,000
Other legacies:	£50,000
Widow:	£168,958
Daughter (£168,958 – £29,369):	£139,589
IHT:	£97,453
	£740,000

It is quite common for executors to ignore these rules and to attempt to distribute residue equally among exempt and non-exempt residuary beneficiaries, effectively charging exempt beneficiaries to tax. Where charities are involved, this will (quite rightly) provoke a sharp reminder of the rules. The executors will have to make good the loss out of their own pocket unless they can recover the over-distribution from the chargeable beneficiaries.

It should be noted that IHT 'grossing-up calculators' can be accessed on HMRC's website at www.hmrc.gov.uk/agents/iht/grossing-up-calcs.htm.

Of course, the executors could refuse to distribute until all the residuary beneficiaries had approved the accounts. The charities will not do so. The executors will be left embarrassed but not out of pocket.

Exempt and non-exempt gifts of residue: Re Benham's Will Trusts and Re Ratcliffe

4.39   The debate on the position of exempt and non-exempt gifts of residue under a will trust originated from *Re Benham's Will Trust* [1995] STC 210. The debate concerns the proper construction of the following commonplace type of clause:

'I give devise and bequeath all my real and personal estate whatsoever and wheresoever not hereby otherwise disposed of unto my Trustees upon trust to sell and convert the same into money with power at their absolute discretion to postpone any such sale and conversion for so long as they shall think fit without being answerable for any loss and after payment thereout of my debts and funeral and testamentary expenses to stand possessed of the residue as to one half part thereof for my children in equal shares absolutely and as to the remainder of my estate upon trust for the following charities ... '

Prior to *Re Benham* it was widely assumed that the proper construction of this type of clause was simply that the children should receive their share subject to IHT. Thus, they would receive less than the charities. The alternative construction, that the testator intended the IHT to be paid and then the residue split, was disregarded. This was because it was prohibited by s 41(b) and so, even if it was intended, it could not be effected.

Re Benham held that there was a third construction which was not prohibited by s 41(b). This third possibility was that the non-exempt beneficiary's share should be grossed up so that after his share bore the IHT, he would receive an equal sum to the exempt beneficiary. This construction results in more IHT being payable.

Re Benham was widely considered to have been wrongly decided. It created uncertainty for executors required to divide the estate in accordance with the will, and to pay the correct amount of IHT. This was so even though HMRC Capital Taxes (as they then were) made clear that their view was that *Re Benham* was distinguishable on the wording of the will (Private Client Business 1996, No 5, p 29). However, that view was not necessarily the view of the exempt or non-exempt beneficiary; indeed certain charities threatened executors with claims if they adopted the calculations required by *Benham*.

The decision of the High Court in *Re Ratcliffe* [1999] STC 262 was therefore particularly welcome. Blackburne J held in *Re Ratcliffe* that the proper construction of the commonplace clause is that the non-exempt beneficiaries receive their share subject to IHT and without grossing up. The learned judge did not follow *Re Benham,* holding that it established no principle of law. The result is that, although *Re Benham* has not been overruled, in the authors' view it has been effectively sidelined, even though the outcome of it may well, occasionally, reflect what a testator might want.

HMRC's Inheritance Tax Manual (at IHTM26131) states that grossing up in accordance with *Re Benham* is 'very rare', but acknowledges (at IHTM26172) that 'It is perfectly possible, though unusual, for you to come across wills deliberately drafted to achieve a *Re Benham* result'. The Manual advises HMRC officers to read the will, and to refer cases of difficulty to their Technical Group after obtaining an explanation of the interpretation suggested by the taxpayer.

The moral is to clarify the position in the will or by way of a variation. The *Benham* decision is defeated if wording such as the following is used:

'I give the capital and income of my residuary estate to my [wife] and my [son] in [equal] shares and the division into shares shall be treated as made before deduction of IHT payable on my death in respect of my residuary estate.'

The *Benham* decision can apply where the wording is to the following effect:

' ... to my [wife] and my [son] in such shares that after deducting IHT payable on my death in respect of my residuary estate the two shares are equal.'

See also *Butterworth's Wills, Probate and Administration Service* (published by LexisNexis).

Planning aspects of ss 36–42

4.40   As already indicated in **4.38** and Example 4.7, there can be complicated grossing and also re-grossing results for legacies given free of IHT when the whole or part of residue goes to an exempt beneficiary (say, the surviving spouse or charity). It is again emphasised: look at the alternatives to legacies given free of IHT and consider switching to either legacies which are subject to IHT or a share of residue instead. Again, the problem need not exist where there is 100% business/agricultural relief.

The aim of s 38 is that the net effect of 'free of tax' and 'subject to tax' legacies are neutral as to the total amount charged to IHT.

Mutual wills

4.41   This is a situation where effectively the testators (usually, but not necessarily, husband and wife) agree, as a matter of contract, that when the first of them dies the survivor will not change his or her will. Usually the ultimate beneficiaries are their children, so they are trying to prevent the survivor having remarried then leaving all their joint assets to the new spouse and possibly then by the will of the second spouse to the children of that spouse. The contrast is between, on the one hand, certainty but inflexibility and, on the other hand, uncertainty and flexibility. It is advisable to state in the will expressly whether the wills are intended to be mutual or not. It is the experience of the authors that non-mutual wills are the norm.

Where the will is silent and a mutual will is not accepted by the court the jurisprudence is complex and will result in one party feeling very aggrieved.

4.41 *Appropriate will planning*

For those interested in the working out of human nature in this context see the contrasting cases of *Healey v Brown* [2002] WTLR 849 on the one hand, and *Charles v Fraser* [2010] WTLR 1489 and *Fry v Densham-Smith* [2011] WTLR 387 on the other.

Chapter 5

Practical aspects of will drafting

DETAILED ASPECTS OF WILL DRAFTING

Survivorship and the rule as to commorientes

Definition of the rule

5.1   The rule as to commorientes set out in Law of Property Act 1925, s 184 provides that:

> 'Where ... two or more persons have died in circumstances rendering it uncertain which of them survived the other or others, such deaths, shall ... for all purposes affecting the title to property, be presumed to have occurred in order of seniority, and accordingly the younger shall be deemed to have survived the elder.'

Statutory relief

5.2   The operation of the commorientes rule could give rise to a double or multiple charge for IHT on such deaths (albeit subject to quick succession relief where there was a chargeable transfer; see s 141). The operation of the commorientes rule can, however, be avoided for IHT purposes. Section 4(2) provides that where it cannot be known which of two or more persons who have died survived the other or others they shall be presumed to have died at the same instant and therefore the estate of the younger is not swollen.

Section 92 covers the different problem of a possible double or multiple charge to IHT on successive deaths. These are deaths which are not, or are not treated as being, simultaneous but which follow within a short period of time and where it is ascertainable which person survived the other, even though only for a relatively short time.

Section 92 provides that where:

• under the terms of the will or otherwise, property is held for any person on condition that he survives another for a specified period of not more than six months, and

- another beneficiary becomes entitled to property by reason of the survivorship condition (ie the original beneficiary not having complied with that condition),

the IHT payable is the same as if that other beneficiary had taken the property direct, without the intervention of the survivorship condition. That beneficiary is deemed to have become entitled from the beginning of the survivorship period. Therefore, no problems remain as to the treatment of the intermediate income, under s 65 in particular. Section 92 also prevents the question of whether a 'settlement' has been created by the survivorship condition from arising in relation to the disposition (see s 43).

Recommended action

5.3   It is for this reason that the survivorship clauses are at least to be considered in all cases of the bequest of an absolute interest as well as of a life interest or an annuity. However, where the transferable nil rate band is in issue, survivorship clauses may be entirely inappropriate, for the reasons explained at **3.25**. Such clauses provide that the gift in question only takes effect if the donee survives the testator by a specified period, say, 30 days or three months (ie contingent gift). If the donee does not survive this period, the gift lapses and no further IHT is payable thereon. The suggested period of three months is usually preferable because it represents an average period in practice for obtaining probate, or used to represent the average period. That period may now be longer because of the extensive inquiries that personal representatives are now obliged to make before lodging the initial IHT return, IHT400.

The important effects of s 92 (subject to complying with the necessary conditions, for example, the six-month period) can be summarised as follows.

- The introduction of the survivorship clause in a will should avoid any double charge.

- It will be possible to prevent assets coming into a beneficiary's estate (ie that of the beneficiary who dies shortly after the testator) in circumstances where it is preferred to make the gift to another party and treat the initial gift as a nullity. This will become particularly relevant if various rates of IHT are re-introduced, ie to prevent the bunching effect.

- It is now generally immaterial whether the gift during the survivorship period carries the intermediate income or not or whether the intended beneficiary is to benefit absolutely, by way of interest in possession or accumulation and maintenance trust.

As between husband and wife, a survivorship condition will affect transfer of the nil rate band of IHT, so the will drafter must think through the effect, as explained at **3.25**.

Example 5.1 – Survivorship clause: poorer surviving spouse

Ann and Bill are married. Ann made lifetime gifts, having used up her nil rate band available on death, and dies on 4 March 2012 leaving an estate of £250,000 to Bill conditionally on his surviving her by three months.

Bill was a spender, who never made any lifetime gifts and who has a nil estate. Bill dies on 7 May 2012. Under the terms of Ann's will, her estate devolves to her three children equally. IHT of £100,000 is payable on the £250,000.

Had Ann not included a survivorship condition, the estate would have passed to Bill and, if he died before spending all of it, it could have passed from his estate to the children at a nil rate of IHT. Thus by arranging for her estate to pass to Bill, preferably under an immediate post-death interest that would protect the fund from dissipation, with remainder for the children to inherit at Bill's death, the IHT could have been washed out by the use of Bill's nil rate band.

Example 5.2 – No survivorship clause: the transferable nil rate band

Colin and Denise are married and successful, with a young family. They are in business together and have a joint estate of £800,000 owned in equal shares. Colin dies on 1 April 2012 and, as it turns out, Denise on 1 May 2012.

Colin made his will before the introduction of the transferable nil rate band. He included no survivorship condition in his will. Under the law as it stood when he made the will, the children, when inheriting on Denise's death, would have suffered IHT of £190,000, ie on the aggregated, bunched estate of £800,000, less her nil rate band of £325,000, at 40%.

Under the transferable nil rate band rules, Colin has not used his nil rate band so on Denise's death both are available, reducing tax on her estate to £60,000 (ie £800,000 − £650,000 = £150,000 at 40%).

Had Colin included an appropriate survivorship condition, and his estate of £400,000 had passed direct to the children and likewise on Denise's death, the same IHT would have been payable.

Note, however, the possibilities available in these circumstances by entering into deeds of variation (see **5.32** onwards).

Statutory anomaly

5.4   The interaction of Law of Property Act 1925, s 184 and IHTA 1984, s 4(2) has an interesting result where spouses die simultaneously (eg in an air crash) or in commorientes circumstances where it is not known which spouse survived the other. If no survivorship condition applies under the terms of the will, no IHT is payable in the estate of the elder, whoever inherits it, on either death. This point is acknowledged in HMRC's guidance (at IHTM12197). This applies to simultaneous deaths in England and Wales; different rules apply in Scotland (see IHTM12193) and in Northern Ireland (IHTM12194).

Therefore if, as between spouses, a survivorship condition is otherwise desirable, the draftsman should exclude its operation for simultaneous deaths in the will of the elder. Alternatively, if the commorientes circumstances in fact arise, exclude the survivorship condition by deed of variation.

Example 5.3 – Simultaneous deaths: no survivorship clause

Ellen is married to Francis, who is her senior by a couple of years. They live in England, and their joint estate, held as tenants in common, is £1,350,000. Neither APR nor BPR is in point. Their wills provide for each other absolutely, not subject to any survivorship condition, with remainder among nephews and nieces. They die in an air disaster on 17 May 2012.

Applying the rule in s 4(2), they are assumed to have died at the same instant. Applying the rule in LPA 1925, s 184, Francis is deemed to have died first, so his estate passes to Ellen, which is an exempt transfer under IHTA 1984, s 18. The nephews and nieces inherit £675,000 from his estate, tax free.

The executors of Ellen's estate have the benefit of the double nil rate band (see IHTM43040), so the nephews and nieces inherit a further estate (£675,000 less nil rate band of £650,000) at a tax cost of £10,000.

Annuities

5.5   As a general rule, a will should not provide for an annuity because:

- this can give rise to additional tax liabilities (especially IHT), because it creates a 'settlement';

- the important income tax relief on the 'capital element' of a purchase life annuity (ie from an insurance company) will not be available under ITTOIA 2005, s 717 (see ITTOIA 2005, s 718(2)); and

- payments out of capital can become taxable as income by reason of the regularity of the payments (see *Brodie's Will Trustees v IRC* (1933) 17 TC 432 and *Cunard's Trustees v IRC* [1946] 1 All ER 159, 27 TC 122).

The doctrine in *Brodie* and *Cunard* has been weakened by the decision of *Stevenson v Wishart* [1987] STC 266. The Court of Appeal there held that, if the trustees, in exercise of their power over capital, chose to make regular payments out of capital to a capital beneficiary rather than release a single sum of a large amount, that did not create an income interest. Apart from their recurrence there was on the facts nothing to indicate that the payments were of an income nature. The annuity problems could also be avoided by advancing funds to a beneficiary under Trustee Act 1925, s 32 even though, instead of a single advance, payments are made by instalments.

As an alternative it is better to give a lump sum to the individual or even a third party upon terms that an annuity be purchased out of that lump sum.

However, an annuity left to a widow may be advantageous.

Discretionary trusts in wills: I – two-year s 144 trusts

5.6   Many people are indecisive about the ultimate destination of their estates (perhaps because the relative needs of possible beneficiaries are in the process of rapid change). To postpone a choice until the very last moment, advantage can be taken of s 144. These provisions allow distributions to be made within two years of the death without any charge to IHT out of assets settled on discretionary trusts by the will.

This facility has become more important for two reasons. First, following FA 2006, trustees may wish to accelerate entitlements of younger beneficiaries so as to avoid the IHT regime that applies to discretionary trusts. Secondly, following the introduction of the transferable nil rate band facility, wills drawn to use the nil rate band on the first death may now be undesirable and a simple appointment of the discretionary fund to the surviving spouse, absolutely or for life, will 'unuse' the band so that it becomes transferable.

In the appropriate circumstances, therefore, the individual could make a will settling his estate (or part of it) on discretionary trusts, specifying in the definition of beneficiaries the whole range of persons who might remotely be considered as candidates for his bounty. The trustees could, within two years of the death, distribute the fund, relying either on any informal letter or memorandum of wishes left behind by the testator in the choice of beneficiaries or using their discretion.

The main *advantages* of a s 144 discretionary will trust are:

- Flexibility: the allocation of assets is left to the wide discretion of the trustees, eg appointment to spouse who then makes PETs. Beware the hostile attitude of HMRC to this sequence of events; see *Lau v HMRC*

207

[2009] WTLR 627 and **5.31**. Contrast the situation of a variation or disclaimer under s 142 where the re-allocation of assets is left to the whim of the person benefiting under the will or intestacy. Some advisers fear that the future viability of s 142 is in doubt, but this might also be the case for s 144.

- There may also be some doubt over whether business and/or agricultural property in the estate qualifies for 100% relief. HMRC will only consider whether relief is due if there may be an IHT liability. A possible solution might therefore be to transfer assets up to the available nil rate band to a s 144 discretionary trust, together with a further specific legacy of the business/agricultural assets (within s 39A(2)). Assuming that the BPR/APR position can be agreed with HMRC within the two-year period in s 144, there is flexibility over how those assets are applied. For example, if no relief is due, consideration could be given to appointing those assets to the surviving spouse. The effect of s 144 will be that the appointment is treated as made under the terms of the will, so that spouse exemption can apply to it.

- As a further example of flexibility, it is currently possible to create an IPDI within the two-year period. Although the IPDI is perhaps thought of mainly as provision for a surviving spouse (probably due to the spouse exemption), that need not be so. It could just as well be a life interest for a young grandchild, which might defer the next IHT charge on the family money for 80 years.

- A s 142 variation is often hampered by the fact that a minor beneficiary's interest cannot, in any way, be reduced without the court's consent. Under a s 144 discretionary trust, as all beneficiaries merely have a hope of benefiting, no such obstacle exists.

- Under s 92, a survivorship condition has to be limited to six months (see **5.2**). A s 144 discretionary trust in effect gives a longer period, ie two years, for achieving a similar result.

- Income tax: if a parent effects a s 142 variation in favour of his minor, unmarried children, he will be regarded as the settlor for income tax purposes under the settlements anti-avoidance provisions (ITTOIA 2005, s 629). To avoid s 631 (dealing with retained and accumulated income), the trustees should not make any payment to the child until he is no longer a minor (ie 18 years) or no longer unmarried, if earlier. This problem does not exist for a s 144 discretionary trust.

- Some testators object to the fact that their bequests can be varied after death under s 142. Under a s 144 discretionary trust, as the beneficiaries merely have a hope of benefiting, a s 142 variation is not possible.

- Stamp duty land tax and stamp duty: distributions out of a s 144 discretionary trust are exempt from stamp duty land tax if no consideration is given (FA 2003, Sch 3, para 1). Similarly, such distributions are exempt from stamp duty and there is no adjudication requirement, provided the appropriate certificate is given; see the Stamp Duty (Exempt Instruments) Regulations 1987 SI 1987/516.

5.7   There are, however, some *disadvantages* to a s 144 discretionary trust, namely:

- Cash flow: IHT is payable in respect of the creation of the trust fund (ie on the estate at death) and would usually have to be reclaimed if appropriated to an exempt party (eg surviving spouse).

- Under s 142, a variation can be made in favour of any person. Under s 144 the beneficiaries are restricted even though the class may be widely defined, including a power to add beneficiaries.

- Discretionary trusts are charged to income tax at the trust rate under ITA 2007, s 9(1) (50% for 2012–13) or the dividend trust rate (42.5% for 2012–13) for dividend income.

- Property transferred within three months of the deceased's death is outside the ambit of s 144. In *Frankland v IRC* [1996] STC 735 it was held that, for an event to be relevant within s 144(1)(a), it had to be an event on which, apart from s 144, tax would have been chargeable, so in effect an occasion for an 'exit' charge. No exit charge can arise under s 65(4) until a complete quarter has elapsed from the deceased's death. See also *Loveday dec'd v IRC* [1997] STC (SCD) 321, where an attempt to use the provisions otherwise for a mere selection of chattels failed. Note that, as a consequence of changes made to s 142 arising out of the FA 2006 amendments to the IHT rules applicable to trusts, certain trust interests (other than absolute interests) created out of a discretionary will trust *will* be 'read back' into the will, even though created within three months of death.

- Distributions/disposals within the two-year period to any beneficiary will not be eligible to the CGT holdover relief under TCGA 1992, s 260 because such distributions are exempt from IHT (although a distribution in the course of administration will result in the beneficiary acquiring the asset at probate value). This is a point that can easily be missed. Thus distributions by personal representatives to legatees, including the trustees of ongoing trusts established by the will, are exempt from CGT (TCGA 1992, s 62(4)).

- Careful consideration must be given, to allow the respective periods of three months and two years to elapse. Take special care where wills have been drafted to the effect that there is an automatic termination shortly prior to the two-year period. Such wills may need to be reviewed and the automatic termination abandoned to allow for the necessary flexibility.

- Any discretionary trust is really only as good as the trustees who manage it. If they are well versed in IHT, all well and good: otherwise mistakes may be made. Most readers of this work will no doubt be able to reassure their clients that, if appointed executor and trustee, they can offer skills in this area.

Discretionary trusts in wills: II – using the nil rate band

5.8   **Chapter 3** examines the changes to the tax treatment of the type of will which establishes a nil rate band discretionary trust from which distributions can be made to the surviving spouse in case of need. As was seen in that chapter, the facility to transfer unused nil rate band has had a significant effect on the decision whether to include such a trust, and on how the discretion is later exercised.

In view of the transferable nil rate band facility, the most likely uses of the structure in future are to:

- protect smaller funds from care fees;

- protect estates from the profligacy of a second spouse or partner; and

- 'slide through' substantial value attracting APR or BPR and 'recycle' the relief by subsequent repurchase of the assets from the trust by the surviving spouse and partner; sometimes called 'double dipping'.

These ideas, and other possibilities, were all considered at **3.16** onwards. An important question is whether an upper limit should be placed on such discretionary trusts in case the nil rate band is increased substantially; and/ or because business/agricultural relief applies at 100%/50%. The answer is probably not, if the surviving spouse is a discretionary beneficiary. The reason is that (s)he can benefit from income or capital distributions within two years of death where s 144 applies. If the trust fund is within the nil rate band, there is no IHT liability for any distributions before the first ten-year anniversary.

Note in this connection that BPR/APR it is not available for calculating the effective rate until the first ten-year anniversary. However, you should explain these issues and obtain specific instructions when making the will and make a note for the executors or trustees not to make distributions to the widow(er) within three months of the death (see **5.7**).

5.9   The surviving spouse can be included in the class of beneficiaries even though (s)he is not intended to benefit absolutely. Either include virtually the entire estate in the discretionary trust and distribute to the surviving spouse before the end of the two-year period relying upon s 144, or before the ten-year period if the trust is only of the value of the nil rate band.

Where the discretionary trust consists of specific gifts of business/agricultural assets only, consider leaving the residue to the surviving spouse (the s 39A rateable apportionment will not then apply because specific gifts of such assets are involved). But do not distribute to a surviving spouse in the first three months following the other spouse's death (see s 65(4) referred to above) unless creating an IPDI, or unless a nil rate band discretionary trust exists and you are not relying on surviving spouse exemption applying.

5.10   There are, however, a number of danger areas to consider:

- Related settlements (s 62: trusts having same commencement dates and same settlor). The value of other property settled by the will (ie the related settlement(s)) could form part of the cumulative total of transfers to which the ten-yearly charges on the discretionary testamentary trust will apply.

- If the discretionary trust continues for more than ten years, IHT ten-year anniversary and interim charges may arise (ss 64–69). This may be more of a nuisance than a disaster if the values do not exceed the nil rate band.

- CGT transfers from a trust do not obtain the relief under TCGA 1992, s 62(4) for testamentary dispositions, although holdover relief under s 260 may be available (but see below).

- IHT distributions to a widow(er) within three months other than by way of IPDI do not give rise to an exit charge (see IHTA s 65(4) and **5.7**).

- No CGT holdover relief for transfers that would be immediately chargeable to IHT in the two-year period from death if s 144 applies.

- Where assets are left to a beneficiary absolutely or by way of a life interest, CGT exemption and market value uplift apply (subject to the restriction in TCGA, s 74 in respect of a life interest where holdover relief has been claimed on creating the trust).

- Discretionary trusts suffer income tax (for 2012–13) at 50% and at 42.5% on dividend income. Tax credits on dividends do not go into the trust tax pool and cannot frank the tax deducted from distributions. As a result, full distribution of trust income requires a 'tax pool adjustment' under which the trustees must pay extra tax to frank the tax deducted from the distribution. These rules are relieved slightly for smaller trusts by ITA 2007, s 491 in respect of the first £1,000 of income. Trustees of larger trusts should bear this in mind when formulating their investment policies.

- Drafting errors, doubts and, for some, surprising results, as arose recently in *RSPCA v Sharp and others* [2010] WTLR 855 ChD, [2011] WTLR 311 CA.

In the *RSPCA* case, a will gave, at clause 3, 'the amount which at my death equals the maximum which I can give … by this my Will without Inheritance

Tax becoming payable in respect of this gift', with residue passing to charity. Had the will contained no other bequests, this clause might have caused little difficulty: there could have been an examination of the lifetime history of chargeable transfers and, absent any, the gift will be of the current nil rate band.

The difficulty arose because clause 4 gave a house to chargeable beneficiaries and directed that 'the Inheritance Tax (if any) payable on my death in respect of the property and all costs of registration of the said [beneficiaries] as proprietors thereof shall be payable out of my residuary estate'. The estate had been administered on the basis that clause 3 gave the nil rate band while clause 4 gave something free of tax, so grossed up, with the charity bearing that tax as a testamentary expense.

The charity argued that clause 3 must be read with clause 4, and merely swept up any unused nil rate band; this in part on reliance on s 4(1) that there is a single transfer on death of the whole estate. That argument would reduce the IHT payable to nil; the deceased must have wanted that.

Peter Smith J in the High Court dismissed the arguments of the charity in quite strong terms, refusing leave to appeal. He noted in particular the use of the words 'if any' in clause 4, which would not be needed if the testator's intention had been that all non-charitable gifts should if possible amount to no more than the nil rate band.

Many might agree with the learned judge: you start at the beginning of the will, you take the clauses in order, and since the gift of the house follows that of the nil rate band, it must be an extra grossed-up gift. However, there is case law to support the principle that you read the will as a whole, not necessarily following its strict order. It did not help that the gift in clause 3 was not of a specified sum, for example by reference to statute.

An argument also runs that 'this gift' in clause 3 did not mean 'this clause 3 gift' but 'this, being part of the gift or transfer of my estate which I am deemed to make under s 4 IHTA 1984'. That may fit the IHT analysis, but is hardly how a layman would read the clause.

But the Court of Appeal, following the view expressed by many learned commentators and practitioners, revised the first decision finding for the charity ([2011] WTLR 311).

Clearly there are lessons here for the will draftsman. The drafting of James Kessler QC in his *Drafting Trusts and Will Trusts* (Thomson Sweet & Maxwell), which is often seen as a benchmark of excellence, contains a clause that would have put the position beyond doubt, if the testator had wanted it:

> 'Any other legacy given by my will or any codicil shall be paid in priority to the Nil rate Sum.'

Practitioners should ask their clients exactly how they wish the burden of tax to fall and draw the will accordingly.

Implied or precatory trusts (s 143)

Precatory trusts

5.11   It has long proved convenient for testators to give assets such as chattels to the personal representatives or other individuals 'in full confidence, but without imposing a binding legal trust or obligation, that they will distribute the same amongst such members of my family living at my death as they shall think fit'. If this informal trust/request is carried out within two years of the testator's death, no additional IHT is payable beyond what was due in respect of the testator's estate.

Section 143 is particularly useful for items of personal use and ornament (eg jewellery), paintings, antiques, etc, thereby avoiding specific mention in the will itself, and also gifts of money. Although this is by no means clear from the words of the statute, the section is interpreted as applying substantially only to chattels: see *Loveday (deceased) v IRC* [1997] STC (SCD) 321.

This benevolent provision had come under threat in the 1989 Finance Bill, but the proposals were withdrawn. These arrangements were upheld in the case of *Re Beatty* [1990] 1 WLR 1503 against a claim by the residuary beneficiaries that the gift was void for uncertainty, notwithstanding the very wide nature of the class of intended beneficiaries and the wide power of delegation. The case also emphasises the importance of the gift to the 'trustees' being a beneficial one, thereby coming within the requirements of s 143.

Secret and half-secret trusts

5.12   In this context, it may become useful to distinguish these precatory arrangements, which are non-binding, from secret trusts which are indeed binding and which therefore can operate without any need for s 143. Under a secret trust, the donee named in the will is bound in equity to transfer to the true beneficiary on whose behalf he acts as trustee only; so that the IHT transfer is direct from the testator to the true beneficiary. There is no transfer for IHT when the trustee discharges the trust by delivering the property to the beneficiary. He is a bare trustee.

A further distinction should be noted within secret trusts themselves. On the one hand, there is the *fully secret trust* where the testator in his will gives property to X absolutely. There is no indication in the will that X does anything but take the property beneficially. However, it is essential, either before or after making the will, that the testator tells X that he is to hold the property so given for Y. X can in these circumstances be compelled in equity to carry out the trust because, either expressly or by silence, he has induced the testator to make the gift or, if already made, not to revoke it.

However, if X hears about the trust only after the death, he cannot be compelled to observe it and is entitled to keep the property for himself. Fully secret trusts are normally used where complete confidentiality is required; as when the testator leaves a legacy to his brother, which excites no interest, but where the brother is obliged to pay it over to the testator's natural son, of whom few people know.

The *half secret trust* is where the testator gives property in his will to X with an express direction in the will itself that X is to hold the property on trust, but without disclosing the terms of the trust. Thus, the testator might leave a sum of money to X 'on the trusts I have already communicated to him'. The testator might, for instance, want to leave the sum between nephews and nieces but in unequal shares, or cutting one out, and not want the world to know. If the trust is notified to X before or at the time the will is made, and the will indicates the trust nature of the gift, X must carry it out. It is doubtful, however, whether a half secret trust can validly be notified after the execution of the will, because the testator would be reserving to himself a power to make testamentary dispositions without due formalities.

In some circumstances it may be preferable, even with chattels, to utilise a secret trust rather than a mere non-binding request.

The matrimonial home

Proposal 1: Outright gift of a share

Is it worth the bother?

5.13 Following the introduction of transferable nil rate bands, many couples will stop worrying about the home. There are many places outside London and the Home Counties where a good family home may be purchased for not much more than one nil rate band and something quite smart for much less than twice that sum, especially after the decline in property values that followed the financial crisis that commenced in 2008. Add the value of some contents and savings, but ignore the value of a pension fund that will not survive the second spouse, and it will be seen that the couple can feel that 'there will be at least something to leave the children' and that they need not therefore put themselves to any great inconvenience to save further tax.

The matrimonial home was previously considered an appropriate asset to use to take advantage of the nil rate band by both spouses, either by placing it into the sole name of one spouse or into joint names depending upon the circumstances. As regards the holding of land and building in joint names, there are two alternatives, namely a holding as 'joint tenants' and as 'tenants in common'. For the former method, the survivor takes absolutely and by operation of law. Hence, it is impossible to make testamentary or lifetime dispositions to third parties.

By contrast in the case of a tenancy in common, disposals of one spouse's shares during lifetime or by will are possible, and hence this method of holding is generally to be recommended as affording greater flexibility. In particular as a tenant in common of part, a widow, as co-owner, would be entitled to occupy the whole. On her death, moreover, her share could be eligible for a discount of between 10% to 15%, subject to the Land Tribunal's agreement (*Arkwright and another (Personal Representatives of Williams, deceased) v IRC* [2004] STC 1323 – see **1.23**). Such a discount is not available (whether as a joint tenancy or tenancy in common) while husband and wife are both alive having regard to the related property provisions (s 161); see *Price v HMRC* [2011] WTLR 161. The discount may apply, however, for the survivor's interest. See also the Land Tribunal decision in *Wight v IRC* (1982) 264 EG 935.

The Valuation Office Agency provides the following general guidelines regarding discounts when valuing an undivided half-share interest (see www. voa.gov.uk/corporate/Publications/Manuals/InheritanceTaxManual/pnotes/ h-iht-man-pn2.html):

- where the other co-owner(s) is (are) not in occupation and the purpose behind the trust no longer exists: 10%;
- where the other co-owner(s) is (are) not in occupation but they have a clear right to occupy as their main residence and the purpose behind the trust still exists: 15%; and
- where the other co-owner(s) is (are) in occupation as their main residence: 15%.

The ability to force a sale

5.14   There was a possible danger area for deaths before 1 January 1997 that the other co-owner(s) may be able to force a sale, as the house would be held on a trust for sale. However, for deaths since 1 January 1997, the TLATA 1996 legislation has meant that there is no longer a duty to sell, and the trustees have a statutory power to postpone the sale (see **4.11** and **6.14** onwards).

In cases where the property is in fact held as joint tenants, but in which it would be preferable for it to be held as tenants in common, it is a relatively simple matter to 'sever' the joint tenancy to make it into a tenancy in common.

A possible structure?

5.15   Assume that the house is worth significantly more than the nil rate band; or that the testator has used that band so that it is not transferable. The testator owns the entire home and wishes to leave the bulk to a chargeable party (eg his son), yet enable his widow to occupy; but he does not want her to have a life interest in the whole property that would be chargeable on her death.

A few years ago, the solution would have been to give the widow an interest in possession with the intention that some time later there would be an appointment by the trustees of an interest in, say, 75% to her son. That would secure spouse relief at the outset and later the widow would occupy the whole by virtue of her trust interest in 25% of the house.

The idea was that the gift of the share in the house, coming as it did from the trustees rather than from the widow, might be sheltered from IHT if she survived seven years, even though she still lived in the house.

Until FA 2006, there was no gift with reservation by the widow because, as a co-owner, the widow was by law entitled to occupy the whole and because the termination was not 'a disposal by way of gift' under FA 1986, s 102. That advantage was nullified by FA 1986, s 102ZA introduced in FA 2006 with effect from 22 March 2006. The termination of the interest in the 'no-longer-possessed property' is now treated as a disposal by way of gift. For that reason, this structure no longer works and should be avoided.

Where, as a variant on the structure, part of the house is not appointed absolutely to children but is instead owned by a relevant property trust, there is an argument that the widow should not be treated as having an interest in possession in it, as well as in the part in which she has an IPDI. This is an area of considerable current interest to HMRC and each case will turn on its precise facts. If, on the facts, the widow enjoys exclusive rights of occupation, she probably will have an interest in possession (see SP 10/79 and *Lloyd's Private Banking* etc). As noted above, in *Judge and another (personal representatives of Walden, dec'd) v HMRC* [2005] STC (SCD) 863 (SpC 506) (see **4.13**), it was held that an interest in possession did not arise even though the widow seemed to have economic control of the dwelling because she could veto sale. In either case, the issue of reservation of benefit must be addressed, which will probably nullify the tax planning.

CGT issues

5.16   If the property in which the widow has a right to live is sold at any time during the widow's lifetime, full CGT private residence exemption should be available by virtue of TCGA 1992, s 225, as the widow is 'entitled to occupy it under the terms of the settlement'. This test is separate from whether the widow enjoys an interest in possession for IHT purposes.

If an individual (eg a widow) is given any right to occupy the matrimonial home in its entirety, this will often, but not always, constitute an 'interest in possession'. As a result, the same IHT will be payable as if the house had been given outright unless the interest terminates more than seven years before such individual's death (ie a PET). To avoid this potential IHT liability, any such occupation must be informal, eg by way of a non-enforceable licence or permission. See *Sansom v Peay* [1976] 3 All ER 375 and IR Press Release 15/8/1979 – SP 10/79.

Sufficient security of tenure is likely to exist in practice if the surviving spouse is an executor or executrix of the will. If she is the only executrix, there must be some doubt as to whether an interest in possession in the house can be avoided: is she really going to exercise her discretion so as to evict herself?

Proposal 2: The home loan/charging method

5.17   This was a way of using the nil rate band on the first death. It will rarely now be used, for the reasons already explained (in particular, see **Chapter 3**), so is mentioned for completeness only.

The spouse would give the nil rate band in his will to chargeable parties by use of a mini-discretionary trust and the residue (ie in particular the home) to the widow. The nil rate band gift would be satisfied by a loan or charge on the property in favour of the trustees of the mini-discretionary trust. The charge would then be a deduction from the widow's estate on her death and she would have had use and occupation meanwhile.

There was an exception where the widow had, during her husband's lifetime, made substantial gifts to him. The loan was not deductible from the widow's estate to the extent that it was property derived from the deceased, that is the widow (FA 1986, s 103). It had been argued that s 103 had no place in the context of spouse-exempt gifts, but *Phizackerley v HMRC* [2007] STC (SCD) 328, SpC 00591 was decided against the taxpayer without that argument being advanced.

'Phizackerley hangover'

5.18   There is one serious issue to address affecting existing schemes where *Phizackerley* may have been in point and may have been sidestepped by the use of a charge imposed on the property by the executors rather than by the surviving spouse, avoiding the problem 'first time round'. Section 103 contains no time limit. The debt which the executors seek to deduct from the estate of the second spouse to die is, see s 103(1):

'… subject to abatement to an extent proportionate to the value of any of the consideration given for the debt or encumbrance which consisted of–

(a) property derived from the deceased; or

(b) consideration (not being property derived from the deceased) given by any person who was at any time entitled to, or amongst whose resources there was at any time included, any property derived from the deceased.'

It does not matter how long ago the property passed from one spouse to the other, it could still be caught. Equally, it matters not that the charge may rest on one asset, where the gift was of another: s 103 can still bite. Clearly, these are matters of proof. Some executors will take a more cavalier approach to their duties in delivering accounts under IHTA 1984, s 216 than they should. If there is any clear link between the debt which is to be deducted from the estate of the surviving spouse and a gift made, however long ago, by that spouse to the first spouse to die, it would seem that *Phizackerley* can apply. This case increases the burden on executors and their advisers, and the risk, now heightened by new legislation, of the penalty for failure to make proper enquiries.

As an alternative to the creation by the surviving spouse of a debt that would fall foul of s 103, many advisers preferred the structure of a life interest, now an IPDI, rather than an outright gift to that survivor. The nil rate band was then not charged on the life tenant's fund; it was in effect a separate fund, carved out of the gift of the share in the house. Since all the value rested with the trustees, there was no need for a charge as such: the trustees held part on one set of trusts and part on another. Knowing what we know now, we can see that this was a more flexible, and better structure.

Practical implications: existing wills and new instructions

5.19   The debt or charge scheme was complicated, both in its establishment and its management. *Phizackerley* tells us that the enquiries to be made before recommending the use of the scheme might have to be more searching than we previously thought. The fact that gifts between spouses are themselves exempt, and that few records may have been kept, does not take those gifts outside the scope of s 103. In practical terms, this increased the cost of preparing wills because of the extra enquiries to be made and, where it was appropriate for the residue of the estate to be left to the surviving spouse on an interest in possession trust rather than absolutely, extra time was needed to explain how s 103 worked and how to avoid the trap that caught the Phizackerley family.

Care must be taken with existing structures. If the trustees just 'sit on their hands' the whole arrangement can be attacked as a sham or on the basis that the widow has an interest in possession in the whole house (or share) without a deduction of the loan. Wherever practicable the widow should not be a trustee of the discretionary will trust, nor have a power of veto, nor a power to 'hire and fire' the trustees. The trustees voting by a simple majority should be able to out-vote the widow. HMRC are likely to call for the professional advisers' letter setting up the arrangement: word it carefully!

Can the whole scheme be challenged under s 268, the associated operations rule? After the success of the taxpayer in *Reynaud v IRC* [1999] STC (SCD) 185 and *IRC v Rysaffe* [2003] WTLR 481, taxpayers generally may have become more confident of the limits of s 268. Its teeth were shown, however, in *Smith and others v HMRC* [2009] WTLR 691 which concerned back-to-back annuities and life policies. It was there held that the different documents need not expressly refer to one another for them to have been taken out with reference to each other. The total package of documents that had been provided by the insurer showed the link, which was enough. It is perhaps in such a way that a challenge might be mounted to show that a surviving spouse had 'incurred' the liability.

Proposal 3: Grant of a tenancy

5.20   Under this arrangement the trustees are not given power to give to the surviving spouse a right to occupy because that would create an interest in possession. Instead, they have power to grant a monthly tenancy at nominal rent. Even though this does create an interest in possession, it will have a low value on the surviving spouse's death.

Note that, if a share in a home is left to a discretionary trust in which the widow(er) is a beneficiary, HMRC may argue that this creates an interest in possession entitlement (see also SP 10/79). The same may apply even if the trustees permit her to occupy without being a specific beneficiary. However, some comfort may be derived from the decision in *Judge and another (personal representatives of Walden, dec'd) v HMRC* [2005] STC (SCD) 863 (SpC 506) (see **4.13**), in which an interest in possession was held not to exist: owing to a mistake of law by the trustees, they had never exercised their discretion in favour of the widow.

Proposal 4: Gift and repurchase

5.21   The husband leaves his half share in the house to his children under his will. On his death the surviving spouse purchases at full market value her husband's half from the children. The husband could give his spouse a market-value option in the will to ensure the spouse can purchase the share. This arrangement will have an SDLT cost and if the half of the house exceeds the nil rate band, an immediate IHT cost. The open market value may well be much less than the value under the related property provisions of s 161.

Alternatively, the half share could be given to the trustees of a will trust (if it is thought that the children will not consent).

Note that some advisers have elaborated a lifetime variant of this idea, which may be fraught with difficulty, involving the sale by one spouse of a share in the home to the other spouse in return for an IOU which the vendor spouse then gives away (eg to the children). Such a plan could fall foul of POAT, and may also infringe s 103 (see 'Using an IOU', *Taxation*, 13 December 2007).

Disclaimer by surviving spouse

5.22   To enable a surviving spouse to be in a position to disclaim his/her interest in the home effectively for IHT (ie not having received any benefit – see **5.38**), consider making a gift of the home conditional on surviving the testator for the maximum period ie six months from the testator's death (s 92).

Finally, it is worth mentioning another proposal that does not work. The deceased leaves assets to his son who by a variation grants a life interest for six months to the deceased's widow, remainder to the son's children absolutely. The intention is that on the deceased's death the surviving spouse exemption applies and the termination of the widow's life interest would constitute a PET.

The trap is that the variation is ineffective if the life interest terminates within two years of the deceased's death (s 142(4)). Avoid the trap by ensuring the life interest does not terminate within two years of the deceased's death.

Reversionary interests and their re-settlement

5.23   A testator may have given a life interest to his widow with remainder to his children. Where any of the children wish to assign their interests in remainder (reversion) to their own children, this can be done without CGT because a disposal of an interest in settled property is exempt where the trust continues (TCGA 1992, s 76). Note that the potential restrictions in s 76(1A) and (1B) should not apply here if the trustees have always been UK-resident and ordinarily resident. For IHT the gift of the reversion is exempt as 'excluded property'.

Once the life tenant has died it will, of course, be too late to effect this useful estate planning (although there may be limited possibilities of disclaiming the interest, and see **5.38**). If the assignor of the reversion retained an interest, eg as a discretionary beneficiary, once the reversion vests in possession, the value of the trust fund will become part of his estate again because he has reserved a benefit. As the assignment is a gift, there should be no SDLT.

The above IHT advantage is subject to an exception (see s 48(1)(b)) where the reversionary interest has previously been owned by the settlor or spouse. It is not then excluded property.

Example 5.4 – Tax on the fund

Adam settles property on his daughter, Jessica, for life, remainder to Adam's wife, Eve. Eve dies before Jessica.

On Eve's death, her reversionary interest is part of her chargeable estate. It must be valued on an actuarial basis.

CGT holdover relief is limited to transfers of business assets under TCGA 1992, s 165; and to other assets where there is a chargeable transfer for IHT under TCGA 1992, s 260, but excluding settlor-interested settlements under the anti-avoidance provisions in TCGA 1992, ss 169B–169G introduced in FA 2004. This makes any transfer that sidesteps the rules for chargeable gains much more interesting.

Avoiding the income tax surcharge under ITA 2007, ss 479 and 493 for pecuniary legatees and residuary beneficiaries

5.24   A problem arises where there is a minor beneficiary entitled to a gift contingently on attaining 18 or a later age. As the beneficiary has only a contingent interest in the income before the age of, say, 18, two main disadvantages result. First, up to the age of 18 the trustees must pay income tax on the accumulated income, in so far as it exceeds (usually) £1,000 at 50% (for 2012–13); and, secondly, there would be no possibility of repayment claims for the beneficiary, except insofar as the income is paid or applied for the beneficiary's maintenance, education or benefit.

The solution could be to give the beneficiary a vested interest in the income as soon as it arises. As a result, although he only has a contingent interest in the capital, the income will be regarded as his. The trustee will only be taxed at 20%.The trustee will issue certificates showing tax deducted at the rates appropriate for the type of income: it is 'streamed'.

Repayment claims may be made on behalf of the beneficiary, whether or not the income is de facto accumulated or paid for his maintenance, education or benefit, though there can be no recovery of tax deemed to have been paid on dividends, any more than the beneficiary could have recovered that tax as a beneficial owner.

Consider the IHT danger if the beneficiary dies before obtaining a vested interest in capital; this involves termination of an interest in possession and consequent IHT liability (which can presumably be cheaply insured against). This will not, however, be a problem if the beneficiary's interest qualifies as a trust for a bereaved minor under s 71A.

For smaller trust funds, the income tax treatment of the trust is a less serious issue, since the first £1,000 of income is exempt from the 50% rate: see ITA 2007, s 491. There have been difficulties of administration, because many trustees have failed correctly to complete returns, but it is understood that this provision, when amended, took about 114,000 trusts out of self-assessment.

The increase in trust income tax rates (apart from the first £1,000) to 50% and 42.5% from 6 April 2010 is likely to have resulted in the trustees of many discretionary trusts considering the creation of revocable interests in possession for beneficiaries (assuming that the settlement deed permits), or possibly creating sub-trusts with interests in possession for different beneficiaries, so that the trust income is taxed at lower rates. However, in most cases this strategy will probably be inappropriate for revocable appointments under a discretionary will trust within the first two years, due to the reading back effect of s 144 (see **5.6**). A modest reduction in the trust rates of tax (to 45% and 37.5%) is due to take effect from 6 April 2013.

Charity, the will and Gift Aid

Background and information

5.25   Under s 143 a gift by a legatee within two years of the death in compliance with a request by the testator is treated as if the gift had been bequeathed by the testator's will. However, in *Loveday deceased v CIR* [1997] STC (SCD) 321, SpC 0140 the trustees who complied with the testator's request could not be treated as legatees because the trustees had exercised fiduciary powers and were not beneficially entitled.

Under the Gift Aid provisions of ITA 2007, s 414 an individual or a close company is entitled to income tax relief for a donation to charity. Gifts can be made net of basic rate tax and the tax is reclaimed from HMRC by the charity. The donor will also be eligible for relief at the higher rate of tax where this applies. The relief cannot apply to gifts by the donor on death.

Example 5.5 – Precatory transfer and Gift Aid

David, in his will, gives £20,000 to a friend George but coupled with a precatory wish for George to make a similar gift to charity (ITA 2007, s 414; IHTA 1984, s 143). There is no other benefit to George under the will.

After David's death and within two years, George, who is a higher rate taxpayer, makes the gift to charity and, in his own right, claims Gift Aid.

The result hoped for is a double tax saving.

		£
IHT saving	Testator's charitable gift 40% (s 143)	8,000
First income tax saving	Beneficiary's higher rate Gift Aid relief (grossed up at appropriate basic rate): £25,000 × (40% − 20%)	5,000
Second income tax saving	Charity recovers basic rate tax on grossed-up amount: ie £20,000, grossed up at 80%, to £25,000	5,000
Total savings		18,000
	As a proportion of the original funds:	90%

See generally HMRC's guidance 'Giving to charity: individuals' on its website at www.hmrc.gov.uk/individuals/giving/index.htm. However, the full relief may not be available: see *St Dunstan's v Major* and *Harris v HMRC* referred to below.

HMRC rely on ITA 2007, ss 416, 417 (previously FA 1990, s 25(2)(e)) to argue that the requisite condition for relief is not satisfied because either the donor or any person connected with him receives a benefit in consequence of making the gift. Whilst some consider that this is an incorrect interpretation, as the benefit must surely relate to a benefit provided by the charity, rather than a separate tax relief, the Special Commissioners upheld the Revenue's view in *St Dunstan's v Major* [1997] STC (SCD) 212.

It was there held that s 25(2)(e) was not confined to benefits provided by the charity itself. Moreover when a benefit was received and the permitted limit was exceeded, the gift was disqualified as a qualifying donation, although the donor's assets would still be diminished by the excess of the donation over the benefit.

On the facts, the residue of the estate became £8,000 more than it would have been had the gift to the charity been made without taking advantage of s 142. Since the donor was the sole residuary beneficiary of the estate, he had in that case, by contrast to the example above, himself ultimately benefited from the IHT saving. Although the residue had been reduced by the amount of the legacy to the charity less the saving of IHT, the Special Commissioner held that the benefit of the IHT saving had greatly exceeded the amount of benefit permitted by s 25(2)(e). That benefit had arisen 'in consequence of making [the gift] to the charity by means of the deed of variation'.

It will be seen that no such 'benefit' should exist if, like George in the example, the beneficiary does not benefit from residue, eg a free of tax legacy; or if the IHT saving is specifically added to the charity's gift.

The principle of the *St Dunstan's* case was followed in *Harris v HMRC* [2011] WTLR 55.

Instead of using the s 143 (precatory trust) route, the legatee could achieve the same result by deed of variation under s 142, namely varying the legacy to himself to a legacy to a charity. This was the route taken in *St Dunstan's*. As the variation operates for IHT, but not for income tax, the Gift Aid advantage should apply. This is because, for purposes other than IHT, the deed of variation does not alter the deceased's will. Thus, the payment to the charity is not made under the will but is a payment of a sum of money by the legatee who has bound himself to make such payment to the charity. HMRC are, however, likely to resist the variation if there had been an arrangement/agreement between the testator and the beneficiary (contrast the precatory trust route).

Personal representatives

Charities

5.26   In an attempt to encourage charitable giving, FA 2012, s 209 introduced (with effect for deaths occurring on or after 6 April 2012) a new 36% rate of IHT on estates, provided a sufficient proportion of the estate is left to charity. The legislation appears in a new Sch 1A to IHTA 1984. While the principle of the legislation is easy to comprehend, the rules for putting that principle into effect are relatively complex.

For the purpose of the legislation, the estate is divided into three components: property that passes by survivorship (called the survivorship component); settled property that the deceased was deemed to own because he had an interest in possession in it (called the settled property component); and the other assets of the estate, excepting gifts subject to a reservation (called the general component).

The value of each component after deducting reliefs other than charity relief is referred to as the 'baseline' amount. In each case, if at least 10% of the baseline amount is given to charity, the 36% rate of tax is applied to the remainder.

Although the test is applied separately to each component, there is the option to elect to merge different components. If the amount given to charity of one component is greater than the amount necessary to qualify for relief, merging that component with another component might enable the other component also to qualify for the lower rate of tax. For this purpose, all property that is (in relation to the deceased) property subject to a reservation is treated as a fourth component which can be merged with any of the other three.

The ability to merge different components will present a practical problem if there are more than two components to the estate. It is yet to be seen how an executor or trustee of a component with 'surplus' charity relief should go about deciding which other component to merge with. Circumstances where this is a consideration will be rare, however.

It is possible to opt out of the lower rate of tax. Doing so will probably be rare. It might be a sensible thing to do if the assets passing to charity are hard to value, and the benefit of the relief is modest in the circumstances. Opting out of the reduced rate would avoid the need to agree a value of the assets in question with HMRC.

Elections should be made: by those taking under survivorship (survivorship component); by the trustees (settled property component); by the PRs (general component); or by the persons in whom the property subject to a reservation is vested (for the purpose of electing to merge such property with another component of the estate). Elections should be made within two years of death and may be withdrawn up to two years and one month from the date of death.

Anyone wishing to take advantage of this reduced rate of tax should consider consulting a competent draftsperson to assist with the preparation of a will. Model will clauses ensure the reduced rate will apply by incorporating into the will a legacy the quantum of which is determined in a formulaic way, incorporating definitions from the relevant legislation. HMRC devote a whole chapter of their guidance (IHTM45000 onwards) to the reduced rate of IHT for charitable gifts, which includes an example of a will clause that HMRC accept will always ensure that a specific legacy to charity meets the 10% test (IHTM45008).

The advantage of the lower rate of tax is also available to an estate that would not otherwise qualify if, post-death, the will is varied (in a manner complying with s 142) so as to leave a sufficient amount to charity. Similarly, if the estate is left wholly or partly on discretionary trusts, the lower rate of tax will be available if a sufficient gift is made to charity in circumstances where s 144 applies. Note, however, that neither of these possibilities can apply to the settled property component; and, if trustees wish to take advantage of the lower rate, they will need to take steps to achieve this prior to the death of their life tenant.

If the minimum necessary payment to charity is made to qualify for the relief, the effect of the lower rate of tax is that the non-charitable beneficiaries lose out by very little compared to the position if no charitable gift had been made. The 'cost' to the non-charitable beneficiaries of including a charitable gift that is just large enough to meet the '10% test' is only 24% of the value of the charitable gift. In other words, tax relief at 76% is given on the amount of the charitable gift.

The situation becomes more interesting if, for example, the estate passes partly to charity, but without quite qualifying for the lower rate of IHT. In such circumstances, the non-charitable beneficiaries should consider taking steps to increase the charitable gift with retrospective effect (by taking advantage of the provisions of s 142 and/or s 144 if possible) so the estate will pass the 10% threshold. After taking into account the reduced IHT burden, the non-charitable beneficiaries will actually receive an increased amount. This course of action is worth considering in any case where the existing charitable disposition exceeds 4% of the baseline amount of any particular component.

Example 5.6 – A better outcome

Mary dies in October 2012 leaving an estate of £525,000. Against this is set the nil rate band of £325,000. Mary has left a legacy of £10,000 to charity and the remainder of her estate to her daughter Elizabeth.

If Elizabeth does nothing, there will be inheritance tax due at 40% on £190,000. After deducting IHT of £76,000, Elizabeth will be left with £439,000.

Suppose Elizabeth varies the disposition of the estate so as to leave an additional £10,000 to charity. The IHT due is reduced to £64,800 (36% of £180,000). Elizabeth is left with £440,200, ie making the deed of variation has left her £1,200 better off.

The situation becomes more complicated when there is more than one component. Bear in mind that, if the charity relief applicable to any one component changes, the allocation of the nil rate band allowance will change also.

Example 5.7 – Two components: Calculating the charitable legacy

The facts are as in Example 5.6, except that Mary's £525,000 estate includes a half share of an investment property worth £103,000, which passes by survivorship to her brother. The nil rate band is allocated rateably.

	Survivorship component (£)	*General component (£)*	*Total (£)*
Value	103,000	422,000	525,000
Gift to charity		(10,000)	(10,000)
Value after reliefs	103,000	412,000	515,000
NRB	(65,000)	(260,000)	(325,000)
Add back charity gift		10,000	
Baseline amount	38,000	162,000	200,000

Elizabeth wants to execute a deed of variation giving just enough extra cash to charity so that the general component will be taxed at 36%. Since the baseline amount of the general component is £162,000 and the general component already includes a charitable gift of £10,000, it might be thought that Elizabeth needs to increase the charitable gift by £6,200 to achieve her objective; but in fact that would be too little. After a little trial and error, the amount she needs to give away can be calculated as £6,282 or thereabouts. This can be proved as follows:

	Survivorship component (£)	General component (£)	Total (£)
Value	103,000	422,000	525,000
Gift to charity		(16,282)	(16,282)
Value after reliefs	103,000	405,718	508,718
NRB	(65,000)	(259,197)	(325,000)
Add back charity gift		16,282	16,282
Baseline amount	37,197	162,803	200,000

A 'side-effect' of Elizabeth increasing the charitable legacy referable to the general component is that the survivorship component benefits from an increased share of the available nil rate band allowance. The tax payable by Mary's brother is reduced by £321 (ie 40% of £803).

In determining whether the lower rate of tax is due, business and agricultural property relief are deducted from the value of the estate for the purpose of calculating the baseline amount. However, business and agricultural assets are included at their full value for the purpose of determining whether a charitable gift that consists of or includes such property has a value not less than 10% of the baseline amount.

Conditional exemption for heritage assets, woodlands relief, and the exemption from IHT on property entering a maintenance fund for historic buildings and the like, are all tax deferral reliefs rather than outright reliefs. Nevertheless, such reliefs are taken into consideration for the purpose of calculating the baseline amount. If the amount subject to relief subsequently falls into charge to IHT, the charge applicable at that time, however, is the full (40%) rate, not the 36% rate.

Potentially difficult and time-consuming calculations may be necessitated where the will includes legacies that are given 'free of IHT'. Such legacies need to be grossed up by the appropriate rate of tax to determine their quantum. In some cases, it is possible that, if the gifts were grossed up at 40%, the conditions for the lower rate of tax to apply would not be met but that, if grossed up at 36%, the conditions would be met. Accordingly, Sch 1A, para 6(1) provides that the calculation is to be carried out assuming that the 36% rate will apply.

Example 5.8 – Grossing up at 36%

Bill died leaving an estate of £525,000. He left chargeable legacies totalling £440,000 free of tax and the remainder to charity. He had made no lifetime gifts.

The baseline amount is £200,000 (ie £525,000 – £325,000).

After deducting the £325,000 nil rate band from the value of the legacies, £115,000 must be grossed up by the applicable rate of IHT to calculate the value of the legacies before tax.

If a rate of 36% is used, the value of the legacies before tax is £504,688. The charitable legacy is therefore £20,312. This is a little more than 10% of the baseline amount, so the lower rate of tax is due.

If a rate of 40% had been used, the value of the legacies before tax would be £516,667. The charitable legacy would be just £8,333, which would be less than 10% of the baseline amount. Without Sch 1A, para 6(1), it would be impossible to decide which rate ought to apply.

HMRC's website helpfully includes calculators to gross up legacies at the 36% reduced rate (www.hmrc.gov.uk/cto/g_up36.pdf) and the 40% full rate (www. hmrc.gov.uk/cto/g_up.pdf) where the estate is partially exempt from IHT and there are free of tax legacies; the calculators are suitable for use in most (but not all) such circumstances.See **5.32** as to the requirement for charities etc to be notified of the existence of instruments of variation in their favour.

Residence

5.27 The residence, ordinary residence and domicile of personal representatives follow that of the deceased for CGT purposes (TCGA 1992, s 62(3)). Therefore if the deceased was non-resident, and assets of the estate increase sharply after death, or if the administration lasts a long time and gains accrue, the executors should sell the assets, ie free of CGT (TCGA 1992, s 2) and distribute the proceeds of sale to the beneficiaries.

By contrast, if the assets have fallen in value following the death, the executors should appropriate the assets *in specie* to the beneficiaries so that, on a sale, the beneficiaries can incur a CGT loss.

Disposal of an interest in an estate before completion of the administration

5.28   During this period (ie during the administration), the residuary legatee merely has the right to require the personal representatives to administer the estate in accordance with the terms of the will. That right is a chose in action (see CG30760), which, it appears, has no base value for CGT (*Marshall v Kerr* [1994] STC 638).

A residuary legatee should therefore wait for the personal representatives to complete the administration, or until they assent the asset to him. That assent is exempt from CGT, but with the advantage of the testator's date of death market value uplift (TCGA 1992, s 62(4)). If the legatee disposes of the asset as a *chose* in action, he is likely to incur a substantial CGT liability unnecessarily (although, if done within two years of death, it may be possible to avoid this by means of a variation to which TCGA 1992, s 62(6) applies). If he waits for the asset to be vested in him, he will be treated as acquiring it at the value agreed with HMRC as at the date of death.

Bare will trusts for minors

5.29   The following points should be considered in relation to bare will trusts for minors.

Income

5.30   The problem identified at **5.24** arises whenever a minor beneficiary is entitled to a gift contingently on attaining 18 or a later age. The solution is again to give the beneficiary a vested interest in the income as soon as it arises, ie on the testator's death.

It has to be recognised that, in theory at least, the beneficiary of a bare trust can at any time direct the trustee how to invest the fund and to pay all income out to him or her, provided that he knows that the fund exists. There are, no doubt, many conspiracies of silence in this area.

Capital

5.31   The bare trust could also extend to entitlement to capital from the testator's death. This would avoid any CGT on the beneficiary satisfying a contingency (eg attaining a specific age). Moreover, any disposals by the bare trustees prior to the beneficiary attaining age 18 will be at the beneficiary's CGT rate, although the rate of CGT for individuals and trustees is currently the same (ie 28% for 2012–13).

The income tax anti-avoidance rules that treat gifts to children as settlor-interested do not apply in this situation because the settlor/testator is dead. Clearly such bare trusts may not be popular with the client testator, as the beneficiary can demand the income, and normally also the capital (see above) at the tender age of 18.

Bare trusts have probably become more popular since the demise of accumulation and maintenance trusts following FA 2006. Apart from the bereaved minor's trust established under s 71A and qualifying trusts for the disabled, all ongoing trusts for children that aim to preserve the capital beyond the age of 18 can incur IHT charges under the regime for discretionary trusts. However, s 43(2), to which the practitioner should refer, defines 'settlement' in such terms that a bare trust is excluded.

VARIATIONS AND DISCLAIMERS – POST-DEATH PLANNING (S 142)

Variations and disclaimers – General

5.32   From the taxpayer's point of view s 142 has been, and continues to be, one of the most useful and popular sections in the IHT legislation, because it allows a two-year breathing space in which to rewrite the provisions of the deceased's will or the passing of property on intestacy. It is indeed useful, but it needs approaching with care. There are hidden snags. The threat of anti-avoidance legislation to be introduced in future Finance Acts has been a staple diet of the media pundits in the run-up to virtually every recent Budget.

This section operates where:

- within a period of two years after the individual's death;

- the destination of any of the assets of his estate (excluding assets charged under the reservation of benefit rules);

- passing by will, intestacy or 'otherwise';

- is varied/altered or the benefits disclaimed by an instrument in writing made by one or more of the original beneficiary(ies); and

- the instrument of variation (IOV) contains a 'statement' that the IOV is to apply for IHT (ie for variations (but not disclaimers) from 1 August 2002).

HMRC have no discretion to extend the two-year period. The section has effect, for IHT and for certain aspects of CGT, as if the variation had been effected by the deceased or, as the case may be, the disclaimed benefit had never been conferred.

If the variation is in favour of a charity, it is only effective, with effect for deaths occurring on or after 6 April 2012, if it is shown that the relevant charity is aware of the variation (s 142(3A)). It is not clear whether the charity needs to be notified within two years of the death, but prudence dictates that it should be.

The 'instrument' is usually effected by way of a deed. This is not essential, but it is helpful as it ensures that the variation is binding as between the original beneficiary and the donee. The IOV must clearly indicate the dispositions that are the subject of it, and vary their destination as laid down by the deceased's will, or under the law relating to intestate estates. Under s 142(6), a variation can apply even though the administration of the estate has been completed and the assets advanced to the beneficiary in accordance with the original dispositions. A variation must not be for a consideration in money or money's worth (unless the consideration is another variation or disclaimer). Therefore, the original beneficiary effecting the variation must not, for example, be paid costs or reimbursed income tax liabilities or have mortgage or other liabilities paid.

If the variation changes the amount of IHT payable, either in the estate of the deceased or in the estate of someone else, the beneficiaries making the variation should send a copy of the variation to HMRC. Note that if the variation results in an additional amount of IHT or CGT being due, the executors or personal representatives must make the statement. They may decline to do so if there are insufficient assets in the estate to cover the extra IHT (s 142(2A)). The personal representatives *must*, within six months, notify HMRC of the amount of any additional IHT payable and send a copy of the variation to them. Practitioners should refer to the useful HMRC IOV checklist IOV2 and HMRC's Customer Guide to Inheritance Tax, which includes 'Can I alter an inheritance following a death?' (www.hmrc.gov.uk/cto/customerguide/page21.htm).

HMRC become very suspicious where an estate is varied so that a chargeable legacy to a child is varied in favour of its mother, the surviving spouse, and so becomes exempt for IHT, whereupon the mother makes a PET to the child. See *Re: Lau* [2009] WTLR 627 where, admittedly, the variation and gift was badly handled on behalf of the taxpayer.

Multiple variations

5.33   There have been some cases in which a number of IOVs have been executed in relation to the same will or intestacy. Whilst HMRC (and their predecessors) emphasise that these cases must be considered on their precise facts, in broad terms their views will be as follows:

'(i)   an election which is validly made is irrevocable;

(ii) an instrument will not fall within s 142 if it further redirects any item or any part of an item that has already been redirected under an earlier instrument; and

(iii) to avoid any uncertainty, variations covering a number of items should ideally be made in one instrument.'

(*Law Society Gazette*, 22 May 1985, p 1454)

Following the decision in *Russell v IRC* [1988] STC 195, beware of trying to take two bites of the cherry. The case decided that, once a deed of variation had been entered into, a further purported redirection to be treated as made by the deceased was not valid in respect of the assets in question; namely, further redirections did not have this retrospective effect.

Changes to an IOV

5.34 Contrast the situation of a further redirection of assets with the decision in *Lake v Lake* [1989] STC 865. The court was completely satisfied that the common intention of the parties, when executing the first deed of variation, had been that the assets specifically bequeathed should bear their own tax. However that deed referred to bequests being 'free of tax', so the court ordered rectification of the first deed.

Reference should also be made to *Matthews v Martin* ChD [1991] STC 8048, where it was discovered that a deed of variation contained errors, but the discovery was not made until after the two-year period. The Revenue took the view that a deed of rectification would not be effective, since the corrections would take effect only from the date of rectification. However, rectification by an order of the court would mean the original deed was varied as from the original execution date. The High Court approved, and the application to vary the original deed was accepted and the order made.

In *Schneider v Mills* [1993] STC 430, rectification was granted of a nonsensical clause whereby the intermediate income, as clearly intended, covered only the period from death to the date of the deed of variation, not for an indefinite period. See also *Racal Group Services Ltd v Ashmore* [1994] STC 416, *Wolff and another v Wolff and others* [2004] STC 1633 and *Allnutt & another v Wilding & others* [2007] EWCA Civ 412 on rectification and its limitations.

Glowacki (deceased) v HMRC [2008] STC (SCD) 188 concerned an IOV which purported to deem a gift of a house to have been made immediately before death; but if the deed did not have the intended effect, the variation was to have no effect, giving the family a second chance of a variation by avoiding the *Russell* rule noted above. HMRC determined that the effect of the deed was to set the available nil rate band against the value of the house in priority to the gift in the will of the nil rate band. The personal representatives appealed, arguing that s 17(a), which provides that a qualifying deed of variation is not a transfer of value, had the effect of taking the house out of the estate before death, so value of £230,000 could still pass under the gift of the nil rate band.

It was held that ss 4 and 17 did not work that way. Section 142 could not remove property from the estate to take it outside s 4. Any variation under s 142 only affected the dispositions on death. The variation therefore failed to achieve its intention. However, HMRC had gone too far in deciding the effect of the deed and in taxing accordingly. They should have decided whether s 142 could be used in the way attempted; and should then have decided whether the deed remained in force as a result. If it did not, they need take matters no further; so part of the determination was quashed.

In *Wills v Gibbs & others*, ChD [2008] STC 808, a variation of the deceased's will was intended to take effect under s 142(1). However, the deed did not contain such a statement, as required by s 142(2). A similar declaration was required for CGT purposes by TCGA 1992, s 62(7), but was not included in the deed of variation. The claimant successfully applied to the court for rectification (the application was not opposed by the defendants). The claimant had not included the relevant statements in the deed because he did not know that they were required in relation to IHT and CGT. The solicitor who drafted the deed had omitted the statements by mistake. The court recognised that the rectification would resolve both fiscal and non-fiscal issues, and therefore rectified the deed.

Example 5.9 – A 'two-bite' situation in practice

(a) Execute a s 142 variation of certain assets into a s 144 two-year discretionary trust.

(b) The assets can then be redirected out of the discretionary trust without further IHT within the two-year period (or up to ten years if the assets are within the nil rate band).

The uses of a variation

5.35   An IOV can cover a wide range of circumstances including:

- divesting assets from a wealthy individual to the next generation;

- a life tenant releasing his interest in one part of the capital to the remainderman, and the remainderman releasing the other part to the life tenant absolutely;

- a redirection of the beneficial interest under a will (eg a widow might renounce a life interest);

- converting 'tax free' legacies into 'subject to tax' legacies adjusted appropriately etc;

- varying the powers of executors, administrators and particularly trustees; and

- correcting defects in a will.

Example 5.10 – IOV and transferable nil rate band

Hugh was married to Jean, who had previously been married to Ken. Ken had died several years ago, leaving all his estate to Jean. On his death in June 2012, having made no chargeable lifetime transfers, Hugh left his estate to Jean for life with remainder to his nephew Lee.

Jean, who has herself made no chargeable transfers, is elderly, lives modestly and is well advised. She realises that her executors will have the benefit of only one transferable nil rate band and that, in effect, the transferable band of either Ken or Hugh will be thrown away. Jean therefore executes an IOV in respect of Hugh's estate, giving an amount equal to the nil rate band to Lee.

Example 5.11 – Variation to remove survivorship condition

Jim practised as a tax adviser. To protect his assets, he and his wife Sally owned their house, worth £600,000, as tenants in common in the proportions Sally 90% and Jim 10%. Their other assets were negligible.

Sally made a will leaving residue to Jim, subject to the usual 28-day clause, with gift over to their daughter Monica. Sadly, both Sally and Jim died in that order in quick succession (but not *commorientes*) in February 2013.

Sally's estate of £540,000 passes to Monica. After the nil rate band of £325,000, the balance of £215,000 attracts IHT at 40%. Jim's estate is only £60,000, so passes to Monica free of tax. The will could have been better drawn.

Could Monica vary Sally's will to remove the 28-day clause, so that Jim's estate on death becomes £600,000 and his executor can claim 200% of the nil rate band, enough to shelter the whole inheritance?

The position is unclear. The variation has not really altered the distribution of the estate within s 142, but merely ensured that it reaches Monica in a more tax-efficient manner. HMRC's guidance (at IHTM35025) states that the destination of the property must be varied. Furthermore, in *Parker's Modern Will Precedents* (Bloomsbury Professional, 7th edition), Michael Waterworth states:

'Both Inheritance Tax Act 1984 s 142(1) and Taxation of Chargeable Gains Act 1992 s 62(6) refer to variations of "dispositions" and it is believed that HMRC is not prepared to accept a Deed of Variation which merely introduces new or additional administrative powers and provisions without altering the disposition of property.'

On that basis, a possible alternative to simply varying Sally's will to remove the 28-day clause might be for her also to vary the destination of her estate so as to create an immediate post-death interest for Jim.

Example 5.12 – Variations and appreciating assets

Suppose that an estate has risen sharply in value since death, as was possible with real property until the recession. The increase might take an individual asset above the nil rate band. The surviving spouse or civil partner might be able to manage without the asset. An IOV can redirect that asset as at the date of death, but effectively redirect the greater value.

The same result can be achieved where the will contains a power for the executors to appropriate an asset at the value that it had at date of death, effectively freezing its value during the administration period and avoiding the rule in *Robinson v Collins* [1975] 1 All ER 321, that appropriation is at current market value, not at probate value.

As to appropriations generally, note that the STEP Standard Provisions (2nd edition) (wider form) admit the possibility of appropriation at probate value. This can facilitate the redirection of greater value noted above.

Example 5.13 – Variations, CGT and income tax

Melanie's estate at the time of her death in August 2010, was worth £400,000 and had been left entirely to her civil partner Nora. Nora was otherwise well provided for. Shares in Melanie's estate rose to such an extent that by March 2012 the (as yet unadministered) estate was worth £600,000.

Nora was content to inherit only £350,000, so executed an IOV that gave her that sum, with residue passing to friends. The £350,000 is exempt as passing to a civil partner, leaving chargeable estate, on probate values, of £50,000. However, the friends will actually get more value than that, with the benefit of the rise in values, free of IHT.

There are two problems for the friends: CGT and market risk. They cannot realise their enhanced inheritance without triggering a liability to CGT, either in the hands of the executors or, following appropriation to them *in specie*, in their own names; but volatility in share prices may encourage them to pay the tax rather than risk losing the rise.

As a separate issue, income tax must be dealt with. No IOV redirects the liability to income tax, so Nora is liable to that tax on income distributed up to the date of the IOV. However, this only applies to income actually paid to the donor of the variation, not to income retained by the executors and paid to the new beneficiaries under the terms of the variation. Residuary beneficiaries are only taxed on a receipts basis (ITTOIA 2005, s 662). Therefore, it should be possible to make a variation retrospective for income tax purposes as well as IHT and CGT, though only to the extent it has not already been distributed to the original beneficiary.

Example 5.14 – Combining the previous idea with a transfer to children

Where a testator has made gifts in excess of the nil rate band to chargeable parties (eg children), these chargeable parties may redirect/vary the will in favour of the surviving spouse, who might subsequently make appropriate PETs.

HMRC routinely challenge, or at least probe, such an arrangement, not so much under the *Ramsay* doctrine or s 268, as on the basis that the variation is for a consideration in money's worth (s 142(3); see **5.42**). In the latter case, the children would have made a PET gift to mother, and mother's transfer would presumably not be a chargeable gift because made without donative intent under a binding obligation; see **5.32**.

Example 5.15 – Extending 'the excluded property' benefit of s 48(3) beyond a single generation where the testator is non-domiciled

Assume that all the assets of an estate are situated outside the UK, but that the beneficiary is, or is deemed to be, domiciled here. The beneficiary varies the will so that the assets go into a discretionary trust in which the individual can be a beneficiary, because the assets are excluded property.

Result: assets remain excluded property beyond beneficiary's death. No ten-year or exit charges should apply as excluded property.

However, as with all foreign structures, extreme care should be taken: in particular note the anti-avoidance provisions of s 80(4) (Initial interest of settlor or spouse (or civil partner)).

Note, in relation to the last example, that the House of Lords decided that it is the *beneficiary* (not the testator) who is treated for CGT purposes as the settlor;

see *Marshall v Kerr* [1994] STC 638, HL. The identification of the settlor for CGT purposes was subsequently given legislative effect by changes introduced in FA 2006 (TCGA 1992, s 68C).

The Revenue (as was) confirmed their view following *Marshall v Kerr* that the decision in that case has no application to IHT. Variations which meet all the requirements of s 142 will continue to be treated for IHT purposes as having been made by the deceased (RI 101 (February 1995)).

For income tax, there is no saving: income is assessable on the UK beneficiary; see ITA 2007, s 721 ('Individuals with power to enjoy income as a result of relevant transactions').

Capital gains tax

5.36   There is a similar power (although somewhat more restricted) to alter dispositions on death for CGT purposes (TCGA 1992, s 62(6)). Such a CGT variation is usually made unless there are assets with losses; where it is wished to use up the small gains exemption; where non-residents are involved; or where the principal residence has risen in value since death. Consider the effect of *Marshall v Kerr*, as just noted at **5.35**.

Whether to include a statement in the instrument of variation

5.37   A separate statement must be included in the instrument of variation that it is intended to apply for CGT purposes (TCGA 1992, s 62(7)). In some cases it can be appropriate for IHT purposes not to vary.

The effect of not varying for IHT is that the beneficiary making the variation is then himself making a transfer of value. This may involve a nil or lower lifetime IHT charge than if the deceased had done this and, as the law stands, after seven years the gift will not be included in the beneficiary's cumulative total.

Where the relationship between the testator and the beneficiary is not an exempt one (eg parent to child), a statement should be included in the variation instrument; otherwise, there may be a double charge, ie once in the testator's estate and again on the transfer by the beneficiary effecting the variation outside s 142, ie as a gift by the beneficiary.

Contrast the situation where there is an exempt disposition by a deceased (eg to his widow). If the widow's cumulative rate of IHT is lower (and bearing in mind that her gift can be a PET or chargeable at one half of the death rate), it will normally be better not to vary for IHT purposes. Instead, let the gift be taxed at her rate and not the deceased's; except where it is wished to use up the deceased's nil rate band.

As to CGT, a statement should normally be included because of the CGT death exemption and market value uplift.

If the statement is *not* made, the IHT treatment is that of a normal transfer of value; for CGT, the variation is a disposal.

Variations and disclaimers contrasted

5.38   The following distinctions should be borne in mind:

- In the case of a variation, the beneficiary redirects the destination of the disposition as he chooses. In the case of a disclaimer he has no choice and his disclaimer merely accelerates the subsequent interests, eg a disclaimed legacy may fall into residue. To overcome this negative character of disclaimers, the will could provide that in the event of any beneficiary disclaiming an interest, the disclaimed asset should fall into a suitable receptacle such as a flexible life interest trust with wide powers of appointment and advancement or a discretionary trust, rather than merely passing to the person entitled in lieu.

- HMRC appear to take the view that as a matter of English law, a partial disclaimer is not possible and that the whole of the interest in settled property (under s 93) must be disclaimed (IHTM16180). The same applies to a disclaimer under a will or intestacy in HMRC's view (IHTM35161).

- However, it was reported (in *Tolley's Practical Tax* Vol 10, No 13, 28 June 1989 at p 102) that Bircham & Co had written to the Capital Taxes Office (as it then was), putting the view that, where the will showed an intention on the part of the testator that a donee should be free to disclaim part only of a single gift, then he could do so, and citing *Guthrie v Walrond* (1883) 22 Ch D 573. The Capital Taxes Office replied that a disclaimer was a matter of general law.

On the footing that *Guthrie* represented good law, s 142 should apply to a partial disclaimer. In reporting this correspondence, Bircham & Co made an additional point; that partial disclaimer may not be confined to cases where the will serves to authorise it. In cases before the courts donees had frequently sought to disclaim the burdensome part of a gift and keep the beneficial part, and it was not surprising that the courts had found a testamentary intention against this; but if the part subject to disclaimer was not burdensome, and was readily severable, it might be that disclaimer could take place. Support for this view came from the opinion stated by Lord Justice Maugham in *Dewar v IRC* [1935] 2 KB 351 at 370–371, that it would always be possible to disclaim part of a cash legacy.

However, as indicated above, it should be noted that HMRC do not accept that such partial disclaimers are possible under English law, although it is possible to accept one gift in a will and disclaim another. In addition, in relation to disclaimers under s 93, HMRC state (at IHTM16180): 'At English law a partial disclaimer is not possible so that the whole of the interest must be disclaimed *(this however is subject to the terms of the trust)*' (emphasis added).

HMRC accept that partial disclaimers of residue are possible under Scots law (Statement of Practice E18).

Example 5.16 – Putting the testator's intentions of permitting and approving part disclaimers beyond any doubt

A suitable clause for inclusion in the will could be as follows:

'I [the testator] HEREBY DECLARE that any gift or other benefit made under or in pursuance of this my Will or any codicil thereto may be disclaimed as to any part of such gift or benefit or as to the whole thereof. I accordingly authorise:

(a)   any person benefiting under this my Will or any codicil thereto; and

(b)   my executors and trustees and any person acting in pursuance of their authority

to deal with and administer my estate in respect of any such (partial or full) disclaimer as hereby authorised.

In furtherance of this authorisation (but not otherwise) all gifts of money or share or shares of residue shall be deemed at any relevant time to be gifts of money in separate denominations of £1 each for the purpose of enabling any relevant beneficiary of this my Will or any codicil thereto to disclaim separate parts divisible in £1 units.'

5.39   With a variation, it makes no difference that the beneficiary may earlier have received some benefit. In the case of a disclaimer, however, it is a condition that before the disclaimer he has received no benefit, although HMRC accept that it may be permissible to accept one gift and disclaim another (IHTM35161). Consider in this connection the use of the survivor provisions in s 92, eg to enable a surviving spouse to disclaim his or her interest in a home effectively for IHT (ie not having received any interim benefit), the gift of the home could be conditional on surviving the testator for the maximum period of six months within the section.

A variation can benefit anyone, not merely another beneficiary or a member of the family. In the case of a minor beneficiary his interest cannot be reduced without the court's consent.

This gives rise to a fine point of will drafting. Where the testator gives a life interest, eg to spouse, the remaindermen should arguably be restricted to the testator's issue *per stirpes* living at his death and not at the death of the life tenant. If the class is left open until the second death, a variation of the testator's will by the remaindermen would be extremely difficult because of the contingent entitlement of future born issue.

5.40   Personal representatives can stand in the shoes of a deceased beneficiary who dies within two years of the testator's death (see RI101 (February 1995)). Within two years, a recipient of the variation can himself effect a further variation if the original beneficiary elected (although HMRC may try to challenge on the basis of multiple variation; see above).

Excluded property etc

5.41   Section 142 applies to excluded property, but not to settled property in which the deceased had a beneficial entitlement to an interest in possession (s 142(5)). Newly granted interests in possession under the will can be disclaimed or assigned. Joint tenancies can be the subject matter of a variation (but not a disclaimer) because the relevant assets are comprised in the deceased's estate (contrast the former requirement of being competent to dispose).

As joint tenancies cannot be disclaimed (*Re Schär, Midland Bank Executor and Trustee Co Ltd v Darner* [1951] Ch 280), appropriate assets held jointly, eg property, valuable chattels, should be severed into tenancies in common. Joint tenancies can, however, be an asset subject to a variation. In the appropriate variation, the joint tenancy should be severed so as to be in a better position to claim a valuation discount (of, say, between 10% and 15%) and thereby increasing the assets within the nil rate band.

No consideration

5.42   A variation or disclaimer must not be for a consideration in money or money's worth, unless the consideration is another variation or disclaimer (ss 93, 142(3)).

For example, the beneficiary effecting the variation must not be paid their costs or reimbursed income tax liabilities or have mortgages or other liabilities paid off.

HMRC are alive to this potential restriction. In *Mrs M Lau (W Lau's Executor) v HMRC* SpC, [2009] WTLR 627, the deceased left legacies of £655,000 each to his stepson (H) and two daughters, free of IHT. The widow (L) was residuary beneficiary under the will. In March 2005, H disclaimed his legacy. In October 2005, L received the residue of the estate (including the disclaimed legacy), and transferred £1 million to H. HMRC determined that H's disclaimer was not effective because it was made for consideration in money or money's worth, within s 142(3). The Special Commissioner dismissed the executor's appeal, and held on the evidence that there was a direct causal link between H's disclaimer of his legacy and the £1 million payment. The disclaimer in this case did not meet the legal requirements of s 142(1) in any event as it was not in writing (L's solicitors were holding it as undelivered).

Gifts with reservation

5.43　Where a testator has died and a beneficiary of the estate effects a variation, eg by varying an outright gift to the beneficiary into a discretionary trust, the fact that the beneficiary is capable of benefiting from the varied gift (eg by being included as a discretionary object) should not constitute a reservation of benefit by the beneficiary. This is because, for IHT purposes, it is the deceased who is deemed to have created the varied gift (eg the discretionary trust). Therefore the reservation of benefit rules (in FA 1986, s 102, Sch 20) do not apply. Contrast this with the situation where the deceased had retained a reservation of benefit. A variation cannot 'cure' this.

An income tax charge on pre-owned assets is precluded where the benefit arises from an instrument of variation. The disposition is effectively ignored for pre-owned asset tax purposes (FA 2004, Sch 15, para 16).

Deeds of variation, s 142 and business/agricultural property relief

5.44　Consider instruments of variation passing down these assets to non-spouses, eg children, grandchildren, or discretionary trusts, rather than to a surviving spouse.

There should be no particular problem in the surviving spouse being a beneficiary of the discretionary trust class.

Re-direction of a beneficial interest under a will

5.45　Consider circumstances where:

(a)   a widow might renounce or assign a life interest granted to her; or

(b)   the executor/trustees might revoke such a life interest by flexible powers in the will.

Under alternative (a), this could be effected by a s 142 variation. Under alternative (b), the arrangement would constitute a PET of the widow's interest, ie the s 142 procedure is not adopted.

Section 142 used to apply even if the widow had died in the two-year period. However, the official view is that the variation must take place in the 'real world'. This approach received some approval in the Special Commissioner's decision in *Soutter's Executory v IRC* [2002] STC (SCD) 385 where Scottish law applied. In essence, the decision was to the effect that once a life interest has ceased with the life tenant's death, s 142 cannot be applied. The case has been criticised because, although logical, s 142 is in essence a deeming provision and retrospective to the testator's, ie the first, death. There is no case under English law to challenge or to affirm the *Soutter* principle.

HMRC's underlying argument is that a variation is a lifetime gift by the original beneficiary. A deceased person cannot make a lifetime gift.

What is not always appreciated is that s 142 can only rearrange interests under a trust created under the will in question, eg not under a lifetime trust.

Income tax

5.46   The power to vary the destination of the estate operates for IHT and CGT only, and not for income tax. In particular, if an adult gives up his share of the estate in favour of his minor unmarried children, he will be regarded as the settlor for income tax purposes (ITTOIA 2005, s 629). The income from that share would be treated as the settlor's, even if accumulated during the unmarried minority of those children. That could have been avoided if the will had contained flexible powers to benefit the children.

Contrast the effect of court orders made under the Inheritance (Provision for Family and Dependants) Act 1975 ('I(PFD)A 1975'), which *are* retrospective to the date of death even for income tax purposes, unlike s 142 deeds of variation. In addition, a court order under I(PFD)A 1975 takes effect for tax purposes even though the normal two-year time limit for variations and disclaimers has passed (see s 146, and I(PFD)A 1975, s 19(1).

Although of great value, therefore, in allowing second thoughts within the two-year period, s 142 is no substitute for regularly reviewing the terms of the will in the light of its relevance to all the circumstances during the lifetime of the testator. For example, an individual with minor children may want to persuade his parent(s) to leave the share direct to the minors (ie to have a grandparent's rather than a parent's trust).

Moreover, any income due to the beneficiary (whether received or not) up to the date of the variation will be that beneficiary's income. Where a deed of variation is to be executed in favour of a charity, it should be done as soon as possible after the death. This is because the charity, unlike the original beneficiary, will be exempt from income tax (see ITA 2007, ss 524–537 and CTA 2010, ss 478–489).

Stamp duty and stamp duty land tax

5.47   Variations are exempt from stamp duty and adjudication requirements, provided the appropriate certificate is given under the Stamp Duty (Exempt Instruments) Regulations 1987 (SI 1987/516) (see Sch, Category M). Disclaimers are also exempt from stamp duty.

For stamp duty land tax purposes, variations are similarly exempt from charge if made within two years of death, and if there is no consideration other than the making of the variation (FA 2003, Sch 3, para 4).

Tax planning and summary

5.48   In considering the effect of the variation, consider the following issues.

- Take account of the identity of property and the needs of various beneficiaries. For example, a widow is likely to need to own the dwellinghouse and liquid assets, but may not need illiquid assets such as shares in the family company.

- Look at the incidence of IHT in particular as to whether to elect or not, the effect of the seven-year cumulation provisions and lifetime as opposed to death rates if there is no election, plus opportunities available for lifetime PETs. If the original gift is to a chargeable party (eg a child of deceased) do elect, because no extra IHT is involved. If extra IHT is involved consider the likely interest charge.

- Consider allocating property entitled to business or agricultural reliefs to non-exempt beneficiaries. Try to allocate appreciating assets to younger individuals and depreciating assets to older individuals.

- Consider the cost involved including additional IHT (and interest thereon), and income tax.

- Bear in mind that a deed of variation or disclaimer is not a substitute for IHT lifetime planning, particularly in the current voluntary PET era which could always be removed in the future by the present or a future government.

Note also the possibility of future restrictions on variations and similar arrangements by amending legislation by a government in the future, though this does at the moment seem to be off the agenda.

GENERAL SUMMARY

5.49   This chapter shows how much can be achieved to preserve estates by the careful preparation of the will (including provision for disclaimers), by taking steps on variation of the will if need be, and how to prepare for the possible closing of that door.

There is a need in current circumstances to prepare wills with the utmost flexibility, and still review them on a regular basis to keep them in maximum effectiveness, thereby averting the need for variations and disclaimers.

A note on intestacy

5.50   The Law Reform (Succession) Act 1995 provides that:

- If the widow(er) does not survive the intestate by 28 days, the intestacy rules apply as if such widow(er) had not survived the intestate: LR(S)A 1995, s 1(1), (3). This will result in the widow(er)'s family not benefiting directly and also ensuring that the intestate's estate benefits from the IHT nil rate band, as well as the widow(er)'s.

- The same rule applies, with effect from 5 December 2005, to civil partners.

The same Act robbed lawyers of another term, of which they were fond, 'hotchpot'. Before 1 January 1996, issue entitled on an intestacy or partial intestacy under a will had to bring into account lifetime gifts from the intestate and would receive less as a result. This was known as 'bringing into hotchpot'. By LR(S)A 1995, s 1(2) this requirement was withdrawn.

Note, in relation to intestacy and claims against an estate under I(PFD)A 1975, the work of the Law Commission in its paper No 191: none of the proposals is yet law but some of them are controversial and practitioners should be aware of them (see **4.10**).

APPENDIX 5.1 – INSTRUCTIONS FOR WILL OR CODICIL CLIENT/S

Notes

1) This form contains questions that will often not apply to a particular client. It is not suitable for sending out to clients to complete.

2) If the user strikes out a question, that may be useful evidence later that at least the will writer gave some attention to the point in issue.

Interview/Telephone call

Date and time:

Persons present:

Client questionnaires – ? Attached – ? (refer below)

Degree of urgency:

Tick the box below that best describes this

1.   *Critical*: client is seriously ill

Unlikely to live more than a few days ☐

2.   *Urgent*: client is seriously ill,

but condition not terminal ☐

3.   *Just in time*: client is not ill at all,

but is going on holiday soon and can afford (and agrees) to pay an enhanced fee for expedition ☐

4.   *Normal*: clear instructions,

no hesitation, no mental problems ☐

5.   *Special*: complicated situation,

tax and family provision issues, fairly good will in place already ☐

6.   *Difficult*: client is hesitant or undecided;

an adequate will is already in place ☐

NB:

1   Are you taking instructions from the *right* person?

2   Has the client accepted the firm's terms and conditions of acting? If this is a case that could be caught by the Cancellation of Contracts Made in a Consumer's Home or Place of Work etc Regulations 2008, has the

cooling-off period expired, or will you wait until it has expired, before preparing the will? Have you explained the delay to the client?

Part I – General

GENERAL DETAILS   (H = Husband   W/CP = Wife or Civil Partner where applicable). Note: this form assumes that instructions are taken from two parties together but later it may be wise to open two files, one each, and put one copy of this form on each.

fot = free of tax   stt = subject to tax   foc = free of charge

1.   *First names*   *Surname*   *Date of birth*
     H:
     W/CP:
2.   Occupation and/or
     Description
     H:
     W/CP:

3.   Address
4.   Domiciled in UK: H   Yes/No
     Domiciled in UK: W/CP   Yes/No
     Resident in UK: H   Yes/No
     Resident in UK: W/CP   Yes/No
5.   Any previous will/s?   H Yes/No
                                                           W/CP Yes/No

     Codicil/s?   H Yes/No
                                                           W/CP Yes/No

     Location of original(s)
     Arrangements for
     destruction:
     but retain made up copy on
     file
6.   Is there now/will be any *foreign property*?
     Concurrent wills? (beware *revocation* trap)
7.   State of health/marriage:
8.   Any other relevant factors:

FAMILY DETAILS

Are any: Adopted   Step   Illegitimate

Is this to make a difference: Yes/No If so, *how*

Previous marriages?

Ask for family tree

A.   CHILDREN:

First Names   Surname   Address   Date of Birth

B.   GRANDCHILDREN:

First Names   Surname   Address   Date of Birth

Are grandchildren born after testator's death to be included as beneficiaries or not?

TECHNICAL DETAILS

Clauses to be included

(tick where applicable)

1.   REVOCATION OF ALL FORMER WILLS AND CODICILS

2.   BURIAL/CREMATION/ANATOMICAL USE

3(a).   EXECUTORS AND TRUSTEES

First Names   Surname   Qualification/Relationship   Details of Gift (if any) – conditional on taking up the *office*?

3(b). GUARDIANS OF MINOR CHILDREN IF SPOUSE/CIVIL PARTNER PREDECEASED

First Names	Surname	Qualification/Relationship	Details of Gift (if any) – conditional on taking up the *office*?

Children Act and 'parental responsibility' aspects:

---

4. SPECIFIC GIFTS eg jewellery: all/residue personal chattels consider distribution in accordance with a list compiled on, and, or after date of will in a *letter of wishes* to surviving spouse/executors). If a business is run from home, are the contents of the home office/studio/workshop/consulting room to be regarded as 'personal chattels'?

First Names	Surname	Qualification/ Relationship (fot/stt)	Details of Gift (if any)

---

5. SPECIFIC DEVISE/BEQUESTS of freehold/leasehold eg Matrimonial Home

First Names	Surname	Qualification/ Relationship (fot/stt)	Details of Gift (if any)

NOTES:

(a) Is a share of the home/property passing to someone other than co-owner? *Beware*! Sever the joint tenancy if there is *any* doubt whatsoever – *do not rely on the client*. See *Carr-Glynn v Frearson* [1998] All ER 225.

(b) Consider mortgage liability: is beneficiary to take subject or free of mortgage. Query existence of life policy to pay off mortgage.

(c) Business/agricultural property – leave *specifically*, *not* as part of residue: IHTA 1984, s 39A.

---

6.   PECUNIARY LEGACIES

First Names	Surname	Qualification/ Relationship (fot/stt)	Details of Gift (if any)

NB: *Charities* – specify with registration number.

---

7.   SHARES IN COMPANIES

Name of Company or umbrella definition	Type of Share	Number of Shares (fot/stt)	Beneficiary

Consider *pre-emption* provisions eg in Articles of Association

---

8.   DISCRETIONARY TRUST OF NIL RATE BAND (AND POSSIBLY BUSINESS/AGRICULTURAL PROPERTY QUALIFYING FOR 100% RELIEF)

Consider: is it still appropriate in the light of the transferable nil rate band facility?

THE BENEFICIARIES:

POSITION OF WIDOW(ER)

LETTER OF WISHES

(eg as to income, loans [capital], absolutely):

consider need for lifetime steps *towards* equalisation/consider severing joint tenancies

---

9.   RESIDUE, ABSOLUTE AND/OR LIFE INTEREST (delete appropriately)

First Names	Address	Relationship to/ Age	Per Stirpes	Per cent
Surname	Qualification	Vest/Bare	at age	or Share
INSTRUCTIONS		–	gross division = *Re Ratcliffe*	
		–	net division = *Re Benham*	

249

10.   SURVIVORSHIP CONDITION eg 1 or 3 months (NB: *excluded* as between spouses in will of *elder* spouse in *commorientes* circumstances!)

---

11.   TECHNICAL CLAUSES TO BE INCLUDED: consider whether to incorporate the *SOCIETY OF TRUST AND ESTATE PRACTITIONERS* Standard Provisions (copy for client) 2nd edition, published October 2011.

Note: if a trust company is appointed executor, it may object to the STEP Standard Provisions, so check.

DETAILS OF CLAUSE	YES	NO	ANY MODIFICATION
FULL INVESTMENT			
APPROPRIATION			
TRUSTEES DELEGATION			
ARE TRUSTEES POWERS TO BE EXTENDED?			
TRUSTEE ACT 1925			
SECTION 31 INCOME			
SECTION 32 CAPITAL			
PARENT OR GUARDIAN OF MINOR TO HAVE			
POWER TO GIVE RECEIPTS TO TRUSTEES			
CHARGING CLAUSE FOR PROFESSIONAL			
TRUSTEES			
INDEMNITY			
TRUSTEES POWERS TO:			
CARRY ON BUSINESS			
TRANSFER BUSINESS			
INTO A COMPANY			
INSURE			
NEGATIVE EQUITABLE RULE			
Re: Apportionment of income			
NB: LIFE INTEREST			
HOTCHPOT and/or IHT INDEMNITIES eg in favour of donees of PETs			

SPECIFIC ADVICE ON CLAUSES
THAT LIMIT THE LIABILITY OF
TRUSTEES

TRUSTEES TO CONSIDER DEED
OF ARRANGEMENT or

VARIATION/DISCLAIMER IHTA
1984 s 142

MISCELLANEOUS

ORIGINAL TO BE RETAINED BY/
SENT TO:

COPIES TO BE SENT TO:

Arrangements for *execution* (beware *Esterhuizen v Allied Dunbar* [1998] 2
FLR 668).

- Consider whether to exclude responsibilities in the *original* letter
  accepting instructions?

- Arrangements as to checking *original*/photostat as to correct execution

DECLARATION TO BE MADE UNDER THE INHERITANCE (PROVISION
FOR FAMILY AND DEPENDANTS) ACT 1975 eg ex-spouse

OTHER PROFESSIONAL ADVISORS = contacts

NB: In nearly all cases the draft will should be *checked* by another fee
earner! (Organise reciprocal help with colleagues.)

---

12. LASTING POWER OF ATTORNEY

H – DoB appoints ....
W/CP – DoB appoints ....

[NOTE: the decision in *McDowall & Others (McDowall's Executors) v CIR
(and related appeal)*, SpC 2003, [2004] STC (SCD) 22 (SpC 382) indicated that
an attorney is not authorised to make gifts of any substance in the absence of
express authorisation, or registration and approval by the Court of Protection.
Procedure is more complicated than it was for an enduring power, but scope is
greater. Existing EPAs remain in force: does client want the new form?]

LIFETIME ESTATE PLANNING measures

– use separate sheets

– separate appointment?

fot = free of tax   stt = subject to tax   foc = free of charge

Part II – Value of estate

Assets of estate for IHT purposes – approximate value

Part III – Type of will

(1)   Absolute interest will:

Gift of estate (whole or part) to one beneficiary or beneficiaries with gift(s) over in case of beneficiary(ies) predeceasing testator/testatrix.

(2)   Disaster will: (where period of survival 30 days or up to six months) thereby negating rule in *commorientes* (where younger deemed to survive older).

(3)   Life interest: whole/part

Notes:

(i)   If spouse immediate post-death interest (IPDI), consider including powers of trustees, eg to make loans in favour of surviving spouse etc.

(ii)   Where surviving spouse has a lease/licence in the matrimonial home, query provide that this spouse is liable for all outgoings, eg insurance.

(4)   Hybrid: IPDI/discretionary plus trustees' powers to advance capital and/or make loans.

(5)   Discretionary: including:

- two-year span s 144;

- using a nil rate band fund; or

- discretionary followed by life interest in part of the home.

[But NB: CGT and IHT trap (two-year and three-month periods respectively – see **5.7**)]

(6)   Any power(s) of appointment exercisable by will or deed in favour of testator/testatrix:

General power   YES/NO

Special power   YES/NO

Details of will or settlement and (if necessary) inspect same.

Part IV – Clauses to be included

(1)   Revocation of all former wills and codicils.

(2)   Guardian of infant children

    (a)   If spouse survives

    (b)   If spouse predeceases

(3)   Executors and trustees:

    (a)   *Relations*: Relationship to testator/testatrix

    (b)   *Professional*: eg solicitors, accountants.

NB: Charging clause (see No (24) below). Inform testator.

[NB: since the judgment of Lightman J in *Rogers (deceased), Re* [2006] EWHC 753 (Ch), if firm has become or is considering becoming an LLP, provide for this possibility in the clause appointing executors.]

    (c)   *Bank or trustee company*: Follow its form of appointment

        –   Consider submitting draft to them for approval

        –   Is the bank nominated joint or sole executor and trustee?

        –   Obtain charging rates/scales

        –   Note STEP Standard Provisions point above

(4)   Specific gifts:

    (a)   Are they to be free of all tax/subject to tax?

        –   Household, furniture and effects

        –   Jewellery, clothes, furs and other personal effects

        –   Motor car (business car?)

        –   Shares in family or other companies (cover amalgamations/ reconstructions)

    (b)   Is spouse to receive all/residue of 'personal chattels': s 55(1)(*x*) Administration of Estates Act 1925?

    (c)   Consider covering by letter of wishes utilising s 143 (see also (25) below).

(5)   Specific devise(s) of freehold property:

    •   Is it/are they to be free of all tax/subject to tax?

    •   Is it/are they to be free of mortgage? Are trustees to discharge mortgage out of residuary estate?

    •   If matrimonial home is specifically mentioned: add 'or other principal residence at the date of my death'.

    •   NB: Burden of IHT (see s 211). Need to specify whether subject to, or free of IHT.

(6)   Specific bequest(s) of leasehold property:

- Is it/are they to be free of all tax/subject to tax?

- Is it/are they to be free of mortgage? Are trustees to discharge mortgage of residuary estate?

[NOTE:

(i)   Banks and other professional trustees may be reluctant to be appointed because of liability under repairing covenants in lease or underlease.

(ii)   Does not bear own IHT unless so provided, ditto freeholds.

(iii)   Consider grant of mere *licence*.]

(7)   Pecuniary legacy(ies) (are they to be free of all tax/subject to tax?) and whether or not in forgiveness of debt(s).

[NB: If to executors and trustees, whether to them 'for their own absolute use and benefit' or for them only if they act as executor and trustee.]

(8)   Annuity(ies) to be provided? Generally: don't.

(9)   Charities, political parties, etc: legacies of whatever size free of IHT (if within ss 23 and 24). Consider whether to include precedent clause ensuring 36% IHT rate will apply.

(10)   Residue:

Is division into specified shares (%) to be subject to a life interest/ protective trust?

(11)   Full investment clause.

(12)   Appropriation clause gives flexibility. Consider adaptation to avoid the rule in *Robinson v Collins* (see Example 5.12). Note STEP Standard Provisions 2nd edition (wider form)

(13)   Power to appoint capital and/or income

Whether a limited or an unlimited power

(14)   Power for trustees to make loans (at whatever rate of interest/interest free in their discretion).

(15)   Power to appoint foreign trustees and administer trust abroad – possibility of saving future CGT and consider in context for excluded property for IHT.

(16)   Negative equitable rule re apportionment of income

Howe v Earl of Dartmouth (1802) 7 Ves 137

Allhusen v Whittell (1867) LR 4 Eq 295

[NB Are you confident that you can explain these rules? If not, include a general clause to negative all equitable apportionments, for example by using the STEP Standard Provisions. What about the duty to hold a balance between capital and income?]

(17) Are the trustees' powers to be extended beyond the provisions of the Trustee Act 1925, ss 31 and 32 as amended, ie appointment of capital and income to infant children or grandchildren?

(18) Power to transfer a business into a company.

(19) Power for trustees to carry on business, for example become directors, receive remuneration (NB: trustees to be free of any liability).

(20) Accruer clause.

(21) Lifetime chargeable gifts and PETs made within seven years of death: provision for (additional IHT). Query – insure or indemnify donee. [NB: clawback can affect gifts: has the donee been warned not to sell the item too soon?]

(22) Parent or guardian of infant beneficiaries to give receipt to trustees so that trustees are fully released.

(23) Charging clause for professional trustees. [NB: this is provided by Trustee Act 2000 anyway and by the STEP Standard Provisions.]

(24) Any special non-legally binding direction to trustees. (Query: by separate letter) [NB: use of precatory implied trusts within two years of death (s 143)].

(25) Trustees' power to insure property, for example, where surviving spouse takes lease/licence in matrimonial home.

(26) General clause that all gifts to be free of all tax or subject to tax. What about the cost of delivery to a distant beneficiary?

(27) Hotchpot, for example adjust IHT liability in respect of earlier gift(s) at lower IHT rate(s). Explain the rule and decide whether or not to exclude it.

(28) Grant options.

(29) Direction to executors to consider application of deed of variation.

(30) Authorising partial disclaimers. (Also consider staggered legacies and gifts of residue.)

(31) Any other provisions.

(32) 'After sales service': eg the implementation of the 'debt or charge' scheme requires an understanding of the issues by the executors and the trustees of the nil rate band trust. Offer an outline of what will be required after the first death?

(33) Seriously consider adopting the *Standard Provisions of the Society of Trust and Estate Practitioners* (STEP) as prepared by James Kessler QC. These cover in the main the common, detailed administrative powers needed in a will *and* lifetime trust. Details are available from STEP at Artillery House (South), 11–19 Artillery Row, London SW1P 1RT 020 7340 0500, or from their website at www.step.org.

These provisions could be adopted by the following wording:

'The Standard provisions (and all of the Special Provisions) of the Society of Trust and Estate Practitioners (2nd edition) shall apply to this will [trust]. Section 11 Trusts of Land and Appointment of Trustees Act 1996 (consultation with beneficiaries) shall not apply.

[If desired by the client and agreed by the trustees] The duty of reasonable care (set out in s 1 Trustee Act 2000) applies to all the functions of the Trustees.'

Part V – Miscellaneous

(1) *Subsequent marriage* (or civil partnership) automatically revokes will unless made in contemplation of that particular marriage which is later solemnised.

(2) Revocation of gifts by *termination of marriage*. Administration of Justice Act 1982, s 18(2), eg divorce or nullity – applies in respect of deaths (on or after 1 January 1983); namely that on the termination of the marriage:

   (i) An ex-spouse ceases automatically to be executor/trustee of the former spouse's will.

   (ii) Gifts to an ex-spouse lapse subject to clearly expressed contrary intention and subject to rights under the Inheritance (Provision for Family and Dependants) Act 1975. For example, if an ex-spouse had been given a life interest in a will, once divorced the ex-spouse's life interest would lapse and the remainder would be accelerated.

   (iii) Other provisions of a will remain valid.

   Having regard to (ii) above, it has been good practice in a will that all gifts to a spouse (or civil partner), whenever made, would provide for a gift over not only in the event of that spouse predeceasing the testator, but also 'if the gift shall fail for any reason'. This would remedy the defect highlighted in the case of *Re Sinclair* [1985] 1 All ER 1066, where a testator gave his estate to his wife contingent on her surviving him for one month and, in default, to charity. The Court of Appeal held that because the marriage had been *dissolved*, both the gift to the former wife (overruling *Re Cherrington* [1984]

2 All ER 285) *and* the gift to charity failed, ie lapsed, and the estate devolved as on *intestacy*. Although the testator had provided for the contingency of the wife not surviving, he had not provided for the alternative contingency of the dissolution of the marriage. This defect was remedied by Law Reform (Succession) Act 1995, s 3 under which such former spouse is deemed to have died as at the date of dissolution etc of marriage for succession purposes. Therefore in the above circumstances the gift in default to the charity would not have failed.

(3)   If the testator has *nominated* any asset (eg national savings or certain friendly society benefits) or made recommendations over any asset (eg death in service pension benefits) give details, as will cannot operate on such asset.

(4)   If the testator has any asset on *hire or hire-purchase*, such asset cannot be given as it is not the testator's to give.

(5)   (a)   If the testator owns *shares* etc in a private limited company:

      Consider the Articles of Association to determine any restriction on disposal thereof (ie pre-emption provisions).

    (b)   If the testator is a *partner* in a business, consider the partnership agreement and ascertain the effect thereof on disposal of his interest.

(6)   Arrangements as to *execution*. Do not *pin* or attach anything to will. Can necessitate affidavit of plight.

Beware of negligence claims if the will has not been properly executed – see *Esterhuizen v Allied Dunbar* [1998] 2 FLR 668. Consider an initial letter of disclaimer.

(7)   Copy of original will to be sent to:

Original will to be retained by:

Original will to be sent to:

(8)   Account, to be sent to:

(9)   Wishes as to burial/cremation.

Eyes and other organs to be left for therapeutic purposes or transplants (not legally binding on executors and trustees).

(10)   Address of beneficiaries:

Note:

(i)   The relationship to the testator/testatrix if any of the beneficiary(ies) should be inserted in the will.

(ii) Where no relationship inserted the address of the beneficiary(ies) should be given.

It is not necessary to insert both (i) and (ii) above as either is sufficient for identification purposes: a record should be taken for the file.

(11) Declaration by spouse under the Inheritance (Provision for Family and Dependants) Act 1975 (this can be included in will or codicil, but preferably by an entirely separate document).

(12) Special form of testimonium and attestation where applicable, for example testator/testatrix blind.

(13) Future scope for deed of variation/disclaimer including the authorisation of partial disclaimers (s 142).

(14) Need to review – when? Diarise.

APPENDIX 5.2 – DEED OF VARIATION ELECTION ALTERNATIVES; PRECEDENT AND NOTES

Introduction

The precedent below covers a situation where, for example, a wealthy father has left the bulk of his estate to his daughter. She does not wish to take all the estate and has set up an appropriate family settlement. She decides to vary her entitlement under her father's will so that a part of the residue (say £325,000 being the 2012–13 nil rate band) goes to the trustees of the said settlement instead of her.

Note that, for income tax purposes, by virtue of ITA 2007, s 472(3) the daughter is settlor of the trust. She is also a beneficiary. Income is therefore taxed on her, at her personal top rate, rather than at the trust rate.

If the variation creates a trust for the daughter's minor children, in view of ITTOIA 2005, s 629, any income should generally be accumulated during the children's minority (or until earlier marriage) but if paid out carries no refundable tax credit: it is simply a gift of money that has already been taxed on mother.

For further precedents of deeds of variation and disclaimers etc, the reader is referred to the following:

- Butterworths *Wills, Probate and Administration Service*
- *Practical Will Precedents* (Sweet & Maxwell)
- Butterworths *Encyclopaedia of Forms and Precedents*: Wills Volumes

- *Halsbury's Laws*: Wills Volume

- Parker's *Modern Will Precedents* (Bloomsbury Professional)

- James Kessler QC and Leon Sartin, *Drafting Trusts and Will Trusts* (Sweet & Maxwell, 11th edition)

- David Endicott and Andrew Jones, *Brighouse's Precedents of Wills* (Sweet & Maxwell, 14th edition).

For the purpose of satisfying IHTA 1984, s 142 and TCGA 1992, s 62, the document need not be a deed, although it often is: the requirement is merely 'an instrument in writing'. This may be relevant to advisers other than solicitors, who are concerned not to commit the offence of preparing a deed for reward. Following *Re Holt's Settlement, Wilson v Holt* [1969] 1 Ch 100, it is likely that this can be formal correspondence, or an order under the Variation of Trusts Act 1958.

Whether to make a statement for IHT purposes

There are circumstances when it is better not to include a statement in a variation that s 142 is to apply, and for the effect of the document to be that the beneficiary under the will or intestacy makes his/her own lifetime gifts.

The table below summarises the main circumstances.

Circumstances	*Recommendation and reason*
Deceased's gift chargeable	Include the statement.
	The alternative of receiving the gift from the deceased, and the beneficiary then making a lifetime gift, could involve a double IHT liability: once on the estate and again on the lifetime gift subject to the PET rules.
Deceased's gift is to exempt beneficiary, who varies in favour of a chargeable beneficiary	Do not, generally, include the statement.
	Assuming beneficiary's estate will be taxed lower than deceased's (and bearing in mind tax on a lifetime gift will be at her life rates or as one or more PETs, subject to seven-year survival). After seven years, beneficiary's gift ceases to cumulate.

Appendix 5.2

Circumstances	*Recommendation and reason*
Deceased's gift is exempt but is of (or up to) the nil rate band and a gift to a chargeable beneficiary is preferred	Do not, generally, include the statement.
	The nil rate band has not been used and is available for transfer and use later. Even if the estate was well in excess of the nil rate band and the surviving spouse did not need it all, it would normally still only be worth making a statement for the nil rate band. Any exempt estate over the nil rate band ceiling could, assuming good health, be disposed of if desired by way of PETs.
Deceased's gift is exempt and is varied in favour of a chargeable beneficiary, where value of estate has risen sharply in the two-year period	Include the statement.
	It should be possible to pass on, free of IHT, the benefit of certain posthumous increases in the value of an estate.
Variations by personal representatives of a deceased beneficiary: 'double death' cases	Include the statement.
	This may achieve posthumous equalisation, though the bunching effect of assets of two estates being assessed in one estate is much less of a problem if the first nil rate band is transferable.
Variations in favour of the estate of a deceased beneficiary	Include the statement.

Circumstances	*Recommendation and reason*
	A beneficiary, eg a son, who inherits from his parents who have both died within the past two years with unequal estates (having made no chargeable lifetime transfers) can equalise those estates thereby reducing the IHT payable. For example, assume parent A left £460,000 to the son, and parent B left £60,000 to the son. The son varies the gift from parent A by redirecting £200,000 to parent B who survived A. Accordingly, no IHT is payable on A or B's estate as to £260,000 each; instead of inheriting from one estate £460,000 (IHT £54,000 (using 2012–13 rates)) and the other estate £60,000 (IHT nil). A saving is thereby achieved in IHT of £54,000; but see Note below.
Variations to apply 100% business/ agricultural property relief	Include the statement.
	The hope is that value may pass down the generations and in suitable cases that the surviving parent may recycle the relief; see further commentary at **15.61**.

Note

HMRC inquire closely into deeds that vary gifts away from chargeable beneficiaries in favour of exempt beneficiaries, and for good reason. Has the exempt beneficiary given consideration for the variation, thus falling foul of s 142(3)? In the example of inheritance from both parents noted above, has there been a true variation? Questions will be asked, such as whether the exempt beneficiary 'needed' the inheritance. Often the answer will be 'yes': a testator may, before transferable nil rate bands, have wished to use his nil rate band to save IHT even where the family circumstances did not really permit it. It will be many years before wills designed to suit the old rules are all replaced or proved.

The precedent

This deed is made the day of 20XX between

Appendix 5.2

1 ABC of (**'the Legatee'**);

2 DEF of and GHI of (**'the Trustees'**); and

3 JKL of MNO of and PQR of (**'the Personal Representatives'**).

Background

A The Trustees are the present Trustees of a Settlement dated .... 20XX (**'the Settlement'**) and made between the Legatee of the one part and the Trustees of the other part principally for the benefit of the Legatee's children.

B By his last Will dated .... (as varied by [two] Codicils dated respectively .... and ....) (together **'the Will'**) STU (**'the Deceased'**) left his residuary estate to the Legatee absolutely.

C The Deceased died on the .... without having varied or revoked the Will.

D The Will was proved in the [Principal] [District] Probate Registry on .... day of .... by the Personal Representatives.

E The Legatee wishes to vary the dispositions of property comprised in the estate of the Deceased so that £325,000 out of the Legatee's share in the residuary estate of the Deceased (**'the Fund'**) is given to the Trustees to be held by them on the trusts of the Settlement.

Operative part

1. The Will shall be deemed to take effect from the death of the Deceased as if it had included in priority to any other gift to the Legatee a gift in the terms set out in the First Schedule and as if the Settlement was then in existence.

2. The Fund shall comprise the assets set out in the Second Schedule hereto.

3. The parties to this variation intend that the provisions of section 142(1) Inheritance Tax Act 1984 [and of Section 62(6) and (7) Taxation of Chargeable Gains Act 1992] shall apply to the variation effected by this deed.

4. The Legatee and the Trustees irrevocably request the Personal Representatives to give effect to the provisions of this deed in lieu of the relevant provisions contained in the Will and hereby indemnify the personal representatives and each of them and their respective estate and effects from and against all claims, demands and expenses arising at any time by reason of their so doing.

5. The Personal Representatives agree to implement the foregoing requests.

6. It is hereby certified that this instrument falls within category 'L' in the Schedule to the Stamp Duty (Exempt Instruments) Regulations 1987 (see Note 3 below).

In witness whereof the parties hereto have set their hands the day and year first before written.

The First Schedule

'I give [subject to tax] the Fund to the Trustees of the Settlement to hold on the trusts of the Settlement and as an accretion for all purposes to the existing sums held on the trusts thereof.'

The Second Schedule

(Assets or cash comprising the £325,000 fund)

Signed and delivered as a deed

by the said [ABC]

in the presence of

Signed and delivered as a deed

by the said [DEF]

in the presence of

Signed and delivered as a deed

by the said [GHI]

in the presence of

Signed and delivered as a deed

by the said [JKL]

in the presence of

Signed and delivered as a deed

by the said [MNO]

in the presence of

Signed and delivered as a deed

by the said [PQR]

in the presence of

Notes on the precedent

1. The parties to the deed must include the original beneficiary making the variation. This would include anyone who is even contingently affected by the deed.

2. *Personal representatives* – not essential to be parties but advisable. However, if as a result of the deed more IHT or CGT is payable, they must join in the variation: see s 142(2A).

3. *Donees* – not essential to be parties, but may well be desirable, as applicable.

4. *Position of minors* – their interests cannot be adversely affected without a court order. Contrast the position if a minor's position is unaffected or improved.

5. It is *not* a requirement that the settlement referred to in recital A need have been in existence on the testator's death, nor that beneficiaries benefiting under the variation were alive on the testator's death.

6. To make a variation, the beneficiary must be of age.

7. Where a will benefits several beneficiaries, a variation can be made by any one beneficiary of his entitlement without the concurrence of the others.

Time limits

Up to two years from the date of STU's death: s 142(1).

The statement

The 'statement' (from 1 August 2002) has to be included in the variation document if s 142 and/or TCGA 1992, s 62 is to apply; and notice must be given to the Board if additional tax becomes payable as a result of the variation. The clause can be adapted to apply only to IHT or CGT or both. If an IOV follows old drafting and refers to an *election*, HMRC will interpret this as a 'statement'; but this statement must be included in the IOV. The previous leeway/flexibility of elections being entered into within six months of the IOV no longer applies.

As there is here clearly a 'variation' (contrast a disclaimer), the 'statement' procedure applies. In some cases it can be appropriate not to apply the 'statement' procedure; see above.

As to CGT, normally apply the 'statement' procedure because of CGT death exemption. *But* consider not electing to get the higher base value at the time of beneficiary's disposal especially if the gain can be mopped up by the beneficiaries' annual exemption (£10,600 for 2012–13); or available losses exist.

Consideration

There must be *no consideration* in money or money's worth (other than consideration consisting of a qualifying reciprocal variation or disclaimer): s 142(3) and TCGA 1992, s 62(8). Payment of legal costs, interest-free loans, or indemnities in favour of the donor of the variation, taking over liabilities, are examples of what can constitute consideration.

Example 5.17 – Reciprocal consideration permitted for IOV purposes

Testator left son Cain a property ('Blackacre'), and son Abel a £75,000 legacy. They enter into an IOV whereby Cain takes, say, £500,000 and Abel acquires Blackacre (as an alternative, Abel might redirect to Cain a share of residue as devised by the testator).

Notes

1. Multiple variations

In *Russell v IRC* [1988] STC 195, it was decided that there cannot be 'two bites of the cherry' in respect of the same asset. Once a variation has been entered into, a further purported redirection deemed to have been made by the deceased in respect of the relevant assets was not valid. See also the reference to *Lake v Lake* [1989] STC 865. After one variation affecting residue, eg carving out a legacy, it may still be possible to carve out a second legacy, but it is always preferable to include all variations in one document.

2. The subject matter of the variation

It is advisable, wherever possible, to use this wording, ie indicating that the deceased's property comprised in the estate immediately prior to his death is being varied. If the variation is extensive and wide ranging, it is likely to be good drafting practice for the variation to adopt a complete substitute will in a schedule to the variation; but some families are reluctant to change a will and like it to be disturbed as little as possible. In addition, if a complete substitute will is adopted, this may preclude a second variation, even of a disposition that is not changed.

It is presumed that the personal representatives have the appropriate power of appropriation, eg under Administration of Estates Act 1925, s 41.

3. Stamp duty

Variations are exempt from stamp duty and provided an appropriate certificate is given under the Stamp Duty (Exempt Instruments) Regulations 1987 (SI 1987/516). Category 'L' is considered to be the correct category, unless there is consideration in the form of a reciprocal variation, which as noted above is not the type of consideration which invalidates an IOV. If this reciprocity does exist, category 'M' is strictly correct, but it seems that HMRC will accept either category.

4. Stamp duty land tax

A transaction varying a disposition on death (whether by will or intestacy) in respect of property is exempt from charge to stamp duty land tax, if the transaction takes place within two years following death and provided that no consideration is given for it other than the making of the variation (see FA 2003, Sch 3, para 4).

Chapter 6

Husband, wife and civil partner

INTRODUCTION

6.1   The IHT planning landscape for spouses and civil partners altered considerably following the Pre-Budget Report 2007 announcement that changes would be introduced in FA 2008 from 9 October 2007 enabling a claim to be made for any unused proportion of the IHT nil rate band on a person's death to be transferred to a surviving spouse or civil partner who dies on or after the above date.

The necessity for IHT planning to utilise nil rate bands on the deaths of spouses and civil partners has therefore diminished following the introduction of ss 8A–8C. The facility to transfer unused nil rate bands on earlier deaths is clearly an important issue, and a separate chapter is therefore devoted to it (see **Chapter 3**).

This chapter deals with the following aspects of estate planning for husbands and wives:

- the IHT exemption: general aspects;

- comparative estates of husband and wife and use of nil rate band;

- channelling of gifts and associated operations;

- matrimonial home and joint ownership; and

- joint bank accounts.

Civil partnerships

6.2   As implied by the chapter heading, following the Civil Partnership Act 2004, from 5 December 2005 registered civil partners are generally subject to the same treatment for IHT purposes as married couples. References in this chapter to 'spouse' should therefore be interpreted to include 'civil partner' where appropriate.

THE IHT EXEMPTION: GENERAL ASPECTS

Importance

6.3   The inter-spouse exemption in s 18 is one of the cornerstones of IHT planning, and is referred to throughout this book. A fundamental aspect of IHT is that liability can be deferred until the death of the surviving spouse (unlike the old ED regime where duty was payable on the *first* death). Absolute transfers between husband and wife whether during lifetime or by will are generally exempt from IHT, subject to the non-domicile aspect dealt with in **6.4**. They each have their separate estates and availability of the nil rate band. Unlike CGT, there is no requirement that the spouses are living together. Although 'spouse' is not specifically defined, 'common law' spouses are not currently covered. On divorce, as opposed to separation, the exemption ceases to apply but relief is likely to be available under s 11 ('Dispositions for maintenance of family'). That topic (including court orders) is discussed at **12.14** onwards.

Under s 18, it is only necessary to show that the value transferred by the one spouse is *attributable* to property which has become the property of the transferee spouse; so that it is not a requirement for exemption that the consequential loss to the transferor spouse must be exactly matched by the increase to the estate of the transferee spouse. This should normally give complete exemption, even in cases where before a transfer the transferor spouse had control of, say, a family company (whether in his own right or as related property) and after the transfer he has not. It is, however, essential that the property becomes part of the donee's estate. As will be seen, practically any lifetime gift into trust made after 22 March 2006, save for a disabled person or a charity, is treated as if it were discretionary. Thus, the donee is not treated as having an interest. Therefore, even a lifetime transfer to a trust for a spouse, fails to enjoy exemption because the spouse is not treated as owning the fund.

It should be noted that the meaning of the word 'spouse' for the purposes of s 18 is restricted to married persons, and not persons living together as husband and wife (*Holland (executor of Holland, deceased) v IRC* [2003] STC (SCD) 43).

The spouse exemption formerly also applied where one spouse settled assets in trust for the other spouse by way of interest in possession, including protective trusts under the Trustee Act 1925, s 33. However, FA 2006 subsequently restricted that. A lifetime transfer to an interest in possession trust (which is not a trust for a disabled person) is a chargeable transfer and the tenant for life does not become entitled to an interest in possession for the purposes of IHT, even though he may be so entitled for income tax and CGT. Since the fund is not treated as forming part of the estate of the life tenant, it does not satisfy the requirements of s 18(1), notwithstanding the terms of s 18(4), which states: 'For the purposes of this section, property is given to a person if it ... is held on trust for him'. By the same token, the exemption is not usually available in the case of a discretionary trust where the trustees appoint to a beneficiary who is the spouse of the settlor (see **6.9**).

Spouse exemption would still be available if the discretionary trust in question was a will trust and a distribution was made in exercise of that discretion, creating an IPDI, within two years of death. In this situation s 144, as amended by FA 2006, would apply. Note that the trap, whereby if an outright distribution is made within three months of death the exemption will not apply, is not in point in the case of an IPDI, thus disapplying *Frankland v IRC* [1996] STC 735 and *Harding (PR of Loveday deceased) v IRC* [1997] STC (SCD) 321 (see **5.7**).

Non-domicile aspect

6.4   If, immediately before the transfer, the transferor but not the transferor's spouse is domiciled in the UK, the exemption is limited (by s 18(2)) to an upper limit. At the time of writing, the upper limit is £55,000 (note: the £55,000 is a cumulative figure taking into account any previous transfers). This is a *separate* fixed exemption (not subject to indexation under s 8) and does not reduce the UK spouse's nil rate band.

However, the government announced in Budget 2012 that it intended to increase the spouse exemption of £55,000 in respect of transfers to a non-UK domiciled spouse or civil partner. In addition, the government announced its intention to allow individuals who are domiciled outside the UK and who have a UK-domiciled spouse or civil partner to elect to be treated as domiciled in the UK for IHT purposes.

Those announced changes were subsequently included in the draft Finance Bill 2013 clauses published on 11 December 2012.

The lifetime limit for exempt transfers is to be increased from £55,000 to the IHT exemption limit at the time of the transfer. Thus if no election is made to be treated as UK domiciled, the overseas assets of the non-UK domiciled spouse would generally continue to be excluded property for IHT purposes, but transfers from their spouse or civil partner would be subject to the increased 'capped' limit.

The effect of making an election in writing to HMRC will broadly be to avoid a possible IHT charge on the first death. However, the worldwide estate of the surviving spouse will be liable to IHT on the second death. An election made while both individuals are alive will take effect from the date the election is made. Elections following a death must be made within two years of the death, where it occurs on or after 6 April 2013.

Elections will be irrevocable, and continue to apply while the electing individual continues to remain resident in the UK. However, an election will cease to have effect if the electing person is resident outside the UK for more than three consecutive tax years. Thus overseas assets may cease to be liable to IHT once more, subject to the person not being actually or deemed domiciled in the UK at that point.

The above election is to be ignored in determining a person's domicile within the deeming provisions of s 267, and s 267 is to be ignored in determining whether a person is eligible to make an election by reason of their domicile status. In addition, the election does not apply for the purposes of other taxes such as income tax, including the remittance basis.

The increased exemption limit is to have effect for transfers of value made on or after 6 April 2013. The first opportunity to make an election will be the date of Royal Assent of Finance Act 2013, although note the above comments regarding elections following a death.

The following points should be borne in mind in considering the restricted £55,000 spouse exemption:

- Any lifetime gifts in excess of the exemption figure nevertheless constitute PETs.

- Gifts made to a spouse whilst non-UK domiciled are not 'cleansed' if the recipient spouse later becomes domiciled here, or is deemed to be so domiciled. Those 'excess' gifts remain on the donor's 'clock' and go against the donor's nil rate band until seven years have expired from their dates.

- The foreign-domiciled spouse is in a position to make gifts of excluded property (see **1.31**) outside the IHT regime. However, here some care should be taken, for if excluded property is gifted to a UK domiciliary its exempt status will, of course, be lost.

- The restricted exemption of £55,000 has a potential effect on the amount of unused nil rate band available to be transferred to the foreign-domiciled surviving spouse. For example, if the deceased spouse's entire estate passes to the surviving spouse, any excess over £55,000 is a chargeable legacy which reduces the unused nil rate band accordingly (see **3.26**).

The various combinations of circumstances are summarised in the table below. Notice that the restricted exemption applies *only* where the transferee spouse is domiciled abroad and the transferor spouse is domiciled in the UK. The £55,000 limit does not apply if both spouses are domiciled outside the UK, or if the *transferor* spouse is domiciled outside the UK but the transferee spouse is domiciled in the UK.

The widened definition of deemed domicile in s 267 (see **17.7**) applies in this context and therefore the transferee spouse, who might be non-UK domiciled for general purposes but is UK domiciled for IHT purposes, has the full exemption available. For example, a change of domicile on emigration within the previous three years will not prevent the full exemption from applying.

Domicile of transferor spouse	Domicile of transferee spouse	Full s 18 exemption	Restricted exemption (£55,000)
UK	UK	Yes	–
UK	Abroad	–	Yes
Abroad	UK	Yes	–
Abroad	Abroad	Yes	–

Notes:

(1)   Restriction *only* applies in the second case (although the excess is treated as a PET in relation to lifetime gifts). Therefore where spouses both have the *same* domicile (wherever it may be), the full unrestricted exemption is available. This will, of course, impact on the available transferable nil rate band.

(2)   A spouse *can* acquire a domicile separate from the other spouse (see **17.4**).

(3)   The restricted exemption of £55,000 is a cumulative lifetime one, at least in HMRC's view (IHTM11033). Thus, transfers made more than seven years before death can reduce or eliminate the restricted exemption. In addition, earlier gifts that were fully exempt within s 18(1) when made are taken into account in terms of the restricted exemption if the transferee spouse subsequently becomes non-UK domiciled.

Conditions

6.5   The inter-spouse exemption is subject to certain conditions set out in ss 18 and 56, namely:

● The transfer or disposition to the spouse must be immediate, ie it must not take effect (presumably in possession) after any period, or when a prior interest terminates (s 18(3)(a)). For example, if a husband gives a life interest, say, to his brother and the remainder after such life interest to his wife, the exemption will not apply. If the gift were the other way round, and absolute, this restriction would not apply to the first gift but a voluntary, unconnected, onward gift by the spouse, perhaps under the terms of mutual wills, would be chargeable under normal principles.

Further, it is provided that the exemption is not lost by reason only that the property is given to a spouse conditionally on surviving the other spouse for a specified period (s 18(3)). This has particular relevance in the context of survivorship clauses, although they are in fact restricted to a six-month period (see s 92).

- The transfer or other disposition must not depend on a condition which is not satisfied within 12 months after the transfer (s 18(3)(b)). It is thought that if it is possible, but not certain, that the condition will be satisfied within 12 months, a 'wait and see' rule should be applied. This second rule would operate in respect of a condition that the surviving spouse acquires an asset for a third party, which is never in fact acquired.

- If property is left to a person (whether surviving spouse or another) subject to a *condition* that the recipient must 'give' certain of his or her own property to another, it seems that this latter transfer is nevertheless a gift and not excluded by virtue of s 10. Although the 'transferee' does not intend to make a gratuitous disposition, as the *first* 'giver' did so intend, it is likely that both transfers are gifts having regard to the phrase 'a transaction intended' within s 10. Accordingly, to comply with the condition in s 18(3)(b) as between spouses the condition of making the second gift should not exceed the 12-month period.

- The inter-spouse exemption does not apply to property given in consideration of the transfer of a reversionary interest, if that reversionary interest does not then form part of the recipient's estate (under s 55) because he has an interest in possession or future interest in the same settled property (see s 56(1)). This provision, intended to counter certain IHT avoidance techniques associated with dealings in settled interests, is of little practical planning effect, other than as a trap to avoid in considering the handling of settlements.

- Where a person acquires a reversionary interest in any settled property for a consideration in money or money's worth, the inter-spouse exemption does not apply on the termination of the prior interest (assuming, for instance, it was held by his wife) when the settled property passes to him as the new reversioner (s 56(2)).

Spouse relief does not apply where a person makes a disposition and thus becomes entitled to a 'settlement power' for money or money's worth (s 55A). A 'settlement power' means (see s 47A), any power over settled property or exercisable over it or over the settlement itself. Section 55A applies not only to the acquisition of a settlement power, but also to the situation where the purchaser can influence the exercise of such a power or restrict its exercise.

Liability of transferee spouse

6.6 Section 203 is a tracing section that deserves to be better known. It provides that when a transferor has made a transfer of value to his spouse, that spouse (to an amount equal to the value of such property at the time of its transfer) is liable for any IHT for which the transferor is liable, in respect of other transfers of value.

This is designed to cover the case where the transferor might wish to avoid liability to IHT having made one or more chargeable transfers, by giving the rest of the assets to his spouse.

Pre-marriage

6.7 Prior to marriage, the parties may wish to buy an asset such as a house and the wealthier party may wish to make a gift of the whole or a share in such asset to the other party. Except to the extent that general exemptions apply, this gift would be a potentially exempt, rather than exempt, transfer.

A useful alternative might be for the wealthier party to lend the other party such additional funds as to make the appropriate purchase and then after the marriage to forgive the loans (ie at a time when the inter-spouse exemption will apply). The waiver should be by deed to avoid any argument by HMRC based on lack of consideration. The loan need not be on commercial terms (but it should be repayable on demand), as although the party making the loan could otherwise have earned interest on that money, the charge to IHT is (by s 3) simply on the decrease in the value of the transferor's estate (of which there is none), rather than on any increase which would otherwise have occurred.

Disposition for maintenance of family (s 11)

6.8 There are important exemptions for inter-family dispositions and particularly in respect of a former spouse, for example on divorce. Details are set out in **12.14**.

Definition of spouse v widow(er)

6.9 On a death, it is clear that the inter-spouse exemption operates in favour of a widow or widower because the estate is valued immediately *before* death (ss 4(1) and 171). In certain other situations, the provisions of ss 53(4)–(6) and 54(2), (3) resolve the position by way of a compromise, ie benefits to a widow or widower are received as 'spouse' for up to two years following the death of their partner ('the settlor spouse'). Instances of the application of this rule are as follows:

Trust interest: reverter to settlor

6.10   Section 54(2) and (3) concern the treatment of an interest in possession that reverts to the settlor or the settlor's spouse who is then domiciled in the UK on the death of the life tenant. If the settlor has died, the reverter will be exempt in favour of the settlor's UK-domiciled widow only if:

- the settlor's death is within two years of the death of the beneficiary with the interest in possession; and

- the widow becomes beneficially entitled to the settled property; and

- neither the settlor nor his spouse had acquired a reversionary interest in the settled property for money or money's worth; or

- where the circumstances are that a reversionary interest has been transferred into settlement after 9 March 1981.

Note the restriction to that rule introduced by FA 2006 as set out in s 54(2A): where a person becomes beneficially entitled to an interest in possession from 22 March 2006, that interest must be a disabled person's interest or a transitional serial interest (TSI). This cuts down the usefulness of the rule.

FA 2006 also introduced s 54(2B), which provides relief if someone with an immediate post-death interest (IPDI) dies within two years of the settlor, and the settlor's UK-domiciled widow(er) becomes beneficially entitled to the settled property. In those circumstances, the value of the settled property is not taken into account in the estate of the person who held the IPDI.

Termination of trust interest: spouse taking

6.11   Section 53(4)–(6) together provide that the same situation arises where the beneficiary with an interest in possession terminates his interest during lifetime, though again the usefulness of this section is cut down by s 53(1A) and (2A) introduced by FA 2006.

The relief is given if the settlor's spouse or (where the settlor has died less than two years earlier) widow(er) becomes beneficially entitled to the settled property, and is UK-domiciled.

It is difficult to understand the logic behind this compromise period of two years. Why should a widow or widower not be able to claim the inter-spouse exemption once the first spouse has been dead for more than two years? This illogicality is perhaps emphasised by the compromise which is not even applied consistently throughout the legislation. For example, in s 80, which treats property as not having become 'settled' where the settlor *or his spouse* retains an initial interest in possession, spouse is defined to include widow or widower without any temporal restriction (though again the general usefulness of s 80 has been restricted by s 80(4), which was introduced in FA 2006 with effect from 22 March 2006).

Note that there is no similar reverter exemption for a distribution charge out of a discretionary trust under the relevant property provisions contained in IHTA 1984, Pt III, Ch III. This is perhaps not surprising as any distribution to the settlor himself would likewise be subject to tax.

A 'pre-owned asset' income tax charge applies in 'reverter to settlor' trust situations (from 5 December 2005), notwithstanding that the property in question is treated as part of the former owner's estate (see **Chapter 13**).

Capital gains tax implications

6.12 For CGT purposes, a tax-free uplift on death of the life tenant is disapplied by TCGA 1992, s 73(1)(b) where settled property reverts to the settlor.

However, as mentioned above, if the property reverts to the UK-domiciled spouse (or widow(er) on the settlor's death within two years), the IHT exemption remains available, and a CGT-free uplift is secured, because the restriction in TCGA 1992, s 73(1)(b) refers to the settlor, but not the settlor's spouse or widow(er).

By virtue of TCGA 1992, s 73(2A), the above exclusion of a chargeable gain (and tax-free uplift) does not apply in respect of interests in possession after 22 March 2006, except where the trust interest was:

- an IPDI;
- a TSI; or
- a disabled person's interest (within IHTA 1984, s 89B(1)(c) or (d)).

Note that the facility of a TSI expired on 5 October 2008. If the death of a beneficiary with a non-qualifying interest in possession results in the trust ending, there is a deemed disposal by the trustees for CGT purposes, and no tax-free uplift. Any settlor who is not a disabled person for IHT purposes may face a CGT disadvantage on becoming entitled to the fund when it reverts.

COMPARATIVE ESTATES OF HUSBAND AND WIFE AND USE OF NIL RATE BAND

No need to equalise

6.13   Many years ago, IHT was charged on an ascending scale which encouraged the equalisation of estates between husband and wife. Since 15 March 1988, however, the position is simpler. After the nil rate band (£325,000 for 2012–13), there is only one single rate of 40% on death (albeit that a lower rate of 36% can apply in respect of estates where charitable legacies are involved; see **5.26**) or half of that, 20%, for lifetime chargeable transfers. This means that, as a general rule, if the nil rate band is already utilised on the first death, there is no longer any *current* advantage for IHT purposes in equalising the estates as between husband and wife. There is always the possibility that the government may reintroduce the progressive rates of IHT.

The facility to transfer unused nil rate bands of spouses (and civil partners) from 9 October 2007 considerably simplified IHT planning, in the sense that it is no longer necessary to ensure that the nil rate band of the first spouse to die has been utilised as far as possible to avoid wastage and a potential increase in IHT liability on the surviving spouse's later death. However, there may be reasons why it is still considered desirable for non-exempt legacies to utilise the nil rate band (see **3.16**).

Husband and wife: rules for other taxes

6.14   Since 6 April 1990, the independent taxation of the incomes of husband and wife has made it good practice to ensure that each spouse has sufficient gross income (either from earnings, or from assets providing gross interest) to soak up the income tax personal allowance for each individual together with the married couple's allowance for one spouse. (Note in this context, however, that the allowance applies only if the claimant is a married man whose wife is living with him, and was abolished for the under 65s with effect from 2000–01.)

Beyond that, the less well-off spouse (income-wise) ought to have income to take advantage of the lower, savings and basic rate bands of income tax. A married spouse can receive bank and building society interest gross if a non-taxpayer, otherwise subject to deduction of savings rate tax.

This is an area of great interest to HMRC: witness their persistence in the *Jones v Garnett* [2006] STC 1536 litigation well beyond the economic value in issue in the particular case. Although outright gifts without conditions between the spouses are successful in diverting income from one to the other, settlements where the settlor retains any kind of interest (eg interest in possession to spouse with reverter to settlor or remainder to children) will not achieve the aim, since the income will be deemed that of the settlor. The general rule is that capital must accompany the income. Thus a gift of shares, carrying rights to dividend but few capital rights will be treated as a settlement: *Young v Pearce*; *Young v Scrutton* ChD 1996, [1996] STC 743. For HMRC's view, see *Tax Bulletin* (April 2003) and TSEM4205 at Example 5.

Income from jointly held assets will normally be split equally between the spouses unless their beneficial interests are not equal and they make a declaration to HMRC of the correct shares. They do not have to make a declaration, in which case the income will be split equally (ITA 2007, ss 836, 837). Note that a declaration cannot be made where a husband and wife or civil partners own property as beneficial joint tenants, as the couple do not own the property in shares but are entitled jointly to the whole of both the property and the income (TSEM9850).

Furthermore, each spouse is entitled to his or her own annual CGT exemption, so that a judicious transfer of chargeable assets showing gains between the spouses can provide further savings if the assets are later sold. Is an inter-spouse transfer just before a disposal likely to be attacked under the Ramsay principle? Probably not, especially in relatively low-value cases. However, it would nevertheless seem sensible to effect the inter-spouse transfer before a third-party sale has been agreed, and/or to spread the transactions over a reasonable period (say, three months) if possible. It is arguable that such a transfer is not in any sense a commercial step. The writers are aware of no published cases taken by HMRC on this particular point. The taking of timely independent advice can obviate the problem: let the recipient spouse hold the asset that will eventually be sold for a while, receive its income and dispose of it only later. There are sometimes reasons not to do this, however.

Example 6.1 – Free gift to the spouse

With an eye to tax planning, the husband had, many years before, given his wife a substantial shareholding in the family company. The company was to be taken over, for many millions of pounds, and the family gathered at the completion meeting. The wife appeared to pay little attention to the precise terms of the various tax warranties and indemnities that she was expected to sign.

'If I sign all these forms', she asked the solicitor, 'do I really receive the sums set opposite my name?'

'Yes: like your husband, you are a shareholder and, provided you agree to all the terms of this Share Sale Agreement, the solicitors for the purchasers will remit to the account, of which you gave me details, the sum shown.'

'Ah.'

She said no more, but looked vacant and signed where she was told. The matter was completed. Neither her family, nor HMRC, ever saw her again; but at least the tax in issue, and lost, was only that attributable to the gain on her shares.

Spouses living together can, however, have only one main residence between them for CGT exemption purposes. Note the position where each had a residence before marriage, and the dwelling was retained (TCGA 1992, s 222(6); see CG64525).

Thus the requirement, subject to separate earnings by each spouse, is to arrange or transfer high income producing assets in favour of the less well-off spouse to use up the income tax personal allowance and lower and basic rate bands; and assets with gains to benefit from the double annual CGT exemption. The adjustment of assets between the spouses is facilitated by the IHT inter-spouse exemption and the CGT inter-spouse no gain, no loss rule (TCGA 1992, s 58). Note, however, in the case of capital gains tax the additional requirement that husband and wife (or civil partners) must be 'living together' in the year of transfer, within the meaning given by ITA 2007, s 1011 (TCGA 1992, s 288(3)).

Adapting to individual circumstances, the aim should be to accommodate these independent taxation requirements within the overall capital objectives for IHT as between husband and wife, such as the use of the nil rate band after every seven years.

One needs to add a word of warning that although currently the IHT concern over the respective size of estates of the spouses covers the nil rate band only, tax law and governments can change. If the one single IHT rate above the nil rate band reverted to a number of ascending rate bands, equalisation of estates might return. Flexibility, with any planning, is thus an important objective.

Use of nil rate band

6.15   In the context of estate planning for spouses and the current IHT circumstances of one positive rate of 40% above the nil rate band (£325,000 for 2012–13), prior to the changes introduced in FA 2008 from 9 October 2007, care was required when dealing with the estates of husband and wife, to ensure that the nil rate band was used in favour of chargeable beneficiaries or donees. Not to use it could cost IHT up to the prevailing nil rate band at 40% when added to the estate of the surviving spouse.

For example, where an individual would normally regard his spouse as the primary beneficiary, he might consider settling by will a sum equivalent to the upper limit of the nil rate band upon a discretionary trust so that the surviving spouse can have the benefit of the fund and at the same time the nil rate band can be utilised and not wasted. Distributions could be made in favour of the surviving spouse in case of need; and if they were of capital any exit charge under the discretionary trust regime in the first ten years would be by reference to the nil rate on the testator's death. Moreover, any distributions might be made by way of loan, which would normally expect to qualify as a deduction against the survivor's estate; or they could instead be income distributions subject to income tax.

The use of the nil rate band for a 'mini-discretionary trust' in this way was very effective, and quite popular. Furthermore, a discretionary trust with a wide class of beneficiaries and wide powers offered a flexible alternative, although there are several points to watch in utilising the nil rate band for a discretionary trust. These are analysed in **5.6–5.10**.

As indicated at **6.1** and in **Chapter 3**, estate planning to utilise nil rate bands in the manner described has assumed less significance following the introduction of the facility to transfer unused nil rate band on the first death (s 8A). However, the use of trusts in wills may still be the preferred option for reasons other than to utilise the nil rate band (eg for asset protection purposes, or for remarried spouses where two nil rate bands are already available).

If a relevant property will trust is preferred such as described in the preceding paragraph, it should be borne in mind in utilising the nil rate band as described above that the nil rate band can normally be expected to increase annually by reference to an indexation factor (s 8), which was previously calculated by reference to the retail price index (RPI), although in recent years it has not. As mentioned at **1.2**, the default indexation factor for all direct taxes, including IHT, changes from the RPI to the consumer price index from 6 April 2015, with the nil rate band being frozen until 2014-15.

FA 2006 set the IHT threshold for 2009–10 at £325,000. FA 2007 further increased the limit to £350,000 for 2010–11, but it was subsequently announced in the Pre-Budget Report 2009 that the nil rate band for that tax year would remain at £325,000. Furthermore, it was announced in the Budget on 24 March 2010 that the nil rate band would remain at £325,000 for the tax years 2011–12 to 2014–15 inclusive (FA 2010, s 8). The government subsequently announced on 5 December 2012 that the nil rate band for 2015–16 would increase by 1% (rounded up) to £329,000.

The testator's will should ensure that the gift matches the ceiling of the nil rate band when he dies. The gift in the will should therefore be of an amount equivalent to the upper limit of the IHT nil rate band in force at the time of the testator's death under IHTA 1984, Sch 1, as amended in accordance with the indexation provisions of s 8, if applicable. Such a formula, while most useful for cash gifts, cannot of course operate in the same straightforward way in the case of specific legacies of assets, particularly where business or agricultural reliefs are involved and changes in values may occur.

Care should always be taken with the nil rate band.

Example 6.2 – Trying to keep it simple

A's will gave an amount up to the available nil rate band to his children, and residue to his wife. The family did not like complicated or technical wording and wished to vary, so as to give specific properties to family members, so they substituted gifts for the more general wording described above.

Unfortunately, it then turned out that a lifetime gift by the deceased, previously unreported, fell within the seven-year period, effectively reducing the available nil rate band. IHT became chargeable as a result. They should have left well alone.

If utilising the nil rate band, the effect of business and agricultural reliefs (**Chapter 15**) is very important. Where relief is at 100% the benefit on top of the nil rate band is unlimited. With relief at 50%, for 2012–13 the nil rate band can become £650,000. Note, however, the trap with 50% (as opposed to 100%) relief under a settlement on discretionary trusts if the assets are then distributed within the first ten years under s 68 (see **7.37**).

As a general principle, because of this multiplying effect on figures, business and agricultural property should be given to chargeable parties rather than to the surviving spouse, to prevent relief being wasted. The same general principle applies whether the earlier spouse dies before or after the transferable nil rate band provisions from 9 October 2007. A further point to bear in mind, however, is that in the case of a partially exempt estate (eg because s 18 applies) the business or agricultural property itself must be given. It is not sufficient merely to create a specific pecuniary legacy payable out of the business or agricultural property. In this latter situation relief is denied on the value of the pecuniary legacy and therefore (at least in part) lost (see s 39A(6)).

In many cases the family home forms the largest part of the joint estates of husband and wife, and the survivor may need such cash or other liquid assets as there are for living purposes. It is still possible to make use of the nil rate band if the first spouse to die by will settles a cash sum equivalent to the nil rate band, say, upon discretionary trusts for children and grandchildren (or absolutely), and leaves the residue of the estate to the survivor. After the death the parties (ie the executors and the surviving spouse) can come together and agree that the cash gift should be charged on the matrimonial home, so that the surviving spouse can continue in occupation. The charge could be registered at HM Land Registry, but might be left as an informal one.

A question arises whether the 'spare' cash in the estate of the first to die of husband and wife may also be released to the surviving spouse or whether the trustees of the nil rate gift should 'collar' anything other than unrealisable assets. Clearly, it supports the reality of the structure if all available securities and cash are transferred to the trustees: they can then decide how much the surviving spouse really needs, bearing in mind the objective of keeping her estate as low as possible to save the later IHT charge.

Arrangements involving the family home purely for the purposes of utilising the spouse's nil rate band were, thankfully, rendered largely unnecessary by s 8A with effect from 9 October 2007. The relative complexity of 'debt' or 'charge' schemes is such that consideration should be given to abandoning those arrangements, such as in existing (pre-9 October 2007) wills that still include them.

CHANNELLING OF GIFTS AND ASSOCIATED OPERATIONS

6.16   The art of timing (whether gifts are into settlement or outright) is for a donor to make a PET or a chargeable transfer to use up the nil rate band while the seven-year survivorship requirement is likely to be satisfied. Thus, where a husband and wife wish to make such gifts to others, for example their children, it may be advisable to 'channel' the gifts through the spouse with the better life expectation or who has not used up the nil rate band.

On the face of it, the associated operations provisions of s 268 would appear specifically designed to counter such channelling transactions. It was made clear, however, when CTT was first being introduced, that in relation to outright gifts the associated operations rules would be used only in blatant or culpable circumstances, or where it was made a condition of the first gift that the other spouse would make a further gift (Mr Joel Barnett, *Hansard*, March 1975, HC Deb, Vol 888, col 56).

It is considered that this assurance also applies to gifts into settlement. This view is supported by the Court of Appeal's decision in *Rysaffe Trustees (CI) Ltd v IRC* [2003] STC 536 (see **1.21**). However, the position may be less clear cut, having regard in particular to the exchange of correspondence between the Institute of Chartered Accountants and the Inland Revenue (as it then was) of September 1985 concerning *Furniss v Dawson* [1984] STC 153 reproduced in ICAEW Guidance Note TR 588 of 25 September 1985. The Revenue's response was as follows:

'I can confirm that we would not seek to disturb existing practices in relation to inter-spouse transfers. It should, however, be borne in mind that the circumstances of such transfers always need to be carefully examined to ensure, among other things, that the transaction has substance as well as form. (For example, an understanding between the spouses on the ultimate destination of the assets would be important in this connection.) In general the terms of the Press Release of 8 April 1975 remain valid as a description of the practice in this area.'

(That Press Release contained notes on FA 1975 on the associated operations provisions of the then s 44, which reflect the *Hansard* statement referred to above.) The Inheritance Tax Manual also confirms (at IHTM14833) that property given unconditionally by one spouse to another and subsequently transferred to a third party cannot be subject to the associated operations provisions.

In certain circumstances, it might be argued by HMRC that the gift into settlement by a spouse, say a wife, who had received a gift from her husband, was a case where the wife was acting merely as a 'conduit'. In other words, the husband never effectively alienated the property given. In these circumstances, the husband might be regarded as the real and only settlor.

Accordingly, various precautionary steps are recommended to reduce the effectiveness of any such HMRC contention:

- The initial gift by the husband should be recorded in a signed memorandum, stressing that the gift is made to the wife as beneficial owner absolutely and unconditionally, eg as follows:

Example 6.3 – Memorandum and deed of gift

MEMORANDUM and DEED that I the undersigned have this day of … 20XX made a gift by way of [share transfer] of … of my Ordinary Shares of £1 each in the capital of … Limited to my wife [name] who has countersigned by way of acknowledgement and receipt.

I RECORD AND CERTIFY that this gift is made as an outright unconditional gift to my wife for her sole absolute use and benefit.

We certify that this deed falls within Category L of the Stamp Duty (Exempt Instruments) Regulations 1987. [NB For gifts of land and property, exemption is claimed under Finance Act 2003, Schedule 3 Paragraph 1.]

IN WITNESS whereof the parties hereto have signed this Memorandum and Receipt as their DEED in the presence of the persons mentioned below this … day of … 20XX

SIGNED and DELIVERED as a deed by

[HUSBAND]

in the presence of:

Witness:

Address:

Occupation:

RECEIPT DATED 20XX

I ACKNOWLEDGE receipt of the above gift upon the terms set out above.

SIGNED and DELIVERED as a deed by

[WIFE]

in the presence of:

Witness:

Address:

Occupation:

- The wife should receive independent professional advice if and when she creates her settlement, and any such advice should be recorded in writing.

- The wife should not in any event settle exactly the same number or quantity of assets (eg shares or cash) given to her initially by her husband.

The wife's gift into settlement, if in fact she decides to make it, should be after a decent interval of time, one month at the very least. Even better, if the gift from the husband produces gross income, let it belong in the wife's name such that the income shows up on her tax returns. If possible (eg in the case of cash), the wife should set up her settlement first, with the husband subsequently, as a separate decision and act, making a gift to the wife of a similar, but not the same, value.

Example 6.4 – Getting it right

Mr A has made previous lifetime chargeable gifts totalling £325,000 gross. He wishes to make a gift of £100,000 gross into a discretionary trust for his son's

283

family. This is a simple lifetime chargeable gift, and the IHT (at half the death rate of 40%) would be £20,000.

His wife, whose estate is worth £200,000, has not used up any of her nil rate band. He suggests to her that she might wish to make the £100,000 gift, which she does at no cost to IHT. Mr A the following year decides to transfer £110,000 to his wife by way of an outright, exempt gift.

It is considered that the wife's gift into the discretionary trust would not, in practice, be taxed as Mr A's under the associated operations rules of s 268.

MATRIMONIAL HOME AND JOINT OWNERSHIP

6.17   The matrimonial home is often the most important asset in a family and will most likely have a value in excess of the nil rate band. This subject of the matrimonial home is treated under three heads:

- mitigation of IHT generally;

- types of ownership; and

- practical and procedural aspects.

Reference should also be made generally to **Chapter 11**.

Mitigation of IHT generally

6.18   For IHT purposes, as between spouses, as in other cases, a life interest in an asset that existed at 22 March 2006 is treated in the same way as an absolute interest (the liability being based on the capital value on the death of the surviving spouse), and accordingly there was no difference for IHT between giving a life interest only in the matrimonial home to the surviving spouse and giving the property to the spouse absolutely. If the gift is by will, that is still true, provided that the spouse receives an immediate post-death interest (IPDI) (which she usually will).

Moreover, for practical reasons it is the wish of the husband and wife in most cases that the survivor should have the matrimonial home absolutely. This does not present the potential difficulties that existed before the facility to transfer unused nil rate band of the first spouse to die was introduced with effect from 9 October 2007. However, in the (perhaps limited) circumstances where it is preferred to utilise the nil rate band, when choosing the family assets with which to do so, other assets may have to be chosen, such as shares in the family company. However, a number of points should be borne in mind.

If the first spouse, for instance, leaves his interest in the home direct to the children, subject to a *right* to occupy in favour of the surviving spouse, it will probably give the survivor an entitlement to the use and enjoyment of the property equivalent to an interest in possession in it (see s 50 and *IRC v Lloyd's Private Banking Limited* [1998] STC 559), thereby shifting IHT on the house from the first death (exempt as passing to the survivor) to the termination of occupation by second. The exact statutory basis is unclear; there is no formal authority for 'deeming' an interest in possession, only that it may reflect economic reality. One is faced with an analogous problem to that raised by SP 10/79 whereby a beneficiary who is allowed by trustees of a settlement to occupy a house, part of the trust assets, on exclusive terms, will normally be regarded as having an interest in possession. SP 10/79 is 'difficult': it is often referred to but, it seems, never actually relied upon in court.

However, no deemed life interest was found in *Judge and another (personal representatives of Walden, dec'd) v HMRC* [2005] SpC 506 (see **4.13**). There, the deceased spouse's trustees had absolute discretion as to whether to permit the surviving spouse to occupy the property for any period (and her economic control over the asset, a veto on sale, was disregarded).

Moreover, if the house was left direct to the children, without the incorporation of conditions so as to secure occupation by the surviving spouse (which in any event seem not to be necessary by reason of the Trusts of Land and Appointment of Trustees Act 1996), the CGT private residence exemption (TCGA 1992, s 225) would be at risk to the extent that all the children as owners did not live there. It may well be preferable, therefore, in many circumstances, to give the survivor the security of his or her own home absolutely, and look at other assets for nil rate band planning. However, see **6.15** for the possibility of charging a nil rate band legacy on the home; and **6.19** for the suggestion of leaving a half share by will to a discretionary trust where the widow is one of the trustees.

Types of ownership

6.19   There are four main types of ownership of the matrimonial home and this involves consideration of ownership in the sole name of one spouse or joint ownership:

- sole ownership of husband;
- sole ownership of wife;
- joint holding as 'joint tenants'; or
- joint ownership as 'tenants in common';

Joint holding as 'joint tenants' is the *only* form of co-ownership capable of existing *in law*, as contrasted with beneficial ownership (ie in equity). Under this method, by reason of the *jus accrescendi* (right of survivorship) rule, the survivor takes the entire interest absolutely by operation of law. Hence, it is impossible (subject to severance which cannot be by will but, as a matter of practice, can be by deed of variation) to make *inter vivos* or death dispositions to third parties because this interest accrues automatically to the survivor.

A joint tenancy can be justified where it has been decided that the surviving spouse should have the entire property absolutely. Note that the difference between a joint tenancy and the other type of joint ownership ('a tenancy in common') is a mere matter of wording (see also **6.38** re severance). If it can be shown that a holding as joint tenants was contrary to the true intention of the parties, the court *may* grant rectification. However, to persuade the court to grant rectification the party seeking it must adduce 'strong irrefragable evidence', see *Countess of Shelbourne v Earl of Inchiquin* (1784) Bro.C.C 338; or see the requirement for 'convincing proof' in *Joscelyne v Nissen* [1970] 2 QB 86. Rectification may be ordered even where tax mitigation is the motive: *Racal Group Services Ltd v Ashmore* [1994] STC 416.

Joint holding as 'tenants in common'

6.20   Since 1925, it is only possible to have a tenancy in common *in equity*. However, this is likely to be of no practical importance as the value of the property will be represented by the respective beneficial interests and not the bare legal title. This type of holding is frequently found to be the most satisfactory from the IHT and practical viewpoints. Each spouse has a separate, say, half share which he or she can separately leave by will or dispose of during lifetime.

A co-owner of a share is entitled at law to occupy the whole of the property in question (TLATA 1996, s 12). Accordingly, there used to be scope for planning by making, say, children co-owners along with their parents. The parents would simply make a gift of an undivided share of their interest in the home. Provided that none of the co-owners was debarred from occupation if they so wished, continued occupation of the whole property by the parents was thought not to give rise to problems in relation to the gift with reservation rules.

This simple planning technique was, however, modified by FA 1986, s 102B introduced by FA 1999 to clarify and make statutory the previous practice which had been 'blessed' by *Hansard* in a statement dated 10 June 1986:

'It may be that my Hon. Friend's intention concerns the common case where someone gives away an individual share in land, typically a house, which is then occupied by all the joint owners including the donor. For example, elderly parents may make unconditional gifts of undivided shares in their house to their children and the parents and children occupy the property as their family home, each owner bearing his or her share of the running costs.

In those circumstances, the parents' occupation or enjoyment of the part of the house that they have given away is in return for similar enjoyment of the children of the other part of the property. Thus the donors' occupation is for a full consideration.

Accordingly, I assure my Hon. Friend that the gift with reservation rules will not be applied to an unconditional gift of an undivided share in land merely because the property is occupied by all the joint owners or tenants in common, including the donor.'

The gift of an undivided share of an interest in land is deemed to fall within the gift with reservation provisions *unless* the donor provides full consideration for his occupation of the property or the requirements of s 102B(4) are met, namely:

- both donor and donee occupy the property together; *and*

- the donor receives no benefit from the donee connected with the gift.

Husband and wife as tenants in common should make provision in their wills concerning their shares in the property. Following TLATA 1996, occupation of the family home by the surviving spouse should be secure even without conferring specific rights. That Act abolished the old rule that interests in land exist behind a statutory trust for sale, imposing upon the trustees an ultimate duty to sell the land. Instead a simple trust for land is created. Sections 12(1) and 13(7) are of particular importance.

Section 12 gives a person 'who is beneficially entitled to an interest in possession in land subject to a trust of land' a statutory right of occupation of the land that was purchased in the first place for his or her occupation. This will invariably be the case with the family home. The right is not, however, absolute, and is subject to restriction by s 13. Nevertheless, s 13(7) provides that the trustees cannot exercise their powers to exclude or restrict occupation by a person who is in occupation of land from continuing to so occupy unless he either consents or the approval of the court is obtained.

Given that the underlying purpose behind ss 12 and 13 has been to give statutory effect to the opinion of Lord Denning in *Bull v Bull* [1955] 1 QB 234 it is thought likely that, should any application be made to the courts, a more flexible approach will be adopted, and relevance given to factors such as the wishes of the person who set up the trust, as well as the welfare of any children.

In November 2007, HMRC provided guidance on interests in possession and SP 10/79 in response to queries raised by STEP and CIOT, which included the following points:

- The circumstances in which HMRC would not regard trustees as having exercised their power to give a beneficiary an exclusive right of occupation (ie so as not to create an interest in possession) are 'rare', but might include instances where there was no evidence of (or significant doubt as to) the intentions of the trustees.

- An SP 10/79 interest in possession generally arises if there is evidence that the trustees have knowingly exercised their powers so as to give a beneficiary exclusive occupation of the property.

- If the trustees have intended to grant a beneficiary the right to occupy a specific, named property owned by the trust, the beneficiary's interest in possession would end when the property was sold.

The guidance on SP 10/79 and interests in possession can be accessed via the STEP website at www.step.org/pdf/874668_1(PCL2).pdf.

Of course, if there remains any doubt about these issues, it will probably be better to leave the share in the house to the surviving spouse, and utilise other assets to take advantage of the nil rate band.

Practical and procedural aspects

6.21 When conveying (unregistered property – deed of gift) or transferring (registered property – deed of transfer) from the sole name of one spouse into the sole name of the other spouse or into the joint names of both spouses, whether as so-called joint tenants or tenants in common, the following practical points should be borne in mind.

(1) Gift of matrimonial home to a donee other than a spouse

6.22 For IHT purposes, the 'reservation of benefit' rules apply to gifts during lifetime (FA 1986, s 102 and Sch 20), and not to wills. If an owner makes a lifetime gift of his house, or part of it, and continues living there, HMRC may claim that by staying there after giving it away the former owner has reserved a benefit, so that the seven-year run off period for outright gifts does not apply (s 3A(4)), and nor does the percentage abatement of IHT on death within seven years of the gift (s 7(4)). The full value of the house remains in the total aggregable estate at death.

There is in fact an exemption under FA 1986, Sch 20, para 6(1)(a) which rules out reservation if the donee leases the property back to the donor for full consideration. Such a gift would then be a PET. It is essential to negotiate arm's-length terms for any tenancy or lease and for each party to be independently advised (see the Revenue letter dated 18 May 1987 to the Law Society in the *Law Society Gazette* dated 1 June 1988 at p 50).

HMRC take the view that full consideration is required throughout the period of any tenancy and the rent should therefore be reviewed at stated intervals, say every three or four years. They do, however, recognise that what is 'full' consideration must lie within a range of normal valuation tolerances and that any amount within that range can be accepted as satisfying para 6(1)(a) (see Revenue interpretation headed 'IHT gifts with reservation' in *IR Tax Bulletin*, Issue 9, November 1993 at p 98).

There are other practical problems apart from reservation: the need for the donor to go on paying a full market rent as his income is perhaps becoming squeezed, and a continuing income tax charge on the rental for the donee. (Consider, in this context, the use of a discretionary trust for family members, eg grandchildren. The rental income could be distributed for the benefit of the grandchildren at a nil or low overall rate of income tax.)

There would also be the question of rights of holding over occupation under the landlord and tenant legislation. If, furthermore, a lease at a market premium was chosen instead of a continuing market rental there would still be the question of income tax on the premium as well as possible rights of enfranchisement under the leasehold reform legislation.

Finally, principal private residence relief from capital gains tax would not be available to the donee should he sell the property, on, say, the donor taking up residence in a nursing home.

All these ideas must also be reviewed in the light of pre-owned assets tax (POAT), which may nullify the savings that had been hoped for (see **Chapter 13**).

Lease carve-outs

6.23   One popular scheme used to be to take the matrimonial home and carve it into two interests: one, a lease under which occupation is retained; and the other, the freehold reversion subject to that lease which is given away. Usually, the transferor would keep the lease (a wasting asset) in his estate, and make an outright gift of the freehold reversion arguing that in those circumstances there had been no reservation of benefit.

A variation of this scheme was subsequently considered and approved by the House of Lords in *Ingram v IRC* [1999] STC 37. In that case, Lady Ingram transferred her property to her solicitor as nominee. The nominee then granted to Lady Ingram a leaseback in order that she could continue to occupy the property. The freehold reversion was subsequently transferred (at Lady Ingram's direction) to the trustees of Lady Ingram's children's trust.

Another variation of the 'lease carve-out' scheme was to grant the lease to the trustees of a life interest trust under the terms of which the settlor was granted an interest in possession, followed by a gift of the freehold.

6.23 *Husband, wife and civil partner*

These types of arrangement have now been largely blocked as an IHT planning technique by FA 1986, s 102A introduced by FA 1999 with effect from 9 March 1999. A gift with reservation of benefit is now deemed to arise if (broadly) the donor or his spouse enjoys a right or interest which entitles or enables him to occupy all or part of the land or to enjoy some right in relation to the land otherwise than for full consideration in money or money's worth.

HMRC accept that there is no gift with reservation if the freehold interest in the house was given away, but a lease was retained or immediately granted at full rent, ie the transfer of the freehold to another individual would be a PET (see IHTM14360).

In addition, there is an exception from the reservation of benefit rules if the right or interest in the land was granted or acquired before the period of seven years ending with the date of gift (s 102A(5)). Accordingly, there appears still to be scope for a lease carve-out, provided any gift of the freehold takes place more than seven years after the creation of the lease under which the donor and/or his spouse will occupy. The result, therefore, is that effective tax planning using this method will now take 14 as opposed to seven years to achieve, such that the right or interest in the land is not 'significant' with s 102A (see s 102A(5)).

However, HMRC apparently consider that *Ingram* schemes effected from 9 March 1999 are still caught by the GWR rules if the lease is not for full consideration (IHTM14360). Alternatively, as noted above, the potential income tax implications under the 'pre-owned assets' regime need to be considered (see **Chapter 13**).

It must also be remembered that even before the changes introduced by FA 1999, there were a number of drawbacks with lease carve-out schemes:

- The donees would not normally benefit from the CGT main residence exemption; and since their acquisition value at the date of gift of the reversion would be low, the ultimate CGT would be likely to be high and to that extent negate the IHT savings. The family might think that they would 'never' sell the house, such that uplift on the death of the donee might relieve the gain, but circumstances change.

- There are potential income tax implications to consider in relation to the lease.

- There is the danger that HMRC might seek to apply the associated operations provisions of s 268, their argument being that the carving out of the lease and the subsequent gift of the freehold reversion were associated transactions (although this danger has diminished following the *Rysaffe* case (*Rysaffe Trustee Co (CI) Ltd v CIR* [2003] STC 536)).

- If the donor, now occupying under the terms of the lease, outlives the duration of the lease, he must either leave his home or pay a full market rent to remain in occupation. Otherwise, the original gift of the freehold reversion will be treated as a gift with reservation of benefit under normal principles (ie within s 102).

- For an example of this difficulty in practice, see *Wolff and another v Wolff and others* [2004] STC 1633, where the original donors had been poorly advised and, upon finding that they would have to pay a rack rent, obtained rectification of the deeds on the ground of mistake. In *Bhatt v Bhatt* [2009] EWHC 734 (Ch) (reported in *STI* 17 April 2009), the claimant was advised by a tax adviser to let her late husband's share of the matrimonial home be put in trust for her children, and to make a new will. However, Mrs Bhatt later became aware that her actions had potentially serious consequences, and issued proceedings for equitable relief. This included rectification of the registered title to the property, and the rescission of a number of documents (a declaration of trust, deed of variation, notice of severance and a transfer of the property to her children). The court held that the documents and the transactions as a whole could be set aside, subject to HMRC being given a reasonable opportunity to contest the outcome.

- However, in *Allnutt & another v Wilding & others* [2007] EWCA Civ 412, the taxpayer intended that a gift of £550,000 into settlement be a PET. However, the gift was an immediately chargeable lifetime transfer. The Court of Appeal rejected an application for rectification, as the settlement correctly recorded the settlor's intention at the time. The fact that the taxpayer's fiscal purpose was not achieved was not considered to be material. By contrast, an application to set aside transfers into trust on the basis of mistake was partly successful in *Ogden and another v Trustees of the RHS Griffiths 2003 Settlement and others* [2008] EWHC 118 (Ch): see **11.45**.

- Subsequently, in *Pitt & another v Holt & another* [2011] EWCA Civ 197, Mr Pitt was very badly injured in a road accident in 1990. The Court of Protection appointed Mrs Pitt as his receiver. A personal injury claim resulted in damages through a structured settlement amounting to £1.2 million, payable as a lump sum and monthly payments. Following professional advice and permission by the Court of Protection, the lump sum and annuity were put into a discretionary trust for the benefit of Mr Pitt, his wife, children and remoter issue during his lifetime, worth £800,000 at the time of transfer. Unfortunately, it was only later realised that an IHT charge of £100,000 arose on creation of the trust, with further liability to exit and ten-year charges. It would have been relatively easy to create the settlement without suffering those IHT consequences, as s 89 excludes this treatment in relation to trusts for disabled persons. Relief was sought on the basis of the rule in *Hastings-Bass* or on the ground of mistake.

- The High Court ([2010] EWCA 45 (Ch)) held that the settlement (and assignment of the annuity) were to be set aside under the *Hastings-Bass* rule. However, HMRC's subsequent appeal was allowed ([2011] EWCA Civ 197). The Court of Appeal held that as there had been no mistake as to the legal effect of the disposition to the settlement, it could not be set aside. In relation to the *Hastings-Bass* rule, Mrs Pitt's actions were not voidable as she was not in breach of her fiduciary duty as a receiver.

- The so-called 'rule in *Hastings-Bass*' is to be the subject of an appeal to the Supreme Court.

- For commentary on the *Hastings-Bass* rule and its application, including the Court of Appeal's decision in the *Futter* case (which was heard at the same time as *Pitt v Holt* above), see **8.20** onwards.

Reversionary leases

6.24   An alternative to the lease carve-out scheme was for husband and wife to retain the freehold and grant a long reversionary lease, eg for 300 years, at nominal rent.

The reversionary lease scheme was generally considered to be effective before 9 March 1999, although the position became less certain following legislative changes from that date. HMRC's guidance states the view (at IHTM14360) that reversionary lease schemes effected from 9 March 1999 are subject to the gift with reservation (GWR) rules, on the basis that the donor's occupation of the freehold (even if held more than seven years before the creation of the lease) is nevertheless considered to be a 'significant right in relation to the land' for GWR purposes (FA 1986, s 102A(3)).

Further HMRC guidance (at IHTM44102) states that reversionary lease schemes established before 9 March 1999 succeed in avoiding the GWR provisions, so long as the lease does not contain any terms that are currently beneficial to the donor (eg covenants by the lessee to, say, maintain the property), but that the donor will consequently be subject to a pre-owned assets income tax charge (under FA 2004, Sch 15, para 3(2)). HMRC also state that the GWR provisions may apply if the lease contains terms currently beneficial to the donor, irrespective of when the freehold interest was acquired.

With regard to reversionary lease schemes established on or after 9 March 1999, HMRC's guidance distinguishes between situations where the donor grants a reversionary lease more than seven years after acquiring the freehold interest, and where the reversionary lease is granted within that seven-year period:

'Where a reversionary lease scheme is established on or after 9 March 1999 it was originally considered that FA86/S102A … would apply because the donor's occupation would be a "significant right in relation to the land". If that were correct, the reservation of benefit rules would apply and there would be no POA charge.

However, where the freehold interest was acquired more than 7 years before the gift ... the continued occupation by the donor is not a significant right in view of FA86/S102A(5), so the reservation of benefit rules cannot apply and a POA charge arises instead.

It follows that if the donor grants a reversionary lease within 7 years of acquiring the freehold interest, FA86/S102A may apply to the gift depending on how the remaining provisions of that section apply in relation to the circumstances of the case – for example, if the donor pays full consideration for the right to occupy or enjoy the land, that would not be a significant right in view of FA86/S102A(3), so the reservation of benefit rules cannot apply and a POA charge arises instead.'

Where the pre-owned assets (POAT) provisions apply (see **Chapter 13**), it may nevertheless be possible to elect out of an income tax charge, and into the GWR provisions instead.

Perhaps the main drawback with this arrangement, apart from the fact that it may be nullified by POAT, is that s 149(3) of the Law of Property Act 1925 may render void any grant of a lease taking effect more than 21 years from the date it is granted, and 21 years might not be sufficient for occupation by the spouses. There is an argument that the 21-year limit only applies on a sale, not a gift. Subject to that, this method, involving one transaction only, would be safe from associated operations; but would produce the same CGT disadvantages for the donees as already discussed.

Both in the case of the lease carve-out and the reversionary lease, the ownership of the freehold and the leasehold interest should not merge, but be held by different parties. This may add a layer of complexity and cost if, say, the (minor) grandchildren are chosen to hold one of the interests, because from 22 March 2006 the creation of a lifetime trust for them of that interest will be a chargeable transfer.

Gift of a share of the home

6.25   It is possible for spouses to retain a share of the matrimonial home, perhaps a third or a quarter, and give the remaining share to their children but the spouses and the other joint owners must all occupy the home. The occupants should pay their proper share of the household running costs. However, the requirement that the donor must not receive any connected benefit (other than a negligible one) does not necessarily mean that the running costs must be shared proportionately. The donor may wish to continue paying all or most of them. Otherwise, the difficulty arises in establishing how much the donee can safely pay, without the donor falling foul of the GWR rules.

This sharing method was originally based on a statement by Mr Peter Brooke, Minister of State HM Treasury, on 10 June 1986 (Standing Committee G Finance Bill) and is preserved by the legislative changes applying to gifts of undivided shares of interests in land contained in FA 1986, s 102B.

It may work very well in the case of an unmarried son or daughter, or even a married child living with the parents. If, however, the children already have their own home, the required element of occupation and sharing is missing. Furthermore, if the children did live there but later moved away, the parents would at that stage have to pay a full rent to avoid a reservation of benefit springing up.

Nothing appears to prevent the use of this arrangement in respect of an unequal share. However, get the paperwork right: HMRC requires all such cases to be referred to its Technical Group (IHTM14332). (Note the alternative of using a s 54 reverter to settlor exemption in **11.28**). This principle could extend to holiday homes and *pieds-à-terre*.

Gift of cash, later invested in a home

6.26   It might be feasible in some circumstances to base an arrangement on a gift of cash. The parents could give their son £150,000 cash outright. At a later stage he could make use of the cash to buy a house where they might all live. However, this may lead straight to a POAT charge, unless it is precisely within the 'son of Hansard' exemption from POAT set out in FA 2004, Sch 15, para 11(5)(c). It would not be appropriate to use the cash to buy the parents' present home since HMRC could attack the arrangement on the grounds of associated operations. The income tax charge on pre-owned assets would need to be considered unless the cash gift was made more than seven years before the house purchase (FA 2004, Sch 15, para 10(2)(c)). It would be simpler for the parents to give the son, say, a third of the house and for him to move in with them.

Reverter to settlor

'Old' (pre-22 March 2006) interests in possession

6.27   It was, until 22 March 2006, possible for a son, out of an earlier cash gift, to purchase and settle a house on a parent for life (by way of interest in possession and PET) with the prospect of reverter to settlor exemption (s 54) on the parent's death.

However, as was noted in an earlier edition of this work, the risk with the scheme, as in the case of any relatively long-term planning, was of changes in the law which might occur. That did of course subsequently happen, even without the change of government that was envisaged. The availability of the reverter to settlor exception is now restricted, such that on the termination of the interest in possession, the property must:

- revert to the settlor during his lifetime; or

- form part of the estate of the settlor's UK-domiciled spouse or civil partner (or surviving spouse or civil partner, where the settlor has died within the last two years).

See ss 53(3), (4) and 54(2), (3), though this result hardly jumps off the page, on a casual reading. FA 2006 affected 'existing' trusts because the property must revert to the settlor or spouse absolutely, or on interests in possession in which they are beneficially entitled. Such qualifying interests in possession were severely restricted from 22 March 2006 (see **6.9**).

All this is relevant because it was usually desirable to take a life interest only, at the time of the reversion, to avoid the CGT position that would otherwise arise on the deemed disposal under TCGA 1992, s 73(1)(b). However, following FA 2006, if the settlement continues it falls outside a qualifying interest in possession under s 49(1). So the reversion must be absolute. If (a big 'if', at the time of writing) property can be considered always likely to rise in value, these considerations may make the scheme unworkable.

Interests in possession on or after 22 March 2006

6.28   As mentioned above, reverter to settlor relief is restricted in respect of trusts created on or after 22 March 2006. The relief applies to DPIs and TSIs to which the person with the interest in possession in settled property became beneficially entitled from that date (s 54(2A)). In addition, the relief can apply where the person with the beneficial interest in the settled property dies, if that interest in possession was an immediate post-death interest (IPDI) throughout. The settlor must have died within two years before the person's death, and on that person's death the settlor's UK-domiciled widow(er) must become entitled to the settled property (s 54(2B)).

Reverter to settlor trust arrangements should be reviewed for POAT purposes, particularly in the light of changes to the POAT legislation introduced by FA 2006, s 80 with effect from 5 December 2005, which were intended to curtail such arrangements (FA 2004, Sch 15, paras 11–13).

Devise of home followed by settlement

6.29   It would not be recommended for a spouse to leave the home in his will to a child on the understanding that the child would then make a s 54 settlement on the survivor, who would no doubt already be living there. Whilst death is not an associated operation, such an arrangement would be open to attack on grounds of artificiality.

Double trust loan scheme

6.30   This idea is still occasionally seen in practice and was discussed in detail in earlier editions of this work. It is no longer effective, in the sense that it has been specifically targeted by POAT. By now, most existing schemes have probably been unscrambled.

POAT imposes a charge where, broadly, the former owner of property, which is no longer in his estate, still occupies it. As a result, taxpayers who implemented the double trust loan scheme some years ago were faced with very real decisions. For many of them, it was necessary to decide, by 31 January 2007, whether they would 'opt back in' to the IHT regime and surrender such tax advantage as they might have secured by the scheme or, in the alternative, start paying the POAT. It was a difficult decision, requiring:

- valuation of the benefit already secured;

- an estimate of life expectancy;

- valuation of the rental on which the POAT would be based; and

- a clear understanding of the scheme and of the options.

There are variations in the application of double trust schemes, such as in respect of the terms of the loan. Where those terms provide that the debt is only repayable after the death of the life tenant, HMRC initially appeared to accept that such schemes were not caught by the GWR rules in respect of the loan. However, HMRC's current guidance states that, in such circumstances, the settlor still obtains a benefit that is referable to the gift. HMRC therefore consider that a GWR charge applies to the loan (the same applies to loans repayable on demand, which were previously considered to be caught). In addition, HMRC consider that a POAT charge arises in respect of the house, on the basis that it is the asset previously owned by the individual (IHTM44105).

In addition to the above approach to the GWR provisions, HMRC's guidance advances the following arguments to negate the intended consequences of IOU schemes (IHTM44106):

'The first is that the provisions of FA86/S103 apply to disallow the deduction of the loan against the trust in which the individual retained a life interest. The sale of the property to the first trust is a disposition and since, in the majority of cases, the trustees had no means with which to pay for the property, the steps they took to fund their purchase created the debt which (through the trustees equitable lien) is an incumbrance against the property. The consideration for the debt was property derived from the deceased and FA86/S103 applies to abate the loan.

Secondly, having regard to the purpose and effect of home loan schemes, the steps taken are a pre-ordained series of transactions, and following the line of authority that is founded on *W T Ramsay v IRC* [1981] 1 All ER 865, the individual steps should be treated as a single transaction comprising a number of elements which when taken together have the effect that the vendor has made a "gift" of the property concerned for the purposes of FA86/S102 and has continued to live there. So reservation of benefit arises in the property.'

The effectiveness of home loan or double trust schemes is likely to be determined through litigation, although no cases have been reported at the time of writing.

If there is a GWR in the property, a POA charge will not arise in respect of it. In that case, HMRC has stated that any POA income tax paid (ie on the basis that no such GWR applied) will be repaid with interest upon a claim being made, irrespective of the time limits for repayment that might otherwise apply (www. hmrc.gov.uk/poa/poa-guidance6.htm).

To assist executors and trustees in the administration of estates, HMRC will provide estimates of the tax that might be payable if HMRC succeeds in future litigation. This would allow executors and trustees to make payments on account to HMRC to mitigate potential interest charges, or to make an appropriate provision out of funds held (HMRC Trusts & Estates Newsletter, August 2012).

Non-trust IOU arrangements

6.31 Loan (or IOU) arrangements can still be effective provided that the debt is created by a transaction between spouses or civil partners. For example, husband sells an investment property to his wife (or civil partner) at market value, the price being left outstanding as an IOU repayable on the death of the survivor. At that point, therefore, the wife holds the property but there has been no increase in her estate because its value is matched by the amount of the loan and remains so during her life.

The husband then gives the IOU to his adult children. The spouses as an economic unit retain ownership of the property (and its rental income) between them but the husband derives no direct benefit, as would be the case with the home. There is a PET of the capital value gifted to the children, and hence the seven-year risk of an IHT liability, although this risk should be insurable.

There is no reservation of benefit between husband and wife, to the extent that the arrangements comprise any gift element (FA 1986, s 102(5)) although, in view of what is said at **6.30**, there may be when the husband gives the IOU to the children. There is no CGT liability on the sale, due to the spouse exemption (TCGA 1992, s 58). The exclusion from POAT for transfers between spouses (or civil partners) applies (FA 2004, Sch 15, para 10(1)(b)).

Care is required to ensure that the loan never becomes disallowable as a deduction from the husband's estate due to the provisions in FA 1986, s 103. Thus the wife should not leave the property to her husband but should leave it direct to the children. If the property came back into the husband's estate s 103 would negate the arrangement. In this example, it should be noted that stamp duty land tax may be in point. This arrangement can also be applied to company shares.

A note of caution should be expressed. As indicated at IHTM44106 in the context of home loan schemes, HMRC could seek to challenge IOU arrangements of this nature along other lines, eg as under the *Ramsay* principle. Such planning should therefore be subject to a suitable 'health warning'.

Proposals concerning the matrimonial home in a will and on death are discussed in **5.13**. Lease carve-out and reversionary lease schemes, in so far as still valid, are discussed at greater length in **Chapter 11**: Gifts.

The various schemes that potentially fall within the POAT provisions introduced in FA 2004 are discussed in **Chapter 13**.

(2) Presumptions of advancement and resulting trust: intention as to beneficial ownership

6.32 Gifts between husband and wife are concerned with two competing presumptions of law in the absence of an express declaration of beneficial interests in the matrimonial home. Although the basis may often be clear, and may even be irrelevant where the spouse exemption is available, some knowledge of the principles may be useful.

Presumption of advancement

6.33 *Purchase in the name of a wife: presumed gift*

This is the presumption that the recipient of an asset is to benefit. It can arise where the husband owns an asset and places it into his wife's name or jointly in the names of himself and his wife, or if he purchases an asset but has the purchase completed by a conveyance into his wife's name.

The presumption of advancement is set to be abolished (by Equality Act 2010, s 199(1)) from a date to be appointed, subject to transitional provisions (s 199(2)).

Not in favour of mistresses

The presumption does not apply between a man and his mistress (*Lowson v Coombes* [1999] 2 WLR 720), even if they later marry: *Austin v Austin* [1978] WLR 46.

Not in favour of husbands

Further, and surprisingly given the date of the decision, the presumption does not operate where the transfer is from a wife to her husband (*Tribe v Tribe* [1996] Ch 107 at 118).

But fiancées are allowed, if later married

Advancement can similarly be inferred where the donor purchases an asset in the name of his intended wife (provided that the marriage is duly solemnised and, it seems, that the transfer of the asset is conditional upon the marriage taking place), see *Moate v Moate* [1948] 2 All ER 486.

Children

This can also apply where a father places an asset in the name of his child or any other person to whom he stands *in loco parentis*.

Contrary evidence

Whilst the law presumes that the husband intends to benefit his wife (or child), this rule can be negatived or rebutted by appropriate evidence as to the husband's intentions at the time of the transfer. An example can be seen in the case of *O'Neill v IRC* [1998] STC (SCD) 110. There, a father put money into an account in the Isle of Man which was a joint account in the name of himself and his daughter. It was held that because the existence of the account had been concealed from the daughter during the lifetime of her father (who had retained de facto control over the account), the account had been set up as a sort of legacy, and the presumption of earlier advancement did not apply. As to joint bank accounts generally, see **6.43**.

In addition, HMRC's stated view on bank accounts is as follows (TSEM9630):

'In the case of bank accounts, the presumption is that the wife or child would get the money in the account on the death of the husband or parent. But until death the beneficial ownership stays with the person who provided the money, and the wife or child is not entitled to any interest accruing before the provider's death.'

Rebuttal of the presumption

The courts will not (see *Gascoigne v Gascoigne* [1918] 1 KB 223) allow evidence of an improper purpose to overturn the presumption, such as an intention to defeat potential creditors: see *Tinker v Tinker* [1970] 1 All ER 540 and *Tribe v Tribe* [1995] 4 All ER 236, CA; but in *Bingeman v McLaughlin* (1973) 1OR (2d) 485 the presumption was not rebutted. On the facts the creditors had not been delayed or harmed. Times are changing, as reflected in *Pettitt v Pettitt* [1970] AC 777, [1969] 2 All ER 385, HL. It has in modern conditions become relatively easy to rebut the presumption. That view is supported by *McGrath v Wallis* [1995] 3 FCR 661, CA.

It all depends on the evidence

However, the presumption is still available to resolve the issue of ownership in the absence of evidence as to the spouse's true intentions at the time of the transfer, and the presumption of joint beneficial ownership has more application as a general rule. A detailed consideration of the subject is beyond the scope of this book, especially where disputes between spouses arise. In *Webb v Webb* [1992] 1 All ER 17, a father had purchased foreign immovable property (a flat in Antibes) in the name of his son. The court rejected the presumption of advancement in favour of the son, declaring that there was sufficient evidence of the father's intention to retain the property for himself. The best advice to clients is to document clearly the basis upon which the transfer is made, whether as a gift, loan, or to be held on trust.

Presumption of resulting trust

6.34   This is the reverse presumption, namely that the recipient of an asset is *not* to benefit, but merely to hold it on trust for the donor. The law on resulting trusts was considered in detail by the House of Lords in *Westdeutsche Landesbank v Islington BC* [1996] AC 669.

Husband a mere nominee

The presumption applies where, for example, the wife owns an asset or contributes towards its purchase, and the asset is placed into her husband's name or jointly between herself and her husband. See for example *Wray v Steele* (1814) 2 Ves & B 388. Equity presumes that the husband is merely the nominee or trustee of his wife as to the appropriate share, unless the presumption is rebutted by appropriate evidence of the wife's intention to benefit the husband at the time of the gift.

She earned a share

This aspect has been extended by way of imputing a constructive trust in favour of a common law wife in the 'sledgehammer' case of *Eves v Eves* [1975] 3 All ER 768, CA. In this case a man and woman cohabited and had children. The house was purchased in the man's sole name, although the woman did a great deal of work in demolishing and later repairing and maintaining the house and the garden. The court imputed a constructive trust in favour of the woman equal to a 25% interest.

Mistress not entitled

The concept of the trust, however, will not always apply to a man and his mistress as much as to a husband and wife. In *Burns v Burns* [1984] Ch 317, the Court of Appeal declared that where the home was bought in the name of the man alone without any substantial contribution by the mistress towards the purchase price, the deposit or the mortgage instalments, then she is not entitled to any share in the house, however hard she may have worked in other directions. The case contains a useful summary of the earlier cases and the common situations.

A luckier mistress

If that case is considered out of line with earlier development, a step forward was taken in *Grant v Edwards* [1986] 2 All ER 426, CA, where a mistress was held entitled to a half share of the home. The case emphasised that the primary question is that of intention. Here there was an intention to share; and the true significance of contributions to the purchase price of the house or to the household expenses was an indication of the intentions of the parties as to beneficial ownership. However, to avoid the principle that equity will not assist a volunteer, the claimant must also demonstrate that she acted on that intention to her detriment.

In *Turton v Turton* [1987] 2 All ER 641 an unmarried couple bought a house in 1972 with an express trust for themselves as joint tenants. They separated in 1975 and the house was sold in 1986. In the absence of any claim to upset it, the declaration of trust was decisive of the couple's respective interests (see *Goodman v Gallant* [1986] 1 All ER 311, CA). Moreover, the date of valuation of the claimant's interest was the date of sale, not the date of separation.

Wife's overriding interest

The issue of ownership arose in *Williams and Glyn's Bank Ltd v Brown* and *Williams and Glyn's Bank Ltd v Boland* [1979] 2 All ER 697 in a way that may occasionally be relevant in IHT situations. In each case the (sole owner) husband had charged the matrimonial home to the bank without the wife's knowledge. Each of the wives had contributed substantially towards the purchase price. The bank sought possession of the property. Held, Court of Appeal, the wives each had an equitable interest in the property; since the wives were in 'actual occupation' that interest constituted an 'overriding interest' (Land Registration Act 1925, s 70(1)(g)), which the banks as mortgagees took subject to, and they were therefore not entitled to obtain possession. That would not apply, see *Lloyds Bank plc v Rosset* [1990] 1 All ER 1111, HL, where the wife's contribution was *de minimis*.

6.34 *Husband, wife and civil partner*

Overreaching of equitable interest

The House of Lords reached the opposite conclusion in *City of London Building Society v Flegg* [1987] 3 All ER 435. Mr and Mrs F and their daughter and son-in-law (Mrs and Mr M-B) bought a house for their joint occupation. The Fs provided a little over half of the purchase price. However, the house was conveyed into the names of the M-Bs as beneficial joint tenants under a trust for sale. Only they were registered as co-proprietors. The M-Bs mortgaged the house unbeknown to the Fs. They defaulted. The building society sought possession. Held, that Fs' rights took effect under the trust for sale, but on creation of the charge their rights to occupy were overreached and thereupon switched to the capital advanced to the M-Bs and the equity of redemption, but subordinated to the legal charge of the building society. They lost their home.

It is thought that, following the commencement of Trusts of Land and Appointment of Trustees Act 1996, although F would now have an interest in land, this would nevertheless remain a situation where the court would order sale under the jurisdiction conferred upon it by s 13. However, the way in which the court will in fact exercise this jurisdiction will have to be tested before any clear opinion can be given.

The effective working of TLATA 1996

Tax practitioners need to be aware of the implications of TLATA 1996, on which can hang the precise nature of the interest of a joint owner in a property. Its value may depend on whether it can be realised. Thus, the following cases, although considering old law, may still be of interest in considering how the court may in practice exercise its jurisdiction under TLATA 1996, s 13.

First, in *Barclays Bank plc v O'Brien* [1993] 4 All ER 417, HL, the indebtedness of the husband's company was secured by a charge over the matrimonial home jointly owned by husband and wife. The bank failed to warn the wife when she signed the security documents of the risk to the home. That failure fixed the bank with constructive notice of the husband's wrongful misrepresentation to her. She was therefore entitled to set aside the legal charge on the home securing the husband's liability.

In contrast, *CIBC Mortgages plc v Pitt* [1993] 4 All ER 433, HL, was a case again of a matrimonial home in the joint names of husband and wife. The husband persuaded his wife to join in taking out a loan for £150,000, secured on the home, which the husband wanted in order to deal on the stock market. The October 1987 crash intervened, and the husband could not keep up the mortgage payments. Although the wife had established undue influence by her husband, the lender was not affected by it because he had been told the purpose of the loan was to buy a holiday home and regarded the loan (paid into their joint account) as a normal advance to a husband and wife for their joint benefit. The wife's appeal was therefore dismissed. It is thought that these cases would be decided the same way, even under the 'new' law.

Dealing with the presumption

6.35   Since there may be good estate planning reasons for placing the matrimonial home into the name of the other spouse or into joint names in order to arrange the estate between husband and wife while attracting the exemption of s 18, it is essential to avoid the operation of the resulting trust where the wife makes the gift or contribution. The instrument effecting the transfer, conveyance or assignment of the property, or an accompanying memorandum, must make the position clear, namely that a gift passing the full beneficial ownership is intended. Where the husband makes the gift it is also advisable that this intention is clearly indicated so that an advancement is not merely presumed but made express.

Intention as to beneficial ownership

6.36   As the courts apply the equitable presumptions less, we have to look more closely at what the parties wanted, especially where the matrimonial home is concerned.

It should be noted that land interests cannot generally be created or disposed of other than by a written instrument. The same broadly applies in respect of declarations of trust in respect of land, and dispositions of pre-existing equitable interest or trust interests. However, there is an exception from the requirement for a written instrument in respect of resulting, implied or constructive trusts (LPA 1925, s 53(2)).

There have been many cases that turn mainly on the facts, so it is impossible to be sure of the law. As a general rule where one spouse, say the wife, has made a substantial contribution towards the purchase of the house either directly or indirectly, the court will apportion to her a beneficial interest in the property.

The principle has been extended to *business profits*. If a wife makes a substantial contribution to her husband's business and receives inadequate emoluments in return, she will be regarded as having an appropriate interest in the matrimonial home or the assets bought out of the profits (*Nixon v Nixon* [1969] 3 All ER 1133 CA).

In the context of marriage breakdown, the Matrimonial Causes Act 1973, ss 23 and 24 give the courts a wide discretion to make financial provision and adjustment of property orders irrespective of how the beneficial interests are expressed, and s 25 of that Act imposes on the court a duty in deciding whether and in what manner to exercise its discretion and to have regard to all the circumstances of the case.

Liability to IHT is concerned with beneficial ownership. The uncertain application of the law referred to above gives rise to difficulties, in particular, whether in any given case a spouse's contribution represents a material interest in the property, whether a gift has been made, or whether a resulting trust has arisen.

This uncertainty can be avoided if the parties will make their intention clear at the time the property is acquired. The court in *Leake (formerly Bruzzi) v Bruzzi* [1974] 2 All ER 1196 declined to go behind the terms of the trust deed which declared in whom the beneficial title vested but regarded such terms as conclusive of the parties' respective beneficial interests in the matrimonial home. In the case of *Heseltine v Heseltine* [1971] 1 All ER 952, CA, where the predominant motive appears to have been to minimise ED, such intention had not been sufficiently declared.

As indicated elsewhere in this book, the legal and beneficial owners of an asset may differ. It is not uncommon for property to be registered in joint names, but for one party to have a greater beneficial interest than the other (eg having contributed more of the purchase price). In those circumstances, the asset may be treated as owned by the parties in accordance with their respective beneficial shares (*Oxley v Hiscock* [2004] EWCA Civ 546, [2005] Fam 211 and *Stack v Dowden* [2007] 2 All ER 929). Following the latter case, HMRC stated that an increasing number of claims had been received that property should be valued at lower than full open market value, on the basis that another individual held a beneficial, but not legal, interest in the property. However, HMRC warned: '… unless there is a case that we consider sufficiently strong that it would be upheld by the courts, the claim will be rejected' in IHT & Trusts Newsletter (December 2007).

More recently, in *Wade v Bayliss* [2010] EWCA Civ 257, a couple commenced living together as man and wife in 1982, but separated in 2005. Following the split, Mr Wade claimed a 50% beneficial interest in the property, even though he had been removed from the deeds in 1986 at his own request. He had apparently made no contribution to the capital cost of the property, and contributed little to the mortgage repayments, although he had worked for free in a business run by Ms Bayliss. The Court of Appeal dismissed Mr Wade's appeal against an earlier decision that Ms Bayliss was the sole beneficial owner of the property in question. It was implicit in the circumstances that both the legal and beneficial interest in the property had been transferred.

Subsequently, in *Kernott v Jones* [2011] UKSC 53, the Supreme Court unanimously held that the beneficial interests of co-habitants in a property can change without their explicit intention. In that case, the co-habitants bought a house in 1985, and jointly owned it, without making any declaration as to how their beneficial interests should be apportioned. The relationship ended, and Mr Kernott moved out after the parties had lived in the property together for more than eight years. Ms Jones had originally contributed £6,000 of the £30,000 purchase price, and the balance had been funded by an interest-only mortgage. Following the separation, Ms Jones continued to live in the property, and assumed sole responsibility for the mortgage and outgoings including repairs and maintenance.

Mr Kernott later demanded his half-share of the house. However, the county court awarded Ms Jones 90% of the equity. Mr Kernott unsuccessfully appealed to the High Court. Subsequently, the Court of Appeal ([2010] EWCA Civ 578) held (by majority) that Mr Kernott and Ms Jones each had a 50% beneficial interest in the property. However, the Supreme Court overturned that decision, stating that an initial presumption of joint tenancy in law and equity can be displaced if the parties changed their intentions, and that a court can deduce their common intention from their conduct.

HMRC appear to attach little importance to the decisions in *Oxley v Hiscock* or *Stack v Dowden* when it comes to considering the beneficial ownership of assets other than residential property. In the Trusts, Settlements and Estates Manual, HMRC state (at TSEM9710):

> 'If taxpayers attempt to rely on the decisions in the cases of *Oxley v Hiscock* [2004] 3 All ER 703) (sole legal title) or *Stack v Dowden* [2007] UKHL 17) (joint legal title), you should point out that those cases relate specifically to the ownership of the matrimonial or quasi-matrimonial home. The cases are likely to be of limited application where it is not ownership of a domestic home that is at issue, but land or buildings rented or personal property.'

The government has declined to follow the Law Commission's recommendations in respect of property interests of unmarried couples, and has indicated that legislation will not be introduced to clarify the law in this area. Sadly, the government's decision will inevitably result in continued uncertainty, complexity and expensive litigation in the future.

(3) Stamp duty and stamp duty land tax

6.37   The 'consideration' in the deed of gift or transfer is not usually valuable, being expressed as the 'natural love and affection of the donor for the donee'. As a result of the Stamp Duty (Exempt Instruments) Regulations 1987 (SI 1987/516) no conveyance or transfer operating as a voluntary disposition *inter vivos* (ie as a gift), is liable to *ad valorem* stamp duty, but is exempt provided an appropriate certificate is included in the instrument (note that this certification requirement does not generally apply to instruments transferring stock and marketable securities otherwise than on sale (following FA 2008, Sch 32), with effect from 13 March 2008).

For stamp duty land tax purposes, a land transaction is exempt if there is no chargeable consideration, eg a gift between spouses (FA 2003, Sch 3, para 1). But note the mortgage trap at (5) below.

(4)   Severance

6.38   The joint tenancy of a property held by husband and wife can be severed so that husband and wife become tenants in common in equity, thereby providing greater flexibility. A simple form of notice of severance will do. An equitable joint tenancy can be severed by a joint tenant giving to the other joint tenant a notice in writing under the Law of Property Act 1925, s 36(2) (proviso) and s 196.

This notice must be given during lifetime because a joint tenancy cannot be severed by will (although it can, in practice, by deed of variation under s 142). It is preferable for a severance to be agreed and signed by both parties.

Example 6.5 – Notice

To [second owner]

I hereby give you notice to sever the joint tenancy that exists between us of [3, Acacia Villas, East Cheam, Surrey]. Please acknowledge this notice by signing the copy. [We will then notify the Land Registry.]

Dated ... 20XX

Signed [first owner]

Acknowledgement

I have received a notice of which the foregoing is a copy. You may notify the Land Registry.

Signed [second owner]

---

(5)   Mortgages and other outgoings

6.39   Frequently, the property is mortgaged; the mortgage may be either legal or equitable. Before a change can take place in the ownership of property subject to such a mortgage, the consent of the mortgagee must be obtained.

In the usual case of property subject to a mortgage with a building society or an insurance company, little difficulty is experienced in practice in obtaining the mortgagee's consent to a transfer between spouses, and therefore the method of transferring the property subject to the mortgage is normally adopted. Alternatively, there is nothing to prevent one spouse conveying or transferring to the other only the equity of redemption *without* the mortgagee's consent.

There is, however, a nasty SDLT trap to beware of. Duty is still payable to the extent of the existing mortgage debt assumed by the donee (FA 2003, Sch 4, para 8). This follows the stamp duty rule in Stamp Act 1891, s 57 (see the Revenue's SP 6/90 of 27 April 1990).

The fact that a husband continues to pay mortgage instalments in respect of his wife's house or share therein should not give rise to any IHT charge because of the available exemptions, for example s 18 (inter-spouse) and s 21 (normal expenditure out of income). The same applies to payment of other outgoings such as insurance, general rates, water rates, and ground rent if the property is leasehold.

(6) Insurance

6.40   If there is any change in the ownership of the legal estate, the relevant insurance company should be notified of such change and an endorsement obtained and annexed to the insurance policy.

(7) Leasehold

6.41   Where the property is leasehold, particular attention must be given to the terms of the lease. Thus, the prior consent of the landlord may be required (although this is unusual for long leases of, say, 99 years); and in any event it is usually necessary to give notice to the landlord of any change of ownership of the legal or equitable interests or mortgage arrangements.

This section of **Chapter 6** has been primarily concerned with a change of ownership of the matrimonial home. On the footing that prevention is better than cure, the decision as to the best method of owning the matrimonial property should, wherever practical, be considered from the outset and before a purchase is completed. In that case the spouses should produce their contributions to the purchase price from their separate funds, a record of this being retained. Otherwise, complications can arise as to the actual beneficial ownership of the parties (see **6.19**).

Even where the spouses have modest means at the time of such purchase, the type of ownership from the IHT angle should be considered. The trend of earnings and wealth is usually upwards.

(8)   Valuation

6.42   In terms of joint property interests involving spouses (or civil partners), when valuing the interest of one spouse it is generally necessary to take account of the other spouse's interest under the related property provisions in s 161, which invariably results in a higher valuation. In *Arkwright and another (Personal Representatives of Williams, deceased) v IRC* [2004] STC 1323 (see **1.24**), the Special Commissioner held that the valuation rule in s 161(4) did not apply to fractional units of property.

However, HMRC subsequently stated: '… HMRC has received legal advice that in some circumstances s 161(4) may, in fact, apply to fractional shares on units'. It is not clear what is meant by 'some circumstances', but HMRC have made it clear that they will apply s 161(4) when valuing shares of land as related property (HMRC Business Brief 71/07; see **1.6**). HMRC will refer any cases involving the application of s 161(4) to litigation (IHTM09737).

JOINT BANK ACCOUNTS

6.43   As a general rule, and as mentioned below, the use of joint bank accounts for substantial sums should be avoided. It robs the family of flexibility in disposing of value, for example a lifetime gift to a trust of the nil rate band, and the law on the treatment of such assets can be uncertain. Where husband and wife have a common fund or pool of assets, for example by way of a joint bank account, the husband's remuneration is treated as earned on behalf of both spouses, being joint property and without regard to the amounts paid in or withdrawn by the party (*Jones v Maynard* [1951] Ch 572, [1951] 1 All ER 802).

This presumption does not apply where it can be shown that the joint account was opened as a mere matter of convenience so that the beneficial ownership remained in one party (*Heseltine v Heseltine* [1971] 1 All ER 952 at 956, CA, per Lord Denning MR). Nevertheless, under the rules for independent income taxation for husband and wife, effective since 6 April 1990, the spouses are treated for the purposes of income tax as beneficially entitled in equal shares to income from joint property; that is, unless they enter into a joint declaration that either one or other is entitled absolutely or that they are entitled in unequal shares (ITA 2007, ss 836, 837).

The courts have also taken note of the way money is treated in other cultures: see (though not a husband and wife case) *Anand v CIR* [1997] STC (SCD) 58. However, in the case of large sums, it may be simpler and clearer for the spouses to have separate bank and building society accounts.

As between husband and wife the use of joint bank accounts for relatively small sums can however be recommended on two grounds. First, as a matter of convenience for day-to-day living expenditure, and secondly to prevent the sums in such accounts being frozen on the death of the first spouse. Substantial sums or assets should not, however, be placed on joint bank or other joint accounts between husband and wife, particularly in the context below. The same applies to joint accounts in general, as was illustrated in *Taylor and another v Revenue and Customs Commissioners* [2008] SpC 704, *MB Smith v HMRC (and related appeals)* [2009] SpC 742, and *Matthews v Revenue & Customs Commisssioners* [2012] UKFTT 658 (TC), (see **1.7**), which were not concerned with the joint accounts of married couples.

Where joint bank accounts are used for making gifts to third parties, serious IHT consequences can follow, having regard to the uncertainty of the treatment by HMRC and with particular reference to the following statutory provisions:

- s 272: the definition of 'property' as including 'rights and interests of any description ...'. Those rights can include, for example, the wife's statutory right to apply for the grant of letters of administration to her husband's estate, and rights to her husband's estate on intestacy: *Daffodil (administrator of Daffodil, deceased) v IRC* [2002] STC (SCD) 224;

- s 5(2): the inclusion in a person's estate of property, over which he has a general power of disposal;

- s 3(3): the deeming provision whereby a chargeable transfer can occur by 'omission to exercise a right'; and

- s 268(1): the inclusion in 'associated operations' of an omission (see also **1.20**).

Moreover, on death, money in the joint account will automatically pass to the surviving spouse as a matter of law through operation of the *jus accrescendi* (right of survivorship) principle discussed in relation to joint ownership of real property in **6.19**. Remember that it is not possible to sever a joint tenancy by will, but only by lifetime notice or (for IHT purposes) by an instrument of variation under s 142.

An application of these IHT provisions could result in a double charge on transfers to third parties. For example, the whole credit balance in a joint account could be treated as part of a deceased spouse's estate even though subsequently the surviving spouse made gifts (eg PETs which became chargeable on the survivor's death within seven years) to third parties out of such account. In addition, the provisions can create anomalies as between the joint owners.

It is, moreover, important to counter any use of the joint account as a sort of testamentary disposition and 'will substitute' as a specific means of providing for the other joint owner on death. The reason, particularly with larger amounts, is the uncertainty of treatment for IHT described above (see for example *O'Neill v IRC* [1998] STC (SCD) 110 discussed at **6.33**).

6.43 *Husband, wife and civil partner*

It is also advisable for husband and wife to have separate bank accounts in the context of claiming the normal expenditure out of income exemption (see **12.4**), making annual exemption gifts (**12.2**) and £250 gifts (**12.3**), as well as making larger PET gifts to use up the respective nil rate bands of each spouse.

Chapter 7

Choice of type of settlement

INTRODUCTION

7.1   As indicated in **Chapter 4**, the making of an appropriate will can lead to useful IHT mitigation; but as wills, by definition, only take effect on death, such mitigation is limited. The position of lifetime settlements requires careful consideration from the estate planning viewpoint. If already existing, should they be retained in their present form or in a varied form or be terminated? Should any new settlement be created?

This is a contentious area of law: HMRC have said, many times, that trusts should in their view not be used to mitigate tax burdens, or to secure tax advantages. They seek a level playing field on which the existence of a trust is tax-neutral. Arguably, the changes introduced by FA 2006 went far beyond that. On the other hand, the yield of IHT probably fell even more than anticipated following the introduction of the transferable nil rate band, with its facility to look back indefinitely into the history of each family. Discussion between HMRC and the professions continues; it is hoped that neither the present government nor any successor will be tempted to introduce radical change just for the sake of it.

Settlements still have many practical advantages. The settlor can choose trustees in whom he has confidence (he may even be a trustee himself); the beneficiaries can be selected with considerable flexibility or, in the case of charitable trusts, the trust's objects may include broad charitable purposes; and most trusts can be established without the beneficiaries' knowledge, this confidentiality preventing any pressure being exerted on the trustees to release funds prematurely, and providing protection against spendthrifts and unstable beneficiaries.

This chapter treats the practical aspects of settlements under the following heads:

- definitions; creation; IHT liability;
- main types of settlement summarised;
- the relevant property trust regime;

- choosing the correct settlement – *interests in possession*;
- choosing the correct settlement – *relevant property*;
- choosing the correct settlement – *other varieties*;

DEFINITION OF SETTLEMENT AND RELATED EXPRESSIONS; CREATION; IHT LIABILITY

Statutory definition

7.2   The IHT definition of 'settlement' is wide, although not quite as extensive as for income tax or capital gains tax (see, for example, ITTOIA 2005, s 624). The term 'settlement' for IHT is defined by s 43(2) (with some modifications for Scottish settlements by s 43(4)). It seems to have worked well; in the FA 2006 'modernisation' of the treatment of trusts for income tax and CGT, aspects of the IHT definition were adopted – see FA 2006, Sch 13, which inserted ITTOIA 2005, s 685A ('Meaning of "settled property"') and s 685B ('Meaning of "settlor"').

It covers any disposition(s) of property, however effected, whereby that property is held in trust for persons in succession or subject to a contingency; or where that property is held on trust to accumulate income or with a power to make discretionary payments of income (whether or not there is also a power of accumulation). It also covers the position when property is charged or burdened with a payment of an annuity or other periodic payment for a life or other limited or determinable period.

Exceptions

7.3   The statutory definition excludes situations where the charge or burden arises from a transaction whereby full consideration is paid in money or money's worth to the disponers. The expression 'full consideration' in this context may be compared with the *dicta* in the income tax cases of *Bulmer v IRC* (1966) 44 TC 1; *IRC v Plummer* [1979] STC 793, HL, and *IRC v Levy* [1982] STC 442, which consider commercial transactions where no element of bounty is intended, and which the courts have excluded from the wide income tax definition of settlement (including 'covenant', 'agreement' or 'arrangement') contained in ITTOIA 2005, s 620(1).

Partnership arrangements, etc

7.4   Partnership assurance arrangements involving each partner taking out a policy in trust for the remaining partners are regarded as settlements for IHT purposes. By concession (ESC F10), such partners' policies effected before 15 September 1976 are not so regarded. However, such policies can have implications under the 'pre-owned assets' income tax regime if the partner retains a benefit for himself (see **Chapter 13**).

Note that a lease of property which is for a life or lives, or for a period ascertainable *only* by reference to a death, or which is determinable on, or at a date ascertainable *only* by reference to a death, is treated as a settlement unless granted for full consideration in money or money's worth (s 43(3)).

Family arrangements and the meaning of 'settlor'

7.5   The definition of settlor is widely (though not exhaustively) defined, including the person who directly or indirectly provides trust funds. See, for example *Crossland v Hawkins* (1961) 39 TC 493, CA. See also *IRC v Mills* [1974] STC 130, where in the House of Lords there is reference to the 'engineer' of the settlement. For another angle see *Butler v Wildin* [1989] STC 22, where there was a nominal subscription for children's shareholding in a development company which *parents* built up. Finally note *Swires v Renton* [1991] STC 49, where the legislation was applied that treats income as being that of the parent settlor, now enacted as ITTOIA 2005, s 629.

More recently, the House of Lords held in favour of the taxpayer in the 'Arctic Systems' case (*Jones v Garnett (Inspector of Taxes)* [2007] UKHL 35. In that case, Mr and Mrs Jones subscribed for shares in a company, of which Mr Jones was the main income earner. Dividends paid to Mrs Jones were held to form part of an arrangement constituting a settlement. However, the exception from the settlement provisions for outright gifts between spouses or civil partners in ITTOIA 2005, s 626 was considered to apply to the arrangement.

HMRC quickly responded to the House of Lords' decision against them by announcing that legislation would be introduced to counter what they regard as 'income splitting'. Draft legislation was produced, then withdrawn, early in 2008 pending further consultation. The new anti-avoidance legislation was originally expected to take effect from 6 April 2009, but its introduction was subsequently postponed. As to the wide definition of the term 'settlor' for income tax, see also ITTOIA 2005, s 620.

In an IHT context the term does, however, have some limit. As noted by the House of Lords in *Fitzwilliam v IRC* [1993] STC 502, there must be at least a conscious association of the provider of funds with the settlement in question; it was not sufficient that the settled funds should historically have been derived from the provider of them.

The expression 'trustees' includes the persons in whom the settled property is vested or who manage it (s 45).

The creation of a settlement

7.6 Since 22 March 2006, the IHT treatment of transfers, during the donor's lifetime, of property into settlement is straightforward. Apart from transfers into a disabled person's trust, which are singled out as PETs, a settlement, whether on pure discretionary trusts or creating an interest in possession, is a lifetime chargeable transfer. Any new 'accumulation and maintenance' trusts created, possibly by error, will be treated as relevant property trusts. Other specialised settlements are chargeable unless (eg charitable trusts) they are given special treatment.

A pre-22 March 2006 trust which gave the settlor an interest in possession did not entail a transfer of value, as the settlor was treated as remaining beneficially entitled to the whole of the trust property. However, FA 2006 gave rise to the concept of a 'non-estate interest in possession' (s 5(1A)), with the result that such a settlor-interested trust is not an automatic 'non-event' for IHT purposes, but may constitute a gift with reservation of benefit instead.

A trust made in the settlor's lifetime giving an interest in possession to the settlor's spouse (having the same domicile) is no longer an exempt transfer under s 18 following FA 2006, because the fund is not treated as part of the estate of the spouse. Lifetime gifts to spouses (or civil partners) should therefore normally be absolute. A pre-22 March 2006 gift in trust for a spouse may constitute a reservation of benefit if the spouse's interest in possession terminates during the donor's lifetime (eg in favour of a discretionary trust) and he either enjoys a benefit from the settled property or the settled property could be applied for his benefit (see FA 1986, s 102(5A) and **1.34**).

The IHT liability for settlements

7.7 The primary liability is on the trustees (s 201(1)). Their liability is restricted to the trust fund itself and they remain solely liable until the due date for payment, normally six months from the chargeable transfer of value or chargeable distribution (for transfers after 5 April and before 1 October in any year; see **2.52**). They can apply to HMRC for a certificate as to their potential liability.

Secondarily liable are persons in whom the property or the income therefrom is vested (ie who have an interest in possession) or in whose favour it has been applied, or any person who is a settlor (while alive) in cases where the trustees are non-resident. This liability of a settlor of a non-resident trust is a very real one because the trustees are unlikely to submit themselves voluntarily to IHT; indeed to do so might constitute a breach of trust. The only satisfaction left to this unfortunate settlor is that the overseas trust fund will remain intact, whereas his assessable estate will be reduced.

MAIN TYPES OF SETTLEMENT

Interest in possession trusts (ss 49–57A)

7.8   A beneficiary with an interest in possession has a specific right to the income or is otherwise entitled to the use or enjoyment of the settled property. In the case of a settlement including real property the beneficiary is given a statutory right to occupy (Trusts of Land and Appointment of Trustees Act 1996, s 12). This type of trust is sometimes called a 'fixed interest' trust.

For IHT purposes, a beneficiary so entitled was formerly treated as beneficially owning the property in which the interest subsisted, not merely an actuarial value of the life interest (this is logical on the basis that the reversionary interest is generally excluded property). That rule remains, but only in relation to those interests that existed at 22 March 2006, or to disabled person's interests, immediate post-death interests or, by limited extension, to interests that replace them under the rules for transitional serial interests (TSIs) (s 49(1A)).

Accordingly as a general rule, subject to reliefs, exceptions and the application of the PET regime, when the beneficiary of an 'old' interest in possession trust, ie one created before the application of FA 2006, dies or makes a disposal of his interest in possession, there is an occasion of charge for IHT purposes. As to the meaning of the expression interest in possession see further **7.14** and **7.15**.

The changes introduced by FA 2006 create a bizarre result: a trust may be treated as a relevant property trust for IHT and yet remain an interest in possession trust for the purposes of general trust law, and for income tax and CGT.

Relevant property trusts (ss 58–85)

7.9   Discretionary trusts have always been classified as 'relevant property' trusts by s 58. FA 2006 greatly widened the type of trust subject to the IHT regime for relevant property trusts. Commonly in such trusts the class of beneficiaries may be drawn widely (eg children and grandchildren, their respective spouses, etc). There is no interest in possession in all or any part of the property.

7.10   *Choice of type of settlement*

The government is consulting on simplification of the IHT rules applicable to relevant property trusts. It is recognised that the current rules are overly complex and can impose a compliance burden out of proportion to the tax due.

The 'entry' charge

7.10   The transfer of value to a relevant property trust is a chargeable transfer unless it falls within one of very few exceptions, such as 'migration' from the status of an accumulation and maintenance trust, which could have arisen under the transitional provisions of FA 2006: see **7.13**.

For many families this is not a problem; the nil rate band may cover the amount of the transfer, particularly where husband and wife jointly settle an asset.

The 'ten-year' charge

7.11   On the tenth anniversary of the commencement of the discretionary trust, and on each subsequent ten-year anniversary, an IHT charge is levied on the value of the settled property (s 64). The rate of tax is reduced by 1/40th for each quarter during the previous ten years in respect of any part of the property where the discretionary trust regime did not apply.

Before FA 2006, this might have been because of changes in the form of the trust, for example, where an interest in possession subsisted during that period. However, the event that terminates the IHT charge will now nearly always be the distribution of property to a beneficiary outright: if the property stays in the trust, it will continue to be taxed in the trust.

Calculation of the tenth anniversary IHT charge is somewhat complicated. IHT is charged at three-tenths of the 'effective rate'. The effective rate is found by first working out the amount of tax, at lifetime rates (at present 20%) the rate being one-half the normal scale in Sch 1, which would be charged on a hypothetical transfer of value. This is one that is equal to:

- the current value of the trust property;
- made by a transferor with a cumulative total equal to that of the settlor in the seven years prior to making the settlement;
- to which is added the value of any property which left the settlement in the ten-year period.

The tax is calculated as a percentage of the value of property on which it is hypothetically charged. As already noted, the rate at which tax is in fact charged on the trust property at the tenth anniversary is three-tenths of this effective rate. Different rules may apply for discretionary trusts set up before 27 March 1974. At present, the maximum effective rate of tax is 6% (being three-tenths of 20%).

The 'exit' charge

7.12   There is also a proportionate interim or 'exit' tax charge when property leaves the discretionary trust during the course of the ten-year cycle (s 65). This charge is a proportion of the full ten-year charge calculated by taking 1/40th of the normal IHT rate for each quarter of a year which has elapsed since the last full charge and then applying that reduced rate to the full amount of the property. There are also provisions for a proportionate tax charge on property leaving the discretionary trust before the first ten-year anniversary. These interim levies are usually called exit charges.

There is no distinction made in the form of these tax charges between UK trusts and overseas trusts. For the detailed provisions, see **7.21**.

Accumulation and maintenance trusts (s 71)

7.13   These were, for many years, the most common 'harmless' trusts, and represented a significant and relatively straightforward opportunity for IHT mitigation. They had many advantages. With the coming into force of FA 2006, they have ceased to have any significant future use. Advisers had until 5 April 2008 to adapt them to the new rules. Most will now gradually wind down, having become interest in possession trusts, where the beneficiaries already had that status before the new rules; or relevant property trusts, where the beneficiaries were on 22 March 2006 too young to be entitled to income and who did not fit the transitional rules.

Occasionally, it was best just to leave them alone and allow the trust fund to 'migrate' to the relevant property regime (without an IHT entry charge).

Distinguishing interest in possession from discretionary settlements

Statute law

7.14   It has already been noted that the general framework of the IHT legislation draws a broad distinction between, on the one hand, settlements in which there is still for IHT purposes an interest in possession, being a disabled person's interest, TSI or an IPDI; and, on the other, settlements where either there is no interest in possession, or creation of the (lifetime) settlement took place after 22 March 2006 and which, therefore, are subject to the relevant property rules.

In practice it can sometimes be difficult to distinguish between an interest in possession trust and a discretionary trust.

Despite the detailed revision of the code in FA 2006, the legislation provides only limited help in distinguishing between the two. Section 51 sets out the IHT position when a person beneficially entitled to a (pre-FA 2006) interest in possession under a settlement disposes of his interest. Section 49(1) declares that a person with an interest in possession in settled property is to be treated for IHT, subject to the qualifications in s 49(1A), as beneficially entitled to the assets in which his interest subsists.

Section 50(1) provides that a person entitled to income produced by a settlement is entitled to an interest in possession in the settled property. Section 50(5) equates an entitlement to the use and enjoyment of property to an interest in possession where there is no entitlement to income produced by settled property. These are all examples of interests in possession in what are sometimes termed 'fixed interest trusts'. The IHT rules for discretionary trusts apply to those settlements, whenever created, where no interest in possession exists, and which are not otherwise excluded from the definition of 'relevant property' in s 58(1); and to virtually all lifetime settlements created after 22 March 2006, whether a beneficiary is entitled to the income or not.

Subject to a limited class of specially favoured settlements, there are therefore two broad categories of settlement:

- pre-FA 2006 fixed interest trusts, with an interest in possession; and the restricted class of interest in possession trusts still permitted by FA 2006 (such as lifetime trusts for the disabled and trusts arising on death (limited to IPDIs, BMTs)) with one set of rules on the one hand; and

- settlements without an interest in possession, and post-FA 2006 fixed interest trusts that do not fall to be dealt with as above, with another set of rules on the other hand.

Unfortunately, save as discussed in the preceding paragraphs, the legislation contains little help in understanding what an interest in possession comprises; and difficulties have arisen in practice in deciding on which side of the line certain cases fall.

Case law: *Pearson*

7.15   The House of Lords in *Pearson v IRC* [1980] STC 318 did a service, therefore, in introducing clear guidelines in the recognition of an interest in possession. Very briefly, the issue in that case turned on the nature of the interest of beneficiaries who were entitled to the income of a fund subject to:

- a power of appointment over capital whereby the current interest of each beneficiary could be removed;

- the trustees' power to apply income towards the payment of taxes, fees and other outgoings; and

- the trustees' power to *accumulate* the income for a period of 21 years, rather than pay it out, as an accretion to the capital of the trust fund.

Was the interest, as the trustees claimed, an interest in possession because the beneficiaries had a right to the income unless and until it was taken away by the trustees in exercise of their power of accumulation or, indeed, their power of appointment over capital? In the context of the power to accumulate, it was conceded by the trustees that if there had been a *duty* to accumulate, then there would not have existed an interest in possession.

The House of Lords (by a bare majority) found for the Revenue; that there was no interest in possession. They held that for there to exist an interest in possession the beneficiaries must have 'a present right to present enjoyment'. In this context there was no difference between a power to accumulate and a duty to accumulate. The power to accumulate prevented a present *right* to present enjoyment from ever arising.

A number of helpful principles emerge from the case, as follows:

- The existence of an overriding power of appointment over capital does not prevent there being a (possible) interest in possession. An overriding power of appointment was analysed as the right to *terminate* a present right of present enjoyment, as opposed to a power to accumulate, which prevented a present right of present enjoyment from ever arising.

- The fact that the birth of further issue might cut down (or even defeat) a beneficiary's interest similarly does not prevent there being a (possible) interest in possession.

- Whether trustees exercise their power to accumulate income or not makes no difference to the decision whether the beneficiary has (or has not) an interest in possession. The mere *power* to accumulate prevents the existence of the interest in possession.

- The case shows that there may be apparent interests in income which are neither future interests nor interests in possession for IHT purposes.

- The power of trustees to pay taxes and other outgoings out of income is an 'administrative' (not a 'dispositive') power, which does not of itself prevent the existence of an interest in possession, represented by the receipt of net income.

- To constitute an interest in possession there must be a present *right* to present enjoyment. (There was no such right in the case of *Trafford's Settlement*, referred to at **7.16**.)

- There was no such right in the *Pearson* case because the trustees could divert the subject matter by deciding to accumulate the income for the benefit of others.

For the wealthy beneficiary, the *Pearson* case can be helpful in avoiding the aggregation of the trust fund with his or her free estate, a situation which applies for pre-FA 2006 interest in possession trusts but not discretionary trusts.

It should perhaps be added, and it fits in with the thinking in *Pearson*, that an infant's contingent interest in a trust fund subject to powers of accumulation does not normally constitute an interest in possession.

Decisions since *Pearson*

7.16   The *Pearson* principle has been followed for income tax purposes in the case of *IRC v Berrill* [1981] STC 784. In that case, additional rate income tax under (what is now) ITA 2007, s 479ff, was chargeable because the beneficiary's life interest in the income was subject to the power of the trustees to accumulate the whole or any part, and hence payable at the discretion of the trustees.

In *Stenhouse's Trustees v Lord Advocate* [1984] STC 195, the trustees had a power to advance the settled funds provided the beneficiaries had attained the age of 22. The trustees resolved to transfer to the three beneficiaries P, H and A their respective shares absolutely; but because A had not attained 22, the trustees resolved that payment out of the trust should not be made until each beneficiary gave an indemnity. They wrote accordingly to the beneficiaries on the same day. The Court of Session held that P and H became entitled to an interest in possession in their shares that same day. Their interests could be severed from that of A, where the trustees had acted *ultra vires*, so that A did not obtain an interest in possession.

Another interesting case was *Re Trafford's Settlement, Moore and Osborne v IRC* [1984] STC 236, where income was held under a discretionary trust for a class of beneficiaries which had not yet closed. There was only one current member of the class. However, because it was possible for a new member of the class to appear before current income fell to be distributed, the present sole member of the class did not have an interest in possession.

The *Lloyds Private Banking* case

7.17   The leading case of *IRC v Lloyds Private Banking Ltd* [1998] STC 559 is of special relevance to schemes to shelter the family home from IHT.

There, on appeal, Lightman J held that an interest in possession existed where a wife left her share in the matrimonial home, by her will upon the following terms:

> 'While my husband remains alive and desires to reside in the property and keeps the same in good repair and insured comprehensively to its full value with Insurers approved by my Trustees and pays and indemnifies my Trustees against all rates, taxes and other outgoings in respect of the property my Trustee shall not make any objection to such residence and shall not disturb or restrict it in any way and shall not take any steps to enforce the trust for sale on which the property is held or to realise my share therein or to obtain any rent or profit from the property.'

Subject thereto the wife left her interest in the property to her daughter absolutely.

The Special Commissioner had decided that an interest in possession had not been created, as the husband and wife had been joint owners, the husband had the right to occupy the whole property in any event (subject, for example, only to an order of the court under Law of Property Act 1925, s 30). Lightman J disagreed, and held that the words in the will were dispositive and conferred upon the husband a determinable interest in possession in the wife's half share of the property. Although as a joint owner the husband had the right to occupy the entire property, he did not have the right to exclusive occupation. His wife's will gave him this right.

Further case law

7.18   The decision in *Lloyds Private Banking* was subsequently applied in the Special Commissioner's decision, *Woodhall v IRC* [2000] STC (SCD) 558. See also *Faulkner (trustee of Adams, deceased) v Inland Revenue Commissioners* [2001] STC (SCD) 112. However, contrast those cases with the decision in *Judge and another (personal representatives of Walden, dec'd) v HMRC* (2005) SpC 506 (see **4.13**), in which the Special Commissioner held that the surviving spouse did not have an interest in possession of a residence because the deceased spouse's trustees had absolute discretion as to whether to permit her to occupy the property for any period, notwithstanding that a sale of the property required the consent of the surviving spouse.

Stow and others v Stow and others [2008] EWHC 495 (Ch) examined the issue of ownership of an interest in a trust arising out of a claim under the Inheritance (Provision for Family and Dependants) Act 1975 at the suit of the widow who had claimed that her late husband had been the beneficial owner of assets held in a trust and that she should inherit more as a result. Mr Stow died in 2005. A year later HMRC issued notices of determination that he had been settlor of each settlement.

The trustees objected. Instead of appealing from the notices of determination, they sought from the High Court a declaration that Mr Stow had not been the beneficial owner of the underlying assets, but that instead they were settled by a Nigerian who had had business connections with Mr Stow. HMRC wanted the case heard by the Special Commissioner, so applied for the High Court proceedings to be struck out.

Not so, held the court, dismissing the application. The issue of beneficial ownership would not only affect the liability of the trustees to IHT, it would also decide a completely different liability, namely whether the estate should pay income tax and whether that liability could be enforced; but neither of these issues was connected to the issue of whether the property was relevant for a claim by the widow under the 1975 Act. Where there is an issue that will affect several liabilities it may be considered by the High Court even though the decision will be relevant to the outcome of a tax appeal.

Statement of Practice 10/79

7.19   HMRC consider that trustees of a discretionary trust with a power to permit a beneficiary to occupy a dwelling house or to use furniture may, if they exercise the power, incur an IHT charge by giving the beneficiary an interest in possession. This is argued for in SP 10/79, though the Statement is yet to be upheld in any decided case. If, which many doubt, it is good law, there is likely to be a further charge when that interest in possession terminates.

Contrast the position if the trustees appoint the property to the beneficiary absolutely: if the beneficiary had a TSI by virtue of his enjoyment of the property, when he subsequently becomes absolutely entitled, there is an exemption from IHT under s 53(2) (see **7.94** onwards). This exemption is, however, limited to the circumstances just described and would not apply where, for example, another limited interest in the fund followed the TSI (see s 53(2A)), except where that further interest came within the restricted definition of a TSI. Note that s 53(2A) was amended by FA 2008, s 140 in such a way that the previous amendment in FA 2006, Sch 20, para 14(3) was treated as never having had effect. This addresses a highly technical issue that arose on the introduction of the new rules (see **7.98**).

Contrast also the position if the beneficiary purchases (or is appointed) some small beneficial interest in the property which he is allowed to occupy. In these circumstances the beneficiary has a *statutory right* to occupy the entire property (Trusts of Land and Appointment of Trustees Act 1996, s 12). *Query* whether the trustees have given the beneficiary an interest in possession to the extent of their *share* by not allowing other beneficiaries to cohabit?

Free loans

7.20   A gratuitous loan of trust property may be regarded by HMRC as being equivalent to allowing the recipient of the loan the use and enjoyment of it and therefore amount to creating an interest in possession. Whilst this is eminently reasonable (from the point of view of HMRC), the precise statutory basis is unclear.

However, in the case of a straightforward loan of money validly made out of the trust property at normal rates of interest, the loan will be represented in the settlement by the corresponding debt due from the borrower just like any other investment or re-investment of the trust property. Whilst in theory it should therefore give rise to no IHT problems, particularly if the loan is repayable on demand, as it should be, the question may arise whether the transaction is more akin to a distribution; for instance, a loan to a young man who 'invests' the proceeds in a red sports car and the cost of its insurance may prove irrecoverable: if there is no reasonable prospect of recovery, was there a loan in the first place?

THE RELEVANT PROPERTY TRUST REGIME AND ANCILLARY PROVISIONS (SS 58–85)

Introduction

7.21   The present IHT regime for taxing relevant property trusts applies (as from 9 March 1982) to 'relevant property', being:

- settled property in which (apart from expressly excluded trusts, see below) *no qualifying interest in possession* subsists (s 58), (see **7.14** on how to distinguish an interest in possession); and

- property comprised in any settlement that falls outside the preferred classes by virtue of FA 2006 (and therefore encompassing most lifetime settlements).

Following the introduction of IHT by FA 1986 the treatment of discretionary trusts remained largely the same, except as follows:

- reduction of cumulation period to seven years from ten years;

- reservation of benefit rules;

- knock-on effect of PETs becoming chargeable (see **7.42**).

The main purpose of the provisions was to maintain a broad balance between the weight of the IHT charge on property held in discretionary trusts and property held in other ways, such as by individuals. However, the steady development of sophisticated structures, including, it must be said, some advocated in earlier editions of this work, led to increasing dissatisfaction on the part of HMRC.

Express exclusions from the definition of 'relevant property'

7.22   Section 58 includes as relevant property any settled property other than:

- charitable trusts;

- pre-FA 2006 accumulation and maintenance settlements, BMTs, 18-to-25 trusts;

- property held in a Treasury-approved maintenance fund;

- certain pension schemes (ie registered, qualifying non-UK and s 615(3) schemes);

- employee trusts;

- protective trusts;

- disabled person's trusts, but subject to qualification (see s 58(1A));

- trade compensation funds; and

- excluded property.

In respect of excluded property (assuming the settlor was non-domiciled on setting up the trusts), no charge arises where property becomes excluded on ceasing to be situated in UK; or if the trustees hold shares in an authorised unit trust or a share in an open-ended investment company by virtue of s 48(3A); or if the beneficiaries are non-domiciled and not ordinarily resident in the UK, where the trustees acquire a holding in exempt gilts by virtue of s 48(4). See **7.35** for a further explanation of the effect of changing investments.

There can be a curious effect on excluded property where, although the settlor was domiciled outside the UK, there is an interest in possession to a UK-domiciled individual followed by discretionary trusts (see **17.14**). This has been tightened up by s 80(4) (as inserted by FA 2006, Sch 20, paras 7 and 23).

A 'qualifying interest in possession' is one to which an individual (or a company whose business is to buy interests in settled property and acquired the interest from an individual for full consideration in money or money's worth) is entitled; see s 59. In the case of an individual who becomes entitled after 22 March 2006, the interest is a qualifying one only if it is an IPDI, a DPI or a TSI; see s 59(1)(a) as amended.

'Relevant property', therefore, which is generally used to refer only to those cases where assets and funds were held on normal discretionary trusts, will increasingly refer to the bulk of trust property. A settlement may be composed of relevant property in part only, eg if the other part is held subject to an interest in possession. A particular example of this caused a temporary but serious difficulty: the pre-FA 2006 accumulation and maintenance trust where some beneficiaries happened to enjoy an interest in possession on 22 March 2006 and others were too young.

Summary of relevant property trust regime

7.23

Item/Charge	*Data*
Entry charge	= settlor's transfer of value
	– subject to seven-year cumulation (ten years for transfers before 18 March 1986)
Ten-year anniversary charge	40 quarters: pro rata charge as appropriate.
	No credit for subsequent distributions.
	Rate = 30% of lifetime scale. Top rate IHT is therefore 6% (= 30% of top life rate of 20%)
Exit charge	Between ten-year charges at previous ten-year anniversary rate; time basis over quarters = maximum 30% × 20% = 6%
Aggregation and cumulation – settlor	*Post*-26.3.74. Full aggregation: (settlor's seven-year cumulation pre-ten-year anniversary and other related settlements of settlor)
	Pre-27.3.74
	(= settlement's ten-year cumulation pre the ten-year anniversary only)
Valuation	Diminution in value
	ss 3(1), 65(1)(b)
	NB 'sound barrier' eg where shareholding control is lost
Reverter to settlor/spouse	No exemption
Accumulation and maintenance settlements	Rapidly disappearing. IHT charge on:
	• depreciatory transactions
	• property leaving trust to non-eligible assignee
	• holding funds beyond 18th birthday of any beneficiary
Special trusts	Charitable/BMT/superannuation/employee/disabled/protective; exempt while conditions satisfied but then subject to a tapered charge

The ten-year charge (s 61) – general

7.24 On the tenth anniversary of the date on which the settlement commenced and on subsequent ten-year anniversaries, a principal charge to IHT is levied on the *then* value of the relevant property comprised therein (as reduced by any available business or agricultural relief). The maximum charge is three-tenths, ie 30%, of the life rate of 20% = 6%. Note that the date, within the ten-year period, on which relevant property first became comprised in the settlement is not the starting date; it is however relevant when calculating the amount of the charge: see **7.26**.

No date before 1 April 1983 could have been a ten-year anniversary, so the first principal IHT charge takes place on the first ten-year anniversary after that, eg for discretionary trusts created before 30 March 1973 the first ten-year charge was 30 March 1993.

The commencement of the settlement

7.25 This, see s 60, takes place when property first becomes comprised in it, which in most cases will be when it is first set up. An event is described in s 80, which can give rise to an IHT charge. If this happens after 22 March 2006 where a settlor (or his spouse) has a 'postponing interest' when the settlement is first set up, the property is only treated as having become comprised in the settlement when it becomes held on trusts under which neither the settlor nor his spouse have a postponing interest. For this purpose a postponing interest must be either an IPDI or a DPI. This provision does not apply to settlements created before 27 March 1974 (s 80(3)). References to the spouse include a widow, widower or civil partner.

Adding funds to a trust

7.26 When a settlor *adds* further assets to an already existing settlement, the addition constitutes a further settlement by the settlor. However, in relation to both the above instances (ie the prior interest in possession and the addition) the ten-year anniversaries of the separate settlements are the same as that of the initial settlement. This is because, with regard to the prior interest in possession, s 61(2) expressly declares that the ten years shall run from the date of the original s 80 settlement; and because, with regard to the addition to the settlement, s 60 states that the commencement of the settlement (ie from which the ten years run: s 61(1)) is the time when property first became comprised in it, ie later additions do not qualify.

Example 7.1 – Pilot trust

A settlor makes an initial £100 settlement to get a trust started, and later adds further property.

The ten years have already started running from the date of the settlement. There will of course be a reduction in the IHT rate of 1/40th for each quarter that the addition is not held throughout the ten years (see **7.30**).

In connection with all references to pre-27 March 1974 settlements it is not a requirement that the trust was discretionary at the outset.

Discretionary will trusts commence from the death. Beware of other settlements created by the same will (except to a spouse), as they are 'related' settlements. The alternative should be considered of a bequest adding to a small lifetime 'pilot' trust.

The ten-year charges – aggregation and the effective rate – post-16 March 1974 settlements, ss 64, 66, 67: the 'effective rate'

7.27   In order to find the appropriate, ie *effective rate,* of tax on the discretionary settlement, a *notional chargeable transfer* is first taken (referable to the trust fund) consisting of the aggregate of the following elements:

● *The fund*

The 'relevant property' forming part or whole of that settlement, valued at the anniversary date. (The strict position is that the charge and the valuation occur 'immediately before' the anniversary.)

If any sale of assets or investment switching may be in prospect, those transactions should take place before the anniversary so that the CGT incurred by the trustees is a liability which can be set against the IHT ten-year charge. Where the settlement has been made by a non-UK domiciled settlor, and subject to certain changes to s 80, IHT is charged only on assets situated within the UK.

Assets outside constitute excluded property. Accordingly, where at the date when assets are put into the settlement the person who is, or who is deemed to be, the settlor is still treated as domiciled outside the UK, steps should be taken in advance of the tax date to see that the settled funds so far as practicable are invested outside the UK. Alternatively, the trustees of the non-domiciled individual's trust should consider holding shares in an offshore investment company, so that those shares will be excluded property even if the underlying company (owned by the trustees) has investments in the UK.

- *Income*

  As regards undistributed and unaccumulated income, the Revenue view (see Statement of Practice 8/86 dated 10 November 1986) is that such income is to be excluded from the ten-year and interim charges.

  The rate of IHT chargeable on accumulated income is calculated as if it were an asset separate from the original trust property. Therefore, such accumulated income only becomes settled property subject to the ten-year and interim charges, from the time the trustees become entitled to the income, not earlier.

- *Non-discretionary assets in the trust*

  Other property, if any, subject to that settlement, in which an interest in possession has subsisted throughout the settlement period, valued at the commencement of the settlement, or immediately after it became comprised, ie *added* to, the settlement, or property held on special trusts otherwise expressly excluded. Following FA 2006, less will fall within this category than before.

- *Related fund property*

  The property comprised in any related settlement valued at commencement of that settlement (ie one made by the settlor on the same day as that settlement, other than charitable trusts) (see s 62).

7.28   *The effective rate of tax* on that notional chargeable transfer, calculated at the *lifetime scale*, is then additionally ascertained by reference to a prior notional cumulative ladder, in order to represent chargeable transfers within the last ten years. This consists of:

- *Transfers on the 'clock' of the settlor*

  These are the values of chargeable transfers made by the settlor in the seven years before the commencement of the settlement (ignoring transfers made on that commencement day); plus

- *Prior trust distributions*

  These are the full amounts that have been subject to interim IHT charges, even at 0%, in the ten years before the anniversary.

In *Rysaffe Trustees (CI) Ltd v IRC* [2002] WTLR 481, the settlor executed five discretionary trusts within 35 days. Private company shares were subsequently transferred to each trust. The Revenue determined that, for the purposes of the ten-year charge, the property comprised in the five trusts should be treated as comprised in a single settlement. The Special Commissioner held in favour of the Revenue, but the High Court allowed the trustees' appeal. The Court of Appeal dismissed the Revenue's subsequent appeal.

The court held that each of the five trust deeds executed by the settlor satisfied the definition of 'settlement' in s 43(2), and it therefore followed that there were five separate settlements. Nevertheless, whilst the settlor intended to create five separate settlements, it would be prudent first to avoid the unfortunate procedural problems that afflicted this case, and secondly to ensure that the terms of each trust were not exactly the same.

There are provisions for adjustments to the total of the 'clock' mentioned above: broadly, on an addition of property to the trust the total *value* of the settlor's chargeable transfers in the seven years preceding the addition will, if it is higher, be substituted, in the calculation of the rate of tax, for the sum of his chargeable transfers in the seven years before the commencement of the settlement (s 67(3) and (4)).

Applying the rate to the trust

7.29   Having thereby discovered the amount of tax on the notional aggregated chargeable transfer, the effective rate on that transfer is then expressed as a percentage by reference to the amount of tax on the aggregated transfer in relation to the transfer itself. The rate of charge on the relevant property in that settlement is then three-tenths of that percentage rate.

Example 7.2 – Ten-year anniversary charge (1)

Tom made a chargeable transfer of £65,000 on 1 May 1996 (having already exhausted his annual gift exemptions). On 1 July 2002 he made two settlements: £150,000 on settlement A on continuing discretionary trusts; and £50,000 on settlement B upon trust for his wife for life (still living July 2012) with remainder on the same trusts as in A (then exempt, s 18).

On 1 July 2012, the IHT ten-year charge becomes payable on settlement A. The funds are then worth £316,000. The notional chargeable transfer is £316,000 (settlement B is ignored since it cannot be treated as a related settlement since it has not yet 'commenced' and will not do so until the discretionary trusts come into being (ss 61(2), 80)).

The notional chargeable transfer is made by a person with a cumulative total equal to that of Tom in the seven years prior to commencement of the settlement (ie £65,000). So the notional chargeable transfer is deemed to be made by a person with an unexpired nil rate band at the then current rates, ie by reference to the current nil rate band of £325,000.

The notional person has available an unused nil rate band of (£325,000 – £65,000) £260,000, so if he were now making a transfer equal to the fund there would be a transfer of (£316,000 – £260,000) £56,000.

Tax attributable to the notional chargeable transfer is thus:

(£316,000 – £260,000) × 20% = £11,200.

The 'effective rate' is £11,200 (tax chargeable) expressed as a percentage of £316,000 (the amount on which it is charged), ie 3.544%.

The rate and IHT on the tenth anniversary of settlement A is therefore 3/10ths of 3.544% = 1.063% of £316,000 = £3,359.

Example 7.3 – Ten-year anniversary charge (2)

Dick made gross chargeable transfers of £40,000 on 1 September 1995, £60,000 on 1 May 1996 and £20,000 on 2 February 1997.

On 1 July 2002 he made:

- a £140,000 settlement, half on discretionary trusts (worth £250,000 on 1 July 2012); half on trust for brother Harry for life (living 2012, with his interest in possession) with remainder as first half; and

- a separate £50,000 accumulation and maintenance settlement (ie on the same day).

An IHT ten-year charge arises on 1 July 2012 on the settlement of £140,000. Rate is 3/10ths of effective rate (as a percentage) on notional chargeable transfer of:

- £250,000 (the current value of the relevant property fund); plus

- £70,000, being half of £140,000 (value at commencement of settlement of interest in possession property fund); plus

- £50,000 (value at commencement of related settlement),

ie £370,000. This is added to Dick's cumulative ladder of (£40,000 plus £60,000 plus £20,000), ie £120,000, to establish the rate. (These were all gifts made by Dick in the seven years before the commencement of the settlement.)

The IHT on life rate scale on a transfer of value of £370,000 by a person who has already made chargeable transfers of £120,000 in the preceding seven years is calculated: the nil rate band on 1 July 2012 was £325,000 so the excess of (£370,000 + £120,000) £490,000 over that band is £165,000, which at 20% would be £33,000.

The 'effective rate' is (£33,000/£370,000), ie 8.92%. This is applied to the relevant property fund.

The rate and tax on relevant property of £250,000 is accordingly 3/10ths of 8.92% = 2.676% = £6,690. No grossing up; this is a notional charge.

The ten-year charge – quarterly reductions on rate (s 66)

7.30   If the relevant property in the settlement at the anniversary date has, for any proportionate period, not been subject to the discretionary trusts throughout the whole ten years (eg because there was an addition to the settlement during the ten years or because there was an interest in possession for part of the time), IHT on that proportion of the settled property is *reduced* by *1/40th* for each successive quarter terminating before the property became subject to the discretionary trusts.

Example 7.4 – Reduction for complete quarters

The value of the relevant property comprised in a discretionary settlement on a ten-year anniversary on 27 June 2012 was £293,000. Full IHT thereon at an overall rate (ie 3/10ths of the effective rate) of 2.40% has been ascertained (after taking into account the settlor's cumulative total at the date of commencement of the settlement, together with the value of related settlements, as demonstrated by Examples 7.2 and 7.3).

£100,000 of the value came from an addition to the settlement on 1 January 2011. The rate of IHT on that addition is reduced by 34/40ths representing the completed number of quarters from 27 June 2002 (commencement of the settlement) to 26 December 2010, before the addition was made on 1 January 2011, so that the calculation of IHT on this part of the fund becomes 6/40ths × 2.40% × £100,000 = £360.

The IHT on the rest of the fund, the original settled property remains at 2.40% × £193,000 = £4,632, so the total IHT payable is £4,992.

The ten-year charge – limited aggregation and the effective rate – pre-27 March 1974 settlements, ss 66(6), 67(4), 68(6)

7.31   The calculation of the notional chargeable transfer to determine the effective rate for the ten-year charge on these pre-CTT/IHT settlements is modified, being *confined solely to the value of the relevant property in the* *settlement* plus the amounts in the ten-year cumulative ladder of that settlement. Other property in the same settlement with a subsisting interest in possession, and related settlements are omitted.

The make-up of the cumulative ladder is also different.

- If it is the *first* ten-year anniversary, the ladder consists of:

  - the amounts of distribution payments from the settlement under the old pre-1982 rules, plus

  - the amounts subjected to interim CTT/IHT charges (see **7.32**), all within the last ten years.

- If it is the *second or subsequent* anniversary, it is the amounts for interim IHT only.

Example 7.5 – An 'old' discretionary settlement

Mr X made a discretionary settlement on 1 January 1974 (ie a pre-27.3.74 trust). On 1 January 1984 (the first ten-year anniversary), the funds then subject to the settlement were worth £60,000. There had been distribution payments to beneficiaries of £10,000 on 1 December 1978 and £20,000 on 1 March 1980. There was also a sum of £40,000 which ceased to be relevant property on being paid out to a beneficiary on 1 September 1982.

On the first ten-year anniversary the effective rate is 17.91% by reference to lifetime CTT of £10,750 on an aggregate of £130,000 less tax attributable to the first £70,000 representing the distributions and the payment out.

The chargeable rate is three-tenths of that 17.91%, ie 5.373%.

The first ten-year anniversary CTT charge on the settled funds is accordingly £3,224 (£60,000 × 5.373%). On the second ten-year anniversary on 1 January 1994, the funds are worth £160,000 (and there have been no distributions etc since 1 January 1984). The charge is 3/10ths of 20% (lifetime rate) on £160,000 after the nil rate band (then £150,000) = £600, an effective rate of 0.375%.

Interim IHT charges (ss 65, 68, 69): 'exit' charges

7.32   IHT is charged *during* the ten-year cycles (ie between the full IHT charges on the ten-year anniversary dates), whenever any part of the property comprised in a discretionary settlement ceases to be 'relevant' (ie discretionary) property. This can happen when:

- the trustees make an advance of capital to a beneficiary, so that the property leaves the trust; or

- under the terms of the settlement or in exercise of the trustees' powers of appointment, the terms of the trust are varied so that a beneficiary becomes entitled to an interest in possession (pre-22 March 2006) or disabled person's interest; or

- (an anti-avoidance provision) if the trustees carry out a value-shifting (depreciatory) transaction which has the effect of reducing the value of the discretionary property, unless no gratuitous intent exists (see s 65(1)(b), (6)).

Consequential loss (s 65(2), (9))

7.33   The amount on which the interim IHT charge is made is quantified as the amount by which the value of the relevant property in the settlement after the event is less than it would be but for the event. Note that this consequential loss formula occurs in the discretionary trust regime with the same effect as diminution in the estate of an individual under s 3(1) (see also Example 1.1).

Trustees are also subjected to an IHT charge similar to that under s 3(3), if they *omit to exercise* a right, unless they can show that it was not deliberate (s 65(9)).

Grossing up (s 65(2)(b))

7.34   If the IHT on an interim charge is paid out of the relevant property remaining in the settlement (ie not directly borne by the beneficiaries), the amount of the tax is added to the consequential loss in a grossing-up operation. Contrast the notional ten-year anniversary charge when there is no grossing up.

Exclusions

7.35   No charge arises on a distribution out of the trust:

- in the *first quarter* from the creation of the settlement or ten-year charge (s 65(4)). In the case of a discretionary will trust, s 144 could not apply (*Frankland v IRC* [1996] STC 735 and *Loveday v IRC* [1997] STC (SCD) 321). Therefore, if a distribution is made to a surviving spouse within this period, the inter-spouse relief is *not* available;

- for *costs and expenses* fairly attributable to the relevant property (s 65(5) (a));

- on a payment which would be *income* for income tax purposes in the hands of a recipient (or would be if he were resident in the UK) (s 65(5)(b));

- for charitable purposes without any time limit (if temporary a tapering charge applies) (s 76);

- if the trust's UK assets become excluded property (ie within s 48(3)(a)) upon becoming located overseas (s 65(7)). Excluded property is not relevant property (s 58(1)(f)). However, note that there is no similar exclusion from an IHT charge if the trustees switch to excluded property in the form of a holding in authorised unit trusts or shares in an open-ended investment company within s 48(3A). An exit charge is therefore imposed because the property has ceased to be relevant property (s 65(1)(a)). HMRC are apparently aware of this anomaly (see 'A Botched Reform' by Chris Jarman, *Private Client Business* (2007) Issue 1).

Amount subject to interim charge (s 65)

7.36 The chargeable amount is arrived at on the basis of the consequential loss formula above, and is grossed up if tax is being paid out of the settlement funds.

Rate of interim charge before first ten-year charge

Post-26 March 1974 trusts (s 68)

7.37 The rate of IHT on the chargeable amount is found in a similar way to that for a ten-year charge (but not precisely in the same way).

Take three-tenths of the effective rate on a notional chargeable transfer consisting of:

- the value at the *commencement* of the property in the settlement; and

- the value at that date of any related settlement;

being a chargeable transfer made by a transferor who is deemed to have made, in the preceding seven years, an aggregate of chargeable transfers equivalent to those made by the settlor in the seven years ending on the day of the settlement, but ignoring transfers on that date. This effective rate comes from the lifetime scale. The rate at which tax is charged is then that rate, multiplied by a fraction consisting of the number of complete quarter-years since the commencement of the settlement, up to 40.

Example 7.6 – Exit before first ten-year anniversary

George set up a £283,000 discretionary settlement on 8 January 2003. He had within the previous seven years made chargeable transfers totalling £70,000.

Also on 8 January 2003 he set up a £65,000 settlement for a disabled relative. On 7 April 2012, the trustees of the discretionary settlement advanced £20,000 to William absolutely. He funded the tax himself.

To find the rate, take the value of the settlement at commencement together with the commencement value of the related settlement: total £348,000. That is the notional chargeable transfer. This notional transfer is deemed to be made by a transferor with a previous cumulative total of £70,000, on the date of the advance to William. So, on the rates in force when the distribution to William is made, the notional transferor has an unused nil rate band of (£325,000 – £70,000) £255,000.

Tax on this notional chargeable transfer (at lifetime rates) is therefore (£348,000 – £255,000) £93,000 × 20% = £18,600, giving an 'effective rate' of 5.345% (ie (£18,600/£348,000) × 100).

The rate of the advance of £20,000, before adjustment, is therefore three-tenths of 5.345% ie 1.603% so the IHT is £320. There are, however, only 32 complete successive quarters from the date of the settlement up to the date of the advance. Accordingly, the chargeable amount of £20,000 is taxed at 32/40 of 3/10 of 5.345% ie 1.283% = £256.

'Mini' and 'tax-free' discretionary trusts

7.38   Discretionary trusts are widely used in situations where no IHT is payable on creation of the trust because the trust fund is within the nil rate band. Moreover, frequently this nil rate band can be 'geared up' by the amount of the business or agricultural relief at 100% or 50%, as the case may be. Keeping a relevant property trust below the IHT threshold can make very good sense: at the lower levels of estate planning, the cost of computing the IHT charges on such trusts can be considerable.

In this connection, a note of warning has to be sounded – a trap for the unwary. Under s 68(4) and (5), in arriving at the rate on interim charges before the first ten-year anniversary, no allowance is made for any business or agricultural relief (note the references in those sub-sections to 'the property then comprised in it'). This does not matter where 100% BPR/APR applies (ie the asset reduces to zero value), but it does matter where only 50% relief applies. Contrast this with calculating the amount of the 'relevant property' in the trust, ie at ten-year anniversaries where business/agricultural relief is given. It is only the rate that does not benefit.

This also applies to the £3,000 annual exemption(s) that may have been obtained on creation of the discretionary trust.

Moreover, this disadvantage only applies for interim charges before the first ten-year anniversary. At the first ten-year anniversary, and at any time thereafter, whether by way of interim charges or ten-year charges, the rate does take account of business and agricultural relief through, so to speak, the back door, because the prior ten-year anniversary rate is the basis of all interim charges thereafter until the next ten-year anniversary.

Rate of interim charge between ten-year charges (s 69)

7.39 The effective rate that applied at the last ten-year charge will apply to the interim charge.

However, if there has been a reduction in the lifetime rate since the previous ten-year anniversary, the effective rate of tax on that anniversary is recalculated using the improved rate (from the point of view of the taxpayer) in force for the purpose of calculating the interim charge (Sch 2, para 3). This procedure applies, for example, to the common situation of an increase in the IHT rate bands in a subsequent tax year (IHTM42115). The taxpayer thus gets the benefit of the reduction in IHT rates.

Example 7.7 – Ten-year anniversary charge

The facts are those in Example 7.6. At the ten-year anniversary on 8 January 2013 the remaining funds subject to the discretionary settlement had grown in value to £280,000. The nil rate band was then £325,000.

To find the effective rate, the aggregate is taken of:

	£
the settled funds	280,000
the value at commencement of the related settlement	65,000
the chargeable transfers in the seven years preceding the date of the discretionary settlement	70,000
and the amount of the advance on which IHT had been paid in 2009	20,000
Total	435,000

By taking the proportion of IHT of £22,000 on £435,000 (ie £435,000 – £325,000 × 20%), the effective rate of 5.057% is produced. Three-tenths of that gives a rate for IHT on the anniversary of 1.517%, so that IHT of £4,247 is payable on the settled funds.

Example 7.8 – Exit after first ten-year anniversary

Fred, who had made no previous chargeable transfers, created a settlement on 29 April 1997 having an initial value of £200,000 (£50,000 thereof being on accumulation and maintenance trusts). The ten-year charge arises on 29 April 2007 when the discretionary fund (excluding the A&M element) was valued at £320,000. The settlement was finally wound up on 30 June 2012, when the discretionary element was worth £400,000.

Ten-year charge 29 April 2007

	£
Chargeable transfer:	
Relevant property	320,000
add: A&M at initial value	50,000
	370,000
IHT on £370,000* =	14,000
effective rate = £14,000 / £370,000 = 3.783%	
3/10 thereof = 1.13%	
£320,000 × 1.13%	3,616
IHT on distribution 30 June 2012	
Re-calculated IHT rate on ten-year anniversary:	
IHT on £370,000**	9,000
Effective rate = £9,000 / £370,000 = 2.432%	
3/10 thereof = 0.73%	
IHT payable = 20/40† × £400,000 × 0.73% =	1,460

*   nil rate band for 2007–08 = £300,000
** nil rate band for 2012–13 = £325,000
20† = completed quarters between 29 April 2007 and 30 June 2012.

New property in the trust

7.40   That rate will be *recalculated* (s 69(2)) if at the time of the interim charge the settlement includes relevant property ('new relevant property') which was not comprised in the settlement at the time of the preceding ten-year charge.

The recalculation takes the form of adding the new relevant property (at the value when it became relevant property) to the property that was subject to the ten-year charge.

Alignment of old trusts

7.41   Where an interim charge arises after the first ten-year anniversary, pre-27 March 1974 settlements are dealt with in the *same way* as post-26 March 1974 settlements, by reference to the effective rate at the last ten-year charge.

The rate on the amount subject to the interim charge is again modified, by being multiplied by the number of complete quarters since the ten-year anniversary, over 40.

No credit for IHT paid on a ten-year anniversary is given for interim charges. This applies whatever the date of creation of the settlement.

Knock-on effect of PETs becoming chargeable transfers

7.42   This can best be explained by an illustration.

Example 7.9 – Death within seven years of a PET

Year 1	Mr A makes a PET
Year 3	Mr A makes a gift into a discretionary settlement
Year 5	The trustees of that settlement make an interim distribution (exit charge) to a beneficiary
Year 6	Mr A dies. The amount of the exit charge is revised/increased because A's cumulative total has risen because the PET proves to be a chargeable transfer.

Liability of trustees

7.43   It was reported (in the *Law Society Gazette*, 12 December 1984, p 3517) that the Law Society had taken up with the Revenue (as it then was) the question of liability of trustees where the settlor of a discretionary trust had been guilty of fraud, wilful default or neglect in matters which affected the rate of IHT (then CTT) on the trust.

In their reply, the Revenue had confirmed that the trustees, once they had paid tax on a distribution, could apply for a certificate of discharge (see s 239). However, whether or not a certificate had been issued, the Revenue would not seek to recover the additional tax (eg on fraud by the settlor) from trustees personally where they had acted in good faith and had insufficient funds left in trust with which to pay.

Special cases (ss 70–76)

7.44   The IHT code for discretionary trusts contains special relieving provisions for certain types of trust, eg employee trusts and charitable trusts. Broadly speaking, trusts of this kind are not liable to the periodic charge while they satisfy certain conditions, and payments out of such trusts are not taxable if made to certain qualifying recipients. However, when the trusts cease to satisfy the conditions or a payment is made to a non-qualifying recipient, there is a charge to tax.

This charge is at a flat rate which tapers over time under s 70(6) (relating to charitable trusts but applied in other cases) as follows:

- 0.25% for each of the first 40 quarters;

- 0.20% for each of the next 40 quarters;

- 0.15% for each of the next 40 quarters;

- 0.10% for each of the next 40 quarters;

- 0.05% for each of the next 40 quarters;

- subject to a maximum rate of 30%.

7.45   The tapered charge will not be levied for periods before 13 March 1975. In the case of special trusts created after 12 March 1975, the charge will not be levied for periods before the date on which the trust was set up or converted into that form.

Example 7.10 – Tapered charge (I)

A charitable trust was set up in March 1975 (or earlier) to terminate in April 1996 (ie a charitable time trust). It has subsisted for 84 quarters (21 years × 4). Therefore, on termination the trust fund will be charged to IHT at 40 × 0.25% = 10% plus 40 × 0.20% = 8% plus 4 × 0.15% = 0.6%: total 18.6%.

Example 7.11 – Tapered charge (II)

A similar trust set up in May 2005 and terminated in June 2012. It will be charged to IHT at 28 (quarters) × 0.25% = 7%.

No tapered charge arises during the period of any complete quarter when the property in question was excluded property.

Maintenance funds for heritage purposes (Sch 4, para 15)

7.46 The Treasury has the power to withdraw a direction, previously made, that a trust should be treated as a maintenance fund if the facts, or the administration of the trust, so warrant. The tapered charge described above applies when property, for whatever reason, ceases to be subject to a maintenance fund.

Planning aspects for relevant property trusts

Avoid related settlements

7.47 Avoid s 62 by arranging for settlements to commence on successive dates. Problems arise if a testator wishes to create more than one trust under his will, one of which is discretionary.

However, since a settlement 'commences' when it is first made, notwithstanding later additions (cf ss 60, 61(1) and 66(2)), it is possible to set up (on different dates) a succession of small 'pilot' settlements (even £10 each) in the testator's lifetime. He can then merely leave property to each of the settlements in his will. Each of them falls to be treated as a separate settlement for IHT purposes (*Rysaffe Trustees (CI) Ltd v IRC* [2003] STC 536). See **7.28**. Possibly, for administrative convenience, the settlements might be merged after the later additions have happened (see **7.82**).

Whilst related settlements should generally be avoided, even if small pilot settlements are created on the same day (and are therefore related settlements), it should be noted that the 'effective rate' used in calculating the ten-year charge is based on the *initial* value of the related settlement (s 66(4)(c)). If their initial value was low (eg £10), the related pilot settlements should therefore not represent too much of a problem for those purposes. Similar comments broadly apply for the purposes of calculating an exit charge before the first ten-yearly charge (s 68(5)). However, it is important that additions to the settlements should be made on the same day, such as on death.

Beware associated operations

7.48 The statutory references, eg s 65(1)(b), to the trustees making a disposition appear to indicate that the associated operations provisions of s 268 may be applied to relevant property trusts (see s 272, defining a disposition to include a disposition effected by associated operations).

Reverter to settlor

7.49   The exemption on reverter to settlor or settlor's spouse is potentially available only to interest in possession trusts, not to relevant property trusts.

Timing

7.50   Where property is *increasing* in value one should appoint as a general rule *before* the next ten-yearly anniversary because the previous ten-yearly anniversary fixes the effective rate. The contrary applies for decreasing values. This is especially true just before the first ten-year anniversary because the funds may initially have been within the nil rate band, such that there would be no exit charge before the first ten-year anniversary: see 'ten-year bonanza' at **7.89**.

Example 7.12 – Increasing values

On 1 August 2003, a tenth anniversary of a discretionary trust, value of trust property = £325,000 (assume brought forward cumulative total is nil).

The IHT rate = 3/10ths of effective rate.

Lifetime scale on (£325,000 – 255,000*) × 20% = £14,000

effective rate is $\dfrac{14,000}{325,000}$ = 4.31%

* Nil rate band for 2003–04

Ten-year anniversary charge = 3/10ths × $\dfrac{14,000}{325,000}$ = 4.202%

If, five years later, on 1 August 2008, the value of trust property had increased to £450,000 and is all appointed out on that date, the IHT is as follows:

Capital appointed £450,000

$\dfrac{3 \times 20}{10 \times 40} \times \dfrac{14,000}{325,000} \times £450,000 = £2,908$

So: appoint before next tenth anniversary, ie at former tenth anniversary effective rate.

Example 7.13 – Decreasing values

On 1 August 2002, a tenth anniversary, trust property = £400,000. Property is decreasing in value and on 1 August 2007 reduced to £250,000. Estimated reduction by 1 August 2012 = £100,000. If the property is appointed on 1 August 2007, the IHT is as follows:

Capital appointed £250,000

Charge on distribution is:

$$\frac{3 \times 20}{10 \times 40} \times \frac{30,000}{400,000} \times £250,000 = £2,812.50$$

So: if the appointment is deferred until after the next tenth anniversary (1 August 2012), there is nil IHT as the fund is by then below the nil rate band (a nil rate would apply to the appointment of any property for the ten years thereafter, even if the property later increases in value).

Payment by instalments

7.51   Trustees may in appropriate cases pay the IHT, either on the ten-yearly charge or on interim charges, by instalments (see **2.32**). Whilst, as a matter of trust law, it may be possible and appropriate to fund such instalments out of income, it is hard to see how that could properly be regarded as a deduction from the income of the trust for the purposes of assessing the primary liability of the trustees.

However, if the use of the trust funds in this way exhausts the available income, tax at the higher rates may be saved.

Why use a relevant property trust?

7.52   There is now no choice in the matter, because since FA 2006 no new lifetime trust which is not a chargeable transfer can be created, except in favour of a disabled person or of a charity. As a result, relevant property trusts, which were in any case preferable where CGT hold-over relief was required (under TCGA 1992, s 260) or where maximum flexibility was desired, will now become much more common.

Prior to legislation in FA 2002 (to counteract the Court of Appeal's decision in *Melville and others v IRC* [2001] STC 1271), this charge could be avoided by giving the settlor, under the terms of the trust, a valuable right to call for the trust property back again, commencing after an appropriate interval. FA 2002 subsequently excluded from the definition of 'property' in IHTA 1984, s 272 a 'settlement power' within s 47A.

Variants of the *Melville* scheme subsequently followed, but were effectively blocked by restrictions in CGT hold-over relief in respect of 'settlor-interested' trusts introduced in FA 2004 (see **1.31**). Another variant seemed possible for a time, in connection with transitional serial interests, but was soon curtailed. It is described in **Chapter 8**. For settlors now, the advice must be to 'get on with it', make gifts within the nil rate band and come back seven years later.

By a strange quirk of fate, the anti-avoidance provisions of FA 2006 opened up an opportunity for a new variation of *Melville*. FA 2010, s 52 closed that opportunity. The legislation made the termination of certain reversionary interests in settled property a chargeable event for IHT. The particular reversioners, called 'relevant reversioners', are those who purchased the reversionary interest for value or the settlor or spouse/civil partner of the settlor who is beneficially entitled to the reversionary interest.

For those individuals there is a deemed chargeable transfer of value of the reversion when a relevant reversion terminates if the relevant reversioner then becomes entitled to an actual interest or if the relevant reversioner assigns his reversionary interest. The PET regime is disapplied so that the transaction becomes an immediately chargeable transfer.

FA 2010, s 53 negates a tax-planning arrangement that could arise on a taxpayer purchasing an interest in a trust. The section works by creating a new category of interest in possession (IHTA 1984, ss 5(1B) and 49(1A)). This interest in possession arises where the life tenant is UK domiciled when he acquired the interest in possession by a transaction that would otherwise be exempt by s 10, ie a transaction not intended to confer a gratuitous benefit. A gift of such an interest in possession will be an immediately chargeable transfer. Additionally, there is a s 53 charge when the interest in possession ends during the purchaser's lifetime by stating that the termination of the interest in possession cannot be a PET.

Avoiding gifts with reservation of benefit provisions

7.53   Prior to legislation introduced in FA 2003 (to counteract the Court of Appeal's decision in *IRC v Eversden and another (executors of Greenstock, deceased)* [2003] STC 822), a popular strategy was for the husband to make a gift to a trust under which the wife takes an initial interest possession. The mechanics of this ingenious idea (which are explained in **1.34**) were effectively blocked by the introduction of FA 1986, s 102(5A)–(5C). Existing schemes potentially fall within the 'pre-owned assets' income tax charge from 6 April 2005 (see **Chapter 13**).

Income tax treatment of discretionary trusts: the tax pool

7.54   This comment applies equally to A&M trusts, for as long as they continue. Discretionary trustees are taxed less favourably than individuals in receipt of dividend income. The reason for this is that, in accounting for tax under ITA 2007, s 493 when a distribution is made out of the trust, although the distribution is still treated as an amount from which tax at the 50% trust rate of tax has been deducted (ITA 2007, s 494), the trustees are entitled to set against this only the tax *actually* paid by them upon receipt of dividend income and not the associated tax credit. The benefit of the tax credit is 'lost' within the trust.

Small trusts are partly sheltered from this rule by ITA 2007, s 491, which disapplies the trust rate from the first £1,000 of income. However, this also reduces the tax flowing into the pool, so effectively the amount that can be distributed without a tax pool adjustment (see ITA 2007, s 497) is even further restricted. Basically, there is no loss; the beneficiary could never have recovered the tax credit anyway. Thus the advice must be to consider making distributions of capital, though no tax will then be recoverable by the beneficiary on that particular receipt.

The tax treatment became even less favourable from 6 April 2010, when the dividend trust rate increased from 32.5% to 42.5%, and the trust rate of tax increased from 40% to 50%.

Capital gains tax

Hold-over relief (TCGA 1992, ss 165 and 260)

7.55   For 'gifts' since 14 March 1989 hold-over deferral has been restricted to:

- gifts of business assets (including certain holdings of unquoted shares in trading companies and of holding companies of trading groups) (TCGA 1992, s 165(2));

- gifts of *all* property which attracts IHT agricultural property relief (ie whether owner occupied or let and including 'hope', development value) (TCGA 1992, s 165(5), Sch 7, para 1);

- gifts of heritage property (s 260(2)(b)(iv));

- gifts to heritage maintenance funds (s 260(2)(b)(iii));

- gifts to political parties (s 260(2)(b)(i));

- gifts on which there is an *immediate* charge to IHT, in particular gifts into lifetime trusts including the nil band and transfers chargeable at the nil rate because, for example, business property relief applies (s 260(2)(a));

- occasions on which a beneficiary becomes *beneficially*, ie absolutely, entitled to trust assets at a time when *no* interest in possession exists. Hold-over relief is specifically available in respect of trusts for bereaved minors and age 18-to-25 trusts, following FA 2006 (s 260(2)(da), (db)).

7.56   Where deferral is not available, TCGA 1992, s 281 allows payment of tax by instalments in respect of gifts of land, controlling shareholdings and minority holdings in unquoted companies (eg investment companies where hold-over relief under TCGA 1992, s 165 is not available), but not free of interest.

Hold-over relief is denied to foreign residents by s 261. Trustees, especially professional ones, must consider their choices carefully, particularly where the trust is likely to be 'exported' (see TCGA 1992, ss 80–98 and Sch 5).

In order to maximise the CGT annual exemption for a trust, husband and wife should create *separate* (*not* joint) trusts. Thereby each trust will be eligible for this exemption, notwithstanding that for CGT purposes generally (and subject to independent taxation since 6 April 1990), husband and wife are treated as one person.

On disposals in 2012–13, all trustees are liable to pay capital gains tax at 28%.

Income tax

7.57   Under the provisions of ITA 2007, s 479, to the extent that income is accumulated, trusts are liable (for 2012–13) at the 50% rate, known as 'the trust rate'. Accordingly, it may be appropriate to distribute the income to low tax paying beneficiaries subject always to the provisions of ITTOIA 2005, s 629 (whereby if the settlement is by a parent for a 'relevant child' the income is treated as that of the parent). The use of trusts by grandparents may therefore be of particular significance, as the provisions of s 629 do not apply.

In addition, the other anti-avoidance provisions in ITTOIA 2005, Pt 5, Ch 5 must be taken into account, including in particular: s 624 settlements where the settlor retains an interest (subject to the exclusions, eg reverter to settlor on death under the age of 25 where beneficiary has a contingent interest – see s 625(2)(e)); the notorious ss 633 and 641 (sums paid to settlor otherwise than as income and capital sums paid by body connected with settlement); and s 629 in relation to parental settlements, as referred to above. Finance (No 3) Act 2010 provided for an adjustment as between settlor and trustees where the settlor's top tax rate is less than 50%. The settlor must pay any resulting tax repayment to the trustees (or any other person to whom income is payable) (see ITTOIA 2005, s 646(4), (5)).

As to the disadvantages associated with the receipt of dividend income by discretionary trustees, see **7.54**.

The rate of income tax payable by trustees in respect of dividends and other income increased from 2010–11 to 42.5% and 50% respectively. This will generally make most trusts less attractive from a tax perspective where the trustees hold significant income-producing assets. The rate is expected to fall slightly (to 37.5% and 45%) from 6 April 2013.

CHOOSING THE CORRECT SETTLEMENT – INTERESTS IN POSSESSION (SS 48–53)

IHT

7.58   FA 2006 changed the IHT landscape for settlements. Interests in possession that existed prior to 22 March 2006 are treated largely according to the old rules: any such interests arising since then are treated differently, depending upon whether the trust was a lifetime settlement, such as are the subject of this chapter, or a trust arising on death, whether by will or by operation of law. A person who was beneficially entitled on 22 March 2006 to an interest in possession in settled property (and see the discussion on the *Pearson* case in **7.15** on what constitutes an interest in possession) is treated as beneficially entitled to the property in which the interest subsists.

Therefore if an individual is entitled to the whole of the income, say as life tenant, the general rule, in the absence of reliefs and exemptions including the application of the PET regime, requires the whole of the trust fund to be assessed to IHT when such life tenant disposes of his interest during his life, or when he dies. Moreover, the value of the trust fund will be added to the individual chargeable transfers of the beneficiary concerned.

A person who becomes entitled to a non-transitional interest in possession in a lifetime trust after 22 March 2006 is treated for IHT (but not for CGT) purposes like the beneficiary of a discretionary trust: the fund is not aggregated with his or her estate on death; and yet main residence relief may be available to shelter a gain arising on the disposal of a residence occupied by a post-FA 2006 tenant for life.

Treatment of 'old' interests in possession

7.59   There is a pro rata liability for a (pre-2006) partial interest. Where a person's entitlement is to income in a specified amount in any period such as an annuity, his interest in possession is taken to subsist in such part of the trust property as produces that amount in that period.

Artificial arrangements to reduce liability by raising or lowering the yield from the trust fund can be countered under the provisions in s 50(4), the Treasury maximum and minimum prescribed rates. Trustees are usually given power to vary investments. Therefore, by switching into high yielding assets when the interest in an annuity is expected to terminate (with the resultant possible PET, and an IHT charge), the annuity would represent a smaller share of the total income. Conversely, with a switch to low yielding assets, the balance of the income would represent a reduced share and therefore save IHT at the time when that balance was disposed of.

The Treasury-prescribed higher and lower rates of yield are imposed to restrict this type of manipulation. Under the Inheritance Tax (Settled Property Income Yield) Order 2000 (SI 2000/174) the Treasury took the step of linking the yields to the FT Actuaries Share Index published in the *Financial Times*. For the higher rate, it will be the yield shown at the relevant date of irredeemables in the FTSE Actuaries Government Securities UK Indices, and for the lower rate, the gross dividend yield of the All-Share actual dividend yield.

The use, occupation and enjoyment of trust assets such as a house can also constitute an interest in possession (s 50(5)) see also the later part of **6.18**, where SP 10/79 is mentioned. It will be noted from the second paragraph of that SP, that the official view is that no interest in possession is created by the grant of a lease at less than full consideration, although there will normally be an IHT charge on the diminution arising in the value of the trust fund.

7.60   As mentioned, the termination of a pre-FA 2006 interest in possession during life or on death would normally give rise to a charge on the capital supporting that interest subject to the PET rules, but there are important exceptions which should enable this type of trust to be used as an appropriate 'harmless' trust.

These exceptions apply when the beneficiary becomes beneficially entitled, either absolutely, or to another interest in possession. In the latter case, unless the new interest has equivalent value to the former interest, there is pro rata exemption only under ss 53(2) and 52(4)(b); to the extent that:

- the disposal is for a consideration in money or money's worth (see s 52(2));

- the trust property reverts to the settlor (ss 53(3) and 54(1));

- the trust property reverts to the settlor's spouse (or his/her/widow(er)) within two years of his/her death (ss 53(4) and 54(2)); and

- in respect of a surviving spouse where estate duty was payable on the first death.

This last exemption applies in the case of a lifetime or death termination of an interest in possession where the first spouse died before 13 November 1974 (Sch 6, para 2), and in these circumstances the trustees should aim for maximum capital growth of the trust fund as the fund will be exempt from IHT. This will involve important investment decisions, for example, that any cash deposits should be used to acquire appreciating assets.

This transitional exemption will of course not apply to any new assets added to the trusts, as the application is in respect of switching investments. In this context consider a widow selling her home to the trustees and remaining with an interest in possession. The gain on the sale and the future gain while in possession will escape CGT (TCGA 1992, ss 222 and 225); meanwhile the widow receives liquid resources which she can spend or use for estate planning. However, a stamp duty land tax charge may arise.

Following changes introduced by FA 2010, an interest in possession which is purchased is treated as forming part of the purchaser's estate, if that person became beneficially entitled to the interest in possession on or after 9 December 2009. The ending of such an interest does not fall within s 52; thus, for example a lifetime termination of the interest is an immediately chargeable transfer, as opposed to a PET. See **7.52**.

Example 7.14 – Estate duty surviving spouse fund

Andrew Vickers died on 30 September 1974 and left £100,000 after payment of estate duty in trust for his wife, Agatha, for life, with remainder to their son. Agatha died on 30 June 2011, having made no lifetime gifts and leaving her entire free estate of £400,000 to her son. Andrew's will trust property was then worth £200,000.

On Agatha's death, IHT of £30,000 is payable (ie (£400,000 – £325,000) × 40%) on the free estate, but the trust passes free of IHT to the son, estate duty having been paid on his father's death (s 273, Sch 6).

Had Andrew died on or after 13 November 1974, no estate duty or IHT would have been payable on the amount left in trust to Agatha (s 18). Andrew's unused nil rate band would have been available and is assumed to be 100%. Agatha's executors would have 200% of the nil rate band available, £650,000, to set against the combined total of her trust and free estate: more than enough to shelter it from IHT.

7.61   There is an anomaly in this retained estate duty surviving spouse exemption with regard to the related property rules in s 161 where, for instance, a widow has private company shares in her own estate, and she has a life interest under her husband's will (estate duty paid on his death) in a fund which includes shares in the same company. If her life interest terminates on her death, the husband's shares, though not liable to IHT, can nevertheless be brought in as related property in valuing the widow's own shares because Sch 6, para 2 provides that the husband's will trust property shall be 'left out of account' on the widow's death; but that does not prevent the husband's will trust shares, to which the widow is deemed to be beneficially entitled under s 49(1), from being brought in, when valuing her *own* shares, as related property.

Contrast the position if the widow releases her life interest in her lifetime. Exemption of the husband's fund is then obtained under Sch 6, para 2, and no question of the valuation of the husband's shares or of her own at that stage arises. It may be appropriate for the widow to release part only of her life interest, eg sufficient of the shares in the husband's fund to bring the combined holding below 50% or, depending on other circumstances, some other level.

However, the release of her life interest, unlike termination on death, will give rise to a CGT charge where a beneficiary becomes absolutely entitled, under TCGA 1992, s 71(1), although this gain may be eligible for hold-over relief under TCGA 1992, s 165 as appropriate for unquoted shares.

7.62   On termination or death there can, exceptionally, be a CGT charge if hold-over relief was claimed when the settlor placed the assets into trust (TCGA 1992, s 74), subject to any further possible hold-over claim.

For the purpose of determining voting control, s 269(3) provides that the interest in possession beneficiary aggregates his own beneficial holding with the trustees' holding. This is a corollary of the basic situation that if an individual owns shares in a company and is life tenant of a trust which also owns such shares, the shares are valued as if the individual owned both holdings.

The effect of the Revenue statement of May 1990 (see **1.24**) is that on the lifetime termination of a pre-FA 2006 interest in possession, the IHT charge under s 52(1) does not require the valuation to be aggregated on a pro rata basis, namely as to the individual's beneficial ownership and the interest in possession entitlement. They are to be valued separately. For example, if the estate owner holds, say, 40% of the ordinary shares in a company beneficially, ie outright, and 40% by way of a life interest, the two 40% holdings are to be valued in isolation on a minority basis, and not as part of an 80% controlling interest.

Therefore, if an estate owner wishes to gift a controlling interest, it may nowadays be better to give two separate minority valued gifts, one beneficially/ absolutely, the other by way of an interest in possession. It would be wise not to make the two gifts contemporaneously having regard to the application of the *Ramsay* principle (notwithstanding the ongoing uncertainty surrounding its precise application) and the associated operations rules in s 268.

'New' interests in possession: the permitted categories

7.63   As noted elsewhere, an 'estate' interest in possession settlement can no longer be created, for IHT purposes, inter vivos, save for a disabled person (a disabled person's interest or 'DPI') under the provisions of s 89 as augmented by ss 89A and 89B introduced by FA 2006.

Research commissioned by HMRC, which was not made public until after the changes in FA 2006, suggested that relatively few trusts are set up for those who fit the tight definition of disability in s 89(4), (5) and (6), namely:

- incapable of managing his affairs; or

- receiving attendance allowance (AA); or

- receiving disability living allowance (DLA) at the middle or highest rate; or

- entitled to AA or DLA, but for certain residence disqualifications; or

- entitled, or would have been, to AA or DLA when the trust was set up but for residence disqualification.

In response to representations, especially by STEP, s 89A extends protection to those who can show that, at the time the trust was set up, they suffered from a condition making it likely that their health would deteriorate and where certain conditions, see s 89A(2) *et seq*, are met.

From 8 April 2013 the government will introduce a new benefit called personal independence payment (PIP) to replace disability living allowance (DLA) for eligible people aged 16 to 64. The definition of a disabled person's trust will need to be amended accordingly with prospective effect.

Interest in possession trusts as PETs as from 17 March 1987

7.64   Since 22 March 2006, the facility to make PETs remains only in respect of disabled persons (IHTA 1984, s 3A, as amended by FA 2006, Sch 20), and a PET can only mean (see s 3A(1A)):

- a gift to another individual;

- a gift to a disabled trust; or

- a gift into a bereaved minor's trust (BMT) on the coming to an end of an IPDI.

Sections 54A and 54B anti-avoidance provisions

7.65   These provisions, which were adapted to suit the new FA 2006 regime, contain complex anti-avoidance rules. The aim is clear, namely to prevent loss of IHT where a settlor by way of a PET had created an interest in possession for a short term on the termination of which a discretionary trust arises. The loss of IHT would result if the life tenant's aggregation of previous transfers in the last seven years was lower than the settlor's, because the life tenant's termination would be the measure of the transfer of value, not the settlor's.

Section 54A applies where:

- there is a termination of an interest in possession (provided, where the person became entitled to the interest after 22 March 2006, it was a DPI or a TSI) on death or in lifetime;

- the whole or part of the value transferred is attributable to property which became settled as a PET by the settlor (on or after 17 March 1987) and within seven years before termination of the life interest;

- the settlor is still then alive; and

- the trust fund then becomes settled property with no qualifying interest in possession (ie held on relevant property trusts).

In such circumstances, IHT is calculated on the higher of:

- the normal charge, ie termination of the interest in possession aggregating the life tenant's chargeable transfers in the previous seven years; and

- the aggregate IHT at the lifetime rates, had the creation of the settlement not been a PET; and taking into account the settlor's chargeable transfers within seven years preceding the creation of the settlement. In other words, the charge can be broadly on the basis of the settlor having created a discretionary trust.

Note that the mischief complained of was not caught where the initial settlement was an accumulation and maintenance trust under s 71; or where an interest in possession thereunder was revoked and a discretionary trust substituted. By contrast, a disabled trust under s 89 is treated like an interest in possession trust when followed by a discretionary trust.

Note also that s 54A(2)(d) provides a let-out from this higher rate anti-avoidance charge if the trust interest lasts for less than six months.

The trustees are primarily liable for the above IHT charge; hence the need for them to retain sufficient assets for up to seven years from the creation of the interest in possession trust. The settlor will, however, also be liable where the trustees have been non-resident between 16 March 1987 and the settlor's death. If the trustees were UK resident at the creation of the settlement and have been non-resident between 16 March 1987 and the relevant death, the settlor's liability does not arise.

Income tax

7.66   A beneficiary who has an interest in possession is entitled to the income as it arises. The income tax liability will depend on the beneficiary concerned, ie his rates and subject to his allowances, except where this rule is overridden by the rules as to settlor-interested trusts (eg by parents for minors) under ITTOIA 2005, s 624.

By definition there is no power to accumulate, hence the trust rate of tax of 50% (for 2012–13) is not in point.

Avoiding income tax on young beneficiaries at the trust rate

7.67   This proposal concerns avoiding tax at the trust rate under ITA 2007, s 479 in respect of certain beneficiaries of lifetime and will trusts; prior to their attaining interests in possession, and obtaining repayment claims. This section does not refer to settlor-interested trusts, where the rules are different.

A problem arises where a minor beneficiary is entitled to a gift contingently on attaining 18 or a later age. As the beneficiary has only a contingent interest in the income before the age of 18, two main disadvantages result. First, up to the age of 18 the trustees must pay income tax at the trust rate; and secondly, there would be no possibility of repayment claims for the beneficiary, except insofar as the income is paid or applied for the beneficiary's maintenance, education or benefit.

A possible solution is to give the beneficiary a vested interest in the *income* as soon as it arises. Then, although he only has a contingent interest in the capital, the income will be regarded as his. The trustees or the beneficiary will only be taxed by deduction up to the basic rate. Repayment claims may be made on behalf of the beneficiary. There is no reason why the appointment of income should not be revocable.

To achieve this, the gift in the (pre-2006) trust deed or will (coming into force at any time) must provide that the beneficiary has a vested right to income before 18 (which income shall belong to the infant absolutely). This chapter does not discuss the FA 2006 regime for will trusts, but it should be noted here that only certain trusts (ie BMTs), avoid the 'relevant property' regime and its related complications.

Further difficulties arise if the gift is a gift by will, such as a contingent *pecuniary* legacy. Such a gift does not normally carry the intermediate income pursuant to Trustee Act 1925, s 31. To avoid the difficulties, the will must specifically provide that the legacy be set aside, invested and that the income produced by the investment of the legacy belongs absolutely to the beneficiary. This will enable the income tax advantages discussed above to apply also to the contingent pecuniary legacies.

Having achieved these income tax advantages one must appreciate the possible risk, perhaps rare both in financial and in mortality terms, namely that the entitlement to income will operate as from the date that the trust commences to operate, and the infant beneficiary will have an interest in possession from then. Accordingly, should he die before he becomes entitled to the capital, an IHT charge arises; but this can generally be easily, and relatively cheaply, insured against. There may also be natural, family objections to giving significant amounts of income to one so young.

As to income tax anti-avoidance provisions applicable to settlements by parents for unmarried minors, see ITTOIA 2005, s 629.

Note that a revocable life interest can be used to avoid the income tax complications of income in a trust being subject to the trust rate, whether or not the beneficiary is a minor.

Capital gains tax

Creation still a disposal

7.68 The mere fact that an interest in possession is granted to the settlor will not prevent the creation of the trust being a disposal for CGT purposes.

Hold-over relief under TCGA 1992, s 165 (and also under s 260) was restricted by the introduction in FA 2004 of TCGA 1992, ss 169B–169G from 10 December 2003. Previously, it was possible for, say, unquoted trading company shares standing at a gain to be transferred to an interest in possession settlement with the benefit of s 165 relief in which the settlor had an interest. This would reset the CGT taper relief 'clock' where the status of the shares had been tainted by a non-business period, and start a new business asset ownership period in the trustees' hands. Taper relief was subsequently withdrawn from 6 April 2008.

Where, in the past, hold-over relief had been claimed, that relief is clawed back if the trust becomes settlor-interested within the following six years (TCGA 1992, s 169C). This presents a significant trap for the unwary and is difficult to explain to the lay client. The rules are widely drawn, and can also apply to arrangements under which the settlor is capable of acquiring an interest. In particular, the widening of the definition of 'settlor interested' so as to include any trust which includes a minor child of the settlor, can cause problems.

Example 7.15 – A costly liaison

Gerald had set up a trust for his adult children into which he had transferred shares in the family trading company at about the time of his divorce, holding over the gain.

He then married Jade, the forceful *femme fatale* in the situation, who had a child aged three who, under the precise terms of the trust, became a beneficiary and who qualified as George's stepchild.

The trust, which had previously not been settlor-interested, changed its nature and hold-over relief was clawed back. The trustees have no liquid funds.

CGT rate

7.69   Trustees of all settlements, whether discretionary or interest in possession, are liable to tax on their capital gains at 28% for 2012–13.

Tax-free uplift on death

7.70   It may be possible to 'wash out' CGT on a death in the circumstances outlined in Example 4.4.

Settlor-interested trusts

7.71   Before the CGT rate was aligned (initially at 18%) for all gains, it was often important to ensure that neither the settlor nor his spouse (or civil partner) could take any interest in the settlement; otherwise the rate of CGT would be that suffered by the settlor, ie a maximum of 40% (TCGA 1992, ss 77–79 before their repeal by FA 2008, s 8 and Sch 20, with effect from 2008–09 and later years).

For those with old cases unresolved, the former provisions were widely drawn (see for example *Trennery v West (and related appeals)* [2005] STC 214). However, in some cases it could actually be beneficial for those anti-avoidance provisions to bite, eg if the settlor's CGT rate was lower than the 40% rate applicable to the trustees. This was also used as a relieving measure in respect of vulnerable beneficiaries by treating them as if they were the settlor under FA 2005, ss 30–39, but those provisions were rendered largely otiose by FA 2008, Sch 2 with effect from 6 April 2008.

What practitioners should appreciate for current compliance work is that, in relation to settlor-interested trusts, the income must be returned as the settlor's but that the gains go on the return made by the trustees. Not every client will understand this.

Set-off under TCGA 1992, s 67

7.72   TCGA 1992, s 67 provides for an allowance against a gain in certain rare circumstances such as where hold-over relief had been claimed under FA 1980, s 79 (which is no longer possible) and the disposal became a chargeable transfer for IHT.

Gifts between spouses

'Unbalanced trusts'

7.73   **Gifts between husband and wife etc** – changes were introduced in the income tax rules (now in ITTOIA 2005, s 624) for income deriving from gifts between husband and wife and for some other settlements. The changes ensured that, with independent taxation (from 6 April 1990), income from simple outright gifts of assets between husband and wife became taxed as income of the recipient.

However the income will generally be treated as the *donor's* for tax purposes if, for example:

- the donor has the right to get the asset back in the future, or to decide what the recipient should do with it; or

- the donor uses a trust to give the income to his or her partner while retaining control over the capital, or passing the capital to a third party. Therefore in a common form life interest trust where a husband settles assets the income from which goes to his wife for life remainder as to capital to the children, the income is not the wife's for tax purposes (see also ITTOIA 2005, s 625(1)).

- Deeds of variation under s 142 were to be very restricted for deaths after the FA 1989 Royal Assent date. Although the Finance Bill provisions were abandoned, anti-avoidance legislation remains a possibility in the future. The use in wills of flexible life interests in favour of spouses with wide powers of appointment in favour of such spouses and/or other beneficiaries should to a degree overcome this problem, but there can be no variation of a lifetime settlement by deed within s 142. Flexible will trusts are therefore to be recommended. Interest in possession trusts which fall within the requirements of an IPDI are generally very useful in wills between husband and wife (see **4.12**).

- Trustees need to watch the distinction between:

  - a distribution by a company of profits akin to a dividend *in specie* and hence income (to which beneficiaries interested in income are entitled); and

  - a company reconstruction where what the trustees receive is capital to be added to the trust fund.

In *Re Lee, Sinclair v Lee* [1993] 3 All ER 926, ICI decided to restructure its activities and placed its pharmaceutical interests into a new company, Zeneca Group plc. They then demerged Zeneca, so that all the shareholders of ICI received shares in Zeneca. In the *Lee* will trust the testatrix had left ICI shares upon trust to pay the income to her husband for life, and on his death to her son absolutely. The court decided that the ICI transaction was a company reconstruction, with two capital assets (shares in ICI and shares in Zeneca) replacing one existing capital asset (shares in ICI). Accordingly, the trustees were to hold the Zeneca shares as capital of the trust fund. As for enhanced scrip dividends received by trustees of interest in possession trusts, see the Revenue SP 4/94 dated 17 May 1994.

Also in this context note the case of *Taube* [2011] WTLR 1 (see **8.9**).

CHOOSING THE CORRECT SETTLEMENT – RELEVANT PROPERTY

Some estate planning aspects involving relevant property trusts

7.74 The term 'relevant property' trust has been used for this section because, whatever the terms of the trust for the purposes of trust law, or income tax, or CGT, a lifetime trust established after 22 March 2006 (save for a disabled trust) falls within the IHT regime that previously applied mainly to discretionary trusts. We therefore have to get used to the different terminology because of the treatment for different taxes or circumstances.

As a result, the formation of a discretionary trust may often now be the best option, for a number of reasons.

The burden of IHT

7.75   Where the settlor has not used his nil rate band at all, the IHT charges on discretionary trusts may well prove manageable. With only one rate, above the nil rate band, IHT for the wealthier family may still be acceptable, though it is really in relation to business and agricultural property that the use of relevant property trusts come into their own.

In return for an entry charge, the moderate periodic and exit charges are a burden that may be carried from the total shareholder return of a reasonably successful investment.

Example 7.16 – Timing capital advances

Mr X has not made previous chargeable gifts. On 1 May 2002 he settles £100,000 on discretionary trusts (no IHT: gifts covered by nil rate band). On the ten-year charge in May 2012 the trust property is worth £400,000. The IHT charge is £4,500 (ie £400,000 less the nil rate band of £325,000, multiplied by 30% of the lifetime rate).

If capital advances had been made *within* the ten years or the trust wound up, the IHT rate applicable would be calculated at 3/10 of the scale of IHT at the time of exit multiplied by 1/40 for every completed quarter to the date of charge from commencement. Based on £100,000, that would inevitably produce a nil charge on exit.

Example 7.17 – Maximum charge 6%

Mr Y settles £200,000 on discretionary trusts on 7 April 2002, having made chargeable gifts of £325,000 within the previous seven years.

On the ten-year anniversary in April 2012, the trust property is worth £500,000 and the IHT charge would be £30,000, which is only 6% of the value of the property.

Even in respect of sizeable distributions, bearing in mind that currently the lifetime rate is 20% (above the nil rate band) and with the ten-year charge at 30% thereof, the maximum ten-year charge can never exceed 6%; and if the property is eligible for the lower business or agricultural relief of 50%, the maximum rate is only 3%, and therefore the annual instalment payable over ten years is only 0.3% per annum.

A settlement of stable value which was not originally within the nil rate band can become a nil rate band trust as the nil rate band increases year by year.

Business property and agricultural reliefs and pitfalls

Transfer into the trust

7.76 Business property and agricultural relief are available on the initial transfer into the settlement, as is the £3,000 exemption (for the current year and, if unused, the previous year).

Example 7.18 – Effect of 50% BPR

Property attracting the lower 50% BPR is transferred to a new discretionary trust. An individual may make the following transfer within his nil rate band (£325,000 for 2012–13), assuming that the annual exemption is available for the current and previous tax year.

	£
Gross	662,000
50% BPR	(331,000)
	331,000
Annual × 2	(6,000)
Balance (covered by nil rate band, if available)	325,000

Both ss 103 (BPR) and 115 (APR) provide that, for the purpose of the relevant property trust rules, references in the reliefs to value transferred by a chargeable transfer include references to the amount on which tax is then chargeable, and that references to the transferor include references to trustees.

So prima facie there is no problem. The hypothetical rate at which IHT is levied at the ten-year anniversary is, by s 66(4), calculated *inter alia* by reference to the value on which tax is charged under s 64. Section 64 charges the value of the property at the time of the charge. So BPR and APR are available because that is 'the amount on which tax is charged'.

Calculation pitfall: exit charge in first decade

7.77 However, the treatment described above does not apply to exit charges within the first ten years. Here, the amount on which the charge is levied is the value leaving the settlement.

This value will qualify for BPR or APR but the 'hypothetical rate' in s 68(1) and (5) is the value, immediately after the settlement commenced, of the property then comprised in it. This is outside the deeming provisions in s 103 and s 115 and so the hypothetical rate in Example 7.18 will be based on £656,000 and not £325,000.

This is an unpleasant pitfall, but is not a problem where the 100% discount applies because the value of the asset is reduced to zero. It will, however, be an issue if relief is available at only 50%, or if the settlement contains both relievable and other property and it is the non-relievable property that is appointed out.

100% BPR/APR and discretionary trusts

7.78 The transfer of business or agricultural assets into such flexible trusts during lifetime or by will is undoubtedly among the best estate planning methods available. In particular:

- Certain business and agricultural assets as outlined above may be held in such trusts indefinitely with 100% relief and will be chargeable neither at the ten-year anniversary dates nor to any interim charges after the first ten-year anniversary charge. At the ten-year anniversary, the trustees will need to satisfy the relevant business or agricultural property conditions. Assuming the 100% relief applies (and any other assets in the trust are within the nil band), the ten-year anniversary charge rate will be zero. Most importantly, that zero rate will continue to apply until immediately prior to the next ten-year anniversary, even though the assets are no longer business or agricultural assets (eg the trust fund consists of the proceeds of sale).

- In a very similar way to what has just been explained, there is a problem for the 50% but not the 100% relief. Under s 68(4) and (5), in arriving at the rate of interim charges before the first ten-year anniversary (but not otherwise), no allowance is made for any business or agricultural relief at the 50% rate. As to the 100% relief, the risk seems to have disappeared because the value of the asset for s 68 purposes is zero, and therefore there is no charge (eg under s 65).

- For lifetime trusts, whether discretionary or not, there is generally no CGT hold-over relief restriction in connection with non-business assets (see TCGA 1992, s 260). There may, of course, be an IHT restriction in respect of 'excepted' assets (IHTA 1984, s 112).

- However, this general rule has been subject to serious qualification, since 10 December 2003. Relief under s 260 is denied if the trust is settlor-interested, and relief already given is clawed back if the trust becomes settlor interested within the following six tax years (TCGA 1992, ss 169B–169C). This can apply where, by virtue of a wide definition of 'settlor-interested', a trust falls within the rules unexpectedly.

- There is also an anti-avoidance rule designed to block claims for both s 260 hold-over relief and private residence relief (under TCGA 1992, s 225), ie on the transfer of a residence to the trustees, and on a subsequent disposal of the residence if occupied by a beneficiary under the terms of the settlement (see TCGA 1992, s 226A).

Example 7.19 – Business and agricultural property

A discretionary trust, set up years earlier, has one of its ten-year anniversary charges on 1 May 2012. At that date, its trust fund consists of:

- £300,000 in cash;

- 26% of the ordinary share capital of Trading Co Ltd; and

- a farm owned and managed by the trustees.

Any distribution of the trust fund in whole or part at any time before the next ten-year anniversary will, in effect, be free of IHT because under ss 68 and 69 the rate at the ten-year anniversary on 1 May 2012 is zero and that zero rate franks interim distributions, ie applies until midnight of 1 May 2022.

This beneficial treatment is neither affected nor altered if, after 1 May 2012, the business property or agricultural property is sold or otherwise disposed of.

Note that the claw-back provisions in ss 113A and 113B (and 124A and 124B) are inapplicable: they could only apply if the settlor died within seven years of creating the trust, and by definition, in this example, ten years or more have elapsed since the trust was set up.

Double IHT relief using discretionary trusts

7.79   Consider the following possibilities:

- Spouse 1 ('H') in his will leaves business/agricultural property to a discretionary trust in favour of the family including Spouse 2 ('W'). On H's death, BPR/APR is obtained for the first time; plus CGT death exemption and market value uplift.

- H leaves W his investment assets or she owns such assets in her own right.

- W purchases, at arm's length (eg under a market value option granted to her in H's will), the business/agricultural assets from the trustees.

- On W's death two years or more after the purchase, her estate should also be eligible for the relief, ie for a second time. Consider insuring the two-year period. CGT exemption and market value uplift apply again.

- Ancillary aspects:

–   Adapt for the farmhouse.

–   W could delegate management responsibilities if wished.

–   W need suffer no loss of income because she is a beneficiary of the discretionary trust.

–   Consider the application of these arrangements by way of deed of variation; but more provocative and potential *Ramsay* implications.

Example 7.20 – 'Doubling up' BPR/APR

Mr Planner, who has made no lifetime chargeable transfers, owns the following assets:

(1)   Stock Exchange securities, building society and bank deposits totalling £1,325,000;

(2)   a 30% holding in Adam Planner Ltd, which manufactures widgets, the shares being valued at £400,000;

(3)   Planner Farm, which Mr Planner has owned and farmed for many years, valued at £600,000.

In his will Mr Planner leaves assets (2) and (3) to a discretionary trust in favour of his widow, children and grandchildren. He also leaves £325,000 of the assets in (1) to the trust. The remaining (investment) assets of £1,000,000 he leaves to his widow, coupled with an option for her to buy the business and agricultural assets from the trust at market value.

Note: The nil rate band for 2012–13 is £325,000.

The effect:

On Mr Planner's death, there is no IHT, and there is CGT exemption and market value uplift. In total over £1.3 million of investments has been transferred into a discretionary trust free of IHT and without any substantial CGT.

On Mrs Planner's death, IHT is limited, assuming she survives two years from the exercise of the option. If, by then, there are still surplus investment assets over the nil rate band, only their value will attract a charge. Any assets in the estate of Mrs Planner at her death will benefit from market value uplift for CGT. Only her own nil rate band will be available to her executors, but her late husband's band has been well used.

Alternatively, Mr Planner could have left all his investment assets to his wife, so she would have had the benefit of an increased nil rate band – that approach may be preferred in some cases.

Flexibility

7.80   A settlor who wishes to take advantage of his own seven-year cut-off can form a discretionary trust and get his seven years running at a time when he is still not sure which of a number of possible beneficiaries should ultimately be absolute owners. Distributions out of a discretionary trust and their timing can be arranged with maximum flexibility.

To the extent that such distributions are out of income, there is no IHT charge because such income distributions, assuming they are liable to income tax, are not chargeable IHT distributions (s 65(5)(b)). However, there would then be a charge to income tax on the trust, applying where appropriate a lower rate to the first slice of the income. The distribution, net of tax, remains taxable but only at the beneficiary's rate, so if the beneficiary pays only at basic rate any excess may be recovered.

Alternatively, and depending upon the precise wording of the trust deed, if income is accumulated it can take on the character of capital. If, on the facts, it does, it then does constitute a chargeable distribution for IHT purposes when it leaves the trust. See also *Carver v Duncan* and *Bosanquet v Allen* [1985] STC 356, HL.

With the coming into force on 6 April 2010 of the Perpetuities and Accumulations Act 2009, settlors gained new flexibility, in that there is no longer a requirement to limit the accumulation period, and the trust itself can now last for 125 years, which is ample for most purposes.

Fragmentation

7.81   Discretionary trusts can be fragmented and the IHT levy substantially reduced. It is important to ensure that a number of separate settlements are created; and (SP 7/84 not being relevant here) to ensure that this is so, the judgment of Lord Wilberforce in *Roome v Edwards* [1981] STC 96 gives the indicia of separate settlements (see also **8.25**).

Methods of fragmentation

7.82   A series of low-value settlements on different dates, followed by additions on the same day. There is scope for growth in the first ten years up to the value of the nil rate band before any IHT is payable (£325,000 for 2012–13) If the initial settlements are of low value, it is not essential to create them on the same day. They will be related settlements under s 62. However, it is only the value of the property in the property when it was created which is aggregated when calculating anniversary charges. If the trusts are set up with, say, £10 each, this should not be too much of a problem.

	1	2	3	4	5
	£	£	£	£	£
Initial settlement	600	600	600	600	600
Added property	64,400	64,400	64,400	64,400	64,400
	65,000	65,000	65,000	65,000	65,000
Cumulative total	–	600	1,200	1,800	2,400
IHT-free growth possible	260,000	259,400	258,800	258,200	258,000
	325,000	325,000	325,000	325,000	325,000

The scope for IHT-free growth in the second and subsequent settlements is less than that for settlement one because, of course, the creation of each preceding discretionary trust uses up part of the settlor's available nil rate band.

The IHT charge when adding the property, ignoring the annual exemption, will be nothing: this stems from s 66(5)(a), s 67(4)(a) and s 68(4)(b). By way of reminder, s 66(5)(a) sets out part of the complicated formula to establish the 'aggregate value' of previous transfers. That formula helps to fix the notional transfer by reference to which the ten-yearly charge is calculated. It provides that one element of this 'aggregate value' is the value transferred by any chargeable transfers made by the settlor in the seven years that end on the date that the settlement was made (disregarding transfers before 27 March 1974, which we would now anyway).

Section 67 concerns property that is added to an existing settlement (after 8 March 1982), but before the ten-year anniversary that is now to be taxed. Section 67(4)(a) deals first with settlements commenced before 27 March 1974. It goes on to provide that where there has been an addition to an 'old' settlement (ie one set up before 27 March 1974), the aggregate transfer for the purposes of s 66(5) must be increased by the value of the transfers by the settlor in the seven years that lead up to the addition, but with two disregards:

- transfers made that day, or before 27 March 1974; and
- values identified in s 67(5), as to which see below.

Section 67 then provides that where the settlor has made, as in our example, two or more chargeable transfers by way of additions to discretionary trusts within s 67(1), s 67(4) applies to 'the transfer in relation to which the aggregate to be added is the greatest'.

Section 68 deals with the charge at the first ten-year anniversary. It postulates a chargeable transfer, assembled from several components. Section 67(4)(b) shows that the deemed transfer is made at the date of the anniversary on the basis that the settlor had, in the previous seven years, made transfers totalling what the settlor had actually made in the seven years before the settlement, but disregarding:

- transfers that day; or

- transfers on or before 27 March 1974.

If the funds settled in this series comprise not cash, but CGT chargeable assets, eg shares in the family company, the separate fragmented disposals will be linked for CGT (the settlor and the trustees of each settlement being connected persons under TCGA 1992, s 286(3)) and, because the disposals are all within the six-year limit, the gain on each disposal will be by reference to the market value of the aggregate shareholding (TCGA 1992, ss 19 and 20).

HMRC may attack this arrangement under the *Ramsay* principle or as associated operations. It now seems clear, from the *Rysaffe* case discussed below, that the associated operations provisions in particular should not be applicable. Those provisions apply only for the purpose of identifying the timing of a transfer of value. Section 60 ('Commencement of settlement') does not operate by first identifying a transfer of value. It merely directs that the date when property first becomes comprised in the settlement is identified. It is important to ensure that the settled funds are properly constituted and become comprised in the settlements, as s 60 requires. Otherwise, there is a danger that the settlements may not have commenced for IHT purposes.

In the *Rysaffe* case ([2002] WTLR 65 SpC, [2002] WTLR 1077 ChD, [2003] WTLR 481, CA; see **7.28**), associated operations were not considered to be applicable to cases where there was no dispute as to the dispositions of property (within s 43). To reduce the scope for challenge (eg on the basis that each addition to the trusts constitutes a new settlement), alter key features of each of the pilot settlements, eg different trustees, accumulation and perpetuity periods, class of beneficiaries, administrative powers etc. Avoid the use of merely nominal sums when creating the pilot settlement, and ensure that each settlement is properly constituted through the receipt of the nominal sum by the trustees.

This remains an aggressive form of IHT planning; more so if there is an intention later to merge the settlements, such as for administrative convenience or to save costs. Whilst the settlements would still be treated separately for IHT purposes (see s 81(1)), such action could provoke HMRC to consider whether they were truly separate in the first place. However, provided adequate care is taken of the sort indicated above, this technique remains worthy of consideration.

On a more general aspect, remember that husband and wife each have their own IHT nil rate band and one spouse may be able to channel shares through the other spouse. HMRC cannot challenge unconditional gifts between spouses followed by subsequent transfers to third parties under the associated operations provisions (see IHTM14833), although there remains the possibility of a challenge on *Ramsay* principles.

This arrangement can be adapted where 100% BPR/APR applies (see **Chapter 15**).

7.83   On the incorporation of a new company, it may be worthwhile in certain circumstances to use new small discretionary trusts to avoid a 'related property' situation. For example:

discretionary trust 1 holds	26% of the shares
discretionary trust 2 holds	26% of the shares
discretionary trust 3 holds	22% of the shares
husband and wife together hold	26% of the shares
	100%

The shares held by the trustees will not be related with those held by the husband and wife; and each holding will become eligible to the 100% business relief.

Note also that s 65(9) (the omission to exercise a right constituting a disposition) and the normal consequential loss formula on any disposition, apply with equal force to trustees as for individuals. Therefore, trustees must, for instance, be prepared to take up favourable rights issues offered to them. The use of discretionary trusts can be particularly appropriate in settling family company shares among a class of children so that the voting powers are retained in the trustees (of whom the settlor may well be one), as opposed to splintering shares among the individual beneficiaries absolutely.

There used to be a disadvantage once the beneficiaries attained an interest in possession because the settlement then became a fixed interest trust, so that upon the death of a beneficiary there was an interest in possession charge under ss 49–50. That facility, and corresponding disadvantage, is much reduced since FA 2006.

However, consider the possible consequences of IHT planning in terms of the availability of the CGT death exemption and market value uplift (TCGA 1992, s 62) and the availability of entrepreneurs' relief. In addition, the income tax charges applicable to dividend income have the broad effect that, in accounting for tax under ITA 2007, s 497 on making a distribution out of the trust, the distribution is still treated as an amount of trust income from which tax at 50% (for 2012–13) has been deducted, but the trustees can only set against their liability tax *actually* paid to HMRC upon receipt of distribution income, and not the associated tax credit. In other words, the benefit of the tax credit is lost.

Overseas situations

7.84   As regards a settlor domiciled outside the UK (meaning neither actually domiciled nor deemed for IHT to be domiciled here), when the settlement is made, provided the assets are also outside the UK the settlement will be, and remain, excluded property for IHT purposes, the domicile of the beneficiaries being irrelevant, as indeed is the residence of the trustees.

However, the excluded property exemption in IHTA 1984, s 48(3) is not available if the interest in the trust property in question was bought on or after 5 December 2005 (s 48(3B)). These anti-avoidance rules were bolstered with effect from 20 June 2012 by FA 2012 which introduced new ss 74A to 74C and a new sub-s 48(3D) into the IHTA 1984 (see **17.14**).

The unfavourable capital gains tax regime (contained in TCGA 1992, s 86), whereby trust gains might be attributed to the settlor of a non-UK resident settlement, will not apply if he has remained domiciled outside the UK throughout the tax year (s 86(1)(c)). Trust gains, however, fall to be attributed to beneficiaries in receipt of capital payments (TCGA 1992, s 87).

Prior to FA 2008, beneficiaries who were UK resident but non-UK domiciled were not liable to a CGT charge under s 87 in respect of capital payments by non-UK resident trustees. However, that exception no longer applies to non-UK domiciled beneficiaries, and a s 87 charge can therefore arise (for 2008–09 and subsequent tax years), subject to a claim for the remittance basis, if applicable (TCGA 1992, s 87B). A non-UK domiciled settlor in receipt of capital payments as a beneficiary is similarly potentially liable to a CGT charge under s 87, following the FA 2008 changes.

HMRC generally still accepts that excluded property cannot be the subject of a reservation of benefit (see IHTM14318). In the case of a non-domiciled settlor who is also a settlement beneficiary, HMRC's guidance (at IHTM14396) includes an example in which the settlor (who was domiciled in New Zealand) later dies whilst domiciled in the UK and without having released the reservation. The guidance confirms that the property is subject to a reservation on death, but that foreign property remains excluded property and is outside the IHT charge. Where the reservation is released during the donor's lifetime, the donor is treated as making a PET (FA 1986, s 102(4)). HMRC's guidance also confirms that provided the property is excluded property when the deemed disposition is made, the assets in which the reservation ceased is excluded from charge (s 3(2)).

Care should be taken where s 80(4) is in point. This was introduced by FA 2006 and may in the fullness of time catch existing excluded property settlements and deprive them of their favoured status. The background is as follows. Section 80(1) postpones, in relation to trusts set up after 27 March 1974, the coming into being of a chargeable transfer where a settlor or his spouse holds an interest in possession in the fund until he or they no longer have that interest. When that happens, the fund is treated as joining a separate settlement. The first time that happens after 22 March 2006, the 'new' rules will apply. The terminology is adapted for the new regime. The effect is that a charge may apply at a time when the settlor is no longer domiciled outside the UK.

Discretionary trusts in reversion

7.85   Reversionary interests are normally excluded property. It is therefore possible to create a discretionary trust of an interest in reversion (ie the right to receive benefit under an existing interest in possession trust on the termination of the prior life interest) with the value of the asset for IHT purposes being nil. The ten-year proportionate relevant property trust charges will not apply.

For CGT purposes the general rule is that the disposal of a reversionary interest by a person who has not purchased it is likewise not taxable (see TCGA 1992, s 76(1)). However, that CGT exemption is disapplied for offshore trusts (see TCGA 1992, s 85).

For the elderly

7.86   Relevant property trusts may prove appropriate vehicles where it is wished to benefit elderly beneficiaries. Prior to FA 2006, if an interest in possession trust was used there would be an early charge on the fund on the death of the beneficiary with that interest, subject furthermore to aggregation with that beneficiary's free estate. There is no aggregation with a beneficiary's estate in the case of a discretionary trust or indeed any lifetime trust since 22 March 2006.

Perhaps the most practical use of discretionary trusts for the elderly is in relation to care fees: a younger relative may wish to give the older person some 'extras' in life whilst not depriving him or her of any state benefits to which the elderly person is entitled. In this connection it might be thought that a trust of a flat, let by the trustees to a person on housing benefit, would be a neat idea. However, note the rules as to 'contrived tenancies' which can effectively deny Housing Benefit in these circumstances.

CGT and IHT – the second home etc

7.87   Prior to changes introduced by FA 2004, a popular asset for discretionary trusts to hold was second homes, whereby the hold-over relief provisions could be exploited to 'wash' a gain using main residence relief. The scheme was curtailed by TCGA 1992, s 226A, which broadly prevents a combination of hold-over relief under TCGA 1992, s 260 and main residence relief being used to wash out gains in this way.

Such an arrangement remains possible in respect of furnished holiday lettings (FHLs). If the second home is a qualifying FHL it is possible to use a combination of gift relief under TCGA 1992, s 165 and main residence relief to wash out gains for gifts between individuals such as family members.

However, it is not possible to make the gift into trust. This is because where both business assets hold-over relief under s 165 and chargeable transfer hold-over relief under s 260 can apply, the latter takes priority (s 165(3)(d)).

Flexible discretionary trust – CGT/IHT mitigation

7.88   Changes were introduced in FA 2002 (following the Court of Appeal's decision in *Melville and others v IRC* [2001] STC 1271) and FA 2004, in order to deal with settlements of investment-type assets ('the assets') carrying unrealised capital gains, where it was not possible to hold over the CGT under TCGA 1992, s 165 (ie not business assets). A flexible discretionary-type trust could be used. This discretionary trust would, after a minimum of three months, terminate initially onto interest in possession trusts for the settlor ('the settlor'). Later, a further interest would be created, say, an interest in possession or (in those days) accumulation and maintenance trust for his children or grandchildren from which he and his spouse would be excluded.

Within this period there would be a time during which the settlor could claim back the trust fund or a part of it. The values of the settlor's retained interests were so substantial that there was little loss to his estate for IHT purposes. The idea was to get massive value into a trust, well over the nil rate band, and to hold over any gains.

Following FA 2002, the settlor's right to reclaim the trust fund is a 'settlement power' explicitly excluded from the definition of 'settlement property' for IHT purposes (see IHTA 1984, ss 272 and 47A), so that there is no IHT loss to the estate (see **1.31**). In addition, following FA 2004, CGT hold-over relief under s 260 is precluded if the trust is settlor interested, or can become one in the following six tax years (TCGA 1992, ss 169B–169C) (see the example of Jade's child at Example 7.15).

Also, see **7.52** for statutory provisions preventing a comeback for *Melville*-type arrangements.

IHT: the ten-year bonanza

7.89   As regards the ten-year anniversary charge for discretionary trusts, the IHT rate continues throughout the period up to just before the first or next ten-year anniversary. This gives rise to tremendous opportunities for IHT planning.

Example 7.21 – Timing trust appointments

Mr Discreet creates a discretionary trust on 1 July 2002 valued at £250,000 (the then nil band). He appoints Messrs Shrewd and Careful the trustees, who invest the fund with skill.

On 1 June 2012, the trust fund is worth £15 million and Messrs Shrewd and Careful appoint the trust fund to Mr Discreet's two adult children absolutely.

No IHT is payable because the original nil rate applies until midnight of 30 June 2012, when the trust fund has to be revalued and IHT (normally at 6%) paid if not previously distributed as above.

Awareness of this timing aspect is clearly of vital importance.

NB Unfortunately, pre-CTT trusts (ie created pre-27 March 1974) do not benefit from this historical valuation, but the distribution charge is based on the market value at that time (s 68(6)).

CHOOSING THE CORRECT SETTLEMENT – OTHER VARIETIES

Inter-spouse settlements

7.90   Since 22 March 2006, the creation of virtually any lifetime trust is a chargeable transfer. Section 58(1B) excludes from this rule only:

- an immediate post-death interest;
- a disabled person's interest; and
- a TSI.

Thus, advisers who were previously used to creating inter-spouse trusts as an extension of the inter-spouse exemption (s 18) and subject to the same conditions must think again. A settlement created by one spouse giving the other an interest in possession is no longer exempt on creation; and the exemption for reverter to settlor or to settlor's spouse does not apply for discretionary trusts or 'relevant property' trusts.

However, trusts of the reverter to settlor type were losing popularity anyway, in view of ITTOIA 2005, ss 624–625 which provide that, unless the settlor has divested himself absolutely from the settled property, the income from it is still to be treated as the settlor's for income tax purposes.

Trusts or dispositions in consideration of marriage (s 22)

7.91   Depending on the relationship between the donor/settlor and the parties to the marriage (or civil partnership), differing amounts will be allowed as exempt transfers for IHT, namely £5,000, £2,500 or £1,000. Such dispositions may be by way of settlement provided the beneficiaries are restricted. The details are summarised in the table below.

Gifts in consideration of marriage or civil partnership (s 22)

1 *Circumstances=gift (in favour of a party to the marriage) by:*	*2* *Exemption limits – outright gifts*			*3* *If disposition is by settlement the exemptions in column 2 apply provided beneficiaries restricted to:*
	£5,000	*£2,500*	*£1,000*	
(i) Each parent	X			parties to marriage; issue of marriage; spouse of such issue;
(ii) Each remoter ancestor		X		certain persons becoming entitled on failure of trusts for any such issue;
(iii) Each party to the marriage		X		subsequent spouse of party to marriage or their issue or spouse of issue; certain 'protective trust' beneficiaries. Trustee's reasonable remuneration allowed;
(iv) Any other transferor			X	beneficiaries restricted as above.

Gifts in excess of the exemption limits in column 2 will normally qualify as PETs.

The following points should be noted in conjunction with the above table:

- The obligation to make the disposition must be made *prior* to and/or *in contemplation of the marriage.*

- The exemptions apply, not only to gifts by individuals, but also to the termination of an interest in settled property in consideration of marriage (s 57(1)–(4)). The life tenant has to give notice to the trustees.

- To the extent that the gift is covered by the exemption, it cannot be taxed under the gift with reservation provisions, although the exemption does not apply to deemed PETs, such as under FA 1986, s 102(4) (see IHTM14191).

Post-nuptial deeds of gift

7.92 It sometimes arises that a deed of gift is entered into *after* a marriage, but in performance of a pre-nuptial agreement. This method should be used sparingly and subject to careful consideration of the following:

- Where a 'gift' remains uncompleted at the death of the donor no deduction from the deceased's estate can be made for IHT in view of s 5(5), which permits deduction of liabilities only where they are incurred for consideration in money or money's worth (eg excluding marriage consideration). Contrast an agreement made in consideration of marriage, to settle specified property actually owned by the settlor which type of arrangement normally created a trust or lien of that property so that the exemption should apply even if the settlor died before transferring the property. Given the low amounts exempted by s 22, it is perhaps unlikely that many will bother with this; it would not cover the cost of the wedding itself.

- For a gift to be exempt it *must* be made in contemplation of the marriage and is normally restricted to gifts made at the time or shortly *before* the marriage.

- Very strict proof would be required where a gift is made *after* the marriage if it is alleged to have been made in consideration of that marriage.

- In *IRC v Lord Rennell* [1964] AC 173, HL (a case on the estate duty exemption), it was stated that the three requirements for exemption are:

  – the gift must be made on the occasion of the marriage;

  – it must be conditional on the taking effect of that marriage;

  – it must be made for the purpose of or with a view to encouraging or facilitating the marriage.

- Therefore a 'gift' taking place, say, several years after the marriage would not comply, especially as the donors would no doubt be retaining the capital and income in the meantime.

- The wording for IHT is less restrictive than it was for estate duty, having regard in particular to the words in s 22(1), '... to the extent that the values transferred by such transfers ...'

- The gift or settlement must therefore be made at the time of, or prior to, the marriage in question which must subsequently take place. HMRC appear to accept that the exemption may be available if the taxpayer can show that the gift was somehow made in contemplation of the marriage (or civil partnership) (IHTM14192). However, gifts made after marriage are not exempt unless made in fulfilment of a binding promise before marriage (IHTM14201).

- Once a couple are engaged, the donor or settlor can make the arrangements. In the case of an outright gift, for example a cheque, the donor should evidence this by dated letter to the donee, making it clear that it is a wedding (or civil partnership) present.

- In the case of a settlement, the settlor can either arrange for the settlement to be created and the asset transferred into it before or on the wedding day or alternatively (but less satisfactory) marriage articles (surely very rare nowadays) can be entered into before the marriage specifying the investments or assets proposed to be settled within, say, six months of the marriage. The trustees can be given the right to accept suitable alternative assets. Until these assets are in fact vested in the trustees, the exempt transfer will not have been made.

The £5,000 limit for a parent is available for each parent; therefore in respect of a bride and groom (or civil partners) both of whose parents are still alive, a total of £20,000 of exempt gifts is available. As in the case of other exemptions, the gift can be of cash or in kind up to the appropriate value.

It is likely, following the *dicta* in *Re Park (No 2), IRC v Park* [1972] Ch 385, CA (another estate duty case), that in the case of an absolute disposition in favour of a party to the marriage the *purpose or motive* of the transferor is irrelevant; and presumably where the disposition is by way of the permitted settlement provisions a sufficient intention of encouraging or facilitating the marriage will have been established.

There is a wide definition of 'child', including illegitimate, adopted and stepchildren. 'Parent' and 'ancestor' are also considered widely (s 22(2)). With respect to circumstance (iii) listed in the table, it is suggested that it would be preferable for the parties to wait until they are married and obtain the inter-spouse exemption (s 18) (meanwhile requisite payments could be covered by loans cancelled subsequent to the marriage). An excess above the stated limits is attributed to the transfers in proportion to the value transferred and will constitute either a PET, or a lifetime chargeable transfer and subject to grossing up if, say, on any form of trust (where the possible beneficiaries are restricted by s 22(4)). There is no grossing up in calculating the exemption limits.

Example 7.22 – Marriage exemption (I)

Eric gave to his unrelated business partner David cash of £3,000 on David's marriage to Sandra.

£1,000 would be exempt under s 22 and the balance, subject to any other exemptions, would constitute a PET.

Example 7.23 – Marriage exemption (II)

Continuing the above, David was given £3,000 by his father, who also gave £3,000 to Sandra.

£5,000 is free of IHT and the balance of £1,000 would be a PET, subject to any other exemptions.

Example 7.24 – Marriage exemption (III)

David's grandmother was going to settle £5,000 on David and Sandra under a normal marriage settlement of which only £2,500 would have been exempt from IHT.

She gave her husband £2,500 instead and each settled £2,500 under the marriage settlement, the whole of which was exempt; HMRC did not consider this should be caught as an associated operation under s 268, but no doubt could have done.

Example 7.25 – Marriage exemption (IV)

David agreed to buy Sandra a Ferrari for a wedding present but prudently waited until after the wedding, which meant that the gift was exempt from IHT within s 18, instead of only £2,500 being exempt within s 22.

Life assurance policies written under MWPA 1882 and other trusts

7.93   The scope for planning in respect of life policies written under Married Women's Property Act 1882 (MWPA 1882) trusts is based on the appropriate use of exemptions and the avoidance of discretionary trusts. The subject is discussed in more detail in **14.10**.

Sections 53 and 54: a possible loophole?

7.94   The FA 2006 changes to interest in possession trusts took some time to work out. One particular area of difficulty was the situation where an existing interest in possession came to an end and was replaced by a new interest under the transitional provisions which expired on 6 October 2008. Some trustees wished the replacement interest to be for the same beneficiary as before. It was thought that this was neutral for IHT.

By s 53(2), there could be no IHT charge when a life interest came to an end and that life tenant became entitled to the fund, either absolutely or for life. As originally drafted, s 53(2A) provided that where a person became entitled to an interest in possession after 22 March 2006 (here not meaning a disabled person's interest), s 53(2) should apply but excluding the provision that allowed for acquiring another interest in possession (ie it only applied if the person became absolutely entitled).

What did this mean? Was it possible, as some thought, for an 'old' interest in possession to be terminated and replaced by another for the same person without IHT? If the words 'or to another interest in possession' did not apply where the person had an 'old' interest in possession there could be no IHT charge on the switchover.

The 'wildebeest' effect

7.95   Few can watch films of the migration of wildebeest across rivers infested with crocodiles without hoping that most of the herd will reach the other side safely. In the same way, there are many trusts that hold substantial gains that the trustees would very much like to 'wash' so that they escape taxation or it is deferred. Often, the trust may hold only shares in, say, a property investment company in respect of which no hold-over of gains is possible under TCGA 1992, s 165.

A scheme was examined for an existing life interest trust under which, after the end of the transitional period, a termination of the life interest would cause the trust to become a relevant property trust, and that would be an occasion for hold-over of gains under TCGA 1992, s 260. However, it was thought that the wording of s 53(2A) did not draw any distinction between the treatment for IHT whether this occurred during the transitional period, or after it had expired.

Assets could be transferred to the life tenant without a large charge to tax provided that the pre-existing, 'old' life interest was replaced with a new one before the transitional period ended. The idea was to distribute the assets from the (now relevant property) trust very soon afterwards, before a quarter had expired, so that there would be no IHT exit charge.

This was curtailed by FA 2008, s 140, which substituted a new s 53(2A). If the interest of a beneficiary such as the life tenant is varied, there will be an IHT charge.

All this did not become immediately clear. HMRC explained that, in their view, s 53(2A) should be interpreted as if the words 'or to another interest in possession in the property' be deleted from s 53(2) regardless of when the life interest arose, so it applied to any interest and there was a potential IHT charge if any transitional serial interest was created for an 'old', ie pre Budget 2006, life tenant. There was much debate. People did not know what to do for the best: whether or not to create transitional serial interests or whether, if they had done, they had done right.

The final result was FA 2008, ss 140 and 141. Section 53(2A) was recast so as to show that it applies only where the tenant for life becomes entitled to a new interest on or after 12 March 2008. Before that date, there is no qualification to s 53(2), so there can be no IHT charge where the 'old' interest ended and a new interest was created for the same person before 12 March 2008, which would have to be a disabled person's interest or a transitional serial interest.

From 12 March 2008 onwards, the rules changed. The termination of a life interest will trigger an IHT charge unless:

• the property vests in the beneficiary absolutely;

• a disabled person's trust is established; or (but see below)

• a transitional serial interest is created.

However, the time limit for creating transitional serial interests, though extended to cover the confusion, has now expired. No ordinary TSI can now be established, save on the death of 'old' life tenants. Unless the life tenant is a disabled person, it is no longer possible to swap an existing life interest for a new one without triggering a charge to IHT.

The extension was only of benefit to trustees of life interests. Those who had not rearranged accumulation and maintenance trusts by 5 April 2008 simply ran out of time. The extension was of great benefit to those who were unaware of the s 53 issue and who, for whatever reason, did not make a decision in time.

Reverter to settlor trusts

7.96 A reversionary interest retained by the settlor (or spouse) is not excluded property, and so remains part of his estate (s 48(1)(b)). If a pre-FA 2006 interest in possession came to an end in the lifetime of the life tenant and during the settlor's life and (see s 53(2)), on the same occasion the property in which the interest subsisted reverted to the settlor or settlor's UK domiciled spouse, IHT was not chargeable under the pre-FA 2006 rules unless the settlor or the spouse had acquired the reversionary interest in the property for a consideration in money or money's worth.

Section 53(2A) limits the scope of that rule where the person becomes entitled to the interest on or after 12 March 2008. If the person becomes entitled to the property itself, it is excluded property; but if the person becomes entitled only to an interest in possession, and that interest is not a disabled person's interest or a transitional serial interest, the general charge under s 52 will apply. Subject to that, the exemption can apply also to the settlor's widow(er), provided the termination is within two years of the settlor's death (s 53(4)).

There are similar provisions in s 54(1), (2) and (3), but now with similar limitations as set out in s 54(2A) and (2B), excluding an IHT charge where there is a reverter to settlor on the death of a person entitled to an interest in possession. The exclusion can now apply only to a disabled person's interest or to a TSI.

The rationale behind excluding the trust property from the life tenant's estate where there is a reverter to settlor becomes a little clearer when it is considered that the creation of the settlement will probably have fallen within the gift with reservation provisions (eg if the settlor can benefit under a power of appointment exercisable by the trustees at any time). For IHT purposes the result is that the property never leaves the estate of the settlor.

Example 7.26 – Reverter to settlor (I)

An individual, before 22 March 2006, settles a house on, say, mother for life: remainder to himself absolutely and he survives his mother. The exemption is available (this was often a useful method of giving an elderly person an interest in possession without incurring a charge on the capital of the trust fund when the beneficiary died, ie an event likely to occur after a relatively short time).

If the settlement was made after that date its creation would be a chargeable transfer and it would be a relevant property trust, so the death of the mother would not be an occasion of charge.

Example 7.27 – Reverter to settlor (II)

It was not uncommon for a father in his will to leave his home (or, say, his half share) to his son to utilise the nil band. Son could, after father's death, grant mother a life interest in the home, with reverter to himself.

As can be seen, this will no longer work, and in any case if the object was only to use father's nil rate band, little tax has been saved. Mother is living in a property in respect of which main residence relief will be available. The settled share of the house she occupies is outside her estate, but the family could now benefit from the transferable nil rate band, which is simpler and may increase over time.

Example 7.28 – Reverter to settlor (III)

The same situation as Example 7.26, but the son does not survive the mother.

The exemption is not available and a charge potentially arises on son's death under the gift with reservation provisions (see above) and/or because the value of the reversionary interest is not an excluded asset.

Example 7.29 – Reverter to settlor (IV)

A grants B an annuity charged on land with remainder to A.

As for Example 7.26 or Example 7.27.

Example 7.30 – Reverter to settlor (V)

A settled house on B for life, subject thereto to C for life, remainder to A.

B dies in 2002, C in 2004, A in 2006.

The exemption is not available on B's death because the asset did not revert to A 'on the same occasion', ie on B's death. The exemption was, however, available on C's death.

Example 7.31 – Reverter to settlor (VI)

If, in Example 7.30, C had died in 2001, ie before B, the exemption would have been available on B's death.

Example 7.32 – Purchase of reversion

S settled a house on X for life with remainder to Y. s purchased Y's remainder in X's lifetime.

The exemption is not available as the reversion has been purchased for a monetary consideration.

377

7.97   A reverter to settlor settlement may give rise to income tax difficulties, eg under ITTOIA 2005, s 624 (subject to possible exceptions in ss 626–627, such as following divorce or separation).

In addition, from 5 December 2005, the 'pre-owned assets' income tax charge (POAT; see **Chapter 13**) applies broadly if the former owner of an asset (or a person who contributed to its acquisition) enjoys the asset under the terms of a trust, and the trust property may in due course revert back to the settlor (or spouse or civil partner) under circumstances eligible for the IHT reverter to settlor exemption (see **13.17**).

Note that the provisions in FA 2004, Sch 15 para 11(11)–(13) (as introduced by FA 2006, s 80) apply to 'estate' interests in possession within s 49(1) generally, and thus have broader potential scope than reverter to settlor trusts.

Notwithstanding the closure of CGT dependent relative relief to transactions after 6 April 1988, it used to be possible to save both IHT and CGT in certain circumstances.

Example 7.33 – 'Old' interest in possession

Albert, before 22 March 2006, gave his mother, Florence, a life interest in a house, which she occupied.

When Florence dies, even after 22 March 2006, she has an 'old' interest in possession so, assuming Albert has outlived her, the property reverts to him free of IHT.

For CGT purposes, the property is taken at a value that gives rise to neither a gain nor a loss.

Example 7.34 – Disabled person's interest

Brian's daughter Emma suffers a mental disorder that prevents her from managing her affairs within the meaning of the Mental Health Act 1983. On 7 July 2009, Brian sets up a trust for her which, whilst not giving her an interest in possession, still provides that not less than half the settled property is applied for Emma's benefit during her lifetime, complying with s 89(1) and thus giving Emma a disabled person's interest within s 89B(1)(a).

The fund is invested in a warden-managed flat and the trustees give Emma a right to live there within the rule in *Sansom v Peay*. No rent is paid. If Brian outlives Emma, 'reverter to settlor' will shelter the fund from IHT (s 54(2A)), and on disposal of the flat no CGT will be payable (TCGA 1992, s 73(2A)).

Pension schemes or funds (ss 58(1)(d) and 151)

7.98   IHT relief applies where appropriate income tax relief is available, for example, in respect of registered pension schemes, qualifying non-UK pension schemes or superannuation funds to which ICTA 1988, s 615(3) applies; see s 58(1)(d), which excludes such pension arrangements from the meaning of 'relevant property' and hence the IHT charges generally applicable to trusts of such property.

For IHT purposes, the death of a pensioner or annuitant gives rise to no IHT charge; likewise when such pension or annuity ends otherwise than on death. However, if the pension or annuity *continues* to be payable after the death (there might, for instance, be a guaranteed period of, say, five years for the pension), the value of the balance of the pension or annuity is taxable as part of the deceased's estate.

If a pensioner gives up part of his own pension to provide a deferred pension to anyone other than his spouse, that disposition will constitute a transfer of value (subject to s 11). Similarly, a member's power or right to dispose of a lump sum, for example, by way of nomination, would be a chargeable transfer. Pension funds may therefore leave such disposal of lump sums on death in service of the member in the discretion of the scheme trustees among a wide class of beneficiaries comprising relatives, dependants and executors. The member may suggest to the trustees the person(s) he wishes to receive the benefit on his death, but this is not binding on the trustees, although normally they would follow the member's wishes unless there were strong reasons to the contrary.

No IHT is payable in normal circumstances on the death in service benefit in these discretionary cases (IHTM17123) (see **9.28**).

The test is whether the rights were part of the estate of the member of the scheme. Thus if, under the arrangements, the member's personal representatives had an enforceable right to the benefit, it must suffer IHT as part of his estate. See SP E3: the disclosure form IHT409 lodged with the IHT400 return extracts the necessary information. See also SP 10/86 referred to in **9.28** which explains the matter (there would be a similar situation in respect of accident insurance schemes; see Inland Revenue Press Release, 6 January 1976, and also s 12).

Accordingly, for such schemes or funds, the ten-year anniversary and interim IHT rules relevant to discretionary trusts will normally not apply (s 58(1)(b)) unless the benefits appropriated out of the scheme or fund are themselves settled on discretionary trusts.

HMRC have stated that s 151 strictly ceases to apply on the member's death, with the result that any distributions of benefits at the trustees' discretion are subject to an IHT exit charge. However, by concession death benefits are treated as remaining held for s 151 purposes, pending the exercise of the trustees' powers for up to two years (IHTM17123). As a result, the wording of many pension trusts requires distribution of the fund within two years.

Note that the rules relating to 'alternatively secured pensions' were revoked from 6 April 2010 by FA 2011, s 65, Sch 16.

One aspect of pension funds has caused considerable difficulty. The cases affected may be FURBS, but the problem may be of more general application.

Suppose that a FURBS has been set up of which Sandra is the main beneficiary. Her personal representatives may receive benefits in the event of her death. The FURBS trustees do not relish paying tax at 50% on the trust income. Sandra does not really need to draw a pension from the fund but would like her children to benefit from it. She realises that the remaining tax benefit of the FURBS is as an IHT shelter.

What can Sandra do? Pulling assets out of the pension fund into new trusts for her children would be treated as the creation of new trusts, so there would be an IHT entry charge. There are some transitional provisions in FA 2004, s 56 and Sch 36, but they are of limited application. There are also income tax charges to be borne in mind unless great care is taken: see ITEPA 2003, s 394 (ie relating to employer-financed retirement benefits).

Should Sandra perhaps do nothing except make a will leaving her estate in part to her children, hoping that, at the discretion of the trustees (as guided by her letter of wishes) they receive the death benefit under the FURBS tax free? This is where the difficulty arises. It has been argued by HMRC in relation to the death benefit that where the personal representatives of the scheme member are included as potential beneficiaries there could be a reservation of benefit. To work, this argument deems the death benefits to be part of the estate of the member on death. The argument is set out at IHTM17504.

This is, put kindly, counter-intuitive. By its very nature the death benefit is not available to Sandra in her lifetime, so how can she reserve any benefit out of it? It is not an asset that she can freely dispose of: The possibility of benefiting from a trust is enough, see *IRC v Eversden* [2003] EWCA Civ 668, for a person to be regarded as 'not excluded from benefit'; but is that really enough? This uncertainty may perhaps be resolved only by a formal decision (the Court of Appeal decision did not deal with this point).

Settlements for the benefit of employees, etc (ss 72, 75, 86 and 87)

7.99   These provisions give relief from IHT to trusts for benefit of employees if, during any period the property cannot be applied otherwise than for the benefit of a class of employees, their relatives or dependants or charities. During that period:

- an interest in possession in less than 5% of the property is disregarded; and

- a payment of the property is not a distribution of 'relevant property' (ie is exempt) unless made to a settlor or to certain defined participators, and exceeds £1,000.

The rate of tax, if any, on distributions ignores aggregation with the settlor. The ten-yearly anniversary charges are inapplicable, and, if a charge does arise, the tapering charge under s 72(2)(a) and (5), bringing in s 70(6), applies, as referred to in **7.44**.

This relief will not normally apply to the so-called 'top hat' schemes, as they are usually for *individual* employees and therefore not 'persons of a class defined by reference to employment'.

7.100   The above provisions give relief while assets are *in* a settlement. Exemption is also available for assets going *into* such a settlement, subject to certain conditions.

Under s 12, relief is available provided the contribution into the trust gave rise to a deduction for income or corporation tax purposes. This is particularly relevant in the case of a contribution into an employee benefit trust by a close company where relief under s 13 (see below) is restricted because participators are included in the class of eligible beneficiaries. As an alternative to s 12, under s 13, where the disposition is by a close company, subject to complying with s 86 and participators being (broadly) excluded from benefit, exemption also applies.

Employee trusts: s 28 exemption

7.101   Where the disposition is by an *individual* and is of shares in the company an exemption under s 28 is available provided the trustees of the employees' trust hold more than half the ordinary shares in the company and have voting control. The trustees must satisfy the control test within one year of the transfer of the shares to them. There must be no agreement affecting the share capital of the company under the terms of which control can be taken away from the trustees (see s 28(2)(b)).

There are restrictions on the trust making dispositions to existing or former participators (within ten years prior to the disposition) with the exception that persons entitled to, or entitled to acquire less than 5% of the issued share capital of any class, or who would be entitled to less than 5% of the company's assets on a winding up are ignored.

CGT relief for such a transfer is given under TCGA 1992, s 239. It is considered that a trust for the benefit of the employees of a *group* of companies, which otherwise satisfies the necessary conditions, enjoys the protection of s 86.

The conditions for individuals remain so harsh as to make the exemption rarely applied in practice. If it is desired, however, to set up an employees' trust but retain control, some of the shares could be transferred to a new company in exchange for shares therein and all the shares in the new company transferred to the employees' trust. A possible disadvantage is that CGT 'roll-over' would be subject to the share exchange rules under TCGA 1992, ss 135–137.

The relief under s 86 is still available (by virtue of s 86(5)) where there is a switch from one employees' trust to another within a one-month period and where the relevant conditions apply to both. Employees of certain newspaper publishing companies also become eligible.

HMRC set out their view on the IHT position in relation to contributions to Employee Benefits Trusts (EBTs) in Revenue & Customs Brief 18/11 (which superseded Brief 61/09 issued on 12 October 2009 Brief 49/09 issued two months earlier). In particular, the Brief describes the circumstances in which HMRC consider that an IHT charge arises under s 94 on contributions to an EBT by a close company (see **9.19**).

Protective trusts (ss 73 and 88) and Trustee Act 1925, s 33

Background

7.102   A protective trust is a trust for the life, or any lesser period, of a principal beneficiary, which terminates on certain events such as the bankruptcy of that beneficiary or a purported sale or alienation of his interest. Thereupon the interest in possession comes to an end and the principal beneficiary together with his family become objects of a discretionary trust.

The termination of the principal beneficiary's interest during the trust period was, under earlier CTT rules, exempt, giving rise to mitigation possibilities such as in *Thomas v IRC* [1981] STC 382. Unsurprisingly, in 1978, the rules were changed so that the principal beneficiary's sale or alienation of his interest is disregarded and he is still treated as beneficially entitled to an interest in possession in the trust assets which, notwithstanding the sale or assignment, are now held on trusts to like effect as those in the Trustee Act 1925, s 33(1). 'Like effect' is treated by HMRC as meaning 'not materially different from s 33(1) in their tax consequences' (SP E7 (originally Revenue letter of 3 March 1976)).

Examples of 'like effect' include:

- *exclusion of spouse* from the class of discretionary beneficiaries;
- power to declare a *full life interest* (ie not merely a protected one);
- power to *advance capital* to the protected life tenant;
- that the protected life interest is *revocable* and that other trusts can be substituted.

Therefore if an individual had (prior to 22 March 2006) set up a protective trust in favour of himself and later purported to sell or alienate his interest, he would in fact have set up a discretionary trust of which he was entitled to income before such sale or alienation without having incurred IHT on its creation; but enthusiasm would be moderated, not only since the individual would be deemed to have an interest in possession so that the assets would remain part of his IHT estate, but also because of the income tax settlement provisions (ITTOIA 2005, Pt 5, Ch 5). If the settlor is also the principal beneficiary, there is no bankruptcy protection for the trust assets as applies in other circumstances.

Protective trusts thus have little merit for IHT planning, but may be useful for non-IHT practical reasons, eg the spouse of a Lloyd's member could give the member a protective life interest by will. It should always be borne in mind that a protective trust will usually add to a beneficiary's IHT estate or in any event not reduce it. A pure discretionary trust may also answer the practical problems, but consider the IHT (and CGT) implications.

Perhaps because there is little scope for IHT mitigation, such trusts were spared some of the changes in FA 2006. Forfeiture of the primary interest in possession did not trigger the discretionary trust regime. Even though a discretionary trust arises under general trust law on the occasion of forfeiture, an 'old' protective trust is unaffected by the new rules (see s 88(3)). The benefit of an interest in possession is not lost, even in the case of a trust created after 22 March 2006, where the interest is an IPDI, a DPI or a TSI. If, however, the requirements for the 'favoured' form of trust are not satisfied, forfeiture will not affect the interest as the protective trust treatment in s 88(2) does not apply to it (see s 88(6)).

If the primary beneficiary had by a mere divesting act triggered off a discretionary trust before the change of rules on 12 April 1978, there is under s 73 an IHT charge when the trust assets cease to be held on the substituted discretionary trusts (either because of the advancement of capital out of the trust other than to the primary beneficiary or because the trustees otherwise make some value-shifting disposition causing the value to go down).

CGT and income tax

7.103   When a protected life interest comes to an end on forfeiture there is *no disposal* for CGT purposes.

On forfeiture of a life interest and automatic substitution of a discretionary trust, the trust rate applies (ITA 2007, s 479), but see above regarding the income tax settlement provisions where the settlor has an interest.

If the settlor is taxable on trust income by virtue of ITTOIA 2005, s 624, an income tax charge potentially arises under the 'pre-owned assets' regime from 6 April 2005 (FA 2004, Sch 15, para 8(1)); see **Chapter 13**.

Trusts for the benefit of mentally or physically disabled persons (ss 74, 89)

Background

7.104 IHT relief is available in respect of a trust for the life of a 'disabled person' (as defined) and which contains no interest in possession, being, for example, a discretionary trust, where not less than half of the settled property applied during his life is for his benefit (ss 74 and 89).

A normal power to advance under Trustee Act 1925, s 32 should not breach this requirement, although a wide power of advancement in favour of persons other than the disabled beneficiary may do so.

The relief consists in deeming the disabled person to have an interest in possession in the trust assets, with the result that there is no IHT on a payment of capital to or for him; but, on an advance of capital to someone other than the disabled person, the termination of the disabled person's interest in possession constitutes a PET.

The IHT position is therefore as follows:

- Property put into the trust by the disabled person is effectively a non-event. For other settlors (eg the parent of the disabled person), the transfer is a PET.

- A payment out of the trust for the benefit of the disabled person is not a taxable distribution, ie it is effectively a non-event.

- When there is a payment/distribution out to someone other than the disabled person, or the property ceases to be held for his benefit, or there is some reduction in the value of the trust estate because of a disposition by the trustees, the trustees have made a PET, and to avoid a charge the disabled person must survive seven years.

This relief has a wider application than might appear at first glance, as it extends to persons resident or present in the UK in receipt of an attendance allowance under Social Security Contributions and Benefits Act 1992, s 64 or disability living allowance under Social Security Contributions and Benefits Act 1992, s 71 (or the equivalent legislation in Northern Ireland), ie the disability can be mental or physical. From 8 April 2013 the government will introduce a new benefit called personal independence payment (PIP) to replace disability living allowance (DLA) for eligible people aged 16 to 64. It is expected that the definition of a 'disabled person' for IHT purposes will therefore be amended.

The IHT regime in respect of trusts for disabled persons was extended by FA 2006, with effect from 22 March 2006. The extended provisions allow for 'self-settlement' by an individual with a condition which is expected to result in a qualifying disability, where there is no interest in possession in the settled property and certain other conditions are satisfied (see s 89A). The extended rules also provide a statutory definition of a 'disabled person's interest' to include an interest in possession from 22 March 2006 in favour of the disabled person, and allow for a self-settled interest in possession from 22 March 2006 by an individual with a condition expected to result in a qualifying disability (s 89B(1)(d)).

It will often be desirable for a trust to fall within the provisions of s 89, such as in terms of avoiding the IHT charges which apply to mainstream relevant property trusts. However, it should be remembered that the disabled person will then be treated as beneficially entitled to an interest in possession in the settled property, which will therefore form part of his estate for IHT purposes. For a case where trustees unsuccessfully argued that s 89 did *not* apply, see *Barclays Bank Trust Company Ltd (as trustees of the Constance Mary Poppleston Will Trust) v HMRC* [2011] WTLR 1489, in which the court considered the construction of s 89 in the context of will trusts for the benefit of a disabled person.

The CGT position is that disabled trusts qualify for the full annual exemption as if the trustees were an individual (TCGA 1992, s 3, Sch 1). For this purpose, half the income must be paid in favour of the disabled beneficiary; unless no income is appointed for the benefit of *any* other person.

However, there is an apparent mismatch between the conditions for the full annual CGT exemption, and those which have to be satisfied in order to attain 'tax favoured' status for IHT purposes. The latter rules require that there be no interest in possession in the settled property.

For CGT purposes, this mismatch arises in TCGA 1992, Sch 1, para 1(1) (b) if income is not accumulated. The disabled beneficiary must be 'entitled' to at least half of the trust income. A trust which ensures that the disabled beneficiary receives at least half the income may satisfy the CGT conditions for a full annual exemption, but in satisfying this requirement it breaches the 'no interest in possession' condition for disabled trust status for IHT purposes.

HMRC are alive to this particular point, stating that 'as a general rule', a disabled trust for IHT purposes will not qualify for the full annual CGT exemption (CG18061A).

Trusts for the vulnerable

7.105 FA 2005 introduced some well-meaning but complex income tax and CGT provisions on trusts with a vulnerable beneficiary.

'Disabled person' is defined for those purposes in similar terms to the IHT definition (FA 2005, s 34). If the beneficiary satisfies the definition, and if the trust qualifies, an election can be made to restrict tax on trust income and formerly on gains to the liability that would arise if the trust property were that of the beneficiary.

The definition of disabled person is less stringent than the conditions in IHTA 1984, s 89, as the latter requires that person to be in receipt of attendance allowance or the disability living allowance care component at the highest or middle rate. By contrast, a disabled person may qualify as a vulnerable person if those benefits are not received due to hospital treatment for renal failure, or if the individual is provided with accommodation (eg in a care home).

There is a mismatch between the requirement:

- for IHT purposes in s 89 that there must be no interest in possession for the disabled person; and

- for vulnerable trust purposes that any income must be applied for the disabled person.

The latter requirement has the effect that only interest in possession trusts are likely to qualify as trusts for the vulnerable. Trusts for the disabled within s 89 only *deem* the disabled person to have an interest in possession for IHT purposes, with income subject to discretionary trusts for a potentially wider class of beneficiaries than the disabled person.

When creating a trust for a disabled person (or varying an existing one), consideration should therefore be given to whether the trust should confer an actual interest in possession for vulnerable trust purposes, or satisfy the conditions in s 89. However, as mentioned above, note that following FA 2006 a disabled person's interest can include a beneficial (as opposed to a 'deemed') interest in possession (s 89B(1)(c), (d)).

Charitable trusts (ss 58(1)(a) and 70)

7.106 In relation to settled property held for charitable purposes only, the discretionary trust provisions including IHT liability for distributions and ten-year charges are excluded. But there is a special IHT charge where assets cease to be held on charitable trusts and are not applied for charitable purposes (other than meeting the normal costs or expenses of the trust) under s 70(2); see **7.44**.

Moreover, under s 76, payments or appropriations *by* discretionary trusts to such charities, or indeed to political parties, national museums etc are not liable to the interim IHT exit charge. Trusts are charitable if they are established for charitable purposes only. Prior to 27 January 2009, this was restricted to UK-established trusts or institutions; see *Camille and Henry Dreyfus Foundation Inc v IRC* [1956] AC 39, HL). However, in *Persche v Finanzamt Lüdenscheid* (CJEC Case C-318/07; [2009] All ER (EC) 673). it was held that German tax law, which prohibited tax relief for donations to a charity based in Portugal, contravened EC law.

Subsequently, FA 2010, Sch 6 changed the law relating to charity exemption and extended the definition of 'charity' to include charities established in the EU and other specified countries. The amending legislation included new conditions to be met from 6 April 2010 for Gift Aid purposes. The FA 2010 changes were introduced for IHT purposes from 1 April 2012 (Finance Act 2010, Schedule 6, Part 2 (Commencement) Order 2012, SI 2012/736) (see **12.21**). However, HMRC will generally apply the territorial extension for charitable gifts made on or after 27 January 2009 for IHT purposes (see IHTM11112). Charities can usefully be included as beneficiaries in a family trust to clear out income otherwise treated as the settlor's in a children's settlement (ITTOIA 2005, s 630).

Certain compensation funds (s 58(1)(e), (3))

7.107 Certain compensation funds such as those administered by the Law Society and The Stock Exchange are excluded from the discretionary trust IHT regime.

Trusts of excluded property (ss 48(3) and 267)

7.108 A trust fund will be excluded property provided:

- the assets are situated abroad (subject to exceptions (in s 48(3A)) in respect of holdings in authorised unit trusts and shares in open-ended investment companies); and

- the settlor was domiciled abroad when the settlement was made (notwithstanding that the beneficiaries are resident and domiciled in the UK), and when any property was added.

Note: see generally, RI166 of February 1997.

Anti-avoidance

7.109 An example of previous 'deathbed' IHT planning involved an individual purchasing an interest in a pre-existing settlement created by a non-UK domiciled individual. Prior to 5 December 2005, a purchased interest in settled property was not precluded from being 'excluded property' for the purposes of s 48(3). However, from that date the exemption in s 48(3) is removed if the interest in trust property has been purchased, resulting in a UK-domiciled individual becoming beneficially entitled to an interest in possession (s 48(3B)). The relevant provisions were bolstered by FA 2012 with effect from 20 June 2012 (see **17.14**).

In the case of a reversionary interest over settled property which is situated abroad, this will be excluded property *provided* that the beneficial owner is domiciled abroad (s 48(3)). At first glance, this appears inconsistent with s 48(1) which provides that a reversionary interest is excluded property (without mention of the geographical location of the property to which it relates), unless it is owned by the person who settled the property, or his spouse, or has at any time been purchased for valuable consideration. This inconsistency can be resolved, however, if s 48(3) is viewed as extending excluded property status to reversionary interests that would not otherwise be treated as excluded property (because they fall within the exceptions set out in s 48(1)). That was certainly the approach taken by the Inland Revenue prior to IHT replacing CTT (cf letter from the Inland Revenue published in the *Law Society Gazette*, 4 February 1976, reproduced at **7.112**).

The extended interpretation of domicile for IHT contained in s 267(1) only applies to property comprised in the settlement on or after 10 December 1974 (s 267(3)). The test as to the time at which property is regarded as having become 'comprised' in a settlement appears to depend on when it was introduced and transferred into the settlement by the settlor, ignoring subsequent switches of property and reinvestment of proceeds of sale.

It follows that it is vital that an individual who is domiciled abroad with assets abroad, and who is considering taking up long-term residence or domicile here, should consider making trusts abroad before coming back, and leaving his assets in the excluded property trust. If he has assets within the UK (other than holdings in an authorised unit trust or shares in an open-ended investment company, which as mentioned are excluded property for a non-UK domiciled individual in any event), or wishes to sell foreign assets and reinvest in the UK, his overseas settlement should own shares in an overseas investment company; and it should be that company which owns the UK assets.

Whether those assets inside the company are abroad or in the UK, the trust assets owned by the trustees will always be the shares in the overseas company, which will be excluded property. There is, perhaps surprisingly, no lifting of the corporate veil for this purpose. Contrast the position of the UK-resident taxpayer in *IRC v Brandenburg* [1982] STC 555. There the veil of incorporation was pierced in so far as the UK taxpayer as sole shareholder of a Jersey company was treated as being beneficially entitled to an interest in possession, not that company to whom the trust fund had, purportedly, been transferred.

7.110 It may be appropriate to utilise so-called 'limbo' trusts with a widely defined beneficiaries clause (the decision in *Re Manisty's Settlement, Manisty v Manisty* [1974] Ch 17, confirmed that this is perfectly feasible). In such a trust the settlor would have been domiciled abroad when the settlement was made; the trust assets would be abroad and to avoid the eventual IHT on their own estate, beneficiaries might become non-resident and non-UK domiciled at the time when the trust fund or an appropriate part was to be appointed to them or when the underlying company decided to make them a loan.

One interesting suggestion in this context is that a trust might be set up with a UK family in mind by a non-resident non-domiciled friend with a small amount of capital and with non-resident trustees. The trustees would acquire shares in the trading company situated abroad to whom genuine orders are passed sufficient to enable the trust-owned company, on a proper commercial basis, to accumulate profits. The discretionary beneficiaries of the trust are overseas residents, possibly overseas charities, but there is power to add further beneficiaries.

Bearing in mind ITA 2007, ss 714–751, if a member of the UK family becomes non-resident at some time in the future, he can be added as a beneficiary and be paid a capital distribution, without incurring IHT as forming part of his estate. There must be no reciprocity between the friend and the family who benefit: it is absolutely essential that the foreign settlor is not directly or indirectly reimbursed by the UK family because any such associated operations would undermine the whole arrangement, as the person generating the funds would then become a settlor within the wide definition of s 44(1).

In addition to ITA 2007, s 714 onwards, it is also important to consider the effects of FA 2009, Sch 17 (which replaced the company migration rules in ICTA 1988, ss 765–767 from 1 July 2009) and TCGA 1992, ss 86–87C in such an arrangement.

Summary

7.111 By way of summary, as regards excluded property, the interaction of the settlement provisions of s 44 and the beneficial ownership concept in s 6(1) gives wide scope for planning.

As regards settled property, it will broadly be excluded property provided it is situated outside the UK and the settlor was domiciled abroad at the time he made the settlement (in which case, the domicile of the beneficiary is irrelevant whether he receives trust assets or makes a disposition of his interest).

Reference should also be made to **Chapter 17** (Foreign domicile) generally.

As regards CGT, the previous benefits applicable to non-UK resident trusts have largely disappeared, unless the individual is domiciled and/or resident abroad.

Reversionary interests and their resettlement

7.112   As indicated at **1.35** and **1.36**, reversionary interests as defined in s 48 are generally excluded property. The following succinct official definition was provided in the *Law Society Gazette* (4 February 1976, at p 89):

'A reversionary interest is excluded property if:

(a)   wherever it is situated it has not been acquired for consideration and it is not expectant on the determination of a lease for life etc. granted otherwise than for full consideration, or

(b)   if the interest itself is situated outside the United Kingdom and is either

   (i)   in the actual beneficial ownership of someone domiciled outside the United Kingdom, or

   (ii)   itself settled property comprised in a settlement made by someone who was domiciled outside the United Kingdom when he made the settlement.'

Note that the element of consideration mentioned in (a) above applies to *any* consideration in money or money's worth, however inadequate and acquired at any time by the person entitled to it, or a person previously entitled to it. Note also that nowadays one would need to include a reversionary interest owned by the settlor or his spouse within the types of reversionary interest that are not excluded property.

The fact that a reversionary interest is generally excluded property is a logical corollary of the basic IHT premise that an individual who has a pre-FA 2006 interest in possession is deemed to own the capital supporting it. To subject the reversionary interest to tax as well would involve a double assessment.

Accordingly, it is normally possible to resettle the reversionary interest, ie an interest that is not yet in possession, without a charge to IHT; but it is no longer possible to make that resettlement by way of an accumulation and maintenance trust under s 71 so as to shelter the fund for another generation. That is precisely the kind of scheme that the Paymaster General had in mind in her comments on Finance Bill 2006 during its passage through Parliament; as if (though this is perhaps unlikely) she had read an earlier edition of this work and had disapproved of it!

Even in those rare cases where a reversionary interest is not excluded property, it may be possible to dispose of it (into trust or otherwise) without a charge to IHT arising if the value of the interest is very small. This will often be the case where the trustees have overriding powers that could be used to defeat the reversioner's interest.

Example 7.35 – Resettling a reversionary interest

The situation described above was particularly appropriate where an individual had a reversionary interest subject to a life interest in favour of, say, his mother.

Where the reversioner was already wealthy, it was often excellent IHT planning for him to resettle his reversionary interest in favour of, say, his own children.

He can still save tax, but only by giving up his interest absolutely, perhaps accelerating the interests of his children under the trust so that they get the money at 18 (or as soon after that age as their grandmother dies).

7.113   Resettlement of reversionary interests must, however, be considered in the light of associated operations (s 268). Further, the device of a trust giving oneself an interest in possession, with a reversion to the spouse, where the spouse then gifts her reversionary interest, say, to the children, does not work. Neither would a trust in favour of one's spouse, with remainder to oneself. In neither case is the reversionary interest treated as excluded property (s 48(1) (b)).

Certain other IHT avoidance devices have been stopped, in particular where an interest in possession in property was created for a short period and the reversionary interest transferred as excluded property into settlement, followed by a tax-free termination of the interest under the former much wider reverter to settlor or settlor's spouse exemption: the interest meanwhile having been acquired for its market value, which was nearly equivalent to the full capital value as the interest in possession was for a very short period, say three months.

Nor does the exemption apply in the case of transfers between spouses or gifts to charities and certain public bodies where the assets are transferred in consideration of a transfer of a reversionary interest being excluded property not forming part of the estate of the person who acquires it. As to the estate planning advantages in assigning a reversionary interest, see **5.23**.

As indicated at **7.52**, anti-avoidance provisions in respect of certain reversionary interests in settled property were introduced in FA 2010, with effect from 9 December 2009. The rules are broadly designed to block arrangements which used reversionary interests to reduce the IHT charge when assets were transferred into trust. They apply if the reversionary interest is held by the settlor or his spouse or civil partner, or to a reversionary interest which has been purchased. If the reversionary interest ends upon the 'relevant reversioner' becoming entitled to an interest in possession in the trust property, the person is treated as making a disposition of the reversionary interest for IHT purposes. IHT is therefore charged based on the value of the reversionary interest immediately prior to its ending.

Aside from blocking a variant of *Melville*-type arrangements, the rationale for this provision appears to be that a purchased reversionary interest or a settlor's reversionary interest in trust property is not excluded property, and therefore forms part of the person's estate (s 48(1)(a), (b)), whereas a post-FA 2006 interest in possession does not normally form part of his estate (s 5(1A)). The vesting of the interest in possession would otherwise result in the reversionary interest no longer being held, thus giving rise to a possible IHT saving.

In addition, it is not possible to avoid an IHT charge by making a gift of the reversionary interest before the interest in possession vests. The anti-avoidance rules also provide that such a gift is an immediately chargeable transfer, as opposed to a PET.

However, the above provisions do not apply to certain interests in possession which are not part of the relevant property regime. Thus, for example, disabled trusts would be excluded from a potential charge.

Further anti-avoidance provisions were introduced in FA 2012 to block a narrow range of specific arrangements relating to settled excluded property, including acquisitions by individuals of certain reversionary interests in settled property which would otherwise be excluded property (see **17.14**).

Trading trusts

7.114 Tax advantages may be gained from operating a business through a trading trust.

An appropriate trust would be chosen. Trustees would be appointed, who would have a right to carry on a trade and appoint qualified managers, etc.

They would be responsible for conducting the business for remuneration. Consider use of a limited partnership under the Limited Partnerships Act 1907.

As to taxation the position would be that:

Trustees could benefit from the 100%/50% business/agricultural property relief (see **Chapter 15**). Subject to this, the creation of the trust triggers IHT on the excess over the available nil rate band.

- The trustees would be assessable to income tax at a maximum of 50%. Contrast the rates of tax for individuals/companies. Be aware of the application of ITTOIA 2005, s 629 in the case of any trust for minor children, or ITTOIA 2005, s 624 where the settlor or his spouse is included as a beneficiary. However, the latter anti-avoidance rule could work in the settlor's favour, if his own income tax rate is lower than the trust rate.

- The distribution of the capital and income of the trust could be with the maximum flexibility, eg accumulating as capital or distributing as income according to the beneficiary's tax position.

- Many of the tax rigours would be avoided, eg transactions in securities (ITA 2007, s 684), benefits in kind, etc.

- As to CGT, hold-over relief (although restricted after FA 1989 and FA 2004) may yet still apply on the creation and termination of the trust since business and agricultural assets are still covered by TCGA 1992, s 165, if the hold-over relief for immediately chargeable transfers in TCGA 1992, s 260 is not available (see s 165(3)(d)). Disposals by the trustees will be liable to CGT at a rate of 28%, although the actual rate may be lower in certain circumstances if entrepreneurs' relief is available (TCGA 1992, s 169J).

- A beneficiary with a pre-FA 2006 life interest in trust property is treated for inheritance tax purposes as owning the underlying assets (IHTA 1984, s 49(1)). If those assets are used in his or her business, they will normally qualify for 100% business property relief (*Fetherstonaugh v IRC* [1984] STC 261). See **15.37**.

Child Trust Fund accounts/Junior ISAs

7.115   Child Trust Funds (CTFs) are unfairly neglected and should be used for as long as they last, albeit that their scope is restricted as they apply to children born between 1 September 2002 and 2 January 2011 where certain conditions are satisfied. The regime offers:

- a UK-based, onshore trust fund;
- for a minor;

- set up without any initial professional charges;

- made expressly subject to strict limits on the administrative charges that may be levied;

- in which the fund itself is allowed to roll up free of income tax;

- and free of CGT;

- into which a third party has paid a nominal sum as a free gift;

- to which the settlor-interested rule for a parent does not apply; and

- to which, if regular, all contributions are free of IHT.

From 1 November 2011, parents, family and friends can add money to the account up to a limit of £3,600 a year. A parent may contribute without falling foul of ITTOIA 2005, s 629, notwithstanding that the income may soon exceed the £100 limit in s 629(3). Alternatively, let an uncle or grandparent add the funds, claiming IHT relief under s 21.

Leave the fund to grow until the beneficiary is 18, by which time the fund, even without reinvested income or any growth, will be significant. Quite simply, all grandparents should consider its use. The money may not be available for private education, but its availability just as the beneficiary might begin further education could be a significant relief to the parents.

Child trust funds were replaced by junior ISAs for any child born on or after 3 January 2011. However, the comments above continue to apply.

Chapter 8

Practical aspects of drafting settlements

RELEVANT PROPERTY TRUSTS

8.1 There are circumstances, as mentioned in **Chapter 7**, when opportunity should be taken to set up new discretionary trusts, but not without looking at all the facts and working out the arithmetic (including the ten-year anniversary charge, and any IHT on establishing the trust arising (because the chargeable value settled is over the threshold) or on potential exit charges).

In particular, remember that in ascertaining the rate for the ten-year charge, it is necessary to look not merely at the anniversary value of the discretionary trust property. The charge is also affected by:

- the settlor's chargeable transfers within the seven years before the settlement was made;

- the value (on formation of the trust) of any property in the settlement in which there has been an interest in possession;

- the value (again on formation) of any property subject to a 'related' settlement, ie one set up on the same day as the settlement in contemplation (this will apply usually to settlements created by will, but note that the order of lifetime settlement creations is most important); and

- the value of any advances out of the settlement in the ten years before the anniversary.

Because of the possible effect on aggregation, it is generally desirable to avoid related settlements and separate fixed and discretionary trusts in the same settlement.

INTERESTS IN POSSESSION

8.2 Remember also the importance of 'getting in first'. For example, in the case of an 'existing' (ie pre-FA 2006) interest in possession trust, the interest in remainder may vest in a distant relative. The life tenant's next of kin, say his children, will be 'hoist' with the aggregation of the trust fund with the life tenant's free estate when he dies. In this type of situation the life tenant should consider disposing of his free estate to his children in his lifetime and before the interest in possession terminates, thereby avoiding this aggregation.

It is often much the better plan for a settlor to make a regular allowance to a poor beneficiary rather than to create an interest in possession in his favour, particularly where the instalments can be treated as normal expenditure out of income within s 21 (see **12.4**).

Suppose that an IPDI has been left by will to a beneficiary who is elderly or who does not need the income. It may be appropriate to vary the will within two years of death under s 142, which will not be a transfer for IHT purposes, so that, even if the variation sets up a relevant property trust, it is not a chargeable transfer by the elderly beneficiary. The variation will not trigger a charge to CGT if an election is made, nor to stamp duty nor SDLT.

For income tax purposes the key is whether, but for the variation, a trust would have existed. In this and the following paragraphs the person who has died is 'the Deceased' and the beneficiary who decides to give up an inheritance is called 'the Varier'. The general rule, see ITA 2007, s 472 ('Settlor where property becomes settled because of variation of will etc'), is that any variation is treated as made by the Varier, so if a trust is created where there would not otherwise have been one, it is the Varier who is deemed both to make the settlement and to provide funds for it. Thus it may be settlor-interested for the purposes of ITTOIA 2005, s 624, though in the case of an elderly Varier it is perhaps unlikely that ITTOIA 2005, s 629 ('Income paid to relevant children of settlor') would be in point.

There is a saving, though, under ITA 2007, s 473 ('Deceased person as settlor where variation of will etc') where a trust already existed. That section depends on whether an election was made, not for IHT purposes but under TCGA 1992, s 62(6): it is therefore quite possible that it would not apply to every deed of variation though many draftsmen, no doubt, will elect under both the IHT and CGT rules without giving the matter serious thought.

Where ITA 2007, s 473 does apply, it treats the settlement as having been made by the Deceased, which is usually preferable to any alternative, especially where the fund is invested in '5% withdrawal bonds' which may trigger chargeable event gains.

Several situations are contemplated by s 473. Section 473(2) concerns:

- settlements that already exist before the death, whether or not the person dying was the settlor; and

- trusts that arise on the death, either by will or on intestacy.

In either case, if property would have become settled, but for the variation, and is so settled, but on different trusts, by virtue of the variation, the Varier is not treated by s 473(2) as the settlor of the new trust: it is made by the Deceased, 'except where the context otherwise requires'.

Section 473(4) applies to a similar situation, where:

- the Deceased was settlor of property; and
- that property, or property derived from it, becomes comprised in another settlement under the variation.

In these circumstances the Deceased, not the Varier, is the settlor for income tax, except as above.

Example 8.1 – Spot the settlor

Martha's will left shares of residue as follows:

- 10% to each of her two daughters;
- 20% to each of her two grandsons who should attain 25, with gifts over; and
- 20% to pay the income equally to her two granddaughters for life, with power for the trustees to advance capital to them after attaining 50, and with gifts over.

One of the daughters has remarried and wishes to benefit a stepchild by carving out a share from her own inheritance. If the share carved out is put in trust, the daughter will be treated as the settlor.

One of the granddaughters is a successful insolvency practitioner who has no need of the fund allotted to her. If she wishes to benefit her less fortunate sister, who used to be in merchant banking, the diversion of her fund will not be a settlement by her, but by her late grandmother.

Subsections (5) and (6) of s 473 concern timing. If the trust arose on the death of the deceased, it was made on his death; but if it is merely treated as having been made by the deceased, it is deemed to have been made just before the death.

Anti-avoidance provisions – depreciatory transactions (ss 52(3), 65(1)(b))

8.3   Transactions between trustees and beneficiaries or persons connected with beneficiaries, designed to depress the value of the trust fund, will be regarded as a transfer of value or a chargeable distribution as the case may be.

This type of provision is particularly designed to counteract transactions such as:

- an artificial sale and purchase price;

- interest-free loan arrangements (where repayment is not until a future specified date; loans genuinely repayable on demand are alright);

- artificial leasing arrangements;

- value-shifting operations where, for example, the trustees agree to a change in the share structure of a company so that their own shares are depressed in value; and

- devices such as the conveyance of a perimeter strip, whereby a strip of land, say a yard wide, entirely surrounding the property, is transferred to a third party in order to reduce the value of the remainder (see also **1.5**).

Note that these anti-avoidance provisions do not apply if 'the transaction is such that, were the trustees beneficially entitled to the settled property, it would not be a transfer of value'. This envisages a commercial or business transaction on the part of the trustees as opposed to a mere gift, and other situations where the trustees sell or realise assets for a good reason, eg to enable a taxation liability to be met; and where no gratuitous benefit is intended.

For relevant property, charitable and (pre-FA 2006) accumulation and maintenance trusts, ss 65(9), 70(10) and 71(5) specifically provide that a disposition can result from an omission to act unless not deliberate. This is in accordance with the 'general' transfer of value rules in s 3.

Loans to beneficiaries

8.4   The question is sometimes raised in this context of a loan of money made by the trustees.

First, it is clear that, if the loan is not merely repayable on demand but that there is some reasonable prospect that the loan will eventually be repaid, there is no (or perhaps negligible) consequential loss to the trust. If the loan is declared to be repayable only at some date in the future, or if it is clear from extrinsic evidence that there is no real possibility of repayment, as where funds are advanced to help out an unlucky gambler or unreformed drug addict, there will be a loss by virtue of a depreciatory transaction, since the present value in the trust of the right to that future repayment is a discounted sum only; and the difference will be subject to IHT.

Secondly, unlike the case where a beneficiary is given exclusive occupation of a house and, as a result, may be treated as having acquired an interest in possession, the loan of money does not produce an interest in possession in the borrower. The distinction can perhaps best be seen by comparing the house, to which the trustees still have legal title and which is still an asset of the trust, with the money which the trustees lend. That money thereupon belongs to the borrower absolutely, although he is under an obligation to repay an equivalent (not the actual) sum. A loan is therefore in essence a re-investment by the trustees. They have, by the lending transaction, ceased to own that money, having converted it into a debt due. The debt is now a trust asset, in place of the cash. The only challenge to this interpretation is where there is no prospect of repayment of the loan by the beneficiary: that it is truly a distribution, not an investment.

Trustees' liability for IHT on termination of an interest in possession

8.5   The trustees will be the persons primarily liable for the payment of IHT on the termination on death of an 'old' interest in possession, ie a TSI, under s 200(1)(b) subject to the limitation in s 204(2), ie, to the extent in broad terms of the property under their control or available to them.

In the case of the termination of a TSI during lifetime by way of a PET which becomes a chargeable transfer on the death of the former life tenant within seven years, the persons primarily liable are the trustees of the settlement (s 199(1) (c)) because, whether or not the settlement continued after the termination, the trustees will have had the trust assets vested in them 'after the transfers'. As the transfer has already taken place they cannot hold for anyone else.

Any absolute beneficiary (s 199(1)(b)) or person with an interest in possession (s 199(1)(c)) will also be liable, but it is the trustees who hold the trust property, and if the settlement comes to an end on the lifetime termination of the interest in possession, the trustees will need to take steps, either by a retention fund or by watertight insurance, to provide for the potential IHT. The personal representatives of the former life tenant are also liable (in view of s 199(2)) but only secondarily because of the limitation in s 204(8).

As to the CGT liability, see TCGA 1992, s 71.

The duty of care

8.6   Historically, trustees were subject to a general duty of care in connection with trust investments: see for example *Bartlett v Barclays Bank Trust Co Ltd* [1980] Ch 515, where bank trustees were liable in negligence to beneficiaries for not preventing two hazardous speculations.

The duty of care to be exercised by trustees received statutory recognition in the Trustee Act 2000. Section 1 of that Act provides that a trustee must exercise:

> 'such care and skill as is reasonable in the circumstances having particular regard to any special knowledge or experience that he has or holds himself out as having and, if he is acting as a trustee in the course or furtherance of a business or profession, to any special knowledge or experience that it is reasonable to expect of a person acting in the course of that kind of business or profession'.

The Act also contains extensive provisions dealing with the trustees' powers of investment.

However, the statutory duty may be excluded by contrary indication in the trust instrument, and it routinely is. See for example the STEP Standard Provisions, 2nd edition. This is mainly because professional trustees are liable in their professional capacity, though many believe it is morally wrong for a person who charges for his services to exclude or restrict liability in this way.

The trustees paying the settlor's capital taxes

8.7 If an individual establishes a trust under the terms of which the trustees are to pay the IHT and/or CGT on the gift into settlement, then that trust may be ineffective for income tax purposes ie the income of the trust may be deemed to be that of the settlor having regard in particular to ITTOIA 2005, s 624 (income arising under settlement where settlor retains an interest) and s 633 (sums paid to the settlor otherwise than as income).

By concession, for IHT purposes the practice of HMRC is not to take this strict view. In SP 1/82 (dated 6 April 1982), HMRC explain the rationale behind this approach as follows:

> 'The inheritance tax legislation (IHTA 1984 s 199) … provides that both the settlor and the trustees are liable for any inheritance tax payable when a settlor puts assets into a settlement. The Commissioners for HMRC have therefore decided that they will no longer, in these circumstances, treat the income of the settlement as that of the settlor for income tax purposes solely because the trustees have power to pay or do in fact pay inheritance tax on assets put into settlements.'

However, practitioners should understand that this Statement of Practice does not appear to apply as regards CGT where the primary liability rests on the settlor (TCGA 1992, s 282), to be contrasted with IHT (s 199(1)) where the liability is placed both on the transferor and the transferee. Where the settlor has taken advantage of the hold-over provisions for CGT under TCGA 1992, ss 165 and 260, the relief falls to be 'clawed back' by virtue of the trust having become 'settlor interested' (s 169C) through the trustees' payment of a liability of the settlor, CGT or otherwise.

It is understood that if the trustees do not have a *power* to pay the CGT as expressed in the trust deed or some supplemental document or other evidence of agreement to pay the CGT (ie if the trustees just pay the CGT ad hoc), HMRC will not seek to apply the income tax anti-avoidance provisions. In that event, the trustees are in all probability committing a breach of trust, ie meeting a liability for which they are not responsible, but HMRC may not necessarily concern themselves on this point. Indeed, it can be argued that they have no *locus standi* to become involved.

Anti-fragmentation provisions for discretionary trusts

8.8   Section 81 ('Property moving between settlements') provides that, where property leaves one settlement and – unless some person in between takes an absolute interest (not an interest in possession) – becomes comprised in another settlement, it shall be treated as still comprised in the first settlement. If, of course, anyone becomes absolutely entitled to the property in the interim, that absolute owner will be a new settlor.

The aim is to discourage fragmentation of such trusts, by rendering ineffective the transfer of property from one settlement to another, so that all capital payments and dispositions by trustees are identified for computational purposes with the original settlement. Another effect is that, if property is transferred out of a UK trust to a non-resident settlement, the UK trustees of the original settlement remain *liable* for any IHT.

Trustees' distributions

8.9   Are they income or capital? When trustees make a distribution of the trust fund, it is often a grey area whether such distribution constitutes capital or income.

It was hitherto always thought that the basic test was whether the distribution was income or capital in the hands of the *recipient* beneficiary. It seemed to follow from cases like *Brodie's Trustees v IRC* (1933) 17 TC 432 and *Cunard's Trustees v IRC* [1946] 1 All ER 159, CA, that the more regular the payments out of the trust, the more likely they would be treated as income in the hands of the beneficiary. Hence the advice was that if the trustees were intent on making capital payments they should make them irregularly and for a clear capital purpose.

In *Stevenson v Wishart* [1987] STC 266, CA, however, it was held that a regular series of payments from the capital of a discretionary settlement in order to pay medical and nursing home expenses of a beneficiary were still capital so far as the beneficiary was concerned. The Court of Appeal declared that if, in their exercise of a power over capital, the trustees chose to make at their discretion regular payments of capital to deal with the special problems of the beneficiary's last year, rather than to realise a single large sum, that did not create an income interest.

This decision appears to make the position somewhat easier. However, it is still safer to err on the cautious side. An irregular large payment will always look better and be more defensible than a series of small payments, particularly if there are no special problems as there were in the *Wishart* case itself. This will be very relevant to the funding of school fees, where income may be insufficient.

Some comfort on the capital and income distinction can perhaps be drawn from HMRC's Trust and Estate Tax Return guide (www.hmrc.gov.uk/worksheets/sa950.pdf): 'Payments out of trust capital including out of accumulated income or deemed income are not usually regarded as the income of a beneficiary irrespective of the purpose for which they are made and should not normally be included'. The guidance adds: 'Exceptionally, payments out of capital are treated as the income of the beneficiary where, by the terms of the trust instrument, payments out of capital must be made, or may be made, in order to supplement income'.

Where a settlement is contemplated and regular payments out might be expected, consideration should be given to making a number of smaller separate settlements instead of one large one. A capital payment can be made on the first occasion out of settlement number 1, on the next occasion out of settlement number 2, and so on. A capital payment thereby occurs as regards any one settlement only at long intervals.

Note that, having regard to the stringent CGT anti-avoidance provisions relating to the surcharge in TCGA 1992, ss 91–98, for CGT purposes, it may prove beneficial to turn capital into income for non-resident trusts, although with a maximum CGT rate of 44.8% where the surcharge applies, this will probably not be so in most cases.

In the strange case of *Taube v HMRC* [2011] WTLR 1, a dividend payment was argued to be a capital receipt of a family settlement and not liable to income tax because it was a 'special dividend' upon a company reorganisation. The court had little difficulty in dismissing the claim.

Trust deeds

8.10   For income tax and capital gains tax purposes, HMRC do not generally ask (as previously) for a copy of every new trust document. Instead they will rely on the information shown by trustees, settlors and beneficiaries in form 41G(Trust) filed when the trust was set up and in their annual tax returns or repayment claims.

When a new trust is created, trustees should obtain form 41G(Trust). The form can be downloaded from HMRC's website (www.hmrc.gov.uk/cnr/41g_trust. pdf). It has been developed over the years and asks for some basic factual information including the identities of the trustees and settlor. This enables the trust office at HMRC to decide on the disclosure required of the trustees including, for example, the relevance of reliefs for vulnerable beneficiaries.

The identity of the settlor will be straightforward in most cases. However, care may sometimes be needed, as the term 'settlor' is broadly defined (in s 44). This definition includes any person by whom the trust was made directly or indirectly, and includes anyone who has provided funds directly or indirectly for the purpose of or in connection with the trust, or has made with any other person a reciprocal arrangement for that other person to make a settlement.

Practitioners should not be lulled into a false sense of security. On the contrary, if they have misinterpreted the type and nature of the trust, this may not be discovered for many years when additional assessments will be raised with possible interest and penalties. For example, an intended life interest may be subject to an (unintended) power to accumulate with the consequent higher rate applicable to trusts applying for income tax and CGT purposes.

Finally, it should be noted that the drafting of the trust deed itself can have unexpected tax consequences. For example, the omission of a default beneficiary (eg a charity) can give rise to a resulting trust for the settlor. Whilst this does not of itself cause the gift with reservation provisions to apply, the retained interest will be included in the estate of the settlor for IHT. There are also potentially unwelcome income tax consequences under the settlements anti-avoidance provisions, and for pre-owned assets tax purposes (see **11.16**).

As regards IHT, however, this practice does not alter the potential scope for examination of deeds by HMRC (see Revenue press release 19 December 1990).

TRUST BUSTING AND VARIATION: (1) BY CONSENT

8.11   Under this first head, particular attention is given to methods of terminating or varying settlements with interests in possession followed by an absolute interest in remainder. As such methods depend upon the beneficiaries' consent, it is assumed that all the beneficiaries can consent to the arrangement being of full age and capacity, ie are *sui juris*.

In addition, consideration should be given to the possible application of the 100% business/agricultural property relief.

Finally, the following points should be noted.

Circumstance 1: Division or partition

8.12   This could be particularly appropriate where it is wished to transfer *appreciating* assets to a remainderman at a stage where a (pre-FA 2006) life tenant may not survive the seven-year period for PET purposes. Moreover, it may be possible to time the partition during a period when the asset value is relatively low.

The value of the gift to the remainderman is frozen at the time of the division/ partition. The same applies to circumstance 2.

Circumstance 2: Enlargement by gift

8.13   This is particularly important from an IHT planning aspect. The holder of a TSI can acquire the remainderman's interest by way of gift free of IHT. The trust is terminated leaving the former life tenant as the absolute owner of the former trust property. A TSI holder should then also be encouraged to make the maximum use of exemptions and reliefs and PETs and use the art of giving as described in detail in **Chapter 11**.

Example 8.2 – Gift of reversionary interest

Freeman has for many years been the life tenant of the Wagner trust.

The remainderman, Rogers, is actually older than Freeman and decides to give to Freeman his reversionary interest in the trust, valued actuarially at £22,000. Freeman, as life tenant, is already treated for IHT as being entitled to the whole capital value of the trust, £100,000, in spite of the fact that the actuarial value of his interest is only £78,000.

The transfer by Rogers is of excluded property and no IHT is payable.

Circumstance 3: The release or surrender by a remainderman

8.14   This might be, for example, a gift by the remainderman to his children, and can result in important IHT savings. This application will be particularly relevant in the case of a surviving spouse exemption where ED was paid on the first spouse's death.

Example 8.3 – Assignment of reversionary interest

John died many years ago, leaving his estate to his wife Frances for life with remainder to his son Richard. Estate duty was paid on the fund on John's death but will not be paid again when Frances dies. She is now aged 92. Richard has just retired from public service and enjoys a substantial pension. His own children are off his hands, but struggling with mortgage commitments.

Richard assigns his interest under John's will to his own children. There will be no IHT on the assignment, as it is of excluded property. Nor will there be a CGT charge if it is a disposal of an interest in a UK trust (TCGA 1992, ss 76 and 85).

Further, there should be no CGT on the death of the life tenant, having regard to the exemption on death (TCGA 1992, s 73).

Circumstance 4: private annuity

8.15   The estate duty decision in *Re Beit, Beit v IRC* [1951] 2 TLR 124; affd [1952] Ch 53, CA, may remain relevant for IHT planning. The arrangement in this case resulted in a settled fund which became valueless on an annuitant's death. The facts were that under the testatrix's will, an annuity was payable out of the residuary estate and the trustees were directed to appropriate a specific capital value to meet the income liability, the remainder of the residue being exonerated.

An arrangement was entered into between the annuitant, the trustees and the residuary beneficiaries, whereby the trustees applied a part of the residuary fund in purchasing from the residuary beneficiaries a covenant to pay an annuity of like amount to the trustees. The covenant by the residuary beneficiaries to pay the income to the annuitant became the sole security for its payment and it was further agreed that the trustees were thereupon free to distribute the remaining residuary estate.

On the annuitant's death it was held that no estate duty was payable because the annuity had not been terminated. There had merely been an appropriation of a specified part of the trust fund in the form of the reversioners' covenants which became valueless on the annuitant's death.

It may well be possible to apply this decision in contending that there is no termination of a pre-FA 2006 interest in possession for the purposes of ss 51 and 52, and, as the similar estate duty associated operations provisions were not applied, it would seem illogical that they should apply for IHT. HMRC may, however, be able to contend successfully that, for IHT purposes, the interest of the annuitant or life tenant has terminated without his becoming absolutely entitled, while the covenant is a retention of interest. The changes in FA 2006 perhaps bring these possibilities to an end.

Circumstance 5: deed of variation

8.16   For will trusts, note the important provisions relating to variations of wills, etc (s 142) (see **5.34** onwards).

Remember that the facility of variation without IHT charge does not extend to the variation of interests under existing trusts: these are not dispositions of 'property comprised in his estate' ie that of the deceased, because trust property is only deemed to be part of that estate.

Circumstance 6: dealings with trust interests

8.17   The following CGT aspects should also be noted:

- minor variations *within* a trust – not a disposal (see SP 7/84);

- no chargeable gain accrues on a disposal of a beneficial interest under a UK trust (TCGA 1992, ss 76 and 85);

- similar treatment for variation under Variation of Trusts Act 1958 (see **8.21** onwards);

- termination of an 'old' life interest on death, ie one existing prior to FA 2006 in respect of the whole trust fund – exempt (but contrast the advantage for IHT purposes of using the lifetime rate or making a PET in respect of a TSI); partial CGT relief where life interest in part of trust fund. But if hold-over relief claimed by settlor on setting up trust under TCGA 1992, ss 165 or 260, that gain crystallises on the death (TCGA 1992, s 74), subject to a possible further hold-over claim, where appropriate;

- a life interest in part – disposal only of *that part* of trust fund – subject to TCGA 1992, s 72(2)–(5);

- section 52(1) ('Charge on termination of interest in possession'). On termination of an interest in possession, eg on partition, consider arranging that the beneficiary pays the CGT so that the CGT is a deduction against the value transferred for IHT purposes (s 165(2)).

Circumstance 7: advancements or appointments

8.18   The trustees may be able to alter or substitute the administrative and even the *dispositive* powers if that is for the overall benefit of the beneficiary in question: see the important cases of *Pilkington v IRC* [1962] 3 All ER 622, HL; *Re Rank's Settlement Trusts* [1979] 1 WLR 1242 and *Re Hampden Settlement Trusts* [1977] TR 177.

TRUST BUSTING AND VARIATION: (2) BY THE COURT

8.19   In the former circumstances it has been assumed that the beneficiaries under the settlement have all been *sui juris* and of full age, so that the arrangements for termination or variation have been effected by consent of all the interested parties involved.

The sanction of the court is necessary where all the parties are not *sui juris* and/ or of full age and cannot therefore give consents binding at law by reason of infancy or other disability, or because their identity has not yet been ascertained.

This second aspect can in appropriate circumstances (ie subject to the terms of the settlement) be overcome without application to the court, by means of advancements by the trustees of all the trust assets to the appropriate beneficiaries of the settlement. Beware the argument that this is a fraud on the power if it is done only to facilitate onward transmission of the funds.

In each case, the trustees must check carefully whether a disposal is constituted or not, because of the CGT implications. See the decisions in *Hoare Trustees v Gardner* [1978] STC 89; *Roome v Edwards* [1981] STC 96, HL; *Bond v Pickford* [1982] STC 403; *Swires v Renton* [1991] STC 490. The law is well summarised in SP 7/84.

Where hold-over relief is not available pursuant to TCGA 1992, s 165 or s 260, it may be appropriate not to create an entirely new trust by the advance but to structure it in such a way that there is no disposal and the trust continues, albeit in a different form, eg by making any appointment or advancement non-exhaustive.

Always take care in drafting assignments of trust interests where the interests of remaindermen have not yet vested, for example because the remainderman must be living at the death of the tenant for life, who, in this scenario, is still alive. The issue is whether the deed of assignment accelerates the interest of the remainderman, such that his interest in remainder becomes an interest in possession.

There are several cases on the issue, notably *Re Guinness's Settlement* [1966] 2 All ER 497; *Re Flower's Settlement* [1957] 1All ER 462; *Re Dawson's Settlement* [1966] 3 All ER 68; *Re Taylor* [1957] 3 All ER 56 and *Re Scott Deceased* [1975] 2 All ER 1033. The problem is essentially one of construction of the principal trust deed and of the deed of assignment. If unsure, as the wealth of authority implies, take specialist advice.

The Hastings-Bass principle

8.20   The courts may set aside the acts of trustees in appropriate circumstances. In *Re Hastings-Bass (deceased) Hastings and others v IRC*, CA [1974] STC 211, Buckley LJ held as follows:

'... where by the terms of a trust ... a trustee is given a discretion as to some matter under which he acts in good faith, the court should not interfere with his action notwithstanding that it does not have the full effect which he intended, unless (1) what he has achieved is unauthorised by the power conferred on him, or (2) it is clear that he would not have acted as he did (a) had he not taken into account considerations which he should not have taken into account, or (b) had he not failed to take into account considerations which he ought to have taken into account.'

The principle has recently produced a plethora of cases, most of them brought by trustees who entered into a transaction which turned out to be a disaster, often involving spectacular amounts of money payable in tax. There has been an equal plethora of articles on the topic, including judges writing on a 'without prejudice' basis. The issue is now at large in two cases, *Futter v Futter* [2010] WTLR 609 and *Pitt v Holt*, but the decision was overturned by the Court of Appeal in favour of HMRC ([2011] WTLR 623). Leave to appeal to the Supreme Court was given but, at the time of writing, there have been no further developments.

In the meantime, the position is broadly that, if trustees act outside the scope of the relevant power, the act is void. However, if the trustees act within their powers but the act is vitiated by a failure to take into account a relevant factor that should have been taken into account (or by taking something irrelevant into account), the act is not void, but it might be voidable. The act would only be voidable if it could be shown that the trustees had breached their fiduciary duty. In that case, the trustees' act could be set aside following a successful application by a beneficiary. However, if the trustees' duty of skill and care had been satisfied by seeking proper professional advice, no breach of trust would be committed, even if that advice turned out to be incorrect.

Note that the court in Jersey has upheld the *Hastings-Bass* principle after the CA decision in *Futter* and *Pitt* so there is now a divergence of judicial attitude. For commentary on the development of the *Hastings-Bass* principle and its application prior to the above cases, readers are referred to the eighth edition of this book. See also **6.19** and **11.45**.

Variation of Trusts Act 1958

8.21   Assuming the court's sanction is necessary, most variations or terminations of settlements are effected under the Variation of Trusts Act 1958 (VTA 1958) as the court's jurisdiction is thereby based on the broadest terms and subject to the widest discretion. Note, however, that this Act does not apply to Scotland or Northern Ireland, although the court's jurisdiction to vary is not confined to trusts to which English law applies.

By VTA 1958, s 1, the court can approve 'any arrangements … varying or revoking all or any of the trusts, or enlarging the powers of the trustees of managing or administering any of the property subject to the trusts'. This does not, however, enable the court to override valid objections, or to dispense with any necessary consents. The trusts need not have arisen since the passing of VTA 1958 and the court's order can be of immediate effect or operative from a future date.

The predominant criterion is the 'benefit' of the person(s) on whose behalf the application is made. The trusts can be in respect of real or personal property 'under any will, settlement or other disposition'.

The court will not entertain an application where the beneficiaries are all of full age and *sui juris* as this must then be a matter of obtaining their consents (*Re Suffert's Settlement, Suffert v Martyn-Linnington* [1961] Ch 1). Nor do discretionary objects as such have power to apply under VTA 1958.

8.22   There are five different kinds of benefits that have been recognised in the many reported cases, namely: financial benefit; moral-social benefit; benefit by removing restriction on contingent interests; facilitating the general administration of the trusts; and widening of investment powers.

The majority of cases brought under VTA 1958 have been designed to reduce tax burdens. Applications have included both the breaking of discretionary trusts and also the enlargement of life tenants' interests. Many of these applications have been successful, but a notable exception was highlighted in the decision of *Re Weston's Settlements, Weston v Weston* [1969] 1 Ch 223, CA, where unusually an application to transfer a trust to Jersey was dismissed as being 'a cheap exercise in tax avoidance', Lord Denning preferring to retain the trusts 'in this our England which is still the envy of less happier lands'.

In the rather similar circumstances of *Re Seales' Marriage Settlement* [1961] Ch 574 and *Re Windeatt's Will Trusts* [1969] 2 All ER 324, transfers of the administration of trusts abroad have been approved.

One particular area of difficulty was compliance with perpetuity and accumulation periods. Fortunately, this is eased under Perpetuities and Accumulations Act 2009 (as to which, see **8.27**), which came into force on 6 April 2010.

Scope of applications; procedure

8.23   The reported cases have covered nearly all aspects concerning the variation and termination of trusts, including: partitioning of the trust assets; re-settlement of interests on discretionary or other terms; variation of provisions as to accumulation of income; inclusion and exercise of powers of advancement; widening of investment powers; transfer of trusts abroad and foreign administration; and many other aspects of 'trust busting' and variation.

The decision in *Re Robinson's Settlement Trusts* [1976] 3 All ER 61 is an example of a case involving CTT where the court's consent was sought for breaking a protective trust and where the amount to be received by an infant beneficiary, albeit that the entitlement was accelerated, was less than the net sum he would receive on the termination of the trust. Templeman J sanctioned the division of the trust subject to a ten-year with-profits policy for £8,000 being taken out for the infant's benefit and payable out of the income of his share.

Procedure before the relevant court (usually the Chancery Division of the High Court) is set out in Ord 93, r 6 of the Rules of the Supreme Court found in Sch 1 to the Civil Procedure Rules 1998. The application is normally made by one or more interested beneficiaries, who join the trustees and any other beneficiaries. The application is commenced by claim form, and is heard in open court unless otherwise directed.

It should be stressed, however, that considerable scope is available by way of self help and, with a little foresight and a carefully drafted trust deed, many somewhat uncertain applications under VTA 1958 should prove unnecessary. See the STEP Standard Provisions, 2nd edition (released in late 2011).

Appointment of foreign trustees; change of proper law

8.24   Specific power should be included in the trust deed to appoint foreign trustees. Indeed the balance of opinion indicates that the normal powers of appointment included in most trust deeds or implied under the provisions of the Trustee Act 1925 enable foreign trustees to be appointed without application to the court.

The ability of foreign trustees to act is supported to a certain degree by the decision of *Re Whitehead's Will Trusts, Burke v Burke* [1971] 2 All ER 1334, namely that there is no legal bar to the appointment of foreign resident trustees and that such an appointment is appropriate provided that 'exceptional circumstances' exist, for example, that the beneficiary is taking up residence in the foreign country.

However, if out of an abundance of caution it is still wished to apply to the court, it is safer to make the appointment of foreign trustees and seek the court's ratification thereto rather than to ask the court to make the appointment itself; because, whereas the court may be ready to ratify, it may be disinclined actively to appoint.

If it is wished, in addition, to change the proper law of the settlement to a foreign country there is no doubt that, in the absence of specific power in the trust deed, application to the court would be necessary. Specific power should therefore be included in the trust deed to cover this aspect as well and also to avoid any doubt arising as to whether the 'exceptional circumstances' as referred to above exist. If a settlement already has a foreign proper law this should be recited in the trust deed. As to the possible disadvantages of appointing foreign trustees, and the risk that the settlor will be left 'high and dry', see **7.7**.

Still on a theme of self-help to avoid the need for application under VTA 1958, draftsmen of modern settlements are generally aware of the desirability of going beyond the narrow powers of advancement in Trustee Act 1925, s 32 and the need to include the widest powers of advancement extending over the whole of the settled funds including powers to appoint on new trusts or other settlements. However, in view of the restricted application of CGT hold-over relief, mainly to transfers of business or agricultural assets or where inheritance tax is chargeable, it may be important in exercising any given power to show that a particular appointment does *not* constitute a new trust and is not therefore a disposal for CGT. (See in particular *Hoare Trustees v Gardner* [1978] STC 89; *Roome v Edwards* [1981] STC 96, HL; *Bond v Pickford* [1982] STC 403; *Swires v Renton* [1991] STC 490; and Revenue Statement of Practice 7/84.)

As to the use of sub-fund settlement elections for CGT purposes, see **8.26**.

Other UK court jurisdictions

8.25   VTA 1958 has become so predominantly used in any application for the court's sanction that other sources of the court's jurisdiction need be mentioned only briefly, including the following:

- the court's inherent jurisdiction, where a compromise of rights in a genuine dispute is sought;

- Trustee Act 1925, s 53, enabling the court to appoint a person to convey property belonging to an infant who is beneficially entitled to the income or capital of trust assets;

- Trustee Act 1925, s 57, for issues relating to management or administration of trust property;

- Settled Land Act 1925, s 64, authorising any transactions affecting or concerning settled land (note, however, the gradual phasing out of the Settled Land Act introduced by the Trusts of Land and Appointment of Trustees Act 1996). For a recent example, see *Sutton v Southgate* [2011] WTLR 1235;

- matrimonial jurisdiction, including maintenance of and financial provision for either party to a marriage and children in cases of divorce, etc (Matrimonial Causes Act 1973, s 24). The application of Married Women's Property Act 1882, s 17 may be preferable to modern matrimonial legislation, because being merely *declaratory* it cannot involve a CGT disposal, whereas orders under modern legislation may do so; transferring and settling property and varying matrimonial settlements; and title to or possession of property between husband and wife.

The jurisdiction of the court can often be of invaluable assistance to beneficiaries and trustees, particularly in the case of settlements created before our present tax structure was envisaged, and to counteract the increasing injustice of retrospective legislation.

Sub-funding

8.26   Many older trusts now have separate funds for each branch of the family, perhaps supervised by separate trustees. However, the funds remain one trust for CGT purposes. To address this, professional organisations encouraged the introduction of sub-funding rules to allow each sub-trust to be treated on its own.

Sadly, when these rules became law in the form of TCGA 1992, Sch 4ZA, the condition of availability was that the operation be deemed to be a disposal of the assets at the time of sub-funding: see para 20. This robs the scheme of any attraction to most trustees, so many will, and do, regard the exercise as a total waste of time. That is a pity: a hold-over facility would have made the legislation much more useful, without putting much tax revenue at risk, merely deferring it until there was a sale of the trust assets.

For that reason, Sch 4ZA is not examined further here: see, however, *Capital Gains Tax 2012/13* (Bloomsbury Professional) at 8.17 for a summary of the requirements of the legislation.

Perpetuities and accumulations

8.27   Whilst a detailed analysis of general law is outside the scope of this book, it is important to note that the rules (in England and Wales) regarding perpetuities and excessive accumulations were amended for new trusts by the Perpetuities and Accumulations Act 2009 ('PAA 2009'), which came into effect on 6 April 2010.

The rule against perpetuities, which dates back to the late seventeenth century, prevents property from being tied up indefinitely in trusts (other than charitable ones), by restricting the time within which future interests in property created by the disposition must vest. However, the old rules were technical and complex.

The new rules end the difficulties involved in determining the perpetuity period, by establishing a single perpetuity period of 125 years for all new trusts from the appointed day (PAA 2009, s 5). The change is intended to eliminate the previous uncertainty of calculating perpetuity periods based on the duration of lives in being, and reduce the difficulties for trustees in administering trust property subject to different perpetuity periods. However, the previous 'wait and see' rule can still apply to trusts with successive interests which breach the rule by the possibility of the trust assets becoming vested outside the trust too late (PAA 2009, s 7).

Trustees of existing trusts that use 'lives in being' to determine the perpetuity period may be able to 'opt in' to the new perpetuities rules if it would otherwise cause uncertainty or be impractical to determine whether the period has ended. The perpetuity period in those circumstances is a fixed period of 100 years (PAA 2009, s 12). There is also a specific exclusion from the perpetuities rule for pension schemes.

In addition, PAA 2009 established a single accumulation period of 125 years for all new non-charitable trusts from the appointed day (PAA 2009, s 13), thus abolishing the previous rule against excessive accumulations. Previously, different accumulation periods were possible (under LPA 1925, s 164, and LPA 1964, s 13), the most common in modern trust deeds being 21 years from the date of the settlement. For charitable trusts, two accumulation periods are available, ie either 21 years, or the life of the settlor (PAA 2009, s 14).

This change to the accumulation period is most welcome from the point of view of large family trusts, where the trustees do not wish beneficiaries to receive too much too soon. Hitherto there came a point when, the accumulation period having expired, the trustees were forced to distribute income that they would have preferred to retain. In future they will have greater freedom. This may also give flexibility in managing the tax pool, which can inadvertently be lost where the accumulation period runs out before all the income has been distributed.

As mentioned, these provisions only apply to England and Wales (PAA 2009, s 23). Note that different provisions apply in Scotland and Northern Ireland.

APPENDIX 8.1 – INSTRUCTIONS/AGENDA FOR IHT ESTATE PLANNING

How to use this form

In a client meeting, many matters will be discussed, some of which may be irrelevant to IHT planning. This form is intended as a guide, which will prompt the person taking instructions to ask extra questions which may open up chances to save tax.

Readers may like to save it electronically and remove, from the final version, any prompts or matters that were not discussed before asking the client to confirm approval of the instructions.

CONFIDENTIAL

CLIENT [*Name*]   [*Tel no*]   [*Date*]

A BACKGROUND & ASSETS

A (1) *Composition of family* (Client, Family, Other dependants)

Member/relationship	*Address*	*Date of birth*	*State of health, occupation and other remarks, eg Dom/ND*[2]
		Husband[3]	Wife/Civil partner[3]
A (2) Present assets and approximate value	Details	£	£
Principal residence:			
– jointly owned?			
– as joint tenants or as tenants in common?			
– subject to mortgage?)			
Shares in family company(ies) (% holding)[4]			
Shares in any partnership (% holding)[4]			
Other properties			

Details	Husband[3]	Wife/Civil partner[3]
Agricultural property and assets		
Stock Exchange securities[5]		
Other investments including:		
EIS, SEIS and VCTs[5]		
National savings products[5]		
Insurance policies[5]		
Interests under settlements		
Cash, bank accounts, building Societies, ISA, etc		
Cars, furniture, jewellery		
Miscellaneous[5]		
Other assets[5]		
TOTAL GROSS ESTATE (Approx)		
LESS: liabilities		
LESS: Mortgages		
LESS: Other loans/debts		
TOTAL approx NET ESTATE		
RELIEFS (see separate calculation prepared after meeting)		
LIFETIME GIFTS (see B below)		
IHT on NET ESTATE		
Estate rate %		
Tax to find		

A (3)   Details of income (£) husband

Earned:

Unearned:

Future alterations, pensions, etc

[Query: surplus for saving, normal expenditure exemption –

please provide copy of latest tax returns for….]

Appendix 8.1

Details of income (£) wife/civil partner

Earned:

Unearned:

Future alterations, pensions, etc

[Query: surplus for saving, normal expenditure exemption –

please provide copy of latest tax returns for....]

A (4)   Expectations: husband

Approximate details/valuations re:

Inheritance(s)

Interests under trusts[5]

(NB Reversions are generally excluded property)

Expectations: wife/civil partner

Approximate details/valuations re:

Inheritance(s)

Interests under trusts[5]

(NB Reversions are generally excluded property)

Notes:
1.   Cross references to relevant parts of book are given in brackets.
2.   Give details, as relevant for example whether married, within a registered civil partnership, single, engaged, names and ages of any children of the family member. If any individual not domiciled or resident in UK, note as ND and/or NR in column.
3.   NB s 161 on related property.
4.   Please indicate rate of likely IHT business property relief and provide latest accounts and, as relevant, Memorandum and Articles of Association.
5.   Give details/separate inventories/copies.
6.   NB Only one year carry forward, ie £3,000 may drop out after 5 April in a particular year. Action?

7.   But beware of the related property rule in s 161(2)(b)(i).

8.   Consider whether any estate assets may be subject to the pre-owned assets income tax charge (see **Chapter 13**).

B WILLS

- B (1) Is inter-spouse exemption to apply (see **Chapter 6**)? If so:

   (a)   Is the nil rate band (NRB) transferable?

   (b)   Is it desired that the NRB be transferred?

   (c)   Is the NRB to be used for the present children, leaving the surviving spouse free to remarry and dispose of his or her remaining assets?

   (d)   Gift to spouse of principal residence and contents?

   (e)   As to other specific gifts in particular consider gifting business/ agricultural assets to chargeable parties, eg into a relevant property trust;

   (f)   As to legacy of £ ...;

   (g)   As to ...% of residue (but advise on double-grossing)

   (h)   Are the *commorientes* provisions to apply? (**5.1**)

   (i)   Consider whether free of tax legacies are advisable (ss 36–42) especially where part of residue to a non-exempt party but advise on grossing-up complications (**4.39**);

   (j)   Application of s 142 – deed of variation etc? – but because of possible introduction of anti-avoidance legislation consider use of disclaimers as less likely to be attacked. NB also the flexibility of immediate post-death interest wills (**4.14**).

- B (2) Will of the other spouse/civil partner

   (a)   If widowed or the survivor of a civil partnership, is there a transferable nil rate band available?

   (b)   If so, what evidence is currently available to support the transfer claim when the time comes?

   (c)   If the transferable band is restricted, how much is left?

- B (3) Instructions for will

Complete separate instruction sheet.

Reduced (36%) IHT rate (charitable legacies within Sch 1A)

(i)   Does the testator wish to leave part of his estate to charity?

(ii)   Is it intended that the estate should qualify for the lower rate of IHT?

(iii)   If so, ensure that the will is worded so that the charitable legacy satisfies the conditions in Sch 1A (see sample wording at IHTM45008).

• B (4) Any existing wills for individual/spouse

Location of originals; their terms; proposals for destruction.

Appropriate use of the nil rate bands of both husband and wife (or civil partners)

(i)   Valuation: note related property rule in (s 161); but otherwise treated as separate individuals (**1.24**).

(ii)   Use the cash-flow advantage of inter-spouse exemption (**6.13**) for survivor especially if younger to make PETs (with new CGT base value; see (4)).

(iii)   Consider assets to be transferred, the principal residence and method of ownership (see also **F** below).

(iv)   CGT: no taxable disposal involved under TCGA 1992, s 62 on death. Contrast the restricted lifetime hold-over under TCGA 1992, ss 165 and 260; merely a deferment.

C GIFTS

The art of giving (**Chapter 11**)

List all previous gifts, noting if any more than seven years previously might be tainted by reservation of benefit. Prepare a cumulative total of chargeable lifetime gifts.

C (1) Attitude and practicality motives; availability of assets and funds.

C (2) Identity of donee(s), order of gifts (**11.9**).

C (3) Identity of assets. Business/agricultural property at 100%/50% discount.

Likelihood of appreciation. Any part to be retained or carved out, for example lease (**11.21**).

C (4) PETs or lifetime chargeable transfers? Watch 14-year cumulation (**1.13**), payment of lifetime IHT by donor (gross up), or donee? Cover liability of personal representatives by indemnity.

C (5) Utilising available exemptions and reliefs (**11.1**). For example:

–   Seven-year cumulation – available instalments (ten years)

–   Business/agricultural property

- – Inter-spouse
- – £3,000 pa[1]
- – £250 pa per donee
- – Normal income expenditure
- – Nil rate band
- – Wedding/civil partnership gifts
- – Excluded property
- – Charities/political parties
- – Works of art, etc*

(and see **I** below)

C (6) Substituting sales for gifts (**11.49**).

C (7) Channelling through the poorer spouse (**6.16**).

C (8) Consider applying the various exemptions and reliefs (see **Chapter 12**).

C (9) Possible use of loans: NB make repayable on demand (**11.53**).

C (10) Exchanging assets between donor (or spouse) and donee **11.51**).

C (11) CGT implications; restricted hold-over relief in lifetime, new base value on death.

C (12) Political climate: likelihood of a change in the generous IHT regime eg PETs; BPR; APR; variations.

Note:

1. NB Only one year carry forward, ie £3,000 may drop out after 5 April in a particular tax year. Action?

D   SETTLEMENTS: Creation

D (1) Fiscal motives: basic trust planning

(a)   Settlor's intentions

IHT life vs death rates

Contrast CGT – death exemption TCGA 1992, ss 62 and 63. Held over gains may revive on death (s 74). Hold-over relief for gifts (if available) or CGT if relief not available. CGT at 18% or 28% for individuals and 28% for trusts.

Query – A trust at all?

(b) Timing

IHT at low cumulative amount.

Channelling husband to wife or vice versa.

IHT and CGT appreciating assets eg insurances, new business.

(c) Choosing/marshalling assets

Business/agricultural property: CGT creation TCGA 1992, s 19 connected: restricted losses.

Sterile assets: IHT and CGT.

Splintering: IHT and CGT valuations.

Creation.

CGT hold-over.

(d) Family company ITTOIA 2005, s 633 *et seq* regarding capital sums; beware in particular s 634 (loans).

Waivers.

Different classes of shares.

(e) CGT entrepreneurs' relief (if applicable) or EIS relief.

(f) Stamp duties: voluntary dispositions generally exempt; but beware taking over liabilities, eg Stamp Act 1891, s 57, but note SP 6/90; and also gift with reservation for IHT.

(g) Settlor's will interrelation with: will trusts.

(h) UK trustees remaining liable.

Overseas trusts: postponement of CGT on beneficiaries, TCGA 1992, s 87 onwards. *But* having regard to TCGA 1992, ss 80–98 it is unlikely to be beneficial for a UK resident and domiciled individual to set up a non-resident trust unless no substantial gains then exist, eg on death.

(i) A nasty trap! If settlor arranges for the trustees to pay his CGT, HMRC may seek to invoke the anti-avoidance income tax provisions of ITTOIA 2005, s 633 onwards, ie trusts may be ineffective for income tax purposes. Particularly if the arrangement is covered by express terms.

D (2) Choice of appropriate type (see generally **Chapter 7**), for example:

– Interest in possession, for trust purposes and for CGT, but treated as a relevant property trust for IHT if created in lifetime except for disabled, etc (ss 49, 49A–49E, 50)

- Reverter to settlor (s 54)
- Inter-spouse (s 18)
- Superannuation (s 151)
- Relevant property trusts (ss 58–85)
- Employee trusts (ss 13, 72, 75, 86)
- Life assurance MWP and other trusts
- Protective trusts (s 88)
- Inheritance trust (see **14.30** onwards)
- Charitable trusts (ss 23, 70)[1]
- Disposition for maintenance of family (s 11) (but note limitation arising from *Phizackerley*)
- Overseas trusts (ss 48(3), 267(3), 271A)
- Reversionary interests (ss 48(1)–(3); 55)

D (3) Details for preparing deed:

(a) Settlor:

Name: [...........................]

Occupation [...........................]

Address [...........................]

AML procedures complied with? [ ]

(b) Type of trust

eg interest in possession;

discretionary trust.

(c) Trustees:

Names [...........................] Occupation [...........................]

Addresses [...........................]

AML procedures complied with? [...........................]

For IHT normally no basic objection in settlor or spouse being trustees but consider having at least one independent (eg professional) trustee, possibly as the first named.

Separate trustees for separate assets?

Power of appointment of new trustees, and investment decisions: such powers can be vested in settlor and if wished on death in surviving spouse and/or legal personal representatives.

Voting: unanimous/or by majority (suggest latter)

(d) Protector:

to be appointed: YES/NO

AML procedures complied with? [..........................]

NB in context of IHT business relief – ie control (*IRC v Barclays Bank Ltd* [1961] AC 509, HL) eg for quoted shares; and the 50% discount for assets used by company and see *Walker v IRC* [2001] STC (SCD) 86 – a casting vote can give control (see **15.34**).

Note:

1. Beware of the related property rule in s 161(2)(b)(i), although see *Arkwright and another (Personal Representatives of Williams, deceased) v IRC* [2004] STC 1323.

(e) Beneficiaries:

Names [..........................] Addresses [..........................]

Class:

Relationship to settlor:

Date of birth:

Power to add additional beneficiaries: YES/NO

Settlor's widow OK for IT but NB IHT

Ultimate default beneficiary (unconditional)

AML procedures complied with? [..........................]

(f) Vesting provisions

Entitlement to:	At age	Irrevocable	Revocable	Gift in default	Other provisions
Income Capital					

NB s 58 *et seq* if applicable

(g) Trust fund to consist of:

Assets   Approx Value
                                                      £

Specify form of assets (eg shares, land) and approximate worth

Memo of addition

Future proposals

Bank accounts

(h)   Full investment powers

(i)   Trustees' indemnity

(j)   Trustees' charging clause

(k)   Exclusion of settlor and spouse.

        Unconditional gift over in default.

(l)   Irrevocability

(m) Trustees' additional powers – and see: Trustee Act 2000, STEP
        Standard Provisions (2nd edn)

        For example:

        –   Vary instruments

        –   Insure, eg gift protection, education etc

        –   Maintenance/advancement

        –   Improve/repair

        –   Accumulation

        –   Wide powers of delegation

        –   Borrow

        –   Lend money to anyone

        –   Act by majority

        –   Appropriation *in specie*

        –   Trade/carry on business

        –   Permit beneficiaries to reside in/use trust assets

        –   Appoint protector (especially if overseas trust)

        –   Administer abroad and appoint foreign trustees

        –   Exclude settlor and settlor's spouse

        –   Other powers: eg consider application of Trustee Act 2000

Notes:

1. Consider adopting the STEP Standard Provisions (2nd edn): saves much length in the document and errors of drafting. See (o) below.

2. Trustee exemption clauses: consider STEP guidelines on notification to settlor? Does he/she fully understand and approve the proposed limitations on the liability of trustees?

    (n) Trusts of Land and Appointment of Trustees Act 1996. Consider excluding or limiting certain provisions, eg consultation with beneficiaries (s 11(11)); appointment and retirement of trustees at instance of beneficiaries (ss 19 and 20 apply to any trusts).

    (o) As to administrative provisions consider including a clause 'The standard provisions *(and all of the Special Provisions)* of the Society of Trusts and Estate Practitioners (2nd edn) shall apply' (see James Kessler QC & Leon Sartin, *Drafting Trusts and Will Trusts*, 11th edn, Sweet & Maxwell).

        Note carefully the provisions referred to in italics.

    (p) Special factors/requirements.

    (q) Transfer document, eg share transfer. Consider pre-emption provisions in Company's Articles of Association. Are waivers necessary?

    (r) CGT hold-over election. Eligible? Desirable?

    (s) Exporting requirements?

    (t) Timing.

    (u) Notices? s 218 (**17.38**)

    (v) Review dates

    (w) Letters of wishes or (preferably) trustees' memorandum of wishes. Consider whether or not to inform beneficiaries

    (x) 'Operator's Manual': will there be any professional trustees or will the family run the trust? If family, do they need a guidance document setting out the main powers, important dates etc?

D (4) Check points and traps

    (a) Gift protection term insurance by trustees/beneficiaries against settlor's death within seven years of disposition; or taken out by settlor on trust (**14.19**).

    (b) Family company share settled; beware capital sums received by settlor or spouse directly or indirectly from settlement (ITTOIA 2005, s 633).

(c) Creation of settlement – may be able to hold over the gain for CGT (NB restrictions TCGA 1992, ss 165, 260 and 169B–169C), ditto on termination; death is exempt (but beware s 74).

Notes:

   (i) Advantage of a cash settlement no gain on 'cash' disposal;

   (ii) Settlor and trustees are 'connected persons' therefore a loss accruing on such disposal will only be allowed against a gain on a further disposal by the settlor to the same trustees (TCGA 1992, s 18(3)).

(d) Stamp duties generally exempt on voluntary dispositions and see **D**(1)(f) above.

(e) Perpetuity period. Note the 125-year perpetuity period in the Perpetuities and Accumulations Act 2009, from 6 April 2010 (see **8.27**).

Accumulation periods: Set out in Law of Property Act 1925, ss 164 and 165 and Perpetuity and Accumulations Act 1964; but generally amended to 125 years by the Perpetuities and Accumulations Act 2009 (see **8.27**).

For overseas settlements, check on local rules re perpetuity period.

(f) Are settlor and spouse excluded fully from benefiting? – income tax, CGT; exclusion of settlor for IHT but not necessarily spouse.

(g) Informal letter of wishes by settlor to discretionary or other trustees or memorandum by trustees.

(h) Administration and keeping of records: trustees to hold regular, eg quarterly, meetings; keep minute book; arrangements for termination or variation of any settlement.

(i) Settlor can remain liable for IHT where foreign resident trustees are appointed (s 201(1)(d)).

(j) Consider effect on settlor's will.

E   SETTLEMENTS: Termination/Variation

E (1) Variation with consent (**8.11**) including:

– Division, partition

– Enlargement by purchase

– Release or surrender by life tenant to remainderman

– Release or surrender by remainderman

- Enlargement by gift: remainderman to life tenant
- Disclaimer of life interest
- Advancement by way of settlement upon new trusts if for benefit of beneficiary(ies) – see *Pilkington v IRC* [1962] 3 All ER 622, HL and Trustee Act 1925, s 32 extended to 100%

    NB

    (i)   Use of IHT life rates.

    (ii)   Remainderman should take appreciating assets.

    (iii) Termination of life interest – CGT hold-over relief position.

    (iv)   Time limit for creating TSIs (under s 49C) expired on 5 October 2008.

E (2) Variation by application to court (**8.21–8.23**), for example under Variation of Trusts Act 1958.

F MAIN RESIDENCE (Chapter 6)

F (1) Consider a joint holding between husband and wife.

NB advantage of 'tenancy in common' over 'joint tenancy' (eg joint tenancy cannot be disclaimed but can be varied), especially where surviving spouse has a mere licence to occupy: avoid right to occupy ie interest in possession.

F (2) Is severance of a joint tenancy appropriate?

F (3) Details of any mortgages – obtain their consent if transfer will be subject to mortgage. Consider possible stamp duty land tax implications.

F (4) Consider a flexible life interest (eg 2nd etc marriages).

F (5) If deceased owns the property, consider a discretionary trust in which the surviving spouse is a potential beneficiary (following *Judge and another (personal representatives of Walden, dec'd) v HMRC* [2005] SpC 506).

F (6) Consider relevant property trust in house or part, up to value of nil rate band for initial two-year period, with rent paid to prevent charge that it is not a discretionary trust, followed by life interest (for CGT), but which is treated as a relevant property trust for IHT; so main residence relief available but no IHT charge on death of life tenant, only ten-year charge.

G BUSINESS INTERESTS (ss 103–114)

NB Business relief: 100% for interest in a business or partnership; 100% for unquoted shares; 50% for property used in company controlled by transferor or a partnership in which he is a partner.

G (1) Shares in [main/family company] Ltd and any other companies (**9.2**).

(a) Consider re-allocation between members of the family etc; but bear in mind CGT rules counteracting division of assets on disposals to connected persons (TCGA 1992, s 19);

(b) Method: for example, gift or sale, subscription, transfer or renunciation bonus issue;

(c) Gift or sale method (see **C.6** above); but beware of clawback of business relief (**15.5**);

(d) Waivers of dividends/remuneration (ss 14, 15) (**9.12** and **9.13**):

(e) Hiving-off to new business (**9.5**);

(f) Freezing operations – bonus issue of deferred ordinary shares; re-organising share capital (**9.6**); keep preference shares with income, give away ordinary shares with high capital value;

(g) Splitting ie separating trading functions (**9.10**);

(h) Watering down operations, for example commercial rights issues (**9.11**);

(i) Takeover: amalgamation, merger; using a financial institution; flotation (**9.22**);

(j) Protection by:

service/consultancy agreement on commercial terms as step one before gift of shares to avoid reservation of benefit; pension arrangements and pension schemes (**9.25–9.28**)

pre-emption provisions in Articles of Association (**9.29**).

(k) Company purchasing own shares (Companies Act 2006, Pt 18, Ch 4 and CTA 2010, s 1033).

Critical review of availability of BPR: has the trade changed over the years? Is this still a trading company, or has it drifted into investment, for example holding let property? Can the tide be turned? Can the investment assets be separated from the trading ones? Could the investments themselves be considered to constitute a business?

G (2) Partnership interests (**10.2** *et seq*)

NB: availability of BPR – beware binding contracts for sale (see **15.86**). Consider using options instead.

(a) Test of reciprocity;

(b) Transfer of interests – *A-G v Boden* [1912] 1 KB 539 (see **10.14**). Beware problems with lifetime disposals; *Rosser v IRC* [2003] STC (SCD) 311 (see **15.66**);

(c) Treatment of goodwill – writing it out;

(d) Gifts especially of land – carve-out: do not re-acquire interest. *Contrast Munro v Stamp Duties Comr* [1934] AC 61 with *Chick v Stamp Duties Comr* [1958] 2 All ER 623;

(e) Re-allocation 'juggling': capital v income rights – watch reservation;

(f) Incorporating a partnership;

(g) Using a limited partnership; or a limited liability partnership under the Limited Liability Partnerships Act 2000;

(h) Reverting to employee status;

(i) Adapting 1(c), (e) and (g) above;

(j) Protection by:

Consultancy

Pension payments by continuing partners

Payments to a registered pension scheme

Life assurance arrangements.

H INSURANCE (Chapter 14)

H (1) MWPA and trust policies, for example as part of normal income expenditure, £3,000 per annum, marriage, etc exemption – use where skipping a generation.

H (2) Joint survivor life policies. Likewise using the relevant exemptions – use where deferring IHT until survivor's death.

H (3) Life of another policies. Check existence of insurable interest.

H (4) Term insurance, for example to cover the seven-year gift period for PETs; seven-year cumulation cut-off problems; and acquisition of foreign domicile s 267.

H (5) Education policies, for example by parents under s 11.

H (6) Modern inheritance trusts, to alleviate the IHT problem while retaining an income.

H (7) Pensions, etc for directors and partners (see I(1)(j) above).

H (8) Quotations to be obtained: From:............... By:....................

I OTHER IHT PLANNING ASPECTS

I (1) Disposition for maintenance of family (s 11) (**12.14**).

I (2) Relief for business agricultural property (ss 103–114; 115–124) (**Chapter 15**).

I (3) Relief for woodlands but aim for 100% business and agricultural property relief (ss 125–130) (**16.1** onwards).

I (4) Works of art, etc (ss 125–130) (**16.12** onwards).

I (5) Gifts for national purposes (s 25) (**12.22**).

I (6) Instalment payment basis (ss 227–229) (**2.28**).

I (7) Quoted securities, etc sold within 12 months of death (ss 178–189) (**2.35**).

I (8) Transfers within seven years before death (ss 131–140) (**2.34**).

I (9) Falls in value of land four years after death (ss 190–198) (**2.37**).

I (10) Sales of related property within three years of a death (s 176) (**2.40**).

I (11) Exempt government securities (ss 6(2), 48(4)) and certain other exempt investments (ss 6(1A) and 48(3A)) (**17.27**).

I (12) Foreign domicile (ss 6(1) and 267) (**Chapter 17**):

    (a)   procedure for acquiring, including intention, choice of country

    (b)   re-allocation of assets abroad

    (c)   no exchange control but other procedural matters

I (13) Electing out of pre-owned assets income tax (see **Chapter 13**) and into gifts with reservation?

I (14) Other matters:

J FURTHER ACTION

ACTION:

BY:

STEPS:

TIMETABLE

Complete the record of lifetime gifts and ensure that all further gifts, whether PETs or chargeable are regularly reviewed and recorded there.

Chapter 9

Business interests – companies

INTRODUCTION

9.1   This chapter is primarily concerned with unquoted, family controlled, close companies, and suggests ways of dealing with the threat of IHT in respect of lifetime transfers, and dispositions on the death of the principal shareholders. The main asset of an individual often consists of substantial or majority holdings of shares in such a company. In many family businesses the value of these shares can be a considerable embarrassment because, although the shares may well have a high face value, the holder reaps little if any benefit from this illiquid asset. The policy adopted was for a long time against declaring dividends, though they have become more popular recently to mitigate the burden of NICs; and the sale of the shares is unlikely if it is wished to retain the business in the family.

Directors often have loan accounts. These should not be forgotten when calculating the estate on death. Such credit balances with the company attract no business property relief.

Occasionally, and perhaps more frequently in a recession than at other times, directors give guarantees to support company debt. It is commonly believed that the amount of any guarantee is deductible from the estate on death, but that is not necessarily so: the true test is whether the guarantee was about to be called upon; and whether, if called in, the director would have been unable to secure reimbursement in full from the company.

If no adequate estate planning is undertaken, the result may well entail the break-up of the company or the sale of its shares on the death of the individual, for financial reasons. Moreover, break-up or sale may well be at an inopportune time, therefore detrimental not only to the individual's estate but also to the company, its other members, directors and employees. The need to gauge the impact of IHT not only on death but also on lifetime transfers highlights the difficulties involved in passing down a business from one generation to another in circumstances where there are valuable illiquid assets but not a great deal of available cash in the hands of individuals.

Nevertheless, it must be said that historically the trend of the IHT legislation has made the task considerably easier, notably under the PET regime, and then through the increase of business (and agricultural) relief to 100% and 50% (from 50% and 30%) from 10 March 1992, followed by the removal of the requirement that in excess of 25% be held in order to qualify for 'full' relief post-5 April 1996. How long will this benign approach survive? That is something about which all advisers will speculate. It may be wise to 'lock into' reliefs while they still exist.

This chapter outlines some of the main aspects of estate planning for these companies, namely:

- IHT planning for directors and shareholders;

- recipients of re-allocated shares, including gifts to members of a family and others; disposal by way of takeover or merger; and sale to financial institutions and the public by way of flotation;

- protection for the individual divesting shareholder.

In the case of gifts of business and agricultural assets where business or agricultural relief is involved, there can be some nasty clawback of relief where assets are disposed of and in trust where changes have occurred: see **15.5**.

As mentioned elsewhere in this chapter, arrangements involving shares can have tax implications extending beyond IHT, most notably for income tax (eg employment-related securities, or the 'settlements' anti-avoidance provisions) and capital gains tax purposes (eg value shifting). A detailed consideration of other taxes is outside the scope of this book, which is primarily concerned with IHT planning issues. Nevertheless, it should be emphasised that planning involving interests in companies (and tax planning in general) should take account of all taxes and duties, in addition to legal and commercial implications.

IHT PLANNING FOR DIRECTORS AND SHAREHOLDERS

9.2   Set out below are some of the possible methods which may overcome the obstacles and difficulties referred to above. The reader's attention is also directed to the wider issues in other chapters, including the art of giving (**Chapter 11**), insurance aspects (**Chapter 14**), special classes of assets including business and agricultural property relief (**Chapter 15**), and emigration (**Chapter 17**).

Whenever a particular estate planning method is under consideration, careful attention must be directed to the anti-avoidance provisions outlined at **1.9** and **1.20** onwards, particularly as regards:

- associated operations (s 268);
- connected persons (s 270);
- restriction on freedom to dispose (s 163);
- related property (s 161);
- tax charges in respect of future payments (s 262); and
- the close company transfer provisions (ss 94–102).

In cases involving business and agricultural property relief, the traps which can trigger a clawback of the relief should be borne in mind. The *Ramsay* approach to statutory construction, as explained by the House of Lords in *MacNiven v Westmoreland* [2001] STC 237 and considered in subsequent cases including *CIR v Scottish Provident Institution* [2005] STC 15, *Barclays Mercantile Finance Ltd v Mawson* [2005] STC 1 and *Revenue & Customs v Mayes* [2011] EWCA Civ 407, must also be taken into account.

It is also important to keep capital gains tax issues in mind, such as to beware transfers into 'settlor-interested' trusts for which hold-over relief is prevented (TCGA 1992, s 169B).

Sales versus gifts

9.3   Assets such as shares of a private company may be particularly suitable for making gifts either outright or into trust, first, if 100% business property relief is available for IHT, and secondly having regard to the possibility of CGT hold-over relief.

It has become possible to seek clearance that shares in a company will qualify for business property relief (www.hmrc.gov.uk/cap/clearanceiht.htm), though only in certain situations. The clearance is not available in respect of PETs because it is time-limited, and the chargeability of a PET may not be tested for seven years. In addition, the clearance is available only in cases of 'material uncertainty', so it is for the adviser to do his or her homework first and, if the legislation or published guidance is clear, to rely on that rather than to seek clearance. Finally, the purpose of the clearance is to facilitate commercial transactions, not to protect advisers from negligence claims, so a good commercial reason for the transaction must be shown (ie that the doubt about tax might frustrate action that would otherwise be beneficial commercially).

Capital gains on disposals by way of gift of family trading company shares fall into the small group of gains which can be held over under the restrictive provisions of TCGA 1992, s 165, although s 260 contains no such asset restrictions. The CGT relief in TCGA 1992, s 165 covers shares and securities in a 'trading company' or the holding company of a 'trading group' (as defined by TCGA 1992, s 165A), where:

- the shares or securities are not quoted on a recognised stock exchange; or

- (assuming the donor is an individual) the company concerned is his 'personal company' (ie at least 5% of the voting rights are held by the donor); or

- there is a non-arm's length disposal for CGT by trustees of a settlement of shares or securities in a trading company or of a holding company of a trading group, where the shares are not listed on a recognised stock exchange or the trustees at that date controlled at least 25% of the voting rights (TCGA 1992, Sch 7, para 2(2)(b)); and

- applies in any other case where business or agricultural property relief (even at the 100% rate) is available (TCGA 1992, s 260). However, remember the restriction in hold-over relief for transfers to settlor-interested trusts.

The donee might subsequently place such shares (or some of them) by lifetime chargeable transfers such as into a relevant property trust, with CGT hold-over relief being available without restriction because an IHT lifetime chargeable transfer is involved (unless the trust is settlor-interested) at low minority value. Beware, however, of the minimum period of ownership requirements applicable for business property relief. Note that HMRC accept that a gift qualifying for 100% business/agricultural relief (and hence of zero value for IHT) is still a chargeable transfer for TCGA 1992, s 260 hold-over relief purposes (CG67041).

Note also that the mere fact that a donor may benefit from a trust that he sets up does not, as might be thought, reduce the value transferred. Thus even though the reservation of a benefit has the effect that, on the death of the donor, the asset will be treated as still in his estate, that is not taken into account by HMRC in valuing the transfer into trust in the first place. Be sure that business property relief is available before entering into the settlement.

In the context of family companies (particularly involving husband and wife), care should be taken to ensure that the receipt of dividends does not inadvertently trigger the settlement provisions. For example, contrast *Young v Pearce; Young v Scrutton* [1996] STC 743 and *Buck v Revenue and Customs Commissioners* [2008] SpC 716 with the case of *Jones v Garnett (Inspector of Taxes)* [2007] UKHL 35. The latter case was decided by the House of Lords in the taxpayer's favour. At the time of writing, HMRC's intended introduction of legislation to counter what it considers to be the undesirable effects of that decision ('income shifting') has been postponed.

If the donor (or his wife) is receiving or continues to receive remuneration or pension benefits from the company, that may constitute the reservation of a benefit out of the gift. Nevertheless, it is unlikely that HMRC will take this view if a service agreement is taken out as a preliminary step and if it is reasonable in providing fixed terms for remuneration (albeit index-linked) and commission on a commercial basis, and similarly with pension provision, and is not open ended.

A further safeguard would be to conclude this service agreement well before the gift of the shares, so that it can be argued that there is no reservation of benefit because the benefit, if any, from the service arrangements has been carved out prior to the gift. HMRC accept that the continuation of existing reasonable commercial arrangements in the form of remuneration and benefits for the donor's services entered into before a gift does not amount to a reservation, provided the benefits are in no way connected to the gift (see IHTM14337).

Reservation is not generally a problem for IHT if 100% business property relief is available *and* maintained (in this context note that 100% business property relief may not always be available), but there are specific circumstances where reservation can be fatal. Consider, for example, where the relief is at 50% on an asset used by a company controlled by the transferor: if the asset passes to a minority shareholder and clawback is in issue, the donee cannot satisfy the requirements of the relief (FA 1986, Sch 20, para 8(1A)(b)). Such a lifetime disposal can also be disadvantageous for CGT, as it sacrifices the market value uplift on death.

There may still occasionally be circumstances when it is desirable to substitute an arm's-length sale and purchase arrangement for a gift. Although potentially triggering a charge to CGT, full entrepreneurs' relief (if available) gives rise to a CGT rate of only 10% on up to £10 million of chargeable gains.

A useful formula may be to agree to a sale of a parcel of shares at such value as shall be agreed by HMRC. This may then overcome the problem occasioned by the 'consequential loss' formula in s 3(1), the arm's-length requirement of s 10 and the 'related property' rule of s 161. There are three hurdles to be overcome to take a sale of such shares outside the IHT provisions of s 3(1) and take advantage of s 10:

- no gratuitous intent in favour of *anyone*;

- the sale is at arm's length on such terms as might be expected to be made in a transaction at arm's length between persons not connected with each other;

- at a price freely negotiated at the time of sale or at a price such as might be expected to have been freely negotiated at the time of sale.

HMRC may try to apply a 'double-standard'. For example, in a transaction between father and son for the 'sale' of a parcel of family company shares, notwithstanding that the value of the shares has been independently valued, HMRC may argue that the father would not have agreed to that transfer on those terms to a stranger.

It was suggested (as far back as 1975) that the sale of part of the controlling holding of a private company's shares just sufficient to deprive the vendor of control would not be an arm's-length transaction within the meaning of what is now s 10. This goes too far because an independent valuation should by definition take into account all available hypothetical purchasers deemed to be in the open market. The key question is how much the vendor would not only want but could expect to get for that parcel of shares if he were selling to a total stranger.

Clearly, the main aim of this type of sale is to enable the estate owner to straddle the point at which the holding is turned from a controlling interest to a minority interest, ie to cross the 50% voting level; the owner will still be entitled (subject to satisfying the conditions) to 100% business property relief if his shares are in an eligible unquoted or AIM company. For IHT purposes, such a transfer would reflect the loss of control, but if one is concerned with an arm's length sale price, one could try to argue that one should look at the percentage holding transferred without reference to the diminution in the transferor's estate.

It would be necessary to watch the anti-fragmentation CGT principles of TCGA 1992, s 19, whereby two or more disposals to connected persons within six years may be added together for valuation purposes.

It might be appropriate as a first step to sell a sufficient number of shares to an independent party, such as a financial institution, just enough to lose control. Thereafter the estate owner could be in a position to transfer minority holdings to members of his family at a minority valuation. This proposal has two serious reservations. First, because s 10 refers to conferring a gratuitous benefit 'on any person' (ie the arrangement could be caught as an indirect gift to such member of the family); and secondly the arrangement could be attacked as an 'associated operation' under s 268 (see **1.21**).

An alternative whereby the necessary number of shares could be given to a charity or exempt body is also made difficult (s 161(2)(b)): these shares remain related property (see also **1.24** and **11.48**). With 100% business property relief, however, such strategies are largely obsolete.

In considering sales versus gifts, there are two other factors to bear in mind:

- the impact of business property relief on a gift (**Chapter 15**); and
- the fact that gains on *sales* of shares involve CGT, whereas gains on *gifts* of unquoted shares in trading companies or shares in family companies (as defined) can generally be held over, unless the transfer is to a settlor-

interested trust. The absence of consequential loss in the transferor's estate for IHT must be weighed against the CGT on sale of the strategic shares at a worthwhile value.

It all comes down to a need to work out the alternatives and an appraisal of factors such as the availability of 100% business property relief and, if not, whether the donor is likely to survive seven years (and the cost of insuring that risk).

Relief for business property (ss 103–114)

9.4   Clearly this relief, at 100% or 50% of the value transferred (depending on the various applicable circumstances), is of fundamental and vital importance in estate planning for the shareholder of the family company. Details of the relief are set out in **Chapter 15**.

One important factor is that the 100% relief for shares in an unquoted trading company, or in a trading company listed on the AIM, applies to all holdings, whatever their size so that the 100% relief is not lost in giving up over 50% voting control.

Hiving-off operations and parallel trading

9.5   Under this method, new developments or operations in a business would be siphoned or channelled to a new business with the existing business remaining static or contracting. IHT planning should therefore receive particular attention on the formation of a business including the expansion of an existing business to new fields. The estate owner might have the controlling or other substantial interest in the existing business and little if any stake in the new business. The valuable contracts and connections might gradually be lost to the existing business and taken up by the new business. The estate would no doubt have 100% business property relief for IHT on the existing company holding.

One could mitigate the CGT position where members of the younger generation take up the shares in the new business at an initial stage, when their value would be unlikely to exceed par value, and then build up their own 100% IHT relief. This idea may indeed be a sound method of handing on a business from an older to a younger generation indirectly, but practical difficulties could arise where the existing business had assets with a substantial value.

Where these practical difficulties do exist, it may be a possibility to undertake a hiving-off operation as to an appropriate part of the business. HMRC could attack the arrangement if there was no adequate commercial basis; if need be in order to preserve commerciality, the operation can be accompanied by a royalty or other fee arrangement. A hiving-off operation of this type will operate more smoothly and be more likely to succeed if an existing business is considering a *new project*, and it is that project that is in fact started off in the new business to be carried on and owned by the younger generation. This is a variant of the principle that estate planning should receive particular attention when a new business is commenced.

Freezing operations, and separate classes of shares

9.6   The aim of these operations is to freeze value in the hands of the owner, or even reduce it over a period, and permit excess value to accrue to other persons (eg the younger generation).

Under the present regime of 100% business property relief (for as long as it lasts) and hold-over relief for capital gains tax, much of what follows in this chapter may be treated as of largely historical interest, the much preferred course at the moment being a simple gift of shares. However, such arrangements may be useful in the context of, for example, family-owned property investment companies. Alternatively, it may be the case that a company initially thought to qualify for BPR in fact does so only in part, on account of the rules as to excepted assets, or fails the 'wholly or mainly' test; in that case, these ideas may be quite helpful.

Besides, time and again the practitioner will be asked to review tax planning effected in the past in the light of the present tax code. In so doing it is often vital to have an appreciation of what the earlier tax planning was trying to achieve, and how.

Freezing operations

9.7   In a 'freezing' operation, the share capital of a company might be divided into, say, two classes where the estate owner (who might otherwise have made a gift or settlement) retains the class (its rights being appropriately reorganised) which absorbs and contains all the *current* value of the company as to both the capital and income rights, without any or with limited growth prospects.

A further new class would be created with little, if any, present value but containing the *future* growth and this new class would normally be allotted in the main to the younger generation or placed into an appropriate settlement, eg a discretionary settlement. Although s 98 aims at charging the 'alteration' or 'extinguishment' of share rights, it is claimed that this freezing operation would not substantially reduce the value of existing shares. Care must however also be taken so as not to offend the capital gains tax 'value shifting' provisions contained in TCGA 1992, s 29.

A more sophisticated freezing operation could involve the formation of a new holding company to acquire all the shares in the existing trading company in which, say, the individual owns all the shares. The individual's children (or their trustees) could subscribe for a modest number of ordinary shares in the holding company at par. The individual would then exchange all his shares in the trading company for, say, preference shares in the holding company. The holding company would then own the trading company as a 100% subsidiary. The preference shares held by the individual could be such that they retained their par value, while the ordinary shares in the holding company, in the hands of the next generation, could reflect in their value all the growth in the underlying trading company.

The question of excluding CGT on the individual's exchange of his shares in the trading company for the new preference shares is, of course, an important factor. Since the operation constitutes an exchange of securities within TCGA 1992, s 135, an advance application for clearance under TCGA 1992, s 138 is important. For income tax purposes, a clearance application in respect of the 'transactions in securities' anti-avoidance rules (ITA 2007, Pt 13, Ch 1) should also be considered (ITA 2007, s 701). In particular, there needs to be a bona fide commercial reason for the transaction.

For IHT purposes, some effort should be made to ensure that the preference shares received fully reflect the market value of the individual's shares in the trading company. In particular, the new holding should carry a dividend level fully in line with current returns. A variant might be to have loan stock instead of preference shares.

It must be said that, while 100% business property relief and hold-over relief for CGT are still available, a simple gift of shares in a trading company or group by the estate owner is much the preferred course in any event.

Dividend waivers

9.8   There are no IHT consequences on a waiver of dividends within a period of 12 months before any right to the dividend has accrued (s 15; see **9.12**); and a policy of waiving dividends may be sound tax planning where some of the shareholders are high taxpayers, while others, such as basic rate taxpayers, are not. A waiver must be by *deed*, as there is no consideration involved.

Some, such as charities and students, may not pay tax at all. The high taxpayers could waive their entitlement to dividends so that more dividends are available to the lower taxpayers. This method should give rise to no CGT charge. However,

HMRC may seek to impose income tax under the 'settlements' anti-avoidance provisions on the waiving shareholders as settlors if other shareholders may benefit as part of an 'arrangement' (such as if the beneficiaries of the 'trust' include minor or unmarried children of these high taxpayers, under ITTOIA 2005, s 629).

Consider also the difficulty where some shares are held by trustees: it will be difficult for them, with a primary duty to maximise their fund, to justify waiving dividends. Specifically, the transfer of shares to a trust in the hope of saving IHT whilst effectively retaining all the income of the company (because there is an understanding that the trustees will regularly waive the dividends on the shares they hold) will not work; that is a reservation of benefit within the expression 'or otherwise' in FA 1986, s 102(1)(b).

Special classes of shares

9.9   The use of separate classes of shares might be considered as opposed to dividend waivers, the low rate taxpayers having shares which entitle them to a high dividend yield. Consideration must, however, be given to the applicability of the value shifting provisions of TCGA 1992, and the employment-related securities provisions of ITEPA 2003, particularly Pt 7, Ch 3B of that Act ('Securities with artificially enhanced market value') and Ch 4 ('Post-acquisition benefits from securities'). If applicable, care must be taken in creating the 'high dividend' shares with the intention of paying them to the low income taxpayers.

A disadvantage of waivers compared with having separate classes of shares (one class being held by, say, trustees) is the fact that waived dividends still produce a dividend history on the shares which could be used by HMRC as support for an increased valuation. Indeed, it might be possible to have a minuted resolution demonstrating an intention on the part of the board and the company never to declare a dividend in respect of the class of shares held by the individuals, in the absence of unforeseen circumstances. Note, however, that long-term waiver of dividends may well give rise to an IHT charge under s 98 and/or a deemed disposal for CGT under the value shifting provisions of TCGA 1992, s 29.

The effect of dividends (and dividend waivers) for valuation purposes must be considered from both a tax and commercial perspective. For example, where there are two classes of shares in issue, one class of, say, preference shares being entitled to all the declared dividend income, the other class of, say, ordinary shares having no entitlement to dividends, this would automatically decrease the value of the latter, without an actual transfer of value. This is, however, subject to the general recommendation that waivers should be undertaken *ad hoc* and not more than one year at a time because a waiver covering several years could constitute a diminution in the individual's estate. In addition, an alteration made to a close company's share (or loan) capital, or rights attaching to them, is treated as a disposition by the participators, whether or not it would normally be treated as such for IHT purposes (s 98(1)). The deemed disposition is specifically prevented from being a PET (s 98(3)), but HMRC accept that any available IHT exemptions may be applied against the resulting transfer of value (IHTM04069).

The existence of onerous contracts and arrangements, for example where the estate owner is the managing director or where pre-exemption provisions are contained in the Articles of Association, might be another method of reducing, containing or restricting the value of an estate owner's shares (but see, in particular, s 163 ('Restriction on freedom to dispose'), the value shifting provision of the CGT legislation, the employment-related securities provisions for income tax purposes, and **1.22**).

Where a controlling shareholder is considering transferring shares but is concerned about losing control, he could (as a first step) arrange to retain a single 'golden share' with rights personal to the holder which would give him overall voting control. Under s 269 ('Control of company'), control is construed as the control of powers of voting on all questions affecting the company as a whole (note under 269(4), where there are other shares with votes limited to the question of winding up, or shares of a specific class with votes only on matters relating to that class, control is determined by powers of voting on all questions except those specific matters). Although the golden share would have a greater value than any of the other shares, its value as only a single share will not be great in real terms, especially if it had no rights (to dividends or on a winding up) other than for voting. It is possible that HMRC might seek to attack such an arrangement on the grounds that the gift of the remaining shares was a gift with reservation. In any event, however, in an era of continuing 100% business property relief, such a single share idea may be regarded as no longer relevant and also an undesirable complication.

On formation of a new company, or at an early stage in its life before share valuation became a concern, the possibility might be considered of having different classes of shares, each class having different rights, say, on voting, dividends, in a winding up. Such different classes might act as an aid in transferring shares down among the family, starting with 'junior' shares and passing through shares with 'medium' rights on to the 'senior' shares as a final step. The question of control of the company at any stage will be determined under s 269. However, as mentioned above, taxes other than IHT should be considered, such as the income tax provisions dealing with employment-related securities.

The valuation of securities in unquoted companies is difficult enough where the rights are simple and conventional. It becomes harder if special rights are included, as was illustrated in the case of *I C McArthur's Executors v HMRC* [2008] SpC 700, reviewed at **15.42**.

Splitting operations

9.10 It may be practical to separate the trading functions among the family. For example, a father might be responsible for the manufacturing side and his two sons dealing respectively with the supply and sale, and the parties could enter into arm's-length restrictive cross-trading agreements. The result of this interdependence should be that each separate branch of the business will have a lower intrinsic value.

Where, for example, a company's business is 'hybrid' in nature, being part trading and part investment, splitting may help to preserve BPR in respect of the company as a whole, provided that the investment business does not predominate.

Watering-down operations

9.11 A favourite former method for reducing CGT and estate duty involved favourable rights issues whereby all the shareholders were issued with provisional allotment letters and the estate owner in question declined to take up his rights, whereas the younger generation eagerly took up theirs.

This proposal looks unattractive initially for IHT, having regard to the provisions of s 3(3) whereby a deliberate omission to act, for example, a failure to take up favourable rights, can constitute a chargeable disposition. However, if the rights issue is commercially viable (and rights issues are usually subject to some discount), the proposal can continue to have practical importance for IHT. Moreover, the estate owner may omit to take up his rights for non-deliberate reasons, for example, lack of funds, absence abroad, etc, but cogent back-up evidence must be available. However, a simple PET gift of original shares is likely to be more straightforward.

Where the estate owner wishes to reduce his holding of ordinary shares but at the same time needs to maintain his income, a proposal on the following lines might be considered. A bonus issue is made on the ordinary shares in the company. The bonus issue consists of fully paid cumulative non-voting preference shares with an ample fixed dividend, but not participating in surplus assets on a return of capital or a winding up. The estate owner might then decide to give away the ordinary shares qualifying for 100% business property relief, but retain the preference shares with their dividend income. On the estate owner's death the preference shares, if still retained, should not have accumulated any further capital value.

As with other strategies mentioned in this chapter, such an arrangement should be considered 'in the round' with other (non-IHT) tax implications in mind.

Waivers of dividends (s 15)

9.12   A person who waives any dividend on shares of a company within 12 months *before* the dividend becomes due does not, by reason of the waiver, make a transfer of value. It is generally accepted by HMRC that the 12-month period ends in the case of a final dividend when it is declared in general meeting and in the case of an interim dividend when it is paid (IHTM04220). This is presumably on the footing that a resolution to pay an interim dividend can be varied or rescinded, and therefore the resolution does not create a debt until the dividend is paid (see HMRC's commentary on company law aspects of dividends at CTM20095, and *Potel v CIR* (1970) 46 TC 658).

For a final dividend declared on 31 December 2012, a waiver would have to have been made within the 12 months beginning 1 January 2012. It appears that HMRC would allow waivers of unascertained dividends and this practice is in line with *Re Gulbenkian's Settlements (No 2), Stephens v Maun* [1970] Ch 408, whereby an individual appears able to disentitle himself from an unascertained right such as a right under a discretionary trust. The waiver must be by deed so as to overcome any contentions by HMRC based on lack of consideration, and also with a view to reducing the force of any HMRC argument that for income tax purposes the right to receive a dividend gives rise to an income tax charge, on the ground that receivability without receipt is nothing.

Beware, however, that a long-term waiver may be considered to fall within the terms of s 98 ('Alteration of rights attaching to shares'). Beware also that HMRC may challenge a dividend waiver as being a transfer of value by associated operations in some circumstances.

Waivers or repayment of remuneration (s 14)

9.13   Such waivers or repayment are similarly exempt from IHT, subject to certain conditions, namely that the remuneration would, apart from the waiver, have been assessed to income tax as employment income (as defined by ITEPA 2003, s 7(2)), and as a result of the waiver or repayment the remuneration will not be treated as a deductible expense for income tax or corporation tax purposes, or is otherwise brought into charge.

For this type of waiver, it is also necessary that the document is in the form of a deed, again to overcome any lack of consideration. There is no time limit on the waiver or repayment (IHTM04210).

In the case of a repayment of remuneration, some HMRC officers might insist upon an income tax liability thereon because there is actual receipt; and so it is better, if possible, to waive future remuneration.

Purchase of own shares by unquoted trading companies (CTA 2010, s 1033)

9.14 Company law generally enables companies, subject to conditions, to purchase their own shares. Prior to Companies Act 2006 being introduced, Companies Act 1985, s 162(1) gave a company the power to purchase its own shares if authorised to do so by its Articles of Association. Companies Act 2006 does not include a requirement in the company's Articles to purchase its own shares, although the members may restrict or prohibit a purchase of own shares through the company's Articles, if they wish.

The redemption or purchase by the company of the shares will not be a taxable distribution (and the shareholder will be liable only tax on a capital gain, if any), provided broadly that:

- the company is an unquoted trading company or in a trading group; and

- *either* the purchase of the shares is for the benefit of the trade (as opposed to tax avoidance (CTA 2010, s 1033(2)) *and* various conditions (in CTA 2010, Pt 23, Ch 3) are complied with (eg the shareholder is UK resident; shares have generally been held for at least five years; and the shareholder's interest in the company is reduced substantially (as defined) as a result of the purchase);

or

- the proceeds from the purchase of the shares are used to settle IHT charged on a death, and are so applied within two years after the death (see below).

In the latter case, CTA 2010, s 1033(3) states that 'the whole or substantially the whole of the payment' (other than any amount applied in paying capital gains tax on the purchase of own shares etc) has to be applied by the person to whom it is made in discharging his liability for IHT charged on a death, and is so applied within the period of two years after the death. It must also be shown that the IHT could not otherwise have been discharged without undue hardship (CTA 2010, s 1033(4)).

There is provision for the company to apply for advance clearance from HMRC (CTA 2010, s 1044).

Concerning the former requirement as to benefiting the trade, useful guidelines where clearance will normally be given are set out in Statement of Practice 2/82, including:

- most cases of a boardroom disagreement;

- an outside shareholder who has provided equity finance and is now withdrawing his investment;

- the proprietor of a company retiring to make way for new management; and

- a shareholder who has died leaving shares in his estate and his personal representatives or the beneficiaries not wishing to keep them. HMRC would normally expect the shareholder's entire interest to be purchased.

These provisions can be useful in cases of illiquid estates, where the main assets constitute shares in a family trading company. Even with the advantage of being able to pay by instalments, the death of a principal shareholder might otherwise necessitate the sale of the company (especially if the company is a property/investment company, such that business property relief is not available) and these provisions may well assist in these circumstances.

The provisions are also useful, for instance, where the shareholder who is disposing can get full CGT entrepreneurs' relief. However, even without this relief, with a top rate of CGT of 28% and a top rate of income tax for 2012–13 of 50% or 42.5% for dividends (reducing to 45% and 37.5% respectively for 2013–14), it will often be better for the shareholder to have the company apply for clearance for a purchase of its own shares (ie clearance that capital treatment applies).

THE RECIPIENTS OF RE-ALLOCATED SHARES

9.15   The shareholder in question, having agreed to reduce his holding, has a wide choice available, as to who should benefit thereby and what action to take. The clawback of business property relief (**15.5**) and the two-year ownership rule (**15.23**) must, of course, both be watched. Possible recipients of re-allocated shares could include the following.

Spouse

9.16   The inter-spouse IHT exemption will normally apply (s 18). To the extent that the spouse exemption does not apply due to the transferee spouse not being domiciled in the UK (see s 18(2)), the transfer of value will be a PET (IHTM11033).

In view of the automatic relief on disposals between spouses living together (TCGA 1992, s 58), any question of obtaining CGT relief would be a matter for the transferee spouse.

Children and issue

9.17 This may give rise to an opportunity for 'skipping a generation'.

Trustees holding

9.18 Discretionary trusts have traditionally been popular, such as in terms of flexibility. However, it is considered unwise to include the donor among the discretionary class, as this will amount to a gift with reservation of benefit, and it is possible that the present very generous business property relief may no longer be available in its existing form at such time as the gift with reservation ceases (on death or otherwise).

The fact that the donor's spouse or civil partner is among the discretionary class of beneficiaries does not, of itself, give rise to a reservation of benefit problem. However, if the enjoyment of a benefit is shared by the donor, the gift with reservation provisions will apply (IHTM14339).

Note also the income tax disadvantages of the trust being settlor-interested (ITTOIA 2005, s 624), and the denial of capital gains tax hold-over relief in those circumstances (TCGA 1992, s 169B), both of which apply if (unlike with the gift with reservation provisions mentioned above) the settlor *or spouse* (*or civil partner*) can benefit.

Moreover, by means of a judicious choice of trustees, an estate owner can in effect safeguard voting control of a company (ie in the knowledge that the trustees will normally vote as the estate owner would have done). Further, there is usually no objection to the estate owner being a trustee.

Employees

9.19 Assets may be settled on trust for the benefit of a company's employees within s 86 ('Trusts for benefit of employees'). Alternatively, the company can make cash contributions to the trust, which could be applied in acquiring shares for appointment to employees, perhaps as part of a share option scheme.

The appropriate IHT exemption while assets are in the trust should apply under s 75 ('Property becoming subject to employee trusts'); and apart from this, an allocation to employees may constitute an arm's-length transaction involving no gratuitous benefit (s 10), or be exempt under the provisions of s 13 ('Dispositions by close companies for benefit of employees'). This provides for exemption when shares (or other assets) are transferred into such an employee's trust. (NB in addition, a transfer of shares by an individual to an employee trust is an exempt transfer if it satisfies the conditions in s 28 ('Employee trusts'); see **7.101**.)

Contributions to employee benefit trusts (EBTs) by a close company may well come under scrutiny from HMRC, in terms of establishing whether an IHT charge arises on the company's participators under s 94. HMRC's view, as stated in HMRC Brief 18/11, is that where a close company makes a transfer of value to an EBT, an IHT charge arises under s 94, unless broadly the disposition is not a transfer of value under ss 10, 12 or 13 and is eligible for relief.

- *No gratuitous benefit (s 10)* – For a disposition to fall within the s 10 exception as not being a transfer of value, HMRC consider that a subjective test and an objective test must both be passed. The subjective test is that there must not be even the slightest possibility of gratuitous intent when the contribution is made. The objective test is broadly that the transaction must either have been made at arm's length between unconnected persons, or have been such as might be expected to be made in a transaction at arm's length between unconnected persons. HMRC consider that 'it will normally be difficult to show that the conditions of s 10 are met'.

- *Allowable for corporation tax purposes (s 12)* – HMRC's view is that the IHT relief in s 12 is only available to the extent that a corporation tax deduction is allowable to the company for the tax year in which the contribution is made. Thus, if a deduction is permanently disallowed (ie under CTA 2009, ss 53, 54) or is deferred (ie by generally accepted accounting practice (UITF32), or is expenditure subject to FA 1989, s 43, or is post 27 November 2002 expenditure subject to CTA 2009, s 1290(2), (3)), s 12 does not apply.

- *Close company dispositions for the benefit of employees (s 13)* – HMRC state that the exclusion from dispositions being transfers of value in s 13 does not apply where (among other things) the contribution is to an EBT which does not satisfy s 86, or the company's participators (and any connected person) are not excluded from benefit under the terms of the EBT (so that s 13(2) applies).

However, HMRC Brief 18/11 points out that business property relief may be due where a transfer of value is attributable to relevant business property, although not if the close company is an investment company.

In addition, HMRC point out that a flat rate exit charge under s 72 can arise in any EBT falling within s 86. Sub-trusts which are not themselves s 86 EBTs fall within the relevant property trust regime, and are liable to ten-year and exit charges.

HMRC operate an 'Employee Benefit Trust (EBT) Settlement Opportunity' to encourage employers and companies who had used EBTs and similar structures to settle tax (including any IHT) and National Insurance contributions without possible litigation by HMRC. Further information is available on HMRC's website (www.hmrc.gov.uk/employers/employee-benefit-trusts.htm), including 'Frequently asked questions' which outline (in section 4) IHT issues in relation to EBTs.

The use of EBTs in tax planning has seemingly been further discouraged through the notoriously complex 'disguised remuneration' provisions for income tax purposes, which were introduced in FA 2011 (ITEPA 2003, Pt 7A 'Employment income provided through third parties'). The general message would appear to be 'caveat planner'.

Charities

9.20   Private (or other) charitable trusts may be a useful method of holding a proportion of the shares of a family company, although this is not a viable method for losing control because the shares of the charity will remain related property with the transferors for five years (s 161(2)).

Financial institutions

9.21   In contrast an allocation to a financial institution or merchant bank may be a useful method of avoiding control as well as finding cash for pending or future IHT liability.

With the increased interest over recent years being shown in fostering small and growing companies, a number of venture capital companies have sprung up, some connected with banks and financial institutions, who are willing to take a stake in suitable circumstances. The proposals tend to vary, some requiring board representation in the company, others (not all of them) naturally looking to their security, in some instances by the creation of preferential stock or shares. These institutions can be useful as a source of support for the company as well as providing funds for suitable expansion. Taking on an institutional partner in this manner can be a first step towards flotation. Although they have varying minimum values for the companies they wish to deal with, all of these institutions are looking for the strong, viable and potentially rewarding company proposition. Once the parties have agreed upon the basic terms, shares are normally purchased from the shareholder(s), thereby providing them with the requisite liquid funds, and further capital may be injected.

The normal activities of the venture capital market are materially boosted by positive incentives from the government:

- The Enterprise Investment Scheme (EIS) has existed for income tax since its introduction by FA 1994, and was extended to capital gains tax by FA 1998 (replacing re-investment relief). Under the Scheme, investors in unquoted trading companies can obtain income tax relief at 30% on investments of up to £1 million (for 2012–13), as well as deferring capital gains (TCGA 1992, Sch 5B). A word of warning, however; the eligibility conditions are tight and extensive. In addition, there is a widely drawn anti-avoidance code. Accordingly great care must be taken if use of the EIS is considered. A full discussion of the scheme is outside the scope of this work but HMRC have published detailed information on its website (www.hmrc.gov.uk/eis/index.htm).

- The Seed Enterprise Investment Scheme (SEIS) was introduced in FA 2012 to incentivise investment in small, early-stage companies (ITA 2007, Pt 5A; TCGA 1992, ss 150E–G, Sch 5BB). SEIS offers investors income tax relief worth 50% of the amount invested on a maximum investment of £100,000, plus capital gains tax (CGT) exemption for gains on shares within the scope of SEIS, and CGT exemption on gains realised from disposals of assets in 2012–13, where the gains are reinvested through the SEIS in the same tax year. Aside from the commercial risks generally inherent in such investments, the legislation is tightly drawn in a similar way to the EIS relief provisions, and great care is therefore needed to avoid the inadvertent restriction or loss of relief. Further information on the SEIS is available on HMRC's website (www.hmrc.gov.uk/seedeis/index.htm).

- A type of investment trust, the Venture Capital Trust (VCT), as a vehicle for investment in unquoted trading companies, with tax benefits (eg income tax relief at 30% on qualifying investments up to £200,000, freedom from income tax on dividends and CGT) for the investor (see ITA 2007, Pt 6, ITTOIA 2005, s 709 and TCGA 1992, s 151A).

Each of these avenues is worth exploring. In addition to the potential income tax and CGT advantages available, some investment 'boutique' firms market EIS investment opportunities in certain 'lower risk' trading activities, with the added incentive of 100% business property relief after two years. Of course, the same tax benefits are potentially available to individual private investors in qualifying owner-managed trading companies, albeit that the commercial risk is not managed in the same way as the marketed EIS opportunities purport.

One other avenue might be explored in relation to a company not qualifying for business property relief where there is a 'friendly' bank, if such still exists. Funds might be raised on the security of the shares, perhaps with repayment deferred for a term that was likely to 'see the donor's time out'. The proceeds could be used to make gifts. If the proceeds of the borrowing could be left with the lender, so that the interest charged was no more than the bank's 'turn' on the money, there could be three benefits:

- A gift might become possible, even where there seemed to be no liquidity with which to make it.

- CGT would not be an issue if the shares themselves were retained.

- There would be an element of 'lock in' because the subject matter of the gift was still held by the bank; so, even without the use of a trust structure, it might be possible to achieve some deferral of enjoyment by the donees of the funds (which is what many donors want).

'Takeover' and 'merger'

9.22 If a partial disposal of shares does not suit the individual, he may be interested in taking more extreme steps by selling or procuring the sale of all or a substantial majority of the shares in the company, thereby obtaining the necessary liquid, or easily realisable, assets to meet IHT in due course. Moreover, by exchanging these shares for other shares in a bona fide commercial arrangement, the CGT liability can be deferred (TCGA 1992, ss 135–138, which includes provision for HMRC clearance in advance). These CGT sections also deal with schemes for reconstruction of companies and amalgamations.

In a situation where there are associated companies with differing shareholders, a merger on commercial terms may result in removing control for particular shareholders in the associated companies. The merger must be without gratuitous intent in view of s 10 and must avoid the close company provisions of s 94. Upon an exchange of unquoted shares (within TCGA 1992, ss 126–136), the new shares are treated as having been held since the original shares were acquired, for the purposes of the business property relief ownership requirement in s 106 (see s 107(4)).

Demergers

9.23 This is the opposite situation to takeover, amalgamation or merger. TCGA 1992, s 192 (for CGT) and CTA 2010, Pt 23, Ch 5 (income tax) contain provisions (hedged about by anti-avoidance conditions) whereby separate trading activities conducted by the same company or group can be segregated into separate independent companies or groups. The transactions resulting in the demerger are (if HMRC approval is given) relieved from CGT, and any distributions are exempt from income tax.

The provisions apply, for instance, where the shares of a company are currently held by two or more sides of a family who do not get on, and there are separate trading activities which can be divided up. Such a demerger can provide a more stable basis for future IHT planning (but watch the anti-avoidance provisions).

Flotation of company

9.24   A note of warning, first of all: business property relief will be restricted if not lost entirely (see further **Chapter 15**). However, there are some advantages to be gained from going public and obtaining admission to the Official List of the London Stock Exchange at the appropriate time.

There are three main advantages as regards IHT:

(1)   The difficulties, delays and uncertainties in negotiating a valuation with HMRC Shares and Assets Valuation that exist in the case of unlisted shares no longer apply. For listed shares, the open market value rule applies (s 160). The recognised practice is to value at a 'quarter up' from the lower figure of closing price on the day of the transfer of value or death (or nearest working day) shown in the London Stock Exchange Daily Official List; or midway between the highest and lowest prices which bargains were recorded on that day, if lower (see IHTM18093 for an example).

(2)   The realisation of shares to pay IHT becomes a much easier and speedier operation. It is true that the listing may itself increase the value of the shares and hence the IHT liability, but in appropriate cases the advantages referred to outweigh such a disadvantage.

(3)   Where shares and securities listed by the London Stock Exchange or holdings in authorised unit trusts are realised by executors or other accountable persons within 12 months of death at a genuinely lower level, they are, subject to conditions, able to claim that the total of the sale price should be substituted for the total of the date of death values of the investments realised (ss 178–189; see **2.35**).

In practice, due to Financial Services Act requirements, only a small proportion of companies are likely to qualify for a full listing on the London Stock Exchange. However, the London Stock Exchange also operates the Alternative Investment Market (AIM) to meet the needs of companies unwilling, or unable, to qualify for a full listing but desiring nevertheless a free market for their securities, whether to encourage investors, or for other reasons. A company may well enter the AIM as a stepping stone to a full listing.

The fact that AIM shares are 'unquoted' brings IHT business property relief benefits: see **15.33**. The same applies to some, but not all, shareholdings in PLUS (formerly OFEX) companies (see IHTM18337). Shares traded on NASDAQ Europe are similarly treated as unlisted at present. However, shares traded on NASDAQ are currently treated as listed for IHT purposes, and BPR does not apply except for controlling shareholdings (IHTM18340–IHTM18341).

In general, if a company is not listed on the UK Stock Exchange, any foreign recognised Stock Exchange or alternative market, its shares and securities will be unquoted (s 105(1ZA)). However, in relation to those companies and generally, it is necessary to consider whether the business carried on makes the shares or securities (or a business interest) eligible for business property relief (see below).

Another alternative (sometimes as a preparation for a later flotation) is to introduce one of the specialist venture capital institutions (see **9.21**).

In planning the above re-allocation of shares, one must beware of a significant drawback: following an official listing, business property relief will no longer be available at the 100% rate (and only at 50% if the transferor had control of the company). This is probably sufficient to counter any of the possible so-called advantages described above.

PROTECTION FOR THE INDIVIDUAL DIVESTING SHAREHOLDER

Loss of voting control

9.25   This involves a difficult decision (and see **Chapter 15** as to business property relief). A controlling shareholder who divests himself of shares carrying voting control has to ensure as far as he is able that the recipients of his shares (be they out-and-out donees or trustees) are sympathetic and reliable. Another safeguard would be to remain as trustee of family settlements of shares. Consider deferring when control passes by using the share arrangement mentioned at **9.6**, but note the danger if 100% business property relief is withdrawn in the future, as is quite possible.

An effective way of giving reassurance to a former controlling shareholder now with a minority holding, who is concerned to be able to keep his directorship, would be for him to arrange, before he reduces his holding, that the Articles of the company give him increased voting rights in respect of his shareholding so as to defeat any resolution being put to remove him from office. The increased votes in this one circumstance should be sufficient to protect him should his holding of shares go down to whatever level he might contemplate. The provision in the Articles should also stipulate an upward movement in the voting rights should his colleagues, for instance, seek to issue more shares to nullify his present voting rights. This gives the transferor the knowledge and comfort that he cannot be ousted from the board against his will and his position as director is safe for as long as he wishes to retain it, preserving his ability to take part and have a full say in the running of the company. This form of voting provision in the articles was declared valid by the House of Lords in *Bushell v Faith* [1970] AC 1099.

However, in an era of 100% business property relief (as well as the employment-related securities provisions for income tax purposes), the most prudent course is to avoid 'fancy shares' and keep the share structure of the company simple. On that footing, rather than giving weighted votes to particular shares, it may be more straightforward merely to have a shareholders' agreement whereby they agree to use their respective best endeavours to keep the existing directors on the board of the company.

Interesting ways of seeking to keep family (or incumbent board) control in publicly listed companies have evolved. In one method, a publicly quoted family company issued bonus preference shares with no voting rights (except in restricted circumstances). Family shareholders in need of cash could sell these preference shares without affecting voting control. The Americans have been particularly inventive with these 'poison pills'. One approach, for instance, where family control was under pressure, has been on lines such as to issue bonus B shares having ten times the votes of each original ordinary share. The B shares could be transferred only to members of the shareholder's family. To be transferred to anyone else, they had first to be converted to ordinaries. Thus a predator could get his hands only on ordinary shares carrying only one vote each. For quoted companies in the UK, on the other hand, there are feelings that non-voting shares, for instance, are inappropriate in the present open era and work against the freedom of the market. Holding 'special' shares with weighted voting rights can affect the availability of business property relief on quoted shares; to achieve a majority, as required by s 105(1)(cc), the shareholder may find that only some of his quoted shares are required to achieve control (the remainder get no relief).

There are further pressures on unquoted private companies in the UK to keep the structure simple. If any restriction of share capital were contemplated, particularly if transfer of shares were to follow, it would be necessary to take into account ITA 2007, s 684 concerning transactions in securities, as well as TCGA 1992, ss 29 and 30 (value shifting) and s 126 *et seq* (reorganisation of share capital). For IHT purposes, s 98 (alteration of share capital) and s 268 (associated operations) would need watching, as well as business property relief implications and gift with reservation dangers.

In addition, ITEPA 2003, Pt 7 (Employment income: income and exemptions relating to securities) includes widely drawn anti-avoidance provisions affecting the issue of restricted and certain other 'fancy' shares, except in certain limited circumstances (eg shares acquired in the normal course of a family relationship). A holistic approach to planning involving shares and securities is therefore essential.

Service/consultancy agreements

9.26 The divesting shareholder/director can be awarded an appropriate service or consultancy agreement on reasonable and adequate terms as to (index linked) remuneration, pensions, etc and this agreement can be for life. However, it should be noted that, under Companies Act 2006, s 188 (re-stating Companies Act 1985, s 319), long-term service agreements require the approval of the company's members by resolution. For IHT and other tax reasons, the terms of the agreement should impose strict, onerous obligations on the individual. In particular, the remuneration ought not to exceed what can be defended as a reasonable return for services rendered (otherwise, the excess might be treated as a company distribution and hence investment income, although currently, with no investment income surcharge, there would be no difference in the individual's income tax. There would, however, be the question of National Insurance contributions).

See **9.3** for the need to get the service contract firmly in place before any transfer of shares, in order to avoid any possibility of a gift with reservation (see also the Revenue letters of February and March 1987 ('Gifts with reservation: director's remuneration')).

Pension arrangements and pension schemes

9.27   Since 6 April 2006 (pensions 'A' day), tax relief has been available for contributions to a registered pension fund whether paid by the employer or employee. However, the pensions regime was amended significantly for tax purposes following FA 2011, affecting (among other things) the annual and lifetime allowance limits.

Tax relief for pension contributions in respect of an active scheme member who is a relevant UK individual is broadly the higher of £3,600 (gross) per annum, or 100% of UK earnings up to the annual allowance (see below), although the annual allowance contribution limit does not apply for any tax year in which a member satisfies an ill-health condition or dies (FA 2004, s 229(3)). Pension inputs in excess of the annual allowance generally give rise to an income tax liability at the individual's marginal rate (FA 2004, s 227(4), (4A)). The pension input limit is measured by reference to the 'pension input period' ending in a tax year.

The annual allowance is £50,000 for 2012–12. However, the government announced at the Autumn Statement 2012 that the annual allowance will be reduced to £40,000 for 2014–15 and subsequent years. Legislation to this effect was published as part of the draft Finance Bill 2013 clauses on 11 December 2012.

Unused annual allowance may be carried forward from the previous three tax years, taking the earliest year's unused amount first (FA 2004, s 228A). This carry-forward facility was introduced by FA 2011 to help compensate for a lower annual allowance, which was reduced from £255,000 in 2010–11 to

£50,000 in 2011–12. As a transitional rule, for carry forward purposes only, the annual allowance for the three tax years preceding 2011–12 are all deemed to be £50,000 (FA 2011, Sch 17, para 30).

In addition to reducing the annual allowance, FA 2011 reduced the lifetime allowance. This was achieved by freezing the allowance for 2011–12 at £1.8 million (ie at the 2010–11 level), and decreasing it to £1.5 million for 2012–13 (FA 2004, s 218(2)), subject to transitional provisions. The standard lifetime allowance is set to decrease further to £1.25 million for 2014–15 onwards, subject once again to transitional protection if certain conditions are satisfied, following the publication of draft Finance Bill 2013 clauses as mentioned above.

Tax relief for employer contributions is subject to the normal rules relating to allowable deductions (eg in ITTOIA 2005, Pt 2, or CTA 2009, Pt 3), but special contributions are subject to spreading (FA 2004, ss 197–198). The employer's contribution will reduce its net assets, and can therefore act as a further IHT planning exercise.

Lump sum death benefits under pension schemes

9.28   In a registered (or, before 6 April 2006, an approved occupational) pension scheme ('the scheme'), if an employee/director dies without starting to draw a pension, or having taken only part of their retirement benefits, the undrawn fund may be used to pay a cash lump sum.

There are generally no limits on the benefits payable either as a lump sum or pension, although in the case of a defined benefits arrangement if the member was aged under 75 when they died, any defined benefits lump sum death benefit (such as where a member dies whilst still in employment and their pension scheme pays out a lump sum based on a multiple of their salary) must be tested against the lifetime allowance, with any excess lump sum being subject to a 55% income tax charge (FA 2004, s 206). If the member was aged 75 or over when they died, the defined benefits lump sum death benefit is not tested against the lifetime allowance, and the lump sum is taxable at 55% (RPSM10106020). Alternatively, if an amount in excess of the lifetime allowance is retained in the scheme to be paid out as a pension, it is subject to a lifetime allowance charge of 25% instead (FA 2004, s 215(2)). If a pension is provided to a dependant, it will count as taxable income of that individual in the normal way.

Uncrystallised funds can similarly be used to provide a pension, which will be subject to income tax. Where the scheme member was aged under 75 when they died, any uncrystallised funds lump sum death benefit is tested against the lifetime allowance, with any benefits in excess of the allowance being liable to a lifetime allowance charge of 55%. If the member was aged 75 or over when they died, the death benefit is not tested against the lifetime allowance, and it may be possible for the entire fund to be paid out, less a tax charge of 55% (FA 2004, s 206; see RPSM10106030).

The special lump sum death benefit charge also potentially applies to other forms of lump sum death benefits, ie pension protection, annuity protection and drawdown pension fund lump sum death benefits. If the scheme member dies after starting to draw a company pension, any such lump sum death benefit paid following death is not tested against the lifetime allowance, and is taxable at the special lump sum death benefits rate of 55% (for deaths from 6 April 2011; previously 35%). The scheme administrator is liable to the special lump sum death benefits charge.

As indicated above, the standard lifetime allowance is set to fall to £1.25 million for 2014–15. However, an amendment will also be made to ensure that where an individual dies before 6 April 2014 but a relevant lump sum is paid on or after that date, the relevant lump sum death benefit will be tested against the standard lifetime allowance at the time of the individual's death. Legislation to that effect was included in the draft Finance Bill 2013 clauses published on 11 December 2012.

The pensions regime as it applies for income tax purposes is potentially very complex, and is outside the scope of this work. Readers are referred to a specialist publication in this area, such as *Tax Efficient Retirement Planning* (Bloomsbury Professional).

FA 2011 replaced the alternatively secured pension provisions with a single drawdown pension (see below and **Chapter 10**).

When the trustees of the scheme distribute the lump sum at their discretion, this should be free of IHT because, although the scheme is discretionary, it is expressly taken out of the IHT settlement regime of s 58(1)(d) by s 151 (see SP 10/86, following up SP E3). However, an IHT charge can arise under s 5(2) if the pension scheme trustees have no discretion over the payment of lump sum death benefits which are paid to the deceased's estate (IHTM17082).

In strictness, the protection afforded by s 151 ceases to apply on the member's death, and any death benefits distributed at the trustee's discretion would be subject to an IHT exit charge. In practice, the pension scheme trustees should normally be able to distribute the lump sum within two years following the member's death under the discretionary powers available to them in the scheme rules, with the death benefits being treated as remaining held for s 151 purposes in the interim. However, as HMRC point out in their guidance, this treatment is concessionary (IHTM17123).

Accordingly, a member of the scheme has an excellent opportunity of mitigating IHT by recommending to the trustees that the lump sum should go to children or grandchildren; or other parties to whom a gift of a lump sum on the member's death would incur IHT.

If, on the other hand, the member recommends his widow, this is not particularly IHT effective because the lump sum will swell her estate for IHT purposes on her death and will not have taken advantage of skipping the generation, as per the suggested route. Clearly, one must temper any IHT mitigation motive with the practical aspect of whether the widow is adequately provided for. The widow could perhaps be 'compensated' by being left the free estate of the member; and, for example, if that estate includes shares of the family company, the beneficiaries of the scheme lump sum could use it (or trustees on their behalf) to purchase shares out of the lump sum, thereby making the widow's assets liquid.

Another alternative might be to request the trustees of the pension scheme to advance the lump sum into a *new* discretionary trust in respect of which the beneficiaries would include the widow (who would thereby have the possibility of income) as well as other members of the family etc. Unfortunately, if the pension trustees do so in the exercise of a discretion over the recipient of the death benefits, the new discretionary trust would not be exempt under s 151 but would come within the settled property regime of s 58 and attract the consequent exit and ten-year anniversary charges, even if made within the two-year period following the pension scheme member's death. However, if the pension trustees have no such discretion (ie they are bound to pay the death benefits to a private discretionary trust), the two-year concessionary period from the member's death transfers to the recipient discretionary trust, and the funds do not constitute relevant property to which s 58 applies, so that no exit charge arises on distributions within the relevant two-year period (IHTM17124).

The interests of others might be taken into account, to whom the scheme member may not have been married, as where for example an individual owed an obligation to another woman and to his children by her. In such a situation it may be best for provision for the widow to come from the (exempt) personal estate whilst the 'other woman' benefits from the pension fund.

Set out below is a suggested letter of wishes in respect of a registered occupational pension scheme:

LETTER OF WISHES

To: The Trustees of the X Ltd occupational pension scheme ('the Scheme')

When exercising the powers and discretion given to you under the Scheme, I request, but without imposing any binding trust or obligation on you, that you have regard to my under-mentioned wishes in respect of any death in service or other lump sum benefits ('the lump sum').

1.	The lump sum should be paid to the under-mentioned in the stated proportions namely:
Names	% of lump sum
2.	[In arriving at a final decision in respect of the payment/ division of the lump sum, I would like you to consult my widow/widower [name] and take into account his/her wishes/ requirements subject always to your overall discretion and the request set out in 1 above].
3.	This request supersedes all previous requests made by me to you or your predecessors.
DATED	20
Signed	

Notes

(a) In respect of the beneficiaries named in para 1, this could include trustees of an appropriate trust (see the commentary above).

(b) It is, of course, perfectly possible to arrange for *part* of the lump sum to go to the widow to cover her needs and requirements and the 'surplus' to go for the benefit of children/grandchildren or other members of the family.

(c) The above letter of wishes should be contrasted with a nomination. For example, an IHT charge may arise (under s 5(2)) if a deceased individual had the power, up to his death, to sign a nomination which bound the pension scheme trustees to make a payment to a person nominated by the deceased (IHTM17083).

Prior to changes introduced by FA 2011 (see below), the freedom from tax of discretionary lump sum benefits on death was cut down considerably because HMRC could use the 'omission to exercise a right' provisions of s 3(3) to produce an IHT claim where an individual postponed taking his pension although entitled to do so, thereby leaving the discretionary lump sum still payable on his death.

In *Tax Bulletin* Issue 2 (February 1992), HMRC commented as follows regarding the scope of s 3(3) claims: 'In practice, the overwhelming majority of pension arrangements are not affected.' In addition: 'We would consider raising a claim … only where there was evidence that the policyholder's intention in failing to take up retirement benefits was to increase the estate of someone else (the beneficiaries of the death benefit) rather than to benefit himself or herself.' However, the possible application of s 3(3) remained a threat hanging over many individuals who had deferred taking their pension benefit entitlements.

In *DM Fryer & Others (Personal Representatives of Ms P Arnold) v HMRC* [2010] UKFTT 87 (TC), TC00398, the executors appealed against a determination by HMRC that the deceased, Ms Arnold, had made a disposition under s 3(3) by deferring her retirement benefits under a pension policy. The normal retirement date under the policy was 8 September 2002 (her 60th birthday), but she was entitled to take benefits at any time between her 50th and 75th birthdays. In April 2002, Ms Arnold was diagnosed with a serious illness, and died on 30 July 2003 without having taken retirement benefits under the policy. The tribunal held, on the particular facts of the case, that Ms Arnold had omitted throughout her lifetime to exercise her pension rights, and that the omission had therefore continued until her death. The burden of proof was on the executors to show that the omission had not been deliberate. However, it was held that the deceased's omission was deliberate, and had diminished her estate. In addition, s 10 did not operate in this case to exempt the omission from a s 3(3) charge. The executors' appeal was dismissed.

IHT charges resulting from s 3(3) should not arise in most cases following changes introduced by FA 2011. Section 12(2ZA) now provides that where a member of a registered pension scheme (or a qualifying non-UK pension scheme, or a s 615(3) scheme) omits to exercise pension scheme rights, no s 3(3) charge applies in respect of the omission.

The circumstances in which a potential s 3(3) charge will no longer be in point (for deaths and omissions to exercise pension rights from 6 April 2011) include the following (www.hmrc.gov.uk/pensionschemes/chapter-9.pdf):

- there is a failure to exercise a right where a pension scheme member who is able to draw retirement benefits chooses not to do so and later dies;

- a scheme member commences income drawdown within two years of death whilst in ill health (so is unlikely to survive to take full benefits, resulting in the balance of the pension fund being paid outside their estate);

- illness intervenes whilst in income drawdown, and the scheme member reduces the level of drawdown (thereby increasing the pension fund value paid to others on death); and

- in certain situations where the scheme member has a right to request ill-health retirement, but does not do so (thereby increasing the pension fund value as above).

Example 9.1 – An active but short retirement

Giles, a widower, could have drawn his pension at age 60 but the annuity rates were so low that he decided not to, and on his retirement he left the fund to grow whilst relying on other resources. The trustees were encouraged to regard his adult children as equal beneficiaries. His passion for offshore yachting sadly exceeded his strength and he succumbed to fatal injuries during bad weather off the Azores, being then aged 61.

The omission by Giles to exercise his pension rights will not give rise to an IHT liability under s 3(3) (note – the pension fund had previously been written into trust, and so did not fall into Giles' estate).

By contrast, if Giles had died before the FA 2011 changes took effect, even though he had been in good health at age 60, his death within two years would probably have caused an HMRC enquiry of his executors to show that he did not defer taking his pension so as deliberately to reduce his estate and benefit his children.

However, registered pension schemes can broadly allow members to draw income from age 55 (from 6 April 2010; previously age 50) onwards, although the member may choose to defer drawing benefits.

The demise of the 'alternatively secured pension' (ASP) was also brought about by FA 2011. Existing ASPs convert to a 'drawdown pension', and no IHT charge generally arises on any lump sum payable following death. However, the lump sum attracts an income tax charge of 55% instead (see above) (FA 2004, s 206).

An IHT charge may still apply if the deceased was entitled to pension scheme payments which are guaranteed and continue after the deceased's death, or if the pension scheme included protected pension rights, and there is no surviving spouse (or civil partner), dependants or nominated beneficiaries so that the lump sum is paid to the deceased's estate (see IHTM17055, IHTM17131).

IHT charges under s 3(1) can still arise as lifetime transfers in respect of contributions to a pension scheme (and on the transfer of pension benefits, eg by transferring from one scheme to another, or by transferring death benefits to a trust), broadly where the contributions are paid or the transfer is made within two years of death whilst the member was in ill health (HMRC Trusts & Estates Newsletter, April 2011). However, HMRC stated (in their draft guidance based on the Finance Bill 2011) that such a charge on contributions will only be considered where an established pattern over several years has been altered in the knowledge that the member would not survive to enjoy the retirement benefit (www.hmrc.gov.uk/budget-updates/march2011/pensions-draft-guidance.pdf).

With regard to pension contributions made by the individual more than two years before death, in circumstances where the death benefits have been transferred outside the estate but the retirement benefits are retained, HMRC will generally accept that any such contributions were not transfers of value on the basis that the individual was in normal health, unless there is clear evidence to the contrary. Where contributions have been made to a pension scheme (approved or unapproved) within two years of the death, the matter is likely to be referred to HMRC's pension specialist (IHTM17042).

459

HMRC consider that there will be a transfer of value if a contribution is made to a separate pension scheme which provides benefits solely for persons other than the contributor (IHTM17043). However, the exemption for normal expenditure out of income or the spouse (or civil partner) exemption will be available in many cases. The relieving provisions of s 151 mentioned above are restricted to registered pension schemes, qualifying non-UK pension schemes or section 615(3) schemes. IHT charges can still arise in respect of 'unapproved' or 'unregistered' schemes such as Employer Financed Retirement Benefit Schemes (EFURBS). Those charges were unaffected by the FA 2011 changes. For example, HMRC generally treat EFRBS as settlements. As such, they fall within the relevant property regime in the same way as any other discretionary trust, and are therefore subject to ten-year and exit charges for IHT purposes.

The government announced on 22 June 2010 that it would end the effective requirement to purchase an annuity by age 75. Following consultation on how to introduce this change, and on draft legislation, this requirement was abolished by legislation introduced in FA 2011. The tax rules for alternatively secured pensions (ASPs) were also repealed, and existing unsecured pensions and ASPs were amalgamated into 'drawdown pensions'. The complex IHT provisions (in ss 151A–151E) which charged IHT on 'left-over' ASP funds on death, and on unauthorised payments from pension schemes and annuities, therefore no longer apply with effect in relation to deaths occurring on or after 6 April 2011, subject to transitional provisions.

Readers are referred to the ninth edition of this book for commentary on the background to ASPs and the IHT rules which applied before the above changes.

As indicated earlier, on death before age 75, it is possible for pension fund capital to pass free of tax into a fund for any surviving dependant. However, if the member had reached age 75, or if a drawdown of cash had already started before then, there will be a 55% income tax charge (FA 2004, s 206(4)). This point is often overlooked.

Pre-emption provisions

9.29   If it is wished to limit the spreading of shareholdings outside the immediate family, pre-emption provisions can be introduced into the Articles of Association. By this method, before the shares can be transferred to non-members, members must first offer their shares to the existing members at a fair price. HMRC may bring in aid the provisions of s 163 ('Restrictions on freedom to dispose') where an IHT valuation advantage is sought. Nevertheless, such pre-emption provisions should, in practice, assist in reducing share valuations.

In the case of *IRC v Crossman* [1937] AC 26, [1936] 1 All ER 762, HL, it was decided that, although one must assume a free market exists *apart* from the pre-emption provisions, the hypothetical purchaser when registered will hold the shares subject thereto. Pre-emption provisions in the Articles of Association attach, of course, to the shares and affect all shareholders, present and future, unless and until the articles are changed.

An alternative way of producing the same effect for the time being is the conclusion of a shareholders' agreement whereby the present shareholders agree to give each other pre-emption rights over the shares. A shareholders' agreement is personal to the shareholders (see, for example, *Gray's Timber Products Ltd v Revenue & Customs Commissioners* [2010] UKSC 4), although HMRC may still resort to s 163. Take care, in drafting such agreements, not to end up with a binding contract of sale within s 113, prejudicing the availability of BPR.

ITA 2007, s 684 ('Transactions in securities')

9.30 A share arrangement may involve a transaction in securities which results in an income tax advantage (see ITA 2007, ss 682–713), so consider whether it would be appropriate to apply to HMRC for clearance under ITA 2007, s 701 that those anti-avoidance provisions are not considered to apply.

Hitherto, the Inland Revenue (as it then was) tended to be more lenient in granting a clearance if the proceeds of a scheme were required to meet pending estate duty commitments. This was, moreover, substantiated in the House of Lords decision in *IRC v Goodwin* [1976] STC 28, where it was held that making provision for estate duty in order to safeguard family control constituted a bona fide commercial reason and therefore no (what is now) s 684 liability existed. The distinction made at the court of first instance between commercial and financial reasons was not followed, although the House of Lords was not decisive as to whether there can be a difference between financial and commercial reasons, its decision being mainly based on upholding the Commissioners' finding of fact.

This case involved the issue of capitalised redeemable preference shares as an estate duty funding scheme and the basic principles and policy are likely to be followed for IHT. While the 100% IHT business property relief era continues, this aspect becomes of less importance, though care must always be taken to ensure that the security in question is actually a 'share' and has not become a mere loan.

The transactions in securities legislation was amended and replaced (by FA 2010) with a view to clearer legislation targeted more effectively at transactions involving tax avoidance. For example, the current transactions in securities provisions include a specific exception from the rules where there is a 'fundamental change of ownership' of a close company (ITA 2007, s 686).

Nevertheless, there still exists the potential for uncertainty as to the application of the anti-avoidance rules, and therefore circumstances in which a clearance application under ITA 2007, s 701 still needs to be considered.

Loans to pay IHT (ITA 2007, ss 403–405)

9.31   Interest on a loan to personal representatives obtained specifically for, and applied in, paying the IHT on an application for a grant of representation to the deceased's estate is allowed for income tax purposes, subject to a maximum period of one year. The same applies to interest on a loan used to repay another qualifying loan. However, a mere overdraft does not so qualify.

To the extent that relief cannot be given in the tax year in which the interest is paid, due to insufficient income in the year, there is a facility for interest relief to be carried back or forward in a specified order (ITA 2007, s 405).

There is no income tax relief for interest on loans to pay lifetime IHT.

Despite 100% business property relief, IHT has to an extent made it more difficult for a business to be passed down from one generation to another. One of the aims of this book, and particularly of this and the next chapter, is to indicate the means and methods by which this common intention can be accomplished.

Chapter 10

Business interests – partnerships and other firms

INTRODUCTION

10.1 Partnerships have long been a popular medium for trading and holding assets and this is likely to continue. In particular, a partnership does not suffer from the dual liability to tax suffered in respect of a company, ie once on its assets and again when the post-tax proceeds are distributed, or otherwise on the shares in the shareholders' hands. For some professions, until fairly recently partnerships have long been the main (if not only) method of carrying on business, though some are now changing to the limited liability partnership (LLP) structure.

Nevertheless, although a new business often starts off as a partnership (if not conducted by a sole trader), it is later usually and by natural progression converted into a company, sometimes for non-tax reasons, the main commercial motivation being limited liability. Shares in a company are, moreover, easier to deal with, transfer, and settle on trust than a share in a partnership.

A company shareholding may benefit from being valued as a minority holding, whereas in the case of a partnership, a share, however small, is based on the net asset value. However, the PET regime gives a certain degree of flexibility in dealing with partnership interests, provided care is taken to avoid falling into the gift with reservation traps which are found in this field.

This chapter treats partnership and other business interests in four main sections:

- general principles relating to IHT with ancillary references to other taxes;

- IHT planning for partnerships (LLPs being a popular choice with professional firms in particular) and businesses;

- protection of an outgoing partner;

- partnerships of 'relatives'.

463

Family limited partnerships ('FLPs' or colloquially 'FliPs') have received some publicity in recent years as an alternative business structure, as well as an alternative to trusts; see for example the work of Zoe Camp in *Private Client Practitioner*, November 2008. They are discussed at **10.30** and following.

GENERAL PRINCIPLES RELATING TO IHT

10.2   For IHT, there are very few specific provisions applying to partnerships (eg ss 107(3), 227(6)(b) and 267A) and the general principles, particularly as set out in ss 3 and 10, apply.

IHT can apply to partnership situations, especially family partnerships, in the following situations:

- on formation;

- on a variation, eg introduction of partners, change in profit/capital shares etc;

- on a lifetime gift of a partnership share of capital or profit;

- on retirement;

- on death while still a partner.

This chapter contains frequent references to business and agricultural property reliefs. It should be read in conjunction with **Chapter 15**, which explains these very generous reliefs in more detail.

Relevance and application of CGT

10.3   Reference should be made to the important HM Revenue & Customs Statement of Practice D12 originally dated 17 January 1975 on Revenue practice in relation to CGT and partnerships. SP D12 was extended by Statement of Practice 1/79 (retired partner: lump sum as well as annuity) and Statement of Practice 1/89, dealing, for as long as it was relevant, with CGT rebasing and indexation. In addition, Revenue & Customs Brief 03/08 'clarifies' HMRC's practice on the CGT treatment of the transfer of an asset to a partnership by means of a capital contribution.

Although the above Statements of Practice do not have the force of law, they are generally helpful to the taxpayer. Thus, in normal circumstances, so long as the partners are not relatives and the balance sheet figures (eg for goodwill) are not increased through revaluation, there is no CGT on the introduction or retirement of a partner, or on a change of profit-sharing ratios, except to the extent that monetary consideration changes hands. Even then there is no CGT if that consideration is the introduction of capital, or the withdrawal of capital, or the grant of annuities within the specified limits.

However, Business Brief 03/08 is perhaps less helpful. Care is required when contributing assets to a partnership. In HMRC's view, if this takes place by means of a capital contribution, for CGT purposes the partner in question has made a part disposal of the asset equal to the fractional share that passes to the other partners. Reference should also be made, if appropriate, to Revenue & Customs Brief 09/09 regarding assets held by a partnership on 31 March 1982 following changes to the rebasing rules in Finance Act (FA) 2008, and how those rules apply to disposals by individuals of partnership assets or changes in partnership asset shares from 2008–09 onwards.

With regard to changes in the partners' profit-sharing ratios, the moral is not to revalue assets beforehand; instead it may be appropriate to make adjustments on a subsequent sale, ie by sharing the proceeds unequally. These rules are modified where partners are 'connected' by family relationship (see **10.55**).

The principle in the above statement (as extended) may be followed for IHT, although one must not assume this too readily because for CGT any benefit is often merely a deferral, for example, where an incoming partner acquires an asset at a lower base value than the market value. For IHT purposes, on the other hand, the legislation aims to assess *each* transaction representing a transfer of value.

Reciprocal arm's-length arrangements

10.4   These arrangements should give rise to no IHT consequences on the basis that, having regard to the existence of reciprocity, no gratuitous benefit is intended (s 10).

This should apply to many aspects of a partnership, including repayment of capital, and rights relating to pensions, annuities, and consultancy, likewise the writing out of goodwill. Many of these rights are contained in the partnership agreement from the outset, on an arm's-length basis, available to all the partners, and a partner's entitlement at a particular time is usually merely a question of chance or 'the luck of the draw'. In the absence of special provisions in the partnership agreement, the actual book values should represent the assessable values.

In each case where partners are 'connected' as relatives, the onus is, however, much more heavily on the taxpayer to demonstrate commerciality (see **10.55**). With a view to discharging this onus, whenever a partnership transaction is undertaken involving a relative, it is preferable to offer (or have offered) a stranger similar terms.

Reservation of benefit

10.5   However, where it is desired to make an outright gift, care must be taken in relation to partnership transfers that constitute PETs and cannot be construed as gifts with reservation. First, on a question of timing, if a gift (eg of a tractor) is made and subsequently the donor goes into a farming partnership with the donees of the tractor this constitutes a reservation of benefit. Contrast the situation where the donor is already in partnership and then makes the gift of the tractor which is already used by the partnership – in which case, there is no reservation.

Reference should be made to the *Munro* and *Chick* cases in **10.20**. Those cases both concerned gifts of land and the distinction just highlighted used to be as valid in relation to gifts of land as it remains in the case of the chattels referred to in the examples. However, save in very limited circumstances, in the case of land the planning opportunities afforded by these decisions were curtailed by FA 1986, s 102 (introduced by FA 1999). This provision is discussed more fully at **11.11–11.45**.

The Inheritance Tax Manual (IHTM14332) contrasts two examples where the reservation of benefit rules would and would not apply.

'Example 4

A farmer, on taking his son into partnership, makes a gift to him of a share of all the partnership assets including the land. They then share the profits and losses in the same proportion as they own the partnership assets at commencement. The farmer dies ten years later.

This is not a GWR. The son has taken possession and enjoyment of the partnership share gifted to him in the form of his share of profits. The father's share of profits is referable to his own partnership share, not the share gifted.

Example 5

Mrs Foster and her son, Gordon, are in partnership. The partnership farms land which belongs to Mrs Foster but there is no formal tenancy agreement and no rent is paid. Mrs Foster gives a half share of the land to her daughter, Harriet, who is not a partner. The partnership remains in rent free occupation of the land until Mrs Foster's death.

This is a GWR. Harriet has not assumed possession and enjoyment of the gifted share of the land to the entire exclusion, or virtually to the entire exclusion, of Mrs Foster.'

Partial gifts: splitting capital from profit

10.6   Problems can also arise where there is a *partial gift*. For example, the donor gives the whole of the partnership capital to the donee but retains, say, half the profit entitlement; this probably constitutes a reservation of benefit.

It may be possible to counter any argument by HMRC that a benefit has been reserved by segregating the partnership shares of capital and profit on the basis that they are *separate assets* and can therefore be the subject of separate gifts.

Achieve 'clean' gifts

10.7   The aim should be to carve out and freeze the interest which the donor wishes to keep, and make an outright gift, without reservation, of the rest (see **10.19**). It might be thought that business relief will be available to shelter the reserved benefit from IHT, but:

- relief is not always at 100%;

- relief is not always available; and

- what was the point of a gift that was ineffective for IHT purposes?

Moreover, any capital sum accruing to the estate on death would of course be chargeable as an asset held on death (s 171(1)). Remember, in this regard, that a 'buy and sell' agreement or a similar arrangement under the partnership provisions whereby the partner's estate is contractually entitled, not to a direct interest in the partnership assets themselves, but to a purchase price, should be avoided because there is no business relief (see **15.86** and the unobjectionable alternative of the *option* method). Care should also be taken with partnership insurance policies, which may fall within the 'pre-owned assets' income tax regime (POAT) if a benefit is retained (as to POAT generally, see **Chapter 13**).

Application of 'free loan' provisions

10.8   In many cases, one or more of the partners is the owner of the freehold or leasehold premises used by the partnership and allows these premises to be used at less than a commercial rent.

Apart from the application of the lower 50% business property relief (and not even this drawback in the case of farmland), no other IHT consequences arise out of this 'free use of asset' type of arrangement, provided that the owner partner can re-occupy at will: there is no effective gift.

A long-term lease arrangement at a low or nil rent could, however, constitute a diminution in the owner's estate for the purpose of s 3(1), on the footing that the estate is left with the discounted value only of the asset, not its full value, unless the owner takes a larger share of the partnership profits in lieu of rent.

Restriction on freedom to dispose

10.9   Reference to the anti-avoidance provision in s 163 ('Restriction on freedom to dispose') was made at **1.22**.

It is very relevant to partnerships, as where favourable options are granted; or artificial restrictions are imposed relating to goodwill. The reciprocity argument referred to in **10.4** may help to avoid a tax charge.

Position of an outgoing partner

10.10   The rights of an outgoing partner are normally set out in the partnership agreement on a reciprocal basis and should therefore give rise to no IHT liability.

Where the ongoing partners will tolerate it, an elderly partner should retain *some* active interest in the partnership rather than retiring. That way he can keep business/agricultural property relief on his capital in the business.

The effect on BPR of retirement whilst leaving money in the business was illustrated by the Special Commissioner's decision in *Beckman v IRC* [2000] STC (SCD) 59, and the taxation of loan accounts is noted at **10.26**. See also the discussion of the Limited Liability Partnerships Act 2000 at **10.28**.

Dispositions allowable for income tax or corporation tax

10.11   Such dispositions are exempt for IHT purposes (s 12). There is no longer any requirement to carry on a trade or business.

The exemption covers, for example, registered pension schemes (or superannuation schemes within ICTA 1988, s 615(3)) from 6 April 2006, or qualifying non-UK pension schemes), plus certain dwelling house rent-free arrangements for employees etc.

IHT planning for partnerships and businesses

10.12   Several proposals have already been dealt with in the previous chapter and can be adapted appropriately. References to these aspects are therefore given by way of heading only. Furthermore, there are many other general planning possibilities available and these are dealt with elsewhere, particularly in **Chapters 11** and **15**.

Relief for business property

10.13   The scale of reductions of the value of business property transferred, frequently 100%, is analysed in **Chapter 15**. Property consisting of a business or interest in a business is covered and business includes profession or vocation (ss 103–114).

Applying and adapting the ratio of *Attorney-General v Boden*

10.14   The idea that a partner might transfer his share in a partnership in return for not having to work so hard might be regarded as a commercial arrangement, not giving rise to any gratuitous benefit. As such, it should be outside the IHT charge.

Attorney-General v Boden [1912] 1 KB 539 (discussed below) was decided for estate duty purposes, but HMRC practice is to follow this decision for IHT. Although this type of arrangement is of historical interest only where 100% APR/BPR is available, it is still important where only 50% relief is available or where a business fails to qualify for BPR because its main trade consists of land dealing or investment.

The *Boden* 'scheme' allows an elderly partner, for example, a father, to dispose of a share in the partnership to a younger partner, for example, his son, whilst avoiding a charge to IHT on the value of the goodwill attaching to that share.

In *Boden*, a father had taken his sons into partnership and disposed of his share to them, effective on his death. The sons were to pay nothing for goodwill but the other assets were paid for at a proper valuation. The partnership agreement provided that the father was not required to devote more time and attention to the business than he should think fit. On the other hand, the sons were bound to devote their full time.

Held, the advantage that had accrued to the father of not having to work was full commercial consideration for the passing of the goodwill in the shares (ie a bona fide purchase within the relevant position). No estate duty was therefore payable on the value of the goodwill on the father's death.

This position should also apply for IHT purposes on lifetime transfers or dispositions on death. A suggested partnership clause to give effect to this *Boden* scheme could read as follows:

> 'During the subsistence of the partnership each partner other than [senior partner] shall devote his whole time and attention to the partnership business but [senior partner] need not devote more but shall devote not less than [one-third] of his time and attention to the partnership business.'

Although the *Boden* scheme had particular reference to avoiding estate duty on goodwill there is no logical reason why the principle should not be extended. See for example *A G v Ralli* (1936) 15 ATC 523, where estate duty assessment on partnership reserve funds was avoided. HMRC are more likely to succeed in resisting such an extension where 'relatives' are involved (and see **10.55**).

A *Boden* arrangement can usefully be effected in stages, for example:

Stage 1 – the senior partner is required to work full time.

Stage 2 – he disposes of *part* of his profit share and partnership interest in exchange for merely giving such time and attention as is necessary for the partnership or, say, four days per week.

Stage 3 – in exchange for a further disposal of his partnership interest, he merely has to give such time and attention as he thinks fit or, say, two days per week.

The form suggested above can be adapted for use in such stages by reducing the minimum time to be devoted by the senior partner at each stage.

Stamp duty considerations

10.15   There should normally be no stamp duty on a *Boden* arrangement. A gift or voluntary disposition is not liable to stamp duty, nor subject to adjudication, provided, in the case of instruments executed before 13 March 2008, that the instrument is certified in the appropriate form (see Stamp Duty (Exempt Instruments) Regulations 1987, SI 1987/516).

In addition, there is normally no *ad valorem* stamp duty payable on a conveyance or transfer on sale of goodwill, or on the transfer of a partnership interest (not involving land) if no monies are paid to the existing or retiring partners.

It would appear that a *Boden* document, although not a voluntary disposition because the son gives full consideration, does not constitute a sale transaction either, so that no stamp duty is payable.

Stamp duty land tax (SDLT) problems

10.16   In the case of partnerships involving land, the complex SDLT rules for partnership transactions contained in FA 2003, Sch 15 may require careful consideration in advance.

In addition to 'ordinary partnership transactions' (ie transactions entered into as purchaser by or on behalf of the other partnership members, other than special transactions), there were, and for some purposes still are, 'special provisions' in respect of the following partnership transactions (Sch 15, para 9):

(a)   the transfer of a chargeable interest to a partnership;

(b)   the transfer of an interest in a partnership (although this is restricted to property-investment partnerships from 19 July 2006 – see below); and

(c)   the transfer of a chargeable interest from a partnership; and for this purpose the transfer of a 'chargeable interest' includes its creation, variation, surrender, release or renunciation.

With regard to (b) above, the transfer of a partnership interest is a chargeable transaction if consideration is given for the transfer and the partnership property includes land. Consideration is provided if the transferee gives money or money's worth, or if a liability is assumed, or if money or money's worth is withdrawn from the partnership for an existing partner reducing his interest or ceasing to be a partner.

The SDLT implications should be fully considered before land transactions involving a partnership are undertaken, and a detailed technical publication in this area should be sought, if necessary. The fact that no consideration is given for the transfer does not necessarily preclude a charge from arising.

In fact, the provisions were initially so complicated, and of such wide application, that many fairly routine structural changes to partnerships, for good commercial reasons, simply did not happen. Farming families were particularly badly affected. All this was ameliorated somewhat by FA 2006 (s 163, Sch 24, para 9), which amended FA 2003, Sch 15, para 14, so that the provisions relating to transfers of partnership interests now applies to a 'property-investment partnership' only, being one whose sole or main activity is investing or dealing in chargeable interests (see para 14(8)).

Even so, FA 2003, Sch 15 remains a minefield. The potential application of anti-avoidance rules (which are framed in very broad terms) must also be borne in mind.

Absence of covenants in restraint of trade

10.17   Partnership businesses are often dependent on the efficiency and merit of the individual partners. This applies particularly to professional partnerships. The goodwill is theirs (ie 'dog' goodwill – see below) and *they* constitute the goodwill in contrast to goodwill which is attached to the premises or location of a firm ('cat' goodwill); for the zoological classification of customers and the type of goodwill they generate, see *Whiteman Smith Motor Co Ltd v Chaplin* [1934] 2 KB 35.

Accordingly, covenants in restraint of trade restricting competition should be included in partnership agreements only if absolutely essential for other, non-tax, reasons (eg if there is concern about a possible future disagreement; but in that case, the parties should consider carefully whether they want to become partners).

From an IHT viewpoint, the absence of any such provision will greatly help in resisting an assessment on the value of a partner's goodwill because if any partner can set up in competition virtually next door without restriction, little if any value can be apportioned to goodwill. By way of exception, if a *Boden* scheme is to be relied on, a restrictive covenant can be imposed on the junior partners, whilst leaving the senior partner free, thereby strengthening the taxpayer's argument by 'feeding' the consideration moving from the junior partners. At a later stage, the junior partners should consider excluding the covenant.

Reallocation of shares in the partnership: carving out an interest to avoid reservation

10.18   The ownership of a partnership, as in the case of a company, is normally based on shares in that partnership.

The holding by a partner of an interest in the partnership usually determines and represents his interest in the capital, profits (and losses), and the right to surplus assets in a winding up. Thus a re-allocation of shares from a more senior partner to a more junior or newly introduced partner may effect useful IHT planning. A more subtle re-arrangement can be undertaken if the three elements of capital, profits and surplus assets are separately treated.

Initially, it is common for parents to admit children to a share of profits only, and even then to a share only of profits of an income nature. This may be out of fear of loss through matrimonial attack or dissolution.

Exactly the opposite arrangement is best for IHT saving. Thus, the (elderly) disposing partner may wish to retain a high ratio of the profits but be perfectly ready to dispose of his interest in the capital and surplus assets. In that case, the partnership is reorganised so that profits are divided between the partners in ratios unconnected with the capital shares. Income tax considerations may conflict with this IHT planning. In any event, business property relief at 100% will apply to the partnership interest in most cases (see **Chapter 15**).

It would be claimed that this re-allocation of the partnership interests is on a reciprocal, arm's-length basis without any gratuitous intention as referred to in s 10.

Partial gifts: retaining a profit share

10.19   Problems for IHT purposes could arise in the case of this sort of partial gift, eg where the donor gives the whole of his share of partnership capital to the donee, but retains, say, half of the profit, because the retention of the profit interest could constitute a reservation of benefit. The same difficulty arises with other types of partnership freezing operations where the donor transfers capital assets, which are intended to appreciate in the hands of the donee, but retains a high profit share.

Alternatively, the donor makes a gift of the farm (land and buildings) but continues to occupy the farmhouse. He might in this latter case be able to 'carve out' and keep the farmhouse, and make a separate outright gift of the land. But beware here the likelihood of losing agricultural property relief on the farmhouse: HMRC take the view that, to qualify for relief, both farmhouse and farmland must be in common ownership. However, this view was not accepted by the First-tier Tribunal in *Hanson v HMRC* [2012] UKFTT 95 (TC) (see **15.67**).

In this general context, it might be of assistance if the partnership agreement were drafted so as to segregate the shares of capital from the shares of profit. It might then be possible to contend that the donor had carved out and retained his interest in the high profit share; and that the gift was of the capital share only.

Gifts with reservation of benefit

10.20   Similar gift with reservation problems may exist in two further situations.

First, where a partner makes a gift of working capital and/or accrued profits to another partner (eg a child or relative) and that recipient partner allows the value of that capital and/or accrued profits to remain in the partnership without the payment of interest on it. The donor partner can certainly be said to derive and to have reserved a benefit. The solution would be for the recipient partner to charge a commercial rate of interest on the capital so re-introduced by him and to negotiate the gradual withdrawal of the capital as trading allows.

Secondly, it may be dangerous for new partners to indemnify existing partners (who transfer shares to the new partners) as to liabilities outstanding when the new partners join, because existing partners could thereby be said to reserve a benefit. It may be possible to counter this argument on the basis that the indemnity is part of the overall commercial deal.

Problems with reservation of interest can also arise in partnership cases where a donor, some time after the gift, re-acquires an interest in the subject matter because reservation then commences. Two contrasting cases illustrate the trap. In *Munro v Stamp Duties Comr* [1934] AC 61, PC, the father's interest in the partnership was already in existence when he made a gift of land. It was therefore a successful case of carving out and there was no reservation of benefit.

On the other hand, in *Chick v Stamp Duties Comr* [1958] 2 All ER 623, PC, the father made an absolute gift of land to his son. Later the father, the son and another formed a farming partnership, and the son brought the land into the partnership. This constituted a reservation of benefit. (It would now be possible to overcome this reservation by entering into a commercial lease: FA 1986, Sch 20, para 6(1)(a). See also the discussion at **10.5** concerning gifts of land in the light of FA 1986, s 102A.)

Reverting to employee status

10.21   A somewhat sophisticated and unusual proposal is that when a partner reaches, say, his mid-fifties, he should revert to an employee status.

This could have dual advantages. First, for IHT there would be no 'capital' asset on his death. Secondly, while so employed, the individual could benefit from appropriate pension arrangements under a registered pension scheme (see **9.27**).

This planning is of course subject to the application of business/agricultural property relief, which will normally be at the rate of 100% (see **Chapter 15**).

Hiving-off operations and parallel trading

See **9.5**.

Splitting operations

See **9.10**.

Incorporating a partnership

10.22   Subject to careful consideration of the many other taxation aspects of turning a partnership into a limited company (and also the relative impact of National Insurance contributions), such a step may be appropriate for IHT planning, if for example:

- shares in the company can thereafter be transferred in appropriate parcels, taking advantage of available exemptions;

- incorporating a partnership and selling minority shareholdings or undertaking 'watering-down' operations along the lines discussed in **9.11**;

- registered (formerly approved) pension schemes can be implemented along the lines indicated in **9.27**.

For some professional partnerships (many of which have adopted limited liability partnership status – see **10.28**), for example, architects or stockbrokers (if they still maintain their independence), a limited or unlimited company could be used. The company itself remains entitled to an indexation allowance for the purposes of corporation tax on chargeable gains.

Incorporation relief

10.23   To obtain roll-over relief upon incorporation, the conditions set out in TCGA 1992, s 162 must be strictly complied with. In particular, *all* the assets of the partnership (with the sole exception of cash) must be transferred to the new company. To the extent that the consideration is in shares in the new company, there is a deferral of the CGT liability.

If the business consists of a property-letting business, relief will probably not be available following the decision in *Ramsay v HMRC* [2012] UKFTT 176 (TC). The decision is not without its critics (see, for example, the article in the July 2012 edition of *Trusts and Estates*), and it is possible that it might be reversed at a later date.

Note also that the company itself acquires the business together with its assets at *market value*: the gains sit within the value of the shares. This creates considerable scope for planning as subsequent disposals can be made by the company with little (if any) liability to tax being triggered.

Hold-over relief

10.24   An alternative route would be to gift assets into the company utilising the hold-over relief for business assets under TCGA 1992, s 165. In this case, it would not be necessary for *all* the assets (other than cash) to be transferred. Under this arrangement, it is the company that inherits the gain whilst the shares are unaffected except that they increase in value because no, or little, consideration has been given for the assets acquired.

An appropriate half-way house might be to set up a service company for the partnership and make appropriate disposals of shares in that company. Such service company would normally deal with the administrative and property holding functions of the partnership making an appropriate arm's-length profit, say, between 5% and 10% on the expenditure incurred by it. However, care should be taken to ensure that any indebtedness of the partnership to the company does not fall foul of the beneficial loan provisions for the individuals, or a liability for the company under CTA 2010, s 455 ('loans to participators') (*Grant v Watton* (and related appeals) [1999] STC 330).

It should, however, be borne in mind that, whereas premises owned by the partnership would obtain 100% business relief, a holding of shares in the service company could, arguably, not qualify for relief on the basis that the company falls within the exception for investment companies contained in s 105(3). Regard must also be given to TIOPA 2010, Pt 5 (ie the 'transfer pricing' provisions) as to artificial prices between 'associated persons'. Note also the rule in *Stephenson v Payne, Stone, Fraser & Co* (1967) 44 TC 507 that excessive profits made by the service company may not be a deductible expense for the partners, yet still be taxable on the company, so that there is no 'symmetry'.

Entrepreneurs' relief

10.25   Entrepreneurs' relief broadly reduces the rate of CGT to 10% on up to £10 million of relevant gains (for 2012–13) in respect of material disposals of business assets.

The incorporation of a partnership business could possibly involve a sale of the business assets to a newly formed limited company, the proceeds being left as an outstanding liability owed by the company, which can be repaid without further CGT or income tax implications for the recipient as and when the company is sufficiently in funds to do so.

Whilst the extraction of company profits at an effective rate of 10% might seem attractive, it should be noted that such a transfer of the business will in most cases trigger an immediate (and perhaps unnecessary in view of the CGT reliefs described above) tax liability.

As to potential IHT disadvantages of incorporation, see below.

Disadvantages of incorporation

10.26   One of the main disadvantages of incorporating a partnership is that the shareholders potentially suffer effective double taxation, once in the company and again on the reflected value in the shares; another is the income taxation (and possible NIC) cost of extracting profits out of the company.

Loans to participators of a company are also subject to charges to tax (CTA 2010, s 455). HMRC may also challenge the existence or valuation of goodwill in appropriate cases (see *Tax Bulletins* 76 and 83), and particularly in incorporations involving the transfer of trade-related property (see www.hmrc. gov.uk/svd/goodwill.htm).

For commercial purposes, a business partner who becomes a shareholder may decide to retain property outside the company. The property qualifies for BPR, however, only if:

- it is used for the purposes of a business carried on by the company;
- the shares held are themselves relevant business property; and
- the transferor controls the company.

Even then, the rate of relief is only 50% (IHTA 1984, s 104(1)(b)).

As discussed at **10.22**, incorporation may involve the sale of business assets to the company with the price left outstanding on loan account. Such a loan to a company does not qualify for business property relief. Whilst the incorporation transactions may lead to a positive balance on a director's loan account, this should not be left in place indefinitely. It gives a means of drawing cash from the company without further tax charge but, if it is still in place when the shareholder dies or wishes to make a chargeable transfer of shares, the value does not qualify for business property relief. The solution may be, if the funds are required in the company and IHT is a concern, to convert the loan into more shares. Of course, the ability to draw down the loan will then be lost and, normally, the shares must be held for two years to earn BPR.

Where a shareholder acquires shares that 'stand in the shoes' of an existing shareholding under the CGT rules applicable to company reorganisations, then for BPR purposes the ownership period of the new shares is deemed to be the same as the period of ownership of the existing shares (IHTA 1984, s 107(4)). This is a potentially helpful strategy in 'deathbed' situations.

In *The Executors of Mrs Mary Dugan-Chapman & another v Revenue & Customs Commissioners* [2008] SSCD 592 (see **15.39**), a business property relief claim relied on the company reorganisations exception to the two-year ownership rule. Mrs Dugan-Chapman (Mrs DC) was allotted one million ordinary shares in the company on 27 December 2002, two days before her death. The issue was broadly whether those shares could be identified for relief purposes with other shares in the company which she had held for at least two years prior to her death. The Special Commissioner dismissed the executors' appeal against HMRC's determination that the value of those shares could not be reduced by business property relief. HMRC had contended that the shares were issued as the result of a simple subscription for shares. There was insufficient evidence or documentation to support the executors' argument that a reorganisation had actually taken place. 300,000 shares allotted to Mrs Dugan-Chapman on 23 December pursuant to a (properly arranged) rights issue did, however, qualify for BPR.

Finally, it should be borne in mind that there is also a possibility of HMRC arguing that a company set up in advance of the incorporation has not 'replaced' the unincorporated business in a strict sense, and that the shares are therefore not 'relevant business property'. However, such an interpretation does seem rather harsh.

Limited partnerships (not LLPs)

10.27 Such partnerships are formed under the Limited Partnerships Act 1907 and are to be distinguished from limited liability partnerships (as to which, see **10.28**). Over the years, these partnerships have had restricted application, although they have been used to an extent in film production ventures and oil and gas exploration. Moreover, ITA 2007, ss 104–105, which apply to limited partners and nullify *Reed v Young* [1985] STC 25, CA, restrict the availability of income tax relief for trading losses. There is also a restriction on the availability of income tax relief for interest paid on borrowings to acquire an interest in limited partnerships generally (ITA 2007, s 399(2)(a)).

Nevertheless, such partnerships still have a useful role, and in utilising them (which would avoid the rigours of close company legislation) there must be at least one general partner who is subject to full unlimited liability, although such general partner might be a limited liability company.

As regards the limited partners, their contribution to the partnership represents the ceiling to their liability. They can assign their shares, but may not take part in the management of the business. (It is claimed that the limited partners can nevertheless be 'active' for the purpose of ITTOIA 2005, Pt 9, so that the income is earned income.)

Given this vehicle, the IHT planning aspects described in **10.14** can be adapted. It might also be a useful method of introducing trustees of appropriate family trusts, as the limited partners. Without the protection of limited liability, it might otherwise be necessary for the trustees themselves to be limited companies.

Limited liability partnerships

10.28 The Limited Liability Partnerships Act 2000 introduced a new corporate entity. Limited liability partnerships became available from 6 April 2001.

A limited liability partnership is treated as a company for most company law purposes and its members' liability is limited. For tax purposes, however, it is largely treated as a partnership. Its separate existence as a corporate entity is ignored, and the income and capital are treated as owned by the individual partners.

Assets held outside, but used in, the partnership are treated for IHT purposes (including business and agricultural property relief) just as the assets of a traditional partnership. The incorporation of a limited liability partnership will not interrupt ownership for the purposes of these reliefs. See *Tax Bulletin* 50 (December 2000).

Setting up a family partnership

10.29 Where a new enterprise is being started up by parents with their children, it may be expected that the parents will contribute the bulk of the capital.

By careful drafting of the partnership agreement, it would be possible to arrange, on the one hand, that profits and losses are divided out as may be agreed, and on the other, that capital profits, on sale or on revaluation of the partnership assets, be shared between the children only. The aim would be to freeze the value of the parents' interest and permit the capital growth to pass to the children.

Family limited partnerships

10.30 There are 'fashions' in tax planning, as in everything. Following the changes to the IHT treatment of trusts in FA 2006, family limited partnerships (FLPs) were suggested as a structure that would replace the family trust.

The problem is this: a family has substantial wealth, but for some reason neither business nor agricultural property relief shelters it. Perhaps land has development value or the investment content of a business now swamps the original business; or relief is restricted to 50% or to the agricultural value only. The value is large enough that a gift into trust of even a modest part would exceed the nil rate band and trigger an immediate IHT charge at 20%. Moreover, the trust will fall within the relevant property regime, giving rise to possible IHT exit and ten-year anniversary charges.

The structure will work well where an existing business has been sold that did qualify for reliefs but the family do not wish to reinvest the sale proceeds in 'risky' assets and cannot therefore benefit from the replacement provisions of s 107 or 118.

479

To address this, the family sets up a limited partnership (under the Limited Partnership Act 1907), in which one person (in our illustration, 'Mum') is the general partner who runs the business. Cash is given to other relatives, who merely invest in the venture. If chargeable assets are transferred upon creation of the partnership, the CGT issues will need to be considered (see HMRC Brief 03/2008), although the inter-spouse CGT exemption (TCGA 1992, s 58) or business asset hold-over relief (s 165) may be of assistance. The arrangement is transparent: it is a contract. For that reason, it will appeal to lawyers and families from civil law jurisdictions, who have such trouble with the trust concept. The partnership is not an entity in itself and has no legal personality.

Capacity

10.31   The main purpose of this structure is to get value down the generations, so members will often be quite young children who, on reaching what passes for adulthood by virtue of Family Law Reform Act 1969, s 1, can decide for themselves whether or not to repudiate the contract.

Children should be separately advised. At age 18, they may become more involved in the venture as an encouragement to leave value in, rather than dissipating it.

Treatment of the interest for law and tax

10.32   The partnership is transparent. If capital to fund a minor unmarried child's purchase of an interest comes from a parent, the income is assessable on the parent (ITTOIA 2005, s 629); but if from a grandparent or as an inheritance the income is the child's. What the child owns is a *chose* in action, ie the right to a share in the assets of the partnership, not to specific assets, so there is no control over such assets. The limited partner cannot interfere in the management of the fund, save by his (limited) right to call for repayment of capital.

A gift of funds to be added to the partnership is a PET, whether the money is paid to the child who then invests it or is paid straight to the partnership bank account for his or her benefit. On the death of the child the share is part of his or her estate. Meanwhile, unlike with a relevant property trust, there are no periodic IHT charges.

Mum, in our example, runs the partnership and controls the flow of income, making reserves for tax and expenses as necessary. She must run it so as to make a profit, not to comply with the requirements of BPR (because if BPR were available this structure might not be used anyway), but so as to show that this is a genuine partnership under general principles. Just holding property or investments together is not enough.

A well-drawn FLP will set out quite definite limits to capital withdrawal, for example a total bar for a fixed period or until reaching a certain age, followed by staged withdrawal or penalties for early encashment of the share.

The general partner

10.33   Although such a partner may be an individual, as in the case of Mum, the general partner could be corporate, which might help to limit liability and would provide cover in the event of death. If an individual, the general partner may require indemnities. If Mum enjoys a substantial estate she may feel vulnerable to claims and the dividing lines of responsibility should be clear.

If the general partner is corporate (ie a family company formed for the purpose), the person who funds gifts to children may wish to own shares in the corporate body to keep control of management. On death, those shares are important strategically but should not pass to the limited partners as a group, since that could make them owners of the whole structure, which might weaken asset protection.

Relatively little jurisprudence has yet accumulated on FLPs so we do not yet know how much Mum may pay herself for the work she does. This commentary shows how control may be reserved, but with that control comes the spectre of reservation of benefit from gifts made to children that are *ab initio* destined to be invested in an FLP.

Another problem for the FLP is regulation. In the UK the management of, dealing with and advising on investments is an activity regulated by the Financial Services Authority (FSA). Mum will be promoting investment, so must be authorised to do so. The FLP will generally be a 'collective investment scheme' within FSMA 2000, s 235. Values must be substantial to justify the regulatory burden, especially if delegated to FSA-authorised advisers.

Attacks on the fund

10.34   The partner, as noted, owns a share, not the underlying assets. That may be difficult to realise to meet liabilities, as in divorce proceedings, but the courts have seldom allowed that to get in the way of doing justice, as they see it, between the parties.

Therefore, although some discount may apply the FLP share will still be one of the resources to which the court may look to provide for the other party to a marriage on the principle that 'you'll find a way to pay'. Much will no doubt turn on recent management of the FLP; if it produces a steady income, this may be used to fund maintenance.

The position is therefore not so different from a discretionary trust, where there is a pattern of income or of capital distributions that the court will take into account in deciding to what extent to regard the fund as an asset or 'resource'. Some protection might be gained by taking the FLP offshore, in the hope that a foreign court would disregard an English court order and refuse to enforce it but the extra compliance costs might not justify such a course. In any case, what will usually be most important is the location of the defendant, who owns the share of the FLP.

PROTECTION OF AN OUTGOING PARTNER

10.35 In the more traditional and bygone partnership era, a retiring partner usually looked to the continuing or new partners for a substantial payment of capital, payable either by a lump sum or by instalments, and used such sums in his retirement and for his widow's benefit.

This method is now relatively unusual, not only for the practical reason that so few persons can provide the necessary capital, but also because such payments are expensive for tax reasons, particularly IHT and CGT.

Therefore, the trend is to replace capital or goodwill payments by payments for consultancy, pensions and/or annuities, and insurance arrangements.

Consultancy and pension payments to the outgoing partner

10.36 On the retirement of a partner, it is fairly common practice to retain him as a consultant and show this position on letterheads, etc, 'below the line'. A consultancy agreement should be entered into whereby the consultant is paid fees on an agreed basis (eg £xx per month). To enable such payments to be allowable deductions of the partnership for income tax purposes, the amounts paid should not be excessive (see ITTOIA 2005, s 34).

References to transfers of shares in the partnership should be kept completely separate and outside the consultancy agreement (see *Hale v Shea (Inspector of Taxes)* [1965] All ER 155, 42 TC 260). Earned income still carries an advantage over unearned, as income supporting pension provision (see **10.41**). Earned income (unlike the assets producing unearned investment income) cannot be transferred between husband and wife, or between civil partners.

Payments to consultants are sometimes expressed as an 'agreed share of profits', because the continuing partners do not wish to commit themselves to a fixed sum irrespective of the partnership's profitability in any year. This method has the advantage of a built-in protection against inflation, but the danger is that such 'consultant' might be deemed for certain purposes still to be a partner, having regard to the definition of a partner in Partnership Act 1890, ss 1 and 2.

Protection against inflation can be more appropriately covered by inserting a clause pegging the consultancy fee and, if wished, any pensions, to the general index of retail prices. These payments should not normally be *charged* on profits, but merely be enforceable by way of personal covenant, because a charge might give rise to a settlement, with all its attendant IHT complications, under s 43(2). If a consultancy agreement is not for life, on its termination the consultancy payment can be substituted by a pension which would normally be somewhat less than the previous consultancy payments. Pension provisions can also be included for the consultant's widow or widower.

These arrangements should be unobjectionable for IHT purposes on the consultant's death, on the basis that they are reciprocal, arm's-length arrangements not conferring any gratuitous benefit.

VAT, PAYE etc

10.37 If payments and other fees of the consultant exceed the VAT-registration threshold, he will have to register for VAT and charge VAT to the firm when billing for his services. It may be possible to avoid these VAT complications by making the consultant a salaried employee taxable on employment income. However, there would then be other difficulties, such as a stricter test for allowable expenses, National Insurance contributions, wrongful dismissal legislation, etc, which should be balanced against the disadvantages of VAT registration.

The complications of VAT and (to a lesser extent) the treatment of partnership pensions as earned income means that consultancy arrangements are somewhat less popular than previously. Whether an ex-partner should be kept on as a consultant or be paid a pension now depends largely on the commercial circumstances of each case.

Annuities/pensions to widows, widowers and dependants of the outgoing partner

10.38 As mentioned above, partnership annuities are a practical alternative to capital or goodwill payments. Moreover, in most cases the payment of the annuities should not give rise to any IHT results. An official letter was published in the *Law Society Gazette*, 2 July 1975 (but not considered important enough to qualify as a Statement of Practice), as follows:

'In the normal case where the partnership agreement can itself be regarded as a commercial transaction the agreement to pay the annuity would itself be covered by the provisions of [s 10] as would the actual payments as and when they became due. The commencement of the annuity on the death of a partner would not itself be an occasion for charge although his share of the partnership would normally be a part of his estate.'

Notwithstanding the above, it is still advisable to secure the payment of such annuities by *personal* covenant not charged on the partnership assets, thus avoiding the potential problem referred to at **10.36**. Continuing annuities should wherever possible be *separate* and distinct and not continuous or for joint lives, as this may further assist in resisting any suggestion that the agreement to pay the annuity gives rise to a settlement for IHT purposes.

Continuing income from the partnership

10.39   This type of arrangement will be particularly suitable in the case of the older members of the partnership whose pension funds have been depleted by market forces or who have simply not paid sufficient premiums under a pension scheme (as considered below) to provide a reasonable income in retirement. It may therefore be necessary to continue to provide an income out of the partnership by means of pensions or annuities from the firm.

Under the pension regime introduced from 6 April 2006, partnership annuities are not subject to the annual or lifetime allowance, and the capital applied in securing them does not count towards the lifetime allowance. Prior to 6 April 2006, a pension paid to a retired partner or his dependants under the partnership agreement or any supplement thereto, was treated as earned income within limits, the main limit being 50% of the average of the partner's profits for the best three (so far as he is concerned) out of the last seven years prior to the partner's death or retirement during which he was required to devote substantially the whole of his time to acting as a partner.

If it is decided to pay partners' pensions from the firm it is sensible to agree them in advance, then record the fact in a supplementary agreement or in the partnership minutes. This will enable the parties to take advantage of the income tax provisions of ITTOIA 2005, s 627(2), which exclude from the scope of the 'settlements' anti-avoidance rules in ITTOIA 2005, s 624 any annual payments made by an individual for commercial reasons in connection with the individual's trade, profession or vocation.

Where a partnership makes annual payments to a retired partner, the capitalised value of those payments may be treated as consideration for the disposal of the partner's share in the partnership assets under TCGA 1992, s 37(3). This will be the case only to the extent the payments exceed what can be regarded as reasonable recognition of the past contribution by the partner to the partnership. An annuity of two-thirds of the average of the best three out of the last seven years is regarded by HMRC as reasonable for a full-time partner with ten years' service (Statement of Practice D12, para 8; and note that Statement of Practice 1/79 extends the practice to a lump sum paid in addition to the annuity).

Capital treatment may be welcomed by the outgoing partner since his effective rate of tax on the payments (after applying entrepreneurs' relief) may be 10%, albeit the tax will be payable 'up front' rather than being deferred over future years. Where the capitalised value of an annuity is treated as consideration received by the retired partner, it will also be regarded as allowable expenditure by the remaining partners on the acquisition of their fractional shares in partnership assets from him.

Disadvantages of the arrangement

10.40   One considerable disadvantage of paying partners' pensions out of the future profits is that the retiring partner is dependent on the continued success of the firm after he has left it and can no longer influence its fortunes. It may also be difficult to introduce new partners where the liability to pay former partners is considerable. It may be necessary to provide that in no circumstances will the total of all pension payments exceed, say, 20% of the profits in any one year. This of course increases the risk which an outgoing partner bears.

It is generally much better therefore to provide pensions so far as possible by means of pension schemes rather than out of future profits. An exception could be made where, for the reasons set out in **10.39**, receipt of the annuity is charged wholly or partly to CGT instead of to income tax. The disadvantage in most cases for the remaining partners is that they will then suffer a larger annual income tax charge on the profits of the business than would otherwise be the case.

Accordingly, pensions from the continuing partners should generally be avoided. Partners should be encouraged to make pension arrangements via commercial pension scheme providers. Appropriate obligations can be written into the partnership agreement.

Pension schemes

10.41   A single pension regime was introduced with effect from 6 April 2006, replacing the various regimes which previously existed, such as those applicable to retirement annuity or personal pension schemes. All too soon, however, new complications were engrafted onto the scheme, for example restricting relief on contributions, which will greatly reduce the attraction of pension provision for some high earners.

A detailed analysis of pension arrangements is outside the scope of this book, and readers are recommended to study a book specifically on this subject, such as *Tax Efficient Retirement Planning* (Bloomsbury Professional). However, key features of the pension regime of potential interest to partners (and others) are broadly summarised below.

Maximum contributions

10.42   The maximum contributions that a partner can make to a registered pension scheme on which tax relief is available is an amount up to his relevant UK earnings for the tax year (FA 2004, s 190), but subject to an upper limit (the 'annual allowance'). The annual allowance is £50,000 (for 2012–13), although it had previously been much higher (£255,000 for 2010–11).

There is no facility to carry back pension contributions to the previous year, unlike previous pension regimes; however, the reduction in the annual allowance to £50,000 by FA 2011 was accompanied by a facility to carry forward any unused allowance for any particular year of assessment by up to three years. There is a strict order in which the annual allowance is used up. The annual allowance in the current tax year is used first, followed by any unused annual allowance from earlier years, using the earliest tax year first.

Contributions are payable net of basic rate income tax, with higher rate relief being claimed through the self-assessment system, if appropriate.

From 6 April 2011, tax relief for pension contributions for high income individuals was to be limited to the basic rate, but this proposal was repealed before it came into force. Anti-forestalling rules were introduced in FA 2009 to prevent excessive additional pension contributions being made from 22 April 2009 in respect of 2009–10 and 2010–11 to avoid the apprehended relief restriction, through the introduction of a 'special annual allowance charge'. This charge had the effect of restricting tax relief on the additional contributions to the basic rate (FA 2009, Sch 35).

Lifetime allowance

10.43   Individual partners are subject to an upper limit in tax-favoured pension funds, beyond which a 'lifetime allowance charge' applies. The lifetime allowance charge was initially set at £1.5 million for 2006–07, increasing in stages to £1.8 million by 2010–11. However, it fell back down to £1.5 million with effect from 6 April 2012. Transitional provisions provided a measure of relief to those who already had, or expected to have, pension funds worth more than £1.5 million; however, the 'price' of accessing the relief is that no further contributions may be made to a money-purchase scheme.

The lifetime allowance charge is measured when pension benefits are taken. The rate of charge is 55% if the excess fund is taken as cash, or 25% if retained and used to provide pension income (FA 2004, s 215). However, it should be noted that the amounts retained would be subject to tax when paid as pension income. The overall rate of tax would therefore be 55% (ie 25% initially, plus 40% on the balance of 75%) for a 40% taxpayer, or (from 2010–11) 62.5% (ie 25% plus 50% on the balance of 75%) for a 50% taxpayer.

Minimum retirement age

10.44   The normal minimum age from which pension benefits can be drawn was increased from 50 to 55 from 6 April 2010.

Tax-free lump sums

10.45   The maximum tax-free lump sum available is broadly 25% of the accumulated pension fund. Whilst many will seize this, as 'tax-free cash', those with guaranteed annuity rates may find it best to take all the benefit as annuity.

Transitional rules may apply to partners who accumulated substantial pension benefits and rights by 6 April 2006. These rules offer some protection from the lifetime allowance charge.

Primary protection – if the partner's pension benefits and rights at 6 April 2006 exceeded the (then) £1.5 million lifetime allowance, and if pension contributions were to continue, he may have opted to apply to HMRC for 'primary protection' in the form of a 'lifetime allowance factor'. For example, if the value of a partner's pension rights at 6 April 2006 was £1.8 million, the primary protection factor is 20% (ie the percentage by which that value exceeds the £1.5 million lifetime allowance).

A subsequent increase in the value of pension rights is measured against the rise in the lifetime allowance, with any excess subject to a lifetime allowance charge. Thus, if ten years later the lifetime allowance is £2.25 million, the primary protection factor increases that limit to £2.25 million × 120% = £2.7 million. If the fund value has increased to £2.8 million, the balance of £100,000 will be subject to a lifetime allowance charge. An election for primary protection had to be made by 5 April 2009 (FA 2004, Sch 36, para 18(6); Registered Pension Schemes (Enhanced Lifetime Allowance) Regulations 2006 (SI 2006/131)).

Enhanced protection – an election for enhanced protection required the partner to have ceased active membership of all pension arrangements by 6 April 2006, and was available irrespective of whether the lifetime allowance was exceeded at that point. Pension benefits are then free from a lifetime allowance charge. An election for enhanced protection must have been made by 6 April 2009, although the decision to cease pension contributions must have been made by 6 April 2006.

Clearly, the earlier in a partner's career a pension is taken out, the longer the period of funding and better the terms available from pension companies. It is quite possible nowadays for partnership agreements to require partners to contribute towards a pension scheme, and this can be coupled with provisions for a compulsory retirement age. In times when capital or goodwill payments are impracticable, such early retirement planning is perhaps of even greater importance.

IHT TREATMENT OF PENSION RIGHTS

10.46   The basic rule, see s 151(2), is that an interest under a pension scheme that ends on the death of the person entitled to it escapes IHT. However, it escapes IHT only if it is an annuity or right to a pension and is not an interest which results from the application of a benefit provided under the pension scheme otherwise than by way of pension or annuity. The provisions of s 151(2) were amended by FA 2008, so as to extend IHT protection to certain overseas pension schemes.

Section 12 of IHTA 1984 operates to prevent employer contributions to registered pension schemes from being treated as transfers of value, and extends the same freedom to an approved scheme under ICTA 1988, s 615(3). Section 12 was amended (by FA 2008, Sch 29, para 18, with effect from 6 April 2006), so as to extend this beneficial treatment to contributions by an employer to a qualifying non-UK pension scheme. A further amendment was made to s 12 in FA 2011 (s 12(2ZA)), so that no disposition is treated as arising if a member of a registered pension scheme, qualifying non-UK pension scheme or a 's 615(3) scheme' omits to exercise pension rights under the scheme (see **9.28**).

The relevant property provisions of s 58 do not catch settled property in pension funds. That relief is extended to qualifying non-UK pension schemes (s 58(1)(d)), and ensures that if a member of such a scheme dies the fund will be protected from IHT provided the funds are, within two years, paid out as a lump sum (IHTM17124). The two years run from the date on which the trustees became aware of the death of the member, or could reasonably have been expected to know of the death.

The exclusion of pension funds from the scope of IHT in most circumstances makes pensions a very effective IHT-shelter. However, the potential liability to income tax on extraction of funds must be borne in mind.

10.47   The key to the IHT charge on the pension fund is whether the member has a general power of disposal over the funds in the scheme. If he has, the funds are treated as part of his estate for IHT purposes. This is rare.

In other circumstances, the pension rights are not included as part of the estate. This includes the more common situation where funds are paid over at the discretion of the pension fund trustee in accordance with a nomination form or other expression of wish made by the pensioner during his or her life.

It is not uncommon for a lump sum payment to be made into trust, rather than to a particular individual. Section 151(5) (as amended by FA 2008, Sch 29) provides that, if the funds become held in a settlement made by someone other than the pensioner, the pensioner is treated as the settlor.

Alternatively secured pension funds (ASPs)

10.48   From 6 April 2006 until 5 April 2011, an important exception to the general exclusion of pension funds from IHT applied to alternatively secured pension funds (ASPs) and certain related forms of provision for dependants. The relevant provisions were set out in IHTA 1984, ss 151A–151C.

The basic structure of the legislation was to bring such funds within the scope of IHT as though the underlying fund was part of the estate of the person who benefited from the funds at the date of his or her death.

With effect from 6 April 2011, any person who, immediately before 6 April 2011, was entitled to an alternatively secured pension is to be treated, on and after that date, as entitled to drawdown pension (FA 2011, Sch 16, paras 51, 86). The provisions for IHT to be levied on ASPs are repealed. Income tax charges are still levied where applicable.

For further explanation of the treatment of ASPs, please see the ninth edition of this book.

Cash options under approved annuity schemes

10.49   Where, under a registered pension scheme or superannuation fund within ICTA 1988, s 615(3) an annuity becomes payable on a person's death to a spouse or dependant of that person, and a capital sum might at the deceased's option have become payable instead to his personal representatives, the deceased is not to be treated as having been beneficially entitled to that sum, with the result that it escapes liability to IHT (s 152).

The scope of this exemption was extended to qualifying non-UK pension schemes by FA 2008, with effect from 6 April 2006.

Overseas pension schemes

10.50   As mentioned above, certain exemptions were extended to 'qualifying non-UK pension schemes' with effect from 6 April 2006. The meaning of 'qualifying non-UK pension scheme' is given in s 271A, which requires the pension scheme to be established in a country or territory outside the UK, and to satisfy the conditions prescribed in the Inheritance Tax (Qualifying Non-UK Pension Schemes) Regulations 2010, SI 2010/51, which came into force on 15 February 2010 but which were deemed to have taken effect on 6 April 2006.

Income tax relief in the UK is not available on a contribution to a qualifying non-UK pension scheme (QNUPS), although (subject to the application of local rules) the other tax benefits usually associated with pension schemes are available. First, there is the opportunity for the funds in the scheme to grow free of taxes (other than taxes withheld at source) until such time as they are withdrawn from the scheme. Second, provided the contribution to the scheme is reasonable in the context of future pension provision for the individual concerned, the funds contributed to the scheme will leave the estate of the individual without giving rise to a transfer of value for IHT purposes, on the basis that there is no intention to confer any gratuitous benefit (s 10). In addition, the scheme itself is not subject to the relevant property regime (s 58(1)(d)).

Hence, contributing to a qualifying non-UK pension scheme may be attractive for certain individuals notwithstanding the lack of tax relief for contributions, eg if the individual making the contribution to the scheme already has a UK pension fund with a value in excess of the lifetime allowance. However, the full tax implications (for IHT and other taxes) of qualifying non-UK pension schemes need to be carefully considered 'in the round' beforehand.

In certain circumstances, eg if an individual is moving abroad from the UK permanently, he or she can arrange to transfer their UK pension scheme fund to a qualifying non-UK pension scheme without incurring a penalty charge. Certain conditions apply. A detailed analysis of the relevant practice and regulations is beyond the scope of this book.

LIFE ASSURANCE

10.51   One of the main problems of a professional partnership is the provision of sufficient cash to repay the capital accounts of an outgoing partner on his death or retirement. Even though there are difficult problems, especially with uneven, larger and changing partnerships, partnership life assurance can often help in these circumstances. It is important to bear in mind the basic practical aims of such assurance, which are:

- to provide cash in the right hands at the right time;

- to ensure the equitable division of cost among the partners;

- to avoid liability to IHT. The greatest problems come with trust policies (see below) where HMRC regard the IHT discretionary trust regime as operating; in other cases the arm's length and reciprocity principles may be relevant in the context of s 10; or one of the other exemptions such as normal expenditure (s 21). Great care should be taken in advance of the implementation of any arrangements;

- to avoid liability to CGT (normally the exemption under TCGA 1992, s 210 will apply); and

- to ensure that any arrangements are flexible and will allow for resignation of partners or the addition of new partners.

There are various means of trying to achieve these ideals.

Trust policies

10.52 Each partner insures his own life for the benefit of his other partners absolutely. A separate policy is usually effected in favour of each partner. These policies are payable at the life assured's retirement date or in the event of his death, enabling the continuing partners to repay his capital. Trust policies for a large partnership usually involve a multiplicity of policies which can be somewhat inconvenient.

Moreover, the IHT dangers of breaching the reciprocity provisions of s 10 must always be watched, as must the 'pre-owned assets' income tax provisions (see **Chapter 13**), where (as is often the case) the settlor retains an interest in the trust policy. It must also be remembered that each trust a person creates can, subject to the commerciality argument below, affect his personal IHT 'clock' and the CGT exemption available on any other trusts he has set up.

Life of another policy

10.53 Each partner effects a policy on the life of his other partners to provide the means to pay for his share of the outgoing partner's capital account. The market value of policies on the lives of the surviving partners would be part of the deceased partner's estate for IHT purposes.

If there is a wide disparity of ages it may be difficult for a young partner to pay the premiums required on the lives of the senior partners, but term assurance could play a part.

General

10.54   Whether the actual policies are endowment, whole life or term depends on whether the actual retirement dates are known with precision, and whether the retirement cover can be afforded. Term assurance may be of great help but would only cover death before the usual retirement date. A mixture of policies may be required.

In conclusion, therefore, financing retirement by life assurance can have various advantages. Reciprocal arrangements can be made as described above, which should constitute commercial arrangements between the partners provided the consideration moves directly between them and there are no trust policies within the IHT charge for discretionary trusts or gifts with reservation, or the income tax 'pre-owned assets' rules.

An extra twist would be to consider a 'critical illness' provision in any such policies, to cover not only the death but also the serious illness (and hence the enforced early retirement) of a partner. Moreover, the payments received under life assurance policies are normally exempt from CGT under TCGA 1992, s 210.

On the maturity of a life policy, the beneficial owner of the cash proceeds may then invest in an annuity and depending on his age at that time, a large proportion of this annuity, constituting in effect a return of capital, will be tax free, under the provisions of ITTOIA 2005, s 717, and only the income element will be taxable. Pensions on the other hand are fully taxable upon the recipient as income except to the extent that the limited lump sum commutation rights are exercised.

PARTNERSHIP OF 'RELATIVES'

10.55   This section concerns an entity that is first and foremost a commercial partnership (within the Partnership Act 1890) and only by coincidence formed of members of a family. Thus, it is quite distinct from the FLP structure described at **10.30**.

IHT planning in partnerships is made more difficult where partners are 'connected persons' within the definition of s 270 by reason of being related. 'Relatives' for this purpose include spouses, father, mother, children and issue, brother, sister, uncle, aunt, nephew and niece and such relatives' spouses. By virtue of the interaction of ss 270 and 10, any disposition between 'relatives' is in effect presumed to be a gift and the onus of rebutting this presumption is on the taxpayer.

The onus will be satisfied if it can be shown that the 'relative' is being treated no more favourably than would be a 'stranger'. On any partnership rearrangement involving a 'relative', it is therefore good tax planning to introduce a 'stranger' on the same or similar terms, if this is otherwise possible; or be able to show that terms previously reached with 'non-connected' partners were on the same or a similar basis.

For IHT purposes, the question of whether a person is a 'connected person' is determined in accordance with TCGA 1992, s 286 (except that 'relative' includes uncle, aunt, nephew and niece, and 'settlement' 'settlor' and 'trustee' carry their meaning for IHT purposes (s 270)). Thus, in the case of non-related partners, they are not 'connected persons', 'in relation to acquisitions or disposals of partnership assets pursuant to bona fide commercial arrangements' (TCGA 1992, s 286(4)).

Accordingly, in these circumstances it is normally possible to show that there was the appropriate element of bona fide commercial arrangement and reciprocity, thereby avoiding any IHT liability.

Similarly, there should be no gratuitous benefit giving rise to an IHT assessment where an individual transfers an asset or pays a sum in consideration of an actuarially equivalent annuity. Moreover, if this annuity comes within the exclusion to the 'settlements' anti-avoidance provisions by virtue of ITTOIA 2005, s 627(2) (eg defined payments under partnership agreements), the annuity should be fully deductible for all rates of income tax by the payer. Before implementing this suggestion, careful consideration should be given to the CGT implications in TCGA 1992, s 37(3) because the consideration for disposal of the asset could be measured by the capitalised value of the annuity subject to Statement of Practice 1/79 dated 12 January 1979.

To the extent that the creation of the family partnership involves funding or the transfer of assets, any transfer of value for IHT purposes will normally constitute PETs to the other family members, in so far as the transfer is not covered by an exemption (eg the spouse or annual exemption). If the partnership is funded with cash (sterling), there should be no immediate CGT issues. Alternatively, a transfer of assets standing at a low or no gain may be appropriate. Another option, if the asset transferred is a business asset standing at a gain, is to claim CGT hold-over relief under TCGA 1992, s 165.

The fact that the partnership is transparent means that income of minor unmarried children will be assessed on their parents, if it was the parents who contributed the partnership assets (ITTOIA 2005, s 629). Partnership assets which are capital growth but non-income producing may therefore be attractive until the children reach age 18.

Further analysis of family general partnerships and their tax implications can be found in an article on the subject in *Tax Adviser* (May 2009).

Chapter 11

The art of giving

INTRODUCTION

11.1 This chapter considers how to make gifts in an IHT-efficient way. It highlights some of the pitfalls of the legislation and deals specifically with the gifts with reservation of benefit provisions. The following topics are covered:

- planning the correct type of gift with particular reference to the nil rate band; and potentially exempt transfers (PETs);

- gifts with reservation with particular reference to the family home, *Ingram* and FA 1999 (and also pre-owned assets – see **Chapter 13**);

- gifts of an interest in land;

- other planning aspects of gifts;

- the donee paying IHT rather than the donor;

- gifts versus sales; and

- gifts versus loans.

In addition to the above IHT planning issues, **Chapter 12**, which covers the use of exemptions and dispositions that are not transfers of value, includes the following:

- gifts in value not exceeding £3,000 per annum (s 19);

- £250 per annum gifts to any number of separate donees (s 20);

- normal expenditure out of income (s 21);

- gifts in consideration of marriage or civil partnership (s 22);

- dispositions for maintenance of family (s 11);

- gifts of excluded property (s 6(1));

- dispositions allowable for income tax and corporation tax (s 12);

- charities (s 23);

- political parties (s 24);

- housing associations (s 24A);

- gifts for national purposes (s 25 and Sch 3);

- gifts subsequently held for public benefit (s 26 (repealed) and s 26A);

- voidable transfers (s 150); etc;

- deathbed situations; and

- gifts by cheque.

PLANNING THE 'CORRECT' TYPE OF GIFT

A reminder of the gift rules

11.2   Under the present regime there are effectively three main rates of inheritance tax: the 40% rate which is chargeable on death (reduced to 36% in certain circumstances involving charitable legacies; see **Chapter 5**), the 20% rate chargeable in respect of lifetime transfers of value (where the transferor does not die within seven years of the transfer), and 0% chargeable in respect of chargeable transfers up to a value of the applicable nil rate band.

The general rule is that the tax is immediately chargeable. Thus, a lifetime gift of £100,000 to any trust, other than for a charity or for a disabled person or on the transition from an IPDI to a BMT; or (for example) a gift to a public company, by an individual who has exhausted his nil rate band is immediately chargeable at the 20% rate (subject to possible relief, such as in relation to 100% business or agricultural property relief – see **Chapter 15**).

The deemed transfer of value made by participators in a close company when the close company makes a transfer of value is also immediately chargeable to tax (see s 94).

Not all transfers of value are immediately chargeable, however. As explained in **Chapter 1**, certain transfers of value are only chargeable if the transferor dies within seven years after the date of the transfer of value. These transfers are referred to as 'potentially exempt transfers' (PETs). A PET is (see s 3A) a 'transfer of value' (see below) made by an individual (after 22 March 2006) to:

- another individual (s 3A(1A)(c)(i));

- another individual where the individual making the transfer makes the transfer of value because his interest in possession has terminated (see s 52, but subject to s 3A(6A) and (7));

- a bereaved minor's trust where the transfer arises on the coming to an end of an IPDI (s 3A(1A)(c)(iii)); or

- a statutory disabled trust.

The cessation of a gift with reservation is also a PET (FA 1986, s 102(4)). However, a purchased interest within s 5(1B) is not a PET; see s 3A(6A). Nor is a transfer of value arising under s 74A ('Arrangements involving acquisition of interest in settled property etc'); see s 74B(1). For further discussion on the concept of PETs, see **Chapter 1**.

The 'transfer of value' must itself satisfy certain conditions. In the case of a 'straight' transfer to an individual, the value transferred by the transfer of value must be attributable to property which becomes comprised in the estate of that individual or, if this is not the case, the estate of that individual must be increased in value by virtue of the transfer. The charge is potentially exempt to the extent of the increase in value of the individual's estate.

In the case of transfers to a BMT or a disabled person's trust the value transferred must be attributable to property which, by virtue of the transfer, becomes settled property to which s 71A or s 89 applies. Again the transfer of value is potentially exempt only to the extent that this condition is satisfied. For the 'IPDI to BMT' transfer to be a PET the following rules apply (see s 3A(3B)):

- L has a life interest;
- that interest is an IPDI;
- the IPDI ends (on or after 22 March 2006);
- L still had the IPDI just before it ended; and
- when the IPDI ends, the fund is still held on trust and is subject to the BMT rules in s 71A.

The above principles are illustrated by the following examples.

Example 11.1 – No PET (1)

An individual transfers assets to a company whose shares comprise the settled property.

Not a PET, because it is the company that benefits, not an individual.

Example 11.2 – No PET (2)

An individual pays the school fees of his grandchildren.

There is no PET, because no other individual's estate is increased by the transfer of value.

Example 11.3 – No PET (3)?

An individual purchases a holiday for his mother.

Arguably not a PET, because the estate of his mother is not increased.

Example 11.4 – No PET (4)?

An individual purchases a holiday for his mother, but on terms that it is not transferable.

Not a PET because her estate is not increased. Some consider this to be too harsh an interpretation: the recipient of a holiday receives a bundle of rights, for example to transport, accommodation and meals, but (in this example, as is common) cannot re-sell those rights.

The solution is to arrange the gift so that a PET is made, if that is the intention.

Thus, in Example 11.2 the individual could gift the cash to the parents (a PET) leaving the parents to arrange the school fees. In Examples 11.3 and 11.4, the individual could give the cash to his mother so that she can purchase the holiday herself. Arguably, the purchase of a holiday may be 'normal expenditure out of income', if a regular occurrence, or alternatively gives the purchaser some rights that he could assign, but it is much simpler just to make a cash gift. It is understood that HMRC do not take the point, but there is little formal guidance. It would be easy for executors to overlook such a gift, especially if made several years before death.

It should be remembered that a PET involves a transfer of value (s 3A(1)). A 'transfer of value' requires a disposition (s 3(1)). A 'disposition' is not defined in IHTA 1984, except that it includes a disposition effected by associated operations (s 272). An interesting point arises in certain situations as to what extent (if any) there is a disposition giving rise to a transfer of value.

For example, an individual invites friends round for dinner, during which the guests drink some very expensive bottles of the host's champagne. What is the IHT position? The host's estate has been diminished by the cost of the bottles of champagne. But does this constitute a disposition, and a transfer of value? If so, it appears that the 'gift' of champagne is more likely to be a chargeable transfer than a PET, as the guest's estate is unaffected by it (s 3A(2)).

The IHT consequences could be far-reaching. Fortunately, in the writers' experience, HMRC do not tend to take the point to extremes.

Using the gift rules

11.3   Lifetime PETs enable the individual to effect a substantial saving of IHT on his death. No charge arises immediately, and none arises if he survives seven years. After seven years, the amount of the gift also drops out of the transferor's current reckoning and cumulative total for future gifts. Even if the transferor dies within seven years of the date of the gift, a saving is possible if the date of death is at least three years after the date of the gift (s 7(4)).

If the transferor does die within the seven-year period, the value of (what is now) a chargeable transfer is the value at the date of the gift. Therefore, it is advisable to give away appreciating assets. In the case of depreciating assets, there is a fallback in s 131(2). This rule, which is not well known, allows the transferee, should the value have gone down by the date of the transferor's death, or should he have sold the asset at arm's length at a loss in the transferor's lifetime, to substitute the reduced value as the taxable amount. Remember the possibility of insurance if there is a known risk of the transferor dying within the seven-year period.

However, making a PET is not always good tax planning. For example:

- A PET may avoid an immediate IHT charge arising at the date of the gift, but it will not reduce the value of the transferor's estate on death if a benefit is retained in the property given away so that the gift with reservation of benefit provisions apply (see FA 1986, ss 102–102C and Sch 20). However, if caught by those rules, the donor is at least spared a 'pre-owned assets' income tax charge (see **Chapter 13**).

- Chargeable assets included in the IHT estate receive a capital gains tax-free uplift on death. This is lost if the asset is given away to a trust or to some other person or persons. This may mean that gifts should be made to the person about to die, not by him.

- A gift to a connected person (or indeed a disposal at undervalue otherwise than at arm's length) is a chargeable event for CGT purposes. The result can be to trigger a CGT liability without necessarily achieving an IHT saving.

Example 11.5 – Late gift for CGT

An individual is near death and his spouse owns chargeable assets which have appreciated in value. If the estate of the deceased, including these assets, would be within the nil rate band (see below), the spouse could gift them to the spouse who is near death.

The assets could then pass under his will back to his surviving spouse free of IHT, but with the benefit of a free uplift in market value for CGT.

Arguably, there is no need for the restriction in value, since there is no limit on gifts between UK-domiciled spouses, but that may be considered provocative. Even if the ailing spouse has lost mental capacity, such that the devolution of his estate is already fixed at the time of the gift and it can be said with certainty where the spouse's property will end up, the associated operations rules cannot apply: death is not such an operation.

If the transaction in Example 11.5 is done the moment before death, it might be said that the assets did not truly form part of his estate within the meaning of IHTA 1984 (see *Westmoreland* and *Ramsay*). There are few examples of the application of the approach in those cases being applied to IHT. However, it is thought that, in the situation just described, there are no associated operations.

Example 11.6 – Gift of asset that has grown in value

Five years ago, a wealthy individual purchased a holiday home for £100,000. It is now worth £300,000, and he gifts it to his adult child. No IHT arises immediately because he has made a PET. But he will be immediately liable for capital gains tax at 28% (for 2012–13) on a deemed chargeable gain of £200,000 (subject to any reliefs).

If the donor dies in the next couple of years, the gift will be set against his nil rate band and there may be no IHT saving. Furthermore, if he reserves a benefit in the house by using it otherwise than for full consideration, the gift with reservation rules may apply so that his estate is charged to IHT on the value of the house notwithstanding the gift (see **11.11**).

Possible solutions

11.4   One can approach this problem in either of two ways. The first is to make a PET (to avoid the IHT) and then rely upon CGT reliefs. For example, the transferor could have made a gift of an exempt asset for CGT purposes, such as a principal private residence, chattels, a car, or cash; or he could have given assets which qualified for 100% business asset hold-over relief under TCGA 1992, s 165. A full discussion of exempt CGT assets is beyond the scope of this book, but it will be seen that, in the event of death soon after the gift, a gain is taxable to CGT that might have benefited from tax-free uplift on death.

The more interesting approach is to make an immediately chargeable transfer for IHT purposes (apparently triggering an IHT charge) so that TCGA 1992, s 260 hold-over relief is available. This approach is very flexible because chargeable CGT assets may generally be given. For example, if the transferor's gift fell within his available nil rate band, or if he was able to claim 100% agricultural or business property relief, he could make a gift to a relevant property (eg discretionary) trust. There would be no IHT charge at the date of the gift, on the gift to the discretionary trust. Although the IHT charge is nil, he has not made a potentially exempt transfer and he may therefore claim s 260 hold-over relief, and defer the CGT charge (possibly indefinitely).

However, see **11.6** for a possible restriction involving hold-over relief and private residence relief for CGT purposes. Also, hold-over relief is only a deferral relief and does not eliminate the latent capital gain attaching to the asset gifted.

Melville schemes

11.5   What if the value of the immediately chargeable transfer of value exceeds the nil rate band and qualifies for no IHT reliefs? Prior to FA 2002, one answer was to make an immediately chargeable transfer of value to a discretionary trust, so that s 260 hold-over relief was available, but depress the value of the chargeable transfer so that the IHT was kept to a minimum. The High Court and Court of Appeal decisions in *Melville and others v IRC* [2001] STC 1271 are examples of this; and, although legislation has now blocked the scheme (see below), some understanding of the case, and of successor 'son of *Melville*' schemes, is still useful.

In *Melville* the transferor made a gift of property to a discretionary trust. Under the terms of the trust, after three months he became entitled to a right to direct the trustees how to deal with the settled property, including the right to direct the appointment of the whole trust fund to himself. This was a valuable right (discounted by the fact that he might die within the three-month period and so not acquire the right at all). Its existence meant that the transfer of value made by him was very low. Therefore, if the scheme worked, full hold-over relief was obtained with a small IHT charge.

The critical issue was whether or not the right constituted 'property' for the purposes of IHTA 1984. The High Court found (without much difficulty) that it was, as did the Court of Appeal. This resulted in a large number of '*Melville schemes*' to minimise the value of a transfer for IHT whilst claiming s 260 hold-over for CGT purposes. Such schemes were countered in FA 2002 by IHTA 1984, s 47A, which introduced the definition of 'settlement power' in relation to trust property, and which amended IHTA 1984, s 272 to exclude a settlement power from the definition of 'property' for IHT purposes.

Subsequently, schemes were devised to sidestep this legislation, until restrictions in hold-over relief introduced in FA 2004 effectively put an end to them (see **1.31** and **1.32**).

11.5   The art of giving

The order in which gifts are made is also a factor which will affect the efficacy of planning by making gifts. See further **11.9**.

Some of the main points mentioned above are further explained in the following three examples.

Example 11.7 – PET and taper

Estate (before gift) of £675,000.

Assume gift (eg outright to individual) of £375,000 made in the seventh year before death (ie more than six but fewer than seven years before death), and death occurring in 2012–13.

	£	£
Inheritance tax payable at death rate on		
First £375,000 (being the potentially exempt transfer)		
First £325,000	Nil	
Next £50,000 at 40%	20,000	
	20,000	
But as donor died in the seventh year		
The tax after taper relief is		
£20,000 × 20%	4,000	
Inheritance tax payable on remaining estate at death:		
£300,000 at 40%	120,000	
Inheritance tax on potentially exempt transfer	4,000	
Total inheritance tax	124,000	
Note:		
If gift in sixth year:		
inheritance tax on £20,000 × 40%		8,000
If gift made in fifth year:		
inheritance tax on £20,000 × 60%		12,000
If gift made in fourth year:		
inheritance tax on £20,000 × 80%		16,000
Otherwise, inheritance tax on first £375,000		20,000
Inheritance tax on next £300,000 (as above)		120,000
Inheritance tax on £675,000		140,000

Example 11.8 – Chargeable transfer and taper

If the gift made in the *seventh year before death* had been into, say, a discretionary trust (no benefit reserved) at 2012–13 rates:

	£
Inheritance tax payable on creation = £375,000 at one-half death rate (one-half of £20,000)	10,000
But taper charge at death rate (as above)	4,000
(No repayment of IHT involved.	
Payment of £10,000 stands)	
If death in the sixth year	
Inheritance tax on creation	10,000
Tapered death charge rate (as above)	8,000
(No repayment of inheritance tax involved.	
Payment of £10,000 stands)	
If death in the fifth year	
Inheritance tax on creation	10,000
Tapered death charge rate (as above)	12,000
Additional inheritance tax due (£12,000 less £10,000 already paid)	
Death charge with credit for inheritance tax paid	2,000
If death in the fourth year	
Inheritance tax on creation	10,000
Tapered death charge rate (as above)	16,000
Additional inheritance tax due	6,000
If death in the third or earlier year	
Inheritance tax on creation	10,000
Untapered death charge rate	20,000
Additional inheritance tax due (half death charge)	10,000

Chargeable transfers and PETs made within seven years of the PET in question which have become chargeable provide special problems.

The complexities of the legislation are illustrated by the remarks of Mr Powell, as reported in *Hansard*, 10 June 1986 at column 401:

'At present, because the seven-year period brings the potentially exempt transfer into the taxation net where the transferor dies within seven years and the potentially exempt transfer cumulates with the gifts made by the transferor in the previous seven years, the effect is that the transferor's chargeable disposals within 14 years of his death are affected by the inheritance tax as opposed to those within three years of his death, with cumulation ten years back, making 13 years in all, under the capital transfer tax system. So for those caught by the tax the new law is slightly worse than the old law.'

The 'knock-on' effect, known as the 14-year backward shadow, is illustrated in the example that follows.

Example 11.9 – Cumulating earlier transfers

1 October 1999	PET	£200,000
1 April 2003	Chargeable transfer	£100,000
3 June 2006	PET	£480,000
11 November 2008	Chargeable transfer	£340,000
1 September 2012	T dies leaving estate of	£500,000

On 1 April 2003, no chargeable transfers had been made in the previous seven years. Therefore, the full nil rate band applicable at the time (£250,000) was available and no tax was payable on the chargeable transfer of £100,000.

On 11 November 2008, there were cumulative chargeable transfers in the past seven years of £100,000. The tax payable on the November 2008 transfer of £340,000 was:

	£
£212,000 @ 0%	Nil
(ie nil rate band of £312,000 less £100,000 of cumulations)	
£128,000 @ 20% (lifetime rates)	25,600
Tax paid:	25,600
Adjustments to be made on death:	

(1) In relation to the potentially exempt transfer of £480,000 on 3 June 2006 (which has become chargeable following T's death within seven years)

Cumulations:	
1 April 2003	100,000
Total	100,000
Nil rate band available	285,000
Less: cumulations	(100,000)

Nil rate band remaining available	185,000
Tax payable on £185,000 @ 0%	Nil
Tax payable on £295,000 @ 40%	118,000
20% taper on transfer more than six but less than seven years before death	23,600
Additional tax payable re PET on 3 June 2006	23,600

(2) In relation to the chargeable transfer of £340,000 on 11 November 2008

Cumulations:

1 April 2003	100,000
3 June 2006	480,000
Total	580,000
Nil rate band available	312,000
Less: cumulations	(580,000)
Nil rate band remaining available	Nil
Tax payable on £340,000 @ 40%	136,000
80% taper on transfer more than three but less than four years before death	108,800
Less: credit for tax paid on lifetime transfer	(25,600)
	83,200
Additional tax payable re chargeable transfer on 11 November 2008	83,200

(3) Estate on death 1 September 2012

Cumulations:

3 June 2006	480,000
11 November 2008	340,000
Total	820,000
Nil rate band available	325,000
Less: cumulations	(820,000)
Nil rate band remaining available	None
Tax payable on £500,000 @ 40%	200,000
No taper relief	

This example actually illustrates four important benefits provided by the IHT legislation:

(a) The chargeable gift is valued at the time it is made, not the value at the date of death. This is useful for appreciating assets and represents a built-in 'freezing' operation. However, difficulties will arise in valuing a gift retrospectively and there is a risk that HMRC may try to apply 'hindsight' to the valuation. In addition, the valuation for CGT purposes can be on a different basis.

(b)   The rates of IHT operating on the death apply.

(c)   For cash-flow purposes, there is no IHT payable until the survivorship condition is breached. Whereas the advantages in (a) and (b) also apply to non-potentially exempt chargeable gifts, this third advantage is peculiar to PETs.

These IHT advantages must clearly be weighed against any CGT charges which may result from the proposed transactions.

(d)   Where the donee of a PET dies before the donor, the possibility of quick succession relief should be borne in mind by the executors of the donee, who may have to wait up to seven years to see if the PET becomes chargeable by the death of the donor. Consider the possibility of insurance.

Use of the nil rate band (s 7)

11.6   An estate owner, especially one who is widowed, should ensure that he takes advantage of the nil rate band (see **Chapter 4**) and keeps this under review because s 8 provides for indexation of all rate bands annually, unless Parliament otherwise determines (as it frequently does). Traditionally, the increase in the retail price index (RPI) in December each year was applied to the rates of chargeable transfers made on or after 6 April in the following year (but see below).

FA 2006 set the nil rate band for 2009–10 at £325,000. FA 2007 further increased the nil rate band, to £350,000 for 2010–11. However, it was subsequently announced in the Pre-Budget Report 2009 that this increase would not take place, and that the nil rate band for 2010–11 would remain at its 2009–10 level of £325,000. Furthermore, FA 2010, s 8(3) provided that this freezing of the nil rate band to £325,000 would be extended to cover the tax years 2011–12 to 2014–15 inclusive as well.

As indicated at **1.1**, the consumer price index (CPI) replaces the RPI as the default indexation factor for all direct taxes including IHT, although this change will not affect the nil rate band until 2016–17 at the earliest, as the government announced on 5 December 2012 that the nil rate band for 2015–16 would be increased by 1% to £329,000.

In the case of spouses and civil partners, the facility to transfer unused nil rate band, which was introduced in FA 2008 (see **Chapter 3**), has perhaps made the use of their nil rate bands on the first death seem less important. However, the use of nil rate bands as part of a lifetime IHT planning exercise should not be overlooked or underestimated. Often in such situations it will be best to preserve the unused transferable nil rate band of the deceased spouse and to use the personal estate of the survivor to fund gifts, since there is a chance that the donor may survive the gifts by seven years, 'refreshing' the nil rate band available.

Although the PET regime (where no IHT is immediately payable and none will be provided the donor survives seven years) improves the outlook for making gifts, for many people the nil rate band may represent a practical limit on IHT planning. Nevertheless, the nil rate band can be useful for making lifetime chargeable transfers (eg a settlement) where, although no IHT is payable because of the nil rate band, hold-over for CGT purposes can be obtained.

Prior to changes introduced in FA 2004, a discretionary settlement within the nil rate band could be a useful vehicle for the owner of a second home with a significant capital gain not eligible for CGT private residence exemption and whose market value was less than, or equal to the owner's available nil rate band.

Example 11.10 – A scheme that no longer works so well

The owner would transfer the property on discretionary trusts claiming hold-over relief for CGT purposes. The trustees of the settlement would permit a suitable beneficiary (eg the son) to occupy the property as a main residence. Then, on a sale of the property they would claim full CGT exemption under the terms of TCGA 1992, s 225 (and see *Sansom v Peay* [1976] STC 494).

However, TCGA 1992, s 226A was introduced (by FA 2004) to block private residence relief in most cases on the disposal of a residence on or after 10 December 2003 by an individual or settlement trustees, if the property's base cost had been reduced following a hold-over relief claim under TCGA 1992, s 260 on an earlier disposal.

Hence, in this example, a s 260 claim by trustees on a transfer of the property to the son prevents private residence relief being claimed by the son on a future disposal (or vice versa), in respect of the beneficiary's (or trustees') period of ownership, including any gain held over.

This treatment is subject to transitional rules if the earlier s 260 disposal was made before 10 December 2003.

Despite the above CGT restriction, it remains possible to use a combination of hold-over relief and main residence relief in one special context, that of furnished holiday lettings.

Example 11.11 – Gift from father to daughter

On the occasion of, say, the gift of a holiday home (where the property qualifies as a furnished holiday letting) from father to adult daughter, a hold-over claim could be made, not under s 260 but under s 165. The daughter would live in the property as her only or main residence for a period of time, before selling it. The entire gain would benefit from main residence relief under s 223.

Although the above anti-avoidance provisions introduced in FA 2004 precluded a combination of hold-over relief under s 260 and main residence relief, the possibility of a hold-over claim under s 165 combined with a main residence relief claim remained.

Note that this arrangement would not have achieved the same tax result if the property had been transferred into trust rather than being gifted to the daughter outright, because where both business assets hold-over relief under s 165 and chargeable transfer hold-over relief under s 260 could apply, the latter takes priority (s 165(3)(d)).

It was originally announced at Budget 2009 that the furnished holiday lettings rules which treat such properties as a trade would be repealed with effect from 2010–11. Fortunately, the abolition of the rules did not subsequently take place, However, the relevant criteria to qualify for treatment as a furnished holiday let were generally tightened with effect from 6 April 2012 following changes introduced in FA 2011, with the result that some properties that qualified under the 'old' provisions may fail to do so under the amended ones.

For a property forming part of a trade under normal principles as opposed to mere letting (eg a small hotel establishment), the combination of hold-over relief and main residence relief potentially remains.

Revocation of hold-over claim

11.7   The above anti-avoidance provision in TCGA 1992, s 226A provides that if a s 260 claim on the earlier disposal is revoked, it is treated as never having applied and private residence relief becomes available (s 226(A)(6)). Declining to make a s 260 claim, or revoking an earlier one, could be considered if the gain since the original transfer into trust has already exceeded the original held-over gain, or is expected to exceed it. This is assuming, of course, that the settlor is content to bear the CGT liability on the property transfer.

However, the ability to revoke a s 260 claim appears to be limited in its scope. Such claims are governed by TMA 1970, s 42 and Sch 1A. The government's stated view is that, if a claim was made within a tax return and the 12-month time limit for amending the return has closed, the claim cannot be withdrawn. The same applies if a claim was made outside the return and the time limit for amending the claim has expired (Hansard, Finance Bill Committee debates 2004, column 355).

Use of seven-year cumulation rule (s 7(1))

11.8   Coupled with a positive attitude to the use of PETs, careful use of the seven-year cumulative ladder can produce staggering results. Seven-year cumulation is really a misnomer. If the donor dies having made a PET just within seven years which is therefore now chargeable, that gift is aggregated for its own ladder with chargeable transfers within the seven years preceding its own date, making 14 years in all.

Nevertheless, a wealthy husband and wife both aged, say, 55 might use the nil rate band and make lifetime chargeable gifts (possibly also entitled to CGT hold-over relief) of £325,000 each (for 2012–13), making a combined total of £650,000. They could repeat that exercise at age 62 and, if they died after age 69, they would each have a further nil rate band – a grand total of £1,950,000, even assuming no increase in the nil rate band during that period.

If the 50% lower business or agricultural property relief was available, that figure would double to £3,900,000. With 100% business or agricultural property relief, the amount would be unlimited. In addition, if they had started making PETs earlier than in their fifties, the saving could be considerably increased. But even at a more modest level, there is a surprising level of saving which can be achieved, particularly if consistent use is made of the annual and normal income exemptions as well.

This aspect is further illustrated below.

Example 11.12 – The eight-year cycle at its best (no previous gifts)

Year(s)	Individual transferor	Reliefs/exemptions		Cumulative	
		Nil rate band	Annual	Total	Total
		£	£	£	£
1	Husband	325,000	6,000	331,000	331,000
2–7	Husband	–	18,000	18,000	349,000
8	Husband	325,000	3,000	328,000	677,000
1–8	Wife	650,000	27,000	677,000	1,354,000

Notes:

(1)   If all property transferred qualifies for the lower 50% business/ agricultural property relief, the cumulative total could be £2,708,000. If 100% relief is available, the cumulative total is potentially unlimited.

(2)   The nil rate band for 2012–13 is £325,000 per individual.

(3)   The table assumes that the individuals concerned start year 1 with a clean slate, ie with no cumulation of chargeable transfers and without having used up the annual £3,000 exemption in the year preceding year 1.

The above table can be summarised in a different way:

	£
Nil rate band £325,000 × 2 =	650,000
Annual exemption £3,000 × 8 =	24,000
Add: assumed annual exemption brought forward £3,000 × 1 =	3,000
	677,000
plus like amount, for the other spouse	677,000
	1,354,000

Notes 1–3 above apply as before.

Order of gifts

11.9   As IHT is a cumulative tax, the nil rate band will be taken up by earlier gifts (whether lifetime chargeable gifts or PETs becoming chargeable). Accordingly, as a general rule, one should make early gifts to those whom one wishes to benefit the most, for example, one's children and issue, so they are either first on the cumulative ladder, or are first to drop out after seven years. Gifts with 100% business/agricultural property relief do not show up at all on the ladder if the property in question is retained by the transferee.

There is one anomalous feature relating to lifetime chargeable transfers where the donor dies within seven years and IHT has to be recalculated on the death rate, with the benefit of taper relief. Under s 7(5), tapering relief cannot be given if the result would be that IHT on death is less than the tax paid in the lifetime. This means that with the death rate at 40%, and half of that rate paid at the lifetime rate of 20% the gift can never get the benefit of taper relief in the earliest two years of the seven-year period (ie the sixth and seventh years) where the reduction in rates is to a percentage of 40% for the sixth year (ie 40% of the death rate of 40% = 16%) or 20% for the seventh year (20% of 40% =

8%). Since both 16% and 8% are below the half rate of 20% paid on the gift in lifetime no reduction can be made.

Where, however, lifetime chargeable transfers are limited to the nil rate band, and PETs are made thereafter rather than before, that anomalous result ought not to arise. If the chargeable lifetime gift has been within the nil rate band, no taper relief is available, as the applicable rate is zero! This point is often overlooked.

If two or more gifts are made on the same day, s 266 prescribes their order. The transfers are treated as made in the order which produces the lowest value chargeable (s 266(1)). This rule was important for lifetime chargeable transfers made on the same day, some grossed up and some not, in former times when there were a number of increasing rates. Subject to that, the transfers are treated as one so they share proportionately the total tax (eg if they use up all or part of the nil rate band and go up into the taxable band) (s 266(2)).

As a general rule, if a donor is contemplating an immediately chargeable gift into a discretionary trust plus PET gifts, the discretionary trust gift should be made on an earlier date so as to ensure that the nil rate band attaches to the gift into the discretionary trust and periodic ten-year charges and interim charges are kept to the minimum.

A further reason for making chargeable transfers before PETs in the same tax year is HMRC's approach to allocating the annual exemption. If an individual makes a PET (eg a gift to a sibling) earlier in the same tax year than a chargeable lifetime transfer (eg a gift to a discretionary trust), the PET will use his annual exemption, even if the gift subsequently becomes an exempt transfer due to the individual surviving for more than seven years. HMRC guidance (at IHTM14143) states: 'apply the exemption first to the *earlier* transfer. It does not matter whether the transfers are PETs or chargeable when made'.

If an individual dies within seven years, the earlier PET becomes chargeable to IHT at the date of that gift. For the purposes of allocating the annual exemption, a chargeable PET is deemed to have been made later than any non-PET made in the same tax year (s 19(3A)). However, HMRC practice (see above) appears to allocate the annual exemption to transfers of value in chronological order. IHT is calculated at the death rates applicable at the time of death, subject to taper relief. In addition, the transfer is cumulated with the death estate, and will also affect the individual's cumulative total of chargeable transfers.

Another appropriate order of giving, where the nil rate band is in point and PETs can drop out after seven years, could be as follows.

(1)   Cash gifts (ie where the reliefs in (2) and (3) below will not apply).

(2)   Gifts where the instalment basis (see **2.27** onwards) is available under s 227, 228 or 229, namely land and buildings; certain shares and securities; businesses or interests therein and timber.

(3)   Followed by assets which will receive the 50% business or agricultural property reliefs so that those reliefs will benefit from the full rate of IHT.

(4)   In theory, gifts with 100% business or agricultural property relief, provided the conditions for relief are maintained, can be left until last since they will not be subject to IHT if death intervenes.

In one other situation, the order of gifts may be important. Suppose that a widow, remarried to a wealthy man whom she survives, enjoys an immediate post-death interest under his will, with remainder to his nephews. Whether or not his nil rate band is transferable, she realises that, on her death, the trust fund will be aggregated with her own free estate so that any available nil rate bands will be spread across the whole. If she makes gifts from her free estate to her own children she in effect secures at least her own nil rate band for their benefit, so that none of it is 'wasted' on her late husband's family.

Making gifts now that are likely to appreciate (and vice versa)

11.10   There is another reason why the correct timing of gifts is of crucial importance. The IHT planner will be primarily concerned that an asset should be transferred at a time when its potential value has not been reached or is in a temporary trough, since the values of both PETs and lifetime chargeable gifts are frozen at the date of gift.

For example, a business might be suffering from a temporary dip in profitability; the market for the asset in question may be currently depressed, for example, property or shares; or the asset may have a built-in acceleration factor (see, for example, the deferred ordinary share bonus issue discussion in **9.6**, or the gift may be of a foal which may one day become a Derby winner). A subsequent increase in value after the gift has been made will not affect the IHT liability so that the question of whether the gift is covered by the annual £3,000 exemption (see **12.2**) is decided on the value at the date of the gift.

Consider also the reverse position, ie that one should *retain* an asset with a current high value which is likely to depreciate; for example, a lease retained by the estate owner, or a middle-aged, petrol-guzzling, high-performance car without pretensions to becoming a classic.

GIFTS WITH RESERVATION OF BENEFIT – THE RULES AND SOME POINTERS (FA 1986, S 102 AND SCH 20)

The general rule in FA 1986, s 102

11.11   FA 1986, s 102 is an anti-avoidance provision, in relation to gifts of property (including land) made on or after 18 March 1986. It applies to an individual ('the donor') who gifts his land, shares, cash and other property to, say, his children or the family trust where:

(a)   possession and enjoyment of the property is not bona fide assumed by the donee (ie the recipient of the gift) at or before the beginning of the relevant period; or

(b)   at any time in the relevant period the property is not enjoyed to the entire exclusion, or virtually to the entire exclusion, of the donor and of any benefit to him by contract or otherwise.

The 'relevant period' is the period ending on the date of the individual's death and beginning seven years before that date, or if it is later, on the date of the gift. For example, where a donor makes a gift ten years before his death which satisfies (a) or (b) above, the relevant period is the seven years before his death. Where the gift was made four years before his death, the relevant period is that four years.

Example 11.13 – Faulty advice

James transferred his flat in London to his son Henry on 6 April 1999, at the same time entering into a lease of it from Henry at the then current market rent. The rent was always paid but never reviewed. In 2011, a golfing pal said 'you've nothing to worry about now, it's been more than seven years since the gift and you didn't reserve a benefit at the time, so I wouldn't bother to go on paying the rent'.

James thought he had heard something about 'pre-owned assets tax' (POAT), so kept on paying his son so as not to be caught by POAT. He was dismayed, on taking proper tax advice in late February 2013 as to whether POAT did apply, to learn that he was well free of POAT; unfortunately, because the rent he was paying was substantially below the current market and had been for some time, he had therefore reserved a benefit out of the gift during the 'relevant period' identified in s 102(1).

Its effect is that the property disposed of is a 'gift with reservation of benefit' (commonly referred to as a 'GROB' or 'GWR') and is treated for the purposes of IHTA 1984 as property to which the individual was beneficially entitled immediately before his death (FA 1986, s 102). The gift is therefore ineffective to reduce the value of his IHT estate.

The proper scope of s 102 is not easy to grasp on first reading. In **11.12** onwards, the meaning and relevance of the important terms are considered. An explanation is also given of how s 102 applies in special circumstances such as gifts into settlement, and gifts of property which is then sold or replaced by the donee.

A pleasant surprise is that, although the provision appears to cover any possible benefit retained or enjoyed, there are limits on its application; see, for example, the decision of the House of Lords in *Lady Ingram* [1999] STC 37, and the statutory exceptions explained at **11.19**. Furthermore, although FA 1999 reversed *Ingram*, FA 1999 provided its own opportunities for tax planning.

'Property'

11.12   The limits on the term 'property' were considered in *Lady Ingram v IRC* [1999] STC 37.

Lady Ingram v IRC

11.13   In 1987, Lady Ingram made a gift to her children of the freehold interest in Hurst Lodge, subject to a leasehold interest which she retained. The leasehold interest was created by two steps: first, a conveyance of her house and land to a nominee; secondly, a grant of a lease for 20 years with a covenant only for quiet enjoyment by the nominee to Lady Ingram. The purpose was to enable Lady Ingram to continue to occupy Hurst Lodge by virtue of the lease without making a gift of the freehold with reservation of a benefit within FA 1986, s 102.

The House of Lords held that Lady Ingram had made an effective gift of the freehold reversion in which no benefit had been reserved. In reaching their conclusion they provided invaluable confirmation as to the scope and meaning of the gift with reservation of benefit provisions.

They confirmed that the provisions apply only if a benefit is reserved in 'property' given away. For this purpose, 'property' is not an object with a physical existence such as Hurst Lodge. It is a specific interest in that object. In Lady Ingram's case, it was the freehold reversionary interest in Hurst Lodge. It followed that Lady Ingram did not reserve a benefit in the property she gave away, even though she continued to enjoy Hurst Lodge by virtue of the lease. She simply gave away one interest in Hurst Lodge in which she reserved no benefit and retained another interest in Hurst Lodge which entitled her to remain in residence.

The House of Lords thus adopted the approach and analysis of the estate duty cases on the original gift with reservation provisions (contained in FA 1894). Lord Hoffmann relied in particular upon *Munro v Stamp Duties Comr* [1934] AC 61.

Their Lordships provided a further insight into what constitutes reserving a benefit. Both Lord Hoffmann and Lord Hutton emphasised that the provisions were concerned with the substance of the gift, not its mere conveyancing form. In the High Court, Ferris J had held that whatever the conveyancing form, 'In terms of substance, Lady Ingram had held her beneficial interests from the very same moment that the trustees and beneficiaries had the property subject to those interests'. The House of Lords agreed. So long as the equitable obligation to hold the freehold subject to the leasehold arose as soon as the freehold was vested in the trustees, the gift by Lady Ingram comprised for the purposes of s 102 only the freehold reversion.

The emphasis on the substance of the gift is noteworthy for two reasons. First, it means that Lady Ingram's scheme would have been effective even if a lease granted by a nominee to a principal was invalid (it was not). Secondly, it rejects *dicta* of the Court of Appeal in *Nichols v IRC* [1975] STC 278 to the effect that a conveyance of land subject to an obligation to grant a lease back is a gift subject to a reservation of benefit.

Following the *Ingram* decision by the House of Lords in the taxpayer's favour, legislation was introduced by FA 1999 with the intention of countering the effects of that decision in respect of gifts of interests in land from 9 March 1999 (FA 1986, ss 102A–102C). See **11.21**.

Difficulties can arise, where the benefit reserved is closely defined, as to whether the entire gift is tainted or only a part.

Example 11.14 – Use of bank account

James made a gift to his daughter Sarah (who was studying in Slovenia) of the use of a bank account. James remained a signatory so that he could arrange remittances whenever Sarah asked. Sarah managed to use most of the account, but James inadvertently used part. There is a reservation of benefit over the whole gift initially, because by remaining a signatory James still has 'power' over the account, so the whole gift is tainted. It is only when Sarah spends the money that the reservation over that part of the account is released.

Example 11.15 – Sporting rights

Jon retires from farming and transfers the estate to his daughter Alex. Jon enjoys shooting, whereas Alex abhors it and is merely glad for vermin to be kept down. The transfer to Alex is therefore worded so as to allow Jon to keep the right to shoot, trap, etc and to have access to the land for that purpose only; and puts on him an obligation to keep, as far as he can, the estate free of rabbits etc. Jon has not reserved a benefit out of the gift of the land itself but has effectively 'shorn' the sporting rights away from the gift. That makes sense anyway, because sporting rights do not of themselves qualify for APR.

Example 11.16 – Cottage

A more difficult example is the gift of a farm which includes cottages. Alice, widowed, transfers to her son Tom the family farm and goes on a series of world cruises. Several years later, and no longer in such good health, she rents one of the cottages as her retirement home. Tom, glad to see his mother again, fails to charge her a full rent, triggering the reservation of a benefit.

The cottage itself was on a separate legal title from the main farm but the gift of it to Tom was contemporaneous with that of the farm itself. FA 1986, s 102(1)(a) refers to 'the property', rather than 'the whole of the property', so it is possible that occupation by Alice will be construed as reservation of a benefit only of the cottage and not of the whole farm. That argument would be strengthened if it could be shown that, for example, the gifts took place on different dates.

'Virtually' … 'no benefit by contract or otherwise'

11.14   There is an argument that the phrase 'or otherwise' must be construed *ejusdem generis* with the phrase 'by contract …' so that it refers only to some enforceable legal right (see *A-G v Seccombe* [1911] 2 KB 688). However, the term 'otherwise' is just as likely to refer to any method which is not contractual, such as an informal arrangement. Indeed, it is widely considered that a benefit is reserved where a donor continues in occupation as a result of an act of kindness by the donee.

HMRC guidance (at IHTM14333) indicates that 'virtually' intends to take gifts outside the reservation of benefit rules where the benefit obtained by the donor is insignificant in relation to the gifted property. It is likely that the odd casual visit by the donor will not prevent the donee enjoying the property to 'virtually' the entire exclusion of the donor. Generally, however, it would be prudent to err on the side of caution here. See also HMRC's Interpretation at RI55 ('Inheritance tax – gifts with reservation').

In *Buzzoni & others v Revenue & Customs* [2012] UKUT 360 (TCC), the Upper Tribunal dismissed an appeal against the decision of the First-tier Tribunal in HMRC's favour. The First-tier Tribunal considered the meaning of 'virtually' for reservation of benefit purposes:

'We think "virtually" is a very high test. To be virtually excluded is to be as good as excluded; to be excluded for all practical purposes. An exceedingly remote chance of benefit or where the benefit is real but very slight might mean a settlor is "virtually" excluded but not otherwise'.

The grant of a future underlease to a trust out of a headlease was held to be a gift with reservation within FA 1986, s 102(1)(b). The underlease did not require the payment of rent, although it did contain covenants, including for the payment of an amount equal to the service charge payable under the headlease. The Upper Tribunal agreed with the First-tier Tribunal that the donor had not been 'virtually' excluded from a benefit. The benefit to the deceased had been in transferring to the trustee of her settlement a liability which she would otherwise have borne.

Substitutions and accretions (Sch 20, paras 2 and 3)

11.15   Where property changes hands after the initial gift, there are complicated rules (based on the estate duty provision, FA 1957, s 38) to determine whether the original subject matter of the gift can be traced and substituted by other assets and valued accordingly. These substitution rules are intended to prevent a simple anti-avoidance trick. For example, A gives Blackacre to B; B exchanges it for Whiteacre which A occupies. The rules mean that A has reserved a benefit by occupying Whiteacre.

However, if the donor gifts cash to his child who buys a holiday home in which the donor is allowed to holiday, the gift of cash cannot be traced into the holiday home (FA 1986, Sch 20, para 2(2)(b)). Likewise if the subject matter of A's gift (Blackacre in the above example) is sold for cash by the donee. This is subject to *Ramsay* and the rules for 'associated operations' although these rules should not be capable of re-characterising the transaction (see *IRC v Brandenburg* [1982] STC 555 at 564b). In any event, the scope of the associated operations rule was diminished by the Court of Appeal in *Rysaffe Trustee Co (CI) Ltd v CIR* [2003] STC 536 (see **1.21**).

Note, however, that the tracing possibilities under POAT may pose problems with this approach; see **Chapter 13**.

Special rules for settled property

11.16   Where a donor makes a gift by way of *settlement*, the type of asset is immaterial: it is the property *comprised* in the settlement that is material. The donor should be excluded from the class of beneficiaries. If there is a power under the settlement to add to the class of beneficiaries, the trustees should be expressly prevented from adding in the donor (see CTO correspondence, *Law Society Gazette* 10 December 1986, and also IHTM14393).

517

The drafting of the trust deed can give rise to important tax issues. For example, the lack of an ultimate default provision raises the question whether there is a resulting trust in favour of the settlor, and therefore a GWR. In a letter dated 18 May 1987, the Inland Revenue (as it then was) confirmed as follows (at para 7):

> 'In the case where a gift is made into trust, the retention by the settlor (donor) of a reversionary interest under the trust is not considered to constitute a reservation, whether the retained interest arises under the express terms of the trust or it arises by operation of general law eg a resulting trust.'

However, if there is no GWR, the question then arises whether there is any income tax charge under the 'pre-owned assets' (POAT) provisions (FA 2004, Sch 15, para 8). The settlor may also be subject to income tax on trust income under the settlements code (see ITTOIA 2005, s 624), although such a liability is taken into account in determining any POAT charge (FA 2004, Sch 15, para 9). The extent of such income tax liabilities will depend on factors including whether the POAT charge is *de minimis* and therefore exempt (see **13.7**), and whether the settlor was UK resident in the tax year (ITTOIA 2005, s 648(2)). Where there is a possibility of a resulting trust in favour of the settlor, consideration could be given to an assignment of his reversionary interest. It should be noted that a reversionary interest is not excluded property if the settlor or spouse is, or has been, entitled to it (s 48(1)(b)), although the interest may be exempt if assigned to a charity. It is good practice to avoid a possible resulting trust in the first instance by including a suitably drafted default clause in the trust deed at the outset.

The suggestion in **11.26** that the donor make a gift of cash to his child who may purchase a holiday home would not work at all if the cash were given not to the child outright but to a settlement.

A gift can be caught under the GWR rules in circumstances where the donor reserves a benefit, eg the donee does not take up exclusive possession, only *after completion of the gift* – see, in particular, the *Chick* decision (referred to in **10.20**).

GWR wrinkles

11.17   The reservation does *not have to emanate from the gift itself* but can be by way of *collateral* arrangements made by or on behalf of donee, eg payment of a covenanted sum to the donor. It is considered, however, that some associated connection with the gift would be required (see *Stamp Duties Comr of New South Wales v Permanent Trustee Co* [1956] AC 512, PC; *A-G v Worrall* [1895] 1 QB 99, CA).

It is *immaterial* that the benefit reserved is small and *not commensurate* with the value of the asset itself or even that the donor is unaware of the benefit (except as to the reference to 'virtually' in FA 1986, s 102(1)(b)). Thus, subject to the possibility of 'splitting' the gift, as in examples of outright gifts in **11.12–11.14**, a gift by a donor of a 1,000 acre farm could be brought back into the estate by s 102 simply because the donor was permitted at a later stage to occupy one room of a small cottage on the edge. Here, the donor should pay demonstrably full consideration for his benefit; see Sch 20, para 6.

It is also immaterial that the benefit reserved to the donor is not detrimental to the donee. The nearest example that can help the taxpayer is in RI55: after a gift of land, say, to a son, the donor may perhaps walk his dogs or ride his horse over the land given away without tainting the gift. However, allowing his horse to graze, or shooting his son's pheasants, would be going too far. To enjoy these extra privileges, the donor should either arrange to pay something to the son (who should really show it in the farm accounts as income) or, as in Example 11.15, should expressly exclude them from the gift made.

It has been argued that a trust for a settlor's children that indirectly benefits him, eg paying school fees, constitutes a gift with reservation. This is probably incorrect on the basis that the benefit is too remote or indirect, and s 11 should in any event exclude any claim.

Full consideration

11.18   Where the donor gives full consideration in money or money's worth there would normally be no reservation. There is a specific rule to this effect for land and chattels in FA 1986, Sch 20, para 6(1)(a) (see **11.19**(b)); but it is not applicable to other types of assets (IHTM14336). Steps should be taken by means of a regular review to ensure that full consideration continues to be paid. Revenue guidance on the meaning of 'full consideration' can be found in Revenue Interpretation 55 (formerly *Revenue Tax Bulletin*, November 1993, p 98), and examples are included in the Inheritance Tax Manual at IHTM14341. It should be noted that there is also a full consideration 'let-out' from the pre-owned assets income tax charge (see **Chapter 13**) in relation to land and chattels, but not intangible property (FA 2004, Sch 15 paras 4(1), 7(1)).

The cessation of a reservation of benefit is itself treated as a potentially exempt transfer by the donor. Therefore, provided that a benefit *ceases* to be reserved outside the seven-year period, no IHT or additional IHT will be payable. It is likely that such cesser is easier to arrange in the case of a series of gifts rather than a large single gift (Sch 20, para 1).

Statutory exceptions to s 102

11.19

(a)   Gifts which are exempt transfers

The reservation of benefit charge does not apply to certain *exempt transfers* as listed in s 102(5) although the exemption provisions have their own built-in requirements and restrictions. The £3,000 annual exemption and normal expenditure out of income exemption are *not* included in the list.

HMRC in their RI55 guidelines (see **11.14**) take the view that, where there is a GWR, and the reservation ceases so that the gift at that point becomes a PET, the £3,000 exemption cannot be set against the PET when the reservation thus ends. However, the £3,000 exemption will be available against other gifts made in that year.

Prior to the introduction of FA 1986, ss 102(5A)–(5C) (by FA 2003), *Eversden* schemes (see **11.25**) used the spouse exemption under s 18 to avoid a gift with reservation of benefit on the gift of an asset (eg a holiday home) to a trust. Such schemes were blocked with effect for disposals from 20 June 2003, and pre-existing schemes are subject to a potential income tax charge under the pre-owned assets regime (see **Chapter 13**).

An alternative arrangement intended to escape the GWR (and pre-owned assets) rules is in relation to discounted gift trusts, which are discussed at **14.32**.

(b)   Full consideration in money or money's worth

FA 1986, Sch 20, para 6 sets out circumstances where the GWR rules do not apply; but the conditions are onerous. For example, in the case of land and chattels the retention of a benefit by the donor is disregarded if the donor is in actual occupation or actual possession and pays full consideration in money or money's worth. The need for actual occupation or possession precludes subletting by the donor. In their RI55 guidelines (see **11.14**), HMRC underline the point that full consideration is required throughout the period, and that regular reviews of rent should take place. However, they recognise that normal valuation tolerances must be recognised in deciding what is 'full' consideration for para 6(1)(a).

The donor's occupation of *land* is expressly disregarded under para 6(1)(b) if it results from:

- unforeseen changes in circumstances (merely getting old is not itself unforeseen); *and*

- the donor is unable to maintain himself through old age, infirmity, etc; *and*

- it represents a reasonable provision by the donee for care and maintenance of the donor; *and*

- the donee is a relative of the donor or his spouse.

These cumulative conditions are onerous. They contrast sharply with HMRC's interpretation of how short the visits of a donor should be after the gift of a house in order to satisfy the 'virtually' *de minimis* test in s 102(1)(b). Some of these limits could well be challenged in specific cases.

If the donor wishes to rely on the 'full consideration' exception above, consider a 'commercial lease' (FA 1986, Sch 20, para 6(1)(a)), pursuant to which the donor pays a full arm's length rent for the lease or tenancy retained. Such a rent would need to be reviewable upwards, say, every three years in the light of changing conditions and preferably inflation, and certified by an independent, qualified surveyor.

The creation of such a new source of taxable, non-deductible income can be very disadvantageous (in the past, the taxable receipt problem was often solved using a grandchildren's accumulation and maintenance trust under s 71). Moreover, the estate owner's income will be reduced. The proposal may be more acceptable for an older estate owner (ie where there would be less emphasis on rent reviews). Note, however, that although the gift with reservation rules will not apply, the PET seven-year requirement for a full rent will apply. Instead of a rent, consider a 'one-off' premium which satisfies the full consideration condition, subject to possible stamp duty land tax considerations.

Avoidance of double charge (s 104)

11.20 The structure of IHT means that in certain circumstances the same property can be charged twice and entered twice into the cumulation of chargeable transfers as a result of a transferor's death. However, the Inheritance Tax (Double Charges Relief) Regulations 1987, SI 1987/1130, provide for relief in these circumstances.

Regulation 5 provides for the avoidance of a double charge where there is a transfer of value by way of gift of property which is or subsequently becomes a chargeable transfer, and the property is (by virtue of the provisions relating to gifts with reservation) subject to a further transfer which is chargeable as a result of the transferor's death. As under regulation 4, whichever transfer produces the higher amount of tax as a result of the death remains chargeable, and the value of the other transfer is reduced by reference to the value of the transfer which produced that amount.

However, this reduction in value does not apply for the purposes of any relevant property trust charges arising before the transferor's death where the transfer by way of gift was chargeable to tax when it was made. Further, provision is made for credit to be given on account of any tax already paid on the transfer by way of gift against so much of the tax payable on the other transfer as relates to the value of the property in question.

Example 11.17 – GWR within seven years of death

A gives B a house (a PET), but reserves the right to continue to live in it rent-free, and does so until he dies five years later. There is a charge on the gift from A to B because it is within seven years of death, but because this is a gift with reservation the house is also charged as part of A's death estate.

Double IHT charge relief is potentially available (SI 1987/1130, reg 5), either by charging the gift with reservation in the death estate and ignoring the PET, or charging the PET and ignoring the gift with reservation; whichever produces the higher amount of IHT remains chargeable.

The regulations helpfully include a schedule with worked examples of the double IHT relief rules as they apply to GWRs, although the examples do not prevail over the rules as stated in the regulations (SI 1987/1130, reg 9).

There is no statutory clearance procedure as to the application of the GWR rules. However, some guidance is available on HMRC's views as to the application of the GWR rules in Revenue Interpretation 55, and also HMRC's Inheritance Tax Manual (in IHTM14301 and subsequent paragraphs).

GIFTS OF AN INTEREST IN LAND

11.21   Consider this example in relation to FA 1986, s 102. The donor owns a freehold house. She grants a 20-year lease of the house to a nominee for herself. Then she gives the freehold subject to the lease to her child. The donor carries on living in the house by virtue of the lease.

The facts in the example are essentially those of *Ingram*. The House of Lords held that the donor's gift is not caught by s 102 because she remained in occupation by virtue of the property retained (the lease), and not by virtue of the property given away (the freehold subject to the lease).

FA 1999 introduced s 102A into FA 1986 with the intention of blocking the *Ingram* scheme. It applies where an individual disposes of an interest in land by way of gift on or after 9 March 1999. It should be noted that pre-9 March 1999 *Ingram* schemes considered effective for IHT purposes are subject to a pre-owned assets income tax charge (see **Chapter 13**).

The rule in FA 1986, s 102A

11.22 Where X disposes of an interest in land by way of gift and FA 1986, s 102 does not apply, the interest in land is property subject to a reservation of benefit (so that the value of the gifted property remains in the donor's IHT estate) broadly if:

- X or his spouse (or civil partner) enjoys a right or interest, or is party to a significant arrangement, in relation to the land; and

- that right, interest or arrangement entitles or enables the donor to occupy all or part of the land, or to enjoy some right in relation to all or part of the land, otherwise than for full consideration in money or money's worth.

The best example of s 102A is *Ingram*: Section 102 did not apply and she enjoyed an interest in relation to the land (the 20-year lease) which entitled her to occupy otherwise than for full consideration in money or money's worth.

However, the rule could also apply to an investment property, such as where X gifts the property to his daughter, but retains a right to receive the rents from the property (NB any CGT and SDLT issues are ignored in this example). By contrast, if X gifts a *share* of the investment property but continues to receive all the rent, FA 1986, s 102B(3)(a) provides that no reservation of benefit arises where the donor does not occupy the land (although the GWR and POAT position following a subsequent sale of the property would need to be considered). Note that the provisions of ss 102 and 102A do not apply in cases to which s 102B applies (s 102C(6)). See also **11.29**.

Application of s 102A to the reversionary lease scheme

11.23 A reversionary lease scheme typically involves the donor granting a 999-year lease over his principal private residence to his children's trust (from which he and his wife are excluded). The lease is to commence in, say, ten years on the basis that the donor has an actuarial life expectancy of nine years (in any event, the period should be less than 21 years to avoid a problem in Law of Property Act 1925, s 149(3) if a rent is to be paid). The period is also fixed to avoid the risk of the grant constituting a deemed settlement under IHTA 1984, s 43.

Does X's retained freehold interest entitle or enable X to occupy all or part of the land, or to enjoy some right in relation to all or part of the land, 'otherwise than for full consideration in money or money's worth'? The answer is surely 'No'. It might have been argued that the occupation must itself be for a rent notwithstanding that full market value was given for the right to occupy on acquisition of the house, although HMRC generally accepted that reversionary lease arrangements effected before 9 March 1999 were not caught by the GWR rules. However, such schemes were one of the targets of the 'pre-owned assets' income tax provisions covered in **Chapter 13**.

HMRC considered that s 102A (which took effect from 9 March 1999) catches reversionary lease schemes, on the basis that the donor's occupation (although acquired more than seven years before creation of the lease) is a 'significant right in relation to the land' within s 102A(3). It is understood that the expression 'significant right or interest' was deliberately chosen as being very wide, equivalent to the lawmaker saying 'Don't even think about doing it' though that may not have discouraged all advisers' inventiveness. See the Inheritance Tax Manual at IHTM14360, which instructs that such schemes should be referred to HMRC's Technical Group.

However, in its pre-owned assets guidance, HMRC appear to contradict the above approach, stating the following (at IHTM44102):

> 'Where a reversionary lease scheme is established before 9 March 1999 ... the arrangement succeeds in avoiding the reservation of benefit provisions so long as the lease does not contain any terms that are currently beneficial to the donor, such as covenants by the lessee to, say, maintain the property. Consequently, the donor will be subject to the POA charge under FA04/Sch15/Para3(2).'

With regard to reversionary lease schemes established on or after 9 March 1999, HMRC's guidance at IHTM44102 distinguishes between situations where the donor grants a reversionary lease more than seven years after acquiring the freehold interest, and where the reversionary lease is granted within that seven-year period:

> 'Where a reversionary lease scheme is established on or after 9 March 1999 it was originally considered that FA86/S102A ... would apply because the donor's occupation would be a "significant right in relation to the land". If that were correct, the reservation of benefit rules would apply and there would be no POA charge.
>
> However, where the freehold interest was acquired more than 7 years before the gift ... the continued occupation by the donor is not a significant right in view of FA86/S102A(5), so the reservation of benefit rules cannot apply and a POA charge arises instead.
>
> It follows that if the donor grants a reversionary lease within 7 years of acquiring the freehold interest, FA86/S102A may apply to the gift depending on how the remaining provisions of that section apply in relation to the circumstances of the case – for example, if the donor pays full consideration for the right to occupy or enjoy the land, that would not be a significant right in view of FA86/S102A(3), so the reservation of benefit rules cannot apply and a POA charge arises instead.'

Where the pre-owned assets provisions apply, it may nevertheless be possible to elect out of an income tax charge, and into the GWR provisions instead. However, the GWR provisions will apply in any event if the lease contains terms which are currently beneficial to the donor.

There are other issues which should briefly be mentioned. The parties must understand the transaction: that was clearly not the case in *Wolff and Wolff v Wolff* [2004] STC 1633, where the elderly couple survived to the date upon which a rack rent became payable under the (badly drawn) reversionary lease and asked for it to be set aside.

Any possibility of a challenge under IHTA 1984, s 268 (associated operations) may be avoided by gifting the freehold retained under the will to someone other than the holder of the reversionary lease. The grant of the lease itself is not an associated operation because it is a single transaction. There is a capital gains tax problem in respect of a residence because the children's trust has an increasingly valuable asset which does not qualify for only or main residence relief for CGT purposes; but see **11.4** regarding hold-over relief claims from a relevant property (eg discretionary) trust.

Exceptions to s 102A

11.24   There is an exception to s 102A where:

- the right, interest or arrangement does not and cannot prevent the enjoyment of the land to the entire exclusion, or virtually to the entire exclusion, of the donor (see s 102A(4)(*a*));

- the right, interest or arrangement does not entitle or enable the donor to occupy all or part of the land immediately after the disposal, but would do so were it not for the interest disposed of (see s 102A(4)(*b*)); or

- the right or interest was granted or acquired before the period of seven years ending with the date of the gift (see s 102A(5)).

The exception under the second bullet point is important because it disapplies s 102A in a case where the donor grants a 20-year rent-free lease to B by way of gift. In such a case, there is a gift of an interest in land and in relation to the land the donor enjoys some right or interest (rights under the lease and as freeholder). The exception applies because those rights do not entitle or enable him to occupy the land immediately after the disposal, but would do so were it not for the interest disposed of.

The effect of the exception under s 102A(5) is that, arguably, the *Ingram* scheme still works if a gap of seven years is left between the date of the purchase of the freehold and the grant of the freehold subject to the lease. Likewise, the reversionary lease scheme (see **11.23**) still works if a gap of seven years is left between the date of purchase of the land and the date of the grant of the lease (so that it may be unnecessary to rely upon the argument that full consideration has been given – if indeed it has). However, as mentioned, there is inconsistency in HMRC's guidance as to whether reversionary lease schemes are still opposed on the basis that the seven-year rule does not apply because there is a 'significant arrangement' in relation to the land. If the arrangement succeeds, POAT may in certain circumstances apply, nullifying the advantage gained.

Note that, although s 102A refers to the donor's spouse, this does not mean that the donor reserves a benefit in gifted land by virtue of his wife receiving a benefit. Rather it is intended to prevent the donor granting a 20-year lease to his wife, then occupying the property by virtue of her lease.

Other statutory exceptions to ss 102 and 102A

11.25   The exception for exempt transfers to spouses in s 102(5) is applied to ss 102A and 102B by virtue of s 102C(2). However, the spouse exemption is limited in its application by s 102(5A)–(5C). Those provisions were introduced to counter the decision in *IRC v Eversden and another (executors of Greenstock, deceased)* [2003] STC 822 (see **1.32**), and prevent the spouse exemption from applying where, for example, a husband makes a gift to a trust under which his wife takes an initial interest in possession, which is subsequently terminated in favour of a discretionary trust in which the husband is a potential beneficiary.

Avoiding s 102A by avoiding gifts of land

(1)   Gifts of cash

11.26   A parent could consider making an outright gift of cash to his child (but with no strings attached). If the child purchased a house in which child and parent live s 102 would not apply because of FA 1986, Sch 20 para 2(2)(b). Section 102A would not apply because there is no disposal of an interest in land. Avoid settling the cash: FA 1986, Sch 20, para 5. However, consider the POAT implications of the proposal.

It is probably too risky for the child to purchase the house in which the parent is living. HMRC guidance (at IHTM14372) suggests that this may constitute a reservation of benefit by associated operations. To reduce the risk of challenge, a suitable length of time should be left between the gift to the child and the purchase of the property from which the donor may benefit.

It should be noted that, although for IHT purposes there is no tracing rule for cash, there is no similar let-out for 'pre-owned assets' income tax purposes, except to the extent that the cash gift was made before 6 April 1998, or (in relation to land or chattels) unless the cash gift was made at least seven years before the property was acquired (FA 2004, Sch 15, para 10(2)(c)); see **Chapter 13**.

(2)   Lifetime debt (IOU) scheme

11.27   Under this once popular scheme, X would sell his principal private residence to his life interest trust for full market value. The purchase price would be paid by the issue of a loan note (or by set-off against a loan from X to the trustees). X then gave the loan note to a life interest trust for his children (or an accumulation and maintenance trust for his grandchildren; this type of trust was prevalent prior to FA 2006). X was wholly excluded from benefit under the second trust.

X remained in occupation of his home by virtue of his life interest under the trust. The value of his IHT estate must be considered in light of the deeming provision in IHTA 1984, s 49. Strictly, s 49 deemed him to be beneficially entitled to the 'property' in which his interest subsists. The residence is 'property', but the debt is not. This was a concern but it was thought sufficient that the trustees had a lien over settled property for the payment of such trust debts which would affect the market value of the property. The concern disappeared if the settled property was encumbered (s 162(4)), but this put X at risk of making a gift of an interest in land.

This scheme appeared to avoid s 102A because, unless the debt was secured by a mortgage on the house at the date of the gift, there was no gift of an 'interest in land'. Furthermore, the purchase price was paid by the trustees albeit by the issue of an IOU, or by set-off against a loan to X. This meant that there was no vendor's lien over land for an unpaid purchase price which, if given by X, could amount to 'a gift of an interest in land'.

The scheme also seemed to avoid s 102 because X gave away a debt with a fixed repayment date (eg one month after the death of X). If the loan was repayable on demand and the donee failed to demand repayment, X would reserve a benefit in the debt by virtue of FA 1986, Sch 20, para 6(1)(c) and IHTA 1984, s 268 (the debt representing the land for the purposes of s 268).

The sale of the property to X's trust gave rise to a stamp duty land tax charge on the whole value of the property: as a result there was a rush to complete schemes just before SDLT came into force, using the old method of 'resting in contract'.

X's occupation of the PPR as beneficiary had the result that the trustees could claim PPR relief on any gain on a sale of the property. There was also a CGT free uplift in the market value of the property on the death of

X if TCGA 1992, s 72 applied. The gift of the loan note was a disposal to a connected party for its (deemed) market value. However, any gain was exempt under TCGA 1992, s 251. The repayment of the debt would be a chargeable disposal by the second trust, but sometimes the debt was acquired direct by the second trust under a 'tripartite loan agreement' rather than by assignment from X (so s 251 would apply to exempt any gain). Note that FA 1986, s 103 was not relevant.

The scheme only reduced the value of X's estate by the value of the debt at the date of death, so any later increase in the value of the house remained in the estate of the original owner.

HMRC never much liked the scheme, but instead of litigation remedied the situation, from their point of view, by legislation, in the form of POAT. That legislation has been described as 'something of a mess' and even at the time of writing has never quite 'settled down'. On the basis that the scheme is effective, for 'pre-owned assets' purposes an income tax charge arises in respect of the residence (see **Chapter 13**).

In addition, in HMRC's view there is a reservation of benefit in respect of the loan (see IHTM44103 and following). This view was originally restricted to loans repayable on demand, but HMRC now apparently consider that the same applies to loans repayable after the life tenant's death (see **6.25**). Any such GWR charge in respect of the loan is separate from any POAT charge on the residence.

The effectiveness of home loan or double trust schemes has been challenged by HMRC, although there has been no reported litigation at the time of writing. If there is a GWR in the property, a POA charge will not arise in respect of it. In that situation, HMRC have stated that any POA income tax paid (ie on the basis that no such GWR applied) will be repaid with interest upon a claim being made, irrespective of the time limits for repayment that might otherwise apply (www.hmrc.gov.uk/poa/poa-guidance6.htm).

In the Trusts & Estates Newsletter (August 2012), HMRC indicated that, in order to allow executors and trustees to deal with the administration of estates held up by litigation over home loan schemes as far as possible, it would provide an estimate upon request of the tax that might be payable if the litigation finds in HMRC's favour. This would allow payments on account to be made (eg to stop interest accruing) on a without prejudice basis, with any overpayments being refunded if the litigation is subsequently decided in favour of the taxpayer.

For those wishing to unravel the scheme and possibly consider other forms of IHT planning instead, the Inheritance Tax (Double Charges Relief) Regulations 2005, SI 2005/3441, prevent a possible double IHT charge from arising.

(3) Fixing a GWR with 'reverter to settlor'

11.28   In the past (ie prior to FA 2006, in particular), where an estate owner had inadvertently reserved a benefit in his settlement of the family home, he could appoint the house to, say, his son absolutely so as to eliminate the GWR. The son (if he so decided) could then settle the house onto interest in possession trusts for the parent and subject thereto for himself (see below for interests in possession created from 22 March 2006).

There was no IHT on the parent's estate on death (assuming the son survived the parent) because of the reverter to settlor exemption (IHTA 1984, s 54). Furthermore, if the trust did not come to an end on the death of the parent but instead the settlor acquired an interest in possession, the house also obtained a CGT uplift in market value (under TCGA 1992, s 72). However, note that there may be CGT and IHT on the appointment to the child.

There are 'pre-owned assets' income tax (POAT) implications (see **Chapter 13**) if a former owner enjoys the asset under a trust, where its terms allow the trust property to revert to the settlor in due course. Legislation introduced in FA 2006 imposes a POAT charge if either:

- the relevant property ceases to be comprised in a person's estate; or

- that person has provided any funds to enable the property purchase, and the relevant (or derived) property is comprised in his estate by virtue of having an interest in possession in it.

In those circumstances, that property is treated for POAT exemption purposes (FA 2004, Sch 15, para 11(1)–(5)) as if it was not included in the person's estate, with the effect that a POAT charge applies (para 11(11)–(13)). These provisions affect not only reverter to settlor trust arrangements, but can apply generally in circumstances whereby property has left the estate of an individual, who subsequently acquires a qualifying interest in possession in the same property. However, the taxpayer can elect into the IHT regime (as an effective GWR) in relation to land or chattels, so that the asset will not give rise to an income tax charge.

There were always limits on the relief:

- the settlor or spouse (or widow(er)) must not have purchased a reversionary interest (see s 53(5)(a)); and

- the settlement of the reversionary interest must be after 10 March 1981 (s 53(5)(b)).

An interesting argument used to arise as to whether the settlement could be, not of the property itself, but of an equitable interest in it. HMRC considered that it must be the property itself, not a mere interest (see the example at IHTM04352).

A particular application of the relief concerned the situation where, perhaps unexpectedly, a child moved out of the family home some time after it had been put into joint names by the parent so as to benefit from the 'joint interest' relief in FA 1986, s 102B(4). If the errant child did nothing, a GWR would arise in respect of the gift to him by the parent of the share of the house that he had been occupying. This could be cured by a reverter to settlor trust of his share. Although technically the previously gifted share came to form part of the estate of the parent, its value did not. The structure was used to avoid POAT, prior to the above anti-avoidance provision.

FA 2006, by effectively preventing the creation of qualifying interest in possession trusts except on death, has stopped the creation of effective trusts to use the reverter to settlor exception, ie the property must revert on trusts where the settlor or spouse becomes beneficially entitled. From 22 March 2006, the only trusts containing a qualifying interest in possession are IPDIs, DPIs or TSIs.

The exception therefore requires:

* that the trust already exists; and

* absolute vesting, when the interest in possession ends, in the settlor; or

* absolute vesting as above, in the spouse or civil partner (see below); or

* a TSI in favour of the settlor (or spouse as above) when the interest in possession ends (although note that the TSI (within s 49C) must have arisen before 6 October 2008).

The spouse or civil partner may take but only if the settlor dies within the last two years.

Clearly, many arrangements will fail to comply exactly with these strict requirements. Existing trusts should be examined to see if the exception still applies.

For commentary on the reverter to settlor exemption in the context of spouses or civil partners generally, see **6.9**.

The rule in FA 1986, s 102B

11.29   FA 1999 extended the scope of the GWR code to gifts of an undivided share of an interest in land, for example, where the sole freeholder gifts half of his interest to another.

Section 102B applies where an individual disposes of an undivided share of an interest in land by way of gift. In that case, the share disposed of is property subject to a reservation; and FA 1986, s 102(3) and (4) apply, except where:

(a)   the donor does not occupy the land; or

(b)   the donor occupies the land to the exclusion of the donee for full consideration in money or money's worth; or

(c)   the donor and the donee occupy the land; and the donor does not receive any benefit, other than a negligible one, which is provided by or at the expense of the donee for some reason connected with the gift.

Where s 102B applies, ss 102 and 102A do not (s 102C(6)).

Example 11.18 – Shared occupation of land

Alf's son Ben lives with him. Alf could give Ben 50% of his interest in the freehold. Ben should not contribute in any way to his father's share of the upkeep and expenses.

Section 102B will apply (not ss 102 or 102A), but there is no GWR because of exclusion (c) above.

There is also an exemption from the 'pre-owned assets' income tax charge in these circumstances (FA 2004, Sch 15, para 11). If Ben moved out, he could charge Alf a market rent (see (b) above).

Notes

(1)   As was noted above, it used to be possible for, say, a son to settle his share onto an interest in possession trust for his father and subject thereto for himself and then his children, but that facility has been lost.

(2)   In the above example, Alf gifted a 50% share of the house to his son. However, FA 1986, s 102B does not contain a requirement to gift an equal share. The donor may therefore wish to consider giving away more than a 50% interest. However, HMRC could contend that, if two individuals occupy a property jointly, the most that can be given away is 50%.

In addition, the Inheritance Tax Manual at IHTM14332 (which provides a number of examples involving joint property) includes the following 'health warning': 'The joint property examples are on the basis that the joint owners take the property in equal shares. Refer any case in which the transferor takes less than an equal share to Technical Group.'

Concluding points

11.30   A stamp duty land tax charge will not arise on any gift of unencumbered property such as land. However, if the land is subject to a mortgage or debt which is assumed by the donee, for SDLT purposes the amount of the debt is treated as consideration so that the conveyance will be stampable with *ad valorem* duty (FA 2003, Sch 4, para 8).

Possible solutions include:

- the donor remains liable for the debt: but this must be made clear in the terms of the gift and is unlikely to be acceptable to a commercial lender;

- repay the mortgage and let the donee mortgage in his own name. However, the two transactions must be independent to avoid a *Ramsay* attack; and

- where the facts permit, the donor could make a series of gifts of interests in the property, each under the SDLT threshold. Each gift must be genuinely independent of the other gifts.

Finally, where the donor gives away his family home, or an interest in it, consider whether it will adversely affect his rights to community care and assistance from the local authority. The area is complex and outside the scope of this book.

Settlor as trustee and GWR

(1) General rule

11.31 It is generally acknowledged that a trustee's duties are entirely of a *fiduciary* nature, since his sole duty and function is to safeguard the interests of the beneficiaries. Thus, as a matter of trust law there is normally no objection to the settlor (or spouse) being one of the trustees (possibly even the first named).

In *Oakes v Comr of Stamp Duties of New South Wales* [1953] 2 All ER 1563, the Privy Council stated 'if property is held in trust for the donee, then the trustees' possession is the donee's possession for this purpose, and it matters not that the trustee is a donor himself' (see also *Stamp Duties Comr of New South Wales v Perpetual Trustee Co Ltd* [1943] 1 All ER 525 and *Oakes v Comr of Stamp Duties of New South Wales* [1953] 2 All ER 1563).

This section considers the effect of the settlor being trustee in the context of the inheritance tax GWR rules.

For the purposes of income tax and capital gains tax, one should consider excluding the settlor and spouse of the settlor from any benefit under the trust whatsoever.

For an example of incorrect management of a trust, see *Lyon's Personal Representatives v HMRC* [2007] SSCD 675 (SpC 616). The settlor gave trustees £2,700,000. He retained a power of revocation and was one of the beneficiaries. He received £15,965 from the trust during his lifetime, dying five years after creating the trust. HMRC issued a Notice of Determination arguing that the gift was subject to a reservation. On appeal, the Special Commissioner held that there had been a reservation, even though the actual benefit to the settlor was small compared with the fund settled. The way that the trust had been operated showed that possession and enjoyment of the property had not been properly assumed by the donee at the outset.

(2)   Trustees' remuneration

11.32   A trustee should ideally receive *no remuneration* at all from the trust if he or she is also a settlor of the trust. Otherwise, the settlor may be reserving a benefit in the property gifted. There is however a possible let out for *reasonable* remuneration under IHTA 1984, s 90 (exemption for a trustee receiving an annuity of a reasonable amount having regard to the duties/services performed). HMRC appear to favour this interpretation, stating that the donor or spouse may receive payment for their services as trustees, provided that the remuneration is not 'excessive' (IHTM14394).

(3)   Settlor/trustee is a paid director of a company whose shares are settled

11.33   Such a situation may also constitute a gift with reservation. Moreover, if the trust deed gives specific dispensation for such entitlement (and from a trust law perspective it is better if it does) this could merely emphasise the existence of the gift with reservation. If there is no dispensation, the trustee would strictly hold such remuneration on behalf of the beneficiaries (see *Barrett v Hartley* (1866) LR 2 Eq 789 and *Re Sykes* [1909] 2 Ch 241, CA).

The reservation of benefit danger is greatest where a settlor settles shares in a company onto a trust (whether or not he is a trustee) and thereafter obtains a paid position as director or employee of the company. Arguably, the fact that he is able to receive payment which derives from settled property means that he has reserved a benefit in that property. The problem is particularly common in cases where the owner of a small family company wishes to settle his shares onto trust, but continue running the business.

The practical solution is to avoid the argument and have in place a service agreement which agrees the remuneration, and the position, independently from, and essentially prior to, the gift of the shares to the trust. The remuneration should be set at a reasonable rate. The settlor then has a credible argument that the remuneration is simply consideration for a service provided to the company and no 'benefit' is received or reserved. The remuneration should not be open ended, but if flexibility is required, consider a fixed amount pegged to the cost of living index and/or subject to a reasonable commission on profits arrangement.

If it is not possible to arrange a service agreement prior to the creation of the trust, the settlor should definitely obtain no more than reasonable remuneration for work done. HMRC accept that the continuation of reasonable commercial remuneration arrangements entered into before the gift does not of itself constitute a reservation, provided the benefits were in no way linked to or affected by the gift. However, a new remuneration package may be challenged as a GWR 'by contract or otherwise' if the gift was taken into account as part of the arrangements (IHTM14395).

In cases of doubt, to be on the safe side the settlor should not be remunerated at all if this is practical.

(4) Settlor settles some shares in a company and retains other shares beneficially

11.34 Again, it could be dangerous from a gift with reservation viewpoint for such a settlor to be a trustee – particularly the first-named trustee with the voting power. The danger is especially apparent if the settlor's beneficial holding and the trust's holding together constitute control, ie the 'marriage' value benefit.

This position is dangerous from a GWR point of view even if the settlor is not a trustee.

Where 100% business/agricultural property relief applies, GWR problems should disappear (see **Chapter 15**).

Remuneration/pension arrangements

11.35 Are remuneration/pension benefits reserved to a 'donor'? Consider this also in the context of the company making additional voluntary pension contributions; and generous 'redundancy'/compensation payments. See *Oakes v Comr of Stamp Duties of New South Wales* [1953] 2 All ER 1563.

The requisite arrangement for remuneration or pension provision should be made as far in *advance* as possible prior to the gift of the shares to avoid any HMRC argument that there is a reservation of benefit. If the arrangements were made *subsequent* to the gift there would prima facie be a gift with reservation.

The arrangements should also be made on a commercial/arm's length basis (*Copeman v William Flood & Sons Ltd* (1940) 24 TC 53 and *LG Berry Investments Ltd v Attwooll* [1964] 2 All ER 126).

Partnership situations

11.36 Gifts made out of partnership interests in the context of the GWR provisions are dealt with at **10.20**.

Paintings and other valuable assets

11.37 Keeping paintings etc in one's house after giving them away is likely to be a gift with a reservation of benefit even where the donor is acting as a caretaker. It is also probable in such cases that possession and enjoyment have not been assumed by the donee (s 102(1)(a)). The solution could be to pay an arm's-length rent.

This issue has become more prominent since POAT, highlighting that there has hitherto been hardly an open market in the leasing of works of art on which to base a fair comparison.

Variations – avoiding the GWR rules

11.38 Where a testator has died and a beneficiary of the estate effects a variation (under s 142), eg by varying an outright gift to the beneficiary into a discretionary trust, the fact that the beneficiary is capable of benefiting from the varied gift, eg by being included as a discretionary object does not constitute a reservation of a benefit by the beneficiary because it is the *deceased* who is deemed to have created the varied gift, eg the discretionary trust.

Health warnings

11.39 Throughout, the practitioner must be aware of three main caveats:

- The application of the 'associated operations' provisions (s 268). Remember, however, that merely because two operations are associated does *not* necessarily entail an IHT charge. Section 268 is merely a definition section and does not itself constitute a charging section; a charging provision would additionally be needed as is in fact the case with GWRs (Sch 20, para 6(1)(c)). Nor can associated operations change the nature of a transaction. The limitations in scope of the associated operations rules were outlined in *Rysaffe Trustees (CI) Ltd v IRC* [2003] STC 536 (see **1.21**).

- The possible application of the *Ramsay* doctrine as laid down in *WT Ramsay Ltd v IRC* [1981] STC 174, HL; *Furniss v Dawson* [1984] STC 153, HL, and subsequently confirmed as a principle of statutory construction by the House of Lords in *MacNiven v Westmoreland* [2001] STC 237(see **1.20** and **2.77**).

- Always consider how a transaction might look 'if things went wrong', as in the following example.

Example 11.19 – Optimism punished

Ben was a scientist with an idea that might one day save the world. Unable to secure commercial funding, Ben worked alone until a large inheritance allowed him to expand his research by creating a small company and employing assistants who shared his enthusiasm.

In 2008, he subscribed for shares in the company, though the majority were held by a former friend who lost interest in the venture. In 2010, he put his house up to guarantee part of the company debt. In September 2012 to comply with banking requirements, he lent money to the company on terms that deferred his right to repayment until the bank had been paid.

The difficult financial climate brought the company to its knees. All finance was withheld and the guarantee was likely soon to be called upon. The worry caused Ben a moment's inattention that in turn resulted in a fatal road accident in February 2013.

The shares held since 2008 are worth little but qualify for BPR. The guarantee had not actually been called in at the date of death, so the executors will probably face tough arguments with HMRC if they seek to claim that it be allowed as a deduction from Ben's estate in full.

The loan to the company could never qualify for BPR, because Ben did not control the company, and in any event it was a mere loan as opposed to a security (s 105(1)(b)). Worse still, there will be a difficulty in valuation. If its commercial value has fallen, in only five or six months, from par to nil, the executors may find that HMRC argue that in September 2012 Ben was throwing good money after bad, lending when he knew, or should have known, that he would never see his money again; so he was in effect making a gift to the company, a chargeable transfer.

OTHER PLANNING ASPECTS OF GIFTS

Avoiding gifts 'donatio mortis causa'

11.40 Such gifts are those made in contemplation of the death of the donor and therefore are conditional and only take effect on the donor's death; and can include land as well as personalty (*Sen v Headley* [1991] 2 All ER 636, CA). Moreover, these gifts are automatically revoked if the donee predeceases the donor or if the donor recovers from the illness. The donor effectively retains the property, and the amount of IHT is thus not affected (IHTA 1984, s 5(2)).

It follows that donors should observe two criteria:

- never make a gift *donatio mortis causa* unless it is genuinely desired that the gift should lapse on recovery;

- if it is wished to make an unconditional gift on a deathbed or in an illness and the gift is likely to be exempt only if made during lifetime (eg the annual £3,000, normal income gift, marriage or an exempt £250) (**1.35**), the presumption that the gift is a *donatio mortis causa* should be firmly rebutted. For example, the donor could accompany the gift with a letter to the donee to the effect that the gift is unconditional, is to take effect forthwith and is not dependent on the donor surviving or any other contingency.

Creating a benefit without a transfer

11.41   It has already been noted that 'an omission to act', notwithstanding the anti-avoidance provision of s 3(3), may still constitute a planning opportunity in appropriate circumstances (see **9.11**). Another possibility would be the provision of opportunities; for example, instead of an estate owner acquiring an adjoining field which would greatly add to the value of his existing land, the adjoining field might be purchased by, say, his son (but not the estate owner's wife, having regard to the related property provisions of s 161).

Similarly, there exist the hiving-off and splitting operations mentioned in **9.5** and **9.10** (remember that hiving-off operations should be commercially based (eg with a licensing or commission arrangement) to avoid any possibility of a transfer of value by the company under s 94(1)). It appears that the entering into of a guarantee would not of itself constitute a disposition on creation, although a call under such guarantee might well give rise to a liability; in any event the associated operations provisions would have to be carefully considered.

Farmers passing their farms on to the next generation may wish to place a covenant on the land preventing its development. The aim is to require consent for development from non-farming family members, who are likely to give their consent only if a capital sum is paid out of the development proceeds to them. Inland Revenue Capital Taxes (as it then was) confirmed some time ago that the imposition of such a restriction does not constitute a GWR (*Tolley's Practical Tax*, 12 May 1993, pp 79–80).

Assuming burdens

11.42   Where the transferee of an asset assumes, in return for the transfer, equivalent or appropriate obligations, the transaction may be one which confers no gratuitous benefits within the context of s 10; and on the footing that there is no gift, there cannot be a gift with reservation.

For example, an ageing parent may transfer a property or an interest therein (say his or her residence, exempt from CGT whether transferred for consideration or not) to a child in exchange for that child assuming the burdens of maintaining and caring for that parent for the remainder of his or her life, including provision of accommodation, care, sustenance and provision of nursing and medical facilities.

In such circumstances, the arrangements should be recorded by an appropriate arm's-length binding agreement. It may be helpful, if tactless, for the parties to record agreement as to the likely value of the services to be undertaken, based on assumptions of life expectancy, the commercial cost of care and the 'underwriting' factor that the carer is assuming a responsibility to the patient on an open-ended basis.

For 'pre-owned assets' income tax purposes, there is a potential exclusion from charge for arm's-length arrangements between connected persons if the disposal consideration is not in money or money's worth (SI 2005/724, reg 5(1)(b)). See **Chapter 13**.

A parent may take his child into partnership, and their respective covenants on time and attention to be given to the business could take advantage of the *Boden* decision (see **10.14**). As a caveat, it is sometimes argued that the assumption of a liability can still be a 'disposition' having regard to the reference in s 3(1) to diminution in the estate. However, s 3(1) first of all defines a transfer of value as a disposition, and a disposition is generally regarded as a transfer of property or a payment over of cash. Moreover, under s 5(3) and (4), a liability is taken into account in valuing an estate only in so far as it has been incurred for valuable consideration.

Some gifts may be better made in kind than in cash

11.43   This is a matter of valuation. For example, instead of the parent making a cash gift of, say, £15,000 on a daughter's marriage, only £5,000 of which would be exempt (the balance being a PET), the parent might have bought furniture, retained and used it, possibly for a short time, and then given it to the daughter (ie at its second-hand value of, say, £5,000). Similarly, instead of giving cash to enable someone to buy a new car, the donor could buy the car himself and then give the asset.

Clearly, the associated operations provisions of s 268 will have to be carefully considered.

The character of exemptions

11.44   Exemptions are generally, but not always, separate and cumulative. The annual £3,000 exemption and the marriage gift exemption are both separate and cumulative. If a father gives his daughter £15,000 on her marriage, the gift is exempt to the extent of £5,000 (marriage: s 22) plus £3,000 (annual: s 19), leaving £7,000 as a PET. By persuading his wife to make similar gifts, the £15,000 could be covered.

Moreover, both the £3,000 and the marriage exemptions are available for settlements where there is an interest in possession which terminates (in the life tenant's lifetime, not on death). Thus, if the father in the example above had a life interest under a trust he may be able to arrange to terminate his interest in £8,000 in favour of his daughter, enabling the marriage and annual exemptions to be claimed by the trustees (s 57).

On the other hand, the £250 exemption for outright gifts to any one person in the year (s 20) applies only where the total of gifts to that person does not exceed that sum. The exemption is not available in order to exempt £250 out of a larger gift to that person (s 20(1)). Nor is this exemption available to trusts.

The exemption for normal expenditure gifts under s 21, available to individuals only, operates separately and apart from the other exemptions. One beneficial use of the s 21 exemption is that a donor, having set up a lifetime trust that uses the available nil rate band, may add to the trust out of his income. Normally, one would advise against making additions to a relevant property trust because of the computational problems that the additions can cause; but, if additions are exempt, that argument no longer applies.

Setting transfers aside

11.45   It is possible for a gift or transfer to be made on the basis of mistake, which can lead to unintended and unfortunate tax consequences. However, in certain circumstances equitable jurisdiction may provide a remedy, with the effect that the transfer can be set aside.

In *Ogden and another v Trustees of the RHS Griffiths 2003 Settlement and others* [2008] EWHC 118 (Ch), pursuant to IHT advice the deceased made various transfers in 2003 and 2004. He was subsequently diagnosed with cancer, and died in 2005. The deceased's executors applied to set aside the transfers, on the basis that the transfers had been made under a mistake about the deceased's health (ie that there was a real chance of him surviving for seven years). Medical evidence indicated that the deceased had been suffering from cancer in February 2004.

The court ruled that equitable jurisdiction could apply if a mistaken fact was sufficiently serious. There was no evidence that the transfers in 2003 were made under a mistake, as the deceased was not ill when the gifts were made. However, the later transfer in 2004 was voidable, because if the deceased had known that he was suffering from lung cancer, he would not have made that transfer.

Two points are worthy of note. First, the IHT payable in respect of the deceased's transfers exceeded £1 million. The court considered that it would be unjust for an unintended liability to be retained for a very substantial amount of IHT. Thus a high standard of seriousness would appear necessary for equitable jurisdiction to apply. Secondly, whilst HMRC were not directly involved in the above case, it is possible that they may seek to intervene in future cases where significant amounts of IHT are at stake, perhaps with a view to opposing applications to set aside gifts or transfers in appropriate circumstances.

The decision in *Ogden* was subsequently followed in *Bhatt v Bhatt* [2009] EWHC 734 (Ch), where a widow accepted tax advice following her husband's death, but later issued proceedings for equitable relief. The court considered that her expectations had been seriously mistaken, and held that the documents and transactions in that case could be set aside.

In *Fine v Fine* [2012] EWHC 1811 (Ch), the High Court accepted an application for rectification in respect of two deeds of appointment, notwithstanding that the ultimate reason for executing the deeds was to avoid the ten-year charge applicable to discretionary trusts. The mistake was as to the legal effect of the documents, which were intended to create interests in possession (such trusts not being subject to ten-year charges before the changes introduced by FA 2006). It was perhaps fortunate that the correspondence and evidence presented to the court made the intentions of Mr and Mrs Fine 'abundantly clear'. This underlines the importance of retaining records such as instructions to professional advisers.

However, there are limitations to the application of equitable relief for mistake, as was highlighted in *Allnutt & another v Wilding and others* [2007] EWCA Civ 412 and *Pitt & another v Holt & another* [2011] EWCA Civ 197 (see **6.19**).

As to court applications to set aside actions under the *Hastings-Bass* principle in relation to trusts, see **8.20**.

DONEE PAYING IHT AND EXPENSES RATHER THAN DONOR

11.46   In the case of a chargeable lifetime transfer, there are advantages to be gained by the donee paying IHT and incidental expenses of transfer, rather than the donor.

These advantages include the following:

- instalment basis of certain assets is only available in respect of lifetime gifts if the donee pays the IHT (s 227(1)(b); for further details as to instalments, see **2.28** onwards);

- there is no grossing up if the donee pays the tax (s 162) (see **1.17**);

- certain expenses incidental to a transfer are deductible from the value transferred (s 164). Although not defined, these expenses should include such items as costs of valuation and professional fees for transferring the asset;

- capital gains tax is deductible from the value transferred if (but only if) it is paid by the donee (whether IHT is paid by the donor or donee) (s 165). Therefore, if there is a chargeable lifetime transfer and the donee contemplates an early sale, do not claim CGT hold-over relief (available for chargeable lifetime transfers) because this will lose the possible CGT deduction against the value transferred for IHT purposes.

On the other hand, if CGT hold-over relief is claimed, and there is a later CGT disposal of the gifted asset by the donee, there will be an allowance against the chargeable gain on that disposal for the lesser of:

- the IHT on the donor's gift to the donee (including any further IHT on a subsequent variation);

- the amount of the gain on the donee's disposal (see TCGA 1992, ss 165(10), s 260(7)); and

- the IHT can therefore wash out the donee's gain, but not give him a loss.

Accordingly, where the donee is intending to retain the asset for the time being, it may be worthwhile, even if there is only a very small gain for CGT purposes on the donor's gift, to elect for hold-over relief, to enable the IHT on the donor's gift to be allowed against a possible large gain on a later CGT disposal by the donee.

11.47   Having established the right to pay by instalments in respect of a chargeable lifetime gift because the donee pays the IHT, an extremely useful method of funding the IHT is for the donor then to proceed to make exempt gifts to the donee regularly in order to enable him to pay the instalments in whole or part, although there should be no undertaking to do so. Such exempt payments could include the £3,000 annual exemption and normal expenditure out of income, etc. This suggestion affords a key planning opportunity in those situations (particularly, subject to the question of BPR or APR, in respect of business and agricultural assets) where IHT can be paid by interest-free instalments.

Moreover, the Revenue (as it then was) confirmed in the *Law Society Gazette* (1 March 1978) that this proposal would not be regarded as an associated operation. Accordingly, annual exemptions can be used to help to fund the IHT on very substantial gifts. Where sums in excess of the annual exemptions are required, the donor could make a loan (interest free and repayable on demand) to the donee, which loan could itself be released or waived in stages by means of annual or other exemptions; but note that any release or waiver should be effected by deed because of the lack of consideration. Alternatively, the donor could make PET gifts.

11.48 Having regard in particular to s 199(1)(a) and (b), which places an equal liability for IHT on the transferor and transferee, it is the generally accepted view that HMRC must accept IHT whether the donor or the donee tenders it and in particular HMRC cannot require the donor to pay rather than the donee in order to obtain the greater amount of tax on the grossed-up basis.

Nevertheless, it is sound practice that when it is intended that the donee should pay the tax, this is recorded in a binding form between the parties (and also note below the inclusion of an appropriate indemnity). This is particularly relevant for PET gifts in case the PET becomes chargeable.

The receipt of the covenant should not constitute a gift with reservation. A suggested form of covenant is set out below, and as there may be no consideration for such covenant it should be in the form of a deed (no stamp duty).

To [Donor]

I the undersigned hereby acknowledge receipt from you this day of [brief details of the asset given] ('the gift') and confirm and agree that the gift is conditional on the covenant, hereby made by me as donee, to pay any IHT, CGT and any other taxes or imposts whatsoever due and payable on or in respect of the gift by the due date(s).

AND I will effectually indemnify you against all claims, demands, actions, proceedings, costs, interest, charges and expenses in respect of or in any way arising out of or in consequence of the said liability to IHT, CGT or any other taxes or imposts whatsoever.

This covenant undertaken by me shall bind my legal personal representatives and shall likewise be enforceable by your legal personal representatives.

Dated ……………………….. 20

SIGNED AND DELIVERED AS A DEED

BY [DONEE] IN THE PRESENCE OF:

GIFTS VERSUS SALES

11.49   Straightforward purchases and sales at arm's length between unconnected persons do not attract any potential IHT liability because they confer no gratuitous benefit within the context of s 10.

However, great care is required in respect of transactions between connected persons, because the relationship might well suggest the possibility of bounty.

In many cases, it may be practical to substitute an arm's-length sale and purchase arrangement for a gift, thereby avoiding any IHT results. Before deciding on a sale rather than a gift, however, there should be weighed in the balance the amount of CGT on a sale compared with the restricted possibility of deferment of CGT on a gift (see TCGA 1992, ss 165, 260). Remember also that on a sale, as contrasted with a gift, no business or agricultural property reliefs are available. SDLT may also be an issue in the case of land and buildings.

A useful formula, if a sale is considered preferable, might be to agree to a transfer of an asset at such price as shall be the value agreed for stamp duty and CGT purposes, by HMRC in the case of a private company's shares, or the District Valuer in the case of land for SDLT purposes.

Moreover, this procedure of selling should overcome the problems occasioned by the consequential loss formula and the 'related property' rules where assets are held by husband and wife or there has been a transfer by either of them to a charity or exempt body (see **12.21–12.23**). An arm's-length sale would avoid any question of gift with reservation. It would also constitute an effective freezing operation, in the case of an appreciating asset.

This proposal could be particularly relevant where an estate owner wishes to transfer shares in a private company which will lose him control.

Where transferors are in reasonably good health and gift term assurance cover is available, PETs may be a better proposition than a sale; particularly for family trading company shares where business property relief is available for IHT and hold-over relief for CGT. Consider the arithmetic; and note the strict requirements of s 10 for sales and the possible application of s 268 (associated operations). Moreover, the PET regime is available even though in the case of family company shares the donor is losing control. The gift is a PET in respect of the larger loss to donor value, as contrasted with the benefit received by the donee, although the significance of this loses its relevance if 100% business property relief is available.

Wasting operations

11.50   This proposal of arranging a sale might, however, be combined with a 'wasting operation'. An asset could be purchased by, say, a son from his father in consideration of an actuarially calculated annuity. This transaction should not constitute a transfer of value under s 10.

For income tax purposes this is known colloquially as a 'reverse annuity operation'; and under ITA 2007, s 904, the annuity instalments must normally be paid gross without deduction of tax and do not constitute a charge in computing the taxable income of the payer.

There are exceptions to this treatment (see ITA 2007, s 904(6)), such as where annuities are paid in consideration of the release of an interest in settled property in favour of a subsequent beneficiary.

Exchanging assets and services

11.51   Where there is an equality of exchange (ie the assets exchanged are of equivalent value), the transaction should result in no IHT (even though it may involve CGT and stamp duty). Where the assets are not exactly equivalent, an appropriate cash balance should be paid.

This method of exchange could be particularly appropriate where a depreciating asset held by a younger generation is exchanged for an appreciating asset held by an older generation, assuming at the date of exchange the assets have equal value.

Note, however, that, although this beneficial principle may be extended to DIY home reversion schemes, an income tax charge under the pre-owned assets (POAT) regime may arise in some circumstances.

Creation of a tenancy and associated operations

11.52   The creation of a tenancy, say, to a relative such as a son, followed by a gift of the freehold reversion, is likely to be caught by the associated operations provisions in s 268. The following proposals should not, however, be subject to such associated operations and, being an arm's-length arrangement, should be outside the IHT net entirely.

First, the freeholder (say, the father) creates a tenancy in favour of the son at full market rent (including adequate rent review clauses, say, every three years). The father later decides to sell the freehold reversion to his son at its investment value, *but* after a period exceeding three years from the creation of the tenancy.

Note that by virtue of s 268(2) the grant of a lease for full consideration is not associated with any operation effected more than three years later. Even though effective for IHT, such an arrangement might have to be rejected because of the income tax liability on the rent received. Note that this arrangement would not work in any event if the lease had been granted in such a way as to allow the father, as donor, to occupy the property, because of POAT.

GIFTS VERSUS LOANS

11.53   Where an individual makes an interest-free loan of cash, or allows another the free use of any asset, such as a property, no IHT liability arises on the notional interest, or rent, etc, forgone. The possibility of an interest-free loan to a prospective beneficiary can be extremely useful as a 'freezing' operation, and the concept has been taken up by life companies as the basis for a continuing, albeit restricted, form of inheritance trust. The face value of the loan is still an asset of the lender's estate because of the liability of the borrower to repay (s 166), but the borrower can utilise the cash to buy an appreciating asset, or go into business, or merely to earn himself interest; and the lender's estate is meanwhile remaining static.

However useful those loans are, they should not take precedence over the use of gifts within the nil rate band or the use of PETs combined with the seven-year cumulation cut-off, annual and other exemptions (which could be used to release a borrower from repayment of part of the loan), and the transfer of appreciating assets.

Loans by trustees of settlements can also be a useful means of making cash available to beneficiaries without necessarily incurring an IHT charge. However, if such loans are on favourable terms, for example, repayable at the end of a fixed period, an IHT liability can arise as a depreciatory transaction, see ss 52(3) and 65(1)(b)).

The question is sometimes raised whether a gratuitous loan of trust property may be regarded as equivalent to allowing the recipient of the loan the use and enjoyment of it and therefore amount to creating an interest in possession. This is not so, because in the case of a straightforward loan of money validly made out of the trust property the loan will be represented in the settlement by the corresponding debt due from the borrower just like any other investment or re-investment of the trust property and should therefore give rise to no

IHT problems. Exercise care in implementing the structure: there must be the expectation at all times that the loan will be repaid. If not, there may be a risk of a 'sham' argument, ie that the transaction is in truth a distribution, not a loan. As an alternative, see the 'diminution in value' argument below.

Contrast the position where the trustees allow a beneficiary exclusive use of a trust asset, eg a dwelling house. Unlike the loan (where the trustees have used the cash to acquire a new asset consisting of the debt due), the trustees still hold the house as a trust asset, and the beneficiary may, by virtue of SP 10/79, be treated as having an interest in possession (see **7.19**).

Whenever loans are made, they should be on terms providing for repayment on demand. If the loan is not repayable until the end of a stated period, HMRC are likely to contend that the lender has replaced his ready cash by a debt due for repayment at some future date; and that the difference between the amount of money advanced, and the present discounted value of the debt, produces a diminution in the lender's estate and constitutes a transfer of value for IHT within s 3(1).

Care should also be taken to ensure that the debt owed to the trustees is situated offshore if the settlement is intended to be an excluded property settlement.

Whether a gift or a loan is to be made, it is important that sufficient information is available to evidence the nature of the advance. For example, in *Silber v Revenue and Customs Commisssioners* [2012] UKFTT 700 (TC), the personal representative appealed against a determination by HMRC charging IHT on the deceased's estate. This was on the basis that (among other things) the sum of £107,210 was advanced as a loan to an unquoted company of which the deceased had been a shareholder. The ground for appeal on this point was that the money was not a loan to the company, but was actually a gift. Unfortunately for the appellant, the available evidence did not support this contention. The tribunal noted in particular that the company's financial statements accounted for the funds as an amount due to a creditor. This was considered to be a prima facie evidence that it was a loan and not a gift. In addition, the IHT account submitted to the Inland Revenue (as it then was) in respect of the deceased's estate showed as an asset of the estate a loan of £107,210 due from the company. The tribunal did not consider that the evidence put forward by the appellant in support of the funds having been a gift to the company was capable of rebutting the prima facie evidence. Accordingly, the tribunal found as a fact that the monies represented a loan to the company, and not a gift. This conclusion is perhaps understandable, given the documentary evidence in support of HMRC's argument, and the relative lack of evidence available to the appellant.

Where loans are subsequently released or waived, perhaps taking advantage of annual exemptions, the release or waiver should always be carried out by deed because of the absence of consideration. It appears that HMRC will not accept that a loan has been waived unless effected by deed, relying on *Pinnel's Case* (1602) 5 Co Rep 117a, although different rules apply in Scotland (see IHTM19100).

The Law Society Revenue Law Committee have previously indicated their view that, while HMRC's contention is not unassailable, unless and until the contention is confirmed or rejected by judicial authority, it must be prudent for clients undertaking IHT planning involving a loan and subsequent waiver to effect the waiver by deed to ensure that the estate of the lender is reduced (*Law Society Gazette*, 18 December 1991, p 40).

The same point is involved in waivers of dividends (**9.12**) and waivers of remuneration (**9.13**). There are stringent anti-avoidance provisions for IHT in respect of artificial loans (FA 1986, s 103) and as will be seen that section even affected the 'debt or charge' scheme in wills, as a result of the decision in *Phizackerley v HMRC* [2007] SpC 00591. A precedent for a deed of waiver is included below.

DEED OF RELEASE AND WAIVER

DATE…………………………………….20XX…

BY [……………..] of [……………..] ('the Lender')

RECITALS

(A)   This Deed is supplemental to a Loan Agreement ('the Loan Agreement') dated …………….. and made between (1) the Lender and (2) ……………… ('the Borrower')

(B)   By virtue of the Loan Agreement the Borrower is obliged to pay the monies owed under the Loan Agreement to the Lender

(C)   The Lender wishes to release the Borrower from all his obligations under the Loan Agreement

OPERATIVE PROVISION

Release of Debt

The Lender HEREBY *releases* the Borrower from all obligations under the Loan Agreement including in particular (but without prejudice to the generality thereof) the amount outstanding as at the date hereof covering all capital and interest (if any) and aggregating the sum of £…………….. plus all future obligations whatsoever.

IN WITNESS whereof this Deed has been duly executed the day and year first before written

SIGNED as a Deed and delivered

By [the Lender] ……………..

In the presence of

[Witness' signature] ……………..

Name ……………..

Address ……………..

Occupation ……………..

LEGAL ASPECTS

11.54 This chapter has dealt with IHT aspects of making gifts. However, in addition to possible implications for other taxes (eg income tax for the gift recipient of an income producing asset), there are potential commercial and legal implications to be addressed. Whilst a detailed consideration of such issues is strictly outside the scope of a book on IHT, it is worth making the general point that IHT planning should be considered 'in the round' with other tax, legal and commercial issues in mind (see **2.80** as to duty of care).

The Law Society has produced a useful practice note 'Making gifts of assets' for solicitors dealing with clients who intend gifting assets. The practice note deals with practical issues such as the gifting of assets to fund future care, and special considerations such as joint donors and multiple donees. The practice note can be accessed via The Law Society website: (www.lawsociety.org.uk/ productsandservices/practicenotes/giftsofassets.page).

Capacity to make a gift

11.55 Apart from tax considerations, difficulties arise where a gift is made by an attorney or where a gift is made late in life to, for example, a carer.

In either case, HMRC may raise issues of capacity, or they may be raised by disappointed family members.

Gifts by attorneys

11.56 Few lasting powers of attorney (LPAs) were initially established following their introduction under the Mental Capacity Act 2005 ('MCA 2005'), for two reasons. First, there was a rush to complete the old form of enduring power of attorney (EPA) before the new rules came into force. Secondly, the procedure for establishing an LPA is slightly complicated, and the officials became rather bogged down. Fortunately, in response to 'customer demand' and with some fairly intense lobbying from the professions, amended and slightly simpler forms of LPA were subsequently introduced.

We shall still, for the foreseeable future, need to take account of MCA 2005, Sch 4, which preserves the rules for EPAs. By Sch 4, para (2), an attorney may make gifts but only subject to strict limitations. First, the EPA itself may forbid the making of gifts, or restrict them; if so, that is the end of the matter.

Even where there is no such limitation, an attorney may benefit himself, or provide for the needs of another person, without having to obtain consent, but only as far as the donor might himself have been expected to provide for those needs. Although the legislation does not say so, saving tax is probably not a 'need'.

The attorney may do whatever the donor might be expected to do to meet those needs. In a masterful, and unofficial, understatement a very senior person charged with administering the rules observed:

> 'When the donor executed the power, she did not thereby agree that her estate could immediately be administered as if she were dead.'

Paragraph (3) of Sch 4 extends the power to make gifts, subject to the terms of the EPA, as follows:

- reasonable seasonal gifts and reasonable gifts on the anniversary of a birth, a marriage or civil partnership, to persons who are related to or connected with the donor (including the attorney); and

- reasonable gifts to any charity to which the donor made gifts or might be expected to make gifts.

For this purpose the value of the gifts must not be unreasonable having regard to all the circumstances and in particular the size of the donor's estate. Note in particular that a series of gifts, unrelated to birthdays etc, designed merely to use the £3,000 pa exemption is not automatically authorised by MCA 2005, Sch 4: it must fall precisely within para 2 or para 3. For an examination of related issues, see also *Curnock v IRC* [2003] SSCD 283 (SpC 365).

One important question is the true meaning of 'seasonal' in the context of gifts. It has been argued, though not yet in a case before the First-tier Tribunal to the authors' knowledge, that an attorney may make regular gifts within the para 3 extension.

In a difficult case application may be made to the Court of Protection for approval of actions taken, or to be taken, by an attorney. Likewise the Court may be approached to approve a proposed course of action where no attorney is acting. The Court will often provide consent to gifts being made for IHT mitigation reasons where it is clear that the person in question would have wanted to make those gifts if they had had capacity to do so, and will not be left with insufficient resources for his or her own requirements.

HMRC certainly regularly take the point and disallow gifts where authority can be questioned, for example after an EPA/LPA has become registered, providing evidence *prima facie* that there is no longer capacity to make gifts.

Gifts to carers

11.57   A particular difficulty arises where a gift is made to a person such as a carer to whom a person may feel beholden late in life. Family may have deserted the potential donor late in life, only to bring their snouts to the trough of his estate after he has died. The carer may be a hardened gold-digger; or may in fact have genuine affection for the donor, which may be reciprocated. It may, in all the circumstances be entirely appropriate, for example, for the residence of the donor to be transferred into the joint names of donor and carer, providing the carer with lasting security.

These are cases where feelings can run high, as implied by the extravagant language of the previous paragraph. The burden of proof, that it was reasonable for the gift to be made, will generally be on the recipient. It may not be enough simply to show that a gift was implemented by a solicitor; there should be clear evidence that the solicitor gave full and independent advice to the donor before the gift, and that the donor fully understood the extent to which his estate and his own freedom of movement would be cut down by the gift.

For an examination of the issue, which is beyond the scope of this work, see *Re Beaney* [1978] 2 All ER 595. The general thrust of MCA 2005 is to presume that a person has capacity to do things, of which making gifts is but one example. If a gift is set aside at the suit of disappointed would-be inheritors, the estate will be increased, so IHT may be increased as a result.

Timely and sound advice, well recorded, might have averted the problem.

APPENDIX 11.1 – TEMPORARY ASSURANCE – GIFT *INTER VIVOS* POLICIES

Provided that the donor is in relatively good health and insurable it is worth considering whether, in the case of IHT, insurance (commonly for PETs) should be effected to cover the IHT payable due to the death of the donor within seven years. Below are very broad annual premium quotations, for illustration purposes only, to give a general idea of the possible cost of an assured sum of £40,000 (being 40% on a cash PET of £100,000) for seven years. The policy should be written for the benefit of the donee.

Age	Male	Female
50	£65.72	£60.00
60	£128.56	£100.32
70	£329.87	£275.93

Note:

The rates shown are for non-smokers.

(Acknowledgement: Robert I Fraser MBE, MBA, MA, FPFS, Senior Client Partner, Chartered Financial Planner, of Towry (www.towry.com)).

Chapter 12

The use of exemptions

INTRODUCTION

12.1   The previous chapter highlighted certain planning points and pitfalls when making lifetime gifts. This chapter covers the use of IHT exemptions. A number of such exemptions are available if the relevant conditions are satisfied, which have the effect of taking transfers of value outside the scope of IHT to the extent of the exemptions.

In addition, the IHT legislation provides that certain dispositions are not to be treated as transfers of value at all, subject once again to certain conditions being satisfied. This chapter highlights two of these in particular, namely dispositions for maintenance of family (s 11) and dispositions allowable for income tax and corporation tax (s 12), as well as considering deathbed situations and gifts by cheque.

GIFTS IN VALUE NOT EXCEEDING £3,000 PER ANNUM (SS 19, 57)

12.2   Transfers of value by a transferor in any one fiscal year (ie 6 April to 5 April) are exempt to the extent that the values transferred by him do not exceed £3,000. Such transfers are also excluded transactions for 'pre-owned assets' income tax purposes (FA 2004, Sch 15, para 10(1)(e), 2(e)). A larger gift can be exempted *pro tanto*, so that a gift of £10,000 could be exempt on the first £3,000, leaving (unless other exemptions were also available) a transfer of value of £7,000.

The annual exemption applies only to lifetime transfers, but is separately and additionally available to other exemptions, subject to compliance with the various conditions. However, HMRC guidance points out that the annual exemption cannot be used in respect of a GWR in the year that reservation by the donor ceases when it then becomes a deemed PET (see IHTM14343).

The exemption can also be used on the lifetime termination of an interest in possession in settled property (s 57). The life tenant has to notify the trustees of the availability of the exemption within six months of the termination. HMRC guidance indicates that a prescribed notice (form 222) is available (IHTM14170), but in practice it is probably seldom used. As far as the writers are aware, the relief was never denied for lack of the form.

The life tenant is deemed to be the transferor; and he has of course only one £3,000 exemption per year to cover both gifts out of his own estate and terminations of interests in possession.

There is a right to accumulate the annual exemption for one further year to the extent that it has not been used in any year (s 19(2)). The exemption for the year of transfer must be used completely before any unused part for the previous year, and if any part left over from the previous year is not used in the current year, it is lost. For example:

Year	Gift	Exemption available	Carry forward
	£	£	£
to 5 April 2011	2,400	3,000	600
to 5 April 2012	2,700	3,600	300
to 5 April 2013	4,000	3,300*	Nil

* (not £3,900)

As in the year to 5 April 2012 a £2,700 gift has been made, there is only a £300 carry-over, and the £600 accumulation from 2011 has been lost.

Note that, under s 19(3A), the annual £3,000 exemption is set against an immediately chargeable transfer and not against a PET made earlier in that year. If the PET becomes chargeable by the death of the donor within seven years it is treated for the £3,000 exemption (and no other purpose) as having been made later than the immediately chargeable gift, which keeps the exemption. Subject to this special rule, earlier transfers are exempt before later ones, although transfers made on the same day are treated pro rata.

As regards PETs, the £3,000 annual exemption is available first against chargeable transfers and then against PETs which become chargeable, as mentioned above. However, HMRC's guidance is rather confusing in this regard. The Inheritance Tax Manual (at IHTM14143) indicates that if tax is payable on two transfers made on different days in the same tax year, the exemption should be applied to the earlier transfer, irrespective of whether the transfers were PETs or chargeable when made. For the avoidance of doubt, chargeable transfers should therefore be made before PETs in the same tax year, if possible.

The following planning aspects should be considered:

- The £3,000 gifts should be made *regularly* so as to ensure that the exemption with the right to accumulate for one year only does not lapse. Husband and wife (or civil partners) together can give away £60,000 under this exemption over ten years; and a couple liable at the 40% rate, by failing to do so, would be giving £24,000 to the Treasury rather than their beneficiaries. It will be appreciated that the exempt gift need not be in cash but can be in assets, such as shares of a company, interests in a property, or a loan account representing the appropriate value.

- The gift should be made, and *shown* to be made, out of *capital* rather than income so as not to reduce the 'normal expenditure' exemption.

- The exemption has particular relevance and use for funding life assurance (see **Chapter 14**), and for annual waivers along the lines indicated in **11.53**.

- As between husband and wife it may be appropriate, as a separate and unrelated transaction, to put funding in place so that each may make gifts. A mere gift to 'channel' assets from one spouse to the other who can thereupon pass on the appropriate gift, eg to a child may be regarded as an associated operation, subject to the comments of Joel Barnett MP reported in *Hansard* 10 March 1975 (see also **6.16**). The terms of a particular gift should always be recorded in writing and where cheque payments are made such cheques should be presented not merely endorsed over.

- Consider adding assets into an appropriate trust: whereas normally relatively small additions to a relevant property trust tend to cause more trouble than they are worth, because they affect the rate of IHT, an addition that is for any reason exempt does not cause such complications.

- It is not enough to create a liability (even by deed) over one's assets in favour of the prospective beneficiary or write him an 'IOU'. There has to be a consequential loss to the estate under s 3(1); and since under s 5(5) a liability can be taken into account only if it has been *incurred* for consideration in money or money's worth, the creation of a liability to pay in these circumstances is not effective.

- If the asset gifted is a loan or capital account with a company or partnership, the correct method is to proceed as follows in order to ensure that there is a properly completed gift.

- Assume that partner A has a loan account with his firm, and he wishes to give B the benefit of it:

  - The firm gives a cheque to A, and A acknowledges receipt. A's loan account is closed or reduced.

  - A pays the cheque into his own bank account and it is cleared.

– A writes a letter to B informing him he wishes to make a gift of £x and encloses his cheque for that amount in B's favour.

– B pays the cheque into his own account and it is cleared.

– B writes a cheque in favour of the firm and accompanies it with a letter saying he is lending the firm the relevant sum. The firm opens a new loan account in favour of B, or increases the balance on any existing account.

Note that a payment by cheque takes effect only when it is cleared (see **12.26**). This formal procedure may, however, not be appropriate if the asset to be transferred is a capital account, rather than a loan account, in a trading partnership and qualifies for business property relief as an interest in a business under IHTA 1984, s 105(1)(a). Where that applies, and by inference the rule in *Beckman v IRC* [2000] STC (SCD) 59 does not apply (see **15.20**) a straight transfer of the capital account itself will be the best course. First analyse the account: has it all been owned by the transferor for two years as required by IHTA 1984, s 106? Recent capital introductions will not qualify, though recent increases that are no more than revaluations of existing assets in the business will do so.

● FA 1986, s 102(5) excludes most exempt transfers from the gift with reservation rules. However, there are two notable exceptions: the £3,000 annual exemption and the normal expenditure out of income exemption (see **12.5**). It would appear therefore that if a gift with reservation exists these exemptions cannot qualify. HMRC consider that the normal income exemption can never apply to a gift with reservation. Furthermore, HMRC take the view (see the November 1993 interpretation guidelines (RI55) referred to at **11.14**) that where, following a gift with reservation, the reservation ceases in the donor's lifetime, whereupon a PET is then treated as made, the £3,000 exemption cannot apply. This represented a change from their former view.

Example 12.1 – Annual exemption: GWR ceasing

On 1 September 2003, A gives his son B his holding of 20,000 shares in publicly quoted XYZ plc. B allows A to retain the dividends. This arrangement ceases on 10 January 2013, A being henceforth excluded, and a PET is treated as made at that time. On 2 March 2013, he makes a gift on discretionary trusts, which is a lifetime chargeable transfer.

The annual £3,000 exemption for 2012–13 cannot be used against the gifted shareholding becoming a PET on 10 January 2013, but is available against the lifetime chargeable transfer on 2 March 2013 (along with any unused part of the 2011–12 annual exemption).

£250 PER ANNUM GIFTS TO ANY NUMBER OF SEPARATE DONEES (S 20)

12.3   A transferor can make any number of separate £250 outright gifts to separate donees in any year to 5 April. Such gifts can be in cash or kind and would cover the normal type of entertainment expenditure disallowed for income tax purposes, which would therefore not strictly be available under the exemption of dispositions allowable for income tax, etc (s 12(1)).

As the gifts must be *outright*, they cannot be used for deemed PETs under the GWR or debts and incumbrances rules (FA 1986, ss 102(4), 103(5)), or those relating to transfers by close companies (s 94). Nor does the small gifts exemption apply upon placing assets *into* settlements, although HMRC accept that the exemption can apply to an absolute gift in trust for a minor (IHTM14180).

The GWR provisions do not apply to gifts falling within the exemption (FA 1986, s 102(5)), even though in strictness the small gifts exemption only applies to outright gifts. HMRC acknowledge '… the mere fact that the donor has reserved a benefit in the gifted property should not, of itself, prevent you from regarding the gift as an outright one' (IHTM14319).

The £250 exemption cannot be used to exempt part of a larger gift (s 20(1)) and only covers donees who have not received more than £250 from the transferor in the year. Thus, if a donor gives £3,250 to a donee, the first £3,000 can be exempted under the annual exemption (see **12.2**); but the £250 exemption cannot be used for the balance. One way of coping with this for, say, a husband and wife with a son and daughter would be for the husband in the present year, to give £3,000 to the daughter and £250 to the son, and the wife vice versa. In the next year they can switch the gifts over. Remember, moreover, that this value is not the value of the property gifted, it is the diminution in the transferor's estate.

NORMAL EXPENDITURE OUT OF INCOME (S 21)

12.4   A gift will benefit from this exemption if, or to the extent that, it complies with certain conditions, ie:

- the gift was part of the *normal expenditure* of the transferor, and

- that (taking one year with another) it was made out of his *income*, and

- that, after allowing for all transfers of value forming part of his normal expenditure, the transferor was left with sufficient income to maintain his *usual standard of living*.

The exemption does not apply to transfers on death or on termination of an interest in possession in settled property, to deemed PETs under the GWR or debts and incumbrance rules, or those relating to transfers by close companies. Nor does the exemption prevent the GWR rules from applying in respect of it (IHTM14231).

The following comments on these conditions may be noted:

Facts and circumstances

12.5   The question whether gifts constitute normal expenditure must be answered according to all the facts and circumstances of each particular case, and is a subjective test.

For example, if a widower, with children grown up, frugal tastes, and no mortgage, regularly saved a high proportion of his income it appears that to give away this proportion would be part of his normal expenditure. Another individual, albeit with a higher income, but with large family commitments and outgoings and no history of savings, may be unable to claim any gift as normal expenditure, as such gift would reduce his standard of living. In the case of a wife who does not contribute to any material extent to the joint standard of living, a higher proportion of her income should be capable of ranking as her normal expenditure.

Where the exemption applies, surplus income can be transferred into a settlement during the settlor's lifetime without the entry charges generally applicable to relevant property trusts.

Pattern

12.6   Following *dicta* in *A-G for Northern Ireland v Heron* [1959] TR 1, a case on the similar ED 'normal and reasonable' exemption, the payments need not necessarily be repetitive, the test of normality being qualitative not quantitative. HMRC guidance indicates that there is no set time span for the purpose of demonstrating a habit of giving, and states: 'It is possible that a number of gifts made by one person may not qualify. It is also possible for a single gift to qualify if it is or is intended to be the first of a pattern and there is evidence of this (IHTM14241).

However, although it seems that a pattern of continuity must be established, the first premium paid under an insurance policy or the first instalment under a deed of covenant may well satisfy this test, on the basis that a payment under a contractual or legal obligation indicates an intention of regularity. As one is now concerned with an annual, lifetime tax, it is possible for HMRC to some extent to adopt a 'wait and see' attitude to this exemption, although their practice is to apply the exemption broadly, usually without the need to undertake an annual analysis of the annual income except in the larger or borderline cases.

HMRC regard 'normal' as meaning habitual (ie conforming to the 'norm' of giving which the transferor has established). HMRC do not, as a matter of practice, seek an IHT return of gifts where they are clearly exempt; nor do they encourage the practice of making returns of the gifts to HMRC and claiming exemption for them at the same time. They are not resourced for that purpose. However, HMRC guidance warns as follows (IHTM06106):

'… the exemption is only available "… to the extent that it is shown …" that the exemption applies. And we interpret "shown" as meaning "shown to the satisfaction of HMRC". It follows therefore that where normal expenditure out of income exemption is in point, a transfer of value remains a chargeable transfer unless and until it is shown to be exempt.'

The guidance goes on to state:

'This requirement to "show" that the exemption is available may suggest that it is necessary to deliver an account in all cases so that the exemption may be agreed. This will defeat the purpose of the regulations.'

However, HMRC then indicate that gifts to which the exemption is considered to apply must be reported on form IHT100 if an IHT liability is otherwise at stake:

'Where denial of the exemption – either in respect of a single gift (whether it is the first of a planned series of gifts or a gift within a series) or cumulatively taking into account earlier transfers – would mean that there is a liability to IHT, an account should be delivered so that the availability of the exemption can be agreed.'

The same point is made elsewhere in HMRC's guidance at IHTM10652, in the context of when form IHT100 is appropriate. HMRC also states the following in the case of lifetime gifts into trust (IHTM14242):

'In rare cases, the exemption may need to be discussed during the transferor's lifetime, for example where a gift is made into trust and would be an immediately chargeable lifetime transfer if the exemption was not available. If … the taxpayer asserts that a first gift is part of an intended series, you can allow the exemption provisionally in the first instance. Make it clear that HMRC proposes to review (and if appropriate disallow) the exemption by reference to the transferor's future gifts if any.'

In any event, it is useful to keep a record of such gifts in case evidence is later called for (see **12.12**).

The term 'normal expenditure' was interpreted in the High Court in *Bennett v IRC* [1995] STC 54. Lightman J held that in the context of s 21, the term 'normal expenditure' connoted expenditure which at the time it took place accorded with the settled pattern of expenditure adopted by the transferor. The existence of such a settled pattern might be established either:

- by reference to a sequence of payments by the transferor out of past expenditure; or

- by proof of a prior commitment or resolution adopted by the transferor regarding his future expenditure.

The facts in *Bennett* were as follows. Mrs Bennett's husband bequeathed, by his will, his shares in a family company and the residue of his estate on trust to pay the income to his widow Mrs Bennett for her life and subject thereto to his three sons, the taxpayers. Following certain transactions the income of the trust increased enormously. Nevertheless, Mrs Bennett lived modestly until her sudden death on 20 February 1990. In 1989, she executed a form of authority addressed to the trustees authorising them to distribute equally between her sons 'all or any of the income arising in each accounting year as is surplus to my financial requirements of which you are already aware'. Payments were made of £9,300 on 14 February 1989 and £60,000 on 5 February 1990.

Lightman J held that the evidence established that Mrs Bennett had made a considered determination for the rest of her life to give to her sons all her surplus income from the trust beyond what she reasonably required for maintenance, and that her determination had been implemented by the execution of the authority requesting the trustees to act accordingly and their so acting. Mrs Bennett had therefore adopted a pattern of expenditure in respect of the surplus income, and the payments to her sons had been made in accordance with that pattern and were accordingly within the meaning of s 21.

Lightman J made a number of additional points:

- first, that if a prior commitment or resolution is shown, a single payment may be within s 21;

- secondly, a commitment towards paying annual premiums on a life assurance qualifying policy gifted to a third party could be a suitable example for s 21; and

- thirdly, there is no need to show that the expenditure is reasonable although it may go to show that as a matter of evidence the relevant pattern of payments exists.

An example of how not to get relief is *Nadin v IRC* [1997] STC (SCD) 107. Mrs Nadin gave away £271,000. Her gross income for the year was £18,605. There was no prior commitment, nor any settled pattern of expenditure. The

Special Commissioner said the evidence pointed to abnormal expenditure. This case looked doomed on the facts, and it was.

Out of income

12.7   As regards the test that the payment must be 'out of income' there is in fact no specific requirement that this means after tax. Nevertheless, insofar as PAYE is deducted from salaries and other employment income, and the general practice for those with investment incomes is to pay the assessed tax out of income as a regular and inevitable outgoing, it follows that looking at the net of tax income merely reflects the general view of what is available income. However, if, say, an individual goes abroad to work for three or four years, suffering little or no tax, he will clearly have little need to take tax into account.

Some inter-spouse transfers of income producing assets (eg from husband to wife) may take place for income tax purposes; and this will enhance the wife's ability to make normal income gifts. Furthermore, where the wife has surplus income and the husband's income is sufficient to maintain the family, separate bank and other accounts should be kept so as to identify the wife's surplus available income.

It has already been noted (**1.27**) that the capital element of a purchased annuity is not regarded as income for IHT purposes. Withdrawals within the annual 5% allowance from single premium policies, as well as withdrawals above that limit which may be liable to higher rate income tax, are still capital withdrawals from a capital asset, and are not available for normal income gifts. Otherwise income refers broadly to income on accounting principles. As capital gains are not the transferor's income, it is not necessary to take into account capital gains tax.

The exemption covers normal *expenditure*; and expenditure connotes payments regarded as expenses or *money* spent. Gifts qualifying for exemption may therefore be expected to have a cash basis out of income. Gifts by an individual of jewellery, stocks or shares out of his estate, or of furniture out of his house, will not count; although regular cash gifts which in fact enable the donee to purchase the jewellery, securities or furniture on an instalment basis may well do. In addition, a specific purchase and gift of the jewellery by the donor out of surplus income may qualify (see IHTM14250).

Partial exemption

12.8   Exemption is granted to 'the extent that' income is available. This means that if, for instance, an individual is paying heavy premiums on a single very large trust policy, the exemption can apply to a proportion of the premiums representing his available income; and the balance of the premiums will be liable to IHT. This ability to split a single gift and exempt one part but not the other removes any need to effect a number of separate staggered policies to ensure that the entire premiums on perhaps the first and second policies are exempted if not the others.

Thus in the case of single large premiums (or other large regular gifts) HMRC will allow a due proportion, ie 'to the extent that'. (The practice of staggering policies may however be advisable for other reasons, see **Chapter 14**.) The balance may qualify for exemption under other provisions (eg the annual exemption).

'Overs' and 'shorts'

12.9   There is a further favourable aspect in the reference to 'taking one year with another' in the context of available income. This expression appears to mean that if an individual, such as an artist or a businessman in hard times, has a widely fluctuating income, the fact that in any one year he has insufficient income should not be a bar to claiming the exemption, where in an earlier year the gift would otherwise be 'normal'. Having said that, HMRC's guidance indicates that claims in respect of income arising more than two years previously will be referred to its Technical Group (IHTM14250).

Further, any attempt to bring income from a later year into an earlier one to support gifts in the earlier year will probably be resisted, though there is actually no statutory authority for denial of exemption on this basis. It is not permissible simply to average income over the seven-year period prior to death to show that there was capacity to make the gifts.

HMRC's guidance devotes a whole page (IHTM14251) to the case *McDowall and others (Executors of McDowall, deceased) v IRC and related appeal* [2004] STC (SCD) 22, in the context of the condition that gifts must be made out of income.

In that case, the deceased (WCM) had formed a habit of making small cash gifts to his children, and had executed a trust disposition and settlement. His habit of making gifts to his children continued until 1991, when he began to suffer from dementia. WCM gave a power of attorney to his son-in-law (M) in 1993. M as attorney made a commitment to distribute a substantial part of WCM's excess income over the amount required for his maintenance. In early 1997, a payment of £12,000 was made to each of WCM's five children. The Special Commissioners held that, on a proper construction of the power of attorney, M had no power to make gifts. The gifts had therefore not been validly made.

However, the Commissioners went on to decide in principle that, had the five gifts of £12,000 been valid, they would have constituted part of WCM's normal expenditure (acting through his attorney), within s 21. The payments were substantial because of the build-up of excess income in previous years. There had been an intention to make regular payments, and a settled pattern had been established by M's prior commitment.

HMRC's guidance at IHTM14251 implies that the *McDowall* case is perhaps less significant and helpful than some taxpayers might expect, pointing out that the Special Commissioners did not consider the meaning of 'taking one year with another' or offer any general guidance on when accumulated income becomes capital. In addition, HMRC warn: 'You may see the argument that *McDowall* provides authority that all income that has not been formally invested retains its character as income indefinitely but that is not what the case established and you should resist any such argument'.

However, it is difficult to reconcile HMRC's approach with the Special Commissioners' decision: 'Our inclination is to conclude that the payments were made out of retained income which remained income in character rather than capital; it was identifiably money which was essentially unspent income and which had been placed on deposit, but not invested in any more formal sense'.

HMRC's 'rule of thumb' income accumulation period of two years will probably be challenged before the tribunal sooner or later. Interestingly, HMRC's guidance points out that the Special Commissioners in *McDowall* did not consider the accumulation period to be a decisive consideration by itself, and that looking at how and for what purpose the income had been accumulated was considered to be more important. Supporting evidence of an intention to accumulate income, with a view to making a gift out of that income, should therefore be helpful in this regard.

Form IHT403, page 6 of which is completed to make the claim, calls for the income and expenditure to be set out year by year and for expenditure to be itemised in considerable detail. Note that the form calls for nursing home fees to be shown as annual, rather than capital, expenditure, which is inconsistent with the decision in *Stevenson v Wishart* (see **12.10**).

Donor's standard of living

12.10   As regards the third condition (maintenance of usual standard of living) the individual should not be obliged to realise capital assets in order to supplement his income. On the other hand, 'exceptional' expenditure can be ignored because it does not reduce the 'usual' standard of living.

Similarly, a change in usual living standards due to reasons outside the donor's control (eg upon redundancy or retirement) will not necessarily be fatal for exemption purposes. In this connection some relief may be allowed where care costs deplete the income. That was no help to the taxpayer in *Nadin*, but the argument was successfully employed in a different context in *Stevenson v Wishart and others (Levy's Trustees)* [1987] 2 All ER 428.

Gift with reservation

12.11   As to the gift with reservation position, see **12.2**.

Procedure

12.12   Negotiations with HMRC will be assisted if, at the time that the gift was made, the circumstances and intentions were recorded by an appropriate memorandum on the following lines:

MEMORANDUM that I the undersigned have this day of 20XX made a gift of £xxx to (Name)

I RECORD AND CERTIFY that this gift is part of my normal expenditure and [taking one year with another] has been paid out of my income. My current and anticipated requirements of life are of a modest nature and this gift together with other similar gifts that I have made and intend making in the future will leave me with sufficient income to maintain my usual standard of living.

Signed ....

RECEIPT (on duplicate)

I ACKNOWLEDGE receipt of the said sum of £

DATED 20XX

Signed ....

Note: The above words in square brackets should if possible be deleted, even though they are included in s 21. The exact meaning of these words is uncertain (see above).

Example 12.2 – Using the exemption

Mr A, aged 70, has a net income after tax of £30,000 per annum, made up of earned income by way of pension and income from investments. Mr A's residence is free of mortgage and he is able to save a regular monthly sum of £700 (ie £8,400 per annum). Mr A has been making regular monthly gifts of

£500 (ie £6,000 per annum or 20% of his net income) divided as to £200 to his sister and £150 each to his son and daughter.

HMRC would no doubt accept that such gifts were part of Mr A's normal expenditure. He could thus still make full use of his annual £3,000 exemption.

Example 12.3 – Partial exemption?

Mr B, aged 45, has a net income after tax (taking one year with another) of £40,000 per annum. He is unable to make any regular savings because his income fluctuates having regard to the profitability of his business, and as he has outstanding commitments on account of mortgage, insurance, education and other liabilities. He is making an allowance of £1,500 per quarter to his son-in-law, who is still training, by dipping into capital.

In this example, HMRC might wish to disallow at least a part of such an allowance as not being part of Mr B's normal expenditure out of income. (The £3,000 annual exemption might also be relevant.) The son-in-law is not within the scope of s 11 ('Dispositions for maintenance of family').

Since the exemption depends so much on individual circumstances, it is not possible to be dogmatic on any particular example, and no special significance attaches to the fraction of income gifted.

Practitioners are recommended to give detailed consideration to this exemption of an individual's normal expenditure, because it represents a useful method of IHT planning, and one which can be applied easily and simply in the appropriate circumstances, especially if a particular gift does not come within the PET regime.

Donors may find HMRC's form IHT403 ('Gifts and other transfers of value') useful on an ongoing basis to record income, expenditure and surplus income each year. The form includes a table ('Gifts made as part of normal expenditure out of income'), which could be used for this purpose. It is otherwise used by personal representatives when accounting for gifts in respect of which exemption under s 21 is claimed. However, note in this connection a small error in the table included in form IHT403. The form contains seven columns, which seems fair enough for recording gifts in the seven years preceding death, but (unless death occurs on 5 April) there will always be eight periods in issue, two part-years and six whole ones. Subject to that observation, and to the point about care costs noted above, the form is helpful in assembling on one sheet all the detail needed to decide if exemption should be allowed.

Remember that a gift outside the seven-year period, unless subject to reservation of benefit, falls out of account, releasing the annual exemption for the year to be applied to any other gifts in that financial year.

Example 12.4 – Combining exemptions

James gave his grandchildren £500 each Christmas and made occasional gifts to his children.

On 17 February 2006, he gave his son Tom £10,000; a few months later (20 June 2006) the same amount to his daughter Daphne. He died on 1 March 2013.

The gift to Tom falls out of account. The grandchildren's gifts are regular.

Against Daphne's gift may be set £6,000, being the exemptions for 2006–07 and 2005–06. Only £4,000 goes against the nil rate band.

Finally, as the preceding paragraphs might suggest, the exercise of determining whether a particular gift falls within the normal expenditure out of income exemption will not be straightforward in many cases, and claims for the exemption may be the subject of enquiries by HMRC. In this context, it is worth noting the following comment in HMRC's own guidance (at IHTM14234): 'In borderline cases you should give the taxpayer the benefit of any reasonable doubt'.

GIFTS IN CONSIDERATION OF MARRIAGE OR REGISTERED CIVIL PARTNERSHIP (SS 22, 57)

12.13   There are two statutory restrictions, first, as to the persons within the marriage or civil partnership consideration, and secondly as to the allowable amount of such gifts or settlements.

The marriage etc exemption can also be used on the lifetime termination of an interest in possession, though perhaps these days the combination of people marrying, and one party enjoying an interest in possession in a trust, is statistically so slight as to be negligible. The life tenant must notify the trustees of the availability of the exemption within six months of the release. The prescribed form for this purpose (form 222) is available from HMRC, but in practice a signed letter should suffice.

The exemption is not considered by HMRC to apply to deemed PETs under the GWR or debts and incumbrances rules (FA 1986, ss 102(4), 103(5)), or in respect of transfers by close companies (s 94). However, to the extent that a gift is subject to the exemption, it cannot also be subject to the GWR rules (IHTM14191).

DISPOSITION FOR MAINTENANCE OF FAMILY (INCLUDING ARRANGEMENTS ON DIVORCE) (S 11)

12.14   It will be noted that the annual exemption, small gifts exemption and wedding or civil partnership exemption are subject to upper monetary limits. However, the IHT regime is more generous in other respects. For example, the normal expenditure out of income exemption is limited only by the donor's personal circumstances.

In addition, the IHT relief for dispositions for the maintenance of family members is not subject to a specified upper limit.

The following dispositions are not transfers of value:

- for maintenance of the spouse or ex-spouse;

- for maintenance, education or training of the child;

- for maintenance or care of a dependent relative.

In *Phizackerley v HMRC* [2007] SpC 00591, the taxpayer was faced with a difficult admission, for the purpose of FA 1986, s 103 because a house had been purchased with funds which 'must have been provided by the Deceased', the husband; counsel argued that such provision, being a roof over the head of the wife, constituted maintenance of the wife. Dr Avery Jones as Special Commissioner rejected the argument, saying that 'the ordinary meaning of maintenance has a flavour of meeting recurring expenses'; it could mean the saving of the burden of paying rent, but he did not allow that construction to apply to the particular facts of the case.

Family members

12.15   In view of the existing inter-spouse exemption (s 18) this exemption has particular relevance to 'ex-spouses', ie as regards financial arrangements on the breakdown of the marriage, particularly on divorce. Counsel for the Revenue noted this in *Phizackerley*.

Where there are alterations or variations of a maintenance order or agreement between the parties, the method employed can be of fundamental importance. So long as the *original* court order or agreement is varied or amended, the IHT exemption of s 11 will apply; but if it is by way of a *new* order or agreement, it is unlikely that the exemption will apply.

Apart from s 11, however, it is probable that a financial arrangement made on a divorce or separation is not in any case a gratuitous transfer, and is accordingly excluded from IHT charge under s 10.

As regards children, the definition is wide and includes illegitimate, adopted, and stepchildren. In certain circumstances, the exemption is available for someone who is not in fact the child of the parent but in the care of the person making the disposition. The exemption can extend beyond the age of 18 if the child then continues in full-time education or training.

HMRC interpret the section as applying only to lifetime gifts and not being available on death, presumably on the footing that s 11 applies to 'dispositions', although this interpretation is not obvious from the section.

Dependent relatives

12.16   In the case of dependent relatives, the exemption applies to the extent that the disposition represents a 'reasonable provision' for his care or maintenance (s 11(3)).

In *McKelvey (Personal Representative of McKelvey Deceased) v Revenue and Customs Commissioners)* [2008] SpC 694, the deceased (D) was a spinster who lived with her widowed mother (M), who was 85 years old, blind and in poor health. D was diagnosed with terminal cancer, and in 2003 gave away two houses that she owned to M. D died in 2005, and M died in 2007. HMRC sought to charge IHT on the value of D's gift of the houses to M of £169,000. D's executor appealed, on the grounds that the transfers were exempt within s 11(3) as dispositions being a reasonable provision for the care and maintenance of a dependent relative. The executor contended that D gave the houses to M so that they could be sold to pay for nursing care.

The executor's appeal was allowed in part. The Special Commissioner held that it was reasonable for D to assume that M would need residential nursing care. The difficulty in this case was in determining what was 'reasonably required' for this purpose. The Commissioner concluded that 'reasonable provision at the time the transfers were made amounted in all to £140,500'. This amount qualified for exemption under s 11, with the balance of £28,500 being a chargeable transfer (s 3A(4)).

HMRC's published view of what represents reasonable provision for the care or maintenance of a dependent relative states the following (at IHTM04177):

> '"Reasonable" would appear to suggest such amount as is reasonably necessary for the purpose of providing care and maintenance (but no more), having regard to the financial and other circumstances of the transferor and the relative and the degree of incapacity or infirmity of the latter.'

567

However, the Commissioner held that, in determining what was reasonably required for M's care: 'It seems to me that the approach adopted in personal injury cases is appropriate.' This was to take a multiplier of 5.5 (being the assumed number of years that M would have required paid nursing care on the evidence) and an annual care cost in M's own home of £21,000. This resulted in a basic sum of £115,500, to which a further sum of £25,000 was added to cover the contingency for higher cost if M was admitted to a home.

HMRC consider that the dependent relative's incapacity needs to be financial as well as physical (IHTM04179). However, contrary to HMRC's guidance in the circumstances of the above case, the Commissioner also held:

> '... I do not think it appropriate to make any adjustment in respect of [M's] own resources since the deceased's evident intention was not to meet a financial shortfall but to provide for the replacement of what she herself had been doing at no cost to her mother.'

A disposition for the maintenance of family members that does not wholly satisfy the relief conditions may be apportioned (s 11(5)) so that, for example, the non-qualifying element of a gift to the family member is separately treated as a potentially exempt transfer, unless covered by other exemptions. However, in HMRC's view (see IHTM04180): '... an apportionment under s 11(5) is appropriate only where the disposition of an identifiable part of the property transferred completely satisfies [Section 11 IHTA 1984]'.

Unfortunately, s 11 does not readily address a problem that may now afflict many families. Grandparents may wish to help out their children who are burdened by massive mortgage repayments and who may be living on much reduced income as a result of redundancy or through family responsibilities: middle class 'Cathy Come Home' situations. Such children are outside the scope of s 11, as are the grandchildren.

This situation can be addressed in two ways: by using s 21 over a period of time, or more radically by the grandparents making an interest-free loan to lift part of the mortgage so as to reduce the repayments to be made by the child.

Other points

12.17

- The s 11 exemption could apply to a non-UK domiciled spouse.

- As regards education policies for IHT, these will be exempt by virtue of s 11 if provided by a parent, but education policies by grandparents and relations other than parents will usually give rise to an IHT charge.

- At first sight the section might be thought to be a useful way of placing sizeable amounts *inter vivos* into a family settlement free of IHT provided the beneficiaries are confined to the defined categories. In particular, as indicated above, under s 11(5) where an identifiable part of the property subject to a disposition (ie specified assets forming part of the total property disposed of) satisfied the conditions of s 11, that part may be exempt, the remainder of the property comprised in the disposition being taxable. However, HMRC practice is to treat the section restrictively, confining its use to the relatively narrow purposes and period in the section and denying relief in so far as the trusts stray at all over the edge.

● Clearly, if a particular gift fails the s 11 exemption test, the gift may nevertheless qualify as a PET.

GIFTS OF EXCLUDED PROPERTY

12.18   The main category of excluded property is property situated outside the UK where the person beneficially entitled to it is an individual domiciled outside the UK (s 6(1)). Therefore, in the case of a gift of cash from abroad, the overseas donor should open a bank account outside the UK in favour of the donee who can then remit free of IHT. On the other hand, if the donor simply sends a cheque which is cashed here, the gift will no longer be one of excluded property.

In the case of settled property, the criterion is that the settlor was not domiciled in the UK at the time the settlement was made, and the trust assets are abroad (but for reversionary interests, see **7.112**) (s 48(3)), or the settled property comprises authorised unit trust holdings or shares in an open-ended investment company (s 48(3A)).

In the case of an individual domiciled abroad with assets abroad who is considering acquiring or re-acquiring a UK domicile (or who is about to become deemed domiciled under s 267(1)(b)), that person should therefore settle those assets abroad *before* the change. In addition, if the size of the case warrants it, and the trust will contain sizeable UK assets, consideration should be given to the trust owning the shares of an offshore investment company (which is situate outside the UK and hence will continue to be excluded property in the hands of the trustees), and the investment company owning the assets including those in the UK.

A reversionary interest is excluded property, unless it has been acquired (at any time before by the present owner or a predecessor) for a consideration in money or money's worth, unless it is one to which the settlor or his spouse is or has been entitled; or it is under a lease for life not granted at a rack rent.

Accordingly, estate owners may wish to concentrate on gifts of this type of asset.

As to the purchase of interests in excluded property trusts by UK-domiciled individuals and anti-avoidance provisions introduced from 5 December 2005, and further anti-avoidance provisions in respect of UK-domiciled individuals acquiring interests in settled excluded property introduced with effect from 20 June 2012, see **17.14**.

For further commentary on foreign domicile and excluded property generally, see **Chapter 17**.

MUTUAL TRANSFERS (FORMERLY SS 148–149)

12.19   These are now of historic interest only, as a means of understanding past transactions. A gift back by a donee to the donor within ten years from the date of the donor's transfer of property up to the value of the donor's chargeable transfer was exempt from CTT in certain circumstances. This exemption was abolished in respect of transfers after 17 March 1986 (FA 1986, s 101, and Sch 19, para 25).

DISPOSITIONS ALLOWABLE FOR INCOME TAX OR CONFERRING RETIREMENT BENEFITS (S 12)

12.20   Seldom encountered in practice (although see **9.19** concerning employer contributions to EBTs), such dispositions are exempt from IHT to the extent that they are allowed in computing the disponer's profits or gains from income tax or corporation tax purposes (eg an *ex gratia* payment to an employee), or would be so allowable if there were any such profits taxable in the UK.

The exemption is extended to contributions to a registered pension scheme, a qualifying non-UK pension scheme or a 'section 615' scheme (or, before 6 April 2006, to approved or comparable pension and retirement schemes). If a member of any such scheme omits to exercise a pension right, the anti-avoidance rule affecting the omission to exercise a right (s 3(3)) does not apply in respect of it (s 12(2ZA)).

CHARITIES, REGISTERED CLUBS, POLITICAL PARTIES AND HOUSING ASSOCIATIONS

12.21   Gifts to charities or registered clubs established in the UK (and extended to charitable organisations located in the EU, Norway and Iceland – see below) are entirely exempt from IHT, whether made in lifetime or on death.

The exemption also applies where property is given to a charity by way of a capital payment out of a relevant property trust. Note the special treatment in **7.106**. Under s 70 the relevant property trust provisions do not apply to charitable trusts except and until property ceases to be so held.

Note that the related property provisions of s 161 (see **1.24**) extend also to charities and public bodies.

This exemption is, however, subject to certain conditions set out in s 23(2)–(5) for charities, partly by way of anti-avoidance and partly to ensure complete vesting. In particular, it should be remembered that:

- a deferred gift to charity is not exempt (s 23(2)(a));

- a conditional gift is not exempt unless the charity becomes absolutely entitled within 12 months of the transfer (s 23(2)(b)); and

- a defeasible gift is not exempt unless it becomes indefeasible within 12 months (s 23(2)(c)).

The conditions in s 23(2)–(5) also apply to ss 24, 24A, 25, 27 (gifts to public bodies), and did apply to s 26 (Gifts for public benefit, now abolished).

Care should be taken to ensure that legacies to charity come into operation on death such that they fall within s 23(1), and not upon some other event such as an appointment by trustees exercising a discretion to do so (*Bailhache Labesse Trustees Limited & others v Revenue & Customs Commissioners* [2008] SpC 688).

Where the value transferred (ie the loss to the transferor's estate as a result of the disposition) exceeds the value of the gift in the hands of the charity, etc, HMRC take the view that the exemption extends to the whole of the value transferred (Statement of Practice E13).

The exemptions under ss 23–27 are all subject to s 56 which excludes exemption in certain situations involving settled property, reserved rights or reversionary interests. Section 56 ('Exclusion of certain exemptions') prevents, *inter alia*, the avoidance of IHT by A settling property on himself for life, remainder to his son where A assigns his life interest to a charity to be used as an intermediary before the benefit passes to A's son. Since the changes to the IHT treatment of trusts that took effect from 22 March 2006, this anti-avoidance rule is largely unnecessary but it remains in place nevertheless.

Prior to changes originally announced in the Budget on 24 March 2010, 'charity' had the same meanings as in the Income Tax Acts (s 272; ITA 2007, ss 989, 430, 446). However, a new statutory definition was introduced (in FA 2010, Sch 6) which includes a four-stage test to determine if an organisation is eligible for UK charity tax reliefs. This includes a jurisdiction condition, which broadly allows the organisation to be located in the UK or an EU member state or specified country including Iceland or Norway (SI 2010/1904). The FA 2010 changes apply for IHT purposes from 1 April 2012 (Finance Act 2010, Schedule 6, Part 2 (Commencement) Order 2012, SI 2012/736); as to transfers before that date, see IHTM11112.

It should be noted that the four-stage test mentioned above includes a 'management condition', which in turn includes a 'fit and proper person' test. This could deprive some organisations of their charitable status. There is no statutory definition of a 'fit and proper' person, although detailed (albeit non-statutory) guidance is available on the HMRC website (www.hmrc.gov.uk/charities/guidance-notes/chapter2/fp-persons-test.htm).

A reduced IHT rate of 36% applies to a deceased person's estate in certain circumstances involving charitable legacies, with effect for deaths on or after 6 April 2012 (Sch 1A). The reduced rate broadly applies where 10% or more of a deceased's net estate (after deducting liabilities, exemptions, reliefs and the nil rate band) is left to charity or a registered community amateur sports club. In such cases, the normal 40% rate is reduced to 36% (see **5.26**).

Gifts to political parties, whether during lifetime or on death, are wholly exempt. To qualify for exemption, the party must have obtained at the last general election either two members elected to the House of Commons or one member and not less than 150,000 votes given to their candidates (see s 24).

Note that where an estate is divisible between a charity or political party or other exempt beneficiary and other beneficiaries who are not exempt, the burden of IHT on the chargeable proportion falls on the non-exempt beneficiaries (s 41) (but note the effect of the *Benham* and *Ratcliffe* decisions outlined at **4.39**).

Example 12.5 – Exempt and non-exempt legacies

A testator dies on 1 January 2013 leaving an estate of £1,100,000, having made no previous transfers. By his will he leaves a legacy of £100,000 to a registered housing association (exempt), a legacy of £370,000 free of IHT to his daughter and the residue as to two-thirds to his son and one-third to charity (exempt). In order to find the amount of IHT chargeable:

(1)   Gross up the legacy of £370,000 to the daughter as if it were the only transfer ie take the nil rate band of £325,000 and multiply the balance of £45,000 by 100/64 (= £70,312) to get the gross figure of £395,312 (ie £370,000 plus £25,312 IHT).

(2)   Work out the chargeable part of the estate with that grossed-up legacy of £395,312. The residue is £1,100,000 less legacies of £100,000 to the housing association and £395,312 to the daughter, ie £604,688. The

son's two-thirds is £403,125, and the charity's one-third is £201,563. The chargeable part of the estate is £798,437 (ie £1,100,000 – (£100,000 + £201,563)).

(3) IHT at 36% (see below) on an estate of £798,437 is £170,437. The daughter's legacy is now grossed up again by multiplying by A/A – B, where A is the chargeable estate and B is the chargeable estate after the tax on it. Thus £370,000 × £798,437/£628,000 = £470,417 which is the daughter's re-grossed-up legacy.

(4) Finally, recalculate the chargeable estate using the daughter's re-grossed-up legacy of £470,417. The son has two-thirds of £1,100,000 less (£470,417 plus £100,000) × 2/3, ie £353,055. The chargeable part of the estate is now £470,417 plus £353,055, ie £823,472, on which tax at 36% is £179,450.

The housing association and the daughter take their legacies of £100,000 and £370,000 respectively. The residue (ignoring costs) is £1,100,000 less £470,000, ie £630,000. The charity takes one-third, ie £210,000, leaving the son to bear the burden of tax on his two-thirds so that he takes £420,000 less £179,450, ie £240,550 (figures rounded).

Notes

(a) The IHT rate of 36% applicable to charitable legacies of 10% or more of the net estate has been applied in the grossing-up calculation, and also the calculation of IHT on the estate, as the 10% requirement is satisfied for the purposes of Sch 1A (see IHTM45030).

(b) A grossing-up calculator at the 36% rate is available on the HMRC website: (www.hmrc.gov.uk/cto/g_up36.pdf).

Note that s 41 applies 'notwithstanding the terms of any disposition', so that the terms of a will or other disposition cannot override the operation of the section. The point applies to any exempt beneficiaries (see **6.13** as to inter-spouse transfers).

Gifts made (after 13 March 1989) to registered housing associations are also exempt transfers (see s 24A). The anti-avoidance legislation applying to charities and public bodies in ss 23–26 also covers gifts to housing associations (eg that the donor must gift his entire interest).

GIFTS FOR NATIONAL PURPOSES (S 25, SCH 3)

12.22 Gifts to certain national institutions as listed are wholly exempt transfers for IHT. These include the main museums, the National Trust, the

Nature Conservancy Council, local authorities, government departments and universities in the UK (as to works of art, see **16.12** onwards). There is no upper limit on the value of the exemption.

A relief is available for CGT purposes in respect of disposals to any of the bodies listed in Sch 3 (TCGA 1992, s 257 'Gifts to charities etc').

A form of relief for income tax, capital gains tax and/or corporation tax purposes was introduced in FA 2012, broadly where individual and corporate donors make qualifying gifts of 'pre-eminent property' (as defined) to the nation (FA 2012, Sch 14). A gift to the nation pursuant to FA 2012, Sch 14 is exempt for IHT purposes (s 25(3)).

GIFTS FOR PUBLIC BENEFIT (S 26) (REPEALED)

12.23   The exemption for gifts for the public benefit (ie gifts to various non-profit-making organisations as approved by the Treasury) was abolished in relation to transfers made from 17 March 1998. The particular asset being transferred to such non-profit-making organisations may have consisted of land, buildings, contents, as well as maintenance funds given as a source of income for the upkeep of such exempted property or works of art, etc. HMRC may have required undertakings in respect of the preservation of the property and access to the public (ss 30(1)(b), 31(1)(d)). If the exemption was not claimed it may well be possible to negotiate a relatively low rate of death value, having regard to the cost of upkeep for example, in the case of historic buildings.

A similar relief was available for CGT purposes (TCGA 1992, s 258).

VOIDABLE TRANSFERS (S 150) AND INHERITANCE (PROVISION FOR FAMILY AND DEPENDANTS) ACT 1975 (S 146)

12.24   A claim for relief is provided by s 150 for IHT where the whole or any part of a chargeable transfer has by virtue of any enactment or rule of law been set aside as voidable or otherwise defeasible. This could apply, for example, in the case of bankruptcy or undue influence, or where a court rules that the donor had no or a defective title. However, it does not appear to apply if the parties elect to set a transfer aside or the court rules that damages should be paid in lieu of setting the transfer aside. In such cases the transfer has not 'by virtue of any enactment or rule of law been set aside'.

The principle is extended by s 146 to the Inheritance (Provision for Family and Dependants) Act 1975. Under s 2 of that Act, the court may order *inter alia* lump sums and/or maintenance payments to be made in favour of a wide class of dependants (which includes 'common law' wives and, from 5 December 2005, civil partners) when an individual has not made reasonable provision for them in his will or in accordance with the intestacy rules.

The property affected by such order is for IHT purposes to be treated as if it had devolved on that individual's death subject to the provisions of the order. Moreover, under s 146(8) the principle covers circumstances where such order stays or dismisses proceedings under the Act on terms. Under s 10 of that Act, the court can require a donee who has received a gift in money or assets from a donor within six years prior to the donor's death, to 'return' the gift in whole or part to the donor's dependants; and any IHT paid is repaid with interest and if not yet paid ceases to become payable. Interest paid to the taxpayer is free of income tax (IHTA 1984, s 236(3)). In respect of settlements or variations thereof, there are corresponding reliefs against capital payments and termination of interest in possession charges.

A claim under the Act must normally be commenced within six months of grant of probate and personal representatives must be careful not to distribute the estate whilst there is a possibility of a claim being made. Testators should be made aware of the effect of the Act when drawing up their wills; it may be appropriate to leave with the will, a letter setting out the testator's reasoned motives for the particular provision he has made, and/or omitted to make (although even then that is no guarantee that a claim will not be made successfully, as was the case in *Ilott v Mitson* [2011] EWCA Civ 346).

Under aborted proposals in the Finance Bill 1989, the 1975 Act was to become the restricted yardstick of what could be achieved by a variation under s 142, but those proposals were dropped.

DEATHBED SITUATIONS

12.25 No individual should leave his IHT planning to his deathbed, but some of course do. There is very limited scope for artificial arrangements such as were once common, and a deathbed marriage of convenience to secure the spouse exemption may not have a wide appeal. Nevertheless, there are a number of steps that can be taken to reduce the burden of IHT or to facilitate further advantageous post-death planning.

- First, advantage should be taken of the exemptions available only during lifetime (see **1.35**). For example, if an individual is life tenant of a fund passing on his death to strangers, he can ensure his own family receive the full benefit of the nil rate band by making PETs to them in lifetime, which become chargeable on death and earlier in the cumulative ladder, leaving the settled fund to bear the full rate of IHT on cumulation after his gifts. Make sure that gifts by cheque are completed (**12.26**); and that all gifts are outright ones, and not *donatio mortis causa*, which are conditional upon the expected death taking place (**11.40**).

- Other important reliefs which have application on death are noted elsewhere, including business relief, agricultural relief (**Chapter 15**), and woodlands and works of art (which exceptionally have no stipulated period of ownership). Check also in the case of partnerships or private company shares that there are no 'buy and sell' arrangements which would exclude business/agricultural relief (**15.86**).

- If there is time, make one or more small discretionary settlements; and let the client settle assets by his will on those trusts. This should also prevent operation of the related settlement provisions. It is also possible to create a settlement giving one's spouse a revocable interest in possession and, subject thereto, upon discretionary trusts; with the result that on revocation of the spouse's interest the rate of IHT will be determined by the spouse's cumulative ladder (s 80). Distributions within two years of death are treated as made under the will (s 144) and this allows more extended thoughts on destination. There is also the two-year precatory trust under s 143 (see **5.11**).

- If there is no time for a fresh will, consider the planning possibilities available in the two years after the death through a deed of variation or disclaimer of the will or intestacy under s 142 (see **5.32** onwards).

- Should the healthier spouse (say, the wife) have chargeable assets showing large capital gains, they can be transferred to the other during lifetime in order to obtain a new base value for CGT on his death, and they can return to the donor exempt from IHT under his will.

- The ailing spouse could also leave his assets to the surviving spouse, thereby obtaining CGT exemption and market value uplift. Thereafter, the surviving spouse may be in a position to make PET gifts to members of the family. Indeed, this may be the correct general formula to adopt where assets show a high CGT liability (eg a low or nominal base value) and hold-over relief is not available. See also **4.16** as to leaving the bulk of one's estate to the surviving spouse and **Chapter 3** as to the facility to transfer unused nil rate band between spouses or civil partners (where the survivor's death is on or after 9 October 2007).

One method whereby a testator before his death might at the same time benefit both a charity and an individual is considered below. This proposal makes use of s 143 whereby, if a legacy is bequeathed by will to a legatee with a non-binding request that the legatee should transfer any of it to other persons, and the legatee carries out the request within two years of the death, the legatee's transfer is treated for IHT as having been made by the testator. If the request was in favour of a charity the benefit is then exempt from IHT. However, for purposes other than IHT, the transfer has been made by the original legatee. He therefore appears able (assuming sufficient taxable income) to take advantage for income tax of the Gift Aid provisions of ITA 2007, Pt 8, Ch 2, whereby a gift of an unlimited amount can be treated as a net amount and qualify for tax relief.

Thus, where a testator leaves, say, £800 to X (a 40% income tax payer) with a non-binding wish that X should give it to charity Y, the following results would, if successful, apply:

- IHT of £320 would be saved on the gift itself (and the deceased's net estate may be subject to a lower rate of IHT (ie 36%) if the charitable legacy satisfies the conditions in Sch 1A);

- the charity would receive £800 net and reclaim basic rate tax of £200 on a gross gift of £1,000;

- X would seek to reclaim higher rate tax of £200 – a total tax saving of £720 on the sum of £800 given in the testator's will.

But see **5.25** for a note of warning about the use of Gift Aid and ss 143 and 142.

It was thought that it would similarly be possible to arrange a variation of a will under s 142 to produce such a non-binding legacy. However, the Special Commissioners in *St Dunstan's v Major* [1997] STC (SCD) 212 upheld the Revenue view that FA 1990, s 25(2)(e) (now ITA 2007, s 416(7)) would disqualify such a scheme. This subsection excludes relief for Gift Aid where either the donor or any person connected with him receives a benefit in consequence of making it, on the grounds that the IHT saving is such a benefit.

Subsequently, the tribunal reached the same view as the Special Commissioner in the *St Dunstan's* case in *Harris (as trustee of the Harris Family Charitable Trust) v HMRC* [2010] UKFTT 385 (TC), where it was held that the IHT exemption resulting from a deed of variation redirecting a gift to charity was a 'benefit' which prevented the gift from qualifying for Gift Aid.

However, the benefit contemplated by ITA 2007, s 416(7) appears to be one provided by the donee charity itself. Furthermore, while a variation operates from the death for both IHT (see **5.32**) and CGT (see **5.36**), it does not do so for income tax purposes, a point upheld by the Special Commissioners in *St Dunstan's*. Accordingly therefore, where a beneficiary of the estate, say the testator's son, provides for s 143 charitable gifts out of his *own* interest (thereby serving to reduce it) within two years of the testator's death, there should be no question of any prior general arrangement among beneficiaries generally which might vitiate the son's claim for income tax relief under the Gift Aid provisions on the subsequent charitable donations by him. See **5.25** for further discussion.

A deathbed planning arrangement involving the purchase of an interest in an 'excluded property' trust was blocked by FA 2006, with effect from 5 December 2005. Previously, a UK-domiciled individual might purchase an interest in an excluded property settlement for, say, £1 million. No transfer of value is made, because the purchase is at full market value. Although he now owns an interest under a trust worth £1 million, its value would not have been included in his chargeable IHT estate on death, because it was excluded property.

However, the excluded property exemption in IHTA 1984, s 48(3) no longer applies, if the relevant interest in trust property was bought on or after 5 December 2005. This change was introduced to prevent UK-domiciled individuals undertaking 'last minute' IHT planning of this nature. However, variations of such 'excluded property trusts' evolved soon after the introduction of s 48(3B)–(3C). The foreign situs assets of a non-UK domiciled individual continue to be excluded property (IHTA 1984, s 6(1)), and an interest in an excluded property trust bought by a non-UK domiciled individual and resettled outside the UK should not be affected by the restriction. As to further anti-avoidance provisions aimed at certain arrangements involving purchased interests in possession and the acquisition by UK-domiciled individuals of interests in settled excluded property, see **1.33** and **17.14** respectively.

GIFTS BY CHEQUE

12.26   Finally in the art of giving, it should be borne in mind that a gift by cheque is not completed until it is paid *and* cleared. Until then, it is simply a revocable authority to the bank which can of course be withdrawn by stopping the cheque.

In *Re Owen, Owen v IRC* [1949] 1 All ER 901, the decision turned on whether gifts by cheque (drawn outside the statutory gift period but cashed within) were subject to estate duty; and it was held the gifts were completed only when the cheques were honoured, so that the gifts were made within the statutory period and were liable to estate duty.

Owen was quoted with approval in *Parkside Leasing Ltd v Smith* [1985] STC 63 where it was held the date of entitlement to income (for Sch D Case III purposes) was not the date the payee received the cheque (even though drawn on the Bank of England and therefore possibly as good as cash) but the date the cheque was cleared, which was in the next accounting period. The same principle was applied in *Barclays Bank plc v Bank of England* [1985] 1 All ER 385 which makes it clear that when a presenting bank (ie that of the payee) receives from him a cheque for collection, its responsibility to him is discharged only when the cheque is physically delivered to the payer's branch for decision whether it should be paid or not.

More recently, in *Curnock v CIR* SpC 36 [2003] STC (SCD) 283, the appellant (under an enduring power of attorney) drew a cheque for £6,000 on the deceased's account in favour of the appellant's son on 21 December 2001, to make use of the annual exemption for the same and preceding year. The deceased died on 22 December 2001, and the cheque cleared on 27 December 2001. The Special Commissioner held that as the cheque had not cleared before the death of the deceased, the gift had not been completed. Furthermore, the cheque was not a debt of the deceased's estate, because it had not been incurred for consideration in money or money's worth (see s 5(5)). However, HMRC must accept a deduction from the estate for any cheques signed for consideration in money or money's worth by the deceased where this is reflected in the assets of the estate, such as if the cheque was intended to pay for building work or goods supplied to the deceased (IHTM28300).

The principle that a gift by way of cheque takes effect only when cleared should be kept in mind where time limits are approaching. HMRC will probably look closely at cheques drawn shortly before such dates, where appropriate (see IHTM14882). It could be relevant, for example, at each yearly stage of taper relief if the time spent in clearing the cheque made the time of the original gift a few days late. It could also be relevant in respect of the running of the seven-year period for PETs and the renewal of the nil rate band.

In cases where time is of the essence the person making the gift should consider executing a declaration of trust of a cash sum in favour of the intended recipient of the gift, at the same time as signing the cheque, since by doing so the intended gift will take effect immediately. The following is an example of a suitable form of wording:

BY THIS DEED I [Name of donor] hereby irrevocably declare that I shall henceforth hold the sum currently standing to my credit at the XYZ bank in account number [number] as follows:

as to £x upon trust for [donee] absolutely and

as to the remainder of such sum for myself

and I declare that I shall henceforth make payment of the said sum of £x to [donee] forthwith.

Signed as a deed and delivered

by [name] ....

in the presence of

[witness] ....

on [date]

Chapter 13

Pre-owned assets

INTRODUCTION

13.1   The pre-owned assets income tax charge (or the 'charge to income tax on benefits received by former owner of property', to be more precise) was originally announced on 10 December 2003, enlarged on in the Budget of 17 March 2004 and press release, and is now embodied in FA 2004, s 84 and Sch 15 and in Treasury Regulations.

In addition, following its introduction, guidance notes ('Income tax and pre-owned assets') were published on the HMRC website, although these have largely been replaced by an expanded version in HMRC's Inheritance Tax Manual at IHTM44000 onwards (even though the pre-owned assets provisions apply for income tax purposes, and not for IHT). The charge operates for 2005–06 and subsequent years, but is retroactive to 18 March 1986!

This chapter provides an outline of the pre-owned assets tax (POAT) rules, including an analysis of what is chargeable, clearly excluded, or potentially excluded from the POAT charge, with reference to subsequent Treasury Regulations and HMRC guidance on the subject.

In essence, the Sch 15 charge is a free-standing income tax charge (under the successor to the former Sch D, Case VI) on 'benefits' received by a former owner of property (including land (especially accommodation), chattels and intangibles in a settlement), following the concept of the benefit-in-kind charge on employees.

The 'prescribed rate' (to be applied to the values of chattels and intangibles when quantifying the cash value of the benefit enjoyed) decreased from 4.75% to 4% with effect from 6 April 2010 (SI 1989/1297, reg 5, as amended by SI 2010/415, reg 2). For land, the chargeable amount is based on the appropriate rental value. Regulations provide, broadly, that land and chattels will be valued every five years, normally as from 6 April.

The reader should bear in mind that this book is primarily concerned with IHT planning. This chapter therefore does not cover the mechanics of the income tax charge in great detail. Readers interested in POAT should refer to separate material on the subject, such as the book *Pre-Owned Assets and Estate Planning* by Emma Chamberlain and Chris Whitehouse published by Sweet & Maxwell). See also *Inheritance Tax 2012/13* (Bloomsbury Professional), chapter 16.

As indicated above, there is a 'cut-off date' for POAT purposes in relation to transactions entered into before 18 March 1986. In addition, outright cash gifts prior to 6 April 1998 may be ignored, ie there is an exclusion from POAT in respect of monetary gifts made at least seven years before the taxpayer occupied or used the relevant land or chattel (FA 2004, Sch 15, para 10(2)(c)), but no earlier than seven years before the introduction of POAT on 6 April 2005.

THE BROAD CONCEPT

General

13.2   The typical circumstance will arise where an individual:

- owned an asset, such as a home;

- disposes of it as a gift or for less than full value (or provides funds for the purchase – but see reference to the seven-year period below); and

- continues to occupy or enjoy the asset in whole or part, but is not subject to IHT as a gift with reservation.

The tax, like IHT, is chargeable on worldwide assets where the individual is UK resident and UK domiciled or deemed domiciled for IHT purposes (see further below). The legislation sets out various formulae for calculating the charge (eg at FA 2004, Sch 15, paras 3–5 (land) and paras 6–7 (chattels)).

Whilst POAT was introduced to catch certain IHT planning arrangements such as *Ingram* and *Eversden* schemes or lifetime double trust home loan ('IOU') arrangements, in practice the rules can catch 'innocent' transactions not intended to avoid IHT: there is no IHT avoidance 'motive test' for these purposes.

Instances of actual payment of the tax seem to be rare: it appears to have achieved its object. Many arrangements that were entered into to avoid IHT have been reversed to avoid paying the tax.

POAT charge

13.3   The POAT charge arises under three main headings:

(1)   land;

(2)   chattels; and

(3)   intangible property.

Separate rules apply under each head of charge for calculating the amount liable to income tax.

Land

13.4   The POAT charge broadly applies if an individual occupies the 'relevant land' (whether solely or jointly), and either the 'disposal condition' or 'contribution condition' are satisfied (see FA 2004, Sch 15, para 3), subject to certain limited exemptions (eg if the land was subject to acceptable 'sharing' arrangements for gifts with reservation of benefit purposes within FA 1986, s 102B(4); see FA 2004, Sch 15, para 11(5)(c)).

HMRC interpret the term 'occupies' widely, to include circumstances where an individual stores possessions in a property, but only if they also had the right to access and use the property, or where they were the only person with access and they used the property from time to time. Occupation is not to be equated with residence, as the latter 'implies a greater level of permanence so a lower threshold is required to satisfy the occupation condition' (IHTM44003).

The chargeable amount in respect of land for POAT purposes is the appropriate rental value, less any payments by the taxpayer to the legal owner of the land in pursuance of a legal obligation (eg a lease or licence) for its occupation (Sch 15, para 4). The 'appropriate rental value' is calculated using a formula (in Sch 15, para 4(2)).

For the purposes of valuing land (and chattels and intangible property) when calculating the deemed POAT benefit, the 'valuation date' is 6 April in the relevant tax year, or if later the first day of the 'taxable period' (Charge to Income Tax by Reference to Enjoyment of Property Previously Owned Regulations 2005, SI 2005/724, reg 2).

Valuations of land (and chattels) at 6 April 2005 applied for 2005–06 and the next four tax years. Subsequent valuations take place at five-yearly intervals. If POAT first applies from a date during the tax year, land is valued at that date (as are chattels), and the same valuation can be used for the following four tax years (SI 2005/724, reg 4).

Chattels

13.5   The POAT rules on chattels are similar to the land provisions. The rules apply if an individual possesses or uses a 'chattel' ie tangible moveable or corporeal property other than money (whether solely or jointly) and either the 'disposal condition' or 'contribution condition' is satisfied (FA 2004, Sch 15, para 6).

Where the POAT charge applies in respect of chattels, the chargeable amount is the appropriate amount less any payments by the taxpayer to the legal owner of the chattel in pursuance of a legal obligation (eg a lease or licence, or perhaps more controversially a deed of covenant) for its possession or use (Sch 15, para 7). The 'appropriate amount' is calculated using a formula in Sch 15, para 7(2).

Whereas the POAT charge on land is based on rental values, for chattels the charge is based on a percentage (represented by a notional amount of interest) of the capital value of the chattel. The prescribed rate of interest is set by regulations (SI 2005/724, reg 3) and is the 'official rate of interest' for employment income purposes in ITEPA 2003, s 181.

As to the valuation of chattels for POAT purposes, see **13.4**.

Intangible property

13.6   The POAT charge on intangible property applies to relevant settled property in which the settlor is treated as retaining an interest (within ITTOIA 2005, s 624), after excluding any interest relating to the settlor's spouse. 'Relevant property' means assets settled or added after 17 March 1986 (FA 2004, Sch 15, para 8).

The charge applies irrespective of whether the settlor derives any benefit from the intangible property, or whether that property generates any income. However, the POAT charge on intangible property does not apply to land or chattels in a settlement. IHT planning, such as *Eversden* arrangements (see **1.34** involving investments such as shares or bank deposits) are potentially caught by the charge.

As with the charge on chattels (see **13.5**), the POAT charge on intangible property applies a percentage in calculating the benefit. The 'chargeable amount' (in FA 2004, Sch 15, para 9) is N minus T, where N represents interest at a prescribed rate on the relevant property, and T is the income tax or capital gains tax payable by the taxpayer under the provisions specified in para 9(1) in relation to the property.

Note that the excluded transactions rules (Sch 15, para 10) do not apply in respect of the POAT charge on intangible property.

The 'prescribed rate' of interest is set by regulations (SI 2005/724, reg 3) and is the 'official rate of interest' for employment income purposes in ITEPA

2003, s 181 (see **13.1**). However, there is no deduction for any payments by the taxpayer for the use or enjoyment of intangible property.

In terms of valuing intangible property for POAT purposes, the 'five year' valuation rule described at **13.4** does not apply. Valuations must therefore be made each year for which the charge applies, either at 6 April in the relevant tax year or (if later) the first day of the 'taxable period' (SI 2005/724, reg 2).

EXCEPTIONS FROM THE POAT CHARGE

13.7   There are some specific and relatively clear-cut exclusions and exemptions from the charge (FA 2004, Sch 15, paras 10, 11). Notable POAT 'let-outs' include the following:

1. Still in donor's estate

The POAT charge does not apply if the relevant property (or property derived from it) is comprised in the individual's estate (FA 2004, Sch 15, para 11(1)).

There is also a proportionate exclusion for property indirectly comprised in the estate, to the extent that its value is derived from the relevant property but is substantially less (para 11(2)).

2. Subject to GWR

Property subject to and remaining within the IHT gifts with reservation charge is not subject to POAT (FA 2004, Sch 15, para 11(5)). Therefore, there should not generally be a double charge to IHT as a gift with reservation and income tax as a pre-owned asset. Practitioners may often find, when dealing with client enquiries as to whether POAT applies, that a structure set up years before to extract value from an estate for IHT purposes has not, in fact, achieved its purpose because a benefit has been reserved.

FA 2004, Sch 15 (at paras 21–23) makes specific provision whereby an individual can elect in a prescribed form (IHT500) to be outside the Sch 15 regime. The election form can be downloaded from HMRC's website (www. hmrc.gov.uk/poa/iht500.pdf). The election must be made (to the Pre-owned Assets Section of HMRC Inheritance Tax in Nottingham, as opposed to the taxpayer's self-assessment office) on or before the 'relevant filing date', which originally means 31 January in the year of assessment that immediately follows the initial year of charge. However, perhaps partly because of limited take-up of this facility, the deadline for election was extended by FA 2007, s 66 (which amended FA 2004, Sch 15, para 23) to allow acceptance of late elections, depending on the particular circumstances of the case. Although effective from 21 March 2007, it applies to elections that were by that date already late.

The taxpayer could nevertheless be worse off by making the election: the overall tax position under both scenarios should be compared beforehand. In some cases (eg the elderly, or those suffering from ill health), it may be sensible to adopt a 'wait and see' approach and defer making the election until the deadline for making it is imminent.

Example 13.1 – Decision not to elect

In April 2002, Alfred and Betty, in their eighties, put in place a double trust loan scheme by which Alfred, the sole owner of their £400,000 home, sold it to Trust A in return for a promissory note. He settled the promissory note for the benefit of his family on Trust B. At the time, Alfred had available the full nil rate band and two annual exemptions: £253,000 in all. The excess, if he died within seven years, of £147,000 would be taxable, subject to abatement depending how long he lived.

Late in 2006, with the prospect looming of having to pay POAT, they reconsidered their position. By then, the house was worth £500,000. If sold by Trust A, the £100,000 gain would be sheltered from CGT by TCGA 1992, s 225 because Alfred at all times held an interest in possession in Trust A. He had that interest at 22 March 2006, so his £100,000 interest in Trust A (the net equity) is aggregable with his free estate.

In considering whether to elect into POAT, Alfred had noted that by April 2007 he would be aged 91, and would have survived the gift by five years, so on his death at that point tax on £147,000 would not be £58,800; it would be reduced to 40% of that, £23,520. The scheme would therefore already have saved the family £35,280, which would be surrendered by making an election. He had also realised that if he lived just two years longer, seven years would have elapsed since he put the scheme in place, and the original value of the house would fall out of account for IHT, potentially increasing the family's saving to 40% of the original value: £400,000 × 40% = £160,000.

Enquiry showed that none of the exclusions applied, so *prima facie* Alfred faced the POAT. The value of the house is apportioned between the part that has, or may have, escaped, and the part still clearly subject to IHT, £100,000. 80% of the value is within POAT. It seems that the full rental value of the house was about £550 per month. 80% of this, £440 per month or £5,280 per annum, is just over the *de minimis* level for POAT. Alfred realised that POAT is self-assessed and that it was for him to decide whether he was within POAT or not. He resolved:

- not to elect, because he had already saved some tax; and

- to look more closely at the valuation issue, to see if the rental value of £550 per month was the right figure.

13.7   Pre-owned assets

It should be noted that HMRC will probably argue that a POAT charge arises in respect of the property, with a separate gift with reservation applying in respect of the IOU (see **13.18**).

Double charge regulations – Charge to Income Tax by Reference to Enjoyment of Property Previously Owned Regulations 2005, SI 2005/724, reg 6 prevents a double liability; for example, in respect of a PET and a GWR, the higher amount of tax is charged.

Presumably, if an election is made in relation to BPR or APR assets subject to relief at the 100% rate, there may be no IHT on death (if the relevant conditions are met) on the taxpayer's death, or upon the reservation ceasing.

3. Disposal at full value

The disposal of whole property by a transaction at arm's length with a person not 'connected' with him is an excluded transaction. For these purposes, the connection rules in ITA 2007, ss 993–994 apply, except that a 'relative' includes uncles, aunts, nephews and nieces, and 'settlement', settlor' and 'trustee' all have the same meanings as for IHT purposes (FA 2004, Sch 15, para 2).

This category also includes a transaction such as might be expected to be made at arm's length between persons not connected with each other. For this and other reasons, the lifetime double trust home loan scheme can no longer be recommended (quite apart from the SDLT liability) (FA 2004, Sch 15, para 10(1)(a)).

4. Gift to spouse or court order in favour of former spouse

A disposal to a spouse (or civil partner) or by court order to a former spouse or civil partner is an excluded transaction (para 10(1)(b)).

Similarly excluded is a disposal by way of gift into trust where the settlor's spouse, or former spouse, remains beneficially entitled to an interest in possession (or alternatively a transfer under a court order to a former spouse) (para 10(1)(c)). This exclusion applies so long as that interest has not come to an end otherwise than on death (para 10(3)). This requirement is designed to prevent *Eversden*-type schemes.

5. 'Old' cases

This exception from POAT applies where the individual ceased to own the asset or an interest in it before 18 March 1986 (when the gifts with reservation provisions were introduced for IHT purposes).

There is also an important relaxation in respect of certain outright gifts of cash made more than seven years before occupation/possession (para 10(2)(c)). For example, father gave son £50,000 ten years ago. Son uses this towards buying a home and invites father to join him. There should be no POAT charge. This applies to land and chattels, but not intangible property.

In addition, it would seem that cash provided for property improvements (as distinct from the acquisition of a property interest) is outside the scope of POAT.

6. Non-residents and non-UK domiciliaries

If the individual is not UK resident for any relevant year of assessment, no POAT charge should arise. If he or she is UK resident, but neither UK domiciled nor deemed to be UK domiciled for IHT purposes, the charge should only arise in respect of property situated in the UK (FA 2004, Sch 15, para 12).

7. Deeds of variation

Changes in the distribution of the deceased's estate within s 17 (eg variations under IHTA 1984, s 142) are within the exclusions, which apply where a beneficiary inherits by will or on an intestacy, and by virtue of these statutory provisions the inheritance is varied within two years of the testator's death. No POAT charge should arise in these circumstances (see FA 2004, Sch 15, para 16), assuming there is no consideration for the variation.

Since Norman Lamont's proposed attack on variations back in 1989, practitioners have often been rather wary of using them. Is there not now a different climate? For example, if a widow is left an asset by her husband absolutely and she gifts the asset into a discretionary trust in which she is a potential beneficiary, that is a gift with reservation; or if it escapes those provisions for any reason, a POAT charge will apply. This is not, and should not, be so where the widow achieves the same result by way of a variation under s 142.

8. 'Small' cases

There is a *de minimis* 'slab' threshold of £5,000 per annum, illustrated at Example 13.1 (FA 2004, Sch 15, para 13).

Therefore, if the benefit is £5,001, the tax will be charged on the entire benefit (not just £1).

Example 13.2 – Caught by the legislation

Suppose the appropriate rental value of a property given away, but still occupied by the donor, is £7,000 per annum, and rent of only £4,000 is paid under a legal obligation, reducing the chargeable amount to £3,000. The *de minimis* rule does not apply, as it is the appropriate rental value which must not exceed £5,000.

However, note that the *de minimis* is potentially available to both husband and wife (ie up to £10,000 in total) in appropriate cases (eg double trust home loan (IOU) schemes).

---

9. Exempt gifts

Certain IHT gifts are exempt from IHT and POAT, namely:

- gifts within the relief for maintenance of the family (s 11) (FA 2004, Sch 15, para 10(1)(d));

- small exempt gifts (s 20); and

- IHT annual exempt gifts (s 19) (Sch 15, para 10(1)(e)).

10. Guarantees

The giving of a guarantee does not of itself incur a POAT charge (Sch 15, para 17).

Restriction in exemption

There is a restriction in the exemptions from charge in FA 2004, Sch 15, para 11 ('Exemptions from charge') in the case of an 'excluded liability' (as defined in para 11(7)). This is presumably aimed at those who successfully executed double trust home loan (or IOU) arrangements; see **13.18**.

If a POAT liability arises under more than one head of charge (eg land and intangible property), the tax charge arises under whichever provision produces the higher amount (Sch 15, para 18).

In addition, if a charge arises under both the POAT rules for land or chattels, and under ITEPA 2003, Part 3 ('Employment income; earnings and benefits etc treated as earnings'), the employment income rules take precedence, and POAT only applies to the extent that the amount chargeable exceeds the amount of employment income (Sch 15, para 19).

OTHER POSSIBLE EXCLUSIONS

13.8   The following are circumstances where a Sch 15 charge may be excluded, but depending on the particular circumstances, and on HMRC and Treasury practice.

Sharing arrangements

13.9   A sharing arrangement envisages cases under FA 1986, s 102B(4) where there is co-ownership and occupation by donor and donee (Sch 15, para 11(5)(c)). Typically this occurs where, say, a widow transfers a share of the beneficial ownership of her home to a son or daughter and they jointly occupy the property, and pay the outgoings in their due proportions.

This arrangement is likely to be outside the POAT charge; but the recommendation is that as a general guide it should be on a 50:50 ownership basis. If the original owner owns only, say, 25% and the donee 75%, a challenge by HMRC and a POAT (or GWR) charge may be more likely! It is less of a grey area in the case of a holiday home where the original owner keeps, say, 25% and three other close relatives have the remaining 75% equally.

Note the following (from a 'Meeting Point' summary by Matthew Hutton in *Taxation*, 22 July 2004, p 436):

'Sharing occupation

Suppose that mother shares her house with her two unmarried daughters. She makes a gift of an undivided share of one third to each of the daughters and all of them continue to live in the house, each paying her share of the expenses. Provided that mother enjoys no other benefit from her continued occupation, reservation of benefit is excluded in relation to the two one-third shares given away (FA 1986, s 102B(4)). Such arrangements are exempted from the new regime under paragraph 11(1)(c) of Schedule 15 to the FA 2004. Chris Whitehouse reported that the Revenue has been arguing that no greater share can be given away than equates to the number of co-owners: in his view that argument is nonsense.

There are interpretation issues as to the meaning of occupation: clearly this need not be continuous, though it should be sufficiently substantive. Amendments to the reservation of benefit regime in 1999, replacing the previous more restrictive Hansard statement in 1986, mean that a property can be protected even if it is not the main family home. However, careful attention should be paid to the sharing of expenses and their documentation. Distinguish between property expenses, that is repairs which can be shared in unequal amounts (according to the shares in the house given away) and living expenses, eg television licence and food bills, which should usually be shared equally between the co-owners. It is acceptable for the donor to pay everything: the problem arises in quantifying how much the donee(s) can safely pay.'

One specific issue arises where accommodation is shared (say, between mother and daughter) as the result of an arrangement that the daughter cares for the mother and in return receives a share in the property. This is not an arm's-length transaction, so its treatment for POAT is difficult, as was highlighted by the joint submission of questions by the Chartered Institute of Taxation (CIOT), and Society of Trust & Estate Practitioners (STEP) and others in July 2005.

HMRC's response was that they 'would need information about how the essential elements of the transaction had been arrived at and for evidence that both parties had sought separate advice and acted upon it'. That may not actually be as unrealistic as it sounds: in dealing with the elderly, some separate advice may be worthwhile, so as to prevent later challenge of the gift by less favoured relatives: see Law Society guidelines on making gifts of assets: (www.lawsociety.org.uk/advice/practice-notes/gifts-of-assets).

Equity release schemes: escape from the POAT regime

13.10   The disposal of property is an excluded transaction if it is a disposal by an individual of his whole interest in the property 'except for any right expressly reserved by him over the property either by an arm's-length transaction or by a transaction such as might be expected to be made at arm's length between unconnected persons' (FA 2004, Sch 15, para 10(1)(a)).

On that basis, provided the sale is of the whole property, the POAT charge will not apply. This was specifically confirmed by HMRC replies to questions raised by CIOT, STEP and others, and is also now covered in HMRC's guidance (IHTM44031).

Example 13.3 – Sale of the entirety

Father sells his house for full value to son subject to a retained lease for, say, ten years at a peppercorn. There will be SDLT implications. Some of the cash received by father could be used to set up a trust for his grandchildren.

It is crucial to obtain independent valuation advice so as to avoid any gratuitous benefit conferred on any person. The lease retained could be for father's life. If granted for full consideration, there is no deemed settlement under s 43(3).

Partial equity release – Regulations also allow for partial arm's-length type equity releases involving land or chattels (Charge to Income Tax by Reference to Enjoyment of Property Previously Owned Regulations 2005, SI 2005/724, reg 5).

This exemption applies to transactions between unconnected persons, which many families think is unfair: provided that the terms are commercial, why should it not be allowable to set up the arrangement within the family, and retain the profit?

In addition, it applies to any disposals between connected persons on arm's-length terms before 7 March 2005, or disposals from that date if the consideration was not in money or readily convertible assets. The latter exemption may assist in cases where an elderly or infirm parent gives an interest in their home to adult offspring in return for the provision of care in the property.

Insurance-based products

13.11   The application of the POAT rules to various products and schemes marketed by life insurance companies is not always certain. Such arrangements generally involve trusts of life policies for which FA 2004, Sch 15, para 8 is the starting point. However, as the basic para 8 test is that any income arising under the settlement (assuming any were to arise) would be taxable on the settlor, it would appear that many insurance-based arrangements will escape.

HMRC's attitude to such schemes initially appeared benign (see for example *Taxation*, 18 November 2004, pp 176–177, the ABI letter analysed by Mike Truman and 25 November 2004, pp 205–208 article by John Woolley).

Subsequent HMRC guidance confirms that, for example, 'straightforward' discounted gift schemes (eg involving a gift into settlement subject to a retained right to an annual income, or to a 'reversion under arrangements') are not caught by para 8, as the trustees hold the retained right on bare trust for the settlor (IHTM44112).

'Gift and loan' arrangements (ie broadly where a small gift (eg a life policy) is settled on trust for the benefit of others, followed by interest-free, repayable on demand loans to the trustees, to enable the trustees to purchase more policies and make partial surrenders in part payment of the loan) are not considered by HMRC to fall within POAT (or the GWR rules). This is on the basis that the settlor is not a beneficiary of the trust, and that the making of the loan is not a settlement for IHT purposes.

However, business partnership policies taken out by a partner who retains a benefit (eg they can cash in the policy during their lifetime for their own benefit) will be potentially subject to a POAT charge under para 8, even if the arrangement is on commercial terms (see IHTM44115).

Pension policies

13.12   Provided that the scheme member cannot benefit from a trust governing death benefits, then (assuming that pension and lifetime benefits for the scheme member are kept separate), HMRC consider that no POAT charge should arise.

In addition, no POAT arises in relation to registered pension scheme arrangements. However, non-registered schemes may fall within the GWR provisions, in which case the POAT rules would not apply (IHTM44114).

'Debt' or 'charge' schemes

13.13 These schemes for the family home on death have become less common since the introduction of the transferable nil rate band facility, because they were commonly used by couples whose wealth did not greatly exceed the average. The arrangement typically utilises the IHT nil rate band legacy (£325,000 for 2012–13) by way of discretionary will trust taking an appropriate loan/charge on the home left to the surviving spouse.

HMRC's guidance includes the following example (IHTM44107):

> 'Jack and Jill own their home in equal shares as tenants in common. Under his Will, Jack leaves property not exceeding the nil-rate band for Inheritance Tax to a discretionary trust, of which Jill is one of the potential beneficiaries. The remainder of his estate passes to Jill absolutely. Following Jack's death, his executors transferred his half share of the property to Jill and, in return, she executed a loan agreement equivalent to the value of the half-share. No Inheritance Tax is payable on Jack's death and when Jill dies, her estate is reduced by the debt and she also has her nil rate band to set against the couple's assets.

> The POA charge does not apply here. As Jill did not own her husband's share at the relevant time and did not dispose of it, the disposal conditions (IHTM44004) in FA04/Sch15/Para3(2) are not met. If she did not provide Jack with any of the consideration given by him for the purchase of his half share the contribution condition (IHTM44005) in FA04/Sch15/Para3(3) will not apply either.

> Even if she had provided him with some or all of the consideration the condition will still not apply as it would have been an excluded transaction (IHTM44032) under FA04/Sch15/Para10(2)(a). Had this been the case, however, the debt would not be allowable as a deduction on Jill's death by virtue of FA86/S103.'

However, beware of two pitfalls of debt or charge arrangements. First, avoid artificial 'sham' arrangements. Second, note the problem of FA 1986, s 103, as highlighted above and in *Phizackerley v HMRC* [2007] SpC 591, which is discussed in some detail in **Chapter 5** (see **5.17** onwards). Moreover, if the arrangement is done via a s 142 variation, this should also be excluded from a POAT charge.

From an SDLT perspective, a charge by the personal representatives prior to the appropriation (plus widow(er) exoneration) should save SDLT (see SDLTM04045) and arguably also sidestep the rule in *Phizackerley* on the death, but not where the original dwelling is disposed of and a fresh charge is taken from the surviving spouse over the replacement property. That second borrowing will be caught by *Phizackerley* (NB remember that the home itself should not be left as an asset of the discretionary will trust).

Following the decision in *Judge and anor (personal representatives of Walden, dec'd) v HMRC* [2005] SpC 506 (see **4.13**), it would seem possible for the deceased's interest in the family home to be left to a discretionary will trust, and for the surviving spouse to occupy it as a beneficiary. Alternatively, following the FA 2006 changes involving IHT and trusts, an interest in possession trust for the surviving spouse may be considered, which is defeasible or allows successive life interests for, say, family members. The trustees should not appoint an actual or deemed (SP 10/79) interest in possession to the surviving spouse within two years following the deceased spouse's demise, as such an interest falls to be treated as an immediate post-death interest by reason of the 'reading back' provisions in IHTA 1984, s 144.

Whilst the popularity of debt and charge arrangements undoubtedly lessened considerably following the introduction of the facility to transfer unused nil rate band between spouses or civil partners from 9 October 2007 (see **Chapter 3**), many such arrangements remain in pre-existing wills.

CAUGHT – IT SEEMS! (IN CERTAIN CIRCUMSTANCES)

13.14   A number of IHT planning arrangements are potentially caught by a POAT charge, as intended. However, some exceptions from charge may still remain, depending on the circumstances.

Reversionary leases

13.15   A popular planning device has been where the freeholder retains the freehold but grants a deferred long lease as a gift, the right of the lessee to occupation under the lease being deferred for, say, 15 to 20 years. Practitioners have regarded this arrangement with considerable confidence, although it must be admitted that it is untested as far as the authors are aware (see **6.24** and **11.23**).

However, FA 2004, Sch 15, para 3(4) states that the creation of a new interest in land out of an existing interest in land is to be taken to be a disposal of part of the existing interest. This brings in the basic charge under that paragraph, which in broad terms, applies where an individual continues to occupy land after a disposal or part disposal of it, otherwise than as an excluded transaction.

HMRC consider that reversionary schemes entered into before 9 March 1999 escape the GWR rules, and are therefore subject to POAT. For later schemes, there was initially some doubt as to whether the GWR rules applied. However, HMRC are now understood to consider that where the freehold interest was acquired more than seven years before the gift, continued occupation by the donor would not be a 'significant right', and that the GWR rules in FA 1986, s 102A cannot apply to the gift. HMRC's POAT guidance has been amended accordingly, and states the following (IHTM44102):

> 'Where a reversionary lease scheme is established on or after 9 March 1999 it was originally considered that FA86/S102A (IHTM14360) would apply because the donor's occupation would be a "significant right in relation to the land". If that were correct, the reservation of benefit rules would apply and there would be no POA charge.
>
> However, where the freehold interest was acquired more than 7 years before the gift (this is the significance of giving the date of Victor's purchase in the example above), the continued occupation by the donor is not a significant right in view of FA86/S102A(5), so the reservation of benefit rules cannot apply and a POA charge arises instead.'

Thus a charge to income tax will apply unless the donor elects into the GWR provisions.

By contrast, if the donor grants a reversionary lease within seven years of acquiring the freehold interest, a GWR may arise under FA 1986, s 102A, depending on the particular circumstances.

Lease 'carve-outs'

13.16 In *Ingram v Commissioners of Inland Revenue* [1999] STC 37 (see **6.23**) a carve-out scheme in relation to the late Lady Ingram's main residence was upheld by the House of Lords. She had transferred the property to her solicitor, who executed declarations that he held the property as her nominee. Thereafter, he granted her a 20-year lease and the freehold was transferred to a family trust.

Ingram-type lease carve-out schemes were blocked by FA 1999, but as with reversionary leases, any pre-1999 carve-out schemes were seemingly caught by the basic POAT charge under FA 2004, Sch 15, para 3, and a review of the list of excluded transactions in para 10 would therefore be necessary to see if they provided assistance in any particular case. For example, there is an exclusion for a disposal to the transferor's spouse, or for a gift into trust in which the spouse (or civil partner) still has an interest in possession (para 10(1) (b), (c)).

Ingram schemes could still operate (with Treasury approval!) over 14 years (FA 1986, s 102A(5); see **11.24**). However, there is no similar exclusion from FA 2004, Sch 15, and therefore such arrangements appear to be caught.

Eversden schemes

13.17   In *Commissioners of Inland Revenue v Eversden* [2002] STC 1109 (see **1.34**), the Court of Appeal upheld the effectiveness against the reservation of benefit rules of an arrangement whereby assets were initially placed into trust for the spouse, but later trusts including the settlor and/or spouse ensued.

HMRC consider that, if assets are held on discretionary trusts of which the settlor is a potential beneficiary, an income tax charge will apply if the settlement was effected before 20 June 2003. The POAT legislation (FA 2004, Sch 15, para 8) is intended to catch these arrangements where the assets in trust are investments.

The income tax charge on pre-owned assets will not operate for so long as the spouse continues to have a beneficial entitlement to an interest in possession in the trust (Sch 15, para 10(1)(c)). However, note that the excluded transaction provisions apply to land and chattels, but not intangible property. The exclusion also applies if the spouse had an interest in possession which ceased on his or her death but not otherwise (Sch 15, para 10(3)).

For settlements effected from 20 June 2003, the property is subject to the GWR rules for IHT purposes (FA 1986, s 102(5A)), so an income tax charge will not apply (FA 2004, Sch 15, para 11(3)). A separate GWR may arise if the spouse's interest in possession is terminated and is treated as a gift under FA 1986, s 102ZA.

Lifetime trust home loan arrangements ('IOU' schemes)

13.18   For example, Mr Smith sold his house to a trust, Trust 1, for £1 million in September 2003, in which he retained a life interest. The trustees gave Mr Smith an IOU for the purchase price. Mr Smith gifted the IOU to a second trust for the benefit of his adult children. He remains in occupation of the property. The outstanding debt reduces the value of the house in Trust 1 for IHT purposes accordingly (the arrangement would not now work because the sale to Trust 1 would incur an SDLT charge and the transfer of the IOU to the second trust would be a chargeable transfer and incur an IHT entry charge on the excess over the nil rate band).

HMRC do not accept that home loan schemes achieve their IHT objective. HMRC's guidance (at IHTM44105) indicates that loans repayable after the life tenant's death are caught under the GWR provisions. This is in addition to loans repayable on demand (see IHTM44104), which were already considered to be caught (see **6.30**). HMRC's general stance appears to be, therefore, that there is a POAT charge in respect of the property, and a GWR in respect of the loan (see **11.27**). The tax treatment of home loan schemes has been the subject of challenges by HMRC, although no litigation has been reported at the time of writing.

The Inheritance Tax (Double Charges Relief) Regulations 2005, SI 2005/3441, provide relief from a double IHT charge for taxpayers who elect into the GWR regime after making lifetime double trust home loan arrangements, where the individual dies after 5 April 2005.

A scheme was mooted under which:

- father, owner of house, sold it to wife;

- the price was satisfied by an IOU, probably interest free; then

- the IOU was given to the children.

It was considered that, if this was not a gift with reservation, POAT would not be in point because the transaction was between spouses. However, it is understood that HMRC have indicated in respect of such arrangements that they would not take the property out of charge to tax if the reservation of benefit was confined to the gift of the IOU. It is the essence of the scheme that any reservation of benefit is so confined.

As a result of the attitude of HMRC, there is at least a risk with such a scheme of a double charge: to IHT on any reserved benefit and to POAT.

Is there a reservation of benefit? If the IOU is free of interest, then quite possibly 'yes'; it seems that HMRC may take the point. That probably means that any sloppily drafted scheme to surface will be the subject of a HMRC Determination. If interest is paid, it will attract income tax: not a popular selling feature for a tax scheme. It was a feature of the schemes that eventually the house and the IOU would end up in the same hands, and that any interest due would be waived.

Should such schemes be unscrambled? The problems of doing so must be carefully considered. For example, where the IOU has increased in value, a CGT charge may apply if the benefit of the IOU is no longer held by the original creditor. The observations of Dawn Primarolo when Paymaster General on the subject of 'burnt fingers' may be apposite here.

Non-trust IOU arrangements

13.19   There still appears to be some scope for IOU arrangements, such as in a non-trust context in relation to investment property. For example, as intimated at **6.31**, a husband may wish to sell an investment property to his wife at full market value, with the sale proceeds being left outstanding as an IOU, which is subsequently gifted to his adult children. POAT does not apply in respect of the rental property, as the husband does not 'occupy' it (within FA 2004, Sch 15, para 3(1)(a)), and in any event transfers between spouses are excluded transactions for POAT purposes (para 10(1)(b)).

Of course, careful consideration must be given to other tax consequences and potential challenges by HMRC, such as SDLT on the property sale, whether there is any reservation of benefit in respect of the loan, and also whether the whole arrangement could be attacked under the *Ramsay* principle.

Reverter to settlor trusts

13.20   For example, son settled a home on his widowed mother for life (prior to FA 2006), with reversion to son on her death (or if he has not survived mother, to son's spouse within two years). This would normally avoid IHT (under ss 53(3) and 54(2)) and no CGT would apply, the reverter being on the mother's death.

However, note that from 22 March 2006, the property must revert to the settlor (or spouse) absolutely to obtain reverter to settlor relief, or to a 'qualifying' interest in possession trust, namely a disabled person's interest, or to a 'transitional serial interest' (until 5 October 2008). This is provided by s 54(2A), which was inserted by FA 2006.

The government blocked reverter to settlor arrangements from 5 December 2005 (the date of the Pre-Budget Review) involving a transfer (say, from mother to son in the above example, notwithstanding that the son might otherwise have inherited the house), followed by settlement of the asset (by the son) for the benefit of the original owner (mother) on a reverter to settlor trust.

The changes were introduced by FA 2006, s 80 amending para 11(9) and inserting sub-paras (11)–(13) into FA 2004, Sch 15, para 11, with effect from 5 December 2005. A POAT charge applies in those circumstances, even though in the above example the home is subsequently in the mother's estate for IHT purposes within s 49(1). However, the chargeable person (mother) can elect (see **13.24**) that the asset will not give rise to an income tax charge, but will be liable to IHT as if the gift with reservation rules applied instead, ie the reverter to settlor exemptions in ss 53(3), 53(4) and 54 do not apply.

As may be expected with anti-avoidance legislation, the relevant provisions, in FA 2004, Sch 15, para 11(9), (11)–(13), are difficult to follow and may have unexpected effects. Basically, there is now an exception to the previous more general exception and double negatives often make for difficult legislation. One scenario (not uncommon among non-UK domiciliaries) concerns self-settlement.

Example 13.4 – POAT problem?

Jennifer settled property on 1 February 2003 on herself for life. She occupies the trust property. POAT ought not to apply upon its introduction, under the general scheme of exemptions (FA 2004, Sch 15, para 11(1)), because the property is in Jennifer's estate.

However, consider FA 2004, Sch 15, para 11(11). This provides that, where at any time the relevant property has ceased to be comprised in a person's estate or (s)he has directly or indirectly funded it, and later the property is aggregated with his estate because (s)he is a tenant for life, para 11(12) comes into play. Paragraph 11(12) prevents relevant property from being treated as comprised in the taxpayer's estate for the purposes of the para 11(1) or para 11(2) exemptions 'at that subsequent time'.

If Jennifer's trust gave her an immediate interest in possession, there is no problem. However, if for example there was an intervening period up to 31 December 2005 during which the trust was a discretionary one, a POAT issue would arise by virtue of these sub-paragraphs from 31 December 2005.

Jennifer may then consider electing into GWR to avoid POAT.

Perhaps the point is now relevant in only a relatively small number of cases, since for IHT purposes the general rule is that no new 'estate' interest in possession trusts can be created except in very limited circumstances (eg for disabled persons, or on death). However, it illustrates the side-effects of certain transactions. Certainly, it gave considerable difficulty when first discovered because the time limit for election into GWR was then very short. That was alleviated by the late election provision introduced in FA 2007.

Where an election is not made in time, POAT will continue until the property is appointed back to the settlor or its enjoyment is terminated by other means.

One specific problem is where a trust owns a company that in turn owns a residence. An election will cause the assets to be treated as part of the taxpayer's estate and could bring assets within IHT by side-stepping the rules as to *situs* that might otherwise have sheltered the assets. Thus the issue is a 'tax tornado': though it may be extremely localised, and of no interest to some provincial practitioners, it may be devastating for those few who are affected by it.

Some of the heat has been taken out of the problem in the situation described at Example 13.4. It seems that in the view of HMRC the words 'at any subsequent time' in para 11(11) do not literally mean 'at any later occasion', but something like 'at any later time after value leaves the donor's estate, thereby reducing his estate, but returns to it because property is purchased with that value and the taxpayer has an interest in possession in the property'. Few advisers would attempt to widen the (fairly) clear words of a taxing statute in that way, so we should perhaps be grateful.

The upshot of all this is that there is probably no difficulty where:

- A settled cash on himself before 22 March 2006; or

- B, being a disabled person, did the same after that date,

and in either case, the trustees:

- bought a house for A (or B, as the case might be) to live in; or

- sold that house and bought another; or

- used some of the proceeds of the house to buy shares, etc.

That leaves only the problem of the discretionary trust that was later appointed onto a qualifying interest in possession trust. There, an election is the only way to avoid POAT.

OPTIONS INVOLVING POAT

13.21   Due to the retroactive nature of POAT, there will doubtless be circumstances in which 'innocent' gifts and arrangements since 18 March 1986 are inadvertently caught by POAT, in addition to the IHT planning arrangements at which POAT was clearly targeted. In either case, a brief window of opportunity existed to avoid POAT altogether by unscrambling the offending arrangements before the introduction of the tax charge on 6 April 2005. Of course, in many cases this would have been impossible or impractical to achieve, or the potential POAT problem may simply not have been recognised in time.

Those faced with a potential POAT charge may therefore wish to consider the following basic planning alternatives, as appropriate.

Pay rent

13.22   Paying rent for land or chattels can reduce or eliminate a POAT charge. Professional valuations should be obtained. For both land and chattels, the rent must be paid under a *legal obligation* (FA 2004, Sch 15, paras 4(1), 7(1)), such as under a lease or licence. Those amounts must be physically paid, ie debts or IOUs would not appear to be acceptable.

As already mentioned in the context of the £5,000 *de minimis* exemption (in Sch 15, para 13), paying sufficient rent to reduce the POAT charge to within the exemption will not work (see **13.7**). In addition, it should be borne in mind that although the payment of rent will reduce the payer's estate for IHT purposes, it may give rise to an income tax liability for the recipient.

However, in some cases the payment of rent may be preferable to the alternatives outlined below, particularly if the affected individual has a short life expectancy (eg if elderly and/or in poor health).

Suppose a taxpayer has entered into a reversionary lease which does not involve reservation of benefit, so that he is within Sch 15, para 3 and POAT on the land is *prima facie* payable. He wants to avoid POAT, but how can he pay rent to himself? The way out prior to FA 2006 was, it seems, for him to transfer the freehold to trustees to hold on interest in possession trusts for himself. HMRC seemed to acknowledge that early in 2006; but since (except as mentioned above) no 'estate' interest in possession trust can generally be created except on death, that avenue is now closed.

Accept the POAT charge

13.23   The potential POAT charge should be quantified and compared with the IHT saving (assuming of course that any planning is successful), and the cost of any viable alternatives, such as paying a market rent for land and chattels. In some cases, it may be cheaper to pay the POAT charge than to pay a full market rent. See Example 13.1.

Elect into the IHT regime

13.24   A POAT charge can be avoided by electing back into the IHT regime (FA 2004, Sch 15, paras 21–23). The effect of the election is to deem the relevant property to be subject to a GWR. The election must be made (on form IHT500; see also Explanatory Notes IHT501) by 31 January following the end of the 'initial year' as defined in paras 21–22 (ie broadly the first year for which a POAT charge applies to the individual in respect of the particular property) (see examples at IHTM44075). However, this deadline may be extended at

HMRC's discretion (para 23(3)), such as if an event beyond the individual's control prevented the submission of the election on time.

The election continues in force until the benefit enjoyed from the relevant (or substitute) property ceases. The election may be withdrawn or amended in writing by 31 January in the tax year immediately following the initial year (Sch 15, para 23(5)), but thereafter is irrevocable.

Whether or not it is beneficial to make the election will depend on the particular circumstances. For example, is the taxpayer willing or able to pay a full market rent in relation to land and chattels? In addition, advisers acting for elderly or infirm clients with a relatively short life expectancy should compare the potential IHT cost of making the election with the estimated POAT charge over the client's likely life, and also consider whether that individual has the resources to pay the income tax charge. If the individual elects back into IHT, but later starts to pay full consideration for the continued use of the land or chattels, there is a deemed potentially exempt transfer, with IHT implications on the individual's death within seven years.

Note that the election does not change what has already taken place (eg for capital gains tax, stamp duty land tax or other purposes, such as potentially exempt transfers, as appropriate). The Inheritance Tax (Double Charges Relief) Regulations 2005, SI 2005/3441, provide relief from a double IHT charge for taxpayers who elect into the GWR regime after making lifetime double trust home loan arrangements (or IOU schemes; see **13.18**), in cases where the individual dies after 5 April 2005 (but not before).

End the benefit

13.25   The practicalities of ending any benefit from the relevant asset (or ensuring that the settlor no longer benefits from intangibles) may require careful consideration.

In particular, if the asset concerned is the family home, ending the benefit may not be a viable option.

Give full consideration

13.26   The giving of full consideration on an arm's-length basis by the donee for an interest in land and chattels can avoid both a GWR and POAT charge (FA 1986, Sch 20, paras 4(1), 7(1); FA 2004, Sch 15, para 10(1)(a)).

Independent valuations should be obtained. If such valuations are not obtained and HMRC successfully contend that less than full consideration was given, the transaction may still avoid POAT on the basis that there is a GWR, for which exemption from POAT applies. If the asset is a chattel, some argument may turn on the true rent. There is little market evidence of such rents, and it may be possible to pay a figure that will be recognised as full, even though it may be less than what the alternative charge would be under POAT for a chattel using the 'prescribed rate' rule.

Unwind the arrangements

13.27 The tax consequences (eg CGT and possibly SDLT) and practicalities of unwinding the arrangements will require careful thought. Circumstances will vary according to the IHT arrangements originally used, but unwinding them may require the co-operation of others, such as donees of land interests in reversionary lease schemes, or trustees in IOU schemes. The most likely occasion for this would be trading down to a retirement flat or other sheltered accommodation.

In an excellent article on TaxationWeb in June 2006, Matthew Hutton explored some of the problems of unscrambling. Different issues will arise with each structure and the tax effect must be analysed. A particular issue is the effect of electing into the GWR regime to avoid POAT. That election removes the threat of POAT, but in the case of pre-existing arrangements leaves the settlor with:

- a possible tax charge on the fund, because he is tenant for life; and

- the GWR charge as part of his estate.

The solution would seem to be to bring the trust to an end. That stops the GWR charge. There remain, however, two potential charges:

- a deemed PET (back to himself) on releasing the reserved benefit; and

- the funds received from the trust.

Fortunately, HMRC will treat one of the charges as nil.

Special problems occur where the settlement is not for the settlor himself but for his spouse. If the life interest is terminated, that is a PET in favour of the settlor which, if a spouse, will be exempt; but what if the capital is instead appointed to the tenant for life? There is then no PET, because the fund would have been aggregated with the life tenant's estate anyway. The reservation of benefit to the settlor-spouse will end, so the appointment has the effect that there is a deemed PET by the settlor. The PET is of the value of the trust assets. However (and this is the catch) there has been no change to the value of the estate of the life tenant, so there is no compliance with s 18(1); and thus no spouse relief under that section. In these particular circumstances, it will be best to ensure that the fund is returned to the settlor.

To some extent these initial problems were later relieved by HMRC's confirmation of their approach. The CIOT, in a letter to HMRC on 13 October 2006, noted the difference between a GWR and the deeming provisions of an election to avoid POAT. They asked for confirmation that where a scheme had been completely unravelled, with the property back in the ownership of the settlor, the election would be ignored for IHT purposes. That would allow the spouse exemption to be available: it was a question of the timing of the transactions. HMRC quickly confirmed that the law would be applied as if there had been an actual gift, making the timing immaterial. This seems to address the problem highlighted by Matthew Hutton above, but in the process illustrates the complexity of the legislation.

The spur for many schemes involving the family home, which spawned POAT as anti-avoidance legislation, was the rise in house prices which, back in 2003, seemed inexorable and greatly exceeded any increase in the nil rate band for IHT. How things have changed in more recent times! Many will need to reappraise their planning strategies with regard to the family home. It may no longer be able to carry the obligations put on it by home reversion schemes. It may no longer exceed in value the double nil rate band that is often available.

More significantly, the relationship between freehold values and rental values may be changing. It was common to argue, in respect of, say, a fine residence in a seaside town on the south coast, that the market rent was around 2% of vacant possession value of the freehold. If true, that had the result that only properties of significant value would exceed two *de minimis* exemptions each of £5,000 for POAT.

If market values have changed significantly, that may affect the choice of paying POAT or electing back into IHT. The problem is the irrevocable nature of an election under FA 2004, Sch 15, para 23: it may be withdrawn only during the lifetime of the chargeable person and before the relevant filing date, being in normal circumstances 31 January following the first year for which POAT is in point.

Chapter 14

Life assurance and other insurance schemes

INTRODUCTION

14.1   Life assurance has a vital role to play in IHT planning. It is a fact that, despite the flexibility of the PET regime (which was curtailed by FA 2006), the presence of IHT makes lifetime giving more difficult, so that making a gift has to a great degree become a conscious, deliberate act, embarked on only after careful thought and advice.

In this atmosphere, a relatively simple means of mitigation or cushioning the effect of IHT is often to take out either: life *assurance* (under which the beneficiary of the policy is *assured* of the benefits at an event *certain*, for example, the end of a specified period or earlier death); or by contingency *insurance* (covering the beneficiary, who is *insured against* a contingency such as death before a particular date).

Examples of life assurance include whole of life and endowment, in each case with or without profits. Such policies, being in essence a savings product, used to qualify for income tax relief on the premiums paid; once that was denied, they reduced in popularity. Examples of life insurance include term insurance, level or decreasing, and convertible term insurance, which can be *converted* into life assurance. Being much cheaper than whole of life assurance, these are more widely used. In addition, there are the special uses of life assurance in such products as modern inheritance trusts, which can play a useful role in planning.

The chapter does not deal with pension provision, which has been discussed in **Chapter 12**, except where linked to other forms of insurance, but examines insurance planning under five heads:

- IHT liability on policies;
- aims and uses;
- main available insurance arrangements;
- insurance and the PET regime; and
- traps for the unwary.

This chapter cannot explore thoroughly the varied possibilities and ways in which insurance schemes can be of benefit. Detailed advice should always be taken from an independent financial adviser who should be an authorised independent intermediary. As a result of the Financial Services Act 1986, the Financial Services Authority (FSA) are responsible for making sure that all persons engaged in carrying on the business of investment (which is widely defined, and includes life assurance and pensions) are authorised, under the regulatory regime.

The objectives are to ensure that all persons so authorised observe high standards of integrity, act with due skill, care and diligence, and deal fairly with their customers. Although there has been some relaxation of the rules, broadly an independent financial adviser (IFA) who is authorised by the appropriate regulatory body (look at his stationery) is not tied to one company's products but is under an obligation to consider and advise on the choice of available products in the market. A 'tied agent' (or company representative) on the other hand is restricted to offering only those products as are supplied by the life office or company to whom he is tied, although he too is under an obligation to give suitable advice in relation to the range offered by his employer. The industry has faced many allegations of mis-selling. To curb this, there is now a movement away from commission and towards fee-based remuneration.

The FA 2006 changes to the IHT treatment of trusts included provisions allowing for settled rights under a contract of life insurance entered into before 22 March 2006 and secured by premiums or an 'allowed variation' from 22 March 2006 to be regarded as having been comprised in the settlement as at that date, if certain conditions are satisfied. These provisions broadly apply to life policies in which there is an interest in possession or which fell within the accumulation and maintenance trust regime at 22 March 2006, and they allow a premium payable under such policies to be treated as PETs, if not covered by the annual or normal expenditure out of income exemptions (IHTA 1984, ss 46A, 46B).

The FA 2006 changes also provided for transitional serial interest treatment to apply to settled property consisting of or including rights under a contract of life insurance in relation to pre-22 March 2006 interests in possession and contracts of insurance, subject to certain conditions being satisfied (IHTA 1984, s 49E).

IHT LIABILITY ON POLICIES

Upon death

14.2   Where a policy becomes payable on death, the principles in s 171 apply so that IHT is charged on the proceeds of the policy. For example, if an individual takes out a life policy on his own life, for the benefit of his own estate (generally a poor planning idea), pays the first premium and then dies, IHT will be payable on the policy proceeds. But if he takes out a policy on the life of another person and then dies, leaving the other person living, then the market value of the policy has to be accounted for in his estate.

There is a ready market in 'second-hand' policies, so we may expect the market value to be greater than the surrender value from the life office (particularly if the life assured was known to be in poor health). However, should the life assured die soon after the proposer's own death, it is nevertheless still only the market value of the policy at his death that needs to be included in the proposer's IHT estate.

The correct valuation of insurance policies is perceived by HMRC to be an area where tax revenue may be at risk, for example, because the executors put forward the surrender value instead of market value. The valuation of life policies is one of the risk areas identified in HMRC's Inheritance Tax Toolkit (www.hmrc.gov.uk/agents/toolkits/iht.pdf).

Lifetime transfers (immediately chargeable and PETs)

14.3   The minimum value of a transfer will be the total premiums paid less any surrenders, the aim being to prevent low artificial values on the surrendering of policies (see s 167(1)). Note also that s 167(2) prevents these artificial rules from applying on death.

These rules do not, see s 167(3)(a), apply to term policies of three years or more; nor, see s 167(4), to unit linked policies which are valued at the value of the quoted units if less than the premiums paid.

This basis of assessment will apply where a policy is taken out by an individual who pays the premiums though the policy is written in trust for dependants absolutely; the value in their hands is linked to the premiums paid. The gifts of premiums are likely to be covered by the available exemptions. This basis will also apply where an individual assigns the benefit of a policy by way of gift or where there is a termination in whole or part of an interest in possession in a trust policy under s 52.

It is often stated that the normal value is the surrender value (if greater than the premiums paid), but this is incorrect, as the market value is to be used which cannot be less than, but could well be more than, the surrender value. However, it is worth pointing out to clients that many policies will currently suffer from depressed valuations, on account of 'smoothing', 'market adjustment' or similar references to the fact that the underlying assets have fallen in value and the fund administrators must limit withdrawals until value is restored. This may therefore be a good time to give away the policy.

AIMS AND USES

Using lifetime exemptions

14.4   These exemptions have already been outlined in **1.35** and **12.2–12.23**. For the purpose of insurance planning, the following exemptions will have particular relevance:

- The £3,000 per annum exemptions (s 19).

- The normal expenditure out of income exemption (s 21). HMRC accept that the payment of one premium alone is sufficient evidence of an intention of normal (ie habitual) expenditure, provided only that the policy is capable of lasting a number of years. This IHT exemption is particularly generous (as noted in **12.4**), in that it is available 'to the extent that' the necessary conditions are satisfied. Where, therefore, there is doubt as to how far the exemption may cover payment of premiums, it is not necessary to have several staggered policies in order that exemption can be given to one or more of them, leaving premiums on the others liable to IHT. Large premiums on a single policy can, if need be, qualify for exemption in part. Moreover, the condition that the expenditure must be 'out of income' is read subject to the words 'taking one year with another'.

- Gifts in consideration of marriage (or civil partnerships) (s 22).

Each of these exemptions (£3,000; normal expenditure out of income; marriage) is separately available, being mutually exclusive.

14.5   Using these exemptions with insurance arrangements has two important advantages as contrasted with making other exempt gifts. First, it provides a convenient method of regular saving; secondly, there is protection in that the problems arising from a premature death are overcome. There is another advantage: taking out a policy may enable a donor, who has already used his nil rate band, to add funds to an existing settlement without an 'entry charge' and without the other computational difficulties that would normally apply to fund additions.

For example, an estate owner may plan to transfer to his children a significant holding of shares piecemeal over a period of years, each transfer being covered by his available exemptions. Should he die before the anticipated actuarial life span, the IHT liability crystallises on the balance of the shares (assuming that no reliefs are in point).

By contrast, if the liability in respect of the shareholding is funded by way of life assurance on his life, the insurance moneys will be payable if his death occurs before his actuarial life span has been exceeded.

Example 14.1 – Endowment to enable purchase of assets

A businessman (whose company does not qualify for business property relief, such as a property investment business) who is aged 50 next birthday takes out a 15-year with-profit endowment policy in favour of his children for a premium of £2,000 per annum. The immediate life cover is £25,000. Levels of bonuses are notoriously unpredictable, but the policy could perhaps produce £50,000 at the age of 65.

The policy proceeds could enable his children, on his premature death to buy the shares or other appreciating assets from his estate. These figures are by way of illustration only and would depend on current economic conditions and interest rates.

This arrangement might allow security to the widow whilst enabling the children to continue to run the business.

The life assurance industry is diverse, and regulated. It is therefore essential to consult a good independent financial adviser.

Deferring IHT between husband and wife (or civil partners)

14.6   For the vast majority of married couples and civil partners, the existence of the spouse exemption enables payment of IHT to be deferred until the second death.

As indicated at **14.8**, appropriate joint life and last survivor policies are specifically designed to fund this liability.

Flexibility of funding

14.7   There are many other occasions when IHT liability will arise that can be appropriately funded, including the death of the first spouse having left assets to the children direct, or where it is wished to have funds available on an endowment basis for a gift intended to be made in the future.

A better alternative to the latter proposal could be to write the endowment policy in trust, paying regular premiums, exempt as normal income gifts, so that the benefit is already in the hands of the donee(s) (otherwise the maturity proceeds will pose a problem as a large gift).

Apart from husband and wife cases, it is frequently simpler in the case of a single person, eg an unmarried aunt or uncle wishing to benefit nephews and nieces but where the principal asset is the residence, to effect a whole life policy in favour of the beneficiaries. The way to look upon policies written in trust is that the estate owner is creating an IHT-free pool of money for the beneficiary(ies), who then either have ready cash towards payment of IHT on death or, the preferable alternative when an endowment matures during lifetime, have the funds to buy appreciating assets from the estate owner himself.

Much of the immediate investment incentive, in the form of income tax relief on premiums paid, has now gone from whole of life and endowment policies. In the short term, many taxpayers adopt the following order of application of surplus income:

- pay down debt; then

- set aside the maximum ISA subscription; then

- make own pension provision; then

- perhaps contribute to Child Trust Funds (ie where any of their children or grandchildren was born between 1 September 2002 and 2 January 2011) or Junior ISAs;

- then set up pension funds for their dependants; and only then

- use long-term traditional savings vehicles.

Another possibility for funding is, when a donor makes a PET gift, to cover by insurance the IHT risk on the donor's death within seven years. There are policies on the market which, if death should occur, provide appropriate sums, reducing with taper relief after three years, from which to pay the IHT.

Care should be taken with the decreasing element: the rules as to taper in s 7(4) are not well understood. It is advisable, however, not to be too rigid with the amounts insured under these policies, but allow some margin for eventualities, particularly where the gift consists, say, of freehold property where HMRC's Valuation Office might argue for a higher value. The policy should, of course, be effected for the benefit of the donee(s).

MAIN AVAILABLE INSURANCE ARRANGEMENTS

Joint life last survivor policies

14.8   These policies are designed for husband and wife (or civil partners) to cover the IHT liability arising on the death of the surviving spouse (or civil partner), ie that spouse's estate including the assets received from the other spouse who died earlier. Thus, to obtain the important cash-flow advantage of deferring IHT until the death of the survivor, a husband and wife may decide to leave each other virtually everything and fund the IHT liability (after any appropriate nil rate bands) by such a joint life and survivor policy written in trust for their beneficiaries. It seems likely that the introduction of the transferable nil rate band has significantly reduced the yield of IHT overall, partly because of its retrospective nature. That must reduce the market for these policies.

Life offices have introduced considerable flexibility into these and other policies, including options for guaranteed future insurability (whereby no future medicals are required) and options for inflation-proof indexing. HMRC accept joint life last survivor policies as qualifying policies (within the meaning of ICTA 1988, Sch 15, Pt 1, in particular) under certain conditions set out below.

Although life assurance premium relief was abolished in respect of qualifying policies effected from 14 March 1984, the qualifying status is still important to preclude the higher rate tax charge arising on the maturity or surrender of a non-qualifying policy. The qualifying policy status will apply in particular where the premiums are paid at yearly or shorter intervals until the survivor's death, or until the first death, or where the policy provides for a minimum of ten years' premiums. The former alternative is the most common and enables the cost of the premium to be kept to a minimum and with a particularly favourable maturity value.

Commercial considerations

14.9   Some advisers feel that the emphasis on these joint life and survivor policies is overplayed. The premiums payable are in effect based on a whole life policy for the *younger* life, ie the premiums payable for a joint life or whole life policy on the younger can often be similar.

In such a case, the whole life policy on the younger may well be preferable, say in the case of a husband with a healthy, younger wife. If the older party dies first, as anticipated, a joint life and survivor policy would not in any case have matured; and if the younger dies first there is the acceleration of the payment of the policy moneys which could then be paid to or for the benefit of the children earlier than would otherwise be the case.

The single whole life policy is, moreover, more flexible, for example as to encashing or (normally a better alternative) selling such a policy with current bonuses. Nevertheless, it has to be remembered that the premiums on a joint life and life of survivor policy will normally be cheaper than those on a single life policy. It pays to do the sums.

Policies written in trust

14.10   An individual can propose for a policy to be written under trust either by statute (Married Women's Property Act 1882, s 11) or by making express provision that the policy on his life is held in trust for a stipulated class of beneficiaries, such as the spouse, children or other members of the family.

The premiums can be funded from income or capital and, as explained above, in many cases it is possible to obtain complete IHT exclusion by use of one or more of the available exemptions. That neatly sidesteps the fact that, since 22 March 2006, a lifetime settlement of the policy will otherwise be a chargeable transfer.

It is often appropriate to write this type of policy on the basis of joint life and survivor, using the proceeds maturing on the death of the surviving spouse to cover IHT on the combined assets then passing. It may be useful to effect a trust policy to mature on the death of the first spouse to die, either to fund IHT if for any reason it was desired to give children benefits over the nil rate band (where the surviving spouse is well provided for); or, perhaps more usually, to establish a discretionary fund to provide benefits for the surviving spouse if need be.

There is, since FA 2006, no point in making the trust comply with the conditions for children's accumulation and maintenance (A&M) trusts, since that regime is closed to new entrants. An IHT charge may become payable when the policy funds in excess of the then current nil rate band arise in the trust. A power to advance the policy funds to an outsider (eg a widow), which used to breach the IHT conditions of A&M trusts, may now be included and may be very welcome to elderly clients, even though it may never, in fact, be called upon. Nowadays a full discretionary trust will often be used, giving unlimited power to allocate money unevenly between the beneficiaries.

Bare trusts: take care

14.11   Alternatively, the policies could be effected by the proposer on bare trust for one or more beneficiaries absolutely and indefeasibly thereby avoiding the settlement provisions. HMRC's present view is that a lifetime gift on trust for a minor absolutely, whether or not the provisions of Trustee Act 1925, s 31 are excluded, is a PET (IHTM16068).

Take care, however: if the trust contains substantive trusts, it will be a chargeable transfer, as where it is wished to make provision by way of a class gift, for example to existing children and children born before the eldest attains 18 or 21. Such a gift is subject to a contingency (that no further children will be born before the eldest child attains that age) and hence gives rise to a settlement

(IHTA 1984, s 43(2)(a)) which, since 22 March 2006, will invariably be a relevant property trust.

Underwriting basis

14.12   These policies are often written on a with profits or unit-linked basis but consideration should be given to the alternative of a without profits policy with guaranteed insurability, whereby the assured is entitled to take out extra cover within limits and at stated intervals without the need for a further medical. This enables the assured to reassess his individual and family circumstances periodically.

It is possible from the point of view of trust law to write the policy in favour of the beneficiaries, so that they have an interest in possession, but at the same time retaining an overriding power of appointment among a class consisting normally of the beneficiaries together with the spouse of the proposer of the policy. This might be done so that, if circumstances change, the interest in the policy can be appointed to the spouse of the settlor. Under the FA 2006 rules, this is a relevant property trust, so the reverter to settlor's spouse exemption previously applicable in trusts where there was an interest in possession (under s 53(4)) is not available.

Note that the settlor himself must not be included among the discretionary beneficiaries because the retention of this interest would make a gift into the policy trust a gift with reservation.

Reservation of benefit?

14.13   HMRC do not generally regard the inclusion of the settlor's spouse among the discretionary objects of a trust as a reservation of benefit to the settlor, unless any actual payments to the spouse were utilised, for instance, in paying household or other expenses for which the settlor was responsible (see IHTM14393). There is a contrary view in relation to the death benefit under funded unapproved retirement benefit schemes, where HMRC do think that reservation of benefit can apply, though the precise justification of that view is certainly open to question. In addition, see **14.29** as to the application of the reservation of benefit provisions in connection with certain life insurance policy products.

Although the interest of the settlor's spouse will bring the case within the settlements provisions of ITTOIA 2005, Pt 5, Ch 5, there will be no income tax consequences because there is no income.

It is possible, where there are likely to be changing views on prospective beneficiaries, to write the policy on normal discretionary trusts for a wide class (again including the spouse of the settlor as some protection for the future). Until 22 March 2006 the price of such greater flexibility would be IHT anniversary and exit charges unless (as may happen in many cases) the nil rate band applied. However, with very few exceptions, all lifetime trusts made since 22 March 2006 are relevant property trusts, and hence this structure will be more greatly favoured than previously.

Payment of policy premiums

14.14   Two points have been raised about the payment of premiums on trust policies which should be mentioned. The first is whether on a strict interpretation of FA 1986, s 102(2), the payment of a renewal premium direct to the life company by the settlor/donor could be treated as a gift with reservation, since possession and enjoyment of the property disposed of by way of gift (ie the cash) had not been assumed by the trustees. HMRC's guidance states: 'Strictly speaking, possession and enjoyment of the property disposed of by way of gift (the cash) has not been assumed by the donee. However, this particular point is not one which should of itself be taken to constitute the gift as one with reservation' (IHTM14453, at Example 1).

The second point arises out of s 3A(3) whereby in dealing with favoured trusts PET treatment on gifts applies 'to the extent that the value transferred … becomes settled property'. HMRC take the view that second and subsequent premiums paid by the settlor/donor to the life office qualify as PETs only to the extent of the additional surrender value which the premium adds to the policy, and the balance is an immediate lifetime chargeable transfer. The same result applies to interest in possession policy trusts under s 3A(2). Most such premiums will be totally exempt anyway under the annual and normal income exemptions, so that no problem arises.

To the extent that the premiums are not thus exempt, however, the official view used to be that full PET treatment on the premiums would be obtained if the settlor/donor, instead of paying the premium direct to the life office, made a transfer to the donee/trustees. In the case of premiums that are too large to qualify for annual or normal income exemption, therefore, the donor must think carefully whether to continue. The addition, to what must now be a relevant property trust, of new capital can generate fiendishly difficult calculations for IHT, the cost of which adds significantly to the administration expense of the trust.

Endowment assurance

14.15   Endowment assurance, whereby a capital sum is received after a given period of years or earlier death, is particularly appropriate when written under trust, say, for children or for grandchildren to build up an IHT-free fund by way of gift. A policy maturing in, say, 10–15 years' time may be suitable. The proceeds, if maturing on the expiry of the policy period, will be useful to the beneficiaries for school fees or for other general purposes.

Bear in mind, however, that contributions to a Child Trust Fund (CTF) account or Junior ISA may be allowed; if so, that may be the preferred first form of saving for children, particularly if the intention is to build up a fund in a tax-efficient manner to meet the costs of the child attending university.

If maturing on the earlier death of the life assured, the proceeds of the policy will be available to cover IHT, either on gifts passing to beneficiaries over the nil rate band or on PETs made to them by the donor within seven years of the death. If the transferor wishes to preserve flexibility, a better alternative is a trust policy. The value of the policy at the time of settlement will rarely exceed the nil rate band, so an immediate IHT charge is generally unlikely.

'Life of another' policies

14.16   These continue to be important. Under such a policy, one individual (say the wife) insures the life of another (say the husband), the latter being the life assured. Provided the person taking out the policy has an insurable interest and pays the requisite premiums from his or her own resources, there should be no IHT payable on the death of the life assured, subject to the anti-avoidance provisions of ss 263 and 268 (as between UK-domiciled spouses, it would not matter who paid the premiums because of the inter-spouse exemption).

Two main aspects must be borne in mind in effecting these life of another policies. The first is insurable interest. The Life Assurance Act 1774 provided that no insurance was to be made on lives by persons having no insurable interest in the life assured. An individual has an unlimited interest in his or her own life and in the life of a spouse or civil partner. Elsewhere, insurable interest must be based on pecuniary interest. The table below summarises, therefore, the main categories where an insurable interest exists.

Person effecting the policy	Life assured	Restrictions of insurable interest
Individual	Own life	Unlimited
Husband	Wife	Unlimited
Wife	Husband	Unlimited
Civil partner	Civil partner	Unlimited
Creditor	Debtor	Amount of debt
Parent	Child	Only if and to the extent that a pecuniary interest exists

Person effecting the policy	Life assured	Restrictions of insurable interest
Fiancé (or vice versa)	Fiancée	The measure of damage resulting from monetary loss should engagement be terminated
Employer	Employee	Value of services ('key man' insurance)
Employee	Employer	Extent of remuneration
Partner	Co-partners	If and to the extent that on a death the continuing partners must purchase the share of goodwill or repay capital and current accounts
Trustees	Beneficiary	If and to the extent that settlement permits plus pecuniary interest (normally the likely amount of any tax on beneficiary's death)
Mortgagee	Mortgagor	The value of the loan plus costs, etc
Donee of gift or beneficiary or trustee under settlement	Donee/settlor	Prospective liability to IHT on gift or settlement (trustee must be empowered)

If insurance is effected without the requisite element of insurable interest, the policy is null and void. However, it is unlikely that a reputable life office would seek to avoid payment on the grounds that insurable interest had not been adequately proven. In practice, life offices require confirmation of insurable interest before accepting a proposal on a 'life of another' basis and, if satisfied initially, it is not necessary for the insurable interest to continue, even though the assurance is a continuing contract.

Moreover, the question of insurable interest can easily be overcome by the life assured effecting the policy for his own benefit and, after payment of one or possibly two monthly premiums, assigning the policy by deed to a beneficiary. The assignee will then have a proper interest in the upkeep of the policy. Any question of IHT will be restricted to the premium(s) paid by the life assured initially plus any further gifts to enable the assignee to proceed with the policy (and it is likely that there will be exemptions available to cover these).

The investment clauses in a settlement should always be drafted to include powers to enable the trustees to effect, invest in and keep up policies; and in the absence of insurable interest, the policy can be effected by the life assured and assigned to the settlement trustees (as in the previous paragraph).

It is of course always possible for an individual to effect a policy on his own life (unlimited insurable interest) *in trust* for beneficiaries.

Note that if an insurance company pays out under a policy, HMRC treat the payment as made in respect of the policy for IHT purposes, notwithstanding any lack of insurable interest (IHTM20085).

Payment of premiums

14.17   The person effecting the life of another policy, or the assignee of a policy effected by the life assured, may well pay the premiums; but, if the life assured pays them, he will for IHT purposes be making successive transfers of value as outlined in **14.3**, although subject to the available exemptions referred to in **14.4**, as well as the inter-spouse exemption.

Application

14.18   Where the donor of property dies within seven years the donee is responsible for any (additional) IHT by reason of the death. The donee should therefore consider insuring the donor's life in respect of this liability.

There is also the problem that if A takes out a policy on his life written in trust for B, B may not know that the policy is in existence and so will not insure against the increased liability due on the premiums (assuming exemptions do not cover them) paid in the seven years before death. A should therefore tell B (if he wants B to know that the original policy exists).

The same position arises in respect of *inter vivos* trusts where the trustees may decide to take out such a policy on the settlor's life to take account of any IHT or increased IHT on death within seven years.

'Life of another' policies may also be relevant to other parties in the context of the seven-year statutory period.

Example 14.2 – 'Life of another' insurance

Gerald gave away his house worth £450,000 on 1 August 2005 to Elena, his young housekeeper, before moving to an old people's home. His remaining estate comprises cash of £50,000 and an aggregable life interest in possession in a trust fund worth £100,000 which passes on his death to his niece Claire.

Claire may on current rates suffer IHT at 40% if Gerald does not survive until 1 August 2012, dying within seven years of the £450,000 gift so that it is subject to cumulation on the death.

Claire may therefore like to consider taking out insurance on Gerald's life to cover this liability.

'Life of another' policies can also be written in trust for dependants such as issue. The death of the life assured does not give rise to any IHT; he is merely the subject of the insurance policy.

The death of a beneficiary of the trust before the life assured likewise gives rise to no IHT liability, assuming the value of the policy is negligible. In any event, if created since 22 March 2006, the trust will be taxed as a relevant property trust; so, even if for trust purposes the beneficiary had an interest in possession in the policy, the IHT treatment will be as for a discretionary trust.

Term insurance

14.19   As an alternative to the life of another policy, term insurance by donees or certain trustees may be appropriate to cover the risk of the donor dying within the seven-year period (see **14.16**).

Term cover is also relevant where an individual decides to acquire an overseas domicile and it is wished to insure against death within the minimum period that it takes to acquire such overseas domicile, namely three years from the date on which it can clearly be shown that foreign domicile has been established (see s 267). A convertible term insurance will enable the donor to convert the term insurance into a whole life insurance if he so wishes without the need for a further medical. The exemption of this type of term insurance under s 167(3) has already been noted.

In undertaking this type of insurance, the usual rules apply:

(1)   The donor/settlor should not effect the insurance for his own benefit because the proceeds would then become part of his own estate. Doubt about insurable interest may necessitate the proposal being made by the donor/settlor at least initially, followed by assignment to the beneficiaries or into trust.

(2)   It is better not to write the policy in trust for the intended donees unless one of the appropriate exemptions will apply to payment of the premiums (such as normal expenditure out of income).

Back-to-back arrangements and associated operations

14.20   This type of scheme has already been referred to in **1.27** and covers circumstances where an individual purchases one or more annuities to enable him to take out one or more life policies written in trust and where the annuity payments feed the premiums for the life policy.

Since, for IHT purposes, the capital element of a purchased life annuity cannot be regarded as income for the normal expenditure exemption (s 21(3)), the scope is restricted. The arrangement may still commend itself, however, where the annuity is purchased out of capital of an estate above the nil rate band since the purchase is 'subsidised' at 40% by the IHT that will no longer be payable on the top slice of that estate representing the purchase price.

Note also the terms of s 263 summarised in **1.27**. If s 263 applies to an annuity purchase coupled to a whole life policy, the IHT position would be restored and the plan wholly ineffective. However, HMRC are prepared to accept that the two contracts are not 'associated operations' if the whole life policy is shown to have been underwritten on the basis of medical evidence without reference to the annuity (Statement of Practice E4; see IHTM20375).

The easiest way to demonstrate that the two contracts were not 'associated' would be to take up the annuity and the policy with separate, unconnected life offices. If the same life office is used, it is vital for the policy to have been issued and the premiums fixed on the basis of full medical evidence.

This point was illustrated in *Smith and others v Revenue and Customs Commissioners* [2007] SpC 605. Husband and wife took out three life assurance policies and three annuities with the same life assurance company. Both spouses completed a medical questionnaire, but only the husband underwent a medical. The Special Commissioner upheld notices of determination that the issue of the life assurance policies at the same time as the annuities, and the vesting of those policies under trust declarations, was a transfer of value by the husband under s 263. The Commissioner held that Statement of Practice E4 did not apply to the policies, as full medical evidence was not obtained in respect of both spouses. The medical questionnaires were insufficient evidence of themselves. The Court of Appeal subsequently upheld the Commissioners' decision ([2008] STC 1649).

Purchased life annuities are split for income tax purposes (ITTOIA 2005, s 717) into a capital element and an income element on the basis of tables agreed with HMRC. Each annuity instalment is thus divided between the capital element on which no income tax is payable (it is considered as a part return of the purchaser's original capital purchase price), and an income element which is taxable. Life offices will quote the capital and income elements if asked. Women, of course, have a greater expectation of life than men; and see **Appendix 1.3** at the end of **Chapter 1**.

Pension and other arrangements

14.21   These have been outlined elsewhere in relation to registered pension schemes (from 6 April 2006; previously superannuation arrangements and director's death in service (**9.27** and **9.28**) and retirement annuities stakeholder and personal pensions). In many cases, death in service lump sums will be free of IHT.

This situation was considered in *Kempe and Roberts (Lyon's Personal Representatives) v CIR* [2004] SpC 424, and the application of that case was subsequently highlighted in the professional press. In *Lyon*, an employee was insured through a company scheme and nominated his sisters as beneficiaries of the policy in the event of death. The sisters appealed from a notice of determination charging IHT on the death benefit. It was held that the deceased had a general power over the policy which allowed him to dispose of it as he liked, so it was part of his estate.

The modern gloss on this case should be approached with caution, since it concerns a situation that did not proceed to trial and the result is not yet the subject of formal acknowledgement of the position of HMRC. It appears that a deceased had lived and worked, and was domiciled, in the UK for many years, leaving an estate of £1,000,000 and aggregable estate of £1,400,000. A personal pension policy was taken out with Norwich Union carrying a death benefit of £200,000. The deceased revocably nominated his sisters as beneficiaries, having neither spouse nor civil partner.

It appears that HMRC took the view, following *Lyon*, that the policy proceeds should attract IHT because they could not pass to an exempt beneficiary. A distinction seems to have been drawn, in favour of the taxpayer in the instant case, between total control of the policy proceeds, as in *Lyon*, and default control, where (as in this case) any revocation of the nomination would cause the proceeds to fall into the estate of the deceased.

The result may seem counter-intuitive. One factor was that, since the deceased was homosexual, he would not have had a spouse and nor at the relevant time could he have had a civil partner. A human rights argument was in prospect on that score. The issue was of concern to several insurers, who had not expected HMRC to take the point.

Education insurance

14.22   Most families, however deeply committed to the expense, find it virtually impossible to pay school fees out of income. For a long time, the traditional alternative source of funds was a grandparental A&M trust, but the lack of dividend tax credit from the tax pool erodes the tax efficiency of that structure, and since FA 2006 it is no longer possible as a PET (though a discretionary trust of up to the nil rate band will go a long way to plugging the gap).

In this context, single premium education insurance policies have proved popular and can be combined with IHT saving. Although the value of education may be intangible, the loss of the capital is now the normal measure of the value of the transfer to which any IHT liability attaches in view of the consequential loss formula in s 3(1).

However, for parents taking out such a policy, the capital sum used will normally be exempt under s 11 for a different reason, ie because the payments will not be treated as transfers of value, being for the maintenance, education or training of a child by the parent (under sub-s (1)). It is also arguable that no gratuitous benefit is conferred under s 10, the parent being under a moral and possibly legal obligation to provide the education.

What constitutes 'maintenance' for the purpose of s 11 was considered (for the purpose of the debt or charge scheme) in *Phizackerley v HMRC* [2007] SpC 591. Dr Avery Jones observed: 'It seems to me that the ordinary meaning of maintenance has a flavour of meeting recurring expenses …'. In the instant case, it did not include the gift of a share in a house, so the case may be distinguishable from the education scenario.

Contrast this with the decision in *McKelvey (Personal Representative of McKelvey Deceased) v Revenue and Customs Commissioners)* [2008] SpC 694 (see **12.16**) in the context of a gift of two houses and the exemption for the reasonable provision for the care and maintenance of a dependent relative for the purposes of s 11(3).

Provision by grandparents and other relatives

14.23   A person having the care of a child can obtain similar exemption under s 11(2). Education policies taken out by other persons such as grandparents or uncles and aunts will fall within the scope of IHT. For those individuals, it may be possible to fund the policies out of income utilising the normal expenditure out of income exemption or other exemptions and reliefs, such as the £3,000 per annum exemption and the nil rate band.

As a general rule, the parent or settlor of the education policy should forgo the right to surrender it from the moment of payment; otherwise, if death occurs before the policy starts paying out, the capital sum would normally be regarded as being an asset of the estate, the estate owner retaining a 'general power' over the capital sum within the meaning of s 5(2).

Moreover, education policies are normally flexible, covering relevant aspects as to transferability, scholarships, death of settlor, abolition of school fees or the possibility that the child does not go to a private school.

As an alternative, education policies can be planned out of income, normally by way of a series of flexible endowment assurance policies which are started when the child is very young and which (perhaps like the child!) mature at intervals during his time at school. The younger the child, the longer the time before the fees become payable, and the more advantageous the policy terms. A period of ten years or more will allow the maximum benefits to be obtained from a series of endowment assurances where the premiums are payable regularly out of income, the policies maturing to produce fees in the relevant future years.

If capital is available, funding arrangements can be made to provide the premiums. Since premiums can vary from time to time (reflecting current investment conditions and interest rates), details of the going rate for the time being should be obtained via an independent financial adviser or direct from school fees specialists. Naturally, the maximum benefit can result from a policy taken out immediately on the child's birth.

Annuities and home income plans

Annuities

14.24 It may be worthwhile considering the purchase of an annuity from a life office in the case of an elderly person (or couple) who are short of income. This is increasingly popular with 'asset rich, cash poor' families who have been alarmed at the incidence of IHT on their 'modest' wealth, though in this wealth bracket the introduction of the transferable nil rate band in FA 2008 may have eased the situation considerably.

The disadvantage is that the purchase moneys disappear out of the estate, but if the estate is over the nil rate band, the loss is reduced by the 40% IHT otherwise payable; and annuities can be capital-protected, giving a guaranteed return if early death occurs.

The rate of the annuity depends on age and current economic circumstances and interest rates, and an escalating annuity can be chosen giving an increase each year, although the starting annuity rate for the same capital will of course be smaller. Since HMRC regard the bulk of the instalments from a purchased life annuity as representing a return of the capital, income tax is payable only on the minor income proportion (ITTOIA 2005, ss 717–724).

Home income plans

14.25 Another possibility where income is required by the elderly is the annuity home income plan. This arrangement enables an individual (or more than one person, eg husband and wife, or sisters) to realise capital on the security of the family home, which is then used for the purchase of an annuity. Again, the greater part of the annuity instalments will escape income tax as a return of the capital, and only the interest part will be taxable.

The interest on the mortgage has to be paid out of the annuity payments; but it can be an interest-only mortgage, and (unlike the general rule) interest relief is still available on a home income loan of up to £30,000 if it was taken out prior to 9 March 1999 (ITA 2007, s 26(1)(a); ICTA 1988, ss 353(1)–(1AA) and 365). On death, the mortgage is paid off out of the sale proceeds from the home.

The mortgage interest should be at a fixed rate to preserve a gap between the amount received and the amount payable. The question is whether the extra income is worth the restriction of the mortgage on the home.

Loan and bond schemes

14.26   The home income plans that have really caused concern have been those where elderly people have raised large loans on their properties out of which they have invested in a unit-linked single premium investment bond. The aim was that the income from the bond would be more than sufficient to pay the mortgage interest and the capital value of the bond would go up.

However, at the end of the 1980s, when interest rates rose, the value of houses fell and the capital invested went down, the individuals faced disaster – see *R v Investors' Compensation Scheme Ltd, ex p Weyell* [1994] 1 All ER 601 for a cautionary tale. Such schemes have effectively been banned, and potential borrowers are well advised to restrict themselves to safe home income plans (SHIPs) by providers of home income schemes.

Pre-owned assets tax issues

14.27   The 'pre-owned assets' income tax charge (POAT) may need to be considered in some circumstances. For example, notwithstanding representations from the professions to the government, partial equity release arrangements involving a connected person (eg a family member) on or after 7 March 2005 are caught, subject to an exemption if the transaction was on arm's-length terms for consideration not in cash or readily convertible assets (SI 2005/724, reg 5; see **Chapter 13**).

This seems most unfair: IHT mitigation may not be the reason for the transaction. The elderly couple, having been discouraged by the bad publicity noted above, would be happy with a deal on identical terms from family members, since any commercial advantage would accrue to family (and no doubt much commission would be saved as well).

Prudence would dictate that the elderly should be very chary of mortgaging their home in any event, and that they should seek to improve their income in other ways. Even so, they will take little comfort from the comments of the Paymaster General when POAT was introduced that 'If one member of a family needs to raise cash, and another member of the family is willing and able to provide it, there are other and more straightforward ways of structuring this than adopting the form of an equity release transaction.'

Fragmenting discretionary trust policies

14.28   It is possible to fragment life assurance policies so that each one represents a nil band value. On that basis, there should be no disadvantage and considerable advantage as regards flexibility in using the discretionary trust form; in particular, a further generation could be skipped. For this purpose, each policy should be taken out at least one day apart (preferably longer) and the beneficiaries under the various trusts should differ to some degree.

HMRC regard the initial premium as constituting the creation of the settlement but see the last paragraph of **14.14** as to the payment of second and subsequent premiums.

Insurance and the PET regime

14.29   Tax schemes come and go. It is worth knowing about old ideas that have since been scotched, so as not to try them again. For example, FA 1986 not only introduced IHT and the PET regime with its increased flexibility in the making of gifts, but also stopped a number of old insurance arrangements.

PETA plans (that linked pure endowment with regular withdrawals and term assurance providing the benefit for the donee) were stopped by FA 1986, Sch 20, para 7 (see IHTM14452).

The deferred premium policy (small first premium in lifetime; covenant to pay second large premium after death, but (then) deductible against the estate; in trust for the beneficiary) met up with s 103(7) disallowing the premium deduction.

Finally, the old-style inheritance trust was stopped under the gift with reservation provisions of s 102 (with a saving for existing cases in s 102(6)).

The old-style inheritance trust in its simple form consisted of a settlement set up by an individual whereby he settled a small sum of cash on flexible trusts (in essence for donees absolutely, with an overriding power of appointment for persons including the settlor). He then lent a substantial sum to the trustees of the settlement, interest free and repayable on demand, and the trustees used the money to buy single premium policies. The trustees then took annual 5% tax-free withdrawals from the policies, and paid them over to the settlor in part repayment of the loan, providing him with a regular flow of cash. On death, the trust fund consisting of the policies less the outstanding loan belonged to the donees (there was a variation known as the 'reverse loan trust' which is explained at IHTM20521 but need not concern us). Under FA 1986, s 102, the arrangement became categorised as a gift with reservation, and appeared to have died (see IHTM14451 onwards).

'New' inheritance trusts

14.30 However, 'new style' inheritance trusts subsequently evolved out of the legislation. The first arrangement (normally termed a retained interest trust or a split trust) proceeds broadly as in the following example.

Example 14.3 – 'New-style' inheritance trust

The individual effects a single premium policy on the joint lives of himself and his wife and the life of the survivor. He declares trusts over the policy whereby he carves out and retains a proportion, say 40%, of the beneficial interest for himself and his wife jointly. The balance is held on trust for a class of beneficiaries including the settlor's wife (but not the settlor).

The husband and wife receive the 5% annual tax-free withdrawals made by the trustees out of the policy. These withdrawals are measured against the whole policy but deducted only against their retained proportion.

It is of course possible, given increased life expectancy and poor investment returns, that the retained proportion becomes exhausted. This will be more likely after the husband's death if his pension dies with him or is much reduced on his death, depending on the widow's needs.

The structure allows for payments to be made out of the trust fund to the widow. The purchase monies for the policy have come from her husband, so there is no gift with reservation by him if appointed sums are paid, even in his lifetime, to his wife, provided that she does not use the sums to pay off liabilities (eg housekeeping) for which he is responsible or otherwise give him some benefit out of the moneys. On the footing that he is excluded, he has made a transfer of value equal to 60% of the value of the policy.

It is noteworthy that this 'new-style' inheritance trust does not contain the feature of the settlor's loan which figured in the 'old style' trust. The reason appears to stem from doubts raised by FA 1986, Sch 20, para 5(4), which at first sight seems to catch property derived from a loan to the trustees of a settlement. However, HMRC confirmed that FA 1986, s 102 and Sch 20 apply only where there is a gift with reservation. Thus, if there is no question of reservation, as there should not be in the initial version of the 'new style' trust as outlined above, there is no place for para 5(4). Accordingly, it follows that the donor is able to lend moneys, interest free and repayable on demand to the trustees of a new style trust out of which they could buy further policies.

'Gift and loan' trust arrangements

14.31   It was no doubt such thoughts as these that have prompted the appearance of a second new-style inheritance trust arrangement. This version is on the lines of the old-style trust but with two new features. The first feature is to set up the trust so as to avoid any question of reservation to the settlor: either with a small sum of cash from which he is rigidly excluded; or by means of an 'empty' settlement where the trustees have no assets until the settlor makes the loan; or (in at least one case) by an initial nominal charitable gift to create the trust into which the interest free loan is made.

Subject to setting up, the trust terms are for individuals absolutely with an overriding power of appointment among a class including in some cases (this is the second new feature) the settlor's wife.

There is a subsequent loan to the trustees, who buy policies and make 5% tax-free withdrawals to repay part of the loan. So the two new features are the segregated original settled cash and the settlor's wife among the discretionary beneficiaries rather than the settlor, both to avoid reservation of benefit.

It appears to be generally agreed that the grant of a loan interest free and repayable on demand does not of itself constitute a gift for IHT purposes, though that may be open to question if there is no realistic prospect that the borrower will ever repay the loan. This scheme, as well as the first new-style one above, has been taken up by those seeking to benefit their families. Both these schemes serve to emphasise that PETs are outright gifts and one must seek at all costs to avoid gifts with reservation.

HMRC guidance (at IHTM20513) confirms that such arrangements are effective in circumventing the gift with reservation provisions in FA 1986, Sch 20, para 5(4):

> 'A revised version of the original scheme which circumvented FA86/ SCH20/para5 (4) was brought out. Under this version the original policy was not put into a settlement but into a bare trust for the absolute benefit of a named beneficiary.

More recent versions of this scheme do not always have the initial gift into trust. Instead the trust is established and the settlor then makes the interest free loan to the trustees, who invest the funds, usually in an insurance bond. These schemes are also not caught by FA86/SCH20/para5 (4). The amount of the loan outstanding remains an asset of the settlor's estate, but usually repayments will be made during the settlor's lifetime to reduce the value to be included in the estate at the date of death.'

In addition, for pre-owned assets income tax purposes, HMRC confirm that a gift and loan trust does not give rise to a charge, as the benefit to the settlor arises in the capacity of a creditor, and not under the trust (IHTM44113).

Nevertheless, it would seem prudent to approach the financial adviser or life office promoting the arrangements for confirmation on the attitude of HMRC towards their particular product. Do not be fobbed off with a mere reference to 'Counsel's Opinion'; ask to see it, noting the date on which it was signed and by whom, and to see the instructions upon which it is based. You will not be able to rely on out-of-date advice.

Discounted gift trust arrangements

14.32   There is a final series of schemes involving a 'carve-out' of benefits retained by the donor and 'discounted' gifts to the donee(s) claimed to be gifts without reservation.

'Version 1' involves a lump-sum investment into an offshore capital redemption policy (not a life policy and therefore claimed to be outside FA 1986, Sch 20, para 7). The donor specifies at the outset the level of income he requires from the bond (the retained portion) and he gives away (under trust) the balance to his beneficiaries.

'Version 2' comprises a series of single premium endowment policies planned to mature at yearly intervals or earlier death. If the donor is alive when each policy matures he takes the benefit himself. If he dies, the proceeds of the remaining policies go to the beneficiaries.

'Version 3' uses a trust of a pure endowment policy. The policy is notionally divided into a 'retained fund', which provides regular payments for the donor, and a 'residuary fund', which is given away and from which the donor is excluded from benefiting. There will be regular drawdowns on the retained fund (up to 5% per annum of the amount invested), but the right to withdrawals dies with the donor. The transfer of value attributable to the gift of the residuary fund can be calculated actuarially at inception; this is essential if the residuary fund is to be held on substantive (rather than 'bare') trusts since, to avoid any IHT charge, the transfer of value arising will need to be kept within the nil rate band. The income benefits payable to the donor are fixed at inception whereas the death benefit which is given away will vary according to the performance of the policy and the amount paid to the donor during the life of the scheme.

Critical analysis of discounted gift schemes

14.33 'Version 3' is particularly complicated and open to argument. No one should take up such a scheme, or indeed any scheme, without careful legal advice and without remembering that success cannot be guaranteed because it may well depend on the law and practice at some future time, say the death of the donor/settlor.

As Chris Whitehouse and Emma Chamberlain explain in *Trust Taxation* (Sweet & Maxwell, 3rd Edition), the discounted gift scheme is viewed as a 'carve-out' or 'shearing arrangement'. Provided it is clear exactly what rights are retained by the settlor, and that the settlor is excluded from all benefit in the trust fund, there is no reservation of benefit.

The intellectual difficulty to be overcome is that a policy is not like land, in which there may be separate interests, such as the freehold and a lease carved out of it. Rights under a policy, being a chose in action, cannot be transferred separately: so the policy or bond must be held within the trust arrangement and the rights in it separated out within the trust. As Chris Whitehouse and Emma Chamberlain remind us, Lord Hoffmann noted, in his judgment in *Ingram v CIR* [1999] STC 37, how important it was to be precise in structuring gifts to achieve an effective carve-out.

Valuing the discount

14.34 There are difficulties in valuing, for IHT purposes, the 'discount' in the transfer. Early in 2007, HMRC issued a technical note on 'Discounted Gift Schemes' involving the gift of a bond from which rights are retained (www.hmrc.gov.uk/cto/dgs-tech-note.pdf), which has been consolidated in its guidance at IHTM20650 onwards. Such transfers are valued on the difference between the amount invested by the settlor and the open market value of the retained rights (within s 160).

HMRC take the view that the value of those rights depends on the settlor's insurability, which is in turn based on such factors as the settlor's sex, age and health. HMRC consider (with some justification) that individuals older than 90 are uninsurable; for this purpose, note that the age of 90 is the actuarially adjusted age to take account of mortality factors. If the settlor's life is uninsurable, there will be no discount element in the gift. Even if the settlor is younger than 90, HMRC's view is that medical underwriting must be obtained at the time of the gift in order to justify any discount claimed.

In the case of joint settlors (eg husband and wife), HMRC consider that the correct approach is to value the retained rights as a whole, before apportioning the value between the joint settlors by reference to the open market value of each settlor's retained rights. The related property provisions (s 161) are applied to the valuation. Care should therefore be taken, as the discount element in these arrangements may be lower than the settlor might expect.

These issues were debated in *Bower and another (executors of Bower) v HMRC* [2009] STC 510. The deceased, then aged 90, had taken out a policy at a cost of £73,000. She was not very well: her notional age for expectancy purposes was 103. She had created a trust and the policy was issued to the trustees. Her reserved rights were a 5% annuity. Five months later, she died. That being within seven years of setting up the arrangement, there was a chargeable transfer of the rights under the policy.

In line with their declared approach as described above, HMRC valued the transfer at £72,750, being the entire value of the purchased annuity less a nominal £250 for the value of the reserved rights. The executors appealed, on the basis that the insurance company had certified that the value of the rights was £7,800, putting the value of the gift at £65,200.

Before the Special Commissioner ([2008] SpC 665), the executors' appeal was allowed in part, on the basis that the open market value of the rights was £4,200. The Commissioner considered that the insurers' figure of £7,800 was too high by one-third. There should also be deducted £1,000 for the likely legal expenses involved. This was not 'palm tree justice'; the Commissioner assumed a sale, to comply with the statutory notion of a willing buyer and a willing seller. The reduction of one-third was a fair assessment of the discount that a buyer would expect to reflect uncertainty; simply adjusting the interest rate would not work when the pay-back time was anticipated to be very short. HMRC appealed.

The High Court allowed HMRC's appeal ([2009] STC 510). In determining the open market value of property under s 160, the question was what a purchaser in the open market would have paid to enjoy the rights attaching to the property. The court held that the Special Commissioner was not entitled to invent possible purchasers or hypothetical speculators. Further, the Commissioner's method of calculation and valuation '... flowed from the erroneous conclusion that he was required or entitled to populate the real market in which the hypothetical sale took place with hypothetical speculators who did not share the characteristics of real buyers'. HMRC subsequently issued Revenue & Customs Brief 21/09, dated 2 April 2009, confirming that cases would be dealt with in accordance with its technical note issued in 2007. The Brief also stated that '... there is nothing in the Inheritance Tax legislation which allows any withdrawals actually taken between the gift date and the date of death of the settlor to be offset against the sum invested'.

It would seem logical that, if a market were to develop in respect of annuities or similar income entitlements of persons aged over 90, the decision in *Bower* would no longer apply. In the meantime, however, despite some ingenious arguments put forward on behalf of the taxpayers, the decision in *Bower* has been followed on similar facts in the subsequent case of *Watkins and Harvey v HMRC* [2011] UKFTT 745 (TC).

The scope for UK life insurers to charge different premiums (or determine different benefits) for males and females based on gender-related factors was removed following a legal challenge to the European Court of Justice by the Belgian consumer's association Test Achats. HMRC subsequently stated that, if the Test Achats decision resulted in changes from the market practice of life companies to take into account the gender of the life assured, HMRC would consult on how best to incorporate that change into its practice of valuing retained rights under discounted gift schemes (Trusts and Estates Newsletter, April 2011).

Other valuation issues

14.35   The *Bower* case revives arguments about valuation immediately before death. The legislation is s 171, 'Changes occurring on death' and in particular the valuation of any interest that is terminated, see 171(2), on death. A 'parallel' interest, such as that of a joint owner, is outside s 171. These issues were examined in *Arkwright v IRC* [2004] STC 89 in relation to interests in the family home.

For example, in valuing the retained fund in a discounted gift scheme policy, is it right to assume, as do HMRC, that, immediately prior to the death of the settlor, it is valueless? Can the valuer enjoy the benefit of hindsight in that way? The comments of Oliver LJ in *Fetherstonhaugh v IRC* [1984] STC 262, at 268 were *obiter*, but he did there say that 'there is nothing in the statute to suggest that the valuation is to be conducted on the basis that the impending demise of the deceased is a known factor which the hypothetical valuer is to take into account'.

The decisions in *Bower* and *Watkins* are potentially of wider application as regards other assets for which there is no ready market. Applying the arguments put forward on behalf of HMRC in those cases, one ought to be able to say that any asset for which there is no ready market can be ascribed, at most, only a nominal value. With a little imagination, the application of this principle could be used as part of an IHT reduction strategy. Whether HMRC would accept that this basis of valuation is to be used in cases where it is beneficial to the taxpayer remains to be seen.

POAT issues

14.36 The impact of POAT on various structures was considered in **Chapter 13**. How, if at all, does it affect discounted gift schemes? Again, research was undertaken by Chris Whitehouse and Emma Chamberlain, who led the examination of the legislation and the discussions that resulted in official guidance. HMRC guidance suggests that the gift with reservation provisions do not apply to the residuary fund, because the settlor does not benefit from it; and that there is no POAT charge on the retained fund in a 'straightforward' case where the settlor has retained a right to an annual income or to a reversion, because it is held on bare trust for the settlor and is therefore not a 'settlement' for IHT purposes (IHTM44112). See also **14.44**.

For as long as this analysis holds, it offers comfort to purchasers of the scheme, even though it may lack intellectual purity.

In the face of all this debate, the authors stand by their cautionary comments expressed earlier. Whilst the retained fund and the residuary fund seem, in the eyes of HMRC, to be valued separately, that basis is uncertain intellectually and, if a scheme were again to be reviewed by the courts, the outcome might surprise us all and upset the insurance companies that have relied on official guidance.

DIY discounted gift schemes

14.37 Many lawyers, perhaps envious of commissions earned by IFAs on insurance products, may wonder if they could replicate the discounted gift structure for clients using trust documents drafted in-house and based on assets that the family already own, thus saving the liquidation of investments – and payment of commission. For example, could a similar arrangement be put in place to hold let property?

Upon acquiring the property, the trust would hold it to pay the donor an income but with absolutely no powers over capital, which would go to the intended residuary beneficiaries of the arrangement. Creating the trust would be a chargeable transfer, so must be limited to the nil rate band. The right to income might well amount to an interest in possession but, since 2006, that would not be fatal to the arrangement; nevertheless care would be needed to define the interest well enough to satisfy Lord Hoffmann that a benefit had not been reserved out of the funds given away (see the note at **14.33**). Any ability for the settlor to occupy the property personally would need to be excluded, to avoid the application of the reservation of benefit provisions which might otherwise apply because of FA 1986, s 102A (unless the trust is funded with cash initially).

Despite the comments above as to the irrelevance of POAT to the reserved fund of a discounted gift scheme when applied to a policy, a 'home grown' scheme might fall foul of POAT. This ought not to be the case while the trust holds let property that is not occupied by the donor, however (FA 2004, Sch 15, para 3(1)). Nevertheless, the mechanics are far from simple to set up and specialist advice would be desirable, increasing the cost. There is also the possibility that such a scheme might in due course become the target of anti-avoidance legislation, eg by extending the scope of POAT.

Personal portfolio bonds

14.38   These are single premium policies where the purchaser retains the ability, in conjunction with his investment adviser, to choose, switch and manage the investments in the fund to which each individual bond is linked.

In *IRC v Willoughby* [1997] STC 995, HL, a case concerned with the anti-avoidance provisions of what is now ITA 2007, s 721 (previously ICTA 1988, s 739), on a transfer of assets abroad, HMRC contended that the underlying reality was that the holder of such a personal portfolio bond continued to benefit from his own portfolio of investments, but was saved from tax by the insertion of the bond structure (the case was concerned with offshore life company bonds).

Lord Nolan, with whom his four colleagues agreed, rejected that argument. He concluded that the bondholder had a contractual right to the benefits promised by the policy alone. Whether this case will ever herald a resurgence of the personal portfolio policy is perhaps doubtful, given the income tax treatment of such bonds (see ITTOIA 2005, ss 515–526).

Flexible reversionary trusts

14.39   An alternative arrangement to discounted gift trusts or gift and loan trusts, the 'flexible reversionary trust' (FRT), has been advanced as an IHT planning structure (Christian Ward, 'An overlooked gem' *STEP Journal*, June 2009; Simon McKie, 'A detailed examination' *Taxation* magazine, 22 October 2009).

The above articles describe a 'traditional' FRT as involving the settlor investing in a series of single premium offshore endowment policies with multiple lives assured. The settlor selects the term of each endowment based on his future 'income' requirements; he then gifts the policies into trust for nominated beneficiaries (eg the settlor's children), on terms such that he retains the right to receive the maturity proceeds of the endowments.

The settlor's 'carved-out' rights are defeasible by the exercise of wide powers vested in the trustees, with the result that the prospective future maturity proceeds have no value unless or until they actually mature. The full value of the endowment policies is therefore taken into account as a chargeable lifetime transfer, without discount for the retained rights (with the result that the settlor will invariably wish to limit the initial gift to his available nil rate band). The extent of the trustees' powers are such that if they exercise their right to extend a policy maturity date, there is no transfer of value by the settlor, as there is no further loss to the settlor's estate in respect of the value of the retained rights.

The FRT is therefore advanced as a flexible long-term vehicle, in which the settlor retains potential access to capital and growth, but with the trustees having the power to prevent unnecessary payments to the settlor. The articles state that, for IHT purposes, HMRC apparently accept that the 'carve-out' of rights is not caught by the reservation of benefit or POAT provisions, and there is no further transfer of value upon the trustees deferring any payments. This is arguably an overly generous interpretation of the law but one that insurance companies are naturally keen to rely on.

Another arrangement created by 'a well-known non-resident insurance company', which has been marketed as the successor to accumulation and maintenance trusts, is aimed at individuals who wish to settle sums on children and young adults but without giving unfettered control over the funds. The arrangement broadly involves a single-premium insurance bond policy and a bare trust. The policy may be assigned to the trustees of the bare trust in which the child, grandchild etc is the beneficiary.

An article (Simon McKie, 'No surrender!' *Trust Quarterly Review*, Volume 7, Issue 1, 2009) describes the arrangements in greater detail, and considers the tax implications. The article points out the possibility that taking out the policy may be an immediately chargeable transfer, on the footing that the value of the policy when made (which involves giving up a right to access the funds invested in it wholly or partly for a period) will almost certainly be less than the initial premium paid in respect of it, and that the transfer of value will not be a PET because it is not a gift to an individual or to a 'privileged trust'. However, the assignment of the policy on bare trust will be a PET.

As with any other policy-linked arrangement, specific financial advice from a suitably qualified and experienced professional and full due diligence are essential. It must always be remembered that HMRC's views of a particular scheme are subject to change and that retroactive or even retrospective legislation is possible.

TRAPS FOR THE UNWARY

Own life, own benefit policies

14.40 An estate owner should be discouraged from taking out whole life policies which upon his death accrue to his estate. Clearly, this merely swells the IHT payable on his death (or, if married, the death of the surviving spouse). It is far better to effect the policies in trust. On the other hand, in the (now rare) case of an endowment policy, an own benefit policy may be desirable, for example, to cater for retirement.

If a policy is to provide the surviving wife with an income-producing fund (as opposed to paying for IHT, not required if passing to her) an own life, own benefit policy could be appropriate but many would now prefer some form of pension policy to secure an immediate tax advantage. In any case, it might be even better, to avoid full IHT on her death, to effect the policy on trusts including the widow among the beneficiaries. She might well be given the bulk of any income, but on the ten-year anniversary date or if the capital were distributed by the trustees following her death, any IHT would be on the favourable '30% of the 20% lifetime rate' basis.

Flexibility

14.41 The enactment of FA 2006, causing the creation of most lifetime settlements to be chargeable transfers, persuaded many settlors to opt for the flexibility of a full discretionary trust, with the advantage that any decision on actual beneficiaries may be deferred.

FA 2006 also had the consequence of removing the benefit of the reverter to settlor or settlor's spouse exemption, such as was available for trusts with an interest in possession created prior to 22 March 2006.

The £250 per annum to any donee exemption

14.42 As a general rule, the small gifts exemption in s 20 should not be used for insurance planning for two reasons:

- the exemption must be by way of an 'outright' gift, so it cannot be used by way of a gift *into* settlement, other than an absolute gift into trust for a minor (see IHTM14180); and

- an estate owner should perhaps keep this exemption in reserve for casual gifts, for example, entertainment and day-to-day presents (particularly since it is not available to exempt part of a larger gift to the donee, nor where other gifts are made to the donee so that together they total more than £250).

Life assurance relief

14.43   Life assurance premium relief was abolished in respect of policies taken out after 13 March 1984, but relief continues to be available for premiums on policies taken out beforehand, and those policies should be kept up in order to continue to get the benefit of the relief. More than 25 years later, there are no doubt still many such policies in existence, and the continued existence of a relief that has not been in existence since before younger practitioners were born will catch some out.

Currently, the relief is given by way of a 12.5% deduction from gross premiums (ICTA 1988, s 266(5), as amended). The payer merely pays over the net premium to the life company (and the life company is then compensated by a refund from HMRC), so that any gift element relates to the net amount handed over only; with the result that the annual £3,000 exemption and other exemptions apply to the extent that they cover the *net* premium.

In the case of policies effected after 13 March 1984, the transfer is of the gross premium and it is the gross amount paid which is the measure for IHT (Revenue Press Release, 17 January 1979).

This chapter has highlighted some of the possible advantages of estate planning through insurance. As the proposals are in the main designed to take advantage of the existing exemptions and reliefs and do not concern themselves with the artificial marketed schemes (apart from explaining them) they are, it is hoped, unlikely to be attacked by the anti-avoidance operations or to be subject to future retrospective or nullifying legislation.

As for any investment, it is important to obtain sound financial advice from a suitably qualified and experienced financial adviser in respect of life insurance and any other insurance-based products.

Pre-owned assets

14.44   HMRC issued guidance, in response to concerns from the insurance industry and others, that arrangements such as those described in this chapter may fall within the 'pre-owned assets' income tax charge. That guidance was subsequently subsumed into the Inheritance Tax Manual at IHTM44000 onwards. The views of HMRC are broadly outlined below.

- *Discounted gift schemes* – As indicated at **14.36**, in 'straightforward' cases of the settlor retaining a right to annual income or to a reversion, HMRC seem content that the arrangement does not fall within the pre-owned assets provisions of FA 2004, Sch 15, para 8 ('Intangible property comprised in settlement where settlor retains an interest'), on the basis that the trustees hold the retained right on bare trust for the settlor. Note the reservations expressed at **14.33**.

- In more complex cases where the settlor's retained rights or interests are themselves held on trust, no tax charge should normally arise (Sch 15, para 11(1)). Any charge that does arise would only be by reference to the settlor's retained rights, rather than the policy value. Reference should be made to the precise terms of the relevant trust.

- *Gift and loan schemes* (ie where the settlor settles a nominal sum on trust for the benefit of others, and then makes an interest-free, repayable on demand loan, which the trustees use to purchase one or more policies and make partial withdrawals to fund loan repayments) – The settlor is not a beneficiary, and the making of the loan is not considered to be a settlement for IHT purposes. No pre-owned assets charge arises under FA 2004, Sch 15, para 8.

- *Business trusts and partnership policies* – If a partner is not a potential beneficiary of his or her own trust, no pre-owned assets charge should arise under Sch 15, para 8. However, if the partner retains a benefit, there is a settlement for purposes of a pre-owned assets charge.

Further information on the pre-owned assets regime generally is contained in **Chapter 13**.

Chapter 15

Estate planning – business and agricultural property

BUSINESS AND AGRICULTURAL ASSETS: INTRODUCTION

15.1   Business property relief (BPR) (ss 103–114) and agricultural property relief (APR) (ss 115–124) operate by reducing the value transferred by a transfer of value. The rate of reduction is 100% or 50%.

BPR was commonly thought to be available only on certain types of assets, described as 'relevant business property'. The decision in *Trustees of Nelson Dance Settlement v HMRC* [2009] EWHC 71 (Ch) (see **15.41**) has put a gloss on that statement. The types of asset or interest qualifying for relief include the following main categories:

- a business or an interest in a business;

- land, buildings, machinery and plant used for the purposes of a business; and

- shares in an unquoted trading company.

The relief is available wherever the business is carried on, but is not available if the business consists wholly or mainly of dealing in securities, stocks or shares, land or buildings, or making or holding investments (see **15.8**).

Originally unquoted shares were eligible for 100% relief only if the transferor held more than 25% of the ordinary shares but, since 6 April 1996, 100% relief has been available whatever the size of the transferor's holding. Shares in trading companies listed only on the Alternative Investment Market (AIM) are regarded as unquoted for BPR purposes. The same applies to some, but not all, shareholdings in PLUS (formerly OFEX) companies (see IHTM18336, IHTM18337). Shares traded on NASDAQ Europe are similarly treated as unlisted at present. However, shares traded on NASDAQ are currently treated as listed for IHT purposes, and BPR does not apply except for controlling shareholdings (IHTM18340, IHTM18341).

Beware: some companies have subsidiary listings on other exchanges which may be 'recognised', thus depriving the shares of BPR status.

The relief is not available to reduce any part of the transfer of value which is attributable to 'excepted assets' (s 112). In general terms, an asset will be an excepted asset if it was *neither:*

- used for the purposes of a business during the preceding two years (or the period of ownership, if less);

- *nor* required at the time of the transfer for future use for those purposes.

Clearances for BPR: official and 'prompted'

15.2   It can often be difficult to know with certainty whether property qualifies for BPR. HMRC therefore introduced, initially for a limited period only, a clearance procedure. It was described in HMRC Brief 25/08 and is non-statutory clearance as to the application of tax law to a specific transaction or event. The trial allowed for clearance where the availability of BPR was material to a transaction, but it seems that very few applications were made, perhaps through lack of publicity of the facility.

HMRC subsequently confirmed (in January 2009) the continuation of the BPR clearance service, and an extension of the scope of the service. HMRC's stated purpose of the clearance service is '… to provide certainty for businesses operating in the UK, as a useful practical service at a level whereby speed of response from HMRC can be reasonably assured'. As part of the extended service, HMRC will also give their view of the tax consequences of a transfer of value that involves a change of ownership of a business (succession) where this transfer, leaving aside the application of BPR, would result in an immediate IHT charge. HMRC state: 'Evidence must be provided that the transfer is commercially significant and is genuinely contemplated'. Clearances in this area will only remain valid for a limited period of six months.

There are various limitations to the procedure. HMRC state that 'Applicants should recognise that the clearance service cannot be used for general confirmation of the business property relief position in the absence of a commercial transaction.' In addition, there must be material uncertainty over the interpretation of the law. If it relates to anything older than the last four Finance Acts, the uncertainty must concern an issue that is commercially significant. The limitations appear to mean that clearance would not be available, for example, to a farmer wanting to give away a two-acre field that might have 'hope value' for development.

HMRC's guidance on the clearance service (www.hmrc.gov.uk/cap/clearanceiht.htm) lists various circumstances in which a clearance application will not be accepted. These include:

- requests for tax planning advice, or comments on such advice;

- where HMRC take the view that the arrangements are primarily to gain a tax advantage rather than primarily commercially motivated;

- where there is not considered to be any uncertainty (eg where the point is covered in HMRC's published guidance); or

- in cases where the disposition of property under a will is conditional on the availability of BPR.

HMRC's guidance sets out specific circumstances in which clearances given will not be binding, including (unsurprisingly) if incorrect or incomplete information is given when the clearance application is made. Application is initially by e-mail, but paper confirmation is given, usually very promptly. It seems to be recognised that the availability of BPR can often be, if not wholly uncertain, at least just enough dependent on the facts of each case for practitioners to worry about it. The clearance allows transactions to proceed that might otherwise be stalled over tax worries. Basically, the procedure does exactly what it sets out to achieve. It cannot help where a PET is contemplated because of the limited duration of the clearance letter itself.

15.3   Where no IHT is presently in point, HMRC will not, as a rule, adjudicate on the availability of BPR. They are not resourced to do so.

The same reluctance can make it difficult for executors to know with certainty what assets to appropriate to the trusts of the nil rate band where they are directed by the terms of the will also to transfer assets qualifying for BPR. If residue passes, say, to the surviving spouse exempt, HMRC will adjudicate on BPR only on the second death. If too much value has been transferred to the trust, because BPR turns out not to be available, that is treated by HMRC as a transfer by the residuary beneficiary. HMRC argue that the executors had power only to transfer such value as would be within the nil rate band, so any excess was not a transfer by them and must have been by the surviving spouse.

It is difficult to get around the problem, but Emma Chamberlain has previously suggested that practitioners might try the following:

- A will could be drawn (or could be so varied by deed of variation) so as to include a discretionary trust.

- A provision of the will or variation specifically gives the target asset to a discretionary trust. (The specific gift takes it outside s 39A.)

- Then include a gift of the nil rate band to the discretionary trust, being defined as such sum as would not attract IHT, but for this purpose ignoring the prior gift of the target property.

The result should be that there is IHT at stake that requires an adjudication of the BPR issue, because the mere existence of the gift of the nil rate band makes any other transfer on the same occasion a chargeable one. If the target asset is worth, say, £200,000 before relief the structure will 'top up' the trust to the nil rate band, if that is desired. If BPR is found to be available, the asset can be appointed out to chargeable beneficiaries such as children. If BPR is refused, and if (which could be a big if) a decision can be reached within two years of death, the trustees still have the option of appointing the asset to the spouse in reliance on s 144 so as to avoid the immediate payment of IHT.

15.4 *Agricultural property relief* is available on 'agricultural property' as defined. This means primarily agricultural land or pasture. It also includes:

- woodland and buildings used for the intensive rearing of livestock or fish, but only if the occupation of that woodland or those buildings is ancillary to the occupation of the agricultural land or pasture – see eg *Williams v HMRC* [2005] SSCD 782 (SpC 500); and

- cottages, farm buildings and farmhouses and the land occupied with them, but only if of a character appropriate to the property.

Following the Lands Tribunal decision in *Lloyds TSB Private Banking Plc (personal representative of Rosemary Antrobus deceased) v HMRC* DET/47/2005 ('*Antrobus No 2*'), the distinction between a 'working' and 'lifestyle' farmer may be significant for the purposes of determining the agricultural value of agricultural property (see **15.43**).

Broadly, the relief is 100% for vacant property, or property subject to a lease created or succeeded to on or after 1 September 1995; and 50% for other tenanted property (s 116(2)). The value to which the reduction applies is the value which the property would have if subject to a perpetual covenant prohibiting its use otherwise than as agricultural property. This will typically be less than the open market value, particularly where there is development potential; but even if the land is pasture, it may command a premium as amenity land. Thus, even 100% APR will not often eliminate the entire transfer of value attributable to the agricultural property in question.

LIFETIME TRANSFERS AND CLAWBACK

The general rules

15.5 If a donor has made a lifetime gift, by way of potentially exempt transfer, of business or agricultural property and dies within seven years, there is a risk that the BPR or APR will be clawed back.

This will *not* generally be the case if the transferee retained the original property from the date of the transfer until the date of death or, if he disposed of it during that period and reinvested the net proceeds of sale in replacement business or agricultural property. In the second case, the reinvestment must take place within three years of the sale of the original property. In contrast to the position for capital gains tax roll-over relief, reinvestment during the 12 months before the disposal of the original property is not permitted.

The replacement property provisions require that 'the whole of the consideration' for a disposal must be applied in acquiring replacement business property (s 113B(1)(b)). HMRC accept that professional costs and capital gains tax may be deducted in computing the net proceeds of sale (IHTM25369).

It appears from *Tax Bulletin* (Issue 14, December 1994) that reinvestment into business property when the original property was agricultural property or vice versa is acceptable.

The rules, apparently, do not allow for a second disposal and re-investment although, if the second piece of replacement property were acquired within three years of the original disposal, it would be capable of 'standing in the shoes' of the original property for the purpose of the provisions.

Where a donor falls seriously ill within seven years of making one or more gifts of business or agricultural property, it will be sensible to review what, if anything, has occurred in relation to those earlier gifts. If the property has been disposed of by the donee, he or she may wish to consider the purchase of replacement property in haste since such replacement property must be owned by the donee at the time of the donor's death (s 113B(3)(a)) in order for relief to be available.

A relaxation of the general rule

15.6   A special rule can apply to a failed PET where the original business property consisted of shares or securities. Whilst the normal rule is that clawback of BPR will apply unless the donee retains the asset and it still qualifies for BPR by reference to the donee, see s 113A(3), the second of these requirements is relaxed where the gift was of:

- quoted securities;
- unquoted securities giving control; or
- unquoted shares.

These categories of asset need not still qualify as relevant business property at the time of the donor's death, or the donee's death if earlier (see s 113A(3)(b),

(3A)). The only time that quoted shares qualify for BPR is when they confer control; see s 105(1)(d).

Chargeable transfer or PET?

15.7   If death within seven years is likely, a chargeable transfer may be preferable to a PET: for a failed PET, there is full clawback of the tax relief, and the now chargeable lifetime transfer is taken into account in computing the nil rate band available in the deceased's estate; for a chargeable transfer, business or agricultural property relief is excluded in calculating the 'additional tax payable'; but, for the purposes of cumulation in the death estate, the lifetime chargeable transfer will still carry the benefit of the relief.

The other advantage may be to 'lock in' relief where it is feared that relief may later be lost, for example on political change.

INVESTMENTS

The 'wholly or mainly' test

15.8   Property will not be 'relevant business property' if the business consists wholly or mainly of making or holding investments. This is so whether the gifted asset is a direct interest in the business concerned, or shares in or securities of a company (s 105(3)). However, this will often be a question of fact.

In *Brown's Executors v IRC* [1997] STC (SCD) 277, the Inland Revenue (as it then was) refused BPR on shares on the grounds that, at the date of death, the business consisted wholly or mainly of making investments. The company had been in the nightclub business but had sold this before the shareholder's death. The proceeds were held on a short-term bank deposit pending acquisition of a new business. The executors appealed successfully to the Special Commissioners.

HMRC now appear to accept that, if a company is wholly or mainly trading, the fact that it owns some investments does not prevent the shares from being relevant business property, though this will be a matter of degree. To determine whether the 'wholly or mainly' test is satisfied, it is legitimate to consider:

- turnover;

- profitability;

- the amount of time that the directors and employees devote to each part of the overall business; and

- underlying asset values, ie the amount of capital devoted to each aspect of the enterprise.

HMRC normally interpret 'mainly' as over 50%. Note, however, that the argument that 'extraneous' assets should not prejudice BPR is much weaker in respect of sole traders and partners than companies. This is because the business of a company is a single entity to which all its assets may contribute, whilst that rule does not apply so strongly to unincorporated businesses, which can be divided into enterprises that are 'proper' trades and non-qualifying ventures or assets.

BPR is a 'snapshot' test, in that the eligibility of, say, shares in a private company is tested at the time of the transfer. This may open up some planning opportunities where the shares in a dormant company have been held by the taxpayer for over two years. However, HMRC will closely examine, and deny relief to, any 'business' that is, frankly, dormant, perhaps because the owner was winding down to retirement or the venture had become no more than a hobby. To support the BPR claim the practitioner must be able to produce clear evidence of trading activity. Whilst *Brown's Executors v CIR* [1996] STC (SCD) 277 shows that BPR may be claimed even in respect of a company that had sold its business, the evidence there was strong that the director was looking for a new venture in which to reinvest the company's ready money.

Where the transfer is on death look, therefore, among the papers of the deceased for minutes of meetings, correspondence about the purchase of equipment or premises or stock, or for other evidence that the entrepreneur was taking risks or laying out time, money and effort to promote the business.

See the further discussion of this issue at **15.17** and **15.18**.

Example 15.1 – Maximising BPR

East Anglian Fabricators Limited was formed by Kevin to make components for agricultural buildings. It owns a substantial freehold site in Norfolk including several acres of pasture.

Agrisite Limited was formed as a sister company to keep Kevin's son Jason occupied after he left school. The idea was that Jason would deliver the components to farmers and help with erection of the buildings, but Jason drifted into conveyancing law and moved to London. Agrisite was mothballed. Farming declined and the construction business stalled.

Hindolveston Pastures Limited had similarly been formed to give an opportunity to Carrie, Kevin's daughter. Carrie was to look after the pasture and keep her horses there, if possible making a little money from her 'horsey' friends.

Carrie exploited the land to the full, gradually building small workshops and industrial units which she let very successfully, returning substantial revenue to Fabricators as landlord.

Kevin realised that, in terms of value, Fabricators was no longer really a trading company: Carrie's efforts swamped the construction business in terms of capital value created, revenue and the use of management time. Even the value of the construction side of the business did not qualify for any relief. Meanwhile Jason, made redundant in the 'credit crunch', had come home and wanted work.

Kevin arranged a sale of the construction business and its freehold premises, (excluding the former pasture, now an industrial estate) to Agrisite so that, if trade improved and Agrisite paid off its inter-company loan incurred on the purchase, any new value in Agrisite would qualify immediately for BPR.

Assets of a business; or used in one?

15.9 It may be difficult to identify the assets used in an unincorporated business, particularly that of a sole trader.

Example 15.2 – A business, or excepted assets?

Alex works from home as a veterinary surgeon but also owns and trains dressage ponies and runs a small riding school. Her establishment comprises a former farmhouse, outbuildings, surgery, tack rooms, paddocks and areas where customers can park their trailers and relax whilst waiting to collect their offspring after riding lessons. The house has five bedrooms but only one 'proper' reception room, the other having been invaded by the administrative functions of the business, whilst much of the former kitchen and dairy has been converted to a surgery with associated reception and store for drugs and dressings.

Horses are Alex's life: she has no family, so most of the bedrooms are full of disused 'horsey' artefacts or business records.

The accounts of the business do not show the house as a capital asset but do include all the historical cost of improvements to it and of conversion of the building for business purposes as well as the cost of erecting stables etc over the years. VAT has been reclaimed on all such works. Alex's (obligatory) 4x4 vehicle, her horsebox and trailers are shown as assets of the business. Alex claims a (substantial) proportion of the running cost of the house as business expenses. The house is free of mortgage.

In these circumstances a strong case can be made out that much of the house and all of the outbuildings, paddocks etc are not merely used for the purposes of the business but are assets of it. The fact that the house is not shown on the balance sheet is not in itself conclusive.

This is relevant for several reasons. Relief may be allowed where part (but not the whole) of a building is used for a business under s 112(4). Relief on an interest in a business is at 100% whilst relief on an asset used in a partnership business is at 50% only, so if Alex took on a partner the issue would have to be addressed. The use of a part of a building also has CGT implications, depriving its owner of main residence relief to the extent that it is used exclusively for a business.

For a further examination of whether a building was itself the business, see *Marquess of Hertford v IRC* [2004] SpC 444, discussed at **15.19**.

The business of a landed estate

15.10   In *Farmer and another (executors of Farmer deceased) v IRC* [1999] STC (SCD) 321, the deceased carried on the business of letting properties as well as the business of farming. The profits of the letting business were greater than the farming profits, but the farming assets, admittedly including the farmhouse itself, were (at death) more valuable than the properties used for letting. The Revenue (as it then was) refused BPR, arguing that because the profits of the letting business were greater than those of the farming the business was wholly or mainly one of making investments.

The executors appealed to the Special Commissioners and won. It was held that the nature of the business had to be considered in the round and that no single factor (such as profitability) should be determinative. On the facts, although the lettings were more profitable than the farm, the overall context of the business, the capital employed, the time spent by the employees and consultants and the levels of turnover supported the conclusion that the business consisted mainly of farming.

The issue of mixed usage in the context of a landed estate was revisited in the Upper Tribunal on appeal in *HMRC v Brander* [2010] UKUT 300 (TCC). The facts were somewhat unusual and 'muddied the waters' to a degree. There were two issues in contention: (a) whether or not there was a single 'business' and (b) whether or not that business consisted mainly of holding investments. The activities carried on included in-hand farming and management of commercial woodlands, however there was also substantial letting activity.

644

At the time of his death, the whole of the estate was owned personally by the deceased; however up until the period shortly before his death part of the estate had been held in a trust of which the deceased was the life tenant. Furthermore, farming activities on the estate had, at certain times, been carried on by the deceased in partnership and at other times on his own account. One consequence of this was that different sets of accounts were prepared for different parts of the business, and this practice continued until the death of the deceased.

Notwithstanding the preparation of separate accounts the tribunal accepted that the land was managed as a single business by the deceased. It was perhaps significant that the deceased had adopted a very 'hands-on' approach and the role of the trustees was largely passive. In deciding whether the business was wholly or mainly an investment business, the tribunal reviewed what it considered to be the main factors of relevance, namely:

(i)   overall context;

(ii)   turnover and net profit;

(iii)   time spent; and

(iv)   capital value.

Having done so, the tribunal accepted that the First-tier Tribunal was entitled to conclude that the business was not mainly a business of making or holding investments, and dismissed HMRC's appeal.

The business of making loans

15.11   In *Phillips and others (Executors of Rhoda Phillips Deceased) v HMRC* [2006] SpC 555, shares in a company which made informal, unsecured loans to related family companies were held to be relevant business property, on the basis that the company's business was making loans, and therefore did not consist wholly or mainly of making or holding investments within s 105(3).

The business of developing land

15.12   In *DWC Piercy's Executors v HMRC* [2008] SpC 687, the Tribunal had to consider a property development company that owned land in Islington on which it had built workshops for letting. The executors of a major shareholder claimed BPR, but HMRC denied it on the ground that the company received substantial investment income and its business was therefore mainly making or holding investments.

The executors claimed that the company was still trading: it still held undeveloped land that it wished to develop for housing but had to wait for uncertainty to be resolved concerning proposals for a new railway line. The Commissioner found that the land was still held as trading stock, not as an investment, and allowed the appeal. A land-dealing company will not qualify for BPR if it is a speculative trader or dealer, but all other land-dealing companies that actively develop land or build on land are outside the exclusion. For a company to be wholly or mainly holding investments, the Commissioner held that it must actually have investments: thus holding the land as trading stock was highly relevant here.

The business of letting property

15.13 The Special Commissioners' decisions in *Martin and another (executors of Moore Deceased) v IRC* [1995] STC (SCD) 5 and *Burkinyoung v IRC* [1995] STC (SCD) 29 should be noted. In these cases, the taxpayers' claims for BPR failed. In *Martin*, the business consisted of owning and letting industrial units on three-year leases at fixed rents. The activities included finding tenants, granting and renewing leases, complying with the landlord's covenants under those leases and managing the premises. To the extent that these activities went beyond straightforward investment activities, they were nevertheless held to be incidents of the business of making or holding investments. Thus, BPR was denied. It was the nature of the business that mattered, not the amount of effort that the owner put into it.

A similar decision to *Martin* was reached in *Burkinyoung*, where the deceased had divided a house into four flats and let them, furnished, on assured shorthold tenancies. Although she was actively involved in the control and management of the let properties, these activities were incidents of the landlord-tenant relationship and accordingly part and parcel of making and holding investments.

Two points clearly emerged from the *Martin* and *Burkinyoung* cases. First, no distinction is to be drawn between investments that are actively managed and those that are passively held. Secondly, in the case of property investment, one must distinguish between activities carried on *qua* landlord and activities which are independent of the landlord-tenant relationship. Activities undertaken by the landlord to ensure compliance with his own obligations under the lease, to enforce compliance by the tenant, or to preserve his investment in the property (eg repairs) are in the first category. The second category consists of activities which are independent of the lease and which are charged for separately. Examples might include heating, cleaning and catering. Even if these services are provided separately, the charges are likely to be insignificant compared to the rental income and thus it will be rare for BPR to be available.

The principles established in *Martin* and *Burkinyoung* were applied in *Clark and another (executors of Clark deceased v HMRC* [2005] STC (SCD) 823, where a company received rents from properties which it owned (ie investment income), plus management charges in respect of a number of dwellings owned by family members (ie non-investment income). Looking at the case in the round, the Special Commissioner held that the company's business consisted mainly of holding investments.

Caravan park businesses; and holiday lettings

15.14   In *Hall (deceased) v IRC* [1997] STC (SCD) 126, the business consisted of a caravan park of 18 acres for 100 caravans and 11 wooden chalets. These were let and various services and facilities were made available to the tenants, eg water, electricity, telephone, refuse disposal and lavatories. Nevertheless, the Special Commissioners denied BPR on the grounds that the business was substantially one of investment, ie the receipt of rents. A similar approach was adopted in another caravan park case, *Powell v IRC* [1997] STC (SCD) 181.

In contrast, in *Furness v IRC* [1999] STC (SCD) 232, the business of running a caravan park was held not to consist wholly or mainly of making or holding investments within s 105(3). However, the business was unusual because over 50% of the net profits came from caravan sales and charges for caravan rallies held at the site. The amount of work carried out on the park by the deceased and his employees was also considered by the Special Commissioner.

In *Weston (executor of Weston deceased) v IRC* [2000] STC 1064, the Special Commissioners held that shares in a company that ran a caravan site were not relevant business property. This decision was upheld by the High Court. The business included buying and selling caravans, buying and selling caravans for commission on behalf of the owners, and granting the right to pitch caravans in return for pitch fees. The question was ultimately one of fact and the Special Commissioner had applied the right test. The 'business' consisted substantially in the ownership and letting of caravan park pitches, ie making or holding investments. Other activities such as selling caravans were subordinate activities.

The Court of Appeal decision in *IRC v George and another (executors of Stedman, deceased)* [2004] STC 147 marked an important victory for the taxpayer. Looked at in the round (à la *Farmer*), this caravan business was clearly a trade and not merely the holding of investments. Lord Justice Carnwarth decided that it was difficult to see why an active family business such as that in this case should be excluded from BPR under s 105(3) merely because a necessary component of its profit-making activity was the use of land. The message for the practitioner is clear: marshal your facts and evidence with great care. In this case, at the time of the death in 1998, there were 167 mobile homes, owned by the occupiers, on the residential park. The company charged a fee to the owners for the use of the site; it also sold caravans, and charged a commission on the sale of caravans by the owners. A profit was also made on the supply of gas, water and electricity to residents.

HMRC guidance (at IHTM25279) provides a useful insight into its approach following the decision in *George*, and is therefore worth repeating here:

'The judgment in *George* is helpful in clarifying what is to be regarded as either investment or non-investment activity. It makes clear that the provision of services under the terms of a pitch agreement is a non-investment activity. This means that in cases where a large part of the business's activities (measured in both time and money) consists of providing services to residents, we would be more likely to consider that the business was neither wholly or mainly investment in nature. However, we need to be satisfied that the figures for pitch fees, for instance, are not artificially depressed in the accounts in favour of inflated figures for wages or other non-investment expenses.

The judgment in *George* also recognises that the time and money spent on maintaining amenity areas is in part designed to maintain the value of the owner's investment. It follows that the taxpayers are entitled to return a reduced level of investment income by offsetting against it part of the maintenance costs. As this could lead to the net investment income being, proportionally, a smaller part of the overall income of the business we might well conclude in a particular case that the business was neither wholly or mainly one of holding investments. On the other hand, we would also need to take into account the time spent by the owner and/or his employees in the maintenance work. When taken together with other work carried out in the business, the evidence might lead us to conclude that the majority of work done is involved in maintaining the value of the owner's investment. If so, then we would seek to deny the claim under Section 105(3) IHTA 1984.

The judgment in *George* also suggests that the holding of land as an investment is separate and distinct from the service element of the business. Finally, when looking at the facts "in the round", trading figures are only a part of the overall picture.

When dealing with a claim for business relief on a caravan park, you will need to obtain detailed business accounts, including breakdowns of both the income and expenditure between the investment and non-investment elements of the business. In addition, you should ask the taxpayers to state precisely what services were provided to the park residents and how long was spent by the deceased (as park owner) and his partners and/or employees providing those services.

After obtaining all the information, you should refer the case to Technical Group.'

Any practitioner dealing with this issue would do well to visit the park site. Generally, such parks may offer space in one or more of the following categories:

- chalets;

- mobile homes;

- pitches for touring caravans that are taken for the season; and

- pitches for 'pull-on tourers', ie cars with towed caravans which visit just for a few days and (increasingly nowadays) campervans passing through.

Of all these categories, it is the last that makes the most work for the site owner. A pitch may be taken for only one night; people arrive late, hoping nevertheless that the site shop will still be open and will have fresh (local) produce left. It must sadly also be said that a slightly less careful attitude to the site may be exhibited by someone who is moving on than by a more permanent resident! Undoubtedly, the letting of a pitch for a whole season is attractive, both in providing reliable cash flow and in securing goodwill for eventual sale of the site. To enhance his claim to BPR, however, the cases show that a site owner should cherish his 'pull on' customers and put up with the work they cause him.

See **15.73** regarding holiday lettings.

The business of producing a crop of grass

15.15 Land may qualify for both APR and BPR but APR is restricted, as noted at **15.4**, to the agricultural value of the land. That was the main issue in *McCall and another (Personal representatives of McLean Deceased) v HMRC* [2009] NICA 12. A parcel of land had an agricultural value, at the date of death, of £165,000 but a market value of £5,800,000 so it was important for the executors to show that there was, at the date of death, a business qualifying for BPR rather than an agricultural interest.

The deceased did not farm the land herself, but let it to local farmers under conacre (or agistment, to be more precise) agreements. The Revenue issued a determination charging IHT on the land, and her personal representatives appealed on the basis that BPR was due. The evidence suggested that the son-in-law of the deceased had spent time looking after the land. It lay on the edge of a town in Northern Ireland and its boundaries were occasionally challenged. For example, a van was driven into the fields and abandoned, resulting in a claim under the Criminal Damage (Compensation) (Northern Ireland) Order 1988 (SI 1988/793).

The work done was:

- walking the land;
- repairing the fencing;
- cleaning drinking troughs;
- clearing the drainage systems of mud and leaves; and
- cutting and spraying weeds.

For these purposes, the son-in-law had a tractor and reaper and a knapsack sprayer. He probably worked no more than 100 hours per year. Some work was contracted out. The grazier fertilised the fields.

Before the Special Commissioner [2008] SpC 678, it was held that the son-in-law's activity of tending the land:

'… was, just, enough to constitute a business … The letting of the land was earnestly pursued, the work tending the land was modest but serious, the letting and tending were pursued with some continuity, the income was not insubstantial, the letting was conducted in a regular manner although the use of [the son-in-law's] time was something which is not a feature of an ordinary business, and the letting of land for profit is a common business. To my mind the Lord Fisher indicia point towards a business.'

A business may be owned even where the sole trader has, as was the case here, lost her mental faculties. The business was more than just the ownership of the land and receipt of its income. The deceased, notwithstanding disability, owned the business constituted by the activities of her son-in-law and the letting of the land. However, the most material point for our present examination was that the Court of Appeal upheld the conclusion of the Special Commissioner that the business consisted wholly or mainly of holding investments, within *s* 105(3). Girvan J stated:

'The agisting farmer had exclusive rights of grazing; he was entitled to exclude other graziers including the deceased; the deceased could not use the land for any purpose that interfered with the grazing and the letting for grazing was the way in which the deceased decided that the grasslands could be used and exploited as uncultivated grassland short of the creation of a lease. The deceased's business consisted of earning a return from grassland whose real and effective value lay in its grazing potential. The activities which were regarded as just sufficient to lead to the lettings of the land being regarded as a business were all related to enabling that potential value to be released.'

Here the deceased was making the land available, not to make a living on it, but from it; the management activities related to letting the land; it was unlike 'hotel accommodation for cattle' as argued by the taxpayer Thus, although the letting of land does not necessarily constitute an investment business, the availability of BPR is likely to depend on the nature and extent of other services also provided.

The decision has caused considerable concern in Northern Ireland, because so much land there is held on the terms that were in point in the case. However, nothing in the case threatens APR on such land, though (see below) the availability of APR on related dwellings is affected.

GROUPS OF COMPANIES

15.16   Groups of companies raise special issues which require the provisions dealing with investment businesses to be adapted. Without special provision, there would be no possibility of BPR for a shareholder in a holding company that held the entire share capital of a trading subsidiary but which itself carried on no business.

This result is initially avoided by s 105(4)(b). This applies to a company whose business consists wholly or mainly in being a holding company, provided that at least one of its subsidiaries carries on a permitted trade. 'Permitted trade' in this context is the writers' shorthand for a business which is not excluded from relief by s 105(3) because of consisting wholly or mainly of dealing in securities, stocks or shares, land or buildings or making or holding investments.

Section 105(4)(b) disapplies s 105(3) in the case of such a holding company. However, s 111 lays down further conditions that are designed to ensure that one or more investment subsidiaries do not effectively benefit from relief purely because a single sister company carries on a permitted trade. On the other hand, the section seeks to preserve relief where the investment subsidiary holds property which is let to its trading sister in circumstances where, had both the property and the trade been held in a single company, relief would have been available. Where relief is not preserved for an investment subsidiary, its value falls to be excluded from the value available for relief.

There is no definition of a group for these purposes, but it has been held by a Special Commissioner that companies do not form a group merely on account of having some or all of their shareholders in common: *Grimwood-Taylor and another (executors of Mallender deceased) v IRC* [2000] STC (SCD) 39. Thus, a company that is merely associated with a group of trading companies by virtue of common shareholders falls to be considered for relief in its own right and not as part of the group.

These provisions mean that group structures and the way in which property is held within those groups require careful consideration. Commonly, but by no means always, the shareholding being transferred, whether on death or otherwise, is in the holding company. Remember the restriction that relief is lost on sale: if the holding is in a subsidiary that may soon be sold for commercial reasons, do not waste time on BPR, which will be lost on sale (except where the replacement provisions apply).

Example 15.3 – Planning with groups

Assume that a holding company owns various trading subsidiaries which operate in valuable buildings. It is desired to insulate these buildings from trade creditors by holding them outside the trading companies.

Assume that the group also owns various buildings which it lets to third parties not in the group. The value of the buildings let to the third parties exceeds the value of the buildings used by the companies.

(1) A single property-holding subsidiary

If all the buildings are placed in one property-holding subsidiary, no relief at all will be available on the value of the properties. The property-holding subsidiary's business does not satisfy s 111(b). It does not consist wholly or mainly of holding land or buildings wholly or mainly occupied by members of the group for permitted trades because the value of the buildings let to third parties exceeds the value of the buildings used by the group members. Thus, the whole value of the property-holding subsidiary is excluded from relief.

(2) Two separate property-holding subsidiaries

This is better: if the properties used by other group members are held in one subsidiary and those let to third parties in a second subsidiary, the first subsidiary will qualify for relief and the second subsidiary will not (s 111(b)).

(3) Properties held by parent company

This could be better still: it may be that relief for all the properties can be obtained if they are held by the parent company. This depends on whether, despite its property interests, its business consists wholly or mainly in being a holding company. This will depend on whether its interest in its trading subsidiaries significantly exceeds its interest in the properties.

Before this strategy is even considered, it should be tested to see whether, by reference to turnover, profitability, the use of management time or underlying asset values, this is a trading group. Even then, there is a risk that the trading activities will diminish or the property values increase so that the 'wholly or mainly' test applied to the holding company ceases to be met. This is a high-risk strategy because it could result in loss of relief on the value of the entire group. The test is the 'business' not the trade: thus arguments as to excepted assets are not in point, only the overall nature of the group is relevant.

(4) Scattering the properties

This suggestion is a combination of (1), (2) and (3) above. The holding company has three subsidiaries. The first is the trading company. The second owns the properties used by the trading company. The third owns some of the properties let to third parties. The remaining properties let to third parties are distributed between the holding company and the second subsidiary. They can be distributed in this way as long as:

- the properties held by the holding company do not prevent its business from consisting wholly or mainly in being a holding company. This is the most important requirement because if it is breached there is a risk that relief on the value of the whole group will be lost (see (3) above). A very large margin of error should be allowed for, particularly where some properties have development value that could materially change the overall values later;

- the properties owned by the second subsidiary consist wholly or mainly of properties occupied by the trading subsidiary for the purpose of its business. A slightly smaller margin of error is required here for two reasons. First, the value of the permitted properties is unlikely to fluctuate dramatically as against the value of the properties let to third parties, unless there are special circumstances. This contrasts with the potential for relative changes in the values of trading subsidiaries and properties, which is a risk in case (3) above, particularly because in (3) the value of the permitted properties is aggregated with the value of the properties let to third parties in applying the wholly or mainly test. Here, that is not so. The second reason that there is a reduced risk in this case is that the worst-case scenario is losing relief on the whole of the second subsidiary. That would have been the case in any event had option (1) been adopted. It should not affect relief for the trading subsidiary.

The third subsidiary holds those properties let to third parties that cannot safely be held by the holding company or the second subsidiary. It is accepted that relief will not be available on the value of the third subsidiary on account of s 111. In that sense, this strategy is equivalent to option (2). However, the value of the third subsidiary on which relief is lost will be diminished by those properties that have been scattered into the holding company and second subsidiary.

The group structure may be deeper than a single holding company with one or more direct subsidiaries. More than one layer of holding company and subsidiary may exist. The legislation provides for the availability of BPR for a group parent company holding shares in a qualifying trading company (s 105(4)(b)), and also for a second layer of holding company by effectively looking through the intermediate company (s 111).

It was initially thought that HMRC may be prepared to accept that a group structure with up to six levels of holding company potentially falls within the BPR regime, subject to meeting the other general criteria regarding qualifying activities and not having excepted assets (see *Taxation*, 1 October 2008). However, it is understood that in subsequent correspondence with the ICAEW, HMRC indicated that there is no limit to the number of intermediate holding companies, but that such companies cannot be ignored or looked through. In practice, HMRC will look at the group as a whole to determine whether it is mainly investment or non-investment in nature, before considering each individual company separately within the group structure to determine whether any relief restriction is necessary in accordance with s 111.

EXCEPTED ASSETS

15.17   Even where the transfer is essentially of relevant business property, the amount of relief may be restricted if the value of that property is partly attributable to excepted assets. These are assets which had neither been used wholly or mainly for the purposes of the business during the two years preceding the transfer, nor were required at the time of the transfer for future use for those purposes.

If the asset was used wholly or mainly for the personal benefit of the transferor or a person connected with him, it is deemed by IHTA 1984, s 112(6) not to have been used wholly or mainly for the purposes of the business concerned.

It should be noted that investment assets will not necessarily be excepted assets. A trading company that includes a business of making or holding investments may qualify for BPR, provided that the investment business does not predominate. A 'wholly or mainly' test applies for these purposes (IHTA 1984, s 105(3)). HMRC accept that a 'hybrid' company that is mainly trading will not be subject to the excepted assets rule in respect of assets used in the investment element of the business (see SVM111220).

However, HMRC consider that a 'business' involves a degree of activity, as noted at **15.8**. For example, the holding of cash normally requires no effort and involves no activity. In *Jowett v O'Neill and Brennan Construction Ltd* [1998] STC 482 (a corporation tax case), the holding of cash on interest-bearing deposit was held not to constitute a business. On the other hand, a holding of investment shares or securities may constitute a business, depending on the size of holdings, the degree of active management and the reason for acquiring them.

Similar principles apply in the context of investment properties. However, in *Salaried Persons Postal Loans Ltd v HMRC* [2005] SpC 504 (another corporation tax case), the company's only source of income was rental income from former business premises. HMRC contended that the company was carrying on a business, but the Special Commissioner allowed the taxpayer's appeal. It was relevant to consider why the company received income and what it actually did to receive the income. The company had merely continued letting its old trading premises, which it had done for nearly 30 years.

15.18   The second condition for the excepted assets restriction to apply (ie that the assets are not required for present or future business use) was the subject of a decision by the Special Commissioners in *Barclays Bank Trust Co Ltd v IRC* [1998] STC (SCD) 125. At the date of the deceased's death, the company held £450,000 in cash. The Inland Revenue (as they then were) accepted that £150,000 of cash was required by the company at that time, but maintained that the remaining £300,000 was an excepted asset. (It should be noted that the undisputed amount of cash represented about 26% of turnover. HMRC recognise that a seasonal business will, at times, hold substantial cash; and that in the downturn at the time of writing, business owners may be more cautious than usual and keep more money in reserve, not least because the banks may refuse to provide working capital, having little of their own.)

The Special Commissioner upheld the view of the Inland Revenue, rejecting the argument that the cash was required for the future purposes of the business. The possibility of using the money in two, three or seven years, should a suitable opportunity arise, was not sufficient. To be required for future use, there must be some imperative that the money will be required for a given project or for some palpable business purpose. For example, money will be required for the future purposes of the business where a company had negotiated the purchase of a business asset and there was a realistic possibility at the time of the transfer that it would buy the business asset with the money.

Contrast the case of *Brown's Executors v IRC* [1997] STC (SCD) 277 (discussed at **15.8**), where the cash proceeds of the sale of a night-club were held on short-term deposit with a bank pending acquisition of a new business. It was argued by the Inland Revenue that the company's business consisted wholly or mainly of making investments and, accordingly, BPR should be denied under s 105(3); but the Special Commissioner was satisfied on the evidence that, had Mr Brown found a suitable nightclub, he would have bought it. Although the issue in that case was a different one, there is clearly no point ensuring that an asset is not an excepted asset if it is not relevant business property in the first place. The later decision in *DWC Piercy's Executors v HMRC* (noted at **15.12**) is consistent with this principle.

15.19   It may be necessary to consider the nature of the asset in determining its value for BPR purposes (s 110(b)). In addition, in the case of land and buildings the excepted assets rule also contains an apportionment provision where part of the asset is not used mainly in the business (s 112(4)). This will commonly apply in relation to a mixed-use building such as a farmhouse.

In *Marquess of Hertford v IRC* [2005] STC (SCD) 177, a stately home (Ragley Hall) was operated as a business. 78% of Ragley Hall was open to the public, and 22% was occupied as a private residence. The Special Commissioner held that the asset attracting BPR was Ragley Hall in its entirety, not just 78% of it. The excepted asset rule in s 112 does not allow for apportionment if a single asset is used mainly for business purposes.

Unfortunately, HMRC appear to view this case as an 'unusual' one, and consider that the judgment cannot be applied to other BPR claims on buildings. This is on the basis that '… it was the nature of the business in this particular case and the part that the physical structure of the hall played in that business that most influenced the Commissioner's decision' (see IHTM25342).

PARTNERSHIP SHARE

Retirement of a business partner

15.20   A partner's share in a partnership may be relevant business property. On retirement, the partner's capital account is converted into a debt owed to him by the partnership. Neither the debt, nor any cash ultimately paid in satisfaction of it, is relevant business property. To preserve BPR, it may be wise to delay retirement, possibly taking on a partner to perform the bulk of the work and retaining only a small share.

Any land, building, machinery or plant which is used for the purposes of the partnership's business will lose the 50% relief on the partner's retirement. In some circumstances, this problem could be avoided by giving away the capital account before the partner retires.

This was illustrated in *Beckman v IRC* [2000] STC (SCD) 59. The deceased ('H') and her daughter ('B') had been business partners until H's retirement in 1993. H's financial interest in the business immediately before her retirement, represented by her capital account, remained the same after her retirement. However, it was held by a Special Commissioner that her legal interest was radically changed on her retirement. Prior to that, she had all the rights of management conferred by the Partnership Act 1890 and all the liabilities of a partner. After retirement, in the absence of any agreement to the contrary, she became simply a creditor of B. Accordingly, on H's death four years later,

BPR on the sum due to her was denied. For the purposes of IHTA 1984, s 105, H's interest in the business ceased when she retired from the partnership that carried on that business.

This unsatisfactory outcome could have been avoided if H had made a gift of the capital prior to retiring, or had remained a partner with a reduced share.

Death of a partner and s 142

15.21   Consider taking the following steps, using an instrument of variation under s 142, to ensure that BPR is not lost on the death of a partner.

Example 15.4 – BPR and instruments of variation

Husband ('H') trades in partnership with his daughter and has both a loan on capital account and separate capital in the partnership. H dies before his wife ('W') and, by his will, leaves her both the loan account and his capital.

In relation to W's estate, no BPR will be available on either asset: the loan account attracts no BPR anyway and W is not a partner, so by reference to her even the capital is only an investment. W effects a variation under s 142, whereby she retains the loan account (which is sheltered by the spouse exemption) but the capital is left by H to the daughter.

BPR will be available on H's death and again in relation to the daughter's estate after two years.

Limited liability partnerships

15.22   In relation to a limited liability partnership (LLP) under the Limited Liability Partnerships Act 2000, the LLP is not to be treated as owned by the individual partners. For IHT (including BPR and APR) purposes, LLP property is treated as that of its members. In addition, the LLP business is treated as carried on by the members (s 267A). There will be no change in the treatment of assets held outside, but used in, the partnership; nor will incorporation into an LLP be regarded as an interruption for these reliefs.

HMRC distinguish between LLPs and other partnerships on the basis that an LLP interest is deemed to be an interest in every asset of the partnership, whereas an interest in a 'traditional' partnership is a 'chose in action'. However, when considering if an LLP is an investment business, HMRC will look at the nature of the LLP's business, rather than the nature of the LLP's assets. For example, if an LLP invests in unquoted shares in a trading company, HMRC consider that BPR is not available on an interest in the LLP, on the basis that the LLP's business is investment in nature, notwithstanding that the underlying assets constitute business property (IHTM25094).

LLPs became available from 6 April 2001. As to the Revenue's views on the tax treatment of LLPs generally, see *Tax Bulletin 50* (December 2000). There is a difference between loans to, and interests in, an LLP; see, for example, the SORP 'Accounting by Limited Liability Partnerships'. Thus, BPR will be available only on the capital (representing a share in the net assets of the business), but probably not on any loans (as a liability of the business, as opposed to an interest in it), in line with the rule in *Beckman v IRC* [2000] STC (SCD) 59.

OWNERSHIP ISSUES

Minimum period of ownership

15.23   Property is not relevant business property unless it was owned by the transferor for two years before the transfer. This is the basic requirement imposed by s 106. It is subject to the provisions of ss 107–109, which deal with replacement property, acquisitions on death and successive transfers respectively.

Enhancement expenditure will immediately qualify for relief provided the asset that has been enhanced has been owned for the requisite period. For example, if a business owner incurs expenditure refurbishing his business premises (which he has owned for more than two years), thus enhancing the value of those premises, he is not required to wait for two years before the expenditure qualifies for relief.

If a business tenant buys in the reversion to his lease, the reversion will merge with the leasehold title ('enhancing' the leasehold interest). By extension of the principle enunciated above, the reversion will not need to be owned for two years to qualify for relief, provided the leasehold interest had been owned for at least two years.

Spouses

15.24   An exception to the minimum period of ownership requirement applies to a transferor who acquired the property on the death of his spouse. Section 108(b) deems the transferor to have owned the property for the period of his spouse's ownership in addition to his own period of ownership. If the aggregate is equal to or greater than two years then the test is satisfied.

This aggregation only applies to periods of ownership falling either side of a transfer on the death of the first spouse. It does not apply if the first spouse made a lifetime gift.

Example 15.5 – BPR and spouse transfers

Wife ('W') acquired the entire issued share capital of Widgets Ltd on 1 January 2009. On 1 January 2011, W made a lifetime gift to her husband ('H') of 40% of her shareholding in Widgets Ltd. On 1 July 2011, W died, leaving her remaining 60% shareholding in Widgets Ltd to H.

On 1 July 2012, H wished to transfer all his shares in Widgets Ltd into a discretionary trust with the benefit of BPR.

H satisfied at that date the minimum period of ownership in relation to the 60% shareholding that he inherited on W's death. In relation to those shares, s 108(b) permitted him to aggregate his period of ownership (one year) with W's period of ownership (two and a half years), giving a total of three and a half years.

However, H did not satisfy the minimum period of ownership in relation to the 40% shareholding which was given to him by W during her life. Because the transfer to him was not on death, H could not aggregate his period of ownership with W's. His period of ownership alone was only a year and a half. He should retain these shares until at least 1 January 2013.

Successions

15.25   A legatee is deemed to have owned the assets from the date of death (s 108(a)).

Where the legacy was from his spouse (or civil partner), the spouse's period of ownership is also deemed to be his (s 108(b)).

If the legatee acquired business property from a person (whether his spouse or not) who satisfied the minimum period of ownership requirement, that requirement is effectively waived on a subsequent transfer by the legatee, as will be seen in the next paragraph.

Successive transfers

15.26   Where there are two successive transfers, and the earlier transferor satisfied the ownership requirements, these requirements are waived for the transferee subject to certain conditions (s 109).

The most significant condition is that at least one of the transfers was on death. It does not matter whether this was the earlier transfer or the subsequent one.

- If A (qualifying for BPR in all respects including minimum period of ownership) leaves his shares to B on death, then B can qualify for BPR on a transfer, even if it occurs less than two years after A's death. Because the transfer by A to B ('the earlier transfer') was on A's death, the transfer by B ('the subsequent transfer') can be either a lifetime or a death transfer and still benefit from s 109.

- If C (again, qualifying in all respects) makes a lifetime gift of his shares to D, D will qualify for BPR on a transfer on his death even if that is within two years of the gift. Because the transfer by C to D ('the earlier transfer') was a lifetime transfer, the transfer by D ('the subsequent transfer') will only benefit from s 109 if it is on D's death. If D wishes to make a lifetime transfer which qualifies for BPR he will need to build up his own period of ownership.

In both of the examples just given, it is irrelevant whether A and B or C and D are spouses, because A and C had each owned the shares for the required period. The special treatment given to spouses would only be relevant if (i) the transferor had not satisfied the minimum period, and (ii) the earlier transfer was on death.

Revisiting the example of A and B, and supposing this time that A had owned the shares for one year only and A was married to B, B could benefit from BPR on a subsequent transfer by holding the shares until a year after A's death. This is by virtue of s 108. Section 108 would have no application if C and D were spouses and C had only held the shares for one year before the gift. This is because the gift by C to D was a lifetime gift and s 108 has no application to lifetime gifts.

Replacements

15.27 The minimum period of ownership requirement will be satisfied if the business property, together with other business property that it directly or indirectly replaced, had been owned by the transferor for a total of two of the five years preceding the transfer (s 107).

If this section is used to satisfy the period of ownership, then there is a limit on the relief. It is limited to the relief that would have been available if the replacement had not been made. In other words, it is limited to the value of the earliest property relied on. This limit does not apply to changes in value resulting from the formation, alteration or dissolution of a partnership, nor from the acquisition of a business by a company controlled by the former owner of the business.

In the Scottish case of *Brander (Representative of Earl of Balfour deceased) v HMRC* [2010] UKUT 300 (TCC), the Earl of Balfour entered into a farming partnership with his nephew in November 2002. In June 2003, he died. HMRC considered that BPR was not due, and the Earl's personal representative appealed. Two issues arose: whether the requirements of *s 107* as to replacement property were satisfied (they were); and whether the business failed the 'wholly or mainly' test of s 105(3). It was held that the lowland landed estate in question fully satisfied the tests for BPR: in particular the late Earl, in managing the tenancies of estate cottages, had selected tenants who could be of service to the estate rather than always going for the highest available rent, so the running of residential property was integrated into the overall business purpose of managing the estate. The decision of the First-tier Tribunal was upheld by the Upper Tribunal on appeal.

Under TCGA 1992, ss 126–136, an original shareholding and a new holding arising from a reorganisation of share capital, a reconstruction or an amalgamation, may be treated as a single asset for capital gains tax purposes. Where those provisions are applied for capital gains tax, and where the new holding consists of unquoted shares, the period of ownership of the new holding for BPR is extended to include the period of ownership of the original holding. However, care should be taken to ensure that the relevant documentation properly records and reflects the reorganisation that has taken place (see **15.40**).

Residuary estates

15.28 A legatee or transferee whose minimum period of ownership requirement has been waived or reduced by ss 108 or 109 must nevertheless hold the property as business (or agricultural) property if he is to get either relief on any transfer that he himself makes. It has been suggested that this might be hindered if the legatee dies or makes a gift before the administration of the estate is complete.

This argument is probably unsustainable in view of s 91 ('Administration period').

Nevertheless, to err on the side of caution, it might be worth vesting the business or agricultural assets in the surviving spouse as soon as possible after the first spouse's death. Alternatively, a deed of variation could specifically vest the assets in the surviving spouse. Such steps must of course only be taken after careful consideration of the solvency of the estate, the potential IHT payable and the assets available for other legatees.

MINORITY SHAREHOLDER – NO RELIEF ON 'MERE ASSETS'

15.29 Where a controlling shareholder owns land or buildings, machinery or plant used by the company to which 50% BPR accrues under s 105(1)(d), that shareholder should consider making a gift of the asset in question before losing control. As a minority shareholder, the 50% relief on those other assets will not apply.

In the context of 'control', see **15.34**.

Consider the IHT advantage of the company owning the assets, thereby bringing them within the net of the 100% relief. Of course, the implications of this action for other taxes (eg CGT and SDLT) must be carefully considered beforehand, and there may be relevant non-tax factors to consider as well.

Example 15.6 – BPR and the effect of gifts

John has for many years owned the land from which his engineering company trades. He has owned 60% of the shares for ten years. His daughters Rachel and Emma hold 20% each. John wants to retire and to pass the business to Rachel and Emma.

If John transfers the shares first, that gift will attract BPR, but there will be no relief on the later conveyance of the land.

If John transfers the land first, 50% relief will initially be available on that gift, subject as below. John can then transfer the shares, with 100% relief. The daughters keep both land and shares.

A problem will arise if John dies within seven years. The clawback rules work by positing a notional transfer of the relevant asset by the donee, testing it for BPR in relation to that person (except for the two-year ownership requirement).

If, as would be usual, John gives his daughters equal shareholdings, neither of them controls the company, so by reference to them the land qualifies for no BPR and the 50% relief previously given will be clawed back even though the daughters 'have done nothing wrong' within the spirit of the relief. This seems most unfair, but follows from s 113A(3)(b).

It would have been better not to make the gifts in the first place: the assets would have qualified for BPR at John's death (though the land might have increased in value, augmenting the IHT charge on the half of its value not sheltered by BPR).

RELEVANT BUSINESS PROPERTY

15.30   To be 'relevant business property', assets must fall within one of the six categories listed in s 105(1). Those within the first three categories, s 105(1) (a), (b) and (bb), potentially qualify for 100% relief.

Those within the next three categories, s 105(1)(cc), (d) and (e), can only qualify for 50% relief.

However, all this should be read in the light of the discussion, at **15.41**, of the *Nelson Dance* case.

Assets qualifying for 100% relief

A business or interest in a business (s 105(1)(a))

15.31   The term 'interest' is not defined, but is likely to mean a proprietary share. Thus, a share in a partnership could potentially qualify for relief under this heading, as could a business run by a sole proprietor.

In the context of partnership freehold and leasehold property, HMRC guidance states (IHTM25104): 'This is a very common item in partnership balance sheets and its inclusion almost certainly means that it is property which belongs to the partnership.'

Nevertheless, it is important to retain evidence (eg a partnership deed) to demonstrate that the land is held as partnership property forming part of a business interest qualifying for 100% BPR. Otherwise, the scope for claiming relief on the land and buildings is restricted (see **15.36**).

There is no limit on the size of the interest or the degree of control held by its owner. The 100% relief applies to Lloyd's special reserves (see also **15.38**).

Unquoted securities giving the transferor control (s 105(1)(b))

15.32   The securities must be unquoted and must give the transferor control of the company, either alone or together with other unquoted securities and any unquoted shares.

Although the transferor must have control of the company immediately before the transfer, the gift need not be of a controlling interest. As to 'control' generally, see **15.34**.

Unquoted shares (s 105(1)(c))

15.33   Transfers of unquoted shares can obtain 100% relief, whatever the size of the transferor's holding.

Note the following:

- The shareholding can be entirely passive. There is no requirement that the shareholder be actively engaged in the business of the company. However, the business of the company itself must not be wholly, or mainly, an investment business (see **15.8**).

- The shareholders need not have voting powers on all questions affecting the company as a whole in order to be eligible for BPR.

- The Alternative Investment Market (AIM) was substituted for the Unlisted Securities Market (USM) from June 1995. The Treasury decided that AIM issues should qualify for all unquoted security tax reliefs, including BPR.

Other reliefs in respect of unquoted shares include: income tax relief on losses on shares subscribed for (ITA 2007, Pt 4, Ch 6); capital gains tax hold-over relief for gifts of business assets (TCGA 1992, s 165); Enterprise Investment Scheme exemption for capital gains tax purposes under TCGA 1992, s 150A(2), or deferral relief – but beware, the shares must be 'eligible shares' (ie generally new ordinary shares) in order to qualify for the relief – see TCGA 1992, Sch 5B, paras 1(2), 19 and ITA 2007, s 173(2); and venture capital trusts (TCGA 1992, s 151A).

Assets qualifying for 50% relief

Quoted shares or securities giving the transferor control (s 105(1)(cc))

15.34   Controlling holdings in fully quoted trading companies or groups qualify for 50% relief, but note that there is no relief for a minority holding in a quoted company.

'Control' is defined by IHTA 1984, s 269, broadly in terms of the exercise of a majority of voting power on all matters affecting the company as a whole. In *Walding and others (Walding's Executors) v CIR* [1996] STC 13, Mrs Walding held 45 out of 100 shares in a company on her death. Her executors claimed that the deceased had control of the company for BPR purposes, on the basis that 24 shares were in the name of her four-year-old grandson, but the court dismissed the executors' appeal against the Revenue's refusal of a BPR claim on factory units owned by the deceased and occupied by the company.

However, a shareholder with a 50% shareholding and a casting vote has control for these purposes. *CIR v BW Noble* KB 1926, 12 TC 911 is authority for this proposition, which was subsequently confirmed by the Special Commissioner's decision in *Walker's Executors v IRC* [2001] SpC 275.

It should be noted that the related property legislation (s 161) applies for the purposes of determining control (s 269(2)). This provision can be helpful if, for example, spouses or civil partners each hold shares in the company which are not controlling holdings in isolation, but are deemed to give control as related property. This situation will be prevalent in unquoted companies in particular (see **15.32** and **15.35**).

Assets owned by a partner and used in the partnership, or owned by a controlling shareholder and used in the company (s 105(1)(d))

15.35   The following points should be borne in mind:

- The assets must be land, buildings, machinery or plant. Otherwise, there is no prospect of relief.

- The relief is only available for as long as the transferor remains a partner in the partnership, or retains control of the company (as already noted).

- The assets must be used for the purposes of a business carried on by the company or partnership.

- The transferor's shareholding or other interest in the business must itself be relevant business property in order for the assets to qualify. This means that the business must amount to a permitted trade. In other words, it must not consist wholly or mainly of dealing in securities, stocks or shares, land or buildings, or making or holding investments.

If the assets are used for the business of a company which is wholly owned by the transferor, there is a clear IHT advantage in arranging for the company itself to own the assets. Their value reflected in the shares can then qualify for 100% rather than 50% relief.

Similarly, there will often be IHT advantages in the partnership rather than the individual partner owning the assets, although this will only be a sensible option where the particular partner's share is a significant one.

15.36   Transferring assets to the company or partnership is complicated by a number of issues:

- The potential dilution of ownership and the risk of an IHT charge on the transfer. The transfer into a company is not a PET and may be charged by virtue of s 3A(1), unless it can be shown that the estate of the transferor has not been diminished or that the transferor had no gratuitous intent and the transaction was one that might have been entered into by parties at arm's length.

- The capital gains tax consequences of a transfer into a company, particularly the potential gain on transfer and the fact that companies are still eligible for indexation allowance.

- The stamp duty land tax implications, such as on transfers of land and buildings to a connected company (FA 2003, s 53).

Settled property in which the transferor had an interest in possession and which was used for the purposes of the transferor's business (s 105(1)(e))

15.37 This provision will rarely apply, particularly following the IHT changes to trusts introduced by FA 2006. If the transferor has a qualifying interest in possession in the assets used for his business, those assets will normally be treated as part of his business and will be entitled to 100% relief (see *Fetherstonaugh v IRC* [1984] STC 261).

The *Fetherstonaugh* case was successfully relied upon in *HMRC v Brander* [2010] UKUT 300 (TCC), in terms of satisfying the two-year ownership test for BPR purposes in s 106 (see **15.10**).

VALUE OF BUSINESS

Liabilities

15.38 The value of a business for the purposes of BPR is determined by s 110. It is the value of the assets used in the business, less the aggregate of the liabilities secured on it or incurred for the purposes of the business (wherever secured).

In *Hardcastle and another (executors of Vernede deceased) v IRC* [2000] STC (SCD) 532, the Lloyd's assets of a non-working Name qualified on established grounds as business property at 100% relief. Moreover, the uninsured underwriting losses were liabilities deductible from the value of the deceased's other estate and not against the deceased's underwriting interests; the losses were not liabilities incurred for the purposes of the business under s 110(b).

Section 110(b) provides that 'the net value' of a business (and similarly under s 110(c) an interest in a business) is the value of the assets used in the business (including goodwill) reduced by the aggregate amount of any liabilities incurred for the purpose of the business. But a trading loss is not a liability for this purpose. Hence, the losses were deductible against the other assets of the trade and reduced the overall IHT bill.

Strictly, it follows that trading profits will not increase the value of a business for the purposes of BPR; nor will trading losses decrease that value. However, the *Hardcastle* case could, in other (more common) circumstances, be disadvantageous to the taxpayer, in that profits at the time of a transfer including a death will not constitute assets for BPR purposes. It is common practice, not usually disputed by HMRC, for executors to have accounts drawn up to the date of death which will take account of profits or losses accrued to that date.

In *IRC v Mallender* [2001] STC 514 the Lloyd's underwriting business, in accordance with well-established principles, constituted BPR under s 110. However, the taxpayer's claim that investment property used to support a security for bank guarantee failed because it was not business property; the land was worth much more than the maximum sum guaranteed. The bank guarantee was an 'asset used in the business', but not the investment property itself; it was a matter of correct apportionment.

Company reorganisation

15.39   Where a company is, and will remain, a trading company and where (as may now frequently happen) it needs to strengthen its balance sheet a good planning opportunity may arise. Section 107(4) treats shares acquired in a capital reconstruction as part of the shareholder's original holding and as having been owned for the same period as the original shares.

An attempt to use this principle to secure BPR very late in the day failed, in large part, however, in *Executors of Dugan-Chapman v HMRC* [2008] SpC 666. Mrs Dugan-Chapman had for many years been a shareholder in Wilton Antiques Ltd. Two days before her death, she decided to participate in a rights issue and increase her shareholding. The company allotted 1,000,000 shares to her. The executors argued that this was a reorganisation and that the new shares be identified with the old, giving a longer deemed period of ownership.

It seems that a promising tax-planning idea fell on its execution. The Special Commissioner examined the documents evidencing the allotment and concluded that the majority of the shares allotted did not satisfy the test in s 107(3) or (4). The new shares could not be identified with the deceased's existing holding, so no BPR was available on them.

To use this tactic, it is necessary to get the facts and the paperwork right. For example:

- Let there be a commercial need for cash, since otherwise the money subscribed for the new shares will be excepted assets within s 112.

- Let the directors record the need for funds for the purposes of the business of the company.

- Execute the rights issue correctly, so that all shareholders can participate and (ideally) several actually do so, in addition to the 'target' shareholder who is flush with cash, elderly and who wishes to shelter an estate from IHT.

Do not attempt to 'water down' the arrangement in any way. The new money must not be a mere loan, nor be seen as such by virtue of 'clever' distinctions as between one class of share and another.

Fall in value relief following dividend

15.40   Fall in value relief will be much in point when administering estates of persons who died during the recent stock market turbulence. It is set out in s 179 but is restricted in several ways; for example, it applies to shares and securities only if they were quoted at the date of death. Section 181 requires any capital payment to be brought into account, being money or money's worth that is not income for income tax purposes. How does this rule apply to special dividends, such as those paid by Ladbrokes plc in 2006, which were equivalent to some 60% of the share value?

HMRC have agreed that, where a company pays a special dividend, satisfied in cash, which carries a right to tax credit as a dividend, that receipt will not restrict fall in value relief. If a company creates B shares so as to return value to shareholders, giving shareholders the option to take a single dividend, following which the shares are converted into (valueless) deferred shares, a similar result may be achieved.

The nature of the property transferred

15.41   By their success before the High Court, the taxpayers in *Trustees of Nelson Dance Settlement v HMRC* [2009] EWHC 71 (Ch) challenged one of the established tenets of the BPR regime, namely that relief is allowed by s 105(1)(a) in respect of an interest in a business, rather than an asset of that business.

Mr Dance, a farmer, transferred land to a settlement. APR was not in issue: the taxpayer wanted BPR, because the land had development value. HMRC denied relief on the basis that what Mr Dance transferred was not an interest in his farming business, but a 'mere asset'.

The taxpayer argued that we must look, not at the specific asset transferred, but at the transfer of value and apply the 'loss to the estate' principle. The estate of Mr Dance was reduced by the transfer: what was reduced was the value of his farming business; he had been in farming for many years; so the transfer of value fell to be reduced by BPR.

The Special Commissioner, in allowing the taxpayer's appeal to the effect that the transfer of farmland qualified for 100% BPR, found a distinction between those cases, such as spouse relief, where the recipient is important, and the present situation, where the basis of relief is the transfer, not the underlying asset, commenting (at para 16):

> 'All these form part of an overall scheme. Everything turns on the loss in value to the donor's estate, rather than what is given or how the loss to the estate arises, except where the identity of the recipient is crucial to a particular exemption.'

HMRC appealed, but the High Court upheld the Special Commissioner's decision. The High Court held that it was sufficient for BPR purposes that the diminution in value of the transferor's estate by reason of the transfer was attributable to the value of relevant business property. As the land had been used in the farming business, its transfer could be regarded as attributable to the value of the business, and BPR was therefore available on the transfer. Sales J stated:

> 'For BPR to be available in respect of a transfer of value relating to a business there is no requirement that the property transferred should be a business which retains its character as a business in the hands of the transferee, or even that the property transferred should itself have the character of a business.'

He added: '... the simple issue in each case is whether the value of the transferor's relevant business property decreased as a result of the transfer of value; the issue is not as to the nature or value of the assets transferred, looked at in isolation'.

The decision is very helpful in IHT terms. Contrast this with the CGT position, where the rules to determine whether a particular asset is a business or a 'mere asset' turn on the line of old cases that used to be relevant to the old CGT retirement relief, then fell into disuse but which have subsequently enjoyed a revival of interest in applying CGT entrepreneurs' relief, for example *McGregor (Inspector of Taxes) v Adcock* [1977] STC 206; *Mannion (Inspector of Taxes) v Johnston* [1988] STC 758; *Atkinson v Dancer* [1988] STC 758 and *Pepper (Inspector of Taxes) v Daffurn* [1993] STC 466. Commentary on those cases is included in the entrepreneurs' relief section of HMRC's Capital Gains Manual at CG64020.

The *Nelson Dance* decision appears to offer planning opportunities for sole traders and partners wishing to transfer business assets into trust with the benefit of BPR (and CGT hold-over relief), whilst continuing to carry on the business. Particularly in the case of trading assets, the decision whether to transfer them into trust must be considered carefully if the business interest would qualify for BPR at 100% in any event. The same may be said of the investment assets of a 'mixed' trading and investment business which is mainly trading (see **15.8**), although a transfer may appear attractive if, for example, the business owner wishes to secure CGT entrepreneurs' relief on all assets of the business, on the basis that investments are excluded from relief (TCGA 1992, s 169L(4)(b)).

In addition, as noted in **Chapter 7**, relevant property trusts are liable to periodic and exit charges. Thus on an exit charge in the first ten years of the trust, BPR is ignored when determining the initial value of the asset. This can be problematic if BPR is not available on exit (see **7.77**), such as if the trustees are not partners in the business. The availability of BPR must also be considered in respect of each ten-year anniversary charge.

The decision in *Nelson Dance* does not seem to accord with HMRC's interpretation of the BPR rules. In the absence of a successful appeal by HMRC, a change in the law is therefore possible, and so any such planning opportunities may be limited.

Remember the limitations of the decision: it focuses on what the estate owner held before the transfer (or deemed transfer). Thus, a transfer to a relevant property trust of, say, land with development value might, within *Nelson Dance*, attract BPR but at the next ten-year anniversary the trustees might be found to hold a mere business asset or a mere investment in respect of which no relief would be available.

Special valuation issues

15.42 A study of the principles of valuation of shares in private companies is outside the scope of this work but, fairly regularly, cases crop up that practitioners should know about. One such is *I C McArthur's Executors v HMRC* [2008] SpC 700, concerning family investment companies.

The taxpayer had held shares in three family investment companies and had made loans to them which carried conversion rights. HMRC taxed them on the basis that the taxpayer had options to acquire further shares, like convertible loan stock and valued on an assets basis. Where the taxpayer had a majority shareholding HMRC allowed 12.5% discount for lack of marketability; and in the third company allowed 45% discount because the deceased held a minority only.

On appeal from the notice of determination, the executors argued that the conversion rights had little value.

Held, there were writs of the debtor to prove the existence of the loans and the conversion rights, so those rights had substantial value. The taxpayer lost.

AGRICULTURAL PROPERTY

Agricultural value

15.43 It must be borne in mind that agricultural property relief is available only against so much of the value transferred as is attributable to the agricultural value of the property.

The agricultural value of the property is the value that it would have if it were subject to a perpetual covenant prohibiting its use otherwise than as agricultural property (s 115(3)). This may be less than its value in the open market without such a restriction. If so, then even if 100% APR is available, a transfer will generate a transfer of value equal to the difference between those two values.

In *Lloyds TSB (personal representative of Antrobus, deceased) v IRC* [2002] STC (SCD) 468 (*'Antrobus No 1'*), the Special Commissioner held that Cookhill Priory farmhouse attracted APR, as being of a 'character appropriate' to the agricultural land and pasture forming part of the estate, within s 115(2) (see **15.67**).

Subsequently, in *Lloyds TSB Private Banking plc (personal representative of Rosemary Antrobus deceased) v HMRC* DET/47/2005 (*'Antrobus No 2'*) (see **15.4**), the Lands Tribunal was required to consider the 'agricultural value' of the farmhouse in *Antrobus No 1* for the purposes of s 115(3). The tribunal concluded that the agricultural value should be determined on the basis that the assumed perpetual covenant in s 115(3) would have prohibited use of the land in any other way.

That was all that the Tribunal had to decide, so any further comments were *obiter* (and were recognised as such by the Special Commissioner in the later case of *McKenna* [2006] SpC 565); but that notwithstanding, HMRC regularly refer to *Antrobus No 2* as if it were authority on the subject of what is a farmhouse, which it is not. Thus, *Antrobus No 2* purported to hold that to be a farmhouse at all for the purposes of s 115(2), it must be occupied by the person who farms the land on a day-to-day basis. This would therefore exclude the '… lifestyle purchaser whose principal reason for living in the house was the amenity afforded by living in it and by the land'.

Returning to the issue to be decided, the tribunal determined that the open market value of the property should be discounted by 30% in arriving at the agricultural value. However, the tribunal also considered that if their interpretation of the law was incorrect and that demand from the lifestyle farmer may be taken into account, the agricultural value of the farmhouse would be only 15% lower than its open market value.

HMRC appear to be making more of this point than it has in the past. It is important to be aware of it if the agricultural property consists of a farmhouse, which may have a greater value as a second home or straightforward residence than it would have if tied to agricultural use. Similarly, part of the value of agricultural land may represent its development potential and HMRC may seek to deny relief on that part of its value. Even bare land may attract a premium if, for example, a small parcel of it would sell well to indulgent fathers of pony-riding daughters, over true agricultural value. If so, that premium attracts no APR.

Availability of relief on farmhouses since Antrobus No 2

15.44   The issue of 'what is a farmhouse?' had been discussed in *Antrobus No 2* even though, as noted, it was no concern of the Lands Tribunal, having already been determined in *Antrobus No 1*.

It was noted, in *McKenna v HMRC* [2006] SpC 565, that the test in *Antrobus No 2* should be approached with caution. What emerges from the many cases on the subject is a gradually hardening attitude of the courts, trying to restrict relief to dwellings of moderate size, occupied by people who are actively engaged in farming operations that are themselves of sufficient extent that there is a viable agricultural business.

Thus, Rosteague House in *McKenna* failed in part because it was 'at the top end' of what might be regarded as a farmhouse locally, in terms of size; although dilapidated it was of exceptional architectural quality; the acreage was moderate, so the house dominated, making it unattractive as a purely agricultural investment; and the actual farming work had in part been moved to another dwelling nearby. The case is considered in detail at **15.69**.

Students of the subject should read in full the decision of Dr Brice who, with characteristic care and attention to detail, has produced a scholarly survey of the law and applied it fairly to the facts before her. Her reasoning clearly establishes an updated set of principles to be applied in future cases.

The following views of HMRC are worthy of note in relation to farmhouses (IHTM24036):

- For a farmhouse to qualify for APR as a farmhouse, it must satisfy two tests, ie the farmhouse must be agricultural property, and it must have been occupied for the purposes of agriculture for the requisite period. HMRC state that both tests can be 'contentious'.

- HMRC officers are instructed to be particularly careful if the deceased farmer had retired and let their land on grazing agreements. However, the guidance also states: 'a temporary cessation of activity (for example, due to ill health) will not, in itself, prevent a residence being a "farmhouse" if, on the precise circumstances of the case, it can properly be considered as *functionally* remaining attached to the farm ...'. Of course, this statement raises the question of what is a permitted period of absence in this regard.

With regard to HMRC's interpretation of the 'character appropriate' test in relation to farmhouses (s 115(2)), see **15.68**. For a review of farmhouse cases, see **15.67**.

Availability of relief on farm buildings

15.45   Agricultural buildings will not qualify for relief if they dominate the land on which they stand: they must be ancillary to it, so that the relief is primarily on the pasture of arable land. It was so held by the Special Commissioner in *Personal Representative of Williams Deceased v HMRC* [2005] SpC 500.

In that case, a broiler house might have qualified for BPR, had the taxpayer carried on the business; but it was let, so APR was the only relief in point. Had the taxpayer retained more land, the building would have qualified for relief; but as it was the area covered by Wells Farm, Malvern, was only 7.41 acres, of which the most relevant part was 2.59 acres on which the broiler houses stood.

Assets qualifying for 100% relief

15.46   The circumstances in which 100% relief is available are set out in s 116(2)(a)–(c):

(1)   Transferor has vacant possession or the right to obtain it within 12 months (s 116(2)(a))

   This provision covers owner-occupied farms and farms where the transferor's interest entitles him to vacant possession or will do within the next 12 months. HMRC by concession (ESC F17) extended this to 24 months.

(2)   Transferor has held his interest since before 10 March 1981 (s 116(2)(b))

'Working farmer' relief is available under this heading if the transferor has held his interest beneficially since before 10 March 1981 and, had he given away that interest before then and made an appropriate claim, FA 1975, Sch 8, para 2 would have applied in computing the value transferred without limitation by paragraph 5. The main elements of these pre-1981 rules, still relevant, are:

- a limit of £250,000 in value and 1,000 acres in area; and

- the requirement that the transferor was wholly or mainly engaged in farming during five out of the previous seven years. The latter test is deemed to be satisfied if not less than 75% of his income was derived from agriculture.

Relief will be denied if at any time between 10 March 1981 and the transfer of value in question the transferor acquired the right to vacant possession, acquired the right to obtain vacant possession within 12 months, or failed to acquire either such right by reason of an act or deliberate omission.

100% relief will be applied to an appropriate *part* of the value transferred if FA 1975, Sch 8, para 5 would have limited the relief available on a transfer before 10 March 1981, but otherwise the conditions for relief under this heading are satisfied. The remaining part will be entitled to 50% relief (see s 116(4)).

(3)   The property is let on a tenancy beginning on or after 1 September 1995 (s 116(2)(c)).

Special provisions relating to tenancies

15.47   The heading identified in **15.46** circumstance (3) applies where the only reason that relief is unavailable under **15.46** circumstance (1) is that the property is let on a tenancy that began on or after 1 September 1995. This relief coincides with the introduction of the Agricultural Tenancies Act 1995 which deregulated the market for let farmland. The policy was to encourage the granting of new agricultural tenancies.

If a tenant dies on or after 1 September 1995 and his tenancy vests under his will or intestacy in another person, that other person's tenancy is deemed to have commenced at the date of death under s 116(5A) for the purposes of determining whether 100% relief is available. Similar provision is made (although this is not applicable to property in Scotland) where, on the death of the surviving tenant on or after 1 September 1995, another person obtains a tenancy under a legislative right.

If a tenant has given notice to retire in favour of a new tenant, but before such retirement takes place the landlord dies, then the new tenant is deemed to have commenced his tenancy immediately before the transfer of value that the transferor is deemed to make immediately before death (s 116(5D)).

The effect of this is to allow the landlord to benefit from 100% relief under this head if he would have benefited had the new tenancy already commenced. This extension of the relief is subject to the condition that the tenant does indeed retire in favour of the new tenant after the landlord's death and within 30 months of the giving of notice.

Traps and guidance

15.48   There are a number of possible traps to be aware of. First, a surrender of an existing lease followed by a re-grant on a non-arm's length basis in order to obtain 100% relief in the future risks amounting to a PET.

Secondly, for capital gains tax purposes the arrangements could constitute dispositions under the value-shifting provisions in TCGA 1992, s 29. This might be avoided if a new lease is granted in an arm's-length transaction on the same property at a different rent but otherwise on the same terms.

HMRC drafted extensive new guidance on the whole subject of APR in March 2009. It is generally well written and pays special attention to all issues affecting tenancies.

Assets qualifying for 50% relief

15.49   50% relief is available on agricultural property which qualifies in all other respects but does not fall within any of the three heads of 100% relief identified at **15.46**.

This will mainly comprise property which has been let since before 1 September 1995 and will not become vacant within the next 12 (or 24) months.

Concessionary reliefs

15.50   In a Press Release dated 13 February 1995, the Inland Revenue (as it then was) published two further extra-statutory concessions relating to IHT.

The first (ESC F17) confirms the practice of HMRC regarding the condition in s 116(2)(a) as satisfied where the transferor's interest in the property immediately before the transfer carried the right to vacant possession within 24 months of the date of the transfer. It also treats the conditions as satisfied where, notwithstanding the terms of the tenancy, the transferor's interest is valued at an amount broadly equivalent to the vacant possession value (see *IRC v Gray (Executor of Lady Fox)* [1994] STC 360, CA).

The second concession (ESC F16) also gives 100% APR in respect of transfers of agricultural property which includes a cottage occupied by a retired farm employee or spouse. This is subject to the occupier being a protected tenant or having a lease for life as part of his contract of employment.

WHAT ARE THE MAIN ESTATE PLANNING LESSONS?

15.51   Business and agricultural property reliefs are currently very generous. They will probably not survive indefinitely. There is always some degree of political uncertainty. There may not be much appetite right now for a 'root and branch' recasting of IHT, but its yield has been eroded rather more, by the introduction of the transferable nil rate band, than the authorities may have anticipated. Any politicians looking afresh at the regime and wanting to make their mark might wish to cut back both APR and BPR or the rates at which they apply.

Because they are available on lifetime gifts as well as transfers on death, those who currently qualify for relief might consider making lifetime gifts to insulate themselves as far as possible against future changes in the law. On the other hand, there are some advantages in delaying making gifts, which need to be considered too.

Shareholdings and partnerships

15.52   Those with shares or interests in partnerships that could qualify for relief should consider the following points:

- Selling the shares, or retiring from the partnership, could cause significant loss of relief. Not only will the possibility of 100% relief on the shares or partnership interest themselves be lost, but so will the 50% relief on assets belonging to the individual and used in the business of the company or partnership.

- If it is likely that shares which qualify for BPR now will cease to do so, or will do so at a less favourable rate, consider making a lifetime gift now. It may be possible to hold over capital gains tax under TCGA 1992, s 165. The downsides to this are: the possibility of clawback (see **15.5**); the lack of capital gains tax exemption on death; and HMRC's view that hold-over relief takes precedence over CGT entrepreneurs' relief, thus potentially affecting claims for the latter (CG64137).

- The gift with reservation provisions must not be ignored where a lifetime gift of business or agricultural property is made. FA 1986, Sch 20, para 8 adapts the gifts with reservation provisions. In general terms, if the donor reserves a benefit, the conditions for relief must continue to be met until the donor's death in order to preserve the relief and reduce the charge on death (see, for example, FA 1986, Sch 20, para 8(1A)(b)).

Use of relevant property trusts

15.53 Business and agricultural property reliefs are both expressly made available to the special IHT regime applicable to 'relevant property' trusts which, as a consequence of FA 2006, comprises nearly all lifetime settlements made since 22 March 2006. In determining whether certain conditions, such as the minimum period of ownership, are met, references to the transferor are treated as references to the trustees (ss 103(1)(b) and 115(1)(b)).

A discretionary trust consisting exclusively of business property that qualifies for the 100% relief can be run in a way that avoids any ten-yearly or exit charges. Although the BPR does not necessarily reduce the *rate* at which tax is charged under the discretionary trust regime, this is not a problem so long as the value transferred is reduced to zero. Note that anything multiplied by zero equals zero!

The position is not so simple when dealing with the 50% relief – or the 100% APR if s 115(3) has prevented the transfer of value from being reduced to zero. In these cases, it is important to remember that, on the ten-yearly charge and on exit charges *after* the first ten-yearly charges, the relief can reduce both the rate of tax and the value transferred. However, before the first ten-yearly anniversary, the relief will only reduce the value transferred. It will not reduce the rate of tax.

Accordingly, to obtain maximum benefit from the relief, distributions during the first ten years should be avoided where possible.

15.54 The transfer of business assets into a discretionary trust by lifetime gift or by will is often one of the best estate planning methods available. In particular, business and agricultural assets can be held in such trusts indefinitely with 100% relief, with no ten-yearly charges (nor exit charges after the first ten-year anniversary).

At the ten-year anniversary, the trustees will need to satisfy the relevant business or agricultural property conditions. Assuming that the 100% relief applies, and that any other assets in the trust are within the nil rate band, the ten-year anniversary charge rate will be zero.

A curious feature of the regime, which may offer scope for tax planning, is that the zero rate will apply until immediately prior to the next ten-year anniversary, even though the assets are no longer business or agricultural assets, for example, because the trust fund consists of the proceeds of sale.

677

Double relief

15.55   Business or agricultural property relief can effectively be obtained twice on the same property in certain circumstances.

Suppose that the first spouse to die leaves business property on discretionary trusts in favour of the surviving spouse and issue. BPR, as well as a capital gains tax free uplift of the base cost to market value, should be obtained on that first spouse's death. The surviving spouse then purchases the business property from the trustees at market value. This could be done pursuant to an option. Subject to surviving the requisite two-year period, he may then obtain BPR a second time, either on his death or on a lifetime transfer. The capital gains tax-free uplift should also be available a second time.

Life assurance is worth considering where, as here, the effectiveness of a plan to minimise inheritance tax depends on a particular individual's surviving for a particular period. One option would be to purchase term cover for the surviving spouse for at least two years. This would be appropriate if the matter is being considered at or after the date of the first spouse's death.

Alternatively, even before the death of the first (business owning) spouse, life assurance could be taken out to cover the risk of the second spouse dying first. Obviously, if that risk materialised, it would prevent the plan for double relief from working. In this case, one would want to cover (i) the risk of the second (non-business-owning) spouse dying first *and* (ii) the risk of that second spouse dying within two years of the first spouse. It should be possible to obtain suitable cover on the second spouse's life for these eventualities. It would be a form of term assurance, but that term would be dependent on the date of death of the first spouse, ie the life of X + 2 years.

Example 15.7 – 'Doubling-up' BPR/APR

Mrs Chambers owns the following assets:

		£
1.	Stock Exchange securities, building society and bank deposits	1,400,000
2.	A 30% holding in Eve Chambers Ltd which manufactures widgets	500,000
3.	Chambers Farm which Mrs Chambers has owned and farmed for many years	800,000

In her will, Mrs Chambers leaves assets numbered 2 and 3 to a discretionary trust in favour of her widower, children and grandchildren. She also leaves so much of the assets in number 1 as are equal in value to the current nil rate band into the trust. The remaining (investment) assets she leaves to her widower coupled with an option to buy the business and agricultural assets from the trust at market value.

On Mrs Chambers' death

Supposing that Mrs Chambers died in September 2012, there will be no IHT. There will also be a capital gains tax free uplift to market value of the base cost of all the assets. The nil rate band for 2012–13 is £325,000 so that amount would, subject to what follows, go into the trust. The remaining £1,075,000 would go to Mr Chambers absolutely. He also, of course, acquires the option to buy the business and agricultural assets from the trust at market value.

On Mr Chambers' death

If Mr Chambers exercised the option to buy the agricultural assets from the trust (drawing on the cash that he inherited absolutely, and having used more of that fund to buy some of the shares in the family company) and survived a further two years from the exercise of the option, there would be no IHT on his death either. The only assets in his estate would be the business and agricultural property.

The number 1 assets (now all in the trust, the majority having been used as purchase money) would no longer be part of his estate. Nevertheless, he could have benefited from the income of those assets during his life as a beneficiary of the trust created by his wife. The business and agricultural property will benefit from a second capital gains tax free uplift of their base costs to market value on Mr Chambers' death.

Use of transferable nil rate band?

15.56   In every case, we must review wills that were drafted before the coming into force of what is now ss 8A–8C. Often it will be best to 'ditch' the nil rate band discretionary trust in a will by appointing the entire fund to the surviving spouse within the two-year period specified in s 144. This will have the effect that the nil rate band of the first spouse to die has not in fact been used on the first death and is available, at current (increased?) rates on the second death.

Note that when dealing with lifetime discretionary trusts the capital gains tax position is different from when they are created on death. There was some uncertainty about the availability of hold-over relief under TCGA 1992, s 260. The concern was that, if 100% relief applied, there was no chargeable transfer.

However, HMRC have confirmed that, in their view, a gift qualifying for 100% business or agricultural property relief is a chargeable transfer for the purposes of s 260 (see Capital Gains Manual at CG67041).

Multiple discretionary trusts: protection against future changes in the reliefs

15.57 The following arrangement uses a number of discretionary trusts to maximise the nil rate band. It can be adapted where 100% business or agricultural property relief applies.

Example 15.8 – Multiple trusts and BPR/APR

Assume that Mr X has surplus business or agricultural assets worth, for the purposes of the appropriate relief, £1,950,000. He creates six discretionary trusts over the course of 2012–13 at staggered intervals. Each trust contains assets worth £325,000. There should be no IHT liability on the transfers into the trusts on the assumption that the 100% relief applies. Capital gains should be held over.

Each trust should be protected by the nil rate band rule, even if the business or agricultural property relief rules are altered in the future and even if the assets cease to be relevant business property or agricultural property. That gives each trust 'a good start in life' in the sense of freedom from IHT entry and exit charges for the first ten years (less one day), but after that the trustees will be subject to the usual rules and if, by then, the fund comprises only cash or assets not qualifying for relief, IHT exit or periodic charges may apply.

There is a risk that a scheme of this sort would be attacked on account of its artificiality. There is also a risk that HMRC may seek to invoke the associated operations rule, although this risk has been curtailed following the decision in *Rysaffe Trustees (CI) Ltd v IRC* [2003] STC 536. These risks can be reduced by ensuring that there are genuine differences between the trusts (eg different trustees and beneficiaries) and that the staggered intervals are as far apart as practicable and are not pre-ordained. Note, however, that HMRC were successful in invoking s 268 to show that life policies, when taken out with annuities, constituted associated operations (see *Smith and Others* [2008] STC 1649).

Other points to be aware of include the possible loss of capital gains tax roll-over relief under TCGA 1992, s 152, and the possible loss of opportunity to claim capital gains tax entrepreneurs' relief if hold-over relief is claimed instead.

Other ways of using business and agricultural property relief

Gifts to elderly relatives as 'peg lives'

15.58   Where valuable assets are eligible for 100% business or agricultural property relief, the main disadvantage of a lifetime gift is the capital gains tax position. Whilst hold-over relief may be available under TCGA 1992, s 165, the tax-free uplift to market value on the death of the owners is clearly the much better alternative.

In appropriate cases, one should now consider whether the asset could be given to an elderly relative, for example a grandparent. The gift to the elderly person would be free of IHT and normally capital gains tax hold-over relief will be available. On the elderly person's death, 100% business or agricultural property relief should be available. The normal minimum period of ownership may also be relaxed under s 109 or s 121. On the death of the elderly relative, the property may then pass under the relative's will to the intended beneficiaries with the benefit of the capital gains tax uplift to market value.

Elderly relative transfers to offshore trust on death

15.59   Alternatively, the elderly person's will could provide for the business or agricultural property to pass into a non-resident trust. The settlor charge would not apply to the trust, he or she being deceased, and the assets would have a base cost equal to market value at death.

A non-resident trust with a deceased settlor accumulates its realised gains as 'trust gains'. These are later potentially taxable on UK resident and domiciled beneficiaries who receive benefits from the trust. Following FA 2008, the same also applies to resident but non-UK domiciled beneficiaries to the extent that chargeable gains are treated as accruing to them, subject to a claim for the remittance basis where applicable, and to transitional provisions in respect of pre-6 April 2008 gains and capital payments.

In both cases, such gains are subject to a capital gains tax 'surcharge' if there is a delay between the realisation of the gain and the benefit. The surcharge can increase the effective tax rate to 44.8% after a six-year delay, so a charge on the settlor at the time of the gain may be thought preferable. Where there are many beneficiaries, and the stockpiled gains are moderate, it is common practice to 'dribble out' the gains by making distributions to each beneficiary of an amount that is within the annual exemption of the beneficiary.

Example 15.9 – Share sale and trust gains

Granfur was a clergyman of otherwise modest means whose offshore trust, established by his will in 2008, included shares in the family company that had been given to him by his (very successful) children and in respect of which the already substantial gain had been held over.

At his death the shares qualified for 100% BPR. The company went public in May 2010 and the trustees made gains of £800,000. Granfur had four children each of whom has four children, and all 20 of them are beneficiaries of the trust.

In the year ended 5 April 2011 the trustees distributed £202,000 divided equally between Granfur's children and grandchildren, none of whom had in that year made any personal gains. All are within the capital gains tax annual exemption, so there is no stockpiled gains charge under TCGA 1992, s 91.

On 30 April 2011, the trustees distributed a further £212,000 on the same basis. If the beneficiaries made no other chargeable gains in excess of their annual exemption, there will again be no stockpiled gains charge. Over half the gains have been washed out.

It is important that the transfer by the children to Granfur was not made for the purpose of making the settlement (TCGA 1992, s 68A(3)).

Use of deed of variation

15.60   If the transfer into the offshore trust is done by way of deed of variation of an outright entitlement, rather than under the elderly relative's will, the beneficiary effecting the variation would be the settlor for capital gains tax purposes (TCGA 1992, s 68C(2), introduced by FA 2006 following the court's decision in *Marshall v Kerr* [1994] STC 638).

This would mean that any gains realised by the trustees would be attributable to and taxable on the donor-beneficiary concerned under TCGA 1992, s 86.

Although the legislation (TCGA 1992, Sch 5, para 6) gives the beneficiary a right of recovery against the trustees, there is some doubt over whether that right is enforceable. With the possible exception of trusts resident in a Brussels Convention country, the better view is that such rights of reimbursement will be unenforceable. Voluntary reimbursement by the trustees is not necessarily a solution, but these complex issues are outside the scope of this book.

Example 15.10 – BPR and CGT hold-over relief

Anne owns 80% of Widget Manufacturing Co Ltd and currently qualifies for BPR. She wants to give 30% of the shares to her daughter Emma. Assume that a 30% holding of these shares is currently worth £600,000 and that there is an inherent gain on such a holding of £500,000 (ie a potential capital gains tax charge of £140,000, ignoring entrepreneurs' relief and the annual exemption).

Anne's father George is still alive, but in his 80s. Anne gives the shares (ie the intended gift to Emma) to George free of IHT as business property. Capital gains are held over. It is then hoped (there must be no prior agreement or arrangement) that George will leave these shares to his granddaughter Emma under his will.

On George's death, there will be no IHT on account of the BPR. That part of the plan could have been achieved by a straight gift by Anne to Emma. However, significantly, there is a capital gains tax-free base cost uplift to market value at the date of George's death. Capital gains tax of up to £140,000 on a future disposal has been saved.

Supplementary points

There are three additional points to make concerning this example:

(1)   It is not essential for George to survive two years from the date of the gift. As long as Anne's period of ownership qualified, and the transfer by George to Emma occurs on George's death, s 109 should ensure that BPR remains available.

(2)   If George did not leave the property to Emma by his will, the beneficiary under the will could execute a deed of variation to achieve the same result. This depends on the co-operation of the beneficiary. Not much can be done if George's will leaves everything to the wicked stepmother or to charity and he fails to change it in time.

(3)   If this plan is adopted instead of an immediate gift to Emma, it means gambling on the continuation of BPR in its current form for George's life. Those involved should be made aware of this risk.

Will planning

15.61   Leaving business or agricultural property to a spouse wastes relief, except in so far as the relief falls short of the full taxable value of the property, for example if it is a farmhouse. A gift to a (UK domiciled) spouse or civil partner is exempt anyway.

Business or agricultural property that may qualify for 100% relief should, for tax purposes, be given to the lower generations (children and grandchildren) or to appropriate trusts. This overcomes the problem that such assets, if left to the surviving spouse, may become investment rather than trading assets; or that on that spouse's death the law may have changed for the worse. Frequently, a surviving spouse does not need the business assets, such as shares in the family company, which may be illiquid. He will need the liquid assets.

If, on the other hand, he may need the business or agricultural assets, those assets can be placed into a 'wait and see' discretionary trust and, if needed, distributed to the surviving spouse more than three months after the first spouse's death but not later than two years after that date (see s 144).

If the testator wants to give business and agricultural assets to chargeable beneficiaries to supplement a nil rate band gift, and leave the residue to the surviving spouse, he must ensure that specific property (eg the shares or the farm) is given to the non-exempt beneficiaries to avoid an apportionment of the relief between them and the exempt surviving spouse under s 39A.

Beware of unfairness between more than one chargeable beneficiary. For example, a gift of shares subject to 100% BPR to the testator's daughter and a gift of an equivalent cash sum to the testator's son would result in an effectively exempt gift to the daughter while the son's gift would be subject to IHT.

As mentioned *passim* in this work, consider whether to take advantage of the transferable nil rate band.

Other advantages of delaying such gifts until death

15.62   If an estate owner is reasonably confident that 100% business or agricultural property relief will be available on his death, there is little incentive to relinquish control or reduce a substantial minority holding by making lifetime gifts. The case of *Rosser v IRC* [2003] STC (SCD) 311 emphasises that it is likely to be preferable to defer gifting business and agricultural property for IHT until death (see **15.66**).

Advantages of delaying gifts until death include the following:

- There is no question of clawback of business or agricultural property relief. This only applies to lifetime gifts that are potentially exempt transfers; see ss 113A, 113B (acquisition of replacement property within three years with whole of consideration of original property) and ss 124A, 124B on business and agricultural property respectively.

- There will be full capital gains tax death exemption and tax-free uplift. Contrast this with capital gains tax hold-over relief which is usually only a deferral of tax.

• The estate owner can retain control of his shareholding.

Deeds of variation

15.63 For death within the two-year period, consider varying (within s 142) the gifts of business or agricultural property subject to 100% relief away from spouses and in favour of non-spouses, such as adult children, grandchildren or discretionary trusts.

Mortgaging or charging agricultural or business assets

Avoid mortgaging or charging a farm

15.64 There are three basic alternatives. First, the farm itself is charged without other security. This should be avoided where possible because, on a transfer of value, the APR will be restricted to the net value of the farm, ie the value of the farm less the mortgage (s 162(4)). If it is not possible to avoid mortgaging the farm, consider charging the farmhouse as opposed to qualifying farmland. If full relief is available for the farmland but relief for the farmhouse may be restricted or denied, it would therefore seem sensible to mortgage the farmhouse.

Secondly, the loan could be secured against some other asset, such as a life policy, or land not occupied for the purpose of agriculture, such as redundant farm buildings, and not the agricultural property itself. In that case, it appears that the indebtedness is set first against the collateral security, leaving the farm and APR unabated by the charge to the extent that the collateral security is sufficient to redeem the charge. This is preferable to the first scenario, even if it means that some relief may be lost.

In *IRC v Mallender and others (executors of Drury-Lowe deceased)* [2001] STC 514, the deceased had given security to a bank over some land in return for the bank providing a guarantee to Lloyd's which was lodged as part of the deceased's underwriting business. Initially, the Special Commissioners had held that the land itself was business property, albeit that its value was several times the value of the guarantee. This decision was overturned by the High Court.

Thirdly, the loan may not be secured on any particular asset. This is less favourable than the second method because the loan may reduce the agricultural value of the farm on a pro rata basis. It may also be unacceptable commercially to the lender.

Avoid mortgaging or charging a business asset

15.65 Almost the same principles apply to business assets as to agricultural assets. Any loan charged on the assets eligible for relief will reduce the amount of relief available and increase the tax on the assets not so eligible. Wherever practicable, loans should be secured on collateral assets.

However, by contrast with APR, for BPR and for payment by instalments (s 227), reliefs such as charging of collateral assets may not work. These reliefs are available only in respect of the 'net value' of the business (ss 110(1) and 227(7)) so, if the proceeds of the borrowing are used for the purposes of the business, they reduce the reliefs for that reason (note the words in s 110: 'reduced by the aggregate amount of any liabilities incurred for the purposes of the business').

The solution could be to interpose a partnership so that the borrowings are used to provide the partnership capital. This problem does not apply to APR, though in a farming situation the two reliefs are often closely linked, so beware. The rule does not apply to a loan to purchase a business since that is not 'for the purpose' of the business itself.

The mortgaging/charging suggestion can be usefully extended. An asset owner could borrow on non-business or agricultural property assets (eg a home) and use the proceeds to invest in assets that should give the relief (eg AIM trading company shares, although this can be risky), or to subscribe for shares in a family company (eg run by the estate owner's children, although again this could be risky).

Tax planning for agricultural property

Agricultural cottages and the farmhouse

15.66 Whether or not the conditions for APR are satisfied, where cottages are occupied by persons employed in agriculture, their valuation will be on the basis that they are only suitable for that purpose. They can therefore be transferred at a low value (s 169).

The reference in s 115(2) to 'agricultural land or pasture' should be given the narrow meaning of the bare land, not the wider meaning under the Interpretation Act 1978 as automatically including buildings on the land (*Starke (Brown's Executors) v IRC* [1995] STC 689, CA). Therefore, for IHT purposes, a farmhouse or building will only qualify for APR if its occupation is ancillary to that of agricultural land. On the facts in *Starke*, a six-bedroom farmhouse on 2.5 acres did not qualify for APR.

Subsequently, in *Williams (personal representative of Williams, deceased) v HMRC* [2005] STC (SCD) 782 (reviewed at **15.45**) it was held that broiler houses were not agricultural property within s 115(2). The broiler houses were not 'ancillary' to the deceased's farm.

Consider an estate owner who gives 85% of his farm to his daughter and retains, say, 15% together with the farmhouse. If the estate owner continues to be involved in the farming business (eg through a partnership), the farmhouse may be eligible for 100% relief. It is a question of degree. One can have a 100% interest in the farmhouse and, say, a 15% interest in the partnership. It is also suggested that a service contract be entered into between the partnership and the 'farmhouse' owner as to the specific administration and other farming duties he must satisfy. The judgment in *Starke* contains *dicta* that admit of the possibility that land may be agricultural property by virtue of some *nexus* other than direct unity of ownership. This was challenged in *Rosser,* as to which see below, where the taxpayer acted in person and the point, to judge from the report, was not fully argued. The point is still not formally decided.

A few farmhouse cases

15.67   In *Harrold v IRC* [1996] STC (SCD) 195, APR was claimed under the seven-year occupation test but, because the farm was unoccupied as dilapidated at the donor's death, no APR was available. See *Atkinson's Executors v HMRC* below as to how a less clear-cut situation was treated.

In *Dixon v IRC* [2002] STC (SCD) 53, a claim for APR failed; in this case, the agricultural use was derisory, comprising only an orchard of 0.6 acres.

The farmhouse must be of a 'character appropriate' to the agricultural property (*Lloyds TSB (personal representative of Antrobus, deceased) v IRC* [2002] STC (SCD) 468; see **15.43**). In that case, a six-bedroom country house situated in approximately 126 acres of agricultural land and pasture, which had been farmed by the Antrobus family since 1907 and had been a working farm was held to be of a character appropriate to the agricultural land and pasture within s 115(2).

By contrast, in *Higginson's Executors v IRC* [2002] STC (SCD) 483, the deceased lived in a lodge on a landed estate. The house was not a typical farmhouse. The Special Commissioner held that the lodge was not a farmhouse within s 115(2). For that purpose, the land and house must be part of an agricultural unit, in which the land predominated. However, in this case the lodge predominated. It was a house with farmland going with it (and not vice versa).

In *Rosser v IRC* [2003] STC (SCD) 311 the estate owners/farmers made lifetime gifts of some 39 out of 41 acres of farmland, retaining the claimed 'farmhouse' and a barn on the relevant death. The claim for APR on the home failed; on the facts it had, clearly, become merely a 'retirement home'. The likely moral is to leave such gifting until death, which also then benefits from the CGT death exemption and market value uplift (TCGA 1992, s 62).

Rosser appeared to confirm the view taken by HMRC in its manuals that, to qualify for relief, a farmhouse must be in common ownership and occupation with the land to which it is 'of a character appropriate'. That was not the approach taken by the First-tier Tribunal, however, in *Hanson v HMRC* [2012] UKFTT 95(TC). The tribunal held that there was no reason to infer from the legislation a requirement for common ownership, and that common occupation alone was sufficient. At the time of writing, it appears likely that the decision will be appealed to the Upper Tribunal.

In *Atkinson's Executors v HMRC* [2010] UKFTT 108 (TC), the tribunal had to consider an issue that often arises in practice. The farmer's health had deteriorated to the point that he was, at the time of his death, living in a care home. Did his residence, a farm bungalow, still qualify for APR, if he was not there?

The deceased had survived his son and was in partnership with his grandson. He owned the farm, which included the bungalow, and had let it all on an agricultural tenancy to the partnership. He became ill, moving first to hospital and thence to a care home. The bungalow remained furnished; his things were there.

At first instance, the tribunal decided that the bungalow was 'occupied for the purpose of agriculture' within s 117: the bungalow, like the whole farm, was occupied by the partnership and, although the deceased was not in residence, he remained a partner, taking an interest in the business of the farm, visiting the bungalow occasionally and keeping his possessions there. On appeal by HMRC (*HMRC v Atkinson* [2011] UKUT 506 (TCC)), however, the Upper Tribunal took a different, rather less generous view. While the partnership may have been in occupation of the property, once there was no prospect of the deceased returning to reside at the property, such occupation did not have a sufficient connection to the farming operations being carried on and hence the occupation was not 'for the purpose of agriculture'.

In *Golding v HMRC* [2011] UKFTT 351 (TC), the First-tier Tribunal was required to decide whether a farmhouse was of a 'character appropriate' to 16.29 acres of agricultural land with adjacent outbuildings. The tribunal decided that the deceased was carrying on a genuine albeit modest farming operation; and the parties had conceded in correspondence that the property in question was a 'farmhouse'. The tribunal had little apparent difficulty in finding that it was appropriate for the deceased to carry on the business from the farmhouse and that it was therefore of a 'character appropriate' to the farm.

The tribunal was apparently swayed by evidence that a report by DEFRA in 2009 showed that there were over 100,000 holdings in England that had an acreage of less than 12.5 acres.

The 'Twiddy list'

15.68 For a farmhouse to be agricultural property, it is largely a question of the purpose of occupation rather than the actual use put to it by the owner or occupier. In an extract of a letter from Peter Twiddy (*Taxation*, 15 June 2000) whilst still the most senior representative of HMRC dealing with this issue, he described the test adopted by Capital Taxes (as it then was) as follows: 'The CTO asks the District Valuer to consider the appropriate test through the eyes of the rural equivalent of the reasonable man on the Clapham omnibus …'.

HMRC now apply the following tests when determining whether a farmhouse is of a 'character appropriate' to the agricultural property (IHTM24051):

- Is the farmhouse appropriate when judged by ordinary ideas of what is appropriate in size, layout, content, and style and quality of construction in relation to the associated land and buildings?

- Is the farmhouse proportionate in size and nature to the requirements of the agricultural activities conducted on the agricultural land? You should bear in mind that different types of agricultural operation require different amounts of land. This is an aspect on which the VOA will be able to give advice.

- Within the agricultural land does the land predominate so that the farmhouse is ancillary to that land?

- Would a reasonable and informed person regard the property simply as a house with land or as a farmhouse?

- Applying the "elephant test", would you recognise this as a farmhouse if you saw it? Although this test involves some subjectivity it can be useful in ruling out extremes at either end of the scale.

- How long has the farmhouse and agricultural property been associated and is there a history of agricultural production? The matter has to be decided on the facts as at the date of death or transfer, but evidence of the farmhouse having previously been occupied with a larger area of land may be relevant evidence.

- Considering the relationship between the value of the house and the profitability of the land, would the house attract demand from a commercial farmer who has to earn a living from the land, or is its value significantly out of proportion to the profitability of the land? If business accounts have been supplied, copies should be forwarded to the VOA. Business accounts can give a useful indication of the extent of the agricultural activity being carried on, although a loss-making enterprise is not on its own considered to be a determinative factor.

- Considering all other relevant factors, including whether land is let out and on what terms, is the scale of the agricultural operations in context?

- There must be some connection or nexus between "such cottages, farm buildings and farmhouses, together with the land occupied with them" and the property to which they must be of a character appropriate. The argument that the nexus must be derived from common ownership rather than common occupation was accepted by the Special Commissioner in *Rosser v Inland Revenue Commissioners* [2003] STC (SCD) 311.'

It is worth noting that the original eight tests were extended to nine in HMRC's revised guidance in March 2009, with the addition of the seventh and ninth bullet points above, and the removal of the following test from the original guidance: 'Weigh up all the factors and consider the matter "in the round".' However, the removal of this test is balanced by the following instruction (in IHTM24052): 'It is not a question of "how many factors have to be failed" in any given case before a house is judged not to be of a character appropriate to the property. It is necessary to consider all the various factors about the house and the land and come to a judgement'.

The 'elephant test', well remembered by students is: something which is difficult to describe but you know one when you see one. However, whereas there may be a consensus as to what is an elephant and what is not, an equivalent measure of certainty will not be present when dealing with a question of fact and degree. Is an animal an elephant if it is half elephant and half lion, supposing such a thing to be possible? Or if it is three-quarters elephant? Or, if it is a dead or deformed elephant? Once the test is adapted to one which involves drawing a line somewhere, it is likely to emerge that we do not all agree on what is an elephant and a more specific test is needed if there is to be some certainty.

The position following *McKenna*

15.69 The most recent, and in many respects the best, authority on farmhouses is *McKenna v HMRC* [2006] SpC 565, where an estate comprised Rosteague House, a lodge, a cottage and a stable flat and 188 acres. 52 acres were coastal slope and 100 acres were agreed to be agricultural land. HMRC denied APR on the house, and the taxpayer's appeal from the decision failed.

The title went back to the thirteenth century and the house itself was part Elizabethan, part eighteenth century, listed Grade II** but, by the relevant time, in very poor condition and in need of very considerable repair. There was evidence of farming from 1365 onwards. During the twentieth century farming was mainly done by others, the owners living in London until retirement to Rosteague in 1978. Thereafter, as long as his health allowed, the estate owner ran the farm from the house but eventually it was managed by an agent. The extent of agricultural activities declined. Mr McKenna relied on a pension, not on the farm, for his living.

The estate was eventually sold, not as a farm, but as residential property. The land was incidental, being mentioned only briefly in the sales literature. Of the sale price of £3,050,000 as much as £2,030,000 might fairly be attributable to the house alone.

The Special Commissioner held that:

- the decision in *Antrobus No 2* as to what constitutes a farmhouse should be approached with some caution;

- one should decide on the basis of the words of s 115(2) rather than apply general principles, though the idea that a farmer is the person who farms the land on a day-to-day basis is a helpful one;

- a farmhouse is a dwelling from which the farm is managed;

- the farmer is the person who farms the land on a day-to-day basis, rather than the person who is in overall control;

- it is not occupation that matters so much as the purpose of that occupation;

- if the premises are 'extravagantly large for the purpose for which they are being used', then even though used for farming they may have become 'something much more grand'; and

- each case turns on its own facts, to be judged by ordinary ideas of what is appropriate in size, content and layout.

On the facts, farming had been reduced and was no longer conducted from the house. The house was too grand for the amount of farming going on. Whilst a farmer need not make a profit, that did not help the taxpayer; on the facts, it was not a farmhouse.

Even if it had been, it was not of a character appropriate: it was 'at the very top end of the size of a farmhouse in Cornwall'. Applying the tests of *Antrobus No 1* in turn, it failed. It also failed the occupation test: neither Mr nor Mrs McKenna occupied for the purpose of farming; they were prevented by ill health from farming.

15.70 There are still some issues unresolved.

Example 15.11 – Farmhouses and APR (I)

Mr and Mrs Gilliam retire and, as in *Rosser*, give their farm to their daughter who takes over the farming, but Mr and Mrs Gilliam stay in the farmhouse. The daughter lives elsewhere. In those circumstances, the farmhouse ceases to be agricultural property, because the daughter runs the farm from other premises. The solution may be for the Gilliams to retain some partnership interest in the overall farm.

Example 15.12 – Farmhouses and APR (II)

Suppose instead that Mr and Mrs Gilliam occupied a farmhouse as life tenants under a pre-FA 2006 life interest trust. The land gets separated from the trust and is now held by the daughter in her own right. The Gilliams give the land to their daughter, retiring into a bungalow nearby. The daughter moves into the farmhouse and runs the farm from there.

The daughter is a farmer of the type favoured by *Antrobus No 2*: she actually farms the land from the farmhouse. It is at least arguable that there is such a close connection between the house and the land that, on the death of Mr Gilliam or of Mrs Gilliam relief should be given on the house, but the point is undecided.

House and pasture

15.71   Following *IRC v Forsyth-Grant* [1943] 25 TC 369, if the grant of a farm business tenancy gives the owner a grant of herbage ('profit a prendre') with responsibility for manuring, seeding and fertilising the land, the 100% APR will apply to that land and may enhance the possibility of relief on the farmhouse (subject to the 'character appropriate' tests set out above).

The potential availability of relief for short-term grazing lets or licences is confirmed in HMRC's manuals (at IHTM24074), where they state, in the context of farmhouses:

> 'It is unlikely that a landowner who has allowed most or all of the agricultural land to be occupied on a grazing licence agreement where he or she does nothing but collect the rent and maintain boundaries, will be considered to be in agricultural occupation of that land. Consequently, as there is no farming activity actually being carried out, any associated house cannot be considered to be a farmhouse and therefore would not be eligible for APR.'

Note that this comment focuses on the house, not on the land itself, the value of which should still qualify for APR.

Whether pasture land was 'occupied for the purposes of agriculture' was considered by the Special Commissioner in *The Executors of Walter Wheatley Deceased* [1998] STC (SCD) 60. He held that grazing by horses such as draught animals could qualify because the horses would have a 'connection with agriculture'. Grazing by horses used for leisure pursuits did not so qualify. Arguably, the issue is the exact basis of occupation. If there is a tenancy, *Wheatley* should apply; but if a licence, the owner-occupier is producing an agricultural crop, grass, whatever eats it.

To avoid the house being an excepted asset within IHTA 1984, s 112(2), because used wholly or mainly for the personal benefit of the transferor (s 112(6)), an arm's-length contract of employment should be considered.

Fallow land

15.72   Fallow land (eg under an EC set-aside scheme) is allowed as agricultural property so long as it is not used for another purpose.

Recently whilst much arable land was not being actively farmed, because of commercial pressures and the entitlement to single farm payment, a question arose whether it was still occupied for the purpose of agriculture; or (as an envious townie might think) only for the purpose of drawing subsidy. The farmer would do well to take seriously his duties to keep the land in good heart, even if he does not grow a crop. Most will no doubt do that anyway: it is their heritage.

The issue is not satisfactorily addressed in the current guidance from HMRC (IHTM24064).

Holiday lettings

15.73   Holiday lettings are not agricultural property but may well qualify for BPR, especially if the landlord contributes active management and services. In other words, it is necessary to show that the activity in question constitutes 'trading' and not 'a mere investment'. See the Special Commissioner's decisions in *Martin* and *Burkinyoung* (discussed at **15.13**).

Until November 2008, HMRC's Inheritance Tax Manual indicated that BPR would normally be allowed if the lettings were short term (eg weekly or fortnightly) and there was substantial involvement with the holidaymakers both on and off the premises. This applied even if the lettings were for only part of the year.

HMRC's guidance (at IHTM25278) was amended in November 2008, to state the following:

'Recent advice from Solicitor's Office has caused us to reconsider our approach and it may well be that some cases that might have previously qualified should not have done so. In particular we will be looking more closely at the *level and type of services*, rather than who provided them.' (emphasis added)

The guidance indicates that cases involving claims for BPR on holiday lettings should be referred to HMRC's Technical Team (litigation). It was clear from the change in guidance that HMRC were taking a more robust approach to this sort of business activity and that a test case was likely.

The test case came in the form of *Pawson (deceased) v HMRC* [2012] UKFTT 51 (TC). The case was significant because the degree of involvement with holidaymakers, and the level and type of services provided, were not extensive; and neither was the business pursued in a particularly earnest manner. Nevertheless, the First-tier Tribunal agreed with the taxpayers that the business was not one that consisted of holding an investment, commenting that an intelligent businessman would regard the business as involving far too active an operation for it to come under that heading.

It is possible that the decision will be appealed. It is certainly difficult to reconcile with some of the 'caravan park' cases described in **15.14**. Notwithstanding the decision in *Pawson*, therefore, the closer the comparison between the holiday accommodation and a hotel in terms of services provided, the better. Owners should therefore consider (for example) the provision of clean linen and towels, regular cleaning of the accommodation, and booking facilities for restaurants and local attractions. The greater the 'level and type' of such services, the better would appear the prospect of obtaining relief.

Milk quotas etc

15.74 Milk and other quotas, for as long as still commercially relevant, will normally qualify for BPR. Notwithstanding the *Cottle* case (see below), HMRC guidance indicates that the value of quotas may alternatively be taken into account in claims for APR.

The revised APR guidance addresses the issue of quotas. In the case of milk quotas, it indicates that if land is used as a dairy farm, milk quota should be valued as part of the land and APR allowed on the full combined value if the land itself qualifies for relief (or alternatively BPR may be available). If freehold land is subject to a tenancy and the tenant has a dairy farm with milk quota, APR may be available on the value of the freehold interest as enhanced by the value of the milk quota, subject to the other APR conditions being satisfied (IHTM24250).

For capital gains tax purposes, there is an apparent conflict. The decision in *Faulkes v Faulkes* [1992] 15 EG 15, where Chadwick J expressed the view that the quota interest was part of and indistinguishable from the land, contrasts with HMRC's original published view that milk quota exists separately from the land for capital gains tax purposes, normally with no base cost (*Tax Bulletin*, Issue 6, page 49).

That official view was supported in the Special Commissioner's decision in *Cottle v Caldicott* [1995] SpC 40. It was held that the taxpayer was not entitled to deduct any part of the cost of the holding of land from the consideration for the milk quota. The milk quota was a personal asset separate from the incorporeal property: TCGA 1992, s 21(1)(a), (b). Following the *Cottle* decision, it is nowadays generally applied and accepted that milk quota is not an interest in land as such.

Diversification

15.75   Diversification to non-agricultural use (eg golf courses) will lose the APR but may well qualify as a business asset. There is no need to own an asset for two years *as business property* for it to qualify for BPR if it was previously owned, for example as agricultural property, and the aggregate is at least two years.

Grant of tenancies etc

15.76   In the 1970s and to a lesser degree in the 1980s, granting tenancies produced substantial tax savings because of the double discount, ie the capital transfer tax agricultural property discount plus the reduction in value from open market vacant possession value. With the 100% discount on vacant possession and let land since 1 September 1995, there is little point in effecting a reorganisation to achieve the double discount and the plan should be to keep matters simple. This, however, does depend on whether one expects any changes in government policy. If the APR discount is going to be reduced, the double discount plan may revive.

In an era where vacant possession gives in effect full exemption, the grant of a tenancy is not generally advisable for IHT purposes. Instead of family-type tenancies, consider a partnership with vacant possession (or at least vacant possession within 12 or 24 months). Licensing arrangements that do not constitute leases or tenancies are fine. Note the European Court of Justice case of *Lubbock Fine & Co v Customs and Excise Commissioners* Case C-63/92 [1994] STC 101, indicating that surrenders of leases are exempt from VAT. However, bear in mind that tenants who currently have security of tenure may be reluctant to agree to a surrender. The income tax and capital gains tax implications of retaining a tenancy should also be taken into account.

For the position on or after 1 September 1995 for new leases and successions, see **15.47**.

Valuation issues: a survey of case law

15.77   Where a person has both freehold land and a share in a partnership to which the land is let on an agricultural tenancy, the question arises as to whether the two interests should be valued on the assumption that they are sold together, and if so, how they should be valued.

In *IRC v Gray (Executor of Lady Fox)* [1994] STC 360, the Court of Appeal decided that, for valuation on death purposes, a freehold reversion in land must be aggregated with a partnership interest which holds a tenancy of that land (following the principle of realising the maximum practicable price without undue expenditure of time and effort: *Duke of Buccleuch v IRC* [1967] 1 506, HL). In other words, it was a single 'natural unit'. The existence of a tenancy can therefore bring about the worst of both worlds. The valuation will be initially on vacant possession principles notwithstanding the tenancy, but, by virtue of s 116(2)(a), only a 50% agricultural property discount will be available rather than 100%. Note that in this case the testatrix was the freeholder and had a 92.5% interest in the partnership which held the tenancy of that freehold estate.

Walton's Executors v IRC [1996] STC 68, CA, concerned the valuation of an agricultural tenancy for capital transfer tax purposes. The W family were the freeholders. They let the farm to a partnership of Mr W and son. On Mr W's death, the Revenue claimed that the capital transfer tax value of the lease was the difference between the value of the freehold with vacant possession and its value subject to the lease. Its reasoning was that, on Mr W's death, there was a hypothetical sale of the tenancy valued at £70,000.

The taxpayer's claim, accepted by the Lands Tribunal and the Court of Appeal, was that there was no hypothetical sale, as the son did not wish to sell but to continue the farming. Therefore, the value of the tenancy was based on a potential profit rental basis (£6,300), ie a real-world situation. This was typically a small value in the absence of any special purchaser, who did not exist in this case.

Partnership land

15.78   Partnership Act 1890, s 22 (which converts partnership property into personal and moveable property) was repealed by the Trusts of Land and Trustees Act 1996. For land held outside a partnership – or company controlled by the taxpayer – and made available as agricultural property, there is 100% relief (s 116). If held as another business asset, 50% relief is available (s 105(1) (d)). Therefore, s 22 need not be specifically excluded from the partnership agreement.

Tenant farmer

15.79   A tenant farmer should consider purchasing the freehold title in order to acquire exempt IHT assets, in contrast with his other assets, reducing his liquid estate not eligible for reliefs. Note that, if the tenant has been in occupation as tenant for a minimum of two years, on a purchase by him the 100% discount becomes immediately available.

Example 15.13 – Hiring followed by purchase

Evan and Ifor are brothers who inherited farms from their father. Evan farmed until his health gave out, at which point he let his farm to Ifor, telling him he would be happy to sell any time it suited Ifor to buy.

Road widening in their Welsh Valley took part of Ifor's farm and injected £300,000 into his bank account shortly before his 75th birthday, which was some consolation not only for the loss of the land but also for the news that, with his own failing health, he should take things easier and consider, at least, giving up Evan's land.

Ifor took the advice both of his doctor and his lawyer. The former told him he had at most 18 months to live; the latter that he should buy the freehold of Evan's land nonetheless. He did, dying much sooner than predicted. No tax fell due on the value of Evan's land.

Farming companies

15.80   Farming companies (s 122) are at a disadvantage: the 100% relief is only available if the transferor controls the company, ie has an interest of more than 50%. Contrast this with BPR, where a 100% discount is currently available whatever the size of the holding.

A holding of 50% or less in a farming company attracts no APR. On the basis that the farm is a business, it may be possible to obtain 100% BPR if the relevant conditions apply.

The shares or securities of a company qualify for APR where the company's assets include agricultural property and the value of the shares or securities can in whole or part be attributed to such property, but only if the transferor of the shares has control of the company within s 269(1) (see ss 122, 123). Note that this control is only required to exist immediately before the transfer, ie the transferor need not have had control for the full two or seven-year period.

In order for the shares to obtain APR, the company must fulfil the same requirements and minimum periods as an individual; and the shareholder transferor must have owned the shares for whichever of the two or seven-year minimum periods is appropriate to the company (s 123(1)).

There are provisions which preserve the relief where the shares replace other eligible property during the relevant period (s 123(3)).

Example 15.14 – Shares in a farming company

On 10 October 2011, Alice, a widow whose late husband had used the nil rate band available to him, gave her farm to her niece by way of a PET. The farm consisted of a house worth £350,000 and 400 acres worth £2,500 per acre, thus having a total value of £1,350,000. Alice had made gifts in the previous seven years which used the nil rate band and her annual exemptions. She had occupied the farm and farmed it herself for 20 years.

The value of the transfer is £1,350,000 reduced by APR of, say, £1,000,000 in respect of the land and of £245,000 for the house: total relief £1,245,000. The chargeable element is £105,000.

The niece farmed the land until Alice's death on 10 February 2012, whereupon the PET became a chargeable transfer with no tapering relief. The niece can pay the IHT of £42,000 over ten years by instalments (s 227), ie annual instalments of £4,200. Interest (see s 234(1)) runs only from the due date of the instalment.

If Alice had rolled over her farming business (including the land) into a company, A Ltd, a year before the transfer in return for 90% of the shares (the other 10% being separately subscribed) the transfer of her 90% shareholding to her niece (together with her niece's retention of the shares and A Ltd's ownership of the farm property up to Alice's death) would still qualify for relief. One could add together the separate occupation of both Alice and A Ltd. IHT would similarly be payable by instalments which, if paid on time, carry no interest.

Habitat schemes

15.81   Certain habitat schemes are (since 26 November 1996) eligible for APR (s 124C). Such schemes are for the protection of the environment and preservation of the countryside and take land out of farming for 20 years. But for this specific inclusion, the land would not qualify for APR.

Special types of farming

Share farming

15.82   The system of share farming has become more popular in the 100% relief era. Its features are:

- a joint contractual venture between the owner of the farmland and the operator (who actually farms the land);
- the owner typically provides land, fixed equipment, machinery and has an agreed share of inputs;
- the operator provides working machinery, labour and inputs; and
- the gross outputs are shared under the agreement.

The results may be summarised as follows:

- no partnership is established;
- there are separate businesses;
- there is no landlord/tenant relationship; and
- IHT: 100% relief should be available (IHTM24081). Both parties should have vacant possession rights. In particular, the owner should be involved in policy-making decisions and exercise rights of inspection.

As to the effect of share-farming arrangements on the availability of APR on the farmhouse, see **15.83**.

HMRC are understood to accept that share farming qualifies for capital gains tax reliefs such as roll-over and entrepreneurs' relief; and constitutes trading as farmers for income tax purposes (ITTOIA 2005, ss 9 and 859(1) for income tax purposes, and CTA 2009, s 36 for corporation tax).

Contract farming

15.83   Consider also contract farming, where the estate owner owns the farm and the actual farming is carried on by sub-contracting, usually to someone who is self-employed. Again, the 100% relief should normally be available. Care must be taken over the invoicing arrangements; for example, the purchase of seed and fertiliser is best undertaken by the owner of the land.

HMRC consider that whether any relief is available on the farmhouse in contract (or share) farming arrangements will depend on such factors as the deceased's degree of financial risk, and his involvement with the everyday agricultural activity (eg the regularity and scope of any meetings with the contractor) and decision-making input (eg the selection, sowing, harvesting and sales of crops) (IHTM24082).

HMRC cite the *McKenna* case (see **15.69**) in support of this approach, but acknowledge that 'these cases can be difficult to decide'.

Single payment scheme

15.84   The single payment scheme (SPS) broadly detached farming subsidies from production, with payment entitlement potentially arising in the hands of farmers and non-farmers. Entitlement to the single payment (SP) is subject to various conditions and standards (eg keeping the land in good agricultural and environmental condition). There was a one-off opportunity in 2005 to receive payment entitlement (PE), which was expected to provide income support for the following eight years. Thereafter, anyone wishing to receive SP must acquire PE from someone entitled to receive it (PE being a tradable asset).

For IHT purposes, PE is subject to the normal IHT rules concerning transfers of value and the death estate. The transfer of PE is liable to IHT as for any other asset. PE is a separate asset falling outside the definition of 'agricultural property' in s 115(2), and cannot therefore qualify for APR (IHTM24254).

By contrast, as mentioned BPR is available for transfers of 'relevant business property', such as a business or interest in a business. Transfers of PE by a farmer who has been farming for at least two years qualify for 100% BPR as an asset of the business. Payments for PE should be used in the business, or be required for future business use. However, transfers of PE by non-traders as an individual asset (as opposed to a business or interest in a business) will not qualify for BPR. For further information on the SPS, see *Tax Bulletin Special Edition*, June 2005.

APR and the EEA

15.85   The scope of APR was extended in FA 2009 to land in states within the EEA but outside the UK, Channel Islands and Isle of Man with effect from 22 April 2009.

The extension applies retrospectively to transfers of value where the tax otherwise payable (or, in the case of instalments, the last instalment) would have been due from 22 April 2009, or was paid or due from 23 April 2003.

Tax already paid can be reclaimed (with appropriate interest), in relation to repayment claims within the time limit for overpayments in s 241(1) (ie within six years after the date on which the payment, or last payment, of tax was made) or 21 April 2010, whichever is the later (FA 2009, s 122(8)).

'Buy and sell' agreements/arrangements

15.86   The trap should be avoided whereby agricultural and business property reliefs are unavailable if the partners or company directors or shareholders have entered into a 'buy and sell' agreement under which, on retirement or the death of one of them before retirement, his personal representatives are obliged to sell and the others are obliged to buy his interest or his shares. Typically, in these arrangements, the funds will be provided through a life assurance policy.

HMRC take the view that such an agreement, entailing an obligatory sale and purchase (not merely conferring an option), constitutes a binding contract for sale within s 124, so that APR is forfeited. The same principle applies to BPR (s 113). See Revenue Statement of Practice 12/80.

A solution is to use the option method. This can achieve the same result if appropriate put and call options are granted. There is a possible argument that cross-options, ie a put and a call, are equivalent in substance to a binding contract for sale on the grounds that the terms will be beneficial to one party or the other and thus a sale is inevitable. In addition, in view of *Ramsay* and *Furniss v Dawson* some disquiet has been expressed as to the use of cross-options. The merits of this argument may be exaggerated, but it may be preferable to include merely a single option (ie either put or call). If cross-options are used, they should be made successive in time and have different exercise periods.

The legal effect of cross options is conditional on the exercise of one or other of them. Until any such exercise takes place, the vendor (or his estate) still has full rights of beneficial ownership in the asset itself (see *J Sainsbury plc v O'Connor* [1991] STC 318, CA). A partnership agreement which does not include this precaution may be cured after its term has expired and it has become a partnership at will, or by variation.

There has also been uncertainty over whether automatic accrual arrangements between members of a partnership may be looked upon by HMRC as binding sale contracts. HMRC's guidance (at IHTM25292) states:

> '... agreements under which ... the deceased's interest passes to the surviving partners, who are required to pay the personal representatives a particular price ... do not constitute contracts for sale. So they do not prevent the interest from qualifying from business property relief by reason of Section 113 IHTA 1984.'

The same approach by HMRC presumably applies for APR purposes as well. This issue does not arise in any event with options, which may therefore be looked upon with favour.

'Accruer' arrangements

15.87   HMRC have confirmed that BPR is available for 'accruer' arrangements (which are not treated as buy and sell arrangements), and where the deceased partner's estate is paid on a valuation or formula basis (see *Taxation Practitioner*, 10 April 1997, p 10).

Chapter 16

Estate planning – woodland, heritage property and Lloyd's underwriters

WOODLANDS – THE RELIEF

16.1   Interests in forestry benefit from favourable income tax treatment. Taxation of the occupation of commercial woodlands used to be assessed to income tax under Schedule B. This regime was abolished with transitional relief provisions by FA 1988, s 64 and Sch 6. Commercial woodlands have been taken out of income tax (ITTOIA 2005, ss 11, 267(b) and 768). Losses on planting are not allowable against other income, and the proceeds of sale of the mature timber are free from income tax.

So far as IHT relief is concerned, a measure of relief for woodlands is contained in IHTA 1984, ss 125–130. The relief applies only to trees and underwood. Although the underlying land is excluded, its value will usually be relatively low and will be eligible for agricultural relief if occupied with, and ancillary to, agricultural land or pasture: see the detailed discussion in *Williams v HMRC* [2005] SpC 500 of the need of cattle for shade. That case is reviewed at **15.45**.

In *Brutus v Cozens* [1973] AC 854, a Schedule D (now 'trading income') case, the court had held that the meaning of an ordinary word of the English language was not a question of law but that it was for the tribunal deciding the case to consider, as fact, whether the words used covered the facts to be proved.

Relying partly on that decision, the court in *Jaggers v Ellis* (see below) upheld the decision of the Commissioner that 'woodlands' meant 'land used for forestry purposes'. The terms 'woodlands' and 'forestry' were not terms of art but were in common usage and to be treated as synonymous. Although woodlands connoted a wood of sizeable area and to a significant extent covered by growing trees, it could not be assumed that any land covered with any trees constituted woodland. The rule of thumb was whether the wood was capable of being used as timber.

There have been two developments in this area. First, a plantation of Christmas trees, which did not have the maturity, height or size to be useful as timber, and which resembled bushes rather than trees, did not constitute woodland: see *Jaggers v Ellis* [1997] STC 1417. The analysis in the judgment provides useful guidance on the meaning of woodland in the IHT legislation.

Second, as reported by the British Christmas Tree Growers Association News, it appears that, in relation to a specific case involving a protected agricultural tenancy, HMRC have acknowledged that the growing of such trees may constitute a 'nursery', and therefore qualify for agricultural property relief. This is because the trees are not grown to maturity and are harvested for sale. This is consistent with the VAT treatment of Christmas tree farms.

Nature of relief

What qualifies?

16.2   IHT relief, on death only, is available if claimed by notice in writing within two years of death or such longer period as the Board will allow (s 125(3)).

The relief is not available for lifetime transfers of woodlands. It applies to woodlands other than agricultural property. The value of the trees or underwood is left out of account at death, but IHT may be payable on disposal (s 126). Growing timber is in fact the only commercial asset in respect of which IHT can be deferred on death.

The occasion of charge

16.3   IHT is payable on a disposal in relation to the last death on which the timber passes. The person entitled to the sale proceeds or who would be entitled if the disposal were a sale is liable to the tax. An inter-spouse (or civil partner) disposal is ignored.

IHT is only charged on the first disposal of the trees or underwood following the death (s 126(3)).

The basis of charge

16.4   IHT is calculated on the net sale proceeds on a sale for full consideration and on the net value at the date of disposal in other cases. The IHT rate scale is the one which would have applied if the chargeable value as above had been included in the estate in relation to the latest death on which it passes and represented the highest part of that estate (s 128).

If the IHT charge crystallises after a reduction in the rates, the reduced rates apply (Sch 2, para 4).

Set-off against BPR

16.5   Where the woodlands were being managed commercially (ie would have qualified as relevant business property for business property relief under ss 103–114) the amount on which IHT is charged under s 126 is reduced by 100%.

However, if there is a woodland postponement election under s 125, only 50% business property relief will be available on a later sale (see **16.7**).

Relief on death only

16.6   The IHT relief is not available on lifetime transfers of woodlands; these will be potentially exempt transfers or lifetime chargeable transfers in the normal way.

Where woodlands relief has been given on death, and the later disposal is also subject to IHT as a chargeable transfer, there will be two computations of IHT. The first will relate to the earlier death and the second to the later chargeable transfer. The IHT relating to the death may be deducted from the value of the chargeable transfer to arrive at the IHT liability on the latter (s 129).

Since, by s 3A(4), a potentially exempt transfer made within seven years of death is a chargeable transfer, presumably the IHT on the earlier death may be deducted not only against lifetime chargeable transfers but also against those potentially exempt transfers that ultimately become chargeable.

Conditions of relief

16.7   Relief is available only if the deceased had held the land beneficially for the five years preceding his death, or had acquired it otherwise than for money or money's worth (s 125(1)(b)). The relief therefore is of no use in deathbed schemes (ie purchasing woodlands shortly before death).

Prior to changes introduced in FA 2009, a requirement for claiming woodlands relief was that the land must be situated in the UK. However, the territorial scope of woodlands relief was extended, so that it is available if the land is in the UK or another EEA state. The extended relief applies in relation to transfers of value where the IHT otherwise payable (or in the case of IHT payable by instalments, the last instalment) either would have been due from 22 April 2009, or was paid or due from 23 April 2003. The FA 2009 provisions also extend the time limit for making a woodlands relief election (and a claim for repayment of IHT if appropriate) where the ability to make the election arises from the changes (FA 2009, s 122). Information on making claims is contained in the HMRC Inheritance Tax and Trusts Newsletter, August 2009. It should be noted that the territorial scope of agricultural property relief (see **Chapter 15**) was similarly extended, so that the relief is available if the property is situated in the UK or another EEA state.

Net values are after selling expenses and expenses of replanting within three years or such longer period as the Board may allow (s 130(2)), except to the extent that these expenses are allowable for income tax (s 130(1)(b)).

Where the woodlands are being managed commercially and would qualify as relevant business property for business property relief under ss 103–114, the amount on which IHT is charged is, as noted above, reduced by 100%.

However, if there is an election under ss 125–127 to leave the value of the woodlands out of account in determining the value of the estate on death, only 50% business property relief will be available under s 127(2) on an eventual sale. Obviously, if at all possible, it is sensible for the owners of woodland to endeavour to manage the woodlands in a commercial and active manner in order to obtain 100% business property relief. Separate accounts should be kept in relation to the woodlands, and these accounts should not be included in the overall farming accounts.

Example 16.1 – Effect of woodlands election

Hawker died on 30 September 1991 and left the following estate, there having been no lifetime transfers:

	£
Sundry assets	300,000
Value of timber	80,000
	380,000
IHT was payable on death on £300,000, less the then nil rate band of £140,000:	
£160,000 × 40%	64,000
On 1 May 2011, the timber was sold for the sum of £200,000 (on which 50% business relief is due) after allowing for selling and replanting expenses so that IHT is payable on	100,000
Other assets at death: assumed	325,000
	425,000

IHT payable (at 2011–12 rates):

First £325,000 @ 0%	Nil
Next £100,000 @ 40%	40,000
	40,000
Less: Payable (at 2011–12 rates) on estate of £300,000 on death	Nil
Payable on sale of timber	40,000

Without election

If no claim had been made, then IHT on death in 1991 would have been (after 50% BPR on the timber, being the rate at that time):

First £140,000	Nil
Next £200,000 @ 40%	80,000
	80,000

The taxpayer will use form IHT100 to report the tax due.

Transfers of woodlands subject to a deferred estate duty charge

16.8   Under the estate duty regime, duty on a death on woodlands could be deferred until the heir felled or sold the timber. If the heir died before the timber was sold, estate duty on his death replaced the earlier deferred charge and could itself again be deferred. Under FA 1986, Sch 19, para 46, any transfer which includes woodlands subject to a deferred estate duty charge is denied PET treatment so that there is an immediate lifetime chargeable transfer and the deferred estate duty is treated as discharged.

As it stands, any single large transfer which includes some small part of woodlands subject to deferred estate duty is refused PET treatment. Extra-statutory concession F15 restricts the denial of PET treatment only to such part of the transfer as consists of the woodlands subject to the deferred estate duty. Thus there is an immediate IHT charge on the woodlands subject to the deferred estate duty, but the remaining part of the transfer constitutes a PET.

WOODLANDS – PLANNING

The decision to elect or not

16.9   In many cases, it will not be advisable to make a s 125 election because, as illustrated in Example 16.1, the eventual IHT liability will be calculated by reference to the value of the woodlands at the time of eventual disposal which will bring into charge any increase in value since the death. By contrast, if an election is not made, the value of the timber will be crystallised at the value at the date of death and the IHT will be payable by instalments.

As a general rule, one should not elect in the case of young softwood (because of the large growth expectation), whereas an election for a mature forest may prove advantageous, subject to the business property relief point referred to earlier. In the case of the former, the ideal situation could be to pay IHT on a death or lifetime gift (if no election is made, there is a low value and the disposition is made in favour of a younger generation who could fell and dispose with no further charge).

Note, moreover, that a s 125 election need not extend to all woodlands in the same estate. It may be appropriate to elect in relation to certain parts only of a deceased's timber estate. Where two or more persons are jointly liable for IHT on woodlands of a deceased, one or more of the co-owners may wish to elect while the others decide not to. Where the conditions are satisfied for 100% business property relief, there will be no need to consider any sort of election.

As already mentioned, the IHT liability, and calculation of the tax, relates to the last relevant death. Accordingly, where the original estate owner had a substantial estate including the timber, it is sometimes possible to save IHT by granting an immediate post-death interest to an elderly impecunious individual by will and then making an election. When that life tenant dies, the IHT liability may fall wholly or partly within the nil rate band. There will be no capital gains tax.

However, the best approach is to aim for business property relief where possible, akin to the approach taken in *Marquess of Hertford v IRC* [2005] STC (SCD) 177 (see **15.19**), although bearing in mind HMRC's view that this case was 'unusual' and decided on the particular facts (IHTM25342).

Use of exemptions

16.10   Instead of using the very restricted relief in s 125, an estate owner should consider transferring his interest in timber by using his available exemptions, particularly the annual exemption, and possibly consider mortgage charging arrangements.

Own use

16.11   It appears that timber felled for use on the owner's property is not a disposal, for example, where used for estate maintenance and repairs. This could be particularly relevant where the estate owner also had agricultural property. There is, however, no specific IHT exclusion (as there was for estate duty).

WORKS OF ART, HISTORIC BUILDINGS ETC

Summary

16.12   The exemption (ss 25–27, 30–35A, 77–79A, Schs 3–5) covers death and lifetime gifts and property held in relevant property trusts. The relief is given by way of conditionally exempt transfer. No claim for conditional exemption in respect of a potentially exempt transfer can be made unless and until the donor dies within seven years.

Gifts to spouses and charities (ie both categories generally exempt from IHT anyway) are outside these conditional exemption rules. Form IHT100 is used to report tax due.

Requirements and conditions

16.13   The requirements for conditional exemption are that:

- the property in question is appropriately designated by the Treasury (under s 31);
- requisite undertakings are given to the Treasury (s 30(1)(b)); and
- for lifetime transfers, the transferor or spouse has held the property for at least six years or inherited it on a death to which conditional exemption (or the estate duty equivalent) applied (s 30(3)).

Details of conditional exemption are given in the HMRC publication 'Capital Taxation and the National Heritage' (formerly leaflet IR67), which is available via HMRC's website (www.hmrc.gov.uk/inheritancetax/conditionalexemption. pdf). This replaces previous guidance on public access to conditionally exempt property in the Inheritance Tax Manual (as to the conditional exemption generally, see IHTM21048).

Claims for exemption usually have to be made within two years of the relevant chargeable event, although the Board may allow a longer period at its discretion (s 30(3BA)).

Designation and scope

16.14   The exemption can apply to pictures, prints, books, manuscripts, works of art and scientific collections where the objects appear to the Board to be pre-eminent for their national, scientific, historic or artistic interest. The exemption may also apply to land and buildings if, in the opinion of the Treasury, they are of outstanding scenic or historic or scientific interest (s 31).

The undertaking that must be given to the Board is to the effect that the property will be kept permanently in the UK with such provisions as to preservation and maintenance and reasonable access to the public as are agreed between the Treasury and the person giving the undertaking (s 31(2)). Slightly different undertakings are given if the property is land or buildings.

Access

16.15 Prior to March 1998, public access to exempt assets usually involved making a prior appointment with the owners of the assets or their agents. Following the changes, owners may no longer elect for public access by prior appointment only. Both future and existing undertakings are open to amendment and owners may be required to publicise their undertakings and disclose relevant information. Owners have six months from the proposal on behalf of the Board to vary an existing undertaking to agree to the variations (s 35A(2)).

If no agreement can be reached and the Tax Tribunal considers the proposed variations to be just and reasonable the Tribunal may make a direction accordingly. Not surprisingly, when introduced these measures were greeted with horror by many owners of valuable assets who had expected to be able to rely upon agreements reached with the Board, and the matter was considered to be highly contentious.

It was argued that variations of existing agreements could be insisted upon by the Board against the wishes of the taxpayer only if the Special Commissioner (which preceded the Tax Tribunal) was satisfied that it was just and reasonable in all the circumstances to direct that the proposed variation be made. The Tribunal ought not to be satisfied that a forced variation of an inherently non-variable agreement (at the time it was entered into, before FA 1998) was just and reasonable. A possible solution is for owners of such works of art to exhibit them in specially arranged public exhibitions.

In *Re Applications to vary the undertakings of 'A' and 'B'* [2005] SSCD 103 (SpC 439), owners A and B had the benefit of conditional exemption for chattels, most of which were kept in the private homes of the owners and their families. HMRC proposed to vary both undertakings and effectively extend the access requirement, which the owners did not agree to. The Special Commissioner held that in the specific circumstances the proposals placed additional burdens on the owners, which would outweigh the benefit to the public to such an extent that they would not be just and reasonable. One particular factor was that one of the owners had been willing to arrange for some access by way of public display, but the local authorities lacked the resources to take up the offer. It was therefore held that the proposals would not take effect.

Management agreements

16.16   An important feature of heritage relief is the requirement that the property or land be well looked after. An undertaking to that effect must be given in respect of land and buildings, set out in a Heritage Maintenance Plan (HMP). Preparing an HMP takes time: HMRC accept that and may in the past have been willing to grant heritage relief whilst the HMP was prepared. That position has changed; conditional exemption will be granted only once an agreed HMP is in place (see HMRC IHT and Trusts Newsletter, December 2007).

HMRC guidance

16.17   It was hoped that future proposals by HMRC to vary undertakings would be fair, equitable and proportionate to the benefits they are intended to provide to the public. There are no further recorded cases. Naturally, each new application for exemption is subject to the more stringent requirements as to access.

The HMRC guidance (published in the IHT and Trusts Newsletter on 18 December 2007) deals with several relevant issues:

- Security: it is reasonable for a visitor to be asked to produce some evidence of ID, such as a passport, on arrival to view heritage items.

- Proof of identity: it is too much to ask for ID to be posted to the heritage owner in advance, but the visitor should arrive with two forms of ID, to show who (s)he is and to confirm the address.

- Charging: owners may make a reasonable charge for allowing visitors to view heritage items, along the lines of what, say, the National Trust would charge; however, many owners make no charge.

HMRC's website also includes a section on 'UK heritage assets – tax exemption', that contains a database of assets exempt from capital taxes, together with information for the public on how to see or visit such property (www.hmrc.gov.uk/heritage).

Chargeable events

16.18   A conditionally exempt transfer becomes liable to IHT on the happening of a chargeable event (s 32). CGT will also be due (TCGA 1992, s 258(5)).

A chargeable event can be breach of an undertaking, death, sale, gift, or other disposition unless the disposition is a sale to an approved institution or the asset is transferred to the Secretary of State in satisfaction of IHT.

A death or gift is not a chargeable event if the transfer itself is a conditionally exempt transfer and similar undertakings are given by the legatee or donee.

The tax payable

16.19   IHT will be payable on a chargeable event on an amount equal to the value of the property at the time of the chargeable event and at the appropriate cumulative lifetime rates, if the transferor is alive, and at the death rate if he is dead, as if it were the highest part of his estate. A sale at an arm's-length value not intended to confer any gratuitous benefit is deemed to take place at the sale price (s 33).

In calculating the value on which IHT is payable, there can be deducted the expenses of any sale (*Tyser v A-G* [1938] Ch 426) and any CGT payable (TCGA 1992, s 258(8)).

HMRC option for higher tax charge

16.20   If there have been two or more conditionally exempt transfers within 30 years of the chargeable event, HMRC need not take the *latest* transfer, but may take any of the previous transfers (s 33(5)). In large part this measure will frustrate much of the planning that might be carried out in its absence; such as arranging for the property to pass on the death of an elderly impecunious individual who has had a life interest in the property.

A chargeable event is treated as part of the transferor's cumulative total. Where conditionally exempt property is comprised in a relevant property settlement, it is exempt from the ten-yearly charge until after a chargeable event has taken place. When a chargeable event occurs, IHT is payable at the special rates specified in s 79(6).

Since conditional exemption was a feature of estate duty prior to the introduction of IHT, there are transitional provisions applicable to conditional exemption granted on a death prior to 7 April 1976 (s 35). There is the possibility that the rate of tax on a chargeable event may be much higher than 40%. Practice in this area requires knowledge of historical rates, and tax systems, that have no relevance anywhere else.

Transferable nil rate band

16.21   It can be seen that the charging regime for heritage property may involve reconsideration of tax on estates where the taxpayer died many years before. The political point could be made that self-assessment is based on dealing with each year on its own and achieving finality; and that arrangements such as the HMRC option for a higher tax charge do not give families finality for very many years. We are, however, stuck with the system that we have.

In the circumstances, a heritage tax charge may well affect the nil rate band usage of a taxpayer long dead and may trigger reworking of IHT on the death of the taxpayer's spouse (though probably not of a civil partner, since the civil partnership legislation is relatively recent) (see **3.6**).

Favoured disposals

16.22 No IHT liability arises on a disposal with the agreement of the Secretary of State in satisfaction of a tax liability, nor in the case of a private treaty sale to a specified national heritage body.

In the latter case, one normally negotiates a price which shares the benefit of the freedom from tax between the vendor and the acquiring institution, the discount from market value being known as the 'douceur'. The national heritage body pays less than the full market price on the one hand, but the vendor receives more than he would have done on a net basis if IHT were payable. The government have advised museums and galleries in general to offer the seller an amount equal to the market value, reduced by 25% of the benefit of the tax exemption but subject to negotiations above or below where flexibility is required. See HMRC publication ('Capital Taxation and the National Heritage') and SP 6/87 ('Acceptance of property in lieu of inheritance tax, capital transfer tax and estate duty').

Both a disposal in satisfaction of tax and a private treaty sale are exempt from VAT (VATA 1994, Sch 9, Pt II, Group 11).

Example 16.2 – IHT charge on later sale

	£
Smith died on 1 May 2011, leaving sundry assets of	345,000
and a painting valued at	85,000

Exemption is claimed on the painting which is subsequently sold by the legatee for net proceeds of £200,000. This sale is a chargeable event and IHT is payable under s 33(1) on the value of the property at the time of the chargeable event. The rate is that which would have applied if the value of the property had been added to the value transferred on death and had formed the highest part of that value.

	£
IHT on death (no lifetime transfers)	
£325,000 @ 0%	Nil
£20,000 @ 40%	8,000
	8,000
IHT on sale (chargeable event)	
£200,000 @ 40%	80,000

Relevant property trusts

16.23   Conditional exemption is given to approved works of art etc held in a relevant property trust when transferred out of the settlement provided that the property has been in the settlement for the whole of the six years ending with the transfer out (s 78(1)).

There is also an exemption from the ten-yearly charge (s 79).

The gift of an interest in land is an exempt transfer for stamp duty land tax purposes (FA 2003, Sch 3, para 1), although the assumption of liabilities such as a mortgage constitutes chargeable consideration for the purposes of such transfers.

Planning

16.24   It may be appropriate for an estate owner to charge other assets in his estate and invest the proceeds in such works of art, etc; or more likely, when raising money for school fees, to keep the artworks as long as possible and sell something else.

Maintenance funds for historic buildings

16.25   A transfer of value for the maintenance, repair or preservation of historic buildings and assets of outstanding scenic, historic or scientific interest etc is, subject to certain conditions, an exempt transfer to the extent that the value transferred by it is attributable to property which becomes comprised in a settlement for a minimum of six years and the Treasury so direct (whether before or after the time of the transfer) (s 27, Sch 4).

Moreover, not only is the transfer into the trust exempt, but so long as the conditions are complied with there is no IHT charge on payment out of the trust for approved purposes or on the ten-yearly anniversary.

Schedule 4 imposes conditions with particular reference to the official directions including:

- that the property is of a character and amount appropriate for the purposes of the settlement;

- a custodian trustee is appointed;

- the application of the capital and income of the trust; and

- the character of the building and land in relation to the national interest and national heritage.

The tax exemption for transfers to approved heritage maintenance trusts must be claimed within two years after the date of the transfer concerned, or within such longer period as the Board may allow (s 27(1A)).

16.26   One small point to watch is the date of the recognition of the fund, described in Sch 4, para 1 as a 'direction'. Maintenance funds can qualify for special treatment for income tax (ie in respect of settlors of such funds; see ITA 2007, Pt 9, Ch 10), but that treatment applies only after the Direction has been given.

Capital gains tax 'hold-over' relief is generally available on a disposal of an asset to a maintenance fund (TCGA 1992, s 260(2)).

LLOYD'S MEMBERSHIP

16.27   Insurance business at Lloyd's is conducted by Lloyd's underwriting members known as 'Names'. They were, and some still are, personally liable as individuals for all claims made on them to the extent of their assets on the basis of unlimited liability (although stop-loss insurance can be effected). Underwriting members are formed into syndicates and each syndicate is managed on a day-to-day basis by managing agents. The acceptance of insurance risk is the basis of Lloyd's activities; and the interest of an underwriting member qualifies both for business relief and for payment of IHT by instalments.

The interest of the typical Lloyd's Name will consist of his Lloyd's Deposit and his contribution to a Special Reserve Fund and to a Personal Reserve Fund. His Lloyd's Deposit comprises investments lodged with Lloyd's as security for the underwriting activities of the syndicate.

The Special Reserve Fund is a 'pot' to which an individual can transfer a proportion of his underwriting profits. Income tax relief is available on payments into the fund, but income tax is payable on any withdrawals.

The Personal Reserve Fund is designed as a practical measure to cater for losses in the current difficult insurance climate.

Other security

16.28   Alongside these funds, the Name will normally seek a stop-loss policy offering protection against losses over and above an agreed specified amount, although recently the cost of such cover has been very high. There may also be an estate protection plan, limiting the liability of his estate in the event of his death and thus easing administration.

The value of syndicate participations and underwriting profits (and losses) will also need to be taken into account for valuation purposes, in respect of open accounts and accounts which are running off.

Bank guarantees

16.29   Increasingly, instead of lodging investments as their Lloyd's deposit, Names have put up bank guarantees in lieu. The bank will normally demand security for the issue of the guarantee and, provided that the assets forming the bank's collateral security are held subject to restrictions on use, business relief should be available on those assets.

However, where the individual has put forward his private residence as collateral security, HMRC may reject business property relief on the grounds that the residence cannot satisfy the 'wholly or mainly for the purposes of a business' test in s 105(1).

Subject to the usual conditions, business property relief at 100% will normally be available at least in part on an individual's Lloyd's underwriting interest. Therefore, it is important to maximise the effect of that relief by giving assets representing the Lloyd's interest (whether during life or on death) to persons other than the exempt spouse (eg children).

Corporate membership of Lloyd's

16.30   Since 1 January 1994, alongside the existing individual members, Lloyd's has allowed corporate members, the shares in which will also normally qualify for 100% business property relief. Also, Scottish Limited Partnerships provide a limited liability option of a partnership registered in Scotland which is a separate legal entity. Corporate members are companies in which investors can take up shares without the risks associated with unlimited liability.

Corporate Names are to be taxed by reference to the time when profits are declared (traditionally, three years in arrears). At the same time, the year of assessment for individual Lloyd's Names is also linked to the year of declaration of profits rather than to the Lloyd's account year. Thus, the profits of account year 2009 will normally be declared in 2012 and will form the basis of assessment for the individual for the year 2012–13.

In the context of Lloyd's, see the two cases concerning business property relief on underwriting businesses: *Hardcastle*, discussed at **15.38**; and *Mallender*, discussed at **15.64**.

As mentioned above, estate protection policies are available to Lloyd's underwriters, to help personal representatives overcome the delay in completing the administration of a deceased Name's estate arising from the three-year accounting system mentioned above.

Chapter 17

Foreign domicile

INTRODUCTION

17.1   Inheritance tax (IHT) is subject to territorial limits. The UK does not seek to tax a transfer where neither the transferor nor the property transferred has a sufficient connection with the UK. The factors used to determine whether a sufficient connection exists are the domicile of the transferor and the place where the property is situated. If both of these are outside the UK, the property is normally excluded from the transferor's estate for IHT purposes.

A separate test is applied to settled property. Whether or not an interest in possession exists in the property, it is the settlor's domicile, together with the place where the property is situated, which determines the scope of IHT. Property which is not taxed on account of its location and the domicile of the owner or settlor is described as *excluded property* and is discussed at **17.11**. This includes certain types of UK property.

Under general UK law, every individual has a domicile, but only one domicile. For IHT purposes, a person is domiciled in the state in which he is domiciled under the general law, but with two exceptions. First, a person who is domiciled outside the UK under general law will nevertheless be deemed to be domiciled in the UK for IHT purposes in specific circumstances (see **17.6**). Secondly, a person may be treated as domiciled elsewhere under the provisions of a double taxation treaty and taxed on the basis of that treaty domicile.

There is a third quasi-exception, in that a person is described in the IHT legislation (and, for convenience, in various parts of this book) as domiciled in the UK or not domiciled in the UK. In reality, a person will be domiciled in, say, England, or Scotland, but cannot be domiciled in the UK as such, because the UK does not have a unified system of law.

Acquiring a non-UK domicile could be described as the most effective form of IHT planning. On the other hand, it is difficult to acquire a domicile of choice which will displace a UK domicile of origin, difficult to know if this has indeed been achieved, and it requires potentially drastic lifestyle changes. These were once considered too drastic to be desirable, but then (for a time) the strength of the pound against both the dollar and the euro subsequently made it much more attractive to sell up and move, usually to warmer climes. Even language is less of a problem than formerly, with increasing numbers of 'ex-pat ghettoes' which cater for the needs of wealthy retirees. Clearly, those who do have, or can with determination acquire, a non-UK domicile can use this to minimise the impact of IHT on their estates.

It should be remembered, however, that domicile is relevant not just to an individual's tax position, but also to other important matters including the law applicable to rights of succession.

DOMICILE UNDER THE GENERAL LAW

17.2 There is no statutory definition of domicile for UK tax purposes (although there is a statutory rule for determining domicile, in Civil Jurisdiction and Judgments Act 1982, s 41, which was considered in a case concerning Roman Abramovich (*Yugraneft v Abramovich* [2008] EWHC 2613 (Comm)). However, HMRC state in their Residence, Domicile and Remittance Basis Manual that the 1982 Act, together with the Civil Jurisdiction and Judgments Act 1991, and the Civil Jurisdiction and Judgments Order 2001, SI 2001/3929, 'use domicile in a narrow and specialised sense that is defined by the legislation' (RDRM20070).

There are three different types of domicile under general law:

- domicile of origin;
- domicile of dependence; and
- domicile of choice.

They are described as different *types* of domicile because they can be acquired and lost in different ways. The country in which a person is domiciled is sometimes described as his permanent home (see *Winans v Attorney General* [1904] AC 287). This can be a useful description, and it is certainly true that domicile requires a degree of permanence which residence, by contrast, does not. On the other hand, it should be borne in mind that both a domicile of origin and a domicile of dependence are acquired by operation of law rather than by choice and that it is possible for a person to be domiciled in a place where he has never been, let alone had a home or lived permanently.

For IHT purposes, a person can be deemed to be domiciled in the UK even though he is domiciled elsewhere under the general law, and thus regarded as non-UK domiciled for income tax and capital gains tax purposes. For example, the settlor-interested, non-resident (or dual resident) trust provisions in TCGA 1992, s 86 do not apply if the settlor was non-UK domiciled throughout the tax year in question.

The taxation of non-UK domiciled individuals for income tax and capital gains tax purposes assumed much sharper focus and greater significance following the rather controversial introduction of changes to the remittance basis rules for the taxation of individuals who are UK resident but not domiciled (or not ordinarily resident) in the UK in FA 2008. Those rules are notoriously complex, and it is therefore perhaps a mercy for the authors of this book that consideration of the remittance basis rules is outside its scope. For commentary on those rules, see *Revenue Law: Principles & Practice* (Bloomsbury Professional). HMRC guidance on the common law principles of domicile and its application of those rules in practice is contained in the Residence, Domicile and Remittance Basis Manual at RDRM20000 onwards.

This chapter is concerned with the IHT rules and consequences of domicile in the UK. First, an individual will be deemed domiciled when he has been resident for (any part of) 17 out of the 20 years of assessment ending with the present one. This rule is the most relevant to someone coming to the UK. Secondly, he will be deemed domiciled if he was domiciled here within the previous three years (IHTA 1984, s 267). This rule will be of relevance when a person leaves the UK to acquire a domicile elsewhere.

The domicile of a child under the age of 16 in Scotland is subject to Scottish law (see RDRM22120).

Domicile of origin

17.3   Everyone acquires a domicile of origin at birth and this remains his domicile until it is replaced by a domicile of dependence or a domicile of choice.

It is important to identify a person's domicile of origin because it can revive when a domicile of choice is lost. This point was illustrated in a non-tax case, *Barlow Clowes International Ltd (in liquidation) and others v Henwood* [2008] EWCA 577 (see **17.5**).

A person's domicile of origin is:

- his father's domicile at the time of his birth, unless

- he was illegitimate, or

- his father died before he was born.

In those other cases, his domicile of origin will be his mother's domicile. Although as a matter of fact it will often be the country in which he was born, this need not be so.

Example 17.1 – A child's domicile

A child might be born in California to parents who had lived there for 20 years. Suppose that the father had an English domicile of origin and that this had not been displaced by a domicile of choice.

In that case, the child would acquire an English domicile of origin at birth, despite the fact that (s)he might never come to England.

In the case of an adopted child, a new domicile of origin is regarded as having been acquired from the relevant adoptive parent, ie the domicile of his child's adoptive father or, if there is no adoptive father, his adoptive mother at the time of his adoption (RDRM22110).

A domicile of origin is the most clinging tenacious form, and will only be displaced if a person acquires a domicile of choice or a domicile of dependence. It will revive if, for example, a domicile of choice is abandoned, unless immediately replaced by a new domicile of choice (*Udny v Udny* (1869) LR 1 Sc & Div 441, HL).

Domicile of dependence

17.4   Domiciles of dependence now only affect children under 16 and persons of unsound mind. Prior to 1 January 1974, this category included married women. Before that date, a woman generally acquired her husband's domicile on marriage and her domicile changed when his did.

This rule was abolished by the Domicile and Matrimonial Proceedings Act 1973 but has some relevance to women who were married before 1 January 1974. On that date, their existing domiciles of dependence were not abandoned, but became domiciles of choice. Thus, a woman may have a domicile of choice on that basis (if it has not been abandoned in the interim) which she would never have acquired on an independent basis. The rule has no relevance to women married on or after 1 January 1974.

Care is needed where the domicile of a parent (upon which a child's domicile is dependent) changed from a domicile of origin to a domicile of choice before the child reaches the age of 16. For example, if the parent had a domicile of origin abroad but subsequently acquired a domicile of choice in the UK when the child was under the age of 16, the child will also become UK domiciled. The child's UK domicile would be retained throughout adulthood, unless replaced by a domicile of choice.

Interestingly, HMRC guidance states: 'This principle is generally accepted, but it should be noted that it has not been applied in every case' (RDRM22210).

Domicile of choice

17.5   A domicile of choice is acquired by both physical presence in another country *and* the settled intention of residing there permanently or indefinitely. It will not be acquired if, for example, that intention is conditional. It will also not be acquired by going to a country for work, even for an extended period, unless there is a definite intention to stay there permanently once the employment has ceased.

A domicile of choice can be lost by leaving the country without any definite intention of returning. A person will acquire a new domicile of choice if he goes to another country with the intention of settling there permanently. If no new domicile of choice is acquired, his domicile of origin will revive.

A person seeking to establish that a domicile of origin has been lost and a domicile of choice acquired has to discharge a heavy burden of proof (ie on a balance of probabilities). The fact that HMRC devote a whole chapter of their guidance on domicile to enquiries into domicile status (RDRM23000) suggests that the task may be difficult. For example, in HMRC's view, 'mere statements [of intention] are generally less important than actual conduct and may carry little weight if the statement does not correlate with actions taken' (RDRM22320). The burden of proof applies equally whether the taxpayer whose domicile of origin is in the UK is arguing that it has been superseded by the acquisition of a domicile of choice, or HMRC are arguing that a taxpayer whose domicile of origin is outside the UK has lost that domicile and acquired a domicile of choice in the UK.

The parties might want to argue either way; such is the flexibility of the tax system.

Example 17.2 – Domicile of spouse

Henry, a fit if somewhat lonely English pensioner and widower, regularly visited Taiwan, eventually returning with Dolly, a hospitality worker many years his junior, whom he married. East Anglian skies (and dialect) did not appeal to Dolly, who wintered in Taiwan.

On Henry's death, his executors would have liked to show that Dolly had become domiciled in the UK to take advantage of s 18 (spouse or civil partner exemption) without the limitation in s 18(2) for non-domiciled transferees. It became a matter of detailed evidence as to whether Dolly had really made her permanent home here.

An example of the type of case where HMRC were arguing in favour of acquisition of domicile of choice came before the Special Commissioners in *F and another (personal representatives of F deceased) v IRC* [2000] STC (SCD) 1. HMRC failed to prove that the deceased had lost his Iranian domicile of origin and acquired a UK domicile of choice.

In *IRC v Bullock* [1976] STC 409, the taxpayer had been brought up in Canada, but had come to live in England in 1932. He married in England and lived there virtually constantly thereafter but was held to have retained his Canadian domicile of origin because his intention, in the event of surviving his wife, was to return to Canada permanently. This meant that he could not be described as having a settled intention of remaining in England permanently.

In *Re Furse, Furse v IRC* [1980] STC 596, on the other hand, the taxpayer had been born in Rhode Island in 1883 and was a US citizen but had a close connection with England throughout his life. He and his wife had a family house in New York and visited it regularly, but they also had a farm in Sussex. It had been bought by the wife in 1924 and the taxpayer lived there until his death in 1963. Unlike the taxpayer in *Bullock*, there was evidence that this taxpayer was happy and contented in the Sussex farm. The only suggestion that he might ever leave England was if and when he was no longer fit enough to lead an active life on the farm. He did not really wish to leave England and was quite settled here. The court accordingly found that he died domiciled in England.

The case of *Re Clore (No 2)* [1984] STC 609 shows how important it is, if there is a settled intention of acquiring a domicile of choice in another jurisdiction, that there is plenty of clear written evidence of that intention and that matters are not just left to the recollections of friends and acquaintances after the death of the individual.

The effect on domicile of the acquisition of British citizenship was illustrated in the case of *Bheekhun v Williams* [1999] 2 FLR 229, CA. Mr Bheekhun had a domicile of origin in Mauritius. He came to the UK to find work in 1960 at the age of 29. When Mauritius became independent he had to choose whether to take British citizenship or Mauritian citizenship. He chose British citizenship, although he retained business links with Mauritius, acquired properties there and later acquired a Mauritian passport. At all times, he continued to live and work in the UK. When he renewed his UK passport, it described him as resident in the UK.

After his death, his separated spouse claimed under the Inheritance (Provision for Family and Dependants) Act 1975 and her claim depended upon establishing that he died domiciled in the UK. The Court of Appeal upheld the decision that he had acquired a domicile of choice in the UK by the time of his death.

It would be wrong to conclude from this decision that citizenship is a determinant of domicile. It is considered that it is not. The choice of acquiring a UK passport is likely to be simply one fact taken into account as evidence of an intention to settle permanently in the UK. The question ultimately remains one of fact. The weight attached to any particular fact will depend on all the circumstances.

In *Moores Executors v IRC* [2002] STC (SCD) 463, a domicile of origin (in USA) was upheld rather than a domicile of choice in the UK. However, in *Surveyor v IRC* [2002] STC (SCD) 501, a domicile of origin in England was held to have been replaced by a domicile of choice in Hong Kong, where the individual's family, social, business and financial ties were situated.

In *Allen and Hateley (as executors of Johnson deceased) v HMRC* [2005] STC (SCD) 614, Mrs Johnson was born in England in 1922, but moved abroad with her husband in 1953. She was diagnosed with Parkinson's disease in 1975. The couple settled in Spain in 1982 and bought a house there. Following her husband's death in 1996, Mrs Johnson moved to England to live with family as a 'visitor' (as she described it) in order to receive the care and support her illness demanded. Apart from clothes and jewellery she left her possessions (including pets) in the Spanish property, which was maintained ready for her occupation. In 2001 she bought the house next door to the family residence, with the intention of renovating it for her needs. However, she was admitted to hospital and died in August 2002 without occupying the property. Mrs Johnson retained the property in Spain until her death, and regarded it as her home.

HMRC issued a notice of determination that Mrs Johnson was domiciled in the UK at the time of her death. The executors appealed. The Special Commissioner held that the Revenue (as it then was) had failed to establish that she ceased to intend residing permanently in Spain. Mrs Johnson had maintained her house there. The purchase of a UK property had been the alternative to moving into a residential care home. The executors' appeal was allowed.

In *Mark v Mark* [2006] 1 AC 98, the House of Lords held, *inter alia*, that unlawful presence is not necessarily a bar to the establishment of a domicile of choice.

In *Agulian v Cyganik* [2006] EWCA Civ 129, the Court of Appeal held that an individual born in Cyprus but who had lived and worked in England for about 43 years between the age of 19 and his death at the age of 63, had not lost his Cypriot domicile of origin and acquired a domicile of choice in England.

The Court of Appeal's approach in *Agulian* was subsequently adopted in *Holliday and another v Musa and others* [2010] EWCA Civ 335, where it was held that an individual (coincidentally also with a Cypriot domicile of origin) who resided in the UK from 1958 until his death in 2006 had, on the facts, intended to settle permanently in England. It is worth noting that the Court of Appeal pointed out that, in considering whether the individual had intended to abandon his domicile of origin, 'any circumstance in a person's life can be relevant'.

In *Barlow Clowes International Ltd (in liquidation) and others v Henwood* [2008] EWCA 577, H was born in England in 1948 but settled in the Isle of Man in 1975, acquiring a domicile of choice there. He bought a substantial property in France in 1988, and in subsequent years H and his wife spent the bulk of their summer months there. H subsequently left the Isle of Man in 1992, and abandoned his domicile of choice there. Following the collapse of the Barlow Clowes bank, H became liable to pay damages.

The company attempted to serve a bankruptcy petition on him, but H contended that he was not domiciled in England and Wales, and that the petition therefore had no effect. The High Court agreed with him, and the company appealed. The company's appeal was allowed. The Court held that after H abandoned his domicile of choice in the Isle of Man in 1992, he did not subsequently acquire a new domicile of choice. H's domicile of origin had therefore revived by default. Note that the decision in this case contains a useful overview of domicile (see the summary at paras 8i–8x and 10–19).

In *Gaines-Cooper v HMRC* (see **17.8**), the appellant claimed to have established a domicile of choice in the Seychelles in 1976, in place of his domicile of origin in England and Wales. However, the High Court upheld the Special Commissioner's decision (based on the relatively long and complicated facts of the case) that he was domiciled in England and Wales in the tax years 1992–93 to 2003–04 inclusive. In the High Court, Lewison J highlighted the potential difficulty in demonstrating the replacement of a domicile of origin with a domicile of choice:

'It is important to remember that a person must always have a domicile; and, conversely, he may only have one domicile at a time. It follows, therefore, that there will (at least in theory) be a particular moment in time at which his domicile changes if he acquires a domicile of choice which replaces his domicile of origin. Before that moment, his domicile will have been his domicile of origin. After that moment it will be his domicile of choice. Locating the moment may be a difficult question of fact. It is also necessary to recall (as Ms Simler submitted) that a person's domicile of origin is particularly "adhesive".'

DOMICILE FOR IHT PURPOSES

17.6   A person who is domiciled outside the UK may nevertheless be treated as domiciled in the UK and taxed accordingly if he falls within the scope of IHTA 1984, s 267. Conversely, although domiciled (or deemed domiciled) here, it may be that he is treated as a non-domiciliary under an applicable double tax treaty and his liability for IHT purposes determined accordingly.

In the IHT context, the legislation refers to a person being domiciled in the UK rather than one of its constituent legal systems, such as England and Scotland. There are cases where, under the general law, a person could be domiciled in, say, Germany, but as a result of the wording of the IHT legislation may be domiciled in the UK for tax purposes. This depends on the proper construction of the words used in the legislation and is discussed at **17.10**.

Note that there is a further form of deemed domicile for IHT purposes, in addition to s 267. The tax status of a person who is a member of the House of Commons or the House of Lords is governed by the Constitutional Reform and Governance Act 2010 ('CRGA 2010'). It provides that a person who is a member of either House for any part of a tax year is generally to be treated as resident, ordinarily resident and domiciled in the UK for IHT (and also income tax and capital gains tax) purposes (CRGA 2010, ss 41, 42).

Deemed domicile under s 267

17.7   A person will be deemed domiciled in the UK for IHT purposes if:

- he was so domiciled within the last three years (commonly referred to as the 'three-year rule'); or

- he was resident in the UK for 17 out of the last 20 years of assessment *ending with the year of assessment in which the relevant time falls* (this is referred to below as the '17/20 rule').

An individual emigrating to the Channel Islands or the Isle of Man is in the same position as someone making a permanent home elsewhere abroad.

In relation to the three-year domicile rule, two points should be noted. First, under the general law, the acquisition of an overseas domicile of choice does not depend on any particular time period. Secondly, the three-year period only starts from the actual change of domicile under the general law. This may of course be later than the date of departure from the UK.

HMRC's guidance on deemed domicile changed in July 2011, and at the time of writing states in the context of the above 'three-year rule' (IHTM13024):

'For the rule to apply the taxpayer must have been domiciled in the UK both on or after 10 December 1974 and at any time within the three *calendar years* before the relevant event (the death or gift)' (emphasis added). However, the legislation refers to the three-year period immediately preceding the 'relevant time' (ie broadly when UK domicile is lost (s 267(1)). It is therefore assumed that HMRC guidance means the third anniversary of the relevant date (and not the alternative interpretation of three calendar years from 1 January to 31 December preceding that date).

Residence

17.8   In relation to the 17/20 rule, two further points should be noted. First, to remain outside that rule effectively means that in any 20-year period there must be at least four full tax years of non-residence. Secondly, the question of whether a person was resident in the UK in any year of assessment is to be determined as for income tax (s 267(4)). For tax years before 1993–94, this was subject to the exception that the 'available accommodation rule' did not apply for this purpose. That rule does not apply (from 1993–94) for income tax purposes either, but obviously the question of deemed domicile may turn on a person's residence in earlier years.

The government announced at Budget 2011 that it would be consulting on the introduction of such a statutory residence test, with a view to introducing a statutory definition of residence and making certain other changes. Consultation documents were subsequently published in 2011 and 2012 respectively. The proposed reforms apply for income tax and capital gains tax purposes, and do not change the general law concept of domicile. The original intention was that a statutory residence test would be included in FA 2012. However, the government later announced that the test was being postponed until 6 April 2013. The draft legislation was subsequently published on 11 December 2012, as part of the draft Finance Bill 2013 clauses.

The introduction of a statutory residence test will no doubt come as a great relief to many tax professionals, in terms of enabling individuals to establish their residence status in the UK with a much greater degree of certainty.

Establishing an individual's residence status has long been difficult. As Malcolm Gunn pithily observed in *Taxation* magazine in 1992:

'Residence is a question of fact. There are very few rules. Cases are decided as and when they arise, without much reference to any other previous decision. The decisions might well conflict with each other but that's just tough luck and there is nothing anybody can do about it.'

Lord Clyde observed in *Reid v IRC* (1926) 10 TC 673 that:

'The result is to make the question of law become (as it were) so attenuated, and the field occupied by the questions of fact become so enlarged as to make it difficult to say that a decision arrived at by the Commissioners with respect to a particular state of facts held proved by them, is wrong.'

Against that background, a string of more recent cases has added to the general uncertainty in terms of establishing whether an individual is resident or ordinarily resident in the UK for tax purposes. Detailed commentary on residence status issues and an analysis of case law on the subject is outside the scope of this book, but readers may wish to note and study recent cases, including:

- *Shepherd v HMRC* [2006] STC 1821;

- *L Barrett v HMRC* [2008] STC (SCD) 268;

- *Gaines-Cooper v HMRC* ([2008] STC 1665 (note, a subsequent application for judicial review was unsuccessful in *R (oao Gaines-Cooper) v HMRC* [2010] EWCA Civ 83). Permission to appeal was granted by the Supreme Court, but that appeal was subsequently dismissed ([2011] UKSC 47);

- *FM Genovese v HMRC* [2009] SSCD 373 (SpC 741);

- *DW Hankinson v HMRC (No 2)* [2009] UKFTT 384 (TC);

- *PG Turberville v HMRC* [2010] UKFTT 69 (TC);

- *LD Grace v HMRC (No 2)* [2011] UKFTT 36 (TC);

- *A Tuczka v HMRC* [2011] UKUT 113 (TCC);

- *Ogden v HMRC* [2011] UKFTT 212 (TC);

- *Broome v HMRC* [2011] UKFTT 760 (TC).

A lack of legislation has caused a significant amount of case law, which in turn contributed to the perceived 'legislation by guidance' in booklet HMRC6 (see below).

The FA 2008 provisions concerning residence and domicile did not change the general rule that an individual is resident in the UK if he or she spends 183 days or more in the UK in any one tax year. What did change was the manner in which days of presence in the UK are counted in determining an individual's residence status for income tax or capital gains tax purposes (ITA 2007, ss 831, 832; TCGA 1992, s 9).

Previously, HMRC practice (by concession) was generally that days of arrival in and departure from the UK were excluded from the residence test day count. However, from 6 April 2008 days are counted if the individual is present in the UK at the end of that day (note this rule is subject to an exception for individuals who are in transit, ie who arrive in the UK as a passenger one day and leave the UK on the next day, and who do not engage in activities substantially unrelated to their passage through the UK). Thus, an individual who arrives in the UK on Monday morning and leaves on Friday evening would count four days under the post-FA 2008 regime, but only three days under the previous one.

For HMRC's views on residence and ordinary residence (eg the 91-day average rule) see the HMRC booklet HMRC6 ('Residence, Domicile, and the Remittance Basis'). This booklet replaced HMRC's previous guidance in IR20. Unfortunately, in the authors' view, HMRC6 does little to clarify the circumstances in which individuals can accurately determine their residence status in many cases.

For IHT purposes, any uncertainty in determining residence status can have a serious 'knock-on' effect. The deemed domicile rule considers the number of years of a person's residence in the UK (ie the '17/20 rule'), with the question of residence in a tax year being determined as for income tax purposes. Thus, for example, a person who leaves the UK and subsequently believes that he has satisfied the 17/20 rule could find to his cost that HMRC disagree, perhaps on the basis that he remained UK resident because he never 'left' the UK in the first place.

The '17/20 rule' is considered in the example below.

Example 17.3 – Planning to prevent deemed domicile

Mr Anglophile arrives in the UK on 1 October 1996 and stays. In the tax year 1996–97, the Inland Revenue (as was) considered him to be resident because he is in the UK for more than six months. He remains resident in the tax year 1997–98 and all later years up to and including 2011–12. On 6 April 2012, at the start of 2012–13 (ie the seventeenth year) he transfers his foreign assets.

Unless he went abroad immediately, so as to be non-resident in 2012–13, the gift would be caught for IHT purposes (although it might only be a PET). To be safer still, he should have left the UK in, say, March 2012 before the start of 2012–13 and stayed out for the whole tax year, making all the dispositions of his foreign assets during his absence.

In order to avoid breaching either of the above rules (namely the three-year and the 17/20 rules), a person leaving the UK with a view to acquiring a domicile elsewhere needs to be aware of the different ways in which the two rules work. Then he can ensure that he does not take any action based on his newly acquired non-domiciled status until he is clear of both rules.

Example 17.4 – 'Losing' deemed domicile

Mr Knowall is aged 50 with an English domicile of origin and has been resident in England all his life. He decides to acquire a domicile of choice in Monaco. He leaves England permanently on 31 December 2008.

If he successfully acquired a domicile of choice in Monaco on arrival under the general law, he will cease to be deemed domiciled for IHT purposes under the 'three-year rule' on 1 January 2012. However, he will not lose his deemed domicile under the '17/20' rule until he has three clear tax years of non-residence behind him and the fourth year has begun.

In this case, Mr Knowall was resident in 2008–09 because he spent six months in England during that year. His three years of non-residence would be 2009–10, 2010–11 and 2011–12. Not until 6 April 2012 (that is, the first day of the fourth clear year, ie 2012–13) will he have lost his deemed domicile.

The deemed domicile rules do not apply for all purposes (see s 267(2)). They do not apply to:

- the exemption for specified government securities in the beneficial ownership of persons who satisfy specific conditions (eg not domiciled in the UK, or not ordinarily resident in the UK (s 6(2));

- certain types of national savings by persons domiciled in the Channel Islands or the Isle of Man (s 6(3)); or

- the interpretation of pre-CTT double taxation agreements still in force by s 158(6); such agreements entered into in the CTT/IHT era contain their own rules for domicile and for resolving the question where both countries claim domicile.

In addition, as indicated at **6.4**, legislation in the draft Finance Bill 2013 clauses published on 11 December 2012 provides for non-UK domiciled spouses to elect to be treated as domiciled in the UK for IHT purposes. In determining an individual's eligibility to make such an election, the deemed domicile rules in s 267 are to be ignored.

With regard to the third bullet point above, reference should be made to the precise words of the treaty in each case.

Example 17.5 – Domicile and double tax treaties

In summer 2011, Noorie wished to make a settlement of foreign assets for the benefit of her children. She had been born in India but was concerned that her residence in Ealing since her marriage in 1995 might make this a chargeable transfer.

The Agreement with India of 3 April 1956 is curious; estate duty has been abolished in India, reducing its effect. Discussions between the two governments thereafter fizzled out. The treaty is stated to relate to estate duty in the UK, but by virtue of s 158(6) it also applies to IHT, even though the FA 1975 repealed the earlier rules.

Article II(2) of the 1956 Agreement provides that domicile at death is determined by reference to the law in force 'in that territory', and Article III(3) prevents duty from being imposed in the UK on non-UK assets on the death of a person who was not domiciled at death in the UK but was domiciled then in India.

Noorie reflected that estate duty had been a tax on death, rather than on lifetime transactions; so, whilst s 158(6) might cover the point, the Agreement might not, in the end, protect the settlement from being taxed as a chargeable transfer (see below).

To be on the safe side, she limited the settlement to assets that qualified for business property relief and that were otherwise within the nil rate band.

In the three instances above, the general law of domicile applies. In circumstances where the assets are located abroad and the actual residence of the parties liable to IHT is abroad, albeit strictly domiciled in the UK for IHT purposes, HMRC may have difficulties enforcing the liability (see *Government of India v Taylor* [1955] AC 491). HMRC are unlikely to be able to enforce IHT abroad, although they may be able to recover from UK-resident beneficiaries.

HMRC accept that domicile issues exclude deemed domicile when considering the double tax agreements (see **17.9**) with France, Italy, India and Pakistan. However, if domicile under general law is in France, Italy, India or Pakistan, the deemed domicile rules can apply to chargeable lifetime transfers (see IHTM13024).

An individual may be able to benefit from the above double tax agreements if at the time of death his assets are located outside the UK and those assets devolve according to non-UK law. A will drafted according to the laws of the relevant jurisdiction is generally advisable. Any remaining IHT problem regarding UK *situs* assets can be overcome by (for example) borrowing against those UK assets (and taking a charge against them) prior to death. The borrowed funds could be deposited offshore (eg Jersey or the Isle of Man). This would result in the offshore funds devolving according to non-UK law, with exposure to

IHT on assets situated in the UK upon death being reduced by the deductible charge against them.

Treaty domicile

17.9   If a person is domiciled or deemed domiciled here under UK law, but is also domiciled in another state under that state's domestic law, then the terms of any applicable double tax treaty should be consulted in order to determine whether or not he will in fact be taxed as a domiciliary.

Typically, a treaty will have a 'tie-breaker' provision which contains a list of factors to determine which country the person will be treated as domiciled in for the purposes of the treaty.

A taxpayer who is neither domiciled nor deemed domiciled in the UK need not be concerned with treaty tie-breaker provisions. These may cause a domiciliary to be taxed as a non-domiciliary but they do not work the other way around. It should be noted that the draft Finance Bill 2013 legislation published on 11 December 2012 provides that the proposed election for a non-UK domiciled spouse to be treated as domiciled in the UK for IHT purposes is to be ignored when interpreting or applying estate duty conventions and double tax agreements which determine an individual's domicile.

However, treaties may still help a non-domiciliary who has some UK situs property. This will depend on the terms of the particular treaty.

Currently, there are capital taxes treaties with France, India, the Irish Republic, Italy, the Netherlands, Pakistan, South Africa, Sweden, Switzerland and the US. Using the US treaty as an example, fiscal domicile for treaty purposes is determined by Article 4, set out below:

'(1)   For the purposes of this Convention an individual was domiciled–

(a)   in the United States: if he was a resident (domiciliary) thereof or if he was a national thereof and had been a resident (domiciliary) thereof at any time during the preceding three years; and

(b)   in the United Kingdom: if he was domiciled in the United Kingdom in accordance with the law of the United Kingdom or is treated as so domiciled for the purposes of a tax which is the subject of this Convention.

(2)   Where by reason of the provisions of paragraph (1) an individual was at any time domiciled in both Contracting States, and

(a)   was a national of the United Kingdom but not of the United States, and

(b)   had not been resident in the United States for Federal income tax purposes in seven or more of the ten taxable years ending with the year in which that time falls,

he shall be deemed to be domiciled in the United Kingdom at that time.

(3)   Where by reason of the provisions of paragraph (1) an individual was at any time domiciled in both Contracting States, and

    (a)   was a national of the United States but not of the United Kingdom, and

    (b)   had not been resident in the United Kingdom in seven or more of the ten income tax years of assessment ending with the year in which that time falls,

he shall be deemed to be domiciled in the United States at that time. For the purposes of this paragraph, the question of whether a person was so resident shall be determined as for income tax purposes but without regard to any dwelling-house available to him in the United Kingdom for his use.

(4)   Where by reason of the provisions of paragraph (1) an individual was domiciled in both Contracting States, then, subject to the provisions of paragraphs (2) and (3), his status shall be determined as follows–

    (a)   the individual shall be deemed to be domiciled in the Contracting State in which he had a permanent home available to him. If he had a permanent home available to him in both Contracting States, or in neither Contracting State, he shall be deemed to be domiciled in the Contracting State with which his personal and economic relations were closest (centre of vital interests);

    (b)   if the Contracting State in which the individual's centre of vital interests was located cannot be determined, he shall be deemed to be domiciled in the Contracting State in which he had an habitual abode;

    (c)   if the individual had an habitual abode in both Contracting States or in neither of them he shall be deemed to be domiciled in the Contracting State of which he was a national; and

    (d)   if the individual was a national of both Contracting States or of neither of them, the competent authorities of the Contracting States shall settle the question by mutual agreement.

(5)   An individual who was a resident (domiciliary) of a possession of the United States and who became a citizen of the United States solely by reason of his–

    (a)   being a citizen of such possession, or

> (b)   birth or residence within such possession,
>
> shall be considered as neither domiciled in nor a national of the United States for the purposes of this Convention.'

Where a person is domiciled in both states as a matter of their respective domestic laws (Article 4(1)), the succeeding sub-paragraphs operate as tie-breakers, to determine in which state he will be treated as domiciled for the purposes of the treaty.

Domicile within the UK

17.10   Property which is not settled property can only be excluded property if the person beneficially entitled to it is an individual *domiciled outside the United Kingdom* (s 6(1)). Settled property can only be excluded property if the settlor was not *domiciled in the United Kingdom* at the time the settlement was made (s 48(3)(a)). The proposed election for a non-UK domiciled spouse to be treated as domiciled in the UK (see **6.4**) does not affect a person's domicile for the purposes of ss 6(2), 6(3) or 48(4) (ie broadly government securities free of tax while in foreign ownership (see **17.26**) and certain other types of saving).

The property must normally be situated outside the UK in order to be excluded property, although there are some exceptions. The *situs* of assets is discussed at **17.18**.

On the domicile point, it is slightly surprising that the legislation refers to domicile in or outside the UK. This is because, under the general law, a person is not domiciled in the UK as such. The UK is not a unified legal system. He will be domiciled in England and Wales or, say, Scotland. This is more than a difference of form.

Consider the following examples.

Example 17.6 – No domicile of choice yet

Beatrice's domicile of origin is in France. She comes to England and takes up residence in Sussex. She is quite certain that she will never return to France and (though she has not yet lived there) she intends to settle permanently in Scotland.

Beatrice has not lost her domicile of origin in France.

Example 17.7 – Domicile of choice acquired

Bertrand's domicile of origin is in France. He comes to England and takes up residence in Sussex. He is quite certain that he will never return to France and he intends to settle permanently in Cumbria.

Bertrand has acquired a domicile of choice in England.

It has been argued that the wording of the excluded property provisions means that Beatrice would be domiciled in the UK for IHT purposes, albeit that she remains domiciled in France under the general law. This argument assumes that the IHT legislation is introducing a new concept of UK domicile, which involves treating the UK as a single jurisdiction and applying the law of domicile to that deemed jurisdiction.

This is probably wrong. The wording of the legislation is not sufficient to create this new concept and HMRC are not known to have taken the point. It is more likely that a person is domiciled in the UK for IHT purposes if she is domiciled (in the real sense) in one of the parts of the UK. She is domiciled outside the UK if she is not domiciled in any of those parts. Beatrice falls into the latter category.

NON-UK DOMICILIARIES – EXCLUDED PROPERTY

17.11   Note that reference is made to the place where property is situated. This is discussed at **17.18**.

Non-settled property

17.12   Property situated outside the UK is excluded property if the person beneficially entitled to it is an individual domiciled outside the UK (s 6(1)). Thus, a Frenchman's *gite* is not subject to IHT.

This rule does not apply if the property is settled. This is so even if there is a person with an interest in possession who is treated as beneficially entitled to the property in which the interest subsists within s 49(1). However the legislation involves double negatives and must be read with care. In particular, reversionary interests are treated differently from current interests (see also at **17.15**).

Section 48(3) concerns foreign property in a trust. Such property, as is described in the next section, is generally excluded unless it is a reversionary interest or unless the settlor was domiciled in the UK when the trust was formed. By s 48(3)(b) the rule in s 6(1) applies to a reversionary interest but not otherwise. That prevents s 6(1) from applying to settled property and, notwithstanding s 49(1), property subject to, say, a life interest remains settled property.

Note, however, the restriction on s 48(3)(b) is itself subject to s 48(3B) (inserted by FA 2006, s 157) so as to remove favoured excluded property status from trust interests purchased after 5 December 2005 (see 'deathbed' planning referred to below). In each case, therefore, it will be necessary to apply each subsection in turn to see if the property is excluded.

In addition, holdings in authorised unit trusts and shares in open ended investment companies are excluded property (from 16 October 2002) if the beneficial owner is a non-UK domiciled individual (s 6(1A)). In addition, see below where those assets constitute settled property.

Settled property

17.13   Property comprised in a settlement and situated outside the UK will be excluded property if the settlor was domiciled outside the UK at the time the settlement was made. The residence of the trustees is irrelevant: what matters is the domicile of the settlor and the situs of the assets. The domicile of the beneficiary is irrelevant, even if he has an interest in possession. Reversionary interests are dealt with separately at **17.15**.

In addition, settled property consisting of holdings in an authorised unit trust or shares in an open-ended investment company is excluded property (from 16 October 2002) if the settlor was non-UK domiciled when the settlement was made (s 48(3A)(a)).

Example 17.8 – Transfer of excluded property

Suppose that a settlor was domiciled in Switzerland and, some years ago, settled assets in France on his UK-domiciled son.

If the settlor's son transfers his interest in the settlement or dies, there will be no transfer of value and accordingly no chargeable transfer. This is because excluded property is simply left out in valuing a person's estate. This means that a person's estate, as defined, is not diminished by a transfer of such property.

Conversely, a settlement made by a UK-domiciled settlor is not excluded property even if all the beneficiaries are domiciled abroad, all the property is situated abroad and the trustees are non-resident. In such circumstances, a distribution to a non-domiciled beneficiary in the hope that he will re-settle will often be advisable. However, care should be taken not to trigger an IHT charge by doing so (eg if the trust is discretionary, an exit charge may result).

Although a settlement made by a non-domiciliary is clearly in an advantageous position from the point of view of IHT, there are a number of points which should be borne in mind when planning for these settlements.

- *'Cat and mouse': failure to retain excluded property status*

  Suppose that the settlor or spouse has an initial interest in possession which is followed by discretionary trusts. If the initial interest was created prior to 22 March 2006, s 80 will treat the discretionary trust as being made by the person with the interest in possession at the time of the termination of that interest. The property in which that interest subsisted is treated as becoming comprised in a new settlement at the date of that termination.

  To be excluded property, the person beneficially entitled to the interest in possession must also have been non-domiciled at the date of termination of his interest (s 82). This condition must be met in addition to those in s 48(3)(a). This rule means that one needs to be wary of these initial interests in possession lest, for example, a deemed domicile is acquired by the spouse who is entitled to the interest before that interest terminates.

  One of the consequences of the wide-ranging changes to the IHT treatment of trusts since 22 March 2006 was to curtail the scope of s 80. FA 2006 added s 80(4), which amends s 80(1) so as to apply only to an interest in possession created on or after 22 March 2006 if it is a 'postponing interest'. A 'postponing interest' is an interest in possession that is an immediate post death interest or a disabled person's interest (s 80(4)).

- *Avoid mixed funds*

  One should not normally mix UK-situated assets and non-UK situated assets in the same discretionary trust. This is because the overseas assets will be taken into account in computing the effective rate of tax applicable to the UK property (IHTM42602).

- *Avoid joint settlors who are domiciled in the UK*

  Do not encourage a UK-domiciled individual to be a joint settlor of an otherwise excluded property settlement. Usually such settlements will be treated as two separate settlements by IHTA 1984, s 44(2). One will consist of excluded property and the other will not.

  However, s 44(2) is qualified. The settlements will only be treated as two separate settlements where '… the circumstances so require'. Although

HMRC accept that the determination of the extent to which overseas assets in a settlement are excluded property by reason of the settlor's domicile will normally be a relevant 'required circumstance' (RI166), this will not invariably be so. In particular, if an attribution of the settled property between the contributions made by each settlor is not feasible, as might be the case where husband and wife contributed joint assets to a trust, this treatment will not be adopted.

To ensure that such attribution is feasible, the trustees must keep careful records. This can become very complicated and time-consuming. The creation of two separate settlements in the first place will normally be a more practicable solution. For similar reasons, a settlor who subsequently becomes UK domiciled should avoid adding assets to the settlement.

- *Gift with reservation – not fatal*

The excluded property character of the settlement overrides the gift with reservation rules. Guidance in the Inheritance Tax Manual created uncertainty on this issue for some time. However, HMRC's guidance (at IHTM14396) was subsequently amended, and now states the following:

'Where the settlor was domiciled outside the UK at the time a settlement was made, any foreign property within that settlement is excluded property and is not brought into charge for inheritance tax purposes.

This rule applies where property is subject to a reservation of benefit even though the settlor may have acquired a domicile of choice in the UK, or be deemed to be domiciled in the UK, at the time the GWR charge arises.'

There is no current objection to the settlor being an object of the discretionary trust, although HMRC guidance created uncertainty for a time (see **17.25**).

The settlor beneficiary should not, however, be excluded subsequently by the trustees from benefiting in his or her lifetime as that will then constitute a deemed potentially exempt transfer under FA 1986, s 102(4).

- *Income tax and capital gains tax treatment*

The creation of the settlement has potential implications for other taxes which need to be carefully considered.

For example, there may be income tax disadvantages as a transfer of assets under ITA 2007, Pt 13, Ch 2 ('Transfers of assets abroad'), or under the settlements code in ITTOIA 2005, Pt 5, Ch 5. Possible capital gains tax implications include the settlor-interested offshore trust provisions in TCGA 1992, s 86 and Sch 5, where the settlor is UK resident or ordinarily resident.

Anti-avoidance

17.14   The potential IHT benefits of excluded property trust status are considerable. However, FA 2006 blocked a once popular IHT 'deathbed' planning arrangement for UK-domiciled individuals with effect from 5 December 2005 (s 48(3B)).

Marketed arrangements involved the sale of excluded property trust interests to UK-domiciled individuals. The purchaser would commonly have a life interest in the settled property, which on death would pass to, say, family members. The purchase of this interest effectively converted funds that would otherwise be liable to IHT into an exempt asset. This exemption was particularly useful if the purchaser's life expectancy was less than the seven-year period required for making PETs, or was perhaps less than the two-year period normally required to qualify for 100% business property relief after the purchase of relevant business property.

However, from the above date, where the trust property interest in question is purchased, the exemption in s 48(3) will not apply. In addition, HMRC have sought to challenge acquisitions before 5 December 2005 in some cases, particularly where non-UK domiciled individuals have settled funds overseas (eg with borrowed cash) with the intention of selling an interest in the trust as part of marketed IHT planning arrangements.

Further marketed arrangements involving variations of those described above subsequently became available following the FA 2006 changes. However, legislation was introduced in FA 2010 to block avoidance in respect of purchased interests in possession (see **1.30**). A degree of caution is advocated in respect of IHT planning arrangements, particularly in view of HMRC's attitude and approach to challenging and blocking them.

Anti-avoidance provisions were also introduced in FA 2012 with effect from 20 June 2012, which were targeted at specific, complicated arrangements of which HMRC had become aware. Those arrangements broadly concerned the acquisition by a UK-domiciled individual of an interest in settled excluded property, involving the giving of consideration in money or money's worth, where a 'relevant reduction' in the individual's estate would otherwise result. The provisions apply where the settlor was not UK domiciled when the settlement was made, or alternatively where a UK corporate settlor settled assets as part of the arrangements, and also affect acquisitions by individuals of certain reversionary interests in settled property which would otherwise be excluded property.

The effect of these anti-avoidance provisions is broadly that the relevant settled property (or a reversionary interest falling within the scope of the provisions) is no longer treated as excluded property. The settlement is treated like a UK trust, and is therefore subject to ten-year anniversary and exit charges (s 48(3D)). Furthermore, the reduction in value of the individual's estate falls to be charged to IHT as if a transfer of value had been made directly to a relevant property trust, ie it is not a PET (ss 74A–74C).

Of course, anti-avoidance provisions targeted at specific arrangements may nevertheless have unforeseen and wider implications than intended. This necessitates at least an awareness of them, and the circumstances in which the provisions could apply.

Reversionary interests

17.15   The circumstances in which a reversionary interest will be excluded property are different from other assets. The general rule is that a reversionary interest is excluded property by definition, irrespective of anyone's domicile (IHTA 1984, s 48(1)). This is the counterbalance to the treatment of a person entitled to a qualifying interest in possession as beneficially entitled to the whole property in which that interest subsists (s 49(1)). If the reversion were not excluded property, the same property would be treated as comprised in more than one person's estate.

There are, however, exceptions to this general rule:

- if the reversionary interest has been acquired at any time for a consideration in money or money's worth (s 48(1)(a));

- if the settlor or his spouse has been beneficially entitled to the reversionary interest (s 48(1)(b));

- if the reversionary interest is expectant on the determination of a lease treated as a settlement by s 43(3) (s 48(1)(c)); or

- if there is a reversionary interest to which an individual is beneficially entitled, and that individual is able to acquire another interest in the relevant settled property, where the anti-avoidance conditions in s 74A(a), (b) and (d) are met (ie in relation to the arrangements involving the acquisition of an interest in settled property, as mentioned at **17.14**).

In relation to the first exception, it applies even if the person currently entitled to the interest did not acquire it for a consideration. It is sufficient to prevent the reversion from being excluded property that a person previously entitled acquired it for money or money's worth.

There are two notable qualifications to the second exception set out above (s 48(2)):

- if the interest is under a settlement created before 16 April 1976, the second point does not apply; and

●   if the person entitled to the reversion acquired it before 10 March 1981, it will not be within the exception if the settlor or spouse was beneficially entitled to it only before that date.

A lease of property is treated as a settlement if the term of the lease is for life or lives or for a period ascertainable only by reference to a death and it is not granted for full consideration in money or money's worth.

The third exception above provides that a reversionary interest in property treated as settled under that definition is not (or not automatically) excluded property.

The fourth exception restricts the scope of excluded property status for reversionary interests in settled property, broadly where a UK-domiciled individual acquires a beneficial interest in settled property in the course of certain targeted arrangements which involve the giving of consideration.

Probably most reversionary interests will be excluded property under the general rule in s 48(1) because they do not fall within one of the four exceptions just discussed. However, even if they do fall within one of those exceptions, they may nevertheless be excluded property under one of the qualifications to those exceptions.

Note the anti-avoidance rule affecting purchased reversionary interests (s 81A), where the interest ends and entitlement to an interest in possession begins (see **1.32**).

Settled reversion

17.16   If the reversion has itself been settled (as opposed to an interest in property beneficially owned), it will be excluded property if the settlor was non-domiciled when it was settled and it is situated outside the UK (s 48(3) (a)). See also HMRC's guidance on reversionary interests (at IHTM04286, IHTM27230).

Note that this rule only applies where the reversion has been settled on other trusts, and that it is the domicile of the settlor of those other trusts that matters. The rule does not apply to a reversion arising under trusts created by a non-domiciliary if it has not been re-settled.

Other reversions

17.17   If the reversion has not been settled, it will be excluded property if the person beneficially entitled to it is non-domiciled and, again, the reversionary interest itself is situated outside the UK (ss 6(1) and 48(3)(b)).

Example 17.9 – Excluded property: reversionary interests

On 1 January 2005, A, who is non-UK domiciled and non-resident, settled some US-registered shares on trustees resident in the Cayman Islands for B for life and thereafter for C. B and C are both domiciled in the UK and the proper law of the settlement is the law of the Cayman Islands.

At this stage, both the shares themselves and the reversionary interest are excluded property. The shares (to which B is treated as beneficially entitled under s 49(1)) are excluded property under s 48(3)(a): they are situated in the US and the settlor (A) was non-domiciled when the settlement was made. The reversionary interest is excluded property under the general rule in s 48(1). It does not fall within any of the exceptions mentioned at **17.15**.

Suppose that C then sells his reversion to a non-domiciliary, D, for a cash sum. In D's hands, the reversion is no longer excluded property under the general rule because it falls within the first exception. It has been acquired for a consideration in money or money's worth. However, it will remain excluded property if, but only if, it is situated outside the UK. In that case, its *situs* combined with D's domicile will make it excluded property under s 6(1).

The law on the *situs* of a reversionary interest is not entirely clear but, unless the property in which the interest subsists is land, the reversion is treated as a chose in action and is situated where it is enforceable. In this case, that is probably the Cayman Islands (see also **17.24** for HMRC's view on the *situs* of reversionary interests).

SITUS

17.18 The following is a very brief summary of the *situs* of some assets under the common law. However, this is a complex subject and, if there is any doubt over the *situs* of an asset, reference should be made to a more detailed work on the subject such as Dicey, Morris & Collins on *Conflict of Laws* (Sweet & Maxwell) or Kessler, *Taxation of Non-Residents and Foreign Domiciliaries* (Key Haven Publications).

Immovables

17.19 Land, buildings on the land and interests in the land are immovable property and are situated where the land itself is situated.

However, the characterisation of property as an interest in land is probably a question for the law of the country where the land itself is situated.

Tangible movables

17.20 These are generally situated in the place where they are physically located at any particular time. Tangible movables include chattels and cash.

Shares and securities

17.21 A share or security whose mode of transfer is an entry in the company's register is situated in the place where:

- that register is kept; or
- the transfer would normally be effected.

Note the illustration of the second of these rules in *Erie Beach Co Ltd v Att Gen for Ontario* [1930] AC 161, and see HMRC's comments at IHTM27123.

A bearer share or security (ie one transferable by mere delivery) is generally situated in the place where it is physically present (*Winans and another v A-G* [1910] AC 27). See also HMRC's comments at IHTM27076.

Debts and choses in action

17.22 These are normally situated in the place where they are enforceable, ie generally where the debtor resides.

A bank account is a debt, which under general law is situated at the branch of the bank where the account is maintained (*R v Lovitt* [1912] AC 212). However, this general rule may be overridden for IHT purposes under the terms of a double taxation convention (s 158(1)).

For debts in Scotland, HMRC state that a specialty debt (eg a debt due under a deed) is also situated where the debtor resides, unlike in England where it is situated where the instrument happens to be (IHTM27092).

Equitable interests

17.23 These must be divided into proprietary interests and rights against the trustees. The former are situated where the underlying property is situated and the latter (as choses in action) where the trustees or executors are resident or, possibly, in the place of the proper law of the trust.

In very general terms, one would expect absolute interests, interests under bare trusts and pre-FA 2006 interests in possession to be treated as proprietary interests and thus situated where the underlying assets are situated; and discretionary interests, interests in unadministered estates and reversionary interests to be choses in action.

Reversionary interests

17.24   HMRC consider that the *situs* or location of a reversionary interest in settled property will normally be determined by the residence of the trustees of the property to which the interest relates (see IHTM04286 and IHTM27230).

IHT PLANNING – NON-UK ASSETS OF NON-UK DOMICILIARY

17.25   A non-domiciliary who has assets abroad would generally be well advised to settle these if there is any risk of becoming UK-domiciled or deemed domiciled. For example, the assets can be settled on discretionary trusts with the settlor as a possible beneficiary and still benefit from excluded property status.

Note that in these circumstances:

- the domicile of the beneficiaries is immaterial; and
- the gift with reservation rules (FA 1986, s 102) should not apply because the excluded property rules prevail.

With regard to the second bullet point above, for a time HMRC's Inheritance Tax Manual included some confusing guidance on this issue, which caused a degree of uncertainty. However, HMRC's guidance (at IHTM14396) was amended in January 2011, and includes the following illustration:

> 'Example
>
> Henry, who is domiciled in New Zealand, puts foreign property into a discretionary trust under which he is a potential beneficiary. He dies five years later having acquired a domicile of choice in the UK and without having released the reservation. The property is subject to a reservation on death but it remains excluded property and is outside the IHT charge.'

In the case of a reservation ceasing during lifetime, HMRC's guidance states that the excluded property position must be considered when the deemed disposition (a PET) is made (under FA 1986, s 102(4)), and indicates that provided the property is then excluded property, IHTA 1984, s 3(2) applies to exclude the assets in which the reservation ceased from charge.

In the case of an individual who has been resident in the UK for 17 or more of the last 20 years, the solution may be for that individual to become non-resident for the period necessary to lose this deemed domicile before making the settlement.

In the table below, the numbers in the columns for Clients A to D show the years that they have been resident in the UK during the 20 years of assessment up to and including 2012–13. The asterisks show the current year of assessment.

- Clients B and C have been resident for at least 17 out of the last 20 years of assessment (the current year in the example being 2012–13). This will be so whether or not either is resident for 2012–13.

- In the case of client B, he will have been resident for 20 out of the last 20 years if he remains resident in 2012–13; and 19 out of the last 20 years if he does not. In either case, he will be deemed domiciled in the UK.

- Client C will have been resident for 18 out of the last 20 years if he remains resident in 2012–13; and 17 out of the last 20 years if he does not. If client C is non-resident in 2012–13 and remains so in 2013–14 and 2014–15, he will lose his deemed domicile under the '17/20 rule' following the end of the latter year.

- Clients A and D, on the other hand, will only be deemed domiciled under the '17/20 rule' if they remained resident for 2012–13. If either became non-resident in that year, they will not be deemed domiciled under the '17/20 rule'.

- In the case of client A, if he remained resident in 2012–13, he will not be able to lose his deemed domicile under this rule until after he has been non-resident for three clear tax years and the fourth has begun, ie until 2016–17.

	Client A	Client B	Client C	Client D
2016–17				
2015–16				
2014–15				
2013–14				
2012–13	*******	*******	*******	*******
2011–12	16	19	17	16
2010–11	15	18	16	15
2009–10	14	17	15	14
2008–09	13	16	14	13
2007–08	12	15	13	12
2006–07	11	14	12	11

17.25   *Foreign domicile*

	Client A	Client B	Client C	Client D
2005–06	10	13	11	10
2004–05	9	12	10	9
2003–04	8	11	9	8
2002–03	7	10	8	7
2001–02	6	9	7	6
2000–01	5	8	6	5
1999–00	4	7	5	4
1998–99	3	6	4	3
1997–98	2	5	3	
1996–97	1	4	2	
1995–96		3	1	
1994–95		2		2
1993–94		1		1

An individual who is neither domiciled nor deemed domiciled, but is likely to become so, should aim to set up an excluded property settlement. If he is not yet clear about whom he wishes to benefit, he can simply create a discretionary settlement with a wide class of beneficiaries (including himself) and with power to add further beneficiaries nominated by him. The trust assets need to remain abroad to ensure that they are excluded property. See also **17.27** regarding certain categories of UK investments which may qualify as excluded property.

Having done this, the trust property will remain excluded property so long as it remains settled and outside the UK. The trustees can appoint life interests to domiciled and resident beneficiaries without incurring any IHT charge at that time or on the later disposal by the beneficiaries of their interests on death or otherwise – again, so long as the property remains settled and outside the UK.

This is subject to an important caveat. If the settlor retains an interest in the property, for example as a discretionary beneficiary, he is treated as making a gift with reservation. This should not matter if he retains his interest in the property until his death. The gifts with reservation charge that would otherwise arise in relation to that property on his death under FA 1986, s 102(3), is apparently accepted by HMRC as inapplicable to excluded property. However, if his interest comes to an end during his lifetime, he is deemed by FA 1986, s 102(4) to make a potentially exempt transfer. As mentioned earlier, HMRC's approach is to consider whether excluded property status applies at the time of that disposition. The risk of a gift with reservation charge can be avoided by ensuring that if the settlor has an initial interest in the property he retains that interest until his death.

There is no need for an excluded property settlement to have non-resident trustees. If there is no real prospect of any of the beneficiaries being non-resident or non-domiciled, it might be simpler to choose resident trustees. On the other hand, non-resident trustees can generally roll up income from foreign property tax-free.

However, UK tax implications need to be considered carefully where there is some connection to the UK. For example, the income tax anti-avoidance rules in respect of transfers of assets abroad by individuals who are ordinarily UK resident (ITA 2007, Pt 13, Ch 2) are complex and wide ranging. Capital gains tax can be deferred until a beneficiary receives a capital payment (TCGA 1992, s 87). Prior to 2008–09 when the capital gains tax rate was 40%, the advantage of doing so tended to be outweighed by the stockpiled gains surcharge (TCGA 1992, s 91), which could lead to an effective tax rate of up to 64%. However, a capital gains tax rate of 28% (for 2012–13, in respect of higher rate taxpayers) means that the maximum effective tax rate for stockpiled gains correspondingly reduced to 44.8%.

If there is some chance that the beneficiaries may become resident or domiciled outside the UK, using non-resident trustees preserves flexibility for the future. However, as indicated above, the tax position must be considered 'in the round', taking into consideration the tax position of the settlor and beneficiaries as well.

Example 17.10 – Keeping it in the family

Erich and Uli were brothers, born in the Rhineland. Erich succeeded to the family winemaking business whilst Uli became a motor engineer in Coventry. They kept in touch and Uli ran a little business on the side selling specialist wines to discerning Midlands families. Sadly, Erich and his wife had no children and the time came to sell up, resulting in a very substantial cash balance which Erich wanted to share with Uli because it was really family money.

Uli and his (British) wife Mary had three grown up sons, all living in England and domiciled there. Uli and Mary were well-enough placed that they did not need extra, which was likely to exceed 5,000,000, but would like to help their boys, who were all settled in the UK and likely to remain there for the foreseeable future. However, Mary did not like the idea of an offshore trust: she thought it 'too grand for the likes of us' and feared that professional fees might erode any benefits of such a structure.

It was therefore agreed that Erich would under no circumstances transfer any money direct to Uli. Instead, Erich would move the money to Switzerland, which recognises trusts more readily than Germany, and Uli and Mary would declare themselves to be trustees of any money that came from Erich. They would keep it in a Swiss bank and in due course invest it outside the UK for the longer term.

That might seem unwise from the perspective of CGT, because any gains would accrue to UK-resident trustees, but Uli and Mary reasoned that some liability to UK tax would arise as soon as the family tried actually to get any benefit from the trust in the UK anyway. Similarly any income arising would attract UK tax; but on distribution to UK-resident beneficiaries that tax would show as a deduction and might in part be recoverable by the beneficiary.

There were two other considerations. As the trustees, Uli and Mary felt that they could better control the professional fees involved in running the trust. Also, in common with some other 'high tax' jurisdictions, the UK compliance requirements in setting up the trust, such as the Money Laundering Regulations, were actually less onerous than in most 'offshore' jurisdictions. That also helped to keep costs down.

The main objective had been achieved; the fund itself was excluded property, so it would not be taxed on the death of any of the sons.

POSSIBLE IHT PLANNING – UK ASSETS OF NON-UK DOMICILIARY

Government securities free of tax while in foreign ownership (ss 6(2), 48(4))

17.26   Certain government securities which are not settled property, and are in the beneficial ownership of persons who satisfy the particular conditions attaching to the securities (eg as to being not domiciled and/or not ordinarily resident in the UK) are exempt from taxation under the provisions of F(No 2) A 1931, s 22(1), or F(No 2)A 1915, s 47. Such securities are excluded property and will therefore give rise to no IHT charge (s 6(2)). However, see below as to legislative changes affecting ordinary residence.

In broad terms, securities issued before 29 April 1996 will be exempt if the beneficial owner is not domiciled or ordinarily resident in the UK. For deaths and other chargeable events from 6 April 1998, all securities issued before that date are excluded property by reference to the ordinary residence (but not domicile) of the beneficial owner (the one exception being 3.5% War Loan 1952 or after, which will only be exempt if the beneficial owner is not domiciled and not ordinarily resident in the UK). The same applies to securities issued on or after that date. A list of FOTRA (Free of Tax to Residents Abroad) securities in issue at 5 April 1998 is included in HMRC's guidance (see IHTM04306).

In the same way, if the exempt gilts are settled property and a person who meets the conditions attaching to the security (as to being non-domiciled and non-ordinarily resident) is entitled to a qualifying interest in possession in them they will likewise be excluded property (s 48(4)(a)). A 'qualifying interest in possession' for individuals is one to which he is beneficially entitled. If beneficial entitlement arises from 22 March 2006, the interest in possession must be an immediate post death interest, a disabled person's interest or a transitional serial interest (s 59(1)(a)).

In the case of a discretionary trust (ie a trust in which no interest in possession subsists), the securities will be excluded property provided that all known persons for whose benefit the settled property or income from it has been or might be applied or who might become beneficially entitled to an interest in possession in it are persons who satisfy the conditions attaching to the security (as to being not ordinarily resident (and not domiciled) in the UK) (s 48(4)(b)).

A charity is not 'a known person for whose benefit the settled property might be applied' because it does not itself benefit and therefore the presence of a UK charity amongst non-domiciled beneficiaries does not mean that the exemption will be lost (*Von Ernst & Cie SA v IRC* [1980] STC 111, CA). *Von Ernst* was a case on the wording of para 3(2) of Sch 7 to FA 1975. Sections 6(2) and 48(4) now refer to a 'person of a description specified in the condition in question' (ie a person who is not ordinarily resident (and not domiciled) in the UK). The case remains relevant in marginally reducing the otherwise wide list of likely beneficiaries.

As an anti-avoidance measure, where property leaves one settlement for another, without having passed through someone's beneficial ownership, the conditions have to be satisfied in respect of both (s 48(5)). This provision was introduced to prevent transfers from one settlement with UK resident and domiciled beneficiaries, to another settlement in which the beneficiaries are foreign individuals.

Similarly, pursuant to s 6(3), certain savings certificates and similar deposits held by persons beneficially entitled to them and domiciled in the Channel Islands or the Isle of Man are excluded property.

In the case of government securities and these savings, the deemed domiciled rules in s 267(1) do not apply (s 267(2)). The exemption could be particularly useful if exchange controls were to be re-imposed and the individual in question was prevented from investing these sterling funds abroad. Similarly, where for future exchange control or other reasons assets have to remain in the UK for a period of time it might then be appropriate for such an individual to charge these assets in the UK and use the proceeds to purchase such exempt government securities or savings as appropriate.

Following legislation published in the draft Finance Bill 2013 clauses on 11 December 2012, the concept of 'ordinary residence' is generally being removed for tax purposes. However, the government's explanatory notes to those provisions point out that the IHT provisions in ss 6(2) and 48(4) will continue to apply to securities issued on the basis of exemption for persons not ordinarily resident provided that the beneficial owner acquired them before 6 April 2013.

Unit trusts and open-ended investment companies (ss 6(1A), 48(3A))

17.27   Further categories of excluded property investments were introduced in FA 2003, from 16 October 2002. Holdings in authorised unit trusts (AUTs) and shares in open-ended investment companies (OEICs) constitute excluded property in the hands of a non-UK domiciled individual (s 6(1A)).

If those categories of investment are settled property, they are excluded if the settlor was non-UK domiciled when the settlement was made (s 48(3A)). However, prior to a change included in the draft Finance Bill 2013 clauses published on 11 December 2012, there was a potential trap for the unwary if switching to such investments from 'relevant property' such as in a discretionary trust. There is a charge when trust property ceases to be relevant property, whether it leaves the trust or not (IHTA 1984, s 65(1)(a)). Excluded property is not relevant property (s 58(1)(f)). The relieving provision in s 65(7) for excluded property within s 48(3)(a) was not extended to include holdings in AUTs or shares in OEICs, and an IHT charge could therefore have arisen in such circumstances.

HMRC were aware of the anomaly in respect of the s 65 charge, which was apparently unintended. Nevertheless, it was some time before any action was taken to remedy the problem. The legislative change in the draft Finance Bill 2013 provides for an exception from the s 65 charge, similar to s 65(7), in respect of relevant property invested in OEICs and AUTs. Consequently, the switching of UK assets in a trust settled by a non-UK domiciled individual to investments in OEICs and AUTs is exempt from IHT charges, with retrospective effect to 16 October 2002 when the above FA 2003 provisions were introduced.

Selling UK assets

17.28   In other circumstances, where a non-domiciled individual wishes to make a gift and has chargeable UK assets, he might consider selling those assets and remitting the proceeds of sale abroad. An arm's-length sale of the assets will not generate an IHT liability, although the CGT consequences should be borne in mind. There should not be any CGT if the individual is neither resident nor ordinarily resident at the time of the sale (TCGA 1992, s 2(1)). However, as indicated at **17.26**, the concept of 'ordinary residence' is generally removed from the UK's primary tax legislation following changes in the draft Finance Bill 2013 clauses published on 11 December 2012. The reference to ordinary residence in TCGA 1992, s 2(1) is therefore removed from 2013–14 and replaced by a 'residence condition'.

Once the proceeds have been remitted abroad, a gift of the cash (or the foreign assets in which it has been reinvested) can be made.

Great care and attention to detail should be exercised when executing tax planning that involves remittances from abroad. Careful planning assumed even greater importance following the FA 2008 rules on the remittance basis of taxation for individuals who are not domiciled or not ordinarily resident in the UK. The reader may wish to refer to a specialist publication or possibly expert advice in this area if such actions are contemplated.

Interposing an overseas investment company

17.29   Owning assets through a company whose shares are situated abroad is a common strategy for non-domiciliaries. The shares in the non-UK company will be excluded property. If a UK-situated asset, such as a house (which is obviously not excluded property) is transferred into such a company, its value is taken outside the scope of IHT. The shares in the non-UK company might be put into a non-resident trust, thereby preserving their excluded property status in the event of the settlor acquiring a UK domicile or deemed domicile in the future.

Aside from IHT issues, a number of tax measures affecting residential property were introduced in FA 2012. The rate of stamp duty land tax (SDLT) on residential properties sold for chargeable consideration of more than £2 million was increased from 5% to 7%, with effect from 22 March 2012 (FA 2003, s 55(2), as amended by FA 2012, Sch 35). Furthermore, a 15% SDLT charge was introduced from 21 March 2012 for the purchase of an interest in a single dwelling where the chargeable consideration is more than £2 million and the purchaser is a company, a partnership one of whose members is a company, or a collective investment scheme (FA 2003, Sch 4A, as inserted by FA 2012, Sch 35).

Unfortunately, the government's attempts to discourage the acquisition of residential property for SDLT and other tax planning reasons do not end there. Legislation was also included in the draft Finance Bill 2013 clauses published on 11 December 2012, which introduces an annual charge on residential properties worth more than £2 million that are owned by certain 'non-natural persons' (ie companies, partnerships with company members and collective investment schemes), subject to a limited range of reliefs (eg in relation to property rental businesses), with effect from 1 April 2013.. Further legislation to be published in January 2013 is expected to extend the CGT regime to gains on disposals by certain 'non-natural persons' (see above) of UK residential property or interests in such property accruing on or after 6 April 2013, if such persons were liable to the above annual residential property tax on the property in question.

Whilst the vast majority of family homes in the UK are worth less than £2 million, the above measures should be borne in mind when considering IHT planning involving UK residential property, such as the family home.

The above strategy will usually be sound for IHT purposes but there are a number of risks associated with it, particularly where property is concerned, if it is occupied by a person who exercises *de facto* control over the company and the trustees. This was dramatically illustrated in *R v Dimsey* [2001] STC 1520; *R v Allen* [2001] STC 1537.There are two principal risks. The first is that the individual is a 'shadow director' whose rent-free occupation of the property is an emolument taxable as employment income. The second is that the company is resident in the UK, which may happen even while the shares remain situated outside the UK for IHT purposes. A non-resident company is nevertheless treated as resident in the UK for corporation tax purposes if its central management and control is exercised in the UK (*De Beers Consolidated Mines Ltd v Howe* [1906] 5 TC 98).

The first risk follows from the House of Lords' finding that a shadow director within ITEPA 2003, s 67(1) is an office holder for the purposes of the benefit in kind rules on living accommodation in ITEPA 2003, Pt 3, Ch 5. A shadow director is someone in accordance with whose directions or instructions the company directors are accustomed to act. The value of his rent-free occupation is treated as an emolument taxable as employment income. Although FA 2008 introduced an exemption from the employment income tax charge for living accommodation (ITEPA 2003, ss 100A, 100B), that exemption only applies to properties situated outside the UK. Such properties are outside the scope of IHT for a non-UK domiciled individual in any event, and so this income tax exemption is not considered further.

At the outset, the individual needs to decide whether to make absolutely certain that he is not a shadow director, or whether to accept that he is a director and mitigate the tax liability. To avoid being a shadow director, he needs to ensure that there is an independent board of directors who do not take instructions from him. These directors must not simply ratify suggestions made by him or, where the shares are held in trust, by the trustees at his direction. The directors must take decisions independently. Unless they disagree with the individual and reject his ideas from time to time, this will be difficult to prove. From the adviser's point of view, it is important to ensure that the client is genuinely prepared to cede control of the company to independent directors without interfering and that he will stick to this throughout the lifetime of the arrangement.

If he is not prepared to do this, he could take the second option of accepting that he is a director but mitigating the income tax liability in one of two main ways. First, if he is also non-resident, he could try to ensure that most of his emoluments (the value of the rent-free occupation) are attributable to duties performed outside the UK. As a non-resident, he will not be taxable on these foreign emoluments. This can be achieved by performing substantial duties outside the UK, such as attending board meetings etc. Whilst it may not be possible to avoid performing *any* duties within the UK (for instance, decorating or repairs may be considered duties), it should be possible to keep these to a minimum. There is a risk that HMRC will argue that the emoluments are exclusively referable to the UK duties, but this risk can be minimised by suitably drafted contracts between the individual and the company.

The second mitigation strategy is to pay a market rent for the period of occupation. In the case of a non-resident, the periods of occupation will be relatively short, but perhaps longer if the individual is UK resident. If the property cost £75,000 or less (improbable these days), then the true cost of paying the market rent would only be the tax payable by the company. However, for properties costing more than £75,000, ITEPA 2003, s 106 treats the occupier as receiving emoluments equal to the appropriate percentage of so much of the cost as exceeds £75,000. The appropriate percentage is the official rate of interest (4% from 6 April 2010). This can lead to a significant charge: on a property worth £1,000,000 a 50% taxpayer would have an annual tax charge of £18,500 under this provision.

The second risk of an offshore company is that it becomes UK resident. If this risk materialises, there are very serious income and corporation tax consequences. The company will be subject to corporation tax on its rental profits and on any chargeable gains it realises. This is particularly unfortunate for a non-resident individual who would himself have been outside the scope of capital gains tax. There will also be an income tax charge on dividends or distributions that are not specifically excluded from income tax. In contrast, if the company is non-resident, there is no UK tax charge on dividends or distributions to a non-resident shareholder. Additionally, even if the individual has avoided being a shadow director, the value of his rent-free occupation will become taxable under CTA 2010, s 1064 if the company is resident, assuming that it is a close company.

To avoid this scenario, the company should be incorporated outside the UK. In addition, there must be absolutely no possibility of the company's central management or control being in the UK (the issue of 'central management and control' or 'place of effective management' has been the subject of a number of cases, including *De Beers Consolidated Mines Ltd v Howe* [1906] 5 TC 198, and more recently *Wood v Holden* [2006] EWCA Civ 26, *News Datacom Ltd and another v Atkinson (Inspector of Taxes)* [2006] SSCD 732 (SpC 561) and *Laerstate BV v Revenue & Customs* [2009] UKFTT 209 (TC). Board meetings should take place outside the UK. Major decisions should be taken at these meetings and they should be properly minuted. The individual must not take any remotely significant decisions or actions in relation to the company whilst in the UK. He may be on the board (although see the discussion above in relation to ITEPA 2003, Pt 3, Ch 5), but he must only perform his duties as director whilst outside the UK.

It may be possible to reduce both of the above risks if the shares are held by non-resident trustees instead of by the individual but this is by no means automatic. Whether central management and control is exercised in the UK and whether the individual is a shadow director are both questions of fact. The interposition of trustees will not itself affect the answer to either question. If the individual takes management decisions, which are effectively conveyed to the board by the trustees, the results will be just as disastrous as if the individual had given instructions to the directors himself. In theory, the trustees may hear suggestions from the individual, then make an independent decision as to whether or not to instruct the directors accordingly. In practice, if the individual's suggestions are invariably adopted, it will be difficult to demonstrate that the trustees' decision is truly independent. The best advice is always to ensure that the individual only makes suggestions outside the UK and, if he does not want to be a shadow director, that he does not make them at all.

It is important that the 'key' decisions affecting a non-resident trust are in fact taken by the trustees. In *Smallwood (and Related Appeal) v Revenue and Customs Commissioners* [2010] EWCA Civ 778, a capital gains tax planning arrangement involved the appointment of a trustee company incorporated and tax resident in Mauritius as trustees, in order that a trust became resident in Mauritius. In the same tax year that share disposals took place giving rise to trust gains, the Mauritius trustees retired in favour of UK-resident trustees.

The success of the above planning arrangement broadly relied upon the terms of a double taxation treaty between the UK and Mauritius, which included a 'tie-breaker' residence clause stating that a person is a resident of the contracting state in which its 'place of effective management' is situated. The Special Commissioner determined that this was the UK (ie as being the place where the realistic, positive management of the trust, or where key management and commercial decisions were in substance made, and the place where actions were determined). The taxpayer appealed.

The High Court, allowing the taxpayer's appeal, held that there had been periods of residence in Jersey, Mauritius and the UK during the relevant tax year.

Mauritius was the state of residence at the time of the disposition, and it held the taxing right under the terms of the treaty, not the UK. However, the Court of Appeal (by a 2:1 majority) allowed HMRC's subsequent appeal. It was held that the place of effective management of the trustees was the UK. The scheme had been conceived in the UK. The replacement of the trustees by a Mauritian trustee and then by UK trustees had been steps in the preconceived scheme of management which went above and beyond the day-to-day management by the current trustees.

Secured borrowings

17.30   Given the potential difficulties associated with ownership of a UK residence via an offshore company, another, less complicated, solution may sometimes be preferred.

Suppose a non-domiciled individual takes a substantial loan from an unconnected third party (eg an offshore bank); if the loan is secured against the individual's UK residence then this will reduce the value of the residence for IHT purposes (s 162(4)).

The borrowed funds can be deposited offshore where they will be excluded property. If funds are deposited with the bank that made the loan then there may be the facility to offset interest charged on the loan against interest forgone on the deposit; in such a case, the arrangement can be quite economical.

Utilising the inter-spouse exemption

17.31   Note that the exemption for inter-spouse transfers is limited to £55,000 (for 2012–13) where the transferor spouse is UK domiciled and the transferee spouse is not (s 18(2)). However, following draft Finance Bill 2013 legislation published on 11 December 2012 this limit is set to increase, broadly to the IHT nil rate band applicable at the time of the transfer. There are also provisions to allow non-UK domiciled spouses to elect to be treated as domiciled in the UK for IHT purposes, so that the inter-spouse exemption is unlimited but electing spouses are then generally subject to IHT on their worldwide estates (see **6.4**).

Non-sterling bank accounts in foreign ownership

17.32   A foreign currency account with a bank in the UK is left out of account for IHT purposes on the death of a person who is neither domiciled, resident nor ordinarily resident in the UK immediately before he dies (s 157(1)). However, following changes included in the draft Finance Bill 2013 clauses published on 11 December 2012, the legislative reference to ordinary residence is removed in relation to deaths on or after 6 April 2013.

This exclusion does not apply to a sterling bank account in the UK. It does, however, apply to a foreign currency account in the UK held on the terms of a settlement in which the non-domiciled, non-resident (and, for deaths before 6 April 2013, non-ordinarily resident) person had a beneficial entitlement to an interest in possession as long as the settlor was non-domiciled when the settlement was made, *and* the trustees were neither domiciled nor resident (or ordinarily resident) in the UK immediately before the beneficiary's death (s 157(3)).

PRACTICAL POINTS

Wills

17.33 On acquiring a new foreign resident status, the individual should either make a new will complying with the relevant foreign law (possibly with a view to a change of domicile) – as well as English law if assets remain situate here – or at least check that his UK will is valid under the foreign law in question.

An alternative is to have more than one will, dealing separately with the assets situated in each jurisdiction on death. This has the advantage that those ultimately applying for probate in the UK will only be concerned with UK assets under the UK will. If there is any likely doubt over whether a person has acquired a new domicile of choice, his relevant intentions should be recited in the will and in any deeds effecting lifetime gifts.

Statutory declaration

17.34 Immediately after taking up foreign residence and domicile, the individual could swear a statutory declaration outlining the facts relevant to this change. Alternatively, a declaration could be sworn immediately before leaving the UK.

Some advisers do not favour this course on the basis that it might raise doubt in the mind of HMRC as to the change of domicile, but the case of *Re Clore (No 2)* [1984] STC 609 (see **17.5**) illustrates the need for clear evidence of the individual's own state of mind and intentions.

Deeds of variation

17.35 A beneficiary under the will of a non-domiciled testator could enter into a deed of variation settling his interest under the will. This will create an excluded property settlement if the assets consist of (or later become) non-

UK situated, whatever the domicile of the varying beneficiary or the other beneficiaries under the settlement.

For IHT purposes (only), the variation (subject to complying with all the conditions of s 142) is treated as made by the testator for all the purposes of IHTA 1984. The interests under the varied settlement could include a life interest for the varying beneficiary or a discretionary settlement for a class of beneficiaries including him. The only possibility of an IHT charge during the lifetime of the settlement is if that trust property becomes situated in the UK and a transfer of value occurs whilst it remains situated in the UK, or if the law changes.

The gifts with reservation rules do not apply because FA 1986 is construed as one with IHTA 1984, and thus the variation is treated as made by the testator, not the varying beneficiary.

However, the capital gains tax and income tax legislation are not so generous. The capital gains tax legislation deems a variation which is effected by written instrument (see s 62(7)) to have been made by the testator for limited purposes. First, TCGA 1992, s 62(6)(a) prevents the variation itself from being a disposal. Secondly, it provides for s 62 itself to apply as if the variation had been effected by the testator (s 62(6)(b)). This means that those benefiting from the variation will be deemed to have acquired the assets on the testator's death at their market value at that date.

Beyond those two specific provisions, the variation has its normal consequences for capital gains tax purposes. In particular, the varying beneficiary will be the settlor for the purposes of TCGA 1992, s 86, in relation to non-UK resident trusts and chargeable on gains accruing to the trustees. See the House of Lords decision in *Marshall v Kerr* [1994] STC 638 and subsequent legislation identifying the settlor in relation to wills or intestacies, in respect of assets becoming settled property (s 68C(2)).

For income tax purposes, similar identification rules apply in respect of variations to which TCGA 1992, s 62(6) applies and so, again, the varying beneficiary will be the settlor (ITA 2007, s 472(2)).

Being the settlor for income and capital gains tax purposes will often put the beneficiary in no worse a position than he would have been had he retained the assets absolutely, in which case it should not deter him from varying a will to create an excluded property settlement. The last statement should be qualified in the case of a non-resident settlement. Whilst the provisions deeming income and gains to be those of the settlor generally include rights of reimbursement against the trustees, the enforceability of these rights against non-resident trustees is somewhat doubtful. See *Government of India v Taylor* [1955] AC 491. If the settlor is not a beneficiary, the trustees may be unable to reimburse him without committing a breach of trust. This problem can be averted by ensuring that the settlor is a beneficiary.

Application to HMRC as to acquisition of new residence

17.36   As soon as a dramatic break with the UK is made, the individual's advisers should contact HMRC explaining the change of residence and domicile as the case may be, with reasons. This is primarily concerned with obtaining the income and capital gains tax advantages.

Form P85 deals with notification of a change of residence upon leaving the UK. It was once normal for HMRC to give provisional agreement that there had been a change of residence (although final confirmation was unlikely before the expiry of at least three years), and to give their view on an individual's domicile status if it was relevant to a possible UK tax liability (but see **17.39**). Unfortunately, these days taxpayers are expected to 'self-assess' their residence and domicile status as part of their tax return submission.

Some commentators have called into question the veracity of HMRC guidance such as HMRC6, leaving many taxpayers in a state of uncertainty on the question of residence and domicile. The introduction of a statutory residence test (see **17.8**) will generally result in greater certainty on residence status, although it appears likely that a lack of certainty on domicile matters will continue.

Transfer of assets abroad

17.37   The income tax consequences of transferring assets abroad (under ITA 2007, Pt 13, Ch 2) (previously ICTA 1988, ss 739–740 *et seq*) must be carefully considered. These provisions apply to persons ordinarily resident in the UK. ITA 2007, s 720 applies to transferors and ITA 2007, s 731 to other persons. HMRC originally considered that ICTA 1988, s 739 (in the 'old' transfer of assets code) applied to both transferors and non-transferors but this view was rejected by the House of Lords in *Vestey v IRC (Nos 1 and 2)* [1980] STC 10. The consequence was the introduction of what is now ITA 2007, s 731.

There are similar provisions for capital gains tax purposes in the form of TCGA 1992, s 86, which taxes settlors, and TCGA 1992, s 87, which taxes those who receive capital payments from the trustees.

Reporting requirements

17.38   Any professional person other than a barrister who is concerned with making a settlement with a UK-domiciled settlor and non-resident trustees must make a return to the Board within three months, giving the names and addresses of the settlor and trustees. A person is absolved from this requirement if someone else has already reported the settlement, or if the settlement is made by will (s 218).

HMRC's information and inspection powers (FA 2008, Sch 36) were extended to IHT with effect from 1 April 2010, replacing the previous information powers in s 219. HMRC have wide powers to obtain information and documents from both taxpayers and third parties, subject to certain restrictions including in relation to privileged communications between lawyers and clients (but not accountants, where legal advice is given on tax matters (*R (oao Prudential plc) v Special Commissioner (and related applications)* [2010] EWCA Civ 1094)).

Testing domicile

17.39   The concept of domicile can be a grey area for a number of reasons and ideally it would often be desirable to test the position with HMRC. There were traditionally two main methods for testing domicile. Unfortunately, their application and usefulness were adversely affected by the FA 2008 provisions regarding the remittance basis, and by HMRC practice.

Seeking to retain non-UK domicile

17.40   This test was (prior to FA 2008) commonly used where, for example, an individual claimed foreign domicile (eg of origin) but UK-resident status, and where it was feared that a UK domicile of choice may have arisen.

With regard to foreign source income, the test involves claiming assessment on the remittance basis (which is available to a non-domiciled (or not ordinarily resident prior to 6 April 2013, under changes included in the draft Finance Bill 2013 clauses published on 11 December 2012) though UK-resident individual), and not on the basis of worldwide income arising. An appropriate amount could be so remitted or retained offshore, and the remittance basis claimed on the self-assessment return, and on the foreign and non-residence supplementary pages of the return completed, as appropriate.

Unfortunately, the introduction in FA 2008 of a £30,000 annual charge for the privilege of claiming the remittance basis, coupled with other drawbacks including the loss of personal allowances, makes this strategy less feasible and much less attractive than before in terms of testing domicile status. The position has potentially worsened following the introduction in FA 2012 of a higher annual charge of £50,000 for non-UK domiciled individuals who claim the remittance basis in a tax year and have been resident in the UK for at least 12 of the previous 14 tax years (ITA 2007, s 809H).

However, in certain circumstances a non-UK domiciled taxpayer can use the remittance basis without paying the £30,000 or £50,000 charge, and without losing their entitlement to personal allowances and the annual exemption for capital gains tax purposes. This applies to such taxpayers if they have less than £2,000 of unremitted foreign income and gains in the tax year, and satisfy the other conditions in ITA 2007, s 809D. If all the conditions are satisfied, the remittance basis applies automatically unless the taxpayer makes an election to the contrary. However, the taxpayer will probably need to complete a tax return in any event due to other income and gains, and will therefore need to make a declaration about his domicile status (see HMRC6, para 5.6). Hence the taxpayer's domicile will still be subject to testing through the normal HMRC enquiry process for self-assessment returns, should they decide to do so.

It was once also possible to submit an application for an HMRC ruling on an individual's domicile status on form DOM1 ('Income and Chargeable Gains – Domicile') in advance of filing the tax return, on the basis that the matter of domicile was 'immediately relevant' to a UK tax liability. Unfortunately, HMRC subsequently announced (in HMRC Brief 17/09) the complete withdrawal of form DOM1. Where an individual had already submitted form DOM1 (or P86) to HMRC and obtained an initial view about their domicile status, HMRC said that it would be 'unusual' for them to open an enquiry on domicile status in the few years after that, unless new information comes to light or there has been a change in circumstances.

Establishing non-UK domicile of choice

17.41 A potentially more difficult situation is where a person who has had a UK domicile (eg of origin) considers he should have acquired a domicile of choice outside the UK, and is non-resident. As he will be non-UK resident, the first method will not help. Instead, a pilot discretionary settlement can be set up with non-UK *situs* assets and somewhat exceeding the IHT nil rate band plus any available annual exemptions. Confirmation would be sought from HMRC that no IHT is payable. If he is non-UK domiciled, the gift into settlement is excluded property; if he is UK domiciled, it is a chargeable lifetime transfer.

If only very little IHT is involved in the use of the pilot settlement, HMRC may well defer a definitive judgment; it is a resources issue. A substantial amount of IHT may therefore have to be put at risk. In HMRC Brief 17/09, HMRC indicated that if an IHT account was submitted by someone setting up the trust on the basis of not being domiciled in the UK, they would only open an enquiry into the return if the IHT at stake made it cost effective for them to do so. The initial IHT limit set was £10,000.

However, HMRC subsequently superseded that guidance in HMRC Brief 34/10, in respect of dispositions after 24 August 2010. The revised guidance states that HMRC will only consider opening an enquiry or making a determination where domicile is an issue if there is a significant risk of loss of UK tax. Unfortunately, HMRC do not consider it appropriate to state an amount of tax that would be regarded as 'significant' for these purposes. Even if an IHT enquiry is opened, it may be stopped at any stage if HMRC consider that it would not be cost effective to continue. The lack of a monetary threshold for an enquiry is an unsatisfactory state of affairs for those individuals seeking certainty about domicile status during their lifetime. However, domicile rulings may be obtained on the individual's death, upon submission of form IHT401 ('Domicile outside the United Kingdom') (see **17.43**).

Finally, on the subject of domicile, an adviser should remember that it will not always be beneficial to a client to establish a non-UK domicile. For example, a non-UK domiciled individual may have established roots in the UK, with assets consisting mainly of business and agricultural property. It may be (and this must of course be checked by reference to the laws of the foreign territory) that he would pay less tax if taxed as a UK domiciliary than if taxed in the present country of domicile. In that case, the advice should be aimed towards losing his domicile in that country (or at least ensuring that he acquires a UK domicile which would override his current foreign domicile under the treaty tie-breaker provisions), subject to obtaining expert advice about the tax implications in the foreign territory.

Pre-owned assets

17.42   The pre-owned assets (POA) income tax regime (see **Chapter 13**) has limitations according to the residence and domicile status of the chargeable person (FA 2004, Sch 15, para 12). The POA regime does not apply for any tax year in which the person is non-UK resident (ie for income tax purposes).

With regard to domicile, POA does not apply to a non-UK domiciled person in the tax year, in respect of foreign *situs* land, chattels, or property comprised in a settlement in which the settlor retains an interest. Only relevant property situated in the UK is subject to a POA charge (para 12(2)).

In addition, settled property which is excluded property of the non-UK domiciled individual (under IHTA 1984, s 48(3)(a)) is disregarded for POA purposes. This disregard applies to a person who was at any time domiciled outside the UK (para 12(3)). Therefore, settled property remains excluded property even if the settlor subsequently becomes domiciled in the UK, provided that no property is added to the settlement after UK domicile is acquired.

For POA purposes, a person is regarded as domiciled in the UK if he would be treated as such for IHT purposes under IHTA 1984 (FA 2004, Sch 15, para 12(4)). This means that the IHT concept of deemed domicile is therefore imported for this income tax purpose.

Compliance

17.43   In line with the stricter rules applied to other taxes, HMRC have taken a more intrusive line on establishing domicile at the date of death, for instance in the changes between forms in the previous IHT200 series and the current IHT400 series. Supplemental schedule IHT401 asks detailed questions as to the residence of the deceased. Questions 7 to 18 inclusive on that form force personal representatives to make much greater disclosure than previously.

In the case of chargeable lifetime transfers or if a settlor was domiciled outside the UK when the settlement was set up, the IHT account (IHT100) is accompanied by form D31 ('Domicile outside the United Kingdom'). This form is rather shorter and less detailed than form IHT401 on death.

HMRC include a schedule of useful information and documents that might be requested during an enquiry about an individual's domicile. It may be helpful to keep and maintain a 'domicile pack' containing as much detail as possible, to support any assertions about the individual's domicile status in the event of an enquiry or dispute with HMRC. The schedule is contained in HMRC's guidance at RDRM23080.

Index

[All references are to paragraph number and appendices]